Fodor's 2013

PARIS

Fodor's Travel Publications   New York, Toronto, London, Sydney, Auckland
www.fodors.com

FODOR'S PARIS 2013

Editorial Contributors: Jennifer Ditsler-Ladonne, Paige Donner, Linda Hervieux, Bryan Pirolli, Heather Stimmler-Hall

Editors: Caroline Trefler (lead editor), Joanna Cantor

Production Editor: Carolyn Roth
Maps & Illustrations: Mark Stroud, Henry Colomb, and David Lindroth, *cartographers;* Rebecca Baer, *map editor;* William Wu, *information graphics*
Design: Fabrizio La Rocca, *creative director;* Tina Malaney, Chie Ushio, Jessica Walsh, *designers;* Melanie Marin, *associate director of photography;* Jennifer Romains, *photo research*
Cover Photo: (River Seine) Jon Arnold/age fotostock
Production Manager: Angela L. McLean

ISBN 978–0–307–92928–0

ISSN 0149–1288

SPECIAL SALES

This book is available at special discounts for bulk purchases for sales promotions or premiums. Special editions, including personalized covers, excerpts of existing books, and corporate imprints, can be created in large quantities for special needs. For more information, write to Special Markets/Premium Sales, 1745 Broadway, MD 3-1, New York, NY 10019, or e-mail specialmarkets@randomhouse.com.

AN IMPORTANT TIP & AN INVITATION

Although all prices, opening times, and other details in this book are based on information supplied to us at press time, changes occur all the time in the travel world, and Fodor's cannot accept responsibility for facts that become outdated or for inadvertent errors or omissions. So **always confirm information when it matters**, especially if you're making a detour to visit a specific place. Your experiences—positive and negative— matter to us. If we have missed or misstated something, **please write to us**. Share your opinion instantly through our online feedback center at fodors.com/contact-us.

PRINTED IN CHINA

10 9 8 7 6 5 4 3 2 1

CONTENTS

MAPS

ABOUT THIS GUIDE

Fodor's Ratings

Everything in this guide is worth doing—we don't cover what isn't—but exceptional sights, hotels, and restaurants are recognized with additional accolades. **Fodor's Choice** ★ indicates our top recommendations; ★ highlights places we deem **Highly Recommended**; and **Best Bets** call attention to notable hotels and restaurants in various categories. Care to nominate a new place? Visit Fodors.com/contact-us.

Trip Costs

We list prices wherever possible to help you budget well. Hotel and restaurant price categories from **$** to **$$$$** are noted alongside each recommendation. For hotels, we include the lowest cost of a standard double room in high season. For restaurants, we cite the average price of a main course at dinner or, if dinner isn't served, at lunch. For attractions, we always list adult admission fees; discounts are usually available for children, students, and senior citizens.

Hotels

Our local writers vet every hotel to recommend the best overnights in each price category, from budget to expensive. Unless otherwise specified, you can expect private bath, phone, and TV in your room. For expanded hotel reviews, facilities, and deals visit Fodors.com.

TripAdvisor ⊙⊙

Our expert hotel picks are reinforced by high ratings on TripAdvisor. Look for representative quotes in this guide, and the latest TripAdvisor ratings and feedback at Fodors.com.

Ratings		Hotels & Restaurants	
★	Fodor's Choice		
★	Highly recommended	🏨	Hotel
☾	Family-friendly	↳	Number of rooms
		🍴	Meal plans
Listings		✕	Restaurant
✉	Address	⌒	Reservations
✉	Branch address	👔	Dress code
📭	Mailing address	▭	No credit cards
☎	Telephone	$	Price
🖷	Fax		
⊕	Website	**Other**	
✎	E-mail	⇨	See also
⊞	Admission fee	☞	Take note
⊙	Open/closed times	🏌	Golf facilities
Ⓜ	Subway		
⊹	Directions or Map coordinates		

Restaurants

Unless we state otherwise, restaurants are open for lunch and dinner daily. We mention dress code only when there's a specific requirement and reservations only when they're essential or not accepted. To make restaurant reservations, visit Fodors.com.

Credit Cards

The hotels and restaurants in this guide typically accept credit cards. If not, we'll say so.

Experience Paris

PARIS TODAY

Bienvenue à Paris! Or, welcome to Paris! Although it may seem as if time stands still in this city—with its romantic, old buildings and elegant 19th-century parks and squares—there's an undercurrent of small but significant changes happening here that might not be immediately obvious.

Today's Paris . . .

. . . is cleaner. Parisians breathe a little easier today as the city moves toward a more eco-friendly lifestyle. And while the image of intellectuals sitting in a café, cigarette in hand, may have been as much a part of the French identity as wine and cheese, that all changed in 2008, when the French government enacted a nationwide smoking ban inside all public buildings, including hotels, restaurants, and bars. The city is also cutting down on smog pollution with its popular Vélib' municipal bikes *(see the "Bicycling in Paris" box in Chapter 3)* and launched the AutoLib' car-sharing service in December 2011 while adding pedestrian, bus, and cycling lanes on roads and extending the métro and tram network. In addition to the gradual replacement of paved streets with more aesthetically pleasing cobblestones and widening the tree-lined sidewalks, the city is also planning an ambitious project to permanently pedestrianize the expressways along the Seine, following the success of Paris Plage, the yearly beach party along the river.

. . . is friendlier. One area where fraternité has evolved is with French service: although North Americans, raised on the principle that the customer is always right, may find servers and store clerks a bit curt (and not always so efficient), Paris has become friendlier than it once was. This can be chalked up to necessity, as the service industry scrambled to compete for tourism dollars after the post-9/11 slump in business, and many of Paris's waiters have discovered that happy American tourists tip better than unhappy ones—even when the 15% service fee is already included in the bill. That's not to say that service is delivered with a smile everywhere; it never hurts to learn a few French phrases, which will almost always reward you with warmer welcomes.

. . . is open in August and on Sunday. As recently as five years ago, Paris was still largely deserted in August when the locals fled to the countryside and beaches, leaving a wake of closed shops and restaurants. Today the city is very much alive

WHAT'S HOT IN PARIS NOW

Did somebody say there's a recession? If so, the hospitality industry has been too busy building new **luxury palace hotels** in Paris to have heard the news. The complete overhaul and opening of the Royal Monceau in October 2010, with decor by Philippe Starck

and management under the Raffles brand, was immediately followed by the opening of a Mandarin Oriental on the Rue St-Honoré and a Shangri-La at Trocadéro.

■ **Green** continues to gain currency in Paris, which is now home to a dozen organic

fast-food chains and juice bars, several eco-label-certified hotels, and the widespread availability of ethical, fair-trade, and organic products at every supermarket chain and open-air market. The trend in rooftop and vertical wall gardens can

throughout the summer, with outdoor music festivals, the beach along the Seine that is Paris Plage, and perhaps even budget constraints keeping more Parisians in town. Although the August exodus was never official policy, the "closed on Sunday" was part of French law until 2009, when the government decided that allowing shops to stay open daily would boost the economy and employment. The Marais, the Avenue des Champs-Élysées and St-Germain-des-Prés are among the liveliest places to go on Sunday, but other neighborhoods aren't the ghost towns they once were.

. . . is even sweeter. Paris has always been a haven for anyone with a sweet tooth, but in the past few years there has been a veritable explosion of sugary temptations, from Ladurée's new tearoom at the Château de Versailles and the stiff competition among the city's *macaron* makers to the widespread craze for Italian gelato shops such as Grom, Amorino, Pozzetto, Deliziefolie, and Gelati d'Alberto. No room for a full dessert? Opt for the Café Gourmand, now served in many trendy cafés, which is an espresso served with an artistic array of minipastries.

. . . is more affordable. It might be hard to believe, but despite the frustratingly strong euro, Paris is actually more affordable today than it was just a few years ago. In 2009 the French government lowered the Value Added Tax on food in restaurants from 19.6% to 5.5% (alcohol and some gourmet foods are still charged the full rate). As a result, many restaurants were encouraged to knock down the price of popular staples such as *un café,* the *plat du jour,* and even the lunch menu. In 2010 slumped economic conditions prompted a relaxation of the strict rules governing sales in France: whereas traditionally there were only two sale periods allowed per year—in January and August—now shops have more flexibility to hold *mini-soldes* when they feel the need to move stock, and consumers can find good deals throughout the year.

be seen in the city's newer buildings, too.

■ Paris also remains an important center for **Contemporary Art,** with the reopening of 59 Rivoli, the famous art squat on the Rue de Rivoli, as well as high-profile exhibitions at the Château de Versailles such

as Jeff Koons and Murakami. Le BAL LAB in Montmartre is a new independent center for documentary images, and in 2011 the historic Gaîté Lyrique reopened as a digital arts center.

PARIS PLANNER

Getting Around

Paris is without question best explored on foot, and thanks to Baron Haussmann's mid-19th-century redesign, the City of Light is a compact wonder of wide boulevards, gracious parks, and leafy squares. When you want a lift, though, public transportation is easy and inexpensive. The métro (subway) goes just about everywhere you're going for €1.70 a ride (a carnet, or "pack" of 10 tickets, is €12.70); tickets also work on buses and trams and the RER train line within Paris.

Paris is divided into 20 *arrondissements* (or neighborhoods) spiraling out from the center of the city. The numbers reveal the neighborhood's location and its age, the 1er arrondissement at the city's heart being the oldest. The arrondissements in central Paris—the 1er to 8e—are the most visited.

It's worth picking up a copy of *Paris Pratique*, the essential map guide, available at newsstands and bookstores.

Saving Time and Money

Paris is one of the world's most visited cities—with crowds to prove it—so it pays to be prepared. Buy tickets online when you can: most cultural centers and museums offer advance-ticket sales, and the small service fee you'll pay is worth the time saved waiting in line. Investigate alternative entrances at popular sites (there are three at the Louvre, for example), and check when rates are reduced, often during once-a-week late openings. Also, national museums are free the first Sunday of each month. There are many within Paris, including the Louvre, Musée d'Orsay, and Centre Pompidou.

A Paris Museum Pass can save you money if you're planning serious sightseeing, but it might be even more valuable because it allows you to bypass the lines. It's sold at the destinations it covers and at airports, major métro stations, and the tourism office in the Carrousel du Louvre (two-, four-, or six-day passes are €39, €54, and €69, respectively; for more info, visit ⊕ *www.parismuseumpass.com*).

Stick to the omnipresent ATMs for the best exchange rates; exchanging cash at your hotel or in a store is never going to be to your advantage.

Hours

Paris is by no means a 24/7 city, so planning your days beforehand can save you aggravation. Museums are closed one day a week, usually Tuesday, and most stay open late at least one night each week, which is also the least crowded time to visit. Store hours are generally 10 am to 7:30 pm, though smaller shops may not open until 11 am, only to close for several hours during the afternoon. Retailers now have the option of doing business on Sunday, although your best bets are department stores, the shops along the Champs-Élysées, the Carrousel du Louvre, and around the Marais, where most boutiques open at 2 pm.

Eating Out

Restaurants follow French mealtimes, serving lunch from noon to 2:30 pm and dinner from 7:30 or 8 pm. Some cafés serve food all day long. Always reserve a table for dinner, as top restaurants book up months in advance. When it comes to the check, you must ask for it (it's considered rude to bring it unbidden). In cafés you'll get a register receipt with your order. *Servis* (gratuity) is always included in the bill, but it's good form to leave something extra if you're satisfied with the service: a few cents for drinks, €1 for lunch, €3 at dinner. Leave 5% of the bill only in higher-end restaurants.

What to Wear

When it comes to clothing, the standard French look is dressier than the American equivalent. Athletic clothes are reserved for sports. Sneakers are not usually worn by adults, but if you pack yours, keep them for daytime only. Neat jeans are acceptable everywhere except at higher-end restaurants; check to see whether there's a dress code.

When to Go

The City of Light is magical all year round, but it's particularly gorgeous in June, when the long days (the sun doesn't set until 10 pm) stretch sightseeing hours and make it ideal to linger in the cafés.

Winter can be dark and chilly, but it's also the best time to find cheap airfares and hotel deals.

April in Paris, despite what the song says, is often rainy.

Summer is the most popular (and expensive) season. Keep in mind that, as in many other European cities, some shops and restaurants close in August for several weeks, though there are still plenty of fun things to do, like free open-air movies and concerts, and the popular Paris Plage, the "beach" on the Right Bank of the Seine.

September is gorgeous, with temperate weather, saner airfares, and cultural events timed for the *rentrée* (or return), signifying the end of summer vacation. In the third weekend in September, scores of national buildings that are normally closed to the public open for visits during the annual Journées du Patrimoine (Patrimony Days).

Paris Etiquette

The Parisian reputation for rudeness is undeserved. In fact, Parisians are sticklers for politesse and exchanging formal greetings is the rule. Informal American-style manners are considered impolite. Beginning an exchange with a simple "Do you speak English?" will get you on the right foot. Learning a few key French words will take you far. Offer a hearty *bonjour* (bohn-zhoor) when walking into a shop or café and an *au revoir* (o ruh-vwahr) when leaving, even if nobody seems to be listening (a chorus may reply). When speaking to a woman over age 16, use *madame* (ma-dam), literally "my lady." For a young woman or girl, use *mademoiselle* (mad-mwa-zel). A man of any age goes by *monsieur* (murh-syur). Always say please, *s'il vous plaît* (seel-voo-play), and thank you, *merci* (mehr-see).

Paris Temps

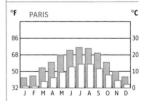

WHAT'S WHERE

These numbers refer to chapters.

2 The Islands. Although they're just a few quick steps from the "mainland," the Ile de la Cité and Ile St-Louis are the heart of Paris. This is where you can find Notre-Dame and Sainte-Chapelle.

3 Around the Eiffel Tower. With the Champs de Mars, Invalides, and the Seine nearby, many lovely strolls give you striking views of Paris's ultimate monument.

4 Champs-Élysées. The Champs-Élysées and Arc de Triomphe attract the tourists, but there are also several excellent museums here, well worth checking out.

5 Around the Louvre. The Faubourg St-Honoré, with its well-established shops and cafés, has always been chic, and probably always will be. Until the 1970s, Les Halles was the "Belly of Paris"—the city's food market.

6 The Grands Boulevards with the Opéra Garnier. Use the Opéra Garnier as your landmark and set out to do some power shopping. There are some good, small museums in the area, too.

7 Montmartre. Like a small village within a big city, Montmartre feels distinctly separate from the rest of Paris—but it's prime tourist territory, with Sacré-Coeur as its main attraction.

8 Marais. The Marais, which used to be Paris's Jewish neighborhood, is now one of the city's hippest destinations. While away the afternoon at the Place des Vosges or shop to your heart's content.

9 Eastern Paris. Canal St-Martin, Bastille, and Oberkampf. If it's new and happening in Paris, you'll find it out here in neighborhoods like Canal St-Martin, Bastille, Oberkampf, and République. The area is filled with trendy restaurants, funky galleries, and cutting-edge boutiques.

10 The Latin Quarter. Leave yourself lots of time to wander the Latin Quarter, known for its vibrant student life.

11 St-Germain-des-Prés. Fabulous cafés and the Musée d'Orsay are here, but make sure you leave time to wander the Jardin du Luxembourg.

12 Montparnasse. Once the haunt of writers and artists—Picasso and Hemingway included—this neighborhood is now known for its contemporary-art scene, as well as the Catacombs.

13 Western Paris. The Bois de Boulogne and the Musée Marmottan Monet are two great reasons to trek out here.

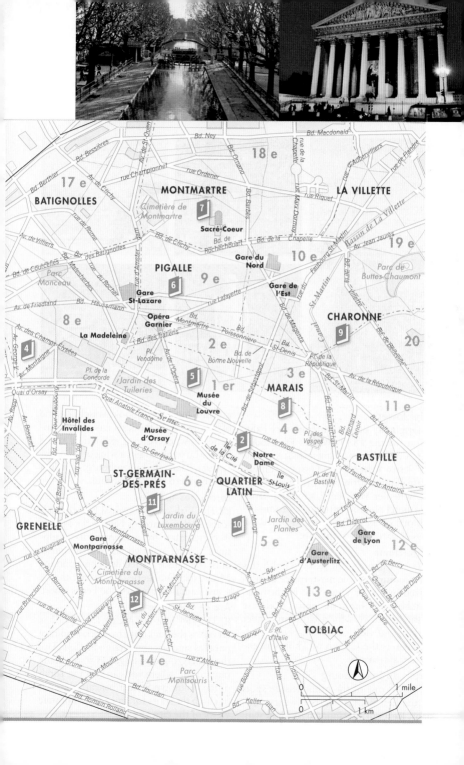

18 e

MONTMARTRE

LA VILLETTE

Bd. Ney

Bd. Ornano

rue Ordener

rue Championnet

Av. de Clichy

17 e

BATIGNOLLES

Bd. Berthier

Bd. Bessières

Av. de St-Ouen

Bd. Macdonald

rue de la Chapelle

rue Riquet

rue d'Aubervilliers

rue de Flandre

Bd. Barbès

Cimetière de
Montmartre

7

Sacré-Coeur

Bd. de Clichy

Bd. de
Rochechouart

Bd. de la Chapelle

Bd. Marx Dormoy

rue Marx Dormoy

Bassin de La Villette

Av. Jean Jaurès

19 e

Parc de
Buttes-Chaumont

Rome

Bd. des Batignolles

Av. de Villiers

Bd. de Courcelles

Parc
Monceau

Malesherbes

rue de Rome

rue d'Amsterdam

rue du Rocher

PIGALLE

6

Gare
St-Lazare

9 e

rue Lafayette

Gare du
Nord

Gare de
l'Est

10 e

St-Martin

rue du Faubourg St-Martin

Bd. de la Villette

Canal St-Martin

CHARONNE

9

rue de Belleville

Av. de Friedland

Av. de Courcelles

Bd. Haussmann

8 e

Opéra
Garnier

La Madeleine

Bd. Montmartre

Bd.
Poissonnière

Bd. des Italiens

2 e

Bd. de
Bonne Nouvelle

Bd. St-Denis

Bd. de Magenta

Bd. de Sébastopol

Pl. de la
République

3 e

Av. de la République

20

11 e

Bd. de Belleville

Av. George V

Av. Montaigne

4

Av. des Champs-Elysées

Pl.
Vendôme

Pl. de la
Concorde

Jardin des
Tuileries

5

1 er

Musée
du
Louvre

MARAIS

8

Pl. des
Vosges

4 e

Bd. Richard Lenoir

Bd. Beaumarchais

Bd. Voltaire

Quai d'Orsay

Av. Bosquet

Bd. de la Tour-Maubourg

**Hôtel des
Invalides**

Quai Anatole France

Seine

Musée
d'Orsay

Bd. St-Germain

7 e

Île
de la Cité

2

Notre-
Dame

rue de Rivoli

Île
St-Louis

Pl. de la
Bastille

BASTILLE

R. du faubourg St-Antoine

Av. Ledru Rollin

Av. Daumesnil

GRENELLE

Bd. de Grenelle

**ST-GERMAIN-
DES-PRÉS**

Bd. Raspail

Bd. St-Michel

6 e

Bd. du Montparnasse

11

Jardin du
Luxembourg

**QUARTIER
LATIN**

rue Monge

10

Jardin des
Plantes

Av. Diderot

**Gare
de Lyon**

12 e

rue de Vaugirard

Av. Emile Zola

rue Paul Barruel

rue de la Convention

**Gare
Montparnasse**

rue du Départ

MONTPARNASSE

Cimetière du
Montparnasse

Av. du Maine

12

Bd. Edgar Quinet

Bd.
St-Michel

Bd.
St-Jacques

Bd. Arago

5 e

Bd. St-Marcel

Gare
d'Austerlitz

Bd. de l'Hôpital

Quai de la Gare

Bd. de Bercy

rue de Dijon

Quai de Bercy

13 e

Bd. Vincent Auriol

rue de Tolbiac

TOLBIAC

Bd. Brancion

rue de la Tombe-Issoire

Av. du Gl-Leclerc

Av. René Coty

rue de la Santé

Bd. A. Blanqui

Pl.
d'Italie

Av. d'Italie

Av. de Choisy

Bd. Brune

Av. Jean Moulin

Bd. Jourdan

14 e

rue d'Alésia

Parc
Montsouris

Av. Reille

Bd. Kellermann

Bd. Romain Rolland

0   1 mile

0   1 km

PARIS
TOP ATTRACTIONS

Eiffel Tower
(A) Originally built as a temporary exhibition for the 1889 World's Fair, today there's no other monument that symbolizes Paris better than Gustave Eiffel's world-famous Iron Lady. It's breathtaking, whether you see it sparkling from your hotel window after dark or join the millions of annual visitors to brave the glass elevator trip to the top.

Notre-Dame
(B) It took almost 200 years to finish this 12th-century Gothic masterpiece immortalized by Victor Hugo and his fictional hunchback. Climb the spiral staircase of the bell towers for a close-up gander at the gargoyles, or have a peek at relics such as the Crown of Thorns in the cathedral treasury.

Jardin du Luxembourg
(C) This is one of the prime leisure spots on the Left Bank for urban-weary Parisians. Relax in a reclining park chair with a picnic lunch or a book, watch a game of *boules* while the kids enjoy a marionette show, or visit an exhibition at the Musée Luxembourg in a wing of the 17th-century Palais de Luxembourg, which is now home to the Paris Senate.

Jardin des Tuileries
(D) The 17th-century formal French landscape of these gardens behind the Louvre is punctuated by contemporary sculptures, a café, and two noteworthy museums: the Musée du Jeu de Paume and the Musée de l'Orangerie. In summer there's a small amusement park and Ferris wheel.

Arc de Triomphe
(E) The 164-foot-tall Arc de Triomphe has served as the backdrop to official military parades since its completion in 1836. Use the underground passageway to reach the monument, where you can visit the Tomb of the Unknown Soldier beneath the arch or climb the stairs for amazing panoramic views of the city.

Musée d'Orsay

(F) After a stunted lifespan as a train station constructed for the 1900 World's Fair, this beautiful Belle Époque building is filled with Art Nouveau objects, Impressionist paintings, vintage photography, and realist sculptures. Don't miss the scale model of the Opéra Garnier or the views of the Seine from the grand ballroom, now housing the museum's restaurant.

Opéra Garnier

(G) Opulent, stunning, and magnificently over the top, Charles Garnier's opera house is one of the outstanding jewels of the Second Empire. Its illustrious marble staircase and ruby-red box seats have been featured in films from *Dangerous Liaisons* to *Marie-Antoinette,* and its backstage corridors are famously haunted by the Phantom of the Opera.

Centre Pompidou

(H) The Pompidou Centre's groundbreaking "inside-out" design is still visually shocking (it opened in 1977). This is also the top destination for modern-art lovers in Paris.

Sacré-Coeur

(I) This wedding-cake white basilica dominates Montmartre's hilltop. Most visitors are content with the views overlooking the city from the basilica stairs, but ambitious sight seekers can climb to the bell tower for an even higher vantage point.

Musée du Louvre

(J) The grandest museum in the world was just a humble fortress in the 12th century, but grew in size and prestige as a sumptuous royal palace until the French Revolution gave it a new lease on life as home to the Republic's art collection. Don't miss the big three—*Mona Lisa, Winged Victory,* and *Venus de Milo.*

PARIS LIKE A LOCAL

To appreciate the City of Light as the locals do, you can start by learning some of the daily rituals of Paris life. These simple, fun pleasures will quickly get you into the swing of being Parisian.

Shop Like a Parisian

Parisians prefer the boisterous atmosphere of bustling street markets to the drab *supermarchés*. Even if you're just buying picnic fixings, you can follow suit. For a full listing of Paris's markets, check out the City Hall website at ⊕ *www.paris. fr*, but these are some of our faves.

Le Marché d'Aligre, just off the Rue du Faubourg St-Antoine beyond the Opéra Bastille, dates back to the 18th century. Open Tuesday through Sunday, the market has fruit, vegetables, cheese, meat, fish, and poultry, as well as a host of other products. The best selection is on the weekend. **Le Marché Mouffetard**, between the Panthéon and the Jardin des Plantes, is a combination of stands and food shops spilling out onto a cobbled pedestrian street. Olive oil, chocolates, books, and wine are available, in addition to fruits, veggies, cheese, and meats (Tuesday–Saturday 9 am–6 pm, Sunday 9 am–1 pm, métro: Censier-Dubenton).

If flea markets are your thing, Paris has three that can satisfy any bargain hunter. **Les Puces des Vanves** (weekends, 8 am to 7 pm, métro Porte de Vanves; Avenue de le Porte de Vanves and Rue Marc Sangnier) is two in one: in the morning, collectors revel among old furniture, stamps, postcards, and almost everything else imaginable; in the afternoon, merchants of new and vintage clothing take over. **Les Puces de St-Ouen** (Saturday, Sunday, and Monday, 9:30 am to 7 pm, métro Clignancourt), otherwise known as the Clignancourt flea market, is a little

more expensive, but a real treasure trove. Bypass the noisy stands near the métro in favor of the buildings beyond the elevated highway, where antiques dealers and vintage-clothing boutiques provide a real blast from the past. You might not *need* to buy flowers, but the flower markets are lovely for wandering, and you can cheer up a budget hotel room with a few daisies in a water glass. Try one of the **Les Marchés aux Fleurs**: at Place de la Madeleine (Tuesday to Sunday, 8 am to 7:30 pm), Place des Ternes (Tuesday to Sunday, 8 am to 7:30 pm), or Place Lépine on the Ile de la Cité (Monday to Saturday, 8 am to 7:30 pm, with the bird market Sunday morning).

Drink Coffee Like a Parisian

Le café in Paris isn't simply a drink that begins the day: it's a way of life. Though Parisians do stop at the counter to order a quick *café expresse, bien serré, s'il vous plaît* ("good and strong, please"), more often people treat the café as an extension of their apartments, with laptops precariously balanced, cell phones ringing, and business being done; in Paris the café is the place to work, read, and chat with friends any time of the day. Think of Simone de Beauvoir, who spent more time at the **Café de Flore** (✉ *172 bd. St-Germain, 6e* ☎ *01–45–48–55–26*) than in her chilly apartment. Choose a café with a patio or good windows for people-watching, or pause at the nearest counter, and you're in for a dose of Parisian café culture. Most locals have their own favorites, and we've listed some of our top choices on the neighborhood Getting Oriented pages; you're bound to find your own preferred haunt(s).

Walk Like a Parisian

Paris was made for wandering, and the French have coined a lovely word for a person who wanders the streets: *le flâneur,* one who strolls or loiters, usually without a destination. In Paris the streets beckon, leading you past monuments, down narrow alleyways, through arches, and into hidden squares. As a flâneur, you can become attuned to the city's rhythm and, no matter how aimlessly you stroll, chances are you'll end up somewhere magical. Some of our suggestions for wandering are along the Seine, into the poetic streets of **St-Germain,** or into the tangled lanes around the **Bastille** and **Canal St-Martin.** Strolling is a favorite Sunday pastime for locals—but you're on vacation, so you can be a flâneur any day of the week.

Eat Baguettes Like a Parisian

The Tour Eiffel might be the most famous symbol of Paris, but perhaps the true banner of France is the *baguette,* the long, caramel-color bread brandished at every meal. Locals take inordinate pride at finding the best *baguette* in the neighborhood. To find a worthy *boulangerie*—a bakery that specializes in bread, as opposed to a *pâtisserie,* specializing in pastries—look for a line outside on weekend mornings. Three faves in Paris are **Arnaud Delmontel** (⊠*39 rue des Martys* ☎*01–48–78–29–33*), **Jean-Pierre Cohier** (⊠*270 rue du Faubourg St-Honoré* ☎*01–42–27–45–26*), and **Boulanger de Monge** (⊠*123 rue Monge* ☎*01–43–37–54–20*). Note that some *boulangeries* follow the traditional three-step customer service protocol: first you place your order at the counter and receive a receipt; then you pay at the *caisse* and get your receipt stamped; finally, you return to the first counter to exchange the stamped receipt for your package of edible art. As you're leaving the bakery, do as many Parisians do— nibble the end of the crust to taste the bread while it's still warm.

Eat Pastries Like a Parisian

High prices are making luxury all the more elusive in Paris, but there's one indulgence most people can still afford, at least occasionally—fine pastries. As you can see when you stop in at any of Paris's extraordinary *pâtisseries* (pastry shops), a wonderful array of French treats awaits. Tops on our list are the deliciously airy and intense *macarons*—nothing like the heavy American macaroons you might be familiar with. **Ladurée** (⊠*16 rue Royale, 8e* ☎*01–42–60–21–79*) claims to have invented these ganache-filled cookies, but two Left Bank *pâtissiers* also have particularly devoted fans of their *macarons*: the flavors at **Gérard Mulot** (⊠*76 rue de Seine, 6e* ☎*01–43–26–85–77*) include pistachio, caramel, and terrific orange-cinnamon, and **Pierre Hermé** (⊠*72 rue Bonaparte, 6e* ☎*01–43–54–47–77*) has exotic ones like peach-saffron, olive oil, and white truffle. The classic opera pastry—almond cake layered with chocolate and coffee cream—can be found at **Lenôtre** (⊠*61 rue Lecourbe, 15e* ☎*01–42–73–20–97*), but devotees also flock to the fine-food emporium **Fauchon** (⊠*26 pl. de la Madeleine, 8e* ☎*01–47–42–60–11*). Another traditional pastry is the *montblanc,* a mini-mountain of chestnut puree capped with whipped cream, best rendered by **Jean-Paul Hévin** (⊠*3 rue Vavin, 6e* ☎*01–43–54–09–85*). And those really in the know watch for anything from the Tokyo-born **Sadaharu Aoki** (⊠*35 rue Vaugirard, 6e* ☎*01–45–44–48–90*); look for his green-tea madeleines and black-sesame éclairs. Many of the sweet spots mentioned here have multiple locations; only the original store is listed.

PARIS WITH KIDS

Paris is often promoted as an adult destination, but there's no shortage of children's activities to keep the young 'uns busy, not to mention that many of the city's top attractions have carousels parked outside them in summer. Make sure to buy a *Pariscope* (found at most newsstands) and check the *enfants* section for current children's events. In addition to what's below, sites of particular interest to children are marked with a rubber-ducky icon (☽).

Museums

Paris has a number of museums that cater to the young and the young at heart. They're a great place to occupy restless minds, especially if the weather is bad. The **Cité des Sciences et de l'Industrie** (the Museum of Science and Industry), at the Parc de la Villette, is an enormous science center, and the children's area is divided into two main sections: one for children from 3 to 5 years of age; another for those from 5 to 12. Interactive exhibits allow kids to do everything from building a house and comparing their body to that of a favorite animal, to learning about communications systems throughout history, from the Tom Tom to the satellite. The **Musée de la Poupée** (the Doll Museum) is a cozy museum in the heart of the Marais, with a collection of more than 500 dolls dating back to the 1800s, complete with costumes, furniture, and accessories. Labels might be in French, but they're not really the point anyway, and the museum features a "Doll Hospital," where "sick" dolls and plush toys come to be repaired; the doctor is in on Thursday, but free estimates are offered throughout the week. The **Palais de la Découverte** (the Palace of Discovery) has high-definition, 3-D exhibits covering everything from chemistry, biology, and physics to the weather, so

there's bound to be some interesting dinner conversation when the day is done. Many of the displays are in French, but that doesn't stop most kids from having a blast; hands down, the choice between this and the Louvre is a no-brainer.

Sites and Shows

A zoo is usually a good bet to get the kids' attention—although you might want to keep in mind that most European zoos aren't as spacious as American zoos. The **Ménagerie** at the Jardin des Plantes is an urban zoo dating from 1794 and home to more than 240 mammals, 400 birds, 270 reptiles, and a number of insects. Unfortunately, the huge **Parc Zoologique**, in the Bois de Vincennes, is closed for renovations until 2014. The **Musée de la Chasse et de la Nature,** in the Marais, is another place to get up close and personal with ferocious lions, tigers, and one in-your-face polar bear—these animals just aren't alive. An impressive collection of taxidermy trophies takes children on a safari to discover how man's relationship with animals through art, stuffed animals, and hunting gizmos. When it comes to spectacles, what child would pass up the circus? There are several in the city *(see the Performing Arts chapter),* and the **Cirque de Paris** has a special feature called a "Day at the Circus"—your kids (and you) can learn some basics like juggling and tightrope walking, then you can lunch with the artists and see a performance in the afternoon. Less interactive are **Les Guignols,** French puppet shows: the original Guignol was a marionette character created by Laurent Mourguet, supposedly in his own likeness, celebrating life, love, and wine. Today the shows are primarily aimed at children, and are found in open-air theaters throughout the city in the warmer months. Check out the

Champs-Élysées, Parc Montsouris, Buttes Chaumont, Jardin du Luxembourg, and the Parc Floral in the Bois de Vincennes. Even if they don't understand French, kids are usually riveted. Of course, the best sight in Paris is the city itself, and a **boat ride** on the Seine is a must for everyone. It's the perfect way to see the sights, rest weary feet, and, depending on which option you choose, lunch or dinner may be part of the treat.

Expending Energy

Most kids are thrilled (at least more than the grown-ups) at the prospect of climbing innumerable stairs to be rewarded with cool views: the **Eiffel Tower** is the quintessential Paris climb, but **Notre-Dame** gets extra points for the gargoyles, and the **Arc de Triomphe** is a good bet, since it's at the end of the Champs-Élysées. When it comes to open spaces for running around, Paris has lots of park options, with extra attractions in summer when kids can work off steam on the trampolines or ride ponies at the **Jardin des Tuileries**. The **Jardin du Luxembourg** has a playground and a pond where kids can rent miniature boats, and the **Bois de Boulogne** has a zoo, rowboats, bumper cars, and lots of wide-open spaces. Ice-skating is seasonal but always a thrill, and from mid-December through February several outdoor Paris sites are turned into spectacular ice-skating rinks with Christmas lights, music, and instructors. The rinks are free to the public; skate rental for adults costs €5. The main rink is at **Place de l'Hôtel de Ville** (the square in front of City Hall).

Underground Paris

There's something about exploring underground that seems to fascinate kids, at least the older ones. **Les Égouts**, the Paris sewer system, has a certain gross factor but isn't actually that disgusting. Keep in mind, though, that the smell is definitely ranker in the summer months. At the **Catacombs**, in Montparnasse, dark tunnels filled with bones are spookily titillating—at least for those not prone to nightmares. For some cheap underground entertainment without the ick factor, the **métro** itself can be its own sort of adventure, complete with fascinating station art such as the submarine decor at Arts-et-Metiers, the colorful Parisian timeline murals at Tuileries, or the Egyptian statues of the Louvre-Rivoli station. A good tip: the Métro lines 1 and 14 feature driverless trains that let you sit at the very front; it's hard to resist the feeling that you're driving.

And for Treats

All that fun will no doubt bring on an appetite, and there's no shortage of special places to stop for a snack in Paris. **La Charlotte de l'Isle** (✉ 24 *rue St-Louis-en-l'Ile*), on the Ile Saint Louis, is a whimsically decorated tearoom known for its hot chocolate—deliciously thick and yummy, unlike what American children are usually used to. Just down the street is **Berthillon**, renowned for its decadent ice cream—though the **Amorino** gelaterias give it a run for its money. And when in need, a pâtisserie selling chocolate croissants is never hard to find. French children adore the pastel clouds of *meringue* (which resemble hardened whipped-cream puffs) that decorate almost every bakery's window, and there are all sorts of cookies to tempt a smile from a tired tot.

GREAT WALK: ARTISTS AND WRITERS OF THE LEFT BANK

Some of the greatest artists and writers of the 20th century were attracted to the winding streets and bustling boulevards of Paris's Left Bank between the end of WWI and the social upheavals of the 1960s.

Winding Streets of the Quartier Latin

The streets around **Place de la Contrescarpe** have hardly changed since they were immortalized in Hemingway's *Moveable Feast*. He lived at 74 rue Cardinal Lemoine (down the street from James Joyce at No. 71) and worked at 39 rue Descartes. George Orwell lived nearby, at 6 rue Pot de Fer, while writing *Down and Out in Paris and London*. The famous bookshop **Shakespeare & Co.** recently lost its owner, George Whitman, in 2011, but his daughter Sylvia continues his legacy in a medieval house at 37 rue de la Bûcherie; many of the Beat Generation writers who frequented it in the '60s, like Burroughs, Ginsberg, and Kerouac, stayed in the **Hôtel de Vieux Paris**, aka the "Beat Hotel," at 9 rue Gît-le-Coeur. Pablo Picasso perfected his cubist style at 7 rue des Grands Augustins from 1936 to 1955.

The Heyday of St-Germain-des-Près

Follow Rue St-André-des-Arts and Rue de Seine to Rue Jacob, home to American writers like Djuna Barnes, who stayed at the Hôtel d'Angleterre at No. 44. On the corner of Rue Bonaparte is **Le Pré aux Clercs**, where Hemingway and Fitzgerald shared many a drink. Henry Miller lived up the street at 24 rue Bonaparte and later at No. 36. Pass the home of Jean-Paul Sartre at No. 42 to the square that now bears his and Simone de Beauvoir's names. Along noisy Boulevard St-Germain are the **Deux Magots, Café de Flore,** and **Brasserie Lipp,** legendary establishments frequented by the couple as well as by Faulkner, Camus, Apollinaire, André Gide, Giacometti, Cocteau, Duras, Hemingway, Fitzgerald, and André Breton. Bookshops like **La Hune** still give the area intellectual character despite the proliferation of fashion boutiques.

Odéon and Luxembourg Gardens

At 12 rue de l'Odéon a plaque commemorating Sylvia Beach's publication of James Joyce's *Ulysses* marks the original location of Shakespeare & Co., which closed in 1944. On Rue de Vaugirard, Faulkner lived at No. 42 and Fitzgerald and his wife Zelda at No. 58. Man Ray's studio is still intact at No. 2 bis, rue Ferou. Hemingway lived at No. 6 for a year, writing often about the **Luxembourg Gardens.**

Montparnasse

Leaving the Luxembourg Gardens, follow Rue du Fleurus, where Gertrude Stein and Alice B. Toklas lived at No. 27, entertaining artists and writers such as Picasso, Matisse, Erik Satie, and *New Yorker* correspondent Janet Flanner. Stein's friends Ezra Pound and Hemingway—who moved a lot—lived nearby on Rue Notre-Dame des Champs (at No. 70 and No. 113, respectively), near Boulevard Montparnasse, the expat epicenter a decade before St-Germain held that distinction. Some of the establishments still here are **Closerie des Lilas** No. 171), **Le Sélect** (No. 99), **Le Dôme** (No. 18), **La Rotonde** (No. 105), and **La Coupole** (No. 102), where Modigliani, Dalí, Samuel Beckett, Colette, and Miró rubbed shoulders. Rue Delambre leads to the **Cimetière du Montparnasse,** the final resting place for many of the illustrious names of the Left Bank, including publishers Hachette and Larousse; artists Man Ray, Kiki de Montparnasse, Brancusi, and Brassaï; and writers like Baudelaire, Ionesco, Sartre et Beauvoir, Beckett, and Duras.

1

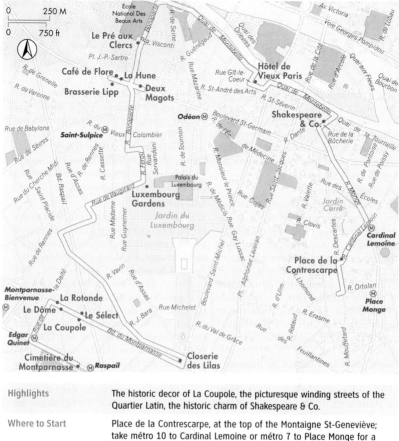

Highlights	The historic decor of La Coupole, the picturesque winding streets of the Quartier Latin, the historic charm of Shakespeare & Co.
Where to Start	Place de la Contrescarpe, at the top of the Montaigne St-Geneviève; take métro 10 to Cardinal Lemoine or métro 7 to Place Monge for a less steep incline.
Length	5.25 km (3.2 miles); duration approximately 2.5–3 hours without stops.
Where to End	At the Cimetère du Montparnasse, just east of the Tour du Montparnasse, next to métro Edgar Quinet (Line 6) and métro Raspail (lines 4, 6).
Best Time to Go	Any time of day when you can see all of the sights in daylight.
Worst Time to Go	Being entirely outside, it's not a good idea to do when it's raining or very cold.
Editor's Choice	Artistic detour to the Musée du Montparnasse (⊠ 21 av. du Maine, Montparnasse or Falguière), the Musée Zadkine (⊠ 100 bis, rue d'Assasm, Notre-Dame-des-Champs), or the Musée du Luxembourg (⊠ 19 rue de Vaugirard, Ⓜ Odéon or St-Sulpice).

GREAT ITINERARIES

Paris is a treasure of neighborhoods and history, and a visit to this glorious city is never quite as simple as a quick look at a few landmarks. These one-day itineraries are mix and match: follow the ones that intrigue you—and leave yourself time to just walk and explore.

Monumental Paris

Begin your day at the Trocadéro métro, where you can get the best views of the Tour Eiffel from the esplanade of the Palais de Chaillot. If you absolutely must ride to the top, now is the best time to get in line. Otherwise, get a Seine-side view of the city's other noteworthy monuments from the Bateaux Parisiens, moored below the Pont d'Iéna. Hour-long cruises loop around the Ile de la Cité, with multilingual commentary on the sights along the way. Afterward you can take the RER to the Musée d'Orsay for lunch in the museum's Belle Époque dining room before tackling the late-19th-century works of art. Then it's a short walk to the imposing Hôtel des Invalides, the French military museum built as a retirement home for wounded soldiers under Louis XIV. The emperor Napoléon Bonaparte rests beneath the golden dome. If the weather's nice, have tea next door in the sculpture gardens of the Musée Rodin (entrance to the gardens €1). If your feet are still happy, cross the gilded Pont Tsar Alexandre III to the Champs-Élysées, passing the Belle Époque art palaces known as the Grand Palais and Petit Palais. You can take Bus 73 from the Assemblée Nationale across the bridge to the Place de la Concorde and all the way up the Avenue des Champs-Élysées to the Arc de Triomphe. Open until 11 pm, its panoramic viewing platform is ideal for admiring the City of Light.

Alternative: Instead of the traditional Seine cruise, try the Batobus, which allows you to hop on and hop off throughout the day with one ticket. The seven Batobus ports include the Eiffel Tower, Notre-Dame, Hôtel de Ville, Louvre Museum, and Musée d'Orsay. Note that there's no commentary on these tours.

Old Paris

Start at the Pont Neuf for excellent views off the western tip of the Ile de la Cité, then explore the island's magnificent architectural heritage, including the Conciergerie, Sainte-Chapelle, and Notre-Dame. The brave can climb the corkscrew staircase to the towers for a gargoyle's-eye view of the city. Then detour to the neighboring Ile St-Louis for lunch before heading into the medieval labyrinth of the Quartier Latin: its most valuable treasures are preserved in the Cluny Musée National du Moyen-Age, including the reconstructed ruins of 2nd-century Gallo-Roman steam baths. At the summit of the hill above the Sorbonne university is the imposing Panthéon, a monument (and mausoleum) of French heroes. Don't miss the exquisite Église St-Etienne-du-Mont next door, where the relics of the city's patron Saint Geneviève are displayed. Follow the Rue Descartes to the Rue Mouffetard for a *café crème* on one of the oldest market streets in Paris. If the sun's still shining, visit the Gallo-Roman Arènes de Lutèce.

Alternative: A different look at the Quartier Latin (Old Paris) can include a visit to the sleek Institute du Monde Arabe, then a relaxing afternoon at the authentic steam baths and tearoom of the nearby Mosquée de Paris.

Royal Paris

Begin at the Place de la Concorde, where an Egyptian obelisk replaces the guillotine where Louis XVI and Marie-Antoinette met their bloody fate during the French Revolution, then escape the traffic in the formal Jardin des Tuileries, which once belonged to the 16th-century Tuileries Palace, destroyed during the Paris Commune of 1871. Pass through the small Arc du Carrousel to the modern glass pyramid that serves as the main entrance to the Louvre, the world's grandest museum, once a 12th-century fortress. When you've built up an appetite, cross the street to the peaceful gardens of the Palais Royal for lunch at a café beneath the stone arcades. From here take métro Line 1 to station St-Paul. To the south you can find the Hôtel de Sens, home to King Henry IV's feisty ex-wife Queen Marguerite, and one of the few surviving examples of late-medieval architecture. Around the corner on Rue Charlemagne is a preserved section of the city's 12th-century fortifications built by King Philippe-Augustus. Cross the busy Rue St-Antoine to Le Marais and enter the Hôtel de Sully, a fine example of the elegant private mansions built here by aristocrats in the early 17th century. Pass through the gardens to the doorway on the right, which leads to the lovely symmetrical town houses of the Place des Vosges, designed by King Henry IV. Many of the old aristocratic mansions in Le Marais have been turned into museums, including the Musée Carnavalet and the Musée Picasso.

Power-Shopping Paris

Get an early start to avoid crowds at Au Printemps and Galeries-Lafayette, two of the city's grandest historic department stores conveniently side by side behind the Opéra Garnier. Refuel at the Place

LOGISTICS AND TIPS

Save time and money with a Paris Museum Pass. Some museums have reduced fees on Sunday and on extended-hour days if you go in the evening.

Keep closing days in mind. Most museums are closed one day a week, on Monday for municipal Museums and the Musée d'Orsay, and Tuesday for national museums such as the Louvre.

de la Madeleine, where gourmet food boutiques such as Hédiard and Fauchon offer light deli foods for shoppers on the move. If the luxury boutiques on the Rue Royale aren't rich enough for you, head down the Rue du Faubourg St-Honoré and the Avenue Montaigne (via Avenue Matignon), where you pass the exclusive couture houses of Chanel, Dior, Hermès, and Yves St-Laurent. ■TIP➜ If you plan on spending more than €175 in one store, bring your passport to get the détaxe forms for your Value Added Tax rebate. Department stores are closed on Sunday, but open late on Thursday. Most small boutiques are closed Sunday and Monday. Le Marais and the Champs-Élysées are the best bets for shopping on Sunday.

Alternative: For a more genteel shopping experience, head to the Left Bank's chic Bon Marché department store, then work your way through the fashion and home decor boutiques around the Église St-Sulpice and St-Germain-des-Prés. Shops get less expensive between métro Odéon and the Quartier Latin.

HANDS-ON PARIS

Sometimes it's not enough to see the sights, shop the boutiques, and sample the regional delicacies: there is the compulsion to really immerse yourself. Taking part in some of Paris's quintessential experiences will allow you to learn more about French culture, and you'll get to meet and mingle with locals and like-minded travelers, creating a far more enriching trip to Paris, whether it's your first or 40th visit! Below are some experiences that we recommend.

Food
Nothing is more French than fine wine and gourmet cuisine. So why not enjoy them hands-on, with cooking classes to perfect your *magret de canard* (duck breast) or to master the art of the soufflé. There are many options, from full-day courses in a Parisian home (in English) that include a market tour to quick lunch lessons with the locals where everyone dines together afterward. In English, except as noted: **Paule Caillat's Promenades Gourmandes** (☎ 01–48–04–56–84 ⊕ *www.promenadesgourmandes.com*). **Cook'n with Class** (☎ 01–42–55–70–59 ⊕ *www.cooknwithclass.com/*). **Marguerite's Elegant Home Cooking** (☎ 01–42–04–74–00 ⊕ *www.elegantcooking.com*). **La Cuisine** (☎ 01–40–51–78–18 ⊕ *www.lacuisineparis.com*), classes in French and English, overlooking the Seine. **Atéliers des Chefs** (⊕ *www.atelierdeschefs.com*), group classes in French.

Wine
And it's no secret that appreciating your wine is greatly enhanced when you know what you're drinking and where it came from. Wine-tasting classes range from fun and casual lessons in English for beginners to more formal dégustations of the finest vintages by seasoned sommeliers.

There's something to fit all budgets and experience levels. **O-Château** (☎ 01–44–73–97–80, 0–800–801–148 toll-free in France ⊕ *www.o-chateau.com*) does wine-tasting lessons in English, vineyard tours, and Champagne cruises on the Seine. **Legrand Filles & Fils** (☎ 01–42–60–07–12 ⊕ *www.caves-legrand.com*) conducts Tuesday night Soirées Dégustation with a bilingual presentation of carefully chosen wines. **Wine Dinners** (☎ 01–41–83–80–46 ⊕ *www.wine-dinners.com*) is a French group hosted by bilingual François Audouze; it organizes gourmet meals (in Michelin-starred restaurants) with a selection of 10 wines.

21st-Century Salons
Parisian salons—where a select group of connoisseurs gathered in a private home to discuss the artistic, literary, political, and philosophical ideas of the time—flourished in past centuries. They're back, in English, and open to anyone who calls to reserve a place. It's an experience not to be missed, and a great way to meet interesting people. **Jim Haynes** (☎ 01–43–27–17–67) hosts an international crowd for Sunday night dinner: informal "standing room only" affairs in his converted artist atelier. **BuffeTime = Talktime** (☎ 01–43–25–86–55 ⊕ *www.meetup.com/TalkTime/*) is a weekly language gathering hosted in a Quartier Latin home by Michael and Veronique. Guests enjoy a buffet dinner while mingling, with half the evening reserved for French conversation, the other half in another language (usually English). **Une artiste à table** (⊕ *unartistealatable.blogspot.com*) is a private gourmet gathering where participants dine in the company of a local artist to discuss their work in Paris.

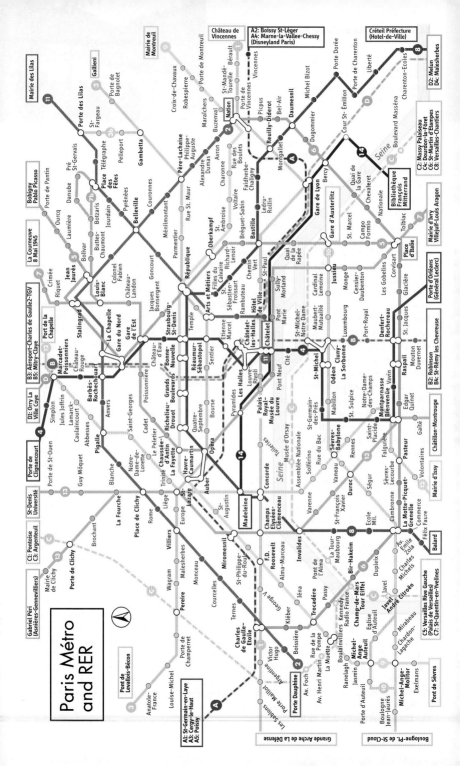

FREE AND ALMOST FREE

It's easy to break the bank in Paris, but those acquainted with the city know where to find the free (or almost free) stuff. Here are some tips.

Free Art

Thanks to the City of Paris's dedication to promoting culture, access to the permanent collections in the city's municipal museums is free, so you can learn about the city's rich history, the characters who contribute to its aura of romance, and the warriors who fought for France's liberation—all without dropping a cent. Setting the example, the **Hôtel de Ville** de Paris (City Hall) in Le Marais regularly runs several expositions at a time, most of which focus on French artists. Past expos have included the "Life of Edith Piaf" and the works of photographers Wally Ronis and Robert Doisneau. The **Maison Européene de la Photographie,** also in Le Marais, is a favorite among flashbulb-poppers and amateur photography buffs alike—and every Wednesday evening, from 5 to 8, this museum opens its doors free of charge. Expositions can cover everything from the history of the camera and the evolution of printing to selections from some of the world's most famous photographers. It's a perfect prelude to cocktail hour. The **Musée Carnavalet**—yup, this is in Le Marais also, near Place des Vosges—puts Paris's history on display with a collection of old signs, relics from bars and cafés, paintings of what the city looked like before it was fully developed (Montmartre was all farmland!), and old keepsakes and letters. It's an excellent place to get a feel for Paris past and present. More free art throughout the year can be found at the **Maison de Balzac,** the **Maison de Victor Hugo, Musée d'Art Moderne de la Ville de Paris,** and the **Petit Palais,** also known as the **Musée des Beaux-Arts de la Ville de Paris.**

Free Music

For free classical music in an ethereal setting, many of Paris's churches host free or almost-free concerts at lunchtime and in the evening. Flyers are posted around the city and outside the churches, or check weekly events listings. The **Église St-Eustache** has free organ recitals every Saturday at 5:30 pm. Also free are *l'Heure Musicale,* medieval music concerts at the **Musée du Moyen-Age** every Friday at 12:30 and Saturday at 4, between October and July. In summer and fall there are free concerts in the city's parks, including the **Jardin des Luxembourg** (classical music), **Parc de la Villette** (world music and jazz), and the **Parc Floral** in the Bois de Vincennes (classical and jazz). During **Paris Plage,** in late summer, there are free nightly pop and rock concerts on the quays of the Seine. When the weather's nice you're also likely to find would-be, wannabe, and even a few real musicians along the *quai* of the **Canal St-Martin,** or in the **Place des Vosges,** guitars in hand for spontaneous song.

Free Serenity

If the hustle and bustle of Paris is getting to you, opt for a free session of **Qi gong** at the **Parc des Buttes-Chaumont** in the 19e arrondissement. Every day at 9 am instructor Thoi Tin Cau leads classes, free of charge, at 7 rue Botzaris, métro Botzaris, on the patch of grass in the middle of the park. Parisians also like to recharge their batteries with an afternoon **catnap** in one of the handy reclined chairs scattered throughout the city's gardens. This is the cheapest option for relaxation, reading, and postcard writing—just make sure your possessions are secure if you're actually going to grab some shut-eye. Perennial favorites for parking yourself, or weary companions, are the **Jardin des**

Luxembourg and the **Jardin du Tuileries,** but one of the most serene venues, buffered from the traffic by the arcaded shops, is the garden at the **Palais Royal,** not far from the Louvre. Any perch along the Seine will also do in a pinch if the busy streets are getting to you: it's amazing how serene a spot by the water can be, so close to the frenetic workings of the city, especially if you find yourself on the incomparably charming **Ile de la Cité.**

Cheap Souvenirs

Perfect for yourself or friends back home, what souvenir retails for just about €0.10 each? The postcard, of course. Go retro (snail mail!) and send some quintessential scenery home with a "J'aime Paris" scribbled on the back, or just bring back a little packet of choice images. For the best prices, check out the news kiosks along Rue de Rivoli and the Grands Boulevards, or visit the bookstore **Mona Lisait** (✉ *9 rue St-Martin, 4e* ☎ *01–42–74–03–02*). For more unusual cards, visit the **Librairie Serge Plantureux** (✉ *4 Galerie Vivienne, 2e* ☎ *01–53–29–92–00*), north of the Palais Royal. **Mondial Art** (✉ *10 rue St-André des Arts, 6e* ☎ *01–55–42–19–00*) has racks of stylish choices, including cards quoting famous French authors. Keep an eye out for vintage postcards, too, sold by the *bouquinistes* along the Seine and by collectors inside Passage des Panoramas. You can buy stamps at any *tabac* as well as at post offices.

(Almost) Free Sightseeing Tours

Imagine passing the Louvre as part of your daily commute. Some of the city's public bus routes are fantastically scenic; hop on the right one and you can get a great tour for just €1.80—sans squawking commentary. The **No. 29** route reaches from the Gare St-Lazare, past the Opéra Garnier, to the heart of Le Marais, crossing the Place des Vosges before ending up at the Bastille. This is one of the few lines that runs primarily on small streets, not major arteries. Hop the **No. 69** bus at the Champ de Mars (by the Tour Eiffel) and ride through parts of the Quartier Latin, across the bridge to the Rive Droite near the Louvre, and on to the Bastille. The **No. 72** bus follows the Seine from the Hôtel de Ville west past the Louvre and most of the big-name Rive Droite sights, also giving you views of the Rive Gauche, including the Tour Eiffel. Bus **No. 73** is the only line that goes along the Avenue des Champs-Élysées, from the Arc de Triomphe through the Place de la Condorde and ending at Musée d'Orsay. You can also take free (though tips are appreciated) walking tours with the enthusiastic guides from **Sandemans** "New Europe Tours" (⊕ *www.newparistours.com*) or with City Free Tour (⊕ *www.cityfreetour.com*).

Free Wine (Tastings)

Here's a tip for getting tipsy: wine stores sometimes offer free or inexpensive wine tastings, generally on the weekends. Check out **La Derniere Goutte** (✉ *6 rue de Bourbon le Château, 6e* ☎ *01–46–29–11–62*) and the prestigious **Caves Taillevent** (✉ *199 rue du Faubourg St-Honore, 8e* ☎ *01–45–61–14–09*) on Saturday afternoons. **La Cave du Panthéon** (✉ *174 rue Saint-Jacques, 5e* ☎ *01–46–33–90–35*), touted for its conviviality, is another destination where wine lovers congregate on Saturday afternoons to learn about—and indulge in—their favorite beverage. If you're lucky, the winemaker hailing from the featured winery of the day may be among those taking part in the tasting.

PARIS MUSEUMS, AN OVERVIEW

There's no shortage of museums in Paris, so it's a good idea to make a plan. This overview includes all the museums listed elsewhere in the book; check the index for full listings.

Major Museums

Ambitious art goers will focus on the Big Three—the **Louvre**, the **Musée d'Orsay**, and **Centre Georges Pompidou**. The Louvre's collection spans from about 7000 BC until 1848, and has its own Big Three: the *Mona Lisa*, the *Venus de Milo*, and *Winged Victory*. The d'Orsay's collection picks up where the Louvre's leaves off, and continues until 1914. The Pompidou has art from the early 20th century to the present.

One-Man Shows

Three major must-sees are **Musée Rodin**, with its lovely sculpture garden; **Musée Picasso** (closed for renovations until mid 2013); and **Musée Marmottan Monet**. There's also **Musée Delacroix, Musée Gustave Moreau, Musée National Jean-Jacques Henner, Musée Zadkine,** and **Musée Maillol**. Dalí enthusiasts will appreciate **Espace Salvador Dalí,** while French chanson fans shouldn't miss the tiny **Edith Piaf Museum**.

House Museums

A house museum is two treats in one: the art and the house itself. **Maison de Victor Hugo** and **Maison de Balzac** are the former homes of writers. **Musée Jacquemart-André** has an intriguing collection of Italian art, and **Musée Nissim de Camondo** has decorative art, mostly from the 18th century. **Musée de la Vie Romantique,** dedicated to the novelist George Sand, was the elegant town house of Dutch-born painter Ary Scheffer, and **Musée Cognacq-Jay** was the home of Ernest Cognacq, founder of the now closed *La Samaritaine* department store. The **Palais Galliera** opens for exhibits on costume and clothing design. The small **Maison de Baccarat** has some Baccarat masterpieces in a Philippe Starck–designed, surrealist building.

Contemporary Art

Excellent venues for modern art include the **Palais de Tokyo** and **Musée d'Art Moderne de la Ville de Paris**. There's also **Fondation Cartier pour l'art contemporain** for emerging artists' work, and **La Maison Rouge,** which shows private collections. The **Pinacothèque de Paris** is a private museum dedicated solely to temporary exhibits, while **Halle St. Pierre** has exhibits of outsider and folk art. **Le 104** is an offbeat art space with artist studios, boutiques, and performance spaces.

French History

Musée National du Moyen-Age has the well-known tapestry *Lady and the Unicorn*. **Musée d'Art et d'Histoire du Judaïsme** documents Jewish history in France. For Parisian history, don't miss **Musée Carnevalet**. Montmartre has its own museum, **Musée de Montmartre**. The new **Cité de l'Architecture et du Patrimoine** presents a history of French architecture, and maritime history is the subject of the **Musée de la Marine** (both are in the Palais Chaillot). The **Musée de la Légion d'Honneur** is an exploration of French and foreign military decoration, and the **Musée de l'Armée,** at the Hotel des Invalides, is a phenomenal military museum. There's also the **Musée Jean-Moulin** in the Jardin Atlantique, focusing on the life of the famous leader of the French Resistance. Architecture buffs might appreciate Google's new permanent exhibit at the Pavillon de l'Arsenal, which traces the entire structural history of the city, including its future.

Best for Kids

Kids love the hands-on science and technology displays at **Cité des Sciences et de l'Industrie** and the **Musée de la Musique**, both in Parc de la Villette. The **Grande Galerie de l'Evolution** and **Musée de la Chasse et de la Nature** have stuffed animals in natural surroundings. The **Palais de la Découverte**, a planetarium, and **Musée Grévin**, a wax museum, are perennial faves. The fabulous **Musée des Art et Metiers** has neat scientific instruments and inventions. For doll lovers, there's the **Musée de la Poupée**. For chocolate lovers of all ages, check out **Chocostory**, the museum of chocolate.

Photography and Design

For a mix of photographs from different artists, your best bet is the **Maison Européenne de la Photographie**. Fondation Henri Cartier-Bresson features works by the well-known French photographer in a building that was also his atelier. The **Musée du Jeu de Paume**, in the Tuileries, showcases modern photography exhibits. For modern design, the **Fondation Le Corbusier** is well worth the trip to the western edge of the city. The **Fondation Pierre Bergé-Yves Saint Laurent** is the designer's atelier as well as an archive and gallery of his work. For those interested in urban planning, visit the free **Pavillion de l'Arsenal** to see the miniature models of Paris neighborhoods. The **Musée des Arts Decoratifs** inside **Les Arts Décoratifs** (which includes **Musée de la Publicité** and **Musée de la Mode**) has one of the world's greatest decorative-art collections.

African, Asian, and Islamic Art

There are two places in town to see Asian art: the **Musée Guimet** is not to be missed, and the **Musée Cernuschi** is a small house museum that holds the personal Asian art collection of Enrico Cernuschi. For Arab and Islamic art and architecture, visit the impressive **Institut du Monde Arabe**, and for African art, try **Musée Dapper**. The **Musée du Quai Branly** features African, Asian, and Oceanic art.

Etc.

Some museums aren't easily classified. The **Musée de l'Erotisme** is a seven-story building dedicated to everything associated with erotic fantasy, while the **Manufacture des Gobelins** traces the history of weaving and tapestry. **Maison de Radio France** presents the history of French radio. The **Musée du Vin** is a history of wine making that also has wine tastings; the **Musée du Parfum rue Scribe** is dedicated to the art of perfume. **La Musée de la Prefecture de Police** is, you guessed it, a museum of the Paris police. The **Musée de l'Orangerie** is a stunning setting for Monet's *Water Lilies*.

Art Galleries

You can find several contemporary-art galleries near the Centre Georges Pompidou, the Musée Picasso, and the Bastille Opéra. The city's hottest avant-garde art scene is on and around the Rue Vieille du Temple in the north Marais. Around St-Germain and the Place des Vosges the galleries are more traditional; works by old masters and established modern artists dominate the galleries around Rue du Faubourg St-Honoré and Avenue Matignon. Carré Rive Gauche, around Rue du Bac in St-Germain, has dozens of art and antiques galleries on its narrow streets.

The **Association des Galeries** (⊕ *www.associationdesgaleries.org*) lists exhibits in more than 100 galleries through the city. **Paris-art.com** (⊕ *www.paris-art.com*) focuses on contemporary art, with reviews, exhibition calendars, and interviews, in French only.

MAKING THE MOST OF YOUR EUROS

Paris has never been cheap, and we know you're going to be looking for some tips on how not to break the bank. Who better to ask than travelers on www.Fodors.com Travel Talk forums?

Get Around Wisely

■TIP➜ Paris is definitely a walking city—take the opportunity to learn the word flâneur (one who strolls)—but when your feet get tired, take the métro or bus instead of a taxi.

"We bought a book at a newspaper stand that had all of the bus routes in it. Very easy to use and it saved us so much time. We also bought the carnet of tickets at metro station. Metro is also great but we wanted to see things outside." —Tdudette

Think with Your Stomach

■TIP➜ There are so many ways to eat well in Paris but still save money: eat picnics, spend your restaurant euros at lunch instead of dinner, have your latté at the counter instead of at a table. You'll save money and probably have a more authentic Parisian experience, too.

"Never buy bottle water at a restaurant: ask for tap water. Lots of savings there." —4totravel

"I would second the suggestion to 'reste au comptoir' in a cafe, vs. sitting at a table. You will save a few coins, and it's a great experience." —petitepois

"There are a number of sandwich shops that sell wonderful sandwiches (goat cheese, tomato, lettuce, and a variety of meats) for takeout for about 4 euros. Pick one up and have a picnic in the park." —FrankS

"I think my big meals of the day will be late lunches and the plat du jour, but most certainly I will go to a couple of nice dinners, within reason." —mahya

■TIP➜ Save money on lodging. Why not rent an apartment instead of shelling out large sums on a hotel? The built-in perk is the money you'll save if you use the kitchen—even just for breakfast. And if you do opt for a hotel, choose your neighborhood with budget in mind. *(See the "Apartment rentals" feature in the Where to Stay chapter.)*

"I was in Paris last year and had a short-term apartment rental. For us, it was the absolute perfect choice. Having a mini-kitchen and Internet access in the apartment was fantastic. There was a small grocery store only a half block away, so we were able to save money by making our own breakfasts, picnic lunches, and some dinners." —likembrave

"People will get much more for their money by staying away from the exact center of the city. It is all very well to want to see the Eiffel Tower from your hotel window or to be a 5-minute walk from the Louvre or Notre-Dame, but that adds a lot of money to the travel expenses." —kerouac

■TIP➜ Note that the jury's still out on whether a Museum Pass will save you money—but everyone agrees it'll save you time because with it, you don't have to wait in lines.

"A two-day pass will cost you 30€. If you plan on visiting more than 3 or 4 places in the two days, you will break even. Even if you don't break even, (in my opinion) the advantage is you get to skip the long lines." —Dejais

THE SEINE

No matter how you approach Paris—historically, geographically, or emotionally—the Seine flows through its heart, dividing the City of Light into two banks, the *Rive Droite* (Right Bank) and the *Rive Gauche* (Left Bank).

The Seine has long been used as a means for transportation and commerce and although there are no longer any factories along its banks, all manner of boats still ply the water. You'll see tugboats, fire and police boats, the occasional bobbing houseboat, and many kinds of tour boats; it might sound hokey, but there's really no better introduction to the City of Light than a boat cruise, and there are several options, depending on whether you want commentary on the sights or not. Many of the city's most famous attractions can be seen from the river, and are especially spectacular at dusk, as those celebrated lights of Paris glint against the sky.

FROM ILE DES CYGNES TO THE LOUVRE

Musée d'Orsay clock

Petit Palais

Pont de l'Alma

Grand Palais

Assemblée Nationale

Pont Alexandre III

Bir Hakeim Bridge

Eiffel Tower

Ile des Cygnes

The **Zouave of the Pont de l'Alma**, sole survivor of the bridge's four original stone soldiers, is used by Parisians to judge water levels.

Whether you hop on a boat cruise or stroll the quays at your own pace, the Seine comes alive when you get off the busy streets of Paris. At the western edge of the city on the **Ile des Cygnes** (literally the Isle of Swans), a small version of the Statue of Liberty stands guard. Auguste Bartholdi designed the original statue, given as a gift from France to America in 1886, and in 1889 a group of Americans living in Paris installed this ¼ scale bronze replica—it's 37 feet, 8 inches tall.

You can get to the Ile des Cygnes via the **Bir Hakeim** bridge named for the 1942 Free French battle in Libya—whose lacy architecture horizontally echoes the nearby **Eiffel Tower**. You might recognize the view of the bridge from the movie *Last Tango in Paris.*

As you make your way downstream you can drool in envy at the houseboats docked near the bronze lamp–lined Pont Alexandre III. No other bridge over the Seine epitomizes the fin-de-siècle frivolity of the Belle Epoque: It seems as much created of cake frosting and sugar sculptures as of stone and iron, and makes quite the backdrop for fashion shoots and weddings. The elaborate decorations include Art Nouveau lamps, cherubs, nymphs, and winged horses at either end. The bridge was built, like the Grand Palais and Petit Palais nearby, for the 1900 World's Fair.

Along the banks of the Seine · *Bouquinistes*

Petit Palais

Place de
la Concorde

Jardin des
Tuileries

Assemblée
Nationale

Louvre

Musée d'Orsay

The average depth of the
Seine within Paris city limits
is 8 m (about 26 feet).

Past the dome of the is the 18th-century neoclassical façade of the **Assemblée Nationale**, the palace that houses the French Parliament. Across the river stands the **Place de la Concorde.** Also look for the great railway station clocks of the Musée d'Orsay that once allowed writer Anaïs Nin to coordinate her lovers' visits to her houseboat, moored below the Tuileries. The palatial **Louvre** museum, on the Right Bank, seems to go on and on as you continue up the Seine.

PERFECT PICNIC PLACES

Paris abounds with romantic spots to pause for a picnic or a bottle of wine, but the Seine has some of the best.

Try scouting out a place on the point of Ile St-Louis; at sunset you can watch the sun slip beneath receding arches of stone bridges.

The long, low quays of the Left Bank, with its public sculpture work, are perfect for an alfresco lunch.

FROM PONT DES ARTS TO JARDIN DES PLANTES

At the water's edge.

Pont des Arts

Pont Neuf

Châtelet Theatres

Hotel de Ville

Institut de France

Ile de la Cité

Conciergerie

Notre-Dame

The Institut de France

Parisians love to linger on the elegant **Pont des Arts** footbridge that streches between the palatial Louvre museum and the Institut de France. Napoléon commissioned the original cast-iron bridge with nine arches; it was rebuilt in 1984 with seven arches.

Five carved stone arches of the **Pont Neuf**—the name means "new bridge" but it actually dates from 1605 and is the oldest bridge in Paris—connect the Left Bank to the Ile de la Cité. Another seven arches connect the Ile and the Right Bank. The pale gray curving balustrades include a row of stone heads; some say they're caricatures of King Henry IV's ministers, glaring down at the river.

On the Right Bank at the end of the Ile de la Cité is the **Hôtel de Ville (City Hall)**—this area was once the main port of Paris, crowded with boats delivering everything from wood and produce to visitors and slaves.

Medieval turrets rise up from **Ile de la Cité,** part of the original royal palace; the section facing the Right Bank includes the **Conciergerie**, where Marie Antoinette was imprisoned in 1793 before her execution.

PARIS PLAGE

Paris Plage, literally Paris Beach, is Mayor Bertrand Delanoë's summer gift to Parisians and visitors. In August the roads along the Seine are closed, tons of sand are brought in and decorated with palm trees, and a slew of activities are organized, from free early-morning yoga classes to evening samba and swimming (not in the Seine, but in the fabulous Josephine Baker swimming pool). Going topless is discouraged, but hammocks, kids' playgrounds, rock-climbing, and cafés keep everyone entertained.

View of the Seine and the Pont des Arts   Paris Plage

Notre-Dame

Also on the Ile de la Cité is the cathedral of **Notre-Dame,** a stunning sight from the water. From the side it looks almost like a great boat sailing down the Seine.

As you pass the end of the island, you'll notice a small grated window: this is the evocative Deportation Memorial.

Next to the Ile de la Cite is the lovely residential **Ile St-Louis**; keep an eye out for the "proper" depth measuring stick on Ile St-Louis, near the Tour d'Argent restaurant.

Sightseeing boats turn near the public sculpture garden at the **Jardin des Plantes**, where you'll get a view of the huge national library, **Bibliothèque François Mitterrand**—the four towers look like opened books. Moored in the Seine near the bibliothèque is the Josephine Baker swimming pool with its retractable roof. Paris used to have several floating pools, including the elaborate Piscine Deligny, which was used in the Paris Olympics in 1924; it inexplicably sank in 1993.

Ile St-Louis

Jardin des Plantes

Bibliothéque Francois Mitterand

PLANNING A BOAT TOUR ON THE SEINE

■ Most boat tours last about an hour; in the winter, even the interior of the boats can be cool, so take an extra scarf or sweater.

■ It never hurts to book ahead since schedules vary with the season and the (unpredictable) height and mood of the Seine.

■ As you float along, consider that Parisians used similar boats as a form of public transportation until the 1930s. Not really like Venice; more like the Staten Island ferry.

■ For optimal Seine enjoyment, combine a boat tour with a stroll—walk around Ile St-Louis, stroll along the Left Bank quays near the Pont Neuf, or start at the quay below the Louvre and walk to the Eiffel Tower, past the fabulous private houseboats.

WHICH BOAT IS FOR YOU?

If you want... lots of information	☎ 01-42-25-96-10 ⊕ www.bateaux-mouches.fr ✉ €11 Ⓜ Alma-Marceau	
	The massive, double-decker **Bateaux Mouches**, literally "fly boats," offer prerecorded commentary in seven languages.	Departs from the Pont de l'Alma (Right Bank) daily April to September: every 20, 30, or 45 min., from 10:15 AM to 11 PM; daily: October through March approximately every hour from 11 AM to 9 PM.
If you want... to do your own thing	☎ 08-25-05-01-01 ⊕ www.batobus.com ✉ €15, €18 *for 2 consecutive days*	
	The commentary-free **Batobus** boat-bus service allows you to hop on and off at any of the eight stops along the river. (Note: there's no service early January through early February.)	Departs from 8 locations: Eiffel Tower, Champs Elysées, Musée d'Orsay, Louvre, St. Germain-des-Pres, Notre-Dame, Hotel de Ville, and Jardin des Plantes.
If you want... to impress a date or client	☎ 01-44-54-14-70 ⊕ www.yachtsdeparis.fr ✉ €198–249 *for dinner cruise* Ⓜ Bastille	
	The **Yachts de Paris** specialize in gorgeous boats—expensive, yes, but glamorous as all get-out, with surprisingly good meals.	Dinner cruises leave from Port Henri IV (near Bastille).
If you want... the Seine, with music	☎ 01-43-54-50-04 ⊕ www.calife.com ✉ €49 *and up for dinner cruise* Ⓜ Louvre-Rivoli	
	Le Calife is the Aladdin's lamp of the Seine, moored across from the Louvre. Jazz, piano music, and evenings devoted to French song makes this a quirky and charming choice.	Departs from the Quai Malaquais, opposite the Louvre and just west of the Pont des Arts footbridge.

The Islands

ILE ST-LOUIS AND ILE DE LA CITÉ

WORD OF MOUTH

"On your first day, consider Ile de la Cité, the epicenter of Paris. It gives you . . . views of Notre-Dame, walks along the banks of the Seine, peeks of 'Old Paris' with narrow winding streets, and access to the left bank."

—Renaud

GETTING ORIENTED

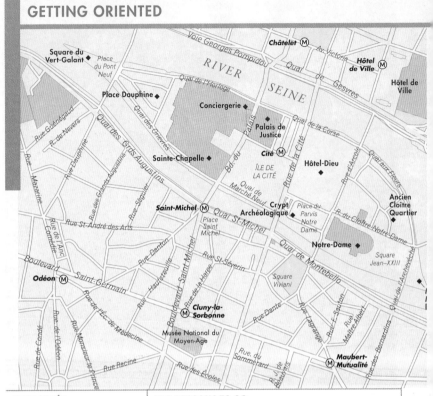

BEST CAFÉS

La Charlotte de l'Isle. Chocolate sculptures and musical events for children give this cozy tea house a whimsical feel. The lusciously thick hot chocolate is the real reason to stop in for a break. ⊠ *24 rue St-Louis-en-l'Ile, Ile St-Louis* ☎ *01–43–54–25–83* ⊘ *2–7:30 pm, Thurs.–Sun.* Ⓜ *Pont Marie.*

Le Saint Régis. This is the most low-key of the cafés huddled on this touristy corner, and attracts more locals than the others. ⊠ *6 rue Jean de Bellay* ☎ *01–43–54–59–41* Ⓜ *Pont Marie.*

TOP REASONS TO GO

Notre-Dame. This towering Gothic cathedral has welcomed visitors to Paris for centuries. Gaze at its famed rose windows, climb the towers to mingle with the gargoyles, or wander around back to contemplate the awe-inspiring architecture from Square Jean-XXIII. At the end of the plaza in front of the cathedral, down the stairs, is the interesting Crypte Archéologique, a museum that allows a look at the city's Roman ruins.

Sainte-Chapelle. Visit on a sunny day to best appreciate the exquisite stained glass in this 13th-century chapel built for King Louis IX.

Strolling the islands. Start with the oldest bridge in Paris, the Pont Neuf, incongruously called the "new bridge," and give a nod to the statue of Henry IV, who once proudly said, "I make love, I make war, and I build." From here, cross to Place Dauphine and make your way to the gorgeous Ile St-Louis, one of the city's most exclusive enclaves.

2

ICE CREAM VS. GELATO

Berthillon. Cafés all over sell this haute couture brand of ice cream, but the headquarters of Berthillon is *the* place to come for this amazing treat. It features more than 30 flavors that change with the seasons, including mouth-puckering *cassis* (black currant) in summer and nutty *marron glacé* (candied chestnut) in winter. Expect to wait in line. The shop and adjacent tea salon is open Wednesday to Sunday 10–8 but closed during the peak summer season, from July 20 to September 1. ⊠ *31 rue St-Louis-en-l'île, Ile St-Louis* ☎ *01-43-54-31-61.*

Amorino. Also popping up all over Paris—there were 22 outlets at this writing—and winning converts faster than you can finish a double scoop, is the Amorino chain of gelaterias. Popular flavors include rich *Bacio* (dark chocolate and hazelnuts) and *spécialités* such as amaretto laced with crunchy biscuits and almonds. The shop is open every day, noon to midnight. ⊠ *47 rue St-Louis-en-l'île, Ile St-Louis* ☎ *01-44-07-48-08.*

MAKING THE MOST OF YOUR TIME

This little area of Paris is easily walkable and packed with sights and stunning views, so give yourself as much time as possible to explore. With Notre-Dame, the Conciergerie, and Sainte-Chapelle, you could spend a day wandering, but the islands are easily combined with St-Germain. The Rue de Buci is a perfect place to pick up a picnic lunch to enjoy at the leafy Square du Vert-Galant at the tip of Ile de la Cité. If you have limited time in the area, just make sure you see Notre-Dame and go for a stroll.

GETTING HERE

Ile de la Cité and Ile St-Louis are in the 1er and 4e arrondissements (the Boulevard du Palais is the dividing line between the 1er and 4e arrondissements on Ile de la Cité). If you're too far away to get here on foot, take the métro to St-Michel station or La Cité.

Sightseeing
★★★★
Dining
★★
Lodging
★★★
Shopping
★★
Nightlife
★

At the heart of Paris, linked to the banks of the Seine by a series of bridges, are two small islands: Ile St-Louis and Ile de la Cité. They're the perfect places to begin a visit to Paris, with picture-perfect views all around. The Ile de la Cité is anchored by mighty Notre-Dame; farther east lies the exclusive Ile St-Louis, dotted with charming hotels, cozy restaurants, and small shops.

At the western tip of Ile de la Cité is regal **Place Dauphine,** one of Paris's oldest squares. The impressive Palais de Justice (courthouse) sits between **Sainte-Chapelle,** the exquisite medieval chapel of saintly King Louis IX, and the **Conciergerie,** the prison where Marie-Antoinette and other bluebloods awaited their slice of history at the guillotine.

The Gothic powerhouse that is **Notre-Dame** originally loomed over a medieval huddle of buildings that were later ordered razed by Baron Georges-Eugène Haussmann, the 19th-century urban planner who transformed Paris into the city we see today. In front of the cathedral is now the Place du Parvis, also known as *kilomètre zéro,* the point from which all roads in France are measured. On the north side of the square is the **Hôtel-Dieu** (roughly translated as "general hospital"), immortalized by Balzac as the squalid last stop for the city's most unfortunate, but which today houses a modern hospital. Just behind the cathedral lies rue du Cloître-Notre-Dame, which cuts through the **Ancien Cloître Quartier,** on whose narrow streets you can imagine the medieval quarter as it once was, densely packed and teeming with activity. At 9–11 quai aux Fleurs, a plaque commemorates the abode that was the setting of the tragic, 12th-century love affair between the philosopher Peter Abélard and his young conquest, Héloïse.

At the farthest eastern tip of Ile de la Cité is the **Mémorial des Martyrs de la Déportation,** all but hidden in a pocket-size park. A set of stairs leads down to the impressive and moving memorial to the more than 200,000 French citizens who died in Nazi concentration camps.

The nearby Pont St-Louis, which seems to be always occupied by an accordion player, leads to the Ile St-Louis, one of the city's best places to wander. There are no cultural hot spots, just a few streets that may make you think you've stumbled into a village, albeit an unusually tony one. Small hotels, restaurants, art galleries, and shops selling everything from cheese to pâté to silk scarves line the main drag, Rue St-Louis-en-L'Ile. There

> ### MONSIEUR GUILLOTIN
>
> Beheading was a popular means of punishment long before the French Revolution, but it was Dr. Joseph-Ignace Guillotin who suggested that there was a more humane way of effecting decapitation than by use of a sword or ax. Not surprisingly, Dr. Guillotin's descendants changed their surname.

were once two islands here, the Ile Notre-Dame and the Ile aux Vaches ("Cow Island," a former grazing pasture), both owned by the Church. Speculators bought the islands, joined them, and sold the plots to builders who created what is today some of the city's most elegant and expensive real estate. Baroque architect Louis Le Vau (who later worked on Versailles) designed fabulous private homes for aristocrats, including the majestic mansions Hôtel Lambert and the Hôtel de Lauzun on the lovely quai d'Anjou.

TOP ATTRACTIONS

Updated by
Bryan Pirolli

Conciergerie. Much of Ile de la Cité's medieval buildings fell victim to wunderkind planner Baron Haussmann's ambitious rebuilding program of the 1860s. Among the rare survivors are the jewel-like Sainte-Chapelle, a vision of shimmering stained glass, and the Conciergerie, the former prison where Marie-Antoinette and other victims of the French Revolution spent their last days.

Built by Philip IV in the 13th and 14th centuries, the Conciergerie was part of the original palace of the kings of France, before the royals moved into the Louvre around 1364; in 1391, it became a prison. During the French Revolution, Marie-Antoinette spent her final 76 days here before her date with the guillotine. There is a re-creation of the doomed queen's sad little cell—and others that are far smaller—with wax figures awaiting their fate behind bars. You can read the names of all the executed, and read letters penned by some of Paris's famous revolutionaries. The chapel's stained glass is emblazoned with the initials M. A.; it was commissioned after the queen's death by her daughter. Outside, in the courtyard, victims of the Terror spent their final days playing piquet, writing letters to loved ones, washing clothes, and waiting for the dreaded climb up the staircase to the Chamber of the Revolutionary Council to hear its final verdict. The building takes its name from the palace's *concierge*, or high-level keeper of the palace. There are free guided tours in French most days at 11 and 3. ⊠ *2 bd. du Palais* ☎ *01–53–40–60–80* ⊕ *www.conciergerie.monuments-nationaux. fr* 🎫 *€7, joint ticket with Sainte-Chapelle €11 or €12.50 during temporary exhibitions* ⊙ *Daily 9:30–6* Ⓜ *Cité.*

Mémorial des Martyrs de la Déportation (*Memorial of the Deportation*). On the eastern tip of the Ile de la Cité lies this extraordinary monument to the more than 200,000 French men, women, and children who died in Nazi concentration camps during World War II. The evocative memorial, inaugurated by Charles de Gaulle in 1962, was intentionally designed to be claustrophobic; a light at the end of the long, narrow tunnel that is the main part of the installation symbolizes hope. The walls are studded with 200,000 pieces of quartz crystal.

> **THE FLOWER MARKET**
>
> Every day of the week except Monday, you can find the flower market facing the entrance to the imposing Palais de Justice (courthouse) on Boulevard du Palais. It's a fragrant detour from the Ile de la Cité, and the Guimard-designed métro entrance to the Cité métro station seems to blend with the greenery on display. On Sunday the place is chirping with birds and other small pets for sale.

🖃 *Free* 🕑 *Mar.–Oct., daily 10–noon and 2–7; Nov.–Feb., daily 10–noon and 2–5* Ⓜ *Maubert Mutualité.*

Fodor'sChoice **Notre-Dame**
★   *See the highlighted listing in this chapter.*

Fodor'sChoice **Sainte-Chapelle**
★   *See the highlighted listing in this chapter.*

WORTH NOTING

Fodor'sChoice **Ancien Cloître Quartier.** Hidden in the shadows of Notre-Dame is this
★   magical, often-overlooked tangle of medieval streets. Through the years lucky folk, including Ludwig Bemelmans (who created the beloved *Madeleine* books) and the Aga Khan have called this area home, but back in the Middle Ages this was the domain of cathedral seminary students. One of them was the celebrated Peter Abélard (1079–1142)— philosopher, questioner of the faith, and renowned declaimer of love poems. Abélard boarded with Notre-Dame's clergyman, Fulbert, whose 17-year-old niece, Héloïse, was seduced by the compelling Abélard, 39 years her senior. She became pregnant and the vengeful clergyman had Abélard castrated; amazingly, he survived and fled to a monastery, while Héloïse took refuge in a nunnery. The poetic, passionate letters between the two cemented their fame as thwarted lovers, and their story inspired a devoted following during the romantic 19th century. They still draw admirers to the Père Lachaise Cemetery, where they're interred *ensemble*. The clergyman's house at 10 rue Chanoinesse was redone in 1849; a plaque at the back of the building at 9–11 quai aux Fleurs commemorates the lovers. ⊠ *Rue du Cloître-Notre-Dame north to Quai des Fleurs* Ⓜ *Cité.*

Palais de Justice. The courthouse complex was built in the 1860s by Baron Haussmann in his characteristically weighty neoclassical style, on the site of the former royal palace of St-Louis that later housed Parliament until the French Revolution. The complex is recognizable from afar with the tower of Sainte-Chapelle, which is inside the

SAINTE-CHAPELLE

✉ *4 bd. du Palais*
☎ *01–53–40–60–97*
🌐 *www.sainte-chapelle.
monuments-nationaux.fr*
🎟 *€8, joint ticket with Conciergerie €11* ⏱ *Mar.–Oct.,
daily 9:30–6; Nov.–Feb., daily
9–5* Ⓜ *Cité.*

2

TIPS

■ To avoid waiting in killer
lines, plan your visit for a
weekday morning, the earlier
the better, though be aware
that sunset is the best time to
see the rose window.

■ Come on a sunny day to
appreciate the full effect of
the light streaming in through
all that beautiful stained glass.

■ You can buy a joint ticket
with the Conciergerie; buy the
ticket there, though, where
the lines are shorter, though
you'll still have to go through
a longish metal detector line
to get into Sainte-Chapelle.

■ The chapel is especially
magical during the regular
concerts held here; call for the
schedule.

■ Free guided tours in English
are offered most days at 2:30.
Call ahead to confirm.

Built by the obsessively pious Louis IX (1226–70), this
Gothic jewel is home to the oldest stained-glass windows in Paris. The chapel was constructed over three
years, at phenomenal expense, to house the king's
collection of relics acquired from the impoverished
emperor of Constantinople. These included Christ's
Crown of Thorns, fragments of the Cross, and drops of
Christ's blood—though even in Louis's time these were
considered of questionable authenticity. Some of the
relics have survived and can be seen in the treasury of
Notre-Dame, but most were lost during the Revolution.

HIGHLIGHTS

The upper chapel is where the famed beauty of Sainte-
Chapelle comes alive: 6,458 square feet of stained
glass is delicately supported by painted stonework
that seems to disappear in the colorful light streaming
through the windows. Deep reds and blues dominate
the background glass, noticeably different from later,
lighter medieval styles such as those comprising Notre-
Dame's rose windows. This chapel is essentially an
enormous magic lantern illuminating the 1,130 figures
from the Bible, to create—as one writer poetically put
it—"the most marvelous colored and moving air ever
held within four walls." You'll no doubt be transfixed
by the stained glass in the upper chapel, but don't miss
the detailed carvings on the columns and the statues of
the apostles. The lowest section of the windows was
restored in the mid-1800s, and a painstaking five-year
renovation should be completed by 2013. The lower
chapel is a bit gloomy and plain, but notice the low,
vaulted ceiling decorated with fleurs-de-lis and cleverly
arranged *L*s for Louis. The dark spiral staircase near
the entrance takes you upstairs.

courthouse complex, peeking out. Black-frocked judges and lawyers can often be spotted taking a cigarette break on the majestic staircase facing rue du Harlay. ⊠ *4 bd. du Palais* Ⓜ *Cité.*

Place Dauphine. The Surrealists loved Place Dauphine, which they called "le sexe de Paris" because of its suggestive V shape. Its origins were much more proper: it was built by Henry IV, who named the square in homage to his successor, called the dauphin, who became Louis XIII when Henry was assassinated. ■TIP→ Snag a table at one of the restaurant terraces here to enjoy one of the best places in Paris to dine en plein air. Ⓜ *Cité.*

Square du Vert-Galant. The equestrian statue of the Vert Galant himself—amorous adventurer Henry IV—keeps a vigilant watch over this leafy square at the western end of the Ile de la Cité while his real head, rediscovered in 2010, sits in a bank vault. The dashing but ruthless Henry, king of France from 1589 until his assassination in 1610, was a stern upholder of the absolute rights of monarchy, and a notorious womanizer. He is probably best remembered for his cynical remark that *"Paris vaut bien une messe"* ("Paris is worth a mass"), a reference to his readiness to renounce Protestantism to gain the throne of predominantly Catholic France. To ease his conscience, he issued the Edict of Nantes in 1598, according French Protestants (almost) equal rights with their Catholic countrymen. The square is a great place to picnic—you can almost dangle your feet in the Seine. ■TIP→ It's also the departure point for the Vedette Pont Neuf tour boats on the Seine (at the bottom of the steps to the right). Ⓜ *Pont Neuf.*

St-Louis-en-L'Ile. You can't miss the unusual lacy spire of this church as you approach the Ile St-Louis; it's the only church on the island and there are no other steeples to compete with it. It was built from 1652 to 1765 to the Baroque designs of architect François Le Vau, brother of the more famous Louis, who designed several mansions nearby—as well as the Palace of Versailles. St-Louis's interior was essentially stripped during the Revolution, as were so many French churches, but look for the odd outdoor iron clock, which dates from 1741. ⊠ *19 bis, rue St-Louis-en-L'Ile, Ile St-Louis* ☎ *01–46–34–11–60* ⊕ *www.saintlouisenlile. catholique.fr* Ⓜ *Pont Marie.*

NOTRE-DAME

Notre-Dame is the symbolic heart of Paris and, for many, of France itself. Napoléon was crowned here, and kings and queens exchanged marriage vows before its altar. There are a few things worth seeing inside the Gothic cathedral, but the real highlights are the exterior architectural details and the unforgettable view of Paris, framed by stone gargoyles, from the top of the south tower.

THE STONE GARGOYLES

Notre-Dame's gargoyles were designed by Eugène Viollet-le-Duc, the architect who oversaw the cathedral's 19th-century renovations. Technically they're chimeras, not gargoyles, as they're purely ornamental; a true "gargoyle" is a carved sculpture that functions as a waterspout.

Begun in 1163, completed in 1345, badly damaged during the Revolution, and restored by the architect Eugène Viollet-le-Duc in the 19th century, Notre-Dame may not be France's oldest or largest cathedral, but in beauty and architectural harmony it has few peers. The front entranceways seem like hands joined in prayer, the sculpted kings on the facade form a noble procession, and the west (front) rose window gleams with what seems like divine light.

The most dramatic approach to Notre-Dame is from the Rive Gauche, crossing at the Pont au Double from quai de Montebello, at the St-Michel métro or RER stop. This bridge will take you to the open square, place du Parvis, in front of the cathedral. (The more direct metro stop is Cité.)

THE WEST (FRONT) FACADE

The three front entrances are, left to right: the Portal of the Virgin, the Portal of the Last Judgment (above), and the Portal of St. Anne, the oldest of the three. Above the three front entrances are the 28 restored statues of the kings of Israel, the Galerie des Rois.

INSIDE THE CATHEDRAL

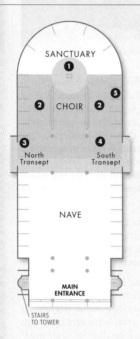

❶ **The Pietà,** behind the choir, represents the Virgin Mary mourning over the dead body of Christ.

❷ **The biblical scenes** on the north and south screens of the choir represent the life of Christ and the apparitions of Christ after the Resurrection.

❸ **The north rose window** is one of the cathedral's original stained-glass panels; at the center is an image of Mary holding a young Jesus.

❹ At the south (right) entrance to the choir, you'll glimpse the haunting 12th-century statue of **Notre-Dame de Paris,** "Our Lady of Paris," the Virgin, for whom the cathedral is named.

❺ **The treasury,** on the south side of the choir, holds a small collection of religious garments, reliquaries, and silver- and gold-plate.

MAKING THE CLIMB A separate entrance, to the left of the front facade if you're facing it, leads to the 387 stone steps of the south tower. These steps take you to the bell of Notre-Dame (as tolled by the fictional Quasimodo). Looking out from the tower, you can see how Paris—like the trunk of a tree developing new rings—has grown outward from the Ile de la Cité. To the north is Montmartre; to the west is the Arc de Triomphe, at the top of the Champs-Elysées; and to the south are the towers of St-Sulpice.

Place du Parvis

Detail of the Gallery of Kings, over the front entrance.

Notre-Dame was one of the first Gothic cathedrals in Europe and one of the first buildings to make use of **flying buttresses**—exterior supports that spread out the weight of the building and roof. At first people thought they looked like scaffolding that the builders forgot to remove. ■TIP→ **The most tranquil place to appreciate the architecture of Notre-Dame is from the lovely garden behind the cathedral, Square Jean-XXIII. By night, take a boat ride on the Seine for the best view—the lights at night are magnificent.**

Place du Parvis is *kilomètre zéro*, the spot from which all distances to and from the city are officially measured. A polished brass circle set in the ground, about 20 yards from the cathedral's main entrance, marks the exact spot.

The Crypt Archéologique (entrance down the stairs in front of the cathedral) is a quick visit but very interesting, especially for kids and archaeology buffs. It gives an "under the city" view of the area, with remains from previous churches that were built on this site, scale models charting the district's development, and artifacts dating from 2,000 years ago.

☎ 01–42–34–56–10
⊕ www.notredame deparis.fr
🎫 Cathedral free. Towers: €8.50. Crypt €4. Treasury €3.
🕐 Cathedral daily 7:45–6:45. Towers Apr.–June and Sept., daily 10 AM–6:30; July and Aug., weekdays 10 AM–6:30, weekends 10 AM–11 PM; Oct.–Mar., daily 10–5:30. Note: towers close early when overcrowded. Treasury Mon.–Fri. 9:30–6 PM. Sat. 9:30–6:30, Sun. 1:30–6:30. Crypt Tues.–Sun. 10–6.

SOMETHING TO PONDER

Do Notre-Dame's hunchback and its gargoyles have anything in common other than bad posture? Quasimodo was created by Victor Hugo in the novel *Notre-Dame de Paris*, published in 1831. The incredible popularity of the book made Parisians finally take notice of the cathedral's state of disrepair and spurred Viollet-le-Duc's renovations. These included the addition of the gargoyles, among other things, and resulted in the structure we see today.

■TIP→ The best time to visit Notre-Dame is early in the morning, when the cathedral is at its brightest and least crowded.

■TIP→ There are free guided tours in English several times a week; check website for times.

Around the Eiffel Tower

WITH INVALIDES

WORD OF MOUTH

"You should visit the Rodin in good weather. The gardens are marvelous, both for the greenery and the sculptures scattered among it."

—Eurocentric

GETTING ORIENTED

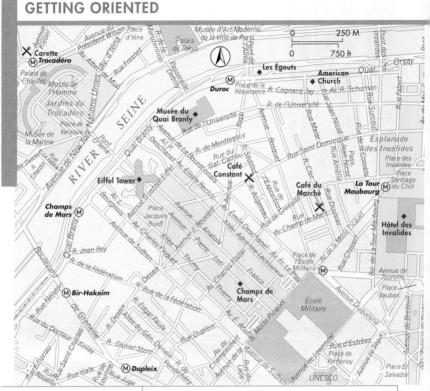

GETTING HERE

This neighborhood covers the 7e arrondissement. The most romantic way to get to the Eiffel Tower is by boat—see the Seine In-Focus section for details. Otherwise, you can head for RER C, station Champs de Mars/ Tour Eiffel. For the best view, get off at the Trocadéro station (métro Line 9 or 6) and make the short walk over the Pont (bridge) d'Iéna to the tower. For the Musée Rodin, get off at Varenne (Line 13). Use this stop, or La Tour Maubourg (Line 8), for Napoléon's Tomb and Hôtel des Invalides.

TOP REASONS TO GO

Eiffel Tower. No question: The ultimate symbol of France is worth a visit at least once in your life.

Musée Rodin. This regal 18th-century *hôtel particulier* (private mansion), once Rodin's workshop, is a must for fans of the master sculptor. The garden makes a perfect setting for Rodin's raw physical sculptures.

Napoléon's Tomb. The golden-domed Hôtel des Invalides is a strikingly fitting place for Napoléon's remains. Military history buffs will appreciate a visit to the adjoining Musée de l'Armée.

A boat ride. Whether you choose a guided tour on the Bateaux Mouches or the unguided Batobus (a water taxi), a ride along the Seine is a relaxing way to see the city's highlights without traffic or crowds. Go after dark to appreciate the lights.

3

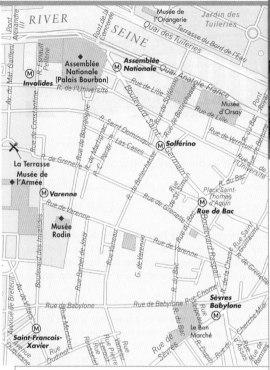

BEST CAFÉS

Café du Marché. On the quaint Rue Cler, this cramped café, popular with locals, serves French classics at good prices. Prepare to wait, as service is slow—you'll have to ask repeatedly for bread and water—but it's all part of the scene. ⊠ *38 rue Cler, Tour Eiffel/Invalides* ☎ *01–47–05–51–27* Ⓜ *La Tour-Maubourg, École Militaire.*

Carette. Tucked into Place du Trocadéro, this grande dame of tea salons has been offering light lunches and sweet treats since 1927. Dive into a *salade composée* of mixed leaves with warm goat cheese, or enjoy a cup of tea and a slice of their famous raspberry charlotte. ⊠ *4 pl. du Trocadero, Trocadéro/Tour Eiffel* ☎ *01–47–27–98–85* Ⓜ *Trocadéro.*

La Terrasse. Of the three well-positioned cafés at busy Place de l'École Militaire, this one is the best choice, with good salads, sandwiches, and French classics like steak tartare. The staff is friendly, too. ⊠ *2 pl. de l'École Militaire, Tour Eiffel/Invalides* ☎ *01–45–55–00–02* Ⓜ *École Militaire.*

MAKING THE MOST OF YOUR TIME

This neighborhood is home to one of the world's great sites, the Eiffel Tower. Depending on the time of year, you can wait a long time to ascend the tower (lines are shorter at night), but even if you stay firmly on the ground, it's worth a trip to see this landmark up close. Afterward, explore Rue St-Dominique's shops, bakeries, and restaurants.

If you're up for a picnic, grab fixings on Rue Cler (between Rue de Grenelle and Avenue de La Motte Piquet), a pedestrian-only market street, and double back to the Champ de Mars, the grassy park at the foot of the tower.

If you have a day to spare, visit the Musée Rodin. If you're pressed for time, do a quick tour of the garden (€1 entry), where many of the best-known sculptures can be seen. From here it's a short walk to Napoléon's over-the-top tomb at the Hôtel des Invalides, which also houses the Musée de l'Armée, devoted to military history. Alternatively, if you're keen on art from Asia, Africa, or the Americas, devote an hour to the Musée du Quai Branly.

Sightseeing
★★★★★
Dining
★★★
Lodging
★★★★★
Shopping
★★★★
Nightlife
★★★

One of Paris's most upscale neighborhoods, the posh 7ᵉ arrondissement is home to the French *bourgeoisie* and well-heeled expats, where nearly every elegant block affords a view of the ultimate symbol of France—the Eiffel Tower.

Lording over the southwestern end of Paris, **the Eiffel Tower** was considered a monstrosity when it opened in 1889. Today it is a beloved icon, especially at night when thousands of twinkling lights sparkle at the top of every hour and the rotating searchlight is a beacon across the Paris night sky.

There are other larger-than-life sights here, too, notably **Hôtel des Invalides,** a sprawling baroque complex with a towering golden dome under which lies the enormous tomb of the pint-size dictator, Napoléon. Along the river, the **Palais Bourbon,** seat of the French Parliament, is an 18th-century homage to ancient Greek architecture. Nearby is the modern, rectangular **Musée du Quai Branly** built by star architect Jean Nouvel. Don't miss the **Musée Rodin,** where the master's outsize sculptures, oozing sensuality, dot the garden and the interior of the Hôtel Biron, the artist's onetime home and workshop.

From the Eiffel Tower east, the walkway along the Seine will take you past one of Paris's most unusual museums, **Les Égouts** (the Sewers— and they are indeed working sewers), and the **American Church.** Cross the **Pont Alexandre III,** the city's most ornate bridge spanning the Seine from Invalides to the Grand Palais. Built between 1896 and 1900, it is bedecked with gilded sculptures, cherubs, and Art Nouveau lamps. It was named for the Russian czar to celebrate Franco-Russian friendship.

TOP ATTRACTIONS

Fodor's Choice
★

Updated by
Paige Donner

Hôtel des Invalides. Les Invalides (pronounced *lehz-ahn-vah-leed*), as this Baroque complex is known, is the eternal home of Napoléon Bonaparte (1769–1821), or more specifically, the little dictator's tomb, which lies under the towering golden dome. There are two churches here: St-Louis des Invalides Church, built between 1677 and 1706, later subdivided into the Église du Dome and the Église des Soldats (Soldiers' Church).

DID YOU KNOW?

For the 200th anniversary of the French Revolution, in 1989, the dome of Les Hôtel des Invalides was regilded using more than 20 pounds of gold.

Louis XIV ordered this complex built in 1670 to house-disabled soldiers, and at one time 4,000 military men lived here. Today, a portion of it remains a veterans' residence and hospital. There's also the Musée de l'Armée, an exhaustive collection of military artifacts from antique armor to weapons. The World Wars Department, also housed here, chronicles the great wars that ravaged Europe.

If you see only one sight here, make it the Église du Dome at the back of the complex. Napoléon's tomb was moved here in 1840 from the island of Saint Helena, where the emperor died in forced exile. Napoléon's body is protected by a series of no fewer than six coffins, one inside the next (sort of like a Russian nesting doll), which is then encased in a sarcophagus of red quartzite. The bombastic tribute is ringed by statues symbolizing Napoléon's campaigns of conquest. To see more Napoléoniana, check out the collection in the Musée de l'Armée featuring the emperor's trademark gray frock coat and huge bicorne hat. Look for the figurines reenacting the famous coronation scene when Napoléon crowns his empress, Josephine. (Notice the heavily rouged cheeks; Napoléon hated pale skin.) You can see a grander version of this scene hanging in the Louvre by the painter David.

For the 200th anniversary of the French Revolution, in 1989, the dome was regilded using more than half a million gold leaves, or more than 20 pounds of gold. Renovations of the church and the museum are ongoing, so parts of it may be closed. The Esplanade des Invalides, the great lawns in front of the building, are favorite spots for pickup soccer and Frisbee games, sunbathing, and dog walking—despite signs asking you to stay off the grass. ■TIP→ The best entrance to use is at the southern end, on Place Vauban (Avenue de Tourville). The ticket office is here, as is Napoléon's Tomb. There are automatic ticket machines at the main entrance on the Place des Invalides. ⊠ *Pl. des Invalides, Tour Eiffel* ☎ *01–44–42–38–77* ⊕ *www.invalides.org* ⊠ *€9* ☉ *Église du Dôme and museums Apr.–Sept., daily 10–6; Oct.–Mar., daily 10–5. Closed 1st Mon. of every month Oct.–June* Ⓜ *La Tour-Maubourg/Invalides.*

Musée du Quai Branly. Paris's newest museum was built by top architect Jean Nouvel to house the state-owned collection of "non-Western" art, culled from several other museums. Despite the interminable queues after the opening in 2006, the museum drew criticism for a seemingly incoherent assemblage of artifacts, from antiquity to the modern age. Critics questioned the connection between funeral masks from Melanesia, Siberian shaman drums, Indonesian textiles, and African statuary. A corkscrew ramp leads from the lobby to a cavernous exhibition space, color coded to designate sections from Asia, Africa, Oceania, and the Americas. The lighting is dim, sometimes too dim to read the information panels (which makes the €5 audioguide a good idea). Renowned for his bold modern edifices, Nouvel has said he wanted the museum to follow no rules. The exterior resembles a massive rust-color rectangle suspended on stilts. There are boxy shapes stuck to the facade facing the Seine, and louvered panels on the opposite side. The colors (dark reds, oranges, and yellows) are meant to evoke the tribal art within. A "living wall" of some 150 species of exotic plants grows on the exterior, which is surrounded by a wild jungle garden with swampy patches—an impressive sight after dark when scores of cylindrical colored lights are illuminated; think numerous minilight sabers poking out of the ground. The name, strangely taken from the street address, is thought by many to be temporary until, after a respectable waiting period, it can be rechristened in honor of its chief backer, former President Jacques Chirac. ■TIP➔ Feel like splurging? Les Ombres restaurant on the museum's fifth floor (separate entrance) has one of the best views of the Eiffel Tower—and prices to match. The budget-conscious can enjoy the garden at Le Café Branly on the ground floor. ⊠ 37 quai Branly, Trocadéro/Tour Eiffel ☎ 01–56–61–70–00 ⊕ www.quaibranly.fr ⊑ €8.50 ☉ Tues., Wed., and Sun. 11–7, Thurs.–Sat. 11–9 Ⓜ Alma-Marceau.

Fodor's Choice
★
Musée Rodin. See the highlighted listing in this chapter.

Fodor's Choice
★
Eiffel Tower. See the highlighted listing in this chapter.

OFF THE BEATEN PATH
Paris's most ornate front door can be found at **29 av. Rapp,** a few minutes' walk from the Pont de l'Alma. The six-story hôtel particulier to which it's attached is an Art Nouveau gem, built in 1901 by Jules Lavirotte, who used brick, stone, and ceramics—the first time ceramics were used to this extent in Paris—to create his whimsical motifs inspired by nature. The historical plaque in front of the building notes that the architect's rebellious style added a "breath of youth and fantasy." Notice the expressions of the pair of nude sculptures: she with a smirk and a jaunty hand on hip; he with a hand cupped to his mouth, calling out to someone. The house was owned by ceramics expert Alexandre Bigot, who frequently teamed up with Lavirotte. The door is the most intriguing feature: carved wood with large oval windows resembling an owl's eyes. The metal handle takes the shape of a curled lizard, its head arching back. Twisting leaves and vines curl around the stone door frame; a woman's head (possibly the architect's wife) is centered at the top, a furry critter crawling down her neck, its pointed nose suspended just above the door. Walk around the corner to 3 Square Rapp to see the house Lavirotte later built for himself.

WORTH NOTING

American Church. Not to be confused with the American Cathedral, across the river at 23 avenue George V, the staff of this neo-Gothic church welcomes English-speaking foreigners. Built in 1927–31, the church hosts free classical music concerts on Sunday from September to June at 5 pm. ⊠ 65 quai d'Orsay, Trocadéro/Tour Eiffel ☎ 01–40–62–05–00 ⊕ www.acparis.org ☉ Mon.–Sat. 9–noon and 1–10:30, Sun. 3–7:30 Ⓜ Alma-Marceau; RER: Pont de l'Alma.

Champ de Mars. This long span of grass, flanked by tree-lined paths, lies between the Eiffel Tower and École Militaire. It was previously used as a parade ground and was the site of the world exhibitions of 1867, 1889 (when the tower was built), and 1900. Today the park, landscaped at the start of the 20th century, is a great spot for picnics, pickup soccer, outdoor concerts, or just hanging out. You can sprawl out on the center

There are more than 20,000 Vélib' bicycles in use as part of Paris's self-service rental-bike program.

span of grass—unusual for Paris. There's also a playground where kids can let off steam. Ⓜ *École Militaire; RER: Champ de Mars.*

⏱ **Les Égouts** (*the Sewers*). Leave it to Paris to make even the sewers romantic. Part exhibit but mostly, well, sewer, this 1,650-foot stretch of tunnels is a fascinating—and surprisingly nonsmelly—look at the underbelly of Paris. Complete with street signs mirroring those above ground, visitors can walk the so-called galleries of this city beneath the city. Walkways flank tunnels of whooshing drain water (wastewater is channeled separately in pipes) that are wide enough to allow narrow barges to dredge sand and sediment. Lighted panels, photos, and explanations in English detail the workings of the 1,300 miles of sewers. Immortalized as the escape routes of the Phantom of the Opera and Jean Valjean in *Les Misérables*, in real life the 19th-century sewers have a florid history. Since Napoléon ordered the underground network built to clean up the squalid streets, the sewers have played a role in every war, secreting revolutionaries and spies and their stockpiles of weapons. Grenades from World War II were recovered not far from where the gift shop now sits. The display cases of stuffed rat toys and "Eau de Paris" glass carafes fold into the walls when the water rises after heavy rains. Buy your ticket at the kiosk on the Left Bank side of the Pont de l'Alma and allow 30 minutes for your visit. Guided tours by friendly *égoutiers* (sewer workers) are available on request, but in French only. ✉ *Opposite 93 quai d'Orsay, Trocadéro/ Tour Eiffel* ☎ *01–53–68–27–81* ⊕ *www.paris.fr* ✉ *€5* ⏰ *May–Sept., Sat.–Wed. 11–5; Oct.–Apr., Sat.–Wed. 11–4; closed last 2 wks of Jan.* Ⓜ *Alma-Marceau; RER: Pont de l'Alma.*

CLOSE UP

Bicycling in Paris

You've seen those 1930s photographs of Paris—men in berets bicycling the streets, a baguette tucked under one arm; elegant women in billowing skirts gliding past the Eiffel Tower on two wheels. Until recently though, it was difficult for visitors to cycle in Paris without signing up for a bike tour. That changed in summer 2007, when the City of Paris introduced **Vélib'**—a bike-rental program.

Vélib' (⊕ www.velib.paris.fr), an amalgam of *vélo* (bike) and *liberté* (liberty), has been a resounding success. You can't miss the silver-and-purple bikes at more than 1,450 docking stations—and growing—all over the city. The environment-friendly intent of the scheme is to complement the public transport system, encouraging people to use the bikes for short trips around town. With more than 60 million trips, the bikes are showing some wear and tear, so check yours over thoroughly.

There are several stands near the Eiffel Tower—one on Quai Branly at Avenue de la Bourdonnaise, another on Bourdonnaise at the corner of Avenue Rapp, and a third at Rue de Grenelle. This neighborhood is ideal for cycling: the roads are wide, there are several bicycle lanes, and most important, the terrain is gloriously flat. Try a relaxing ride across the Champs de Mars, along Rue St-Dominique, and around the Invalides, for starters.

You'll pay €1 a day, or €5 for a seven-day pass, to use Vélib'. If you ride for less than 30 minutes at a time, there's no additional fee (you get a code to use through the day, which allows you to take out a bike whenever you want one). If you keep a bike for more than 30 minutes, you pay an additional €1, then €2 for the next 30 minutes, and then €4 for each half hour on top of that. If you're spending a lot of time in Paris, opt for the €29 annual pass, which has no daily fee. (There is also a combination métro/bike pass available.) The system accepts debit or credit cards that contain an electronic chip that can be read by the French system; not all cards work, but American Express does. If your card is rejected, don't despair: **Fat Tire Bike Tours** (☎ 01–56–58–10–54 ⊕ www.fattirebiketours.com/paris) offers inexpensive rentals.

Regardless of how you get around, here are some rules to remember: Stop at red lights (or risk a fine), and watch for vehicles turning right, which may not see you. Cyclists are allowed in most, but not all, bus lanes (watch for no-cycling signs).

The French cycle in high-heeled boots and miniskirts, business suits and loafers—so don't worry if you didn't pack the right biking clothes. Helmets are almost never worn (except by kids) and Vélib' rentals don't include them.

Palais Bourbon. The most prominent feature of the Palais Bourbon—home of the **Assemblée Nationale,** the French Parliament, since 1798—is its colonnaded facade, commissioned by Napoléon to match that of the Madeleine, across the Seine. Jean-Pierre Cortot's sculpted pediment portrays France holding the tablets of Law, flanked by Force and Justice. There are sometimes outdoor photo exhibitions here, on the Assemblée's railings. ⊠ *Pl. du Palais-Bourbon, St-Germain-des-Prés* ☉ *During temporary exhibits only* Ⓜ *Assemblée Nationale.*

MUSÉE RODIN

✉ *79 rue de Varenne, Trocadéro/Tour Eiffel* ☎ *01–44–18–61–10* ⊕ *www.musee-rodin.fr* 🎟 *€6; gardens only, €1; free 1st Sun. of month* ☉ *Tues.–Sun. 10–5:45* Ⓜ *Varenne.*

TIPS

■ For €1, you can enjoy the 7 acres of gardens.

■ If you want to linger, the Café du Musée Rodin serves meals and snacks in the shade of the garden's linden trees.

■ As you enter, a space on the right houses temporary exhibitions. A combination ticket is €10.

■ An English audioguide (€4) is available for the permanent collection and for temporary exhibitions.

■ Skip the line by buying a joint ticket (must be used the same day) with the Musée d'Orsay for €12.

Auguste Rodin (1840–1917) briefly made his home and studio in the Hôtel Biron, a grand 18th-century *hôtel particulier* (private mansion) that now houses the museum dedicated to his work. He died rich and famous, but many of the sculptures that earned him his place in history were originally greeted with contempt by the public, which was unprepared for his powerful brand of sexuality and raw physicality. A major renovation will close parts of the Hôtel Biron throughout 2012.

HIGHLIGHTS

Most of Rodin's well-known sculptures are in the gardens. The front garden is dominated by *The Gates of Hell* (circa 1880). Inspired by the monumental bronze doors of Italian Renaissance churches, Rodin set out to illustrate stories from Dante's *Divine Comedy*. He worked on the sculpture for more than 30 years, and it serves as a "sketch pad" for many of his later works. Look carefully and you can see miniature versions of *The Kiss* (bottom right), *The Thinker* (top center), and *The Three Shades* (top center).

The museum's interior, though showing its age, still serves as an elegantly creaky setting for two floors of Rodin's work including *The Bronze Age*, inspired by a pilgrimage to Italy and the sculptures of Michelangelo; the work was so realistic, critics accused Rodin of having cast a real body in plaster.

There's also a room of impressive works by Camille Claudel (1864–1943), Rodin's student and longtime mistress, a remarkable sculptor in her own right. Her torturous relationship with Rodin eventually drove her out of his studio—and out of her mind. In 1913 she was packed off to an asylum, where she remained until her death.

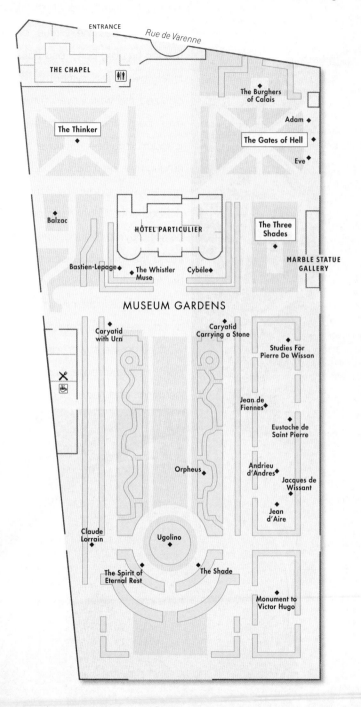

ENTRANCE
Rue de Varenne

THE CHAPEL

The Burghers
of Calais

Adam ◆

The Thinker
◆

The Gates of Hell ◆

Eve ◆

3

Balzac
◆

HÔTEL PARTICULIER

The Three
Shades
◆

MARBLE STATUE
GALLERY

Bastien-Lepage◆ ◆ The Whistler
Muse

Cybéle◆

MUSEUM GARDENS

Caryatid
with Urn
◆

Caryatid
Carrying a Stone
◆

Studies For
Pierre De Wissan
◆

Jean de
Fiennes◆

Eustache de
Saint Pierre
◆

Andrieu
d'Andres◆

Orpheus ◆

Jacques de
Wissant
◆

Jean
d'Aire
◆

Claude
Lorrain
◆

Ugolino
◆

The Spirit of
Eternal Rest ◆

The Shade ◆

Monument to
Victor Hugo
◆

New York has the Statue of Liberty, London has Big Ben—and Paris has the Eiffel Tower. This symbol of Paris, recognized the world over, did not, however, begin life as the beloved icon it is today. Engineer Gustave Eiffel's iron creation for the 1889 World's Fair was greeted with disgust by Parisians, who dubbed it the Giant Asparagus. French author Guy de Maupassant supposedly hated the tower so much that he often ate lunch there, explaining that it was the only place in the city where he could avoid seeing it. Parisians eventually warmed to the tower, an inescapable part of the landscape that has captured the minds and hearts of generations.

Total height: 1,063 feet

■ The 200 millionth visitor went to the top of the Eiffel Tower in 2002.

■ To get to the first viewing platform, Gustave Eiffel originally used avant-garde

■ Every 7 years the tower is repainted. The job takes 15 months and uses 60 tons of "Tour Eiffel Brown" paint in three shades—lightest on top, darkest at the bottom.

LA TOUR EIFFEL

hydraulic cable elevators designed by American Elisha Otis for two of the curved base legs of the tower. French elevators with a chain-drive system were used in the other two legs. During the 1989 renovation, all the elevators were rebuilt by the Otis company.

■ An expensive way to beat the queue

is to reserve a table at **Le Jules Verne**, the restaurant on the 2nd level, which has a private elevator. Taken over by star chef Alain Ducasse, count on a dinner bill of €450 for 2 with wine, though there's an €85 prix-fixe menu at lunch (without wine). ⊕ *www.lejulesverne-paris.com* ☎ *01–45-55-61-44.*

■ If you're in good shape, you can take the stairs to the 2nd level. If you want to go to the top you have to take the elevator.

■ The tower nearly became a giant heap of scrap in 1909, when its concession expired, but its use as a radio antenna saved the day.

■ The tower is most breathtaking at night, when the girders are illuminated. The light show, conceived to celebrate the turn of the millennium, was so popular that the 20,000 lights were reinstalled for permanent use in 2003. It does its electric shimmy for 5 minutes every hour on the hour (cut from 10 to save energy) until 1 am.

NEED A BITE?
58 Tour Eiffel, the restaurant on the first level, serves a good-value, self-service lunch. There is table service at dinner.

Le Café Branly, in the nearby Musée du Quai Branly (✉ *27 Quai Branly, Trocadéro/Tour Eiffel* ☎ *01-47-53-68-01*) is a good choice for lunch or a late-afternoon snack.

The base formed by the tower's feet is 410 by 410 feet.

☎ 01-44-11-23-23

⊕ www.tour-eiffel.fr

🎫 By elevator: 1st and 2nd levels €8.20, top €13.40; By stairs: 1st and 2nd levels only, €4.50

☉ mid June through Aug., daily 9 AM–12:45 AM* (11:30 PM for summit);

Sept.–May, daily 9 AM–11 PM* (10:30 for summit); Stairs close at 6 PM in winter

*LAST TICKET SOLD

Ⓜ Bir-Hakeim, Trocadéro, Ecole Militaire; RER Champ de Mars

■TIP→ Beat the crush by reserving your tickets online.

AT A GLANCE

Dining at a Glance

For full reviews
⇨ *Chapter 14.*

INEXPENSIVE DINING
Le Café Constant,
Bistro, 139 rue
St-Dominique

Les Cocottes de
Christian Constant,
Modern French, 135 rue
St-Dominique

MODERATE DINING
Afaria, *Bistro,*
15 rue Desnouettes

D'Chez Eux, *Bistro,*
2 av. de Lowendal

Jadis, *Bistro,* 208 rue
de la Croix-Nivert

L'Ami Jean, *Spanish,*
27 rue Malar

La Table Lauriston, *Bistro,* 129 rue de Lauriston

Le Petit Rétro, *Bistro,*
5 rue Mesnil

Thoumieux, *Brasserie,*
79 rue St-Dominique

EXPENSIVE DINING
Au Bon Accueil, *Bistro,*
14 rue de Monttessuy

Hiramatsu, *French*
Fusion, 79 rue
St-Dominique

Il Vino, *French*
Fusion, 13 bd. de La
Tour-Maubourg

L'Arpège, *Modern*
French, 84 rue de
Varenne

L'Astrance, *Haute*
French, 4 rue Beethoven

Le Jules Verne, *Modern*
French, Tour Eiffel

Le Troquet, *Modern*
French, 21 rue
François-Bonvin

Le Violon d'Ingres,
Modern French, 135 rue
St-Dominique

The Champs-Élysées

WORD OF MOUTH

"If the Champs-Élysées is on your 'must see' list, take the metro to one of the stops partway along the Champs and walk up to the Arc de Triomphe . . . the views from [the top of the Arc] are excellent, and you'll be fascinated to see the 5 lanes of traffic swirling around the base."

—di2315

GETTING ORIENTED

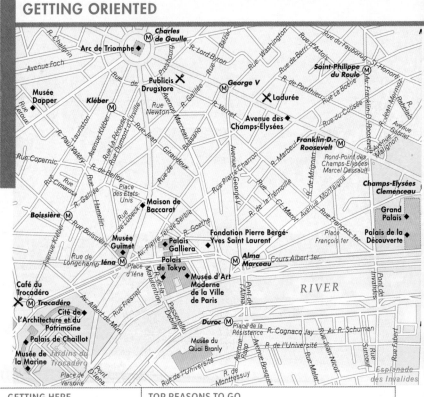

GETTING HERE

This neighborhood includes the 8e and 16e arrondissements. For the top of the Champs-Élysées/Arc de Triomphe, take métro Line 1, 2, or 6, or the RER A, to Charles-de-Gaulle–Étoile. For the bottom of the avenue, near the Grand Palais, go to the Champs-Élysées–Clemenceau métro station (Line 1). For the Palais de Chaillot, use the Trocadéro métro station on lines 6 and 9.

TOP REASONS TO GO

The Champs-Élysées. One of the best times to stroll the wide sidewalks of this famous avenue is at dusk as the famous lights are coming on. Great if you can splurge in the upscale boutiques on and around the avenue, but many will, instead, practice the fine Parisian art of *lèche-vitrines*, or window shopping (literally, "window licking").

Palais de Chaillot. A favorite of fashion photographers, this statue-lined plaza-terrace at the Place du Trocadéro boasts the city's best view of the Eiffel Tower.

Musée Guimet. One of the city's finest smaller museums with a world-class collection of art from all over Asia. Don't miss the rare Khmer sculptures from Cambodia.

A *macaron* from Ladurée. Is it worth lining up for 30 minutes for a little taste of heaven? It's up to you to decide, but rest assured that the *macarons* (meringue cookies) made by this famous *pâtissier* since 1862 are as good as ever. They come in more than two-dozen flavors.

4

BEST CAFÉS

Café du Trocadéro. Of the cafés that ring this square, this is the only one with a view of the Eiffel Tower. The friendly staff and good food make it a solid choice. ✉ 8 pl. du Trocadéro, Trocadéro ☎ 01–44–05–37–00 Ⓜ Trocadéro.

Ladurée. This jewel-box tea salon—the most opulent branch of the Ladurée empire—is worth the splurge for lunch (reserve a table), or come for afternoon tea and dessert. ✉ 75 av. des Champs-Élysées, Champs-Élysées ☎ 01–40–75–08–75 Ⓜ George V.

Publicis Drugstore. At the top of the Champs, this funky spot is part restaurant, part mini-department store stocked with high-end items like Dior baby clothes. Fine wine and cigars (and public toilets) are on the first floor. Prices are moderate (Note: The prix fixe is still €19–€23.50) if you order the prix-fixe menu and the food is good. ✉ 133 av. des Champs-Élysées, Champs-Élysées ☎ 01–44–43–77–64 Ⓜ Charles-de-Gaulle–Étoile.

MAKING THE MOST OF YOUR TIME

This neighborhood is an essential stop for every first-time visitor to Paris, and returning travelers will find plenty to do, too. Try to leave yourself a long day to tour some museums around Place du Trocadéro before heading to the Champs-Élysées, worth a walk from end to end. Stop for lunch or dessert at one of the cafés or tea salons. And try to detour down the Avenue Montaigne, Paris's answer to Rodeo Drive. If your time is limited, you can just come for a stroll at night, when the Champs is alight: there are bars and nightclubs for all tastes, or you can keep it low key and head to one of the big movie houses with cushy seats showing English-language films (look for v.o. for *version originale*).

Sightseeing
★★★★★
Dining
★★★
Lodging
★★★★★
Shopping
★★★★
Nightlife
★★★★★

Welcome to bling-bling Paris. Make no mistake, the Champs-Élysées, while ceding some of its elegance in recent times, remains the city's—if not the world's—most famous avenue. Like New York's Times Square, or London's Piccadilly Circus, the Avenue des Champs-Élysées inspires boldness. Parisians complain that fast-food joints and chain stores have cheapened the avenue, but others are more philosophical, noting there is something here for everyone: if you can't afford lunch at Ladurée, there's always McDonald's (and the view from the second floor is terrific).

Anchoring the Champs is the mighty **Arc de Triomphe,** Napoléon's monument to himself. At the other end, the exquisitely restored **Grand Palais** plays host to some of the city's grandest art exhibitions. Across the street, the permanent art collection is free at the **Petit Palais,** and there's also a quiet garden café. Between here and **Place du Trocadéro,** a busy traffic circle, you can find several museums housed in some of the city's most impressive buildings: at the **Palais de Chaillot** complex is the **Cité de l'Architecture et du Patrimoine,** a must for architecture buffs, and across the plaza is the charming **Musée de la Marine.** Farther on, the Asian art collection is tops at the **Musée Guimet.** For 20th-century art, the **Musée d'Art Moderne de la Ville de Paris,** on Avenue du Président-Wilson, has an impressive free permanent collection. Contemporary-art lovers should also check out what's showing next door at the trendy **Palais de Tokyo.** These twin buildings were built for the 1937 World's Fair, and are impressive simply for their monumental facades. Across the street is the **Palais Galliera,** a museum framed by a lovely garden; showing fashion-theme special exhibitions.

DID YOU KNOW?

The magnificent Grand Palais, with its enormous glass roof, is known for its provocative and crowd-pleasing temporary art exhibits.

TOP ATTRACTIONS

Updated by
Paige Donner

Arc de Triomphe

See the highlighted listing in this chapter.

Avenue des Champs-Élysées. Marcel Proust lovingly described the genteel elegance of this storied avenue, the Champs-Élysées (pronounced chahnz-eleezay, with an "n" sound instead of "m" and no "p"), during its Belle Époque heyday, when its cobblestones resounded with the clatter of horses and carriages. Today, despite unrelenting traffic and the intrusion of chain stores and fast-food restaurants, the avenue still sparkles. There's always something happening here: the stores are open late—and many are open on Sunday (a rarity in Paris), the nightclubs remain top destinations, and the cafés offer prime people-watching—though you'll pay for the privilege: after all, this is Europe's most expensive stretch of real estate. Along the 2-km (1¼-mi) stretch, you can find the marquee names in French luxury, including Cartier, the perfumier Guerlain, and Louis Vuitton. Newer arrivals, like the cavernous Sephora are fun to check out because, in the bigger-is-better spirit of the Champs, there are often events and giveaways. Car manufacturers try to out-bling each other with space-age showrooms. Old stalwarts are still going strong, if a bit faded, like the Lido cabaret and Fouquet's, whose celebrity clientele extends from James Joyce to President Nicolas Sarkozy, who celebrated his election night victory at this restaurant in May 2007. The avenue is also the setting for the last leg of the Tour de France bicycle race (the third or fourth Sunday in July), and ceremonies on Bastille Day (July 14) and Armistice Day (November 11). The Champs-Élysées, which translates as "Elysian Fields" (the resting place of the blessed in Greek mythology), began life as a cow pasture and in 1666 was transformed into a park by the royal landscape architect André Le Nôtre. Traces of its green origins are visible near Concorde, where elegant 19th-century park pavilions house the historic restaurants Ledoyen, Laurent, and Le Pavillon Élysées Lenôtre. Ⓜ *Champs-Élysées–Clemenceau, Franklin-D.-Roosevelt, George V, Étoile.*

> **DID YOU KNOW?**
>
> The monument at the Place de l'Alma, at the bottom of avenues Montaigne and George V, along the Seine and just next to the Bateaux Mouches boarding dock, has become Princess Diana's unofficial shrine, where bouquets and messages are still placed by her admirers—city workers regularly clean up flowers, graffiti, and photographs. The replica of the Statue of Liberty's flame predates Diana's car accident though: it was donated by Paris-based American companies in 1989 in honor of the bicentennial of the French Revolution.

> **WORD OF MOUTH**
>
> "First stop: Arc de Triomphe. We decide to go to the top. We mistakenly enter the long, winding staircase instead of the elevator and walk 284 painful steps to the stop along a narrow, winding staircase. Enjoyed the views especially the streets that look like the spokes of a wheel. Got near dizzy going down those steps again!"
>
> —ramekin4

ARC DE TRIOMPHE

✉ *Pl. Charles-de-Gaulle,*
Champs-Élysées
☎ *01–55–37–73–77*
⊕ *www.arc-de-triomphe.*
monuments-nationaux.fr/
💶 *€9, free under 18* ⊗ *Apr.–*
Sept., daily 10 am–11 pm;
Oct.–Mar., daily 10 am–10:30
pm Ⓜ *Métro or RER: Étoile.*

4

TIPS

■ France's Unknown Soldier is buried beneath the arch; the flame is rekindled every evening at 6:30, which is the most atmospheric time to visit. To beat the crowds, though, come early in the morning or buy your ticket online (€1.60 service fee).

■ Be wary of the traffic circle that surrounds the arch. It's infamous for accidents—including one several years ago that involved the French transport minister. Use the underground passage from the northeast corner of the Avenue des Champs-Élysées.

Inspired by Rome's Arch of Titus, this colossal, 164-foot triumphal arch was ordered by Napoléon—who liked to consider himself the heir to the Roman emperors—to celebrate his military successes. Unfortunately, Napoléon's strategic and architectural visions were not entirely on the same plane, and the Arc de Triomphe proved something of an embarrassment: although the emperor wanted the monument completed in time for an 1810 parade in honor of his new bride, Marie-Louise, the arch was still only a few feet high, and a dummy arch of painted canvas was strung up to save face. Empires come and go, but Napoléon's had been gone for more than 20 years before the Arc de Triomphe was finally finished, in 1836.

HIGHLIGHTS

The Arc de Triomphe is known for its magnificent sculptures by François Rude, including *The Departure of the Volunteers in 1792,* better known as *La Marseillaise,* to the right of the arch when viewed from the Champs-Élysées. Names of Napoléon's generals are inscribed on the stone facades—the underlined names identify the hallowed figures who fell in battle.

The traffic circle around the Arc is named for Charles de Gaulle, but it's known to Parisians as "L'Étoile," or the Star—a reference to the streets that fan out from it.

Climb the stairs to the top of the arch and you can see the star effect of the 12 radiating avenues and the vista down the Champs-Élysées toward Place de la Concorde and the distant Musée du Louvre.

There is a small museum halfway up the arch, devoted to its history.

CLOSE UP

Hemingway's Paris

There is a saying: "Everyone has two countries, his or her own—and France." For the Lost Generation after World War I, these words rang particularly true. Lured by favorable exchange rates, free-flowing alcohol, and a booming arts scene, many American writers, composers, and painters moved to Paris in the 1920s and 1930s, Ernest Hemingway among them. He arrived in Paris with his first wife, Hadley, in December 1921 and made for the Rive Gauche—the Hôtel Jacob et d'Angleterre, to be exact (still operating at 44 rue Jacob). To celebrate their arrival the couple went to the Café de la Paix for a meal they nearly couldn't afford.

Hemingway worked as a journalist and quickly made friends with expat writers such as Gertrude Stein and Ezra Pound. In 1922 the Hemingways moved to 74 rue du Cardinal Lemoine, a bare-bones apartment with no running water (his writing studio was around the corner, on the top floor of 39 rue Descartes). Then, in 1924, the couple and their baby son settled at 113 rue Notre-Dame des Champs. Much of *The Sun Also Rises*, Hemingway's first serious novel, was written at nearby café La Closerie des Lilas. These were the years in which he forged his writing style, paring his sentences down to the pith. As he noted in *A Moveable Feast*, "hunger was good discipline." There were some especially hungry months when Hemingway gave up journalism for short-story writing, and the family was "very poor and very happy."

They weren't happy for long: in 1926, as *The Sun Also Rises* made him famous, Hemingway left Hadley and the next year wed his mistress, Pauline Pfeiffer, then moved to 6 rue Férou, near the Musée du Luxembourg.

For gossip and books, and to pick up his mail, Papa would visit Shakespeare & Co., then at 12 rue de l'Odéon, owned by Sylvia Beach, who became a trusted friend. For cash and cocktails Hemingway usually headed to the upscale Rive Droite. He collected the former at the Guaranty Trust Company, at 1 rue des Italiens. He found the latter, when he was flush, at the bar of the landmark Hôtel de Crillon, just on the Place de la Concorde and next to the American Embassy, or, when poor, at the Caves Mura, at 19 rue d'Antin, or Harry's Bar, still in brisk business at 5 rue Daunou. Hemingway's loyal and legendary association with the Hôtel Ritz was sealed during the Liberation in 1944, when he strode in at the head of his platoon and "liberated" the joint by ordering martinis all around. Here Hemingway asked Mary Welsh to become his fourth wife, and here also, the story goes, a trunk full of notes on his first years in Paris turned up in the 1950s, giving him the raw material for writing *A Moveable Feast*.

★ **Cité de l'Architecture et du Patrimoine.** It took 10 years and $114 million to transform the City of Architecture and Heritage into one of the world's great architectural museums. Reopened in September 2007 to much fanfare, the former French Monuments Museum's three cavernous galleries (86,000 square feet) contain some 350 plaster-cast reproductions of the greatest gems of French architecture. Copies include partial facades of the most important Gothic churches, massive carved doors, and the curved 16th-century staircase to the organ loft at St-Maclou church in Rouen. The famous stained-glass windows of the Chartres cathedral are represented, along with an assembly of gargoyles practically leaping off the back wall of the soaring first-floor gallery. Just below it is the door to an interactive room for children. The video-game set will love the video monitors, with joysticks, that allow a 360-degree view of some of the most impressive cathedrals. The upper-floor gallery is devoted to modern architecture, with models and video explainers of myriad building projects, as well as a life-size replica of a postwar apartment in Marseille designed by the urban-planning pioneer Le Corbusier. Don't miss the gallery of murals with stellar reproductions of frescoes and windows of medieval chapels and other buildings through the ages. Some critics have griped that reproductions are not so impressive in a country with plenty of the real thing, but this museum has nevertheless succeeded in amassing a fine "best of" collection under one roof. ■ TIP→ Allow 1½ to 3 hours for a visit and spring for the €3 English "visioguide," an excellent audiovisual guide to the collection. ✉ 1 pl. du Trocadéro, Trocadéro/Tour Eiffel ☎ 01–58–51–52–00 ⊕ www.citechaillot.fr ☞ €8; €10 with temporary exhibits ⊙ Fri.–Mon. and Wed. 11–7, Thurs. 11–9, closed Tues. Ⓜ Trocadéro.

> **WORD OF MOUTH**
>
> "The Cité de l'Architecture et du Patrimoine is off the tourist track, since it is a huge national museum that you can see all by yourself instead of being trampled by the crowds. I also recommend it to people who just can't see everything in France during their visit, or are looking for things to go and see in person during their next visit. I know that the idea that everything in this museum is a copy is what is most off-putting, but you really have to see it for yourself to understand its importance. So please give the Cité de l'Architecture et du Patrimoine a chance next time you are at Place du Trocadéro."
>
> —kerouac

Grand Palais. With its curved-glass roof and gorgeous restored Belle Époque ornamentation, you can't miss the Grand Palais whether you're approaching from the Seine or the Champs-Élysées. It forms an elegant duo with the Petit Palais across Avenue Winston-Churchill: both stone buildings, adorned with mosaics and sculpted friezes, were built for the 1900 World's Fair, and, like the Eiffel Tower, were not supposed to be permanent. The art shows staged here are often the hottest ticket in town. Previous popular shows include "Marie Antoinette" and "Picasso and the Masters." To skip the long lines, it pays to book an advance ticket online, which will cost you an extra euro. ✉ Av. Winston-Churchill, Champs-Élysées ☎ 01–44–13–17–17 ⊕ www.grandpalais.fr, www.rmn.fr for reservations ☞ €12 ⊙ Wed.–Mon. 10–10, Thurs. 10–8 Ⓜ Champs-Élysées–Clemenceau.

Musée d'Art Moderne de la Ville de Paris (Paris Museum of Modern Art). Although the city's modern-art museum hasn't generated a buzz comparable to that of the Centre Georges Pompidou, it can be a more pleasant experience because, like many smaller museums, there are often no crowds. The building reopened after a long renovation in February

2006, and its vast, white-walled galleries make an ideal backdrop for the museum's temporary exhibitions of 20th-century art. The permanent collection on the lower floor takes over where the Musée d'Orsay leaves off, chronologically speaking: among the earliest works are Fauvist paintings by Maurice Vlaminck and André Derain, followed by Pablo Picasso's early experiments in Cubism. Other highlights include works by Robert and Sonia Delaunay, Chagall, Matisse, Rothko, and Modigliani. ⊠ *11 av. du Président-Wilson, Trocadéro/Tour Eiffel* ☎ *01–53–67–40–00* ⊕ *www.mam.paris.fr* ✉ *Permanent collection free, temporary exhibitions €5–€12* ⊙ *Tues.–Sun. 10–6, Thurs. until 10 for temporary exhibits* Ⓜ *Alma Marceau, Iéna.*

★ **Musée Dapper.** A well-curated museum dedicated to African art, the Dapper is famous for its stunning temporary mask exhibitions. Created by Christiane Falgayrettes-Leveau and her husband, Michel Leveau, in 1986, it's a calm place to visit, and makes a good pairing with a stop at the nearby Musée Guimet. Most of the visitor information is in French, but see the website for English descriptions of current exhibitions (there is no permanent collection). ⊠ *35 bis, rue Paul Valéry, Champs-Élysées* ☎ *01–45–00–91–75* ⊕ *www.dapper.com.fr* ✉ *€6* ⊙ *Wed.–Mon. 11–7; usually closed mid-July–Sept.* Ⓜ *Charles-de-Gaulle–Étoile.*

Fodor's Choice
★ **Musée Guimet.** One of the best smaller museums in Paris, the Guimet National Museum of Asian Arts has a world-class collection that traces its roots to the Lyonnais industrialist Émile Guimet. His extensive travels in the late 19th century resulted in a priceless collection of Indo-Chinese and Far Eastern treasures. The collection, enriched by the state's vast holdings, is laid out geographically in airy, light-filled rooms, thanks to a top-end renovation (1998–2000). Just past the entry, you can find the largest collection of Khmer sculpture outside of Cambodia, including astonishing 12th-century statues of female divinities. The second floor has statuary and masks from Nepal, ritual funeral objects from Tibet, and jewelry and fabrics from India. Peek into the old library rotunda, with wood-paneled walls and ionic columns topped with carytids: this is where Monsieur Guimet used to entertain the city's notables; and Mata Hari danced here in 1905. The China collection is comprehensive, spanning the dynasties. On the third floor is an 18th-century model of a Chinese pavilion in delicately sculpted ivory, with tiny figurines. Up the stairs is the China Laquer Rotunda with two large screens from the Qing dynasty with flora and fauna motifs. (There's also a nice view of Paris.) Pick up a free English-language audioguide and brochure at the entrance. If you need a pick-me-up, stop at the basement café, Salon des Porcelaines, for a ginger milk shake. ■ **TIP→ Don't miss the Guimet's impressive Buddhist Pantheon, with two floors of Buddhas from China and Japan, and a Japanese garden. Admission is free and it's just up the street at 19 avenue d'Iéna.** ⊠ *6 pl. d'Iéna, Trocadéro/Tour Eiffel* ☎ *01–56–52–53–00* ⊕ *www.museeguimet.fr* ✉ *€7.50; €9.50 with temporary exhibition* ⊙ *Wed.–Mon. 10–6* Ⓜ *Iéna, Boissière.*

Palais de Chaillot. This honey-color Art Deco cultural center on Place du Trocadéro was built in the 1930s to replace a Moorish-style building constructed for the World's Fair of 1878. The plaza-terrace is a top draw for camera-toting visitors intent on snapping the perfect shot of

The Musée Guimet features Asian art and an auditorium for concerts and other events.

the Eiffel Tower. In the building to the left is the Cité de l'Architecture et du Patrimoine—an excellent architecture museum—and the Théâtre National de Chaillot, which occasionally stages plays in English. Also here is the Institut Français d'Architecture, an organization and school. The twin building to the right contains the Musée de la Marine, an excellent small museum with a nautical theme; and the Musée de l'Homme, which is closed for renovation and set to reopen, as the Musée de l'Humanité, in 2012 or beyond. Also here is the cozy Café de l'Homme, which has a fantastic view of the tower but a pricey menu that is not nearly as stellar. The garden leading to the Seine has sculptures and dramatic fountains and is a dramatic staging ground for fireworks on July 14, Bastille Day. ⊠ *Pl. du Trocadéro, Trocadéro/ Tour Eiffel* Ⓜ *Trocadéro.*

Palais de Tokyo. In a space that was derelict for more than a decade, this Art Nouveau twin of the Musée d'Art Moderne reopened in 2002 as a trendy, stripped-down space for contemporary arts with unorthodox, ambitious programming. There is no permanent collection; instead, dynamic temporary exhibits spread over a large, open area reminiscent of a construction site, with a trailer for a ticket booth. Instead of traditional museum guards, young art students—most of whom speak at least some English—are on hand to help explain the installations. The cultural programming extends to debates, concerts, readings, and fashion shows. Following an extensive renovation in early 2012, there are now even more funky restaurants and offbeat shops. ⊠ *13 av. du Président-Wilson, Trocadéro/Tour Eiffel* ☎ *01–47–23–54–01* ⊕ *www. palaisdetokyo.com* 🖼 *€6* ⊘ *Tues.–Sun. noon–midnight* Ⓜ *Iéna.*

NEED A BREAK?

Tokyo Eat. For an inexpensive bite, check out the Palais de Tokyo restaurant, Tokyo Eat, the only museum café in town with tables filled with hip locals, especially at lunch. ✉ *13 av. du Président-Wilson, Trocadéro/Tour Eiffel* ☎ *01–47–20–00–29.*

WORTH NOTING

Fondation Pierre Bergé–Yves Saint Laurent. With his business partner, Pierre Bergé, the iconic late fashion designer Yves Saint Laurent reopened his former atelier in 2004 as a gallery and archive of his work. Unfortunately, YSL's private collection of dresses can be viewed only on private group tours booked in advance. What you can see here are temporary exhibits that change every few months, most with themes related to the fashion house, such as retrospectives on fashionista doyenne Nan Kempner, and another on YSL photographer David Seidner. ✉ *3 rue Léonce Reynaud, Trocadéro/Tour Eiffel* ☎ *01–44–31–64–31* ⊕ *www.fondation-pb-ysl.net* ✑ *€7* ☉ *Tues.–Sun. 11–6* Ⓜ *Alma-Marceau.*

Maison de Baccarat. Designer Philippe Starck brought an irreverent *Alice in Wonderland* approach to the HQ and museum of the venerable Baccarat crystal firm. Relocated to the 16ᵉ arrondissement in 2003, Starck played on the building's surrealist legacy: Cocteau, Dalí, Buñuel, and Man Ray were all frequent guests of the mansion's onetime owner, Countess Marie-Laure de Noailles. At the entrance, talking heads are projected onto giant crystal urns, and a lighted chandelier is submerged in an aquarium. Upstairs, the museum, which is a generous term for the splendid but rather small collection, features masterworks created by Baccarat since 1764, including soaring candlesticks made for Czar Nicholas II and the perfume flacon Dalí designed for Schiaparelli. The museum is located on the beautiful place des États-Unis, so be sure to set aside a few moments to enjoy the pretty little park and the fine statue of Washington and Lafayette. ✉ *11 pl. des États-Unis, Trocadéro/Tour Eiffel* ☎ *01–40–22–11–00* ⊕ *www.baccarat.fr* ✑ *€5* ☉ *Mon. and Wed.–Sat. 10–6:30* Ⓜ *Iéna.*

♔ ★ **Musée de la Marine** (*Maritime Museum*). Inside this charming, little-known museum is a treasure trove of sculpture and art with a nautical theme. There are impressive models of vessels from 17th-century flagships to modern warships. Kids can climb a step to get a closer look at a model aircraft carrier, cut in half, with its decks exposed. The main gallery features several figureheads recovered from sunken ships, including a giant Henri IV, with hand on heart, miraculously saved from a shipwreck in 1854 during the Crimean War. Another enormous representation of Napoléon, in his favored guise as a Roman emperor, was taken from the prow of the frigate *Iéna* in 1846. There is also a metal diving suit from 1882, and the menu from a 1935 voyage of the SS *Normandie* cruise ship (halibut and fresh peas were served). There are usually two temporary exhibitions, one focusing on artwork taken from the museum's collection, the other of borrowed works. Audio guides are included in the admission price. ✉ *17 pl. du Trocadéro, Trocadéro/Tour Eiffel* ☎ *01–53–65–81–32* ⊕ *www.musee-marine.fr* ✑ *€7; €9 temporary exhibitions* ☉ *Wed.–Mon. 10–6* Ⓜ *Trocadéro.*

Palais de la Découverte (*Palace of Discovery*). This science museum and planetarium behind the Grand Palais has a wide variety of exhibits on subjects from electricity to climate change to nuclear physics. After a merger with Cité des Sciences in 2009, the Palais's days were said to be numbered but, as of this writing, the museum is still open. Built for the 1937 World's Fair, the museum bills itself as the first interactive museum. There's also a planetarium with several shows daily. ⊠ *Av. Franklin-D.-Roosevelt, Champs-Élysées* ☎ *01–56–43–20–20* ⊕ *www.palais-decouverte.fr*

⊠ *€7; planetarium additional €3.50* ◷ *Tues.–Sat. 9:30–6, Sun. 10–7* Ⓜ *Champs-Élysées–Clemenceau.*

Palais Galliera. This regal mansion, built from 1878 to 1894, is closed for renovation until spring 2013. It is home to the Musée Galliera, also called the Musée de la Mode (Fashion Museum), though it opens only for temporary exhibitions on costume and clothing design. Past shows have featured the city-owned museum's vast collection of dresses organized under various themes, such as the "high-tech" crinoline styles of the Second Empire (1852–70). The 2003 Marlene Dietrich show was credited with influencing designers, who incorporated the looks in their runway collections. The lovely 19th-century style garden along Avenue du Président-Wilson is open during the renovation. ⊠ *10 av. Pierre-1er-de-Serbie, Trocadéro/Tour Eiffel* ☎ *01–56–52–86–00* ⊕ *www.galliera. paris.fr* ⊠ *€7, admission varies* ◷ *Tues.–Sun. 10–6 during temporary exhibits only* Ⓜ *Iéna.*

Petit Palais. The little cousin of the Grand Palais across the street has a free permanent collection of French painting and furniture, with canvases by Courbet and Bouguereau. The temporary exhibitions are often excellent, and the building itself—a 1902 cream puff of marble and gilt, with huge windows overlooking the Seine—is worth a look. Outside, keep an eye out for two excellent sculptures: French World War I hero Georges Clemenceau, facing the Champs-Élysées; and Jean Cardot's resolute image of Winston Churchill, facing the Seine. ∎TIP➜ Tucked in the courtyard is a quiet garden with palm trees and a café—an ideal spot to rest weary feet. ⊠ *Av. Winston-Churchill, Champs-Élysées* ☎ *01–53–43–40–00* ⊕ *www.petitpalais.paris.fr* ⊠ *Permanent collection free; temporary exhibit entry fees vary* ◷ *Tues.–Sun. 10–6, Thurs. until 8 for temporary exhibits* Ⓜ *Champs-Élysées–Clemenceau.*

AT A GLANCE

Dining at a Glance

For full reviews
⇨ *Chapter 14.*

INEXPENSIVE DINING
Au Petit Verdot du 17e, *Bistro,* 9 rue Fourcroy

Le Hide, *Haute French,* 10 rue du Général Lanzerac

MODERATE DINING
Chez Savy, *Bistro,* 23 rue Bayard

L'Huîterie, *Seafood,* 16 rue Saussier-Leroy

La Fermette Marbeuf 1900, *Brasserie,* 5 rue Marbeuf

Mini Palais, *Modern French,* 3 av. Winston Churchill

Rech, *Seafood,* 62 av. Des Ternes

EXPENSIVE DINING
Alain Ducasse au Plaza Athénée, *Haute French,* Hôtel Plaza Athénée, 25 av. Montaigne

Dominique Bouchet, *Bistro,* 11 rue Treilhard

Guy Savoy, *Haute French,* 18 rue Troyon

Kifuné, *Japanese,* 44 rue St-Ferdinand

L'Arôme, *Modern French,* 3 rue St-Philippe du Roule

La Table du Lancaster, *Haute French,* Hotel Lancaster, 7 rue de Berri

Le Bristol, *Haute French,* Hôtel Bristol, 112 rue du Faubourg St-Honoré

Le Cinq, *Haute French,* Hôtel Four Seasons George V, 31 av. George V

Le Cristal Room, *Haute French,* 11 pl. des États-Unis

Ledoyen, *Haute French,* 1 av. Dutuit, on Carré des Champs-Élysées

Pierre Gagnaire, *Haute French,* 6 rue de Balzac

Stella Maris, *French Fusion,* 4 rue Arsène-Houssaye

Taillevent, *Haute French,* 15 rue Lamennais

Around the Louvre

WITH LES HALLES AND FAUBOURG ST-HONORÉ

WORD OF MOUTH

"We went [to the Louvre] with a 9- and 12-year-old. We basically took the brochure, which has a dozen (or more?) photos on it, and turned it into a scavenger hunt to see if we could find them . . . I think that helped and made it more fun."

—indy_dad

GETTING ORIENTED

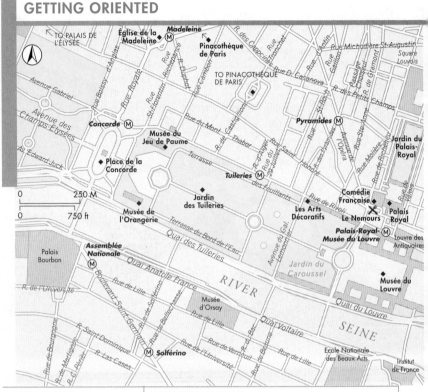

GETTING HERE

The neighborhoods in the Around the Louvre chapter include the 1er and 2e arrondissements, from the Faubourg St-Honoré to Les Halles. If you're heading to the Louvre, take the métro Line 1 to the Louvre/Rivoli or Palais-Royal/Musée du Louvre stop. For the Tuileries, use the Tuileries stop on the same line. For Place de la Concorde, use the Concorde stop on Line 1, 8, or 12. This is a good starting point for a walk on Rue St-Honoré. If you're going to Les Halles, take the Line 4 to Les Halles or the Line 1 to Châtelet.

TOP REASONS TO GO

Musée du Louvre. The world's first great art museum is worth a long visit to see some of the most renowned works of art, from the serenely smirking *Mona Lisa* to the statuesque *Venus de Milo.*

Tuileries to Place de la Concorde. For centuries, Parisians and visitors alike have strolled the length of this magnificent garden to the gold-tipped obelisk at the Place de la Concorde.

Galerie Vivienne. The prettiest 19th-century glass-roofed shopping arcade left in Paris, this *passage* is worth a stop for shopping, lunch, or afternoon tea.

Palais-Royal. Visit these arcades and the romantic garden and understand why the French writer Colette called the view from her window "a little corner of the country."

Rue Montorgueil. This historic market street, lined with food shops and cafés, is at the heart of one of the city's trendiest neighborhoods.

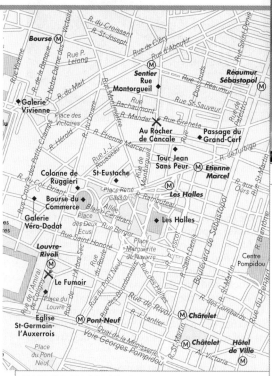

BEST CAFÉS

5

Au Rocher de Cancale. As its impressive old facade attests, this café dates to 1846, when Rue Montorgueil was the place to buy oysters (Cancale is a famous oyster town in Brittany). Today the terrace is a perfect spot for lunch. Try one of the huge salads. ⊠ *78 rue Montorgueil, Beaubourg/Les Halles* ☎ *01–42–33–50–29.*

Le Fumoir. Equal parts café, bar, and restaurant, Le Fumoir is a timelessly popular place to sip coffee and read the paper, or enjoy a cocktail before settling into the back salon for dinner. Reservations are a good idea for dinner and Sunday brunch (€22). ⊠ *Pl. du Louvre, 6 rue de l'Amiral-Coligny, Louvre/ Tuileries* ☎ *01–42–92–00–24* Ⓜ *Louvre.*

Le Nemours. Adjacent to the Palais-Royal and steps from the Musée du Louvre, this café with rows of tables on a lively plaza is a great place to map out your day over a croissant and *café crème.* ⊠ *2 pl. Colette, Louvre/ Tuileries* ☎ *01–42–61–34–14.*

MAKING THE MOST OF YOUR TIME

Try to devote two days or more—one alone for the Louvre—to these vastly different neighborhoods. The narrow sidewalks of the Faubourg St-Honoré are lined with some of the city's finest boutiques. The Place de la Concorde is the gateway to the Tuileries garden. At the eastern end, the old market district, Les Halles, is booming with trendy shops and restaurants popping up around cobbled Rue Montorgueil, where traffic is mercifully restricted.

If you're headed to the mammoth Musée du Louvre, it's best to have a game plan in mind. First step: avoid the lines at the main entrance under the pyramid by using the underground entrance in the Carrousel du Louvre, 99 rue de Rivoli. Buy your ticket at one of the machines.

Sightseeing
★★★★
Dining
★★
Lodging
★★★★
Shopping
★★★★★
Nightlife
★★

The neighborhoods in this chapter, from the Faubourg St-Honoré to Les Halles, are a study in contrasts, from très chic to trendy, with the Louvre in the midst of the bustle.

The impossibly posh **Rue Faubourg St-Honoré** has been a fashionista destination for three centuries, as popular now as it was when royal mistresses shopped here. Just about every chic boutique has a branch here, and this is where you can find some of the city's best hotels. Once the stomping ground of kings and queens, today it's home to the French president and the American and British ambassadors. To the east, **Les Halles** has risen from its roots as the city's vermin-infested wholesale food market to a booming quarter with expensive apartments and shops, cafés, and bars centered on Rue Montorgueil, one of the city's oldest market streets and today the epicenter of one of the city's hottest neighborhoods.

In between, you can find some of Paris's top draws, namely the mighty **Musée du Louvre** and, next door, the majestic **Jardin des Tuileries.** The garden is home to the **Musée de l'Orangerie,** with its curved galleries showcasing Monet's *Water Lilies,* while the nearby **Musée des Art Décoratifs** is a must for design buffs. In the Place Colette, the stately theater, the **Comédie Française,** is still going strong after 400 years, and at the edge of the square is the psychedelic sculpture—doubling as a métro entrance—of the *kiosque des noctambules* (kiosk of the night-crawlers), designed by artist Jean-Michel Othoniel.

Hidden just off Place Colette is the **Palais-Royal,** a romantic garden ringed by arcades with boutiques selling everything from antique war medals to the latest frock by Stella McCartney. A stone's throw away is the **Galerie Vivienne,** the exquisitely restored 19th-century shopping arcade.

Recalling the area's history as a food hub, there's a small cluster of shops stocking everything a well-dressed kitchen needs (during her years in Paris, American chef Julia Child was a regular at the legendary E. Dehillerin, at 18–20 rue Coquillière). This is the gateway to **Les Halles** (pronounced leh-*ahl*), which was until 1969 the city's wholesale food market, but has since flailed for an identity. A sweeping multiyear renovation is now under way that promises a much-needed face-lift of the plaza above ground and the vast shopping mall below.

TOP ATTRACTIONS

Updated by
Bryan Pirolli

★ **Galerie Véro-Dodat.** A lovely 19th-century passage, gorgeously restored, the Véro-Dodat has a dozen artsy boutiques selling art, furniture, and accessories. The headliner tenant is Christian Louboutin, at Rue Jean-Jacques Rousseau, whose red-soled stilettos are favorites of Angelina and Madonna as well as other members of the red-carpet set. On the opposite end, at the Rue du Bouloi entrance, star cosmetics maker Terry De Gunzburg has a boutique, By Terry. ⊠ *19 rue Jean-Jacques Rousseau, Louvre/Tuileries* Ⓜ *Palais-Royal.*

★ **Galerie Vivienne.** The grande dame of Paris's 19th-century *passages couverts*, or covered arcades, this beautifully restored gallery, with its tiled floor, will send you back to a time of gaslights and horse-drawn carriages. Parisians came to passages like this one to escape the muddy streets, and to see and be seen browsing the boutiques under the glass-and-iron roofs—the world's first shopping malls. Today, the Galerie Vivienne still attracts top-flight shops such as **Jean-Paul Gaultier** (6 rue Vivienne) and the high-quality secondhand clothes seller **La Marelle** (No. 21), as well as boutiques selling accessories, housewares, and fine wine. ∎TIP➔ The Place des Victoires, a few steps away, is one of Paris's most picturesque squares. In the center is a statue of an outsized Louis XIV (1643–1715), the Sun King, who appears almost as large as his horse. ⊠ *Main entrance at, 4 rue des Petits-Champs, Louvre/Tuileries* Ⓜ *Palais-Royal/Bourse.*

NEED A
BREAK?

A Priori Thé. A Priori Thé has been comforting travelers for over 30 years. Come for lunch or afternoon tea featuring delicious scones, cakes, or cheesecake created by American owner Peggy Hancock. ⊠ *35 Galerie Vivienne, Louvre/Tuileries* ☎ *01–42–97–48–75.*

Ⓒ **Jardin des Tuileries.** *See the highlighted listing in this chapter.*

Fodor'sChoice
★

★ **Les Arts Décoratifs.** Sharing a wing of the Musée du Louvre, but with a separate entrance and admission charge, the Musée des Arts Décoratifs is home to a stellar collection of decorative arts. Spread across nine floors, the vast holdings include altarpieces from the Middle Ages and furnishings from the Italian Renaissance to the present day. There are period rooms reflecting the ages, such as the early 1820s salon of the Duchesse de Berry, who actually lived in the building, and several rooms reproduced from designer Jeanne Lanvin's 1920s apartment. Don't miss the gilt-and–green velvet bed of the Parisian courtesan who inspired the boudoir in Émile Zola's novel *Nana.* You can hear Zola's description of it on the free English audioguide, which is highly recommended. Don't miss the impressive jewelry gallery on the second floor.

The arts center comprises two other museums—more aptly called departments—which play host to temporary exhibitions. The Musée de la Mode et du Textiles (Museum of Fashion and Textiles), for instance, spotlights designers such as Sonia Rykiel. The other department, the Musée de la Publicité, is dedicated to advertising and publicity. Temporary exhibitions are staged in the Nef (nave). There is also a quiet

5

DID YOU KNOW?

La Fontaine des Mers (the Fountain of the Seas) is one of two fountains flanking the towering stone obelisk on the Place de la Concorde.

restaurant, Le Saut du Loup, with an outdoor terrace that serves lunch even on Monday when the museum is closed. A joint ticket is available with the exquisite Musée Nissim de Camondo. ■ TIP→ If you're combining a visit here with the Musée du Louvre, note that the museums close on different days, so don't come on Monday or Tuesday. ✉ *107 rue de Rivoli, Louvre/Tuileries* ☎ *01–44–55–57–50* ⊕ *www.lesartsdecoratifs.fr* ✂ *€9; €13 temporary exhibitions; €11.50 joint ticket with the Musée Nissim de Camondo* ⊙ *Tues.–Sun. 11–6, Thurs. 11–9* Ⓜ *Palais-Royal.*

Les Halles. For 801 years, this is the district that fed Paris, with acres of food halls overflowing with meats, fish, and vegetables. Sensuously described in Émile Zola's novel *The Belly of Paris,* Les Halles was teeming with life—though not all of it good: hucksters and homeless shared these streets with prostitutes (who still ply their trade—though in diminishing numbers—on nearby Rue St-Denis). And the plague of cat-size rats didn't cease until the market moved to the suburbs in 1969. Today, you can still see stuffed pests hanging by their tails in the windows of the circa-1872 shop Julien Aurouze (8 rue des Halles) whose sign, *Destruction des Animaux Nuisibles* (in other words, vermin extermination), says it all. All that remains of the 19th-century iron-and-glass market buildings, designed by architect Victor Baltard, is a portion of the superstructure on the southern edge of the Jardins des Halles, which was turned into an unattractive plaza and garden. The Fontaine des Innocents, sculpted in 1550, at rues Berger and Pierre Lescot, marks the site of what was once a vast cemetery before the bones were moved to the Catacombs. After years of delays, Les Halles is undergoing one of the city's most ambitious public works projects: A sweeping €500 million renovation that will transform the plaza, and the much-maligned underground concrete mall the Forum des Halles, into a place where Parisians actually want to go. In an echo of the past, a 48-foot vast iron-and-glass canopy will cover a sweeping garden and plaza, flooding light into the stores below. While the project has not been without opponents, most Parisians are happy about the prospect of a prettier Les Halles, even if they have to wait until 2016 to see it. The plaza is closed during construction, though the mall will remain open, with partial closures. Looming over the construction site is the magnificent church of St-Eustache, a Gothic gem. Film buffs may want to check out the recently renovated Forum des Images, with some 7,000 films available for viewing on individual screens. To find it, enter the mall on the side of the church at the Porte St-Eustache.

The streets surrounding Les Halles have boomed in recent years with boutiques, bars, and restaurants galore that have sent rents skyrocketing. Historic rue Montorgueil, is home to small food shops and cafés. Running parallel, rue Montmartre, near the church, still has specialty shops selling foie gras and other delicacies, though these merchants, like the butchers and bakers before them, are slowly being pushed out by trendy clothing boutiques. ✉ *Plaza/garden closed during renovation. Mall entrances on Rue Pierre Lescot, Rue Berger, and Rue Rambuteau, Beaubourg/Les Halles* ⊕ *www.forum-des-halles.com* ⊙ *Mall, Mon.–Sat. 10–8* Ⓜ *Les Halles; RER: Châtelet Les Halles.*

Fodor's Choice **Musée de Louvre.** *See the highlighted listing in this chapter.*
★

JARDIN DES TUILERIES

✉ *Bordered by Quai des Tuileries, Pl. de la Concorde, Rue de Rivoli, and the Louvre* ☎ *01-40-20-90-43* 🎟 *Free* 🕐 *June, July, and Aug., daily 7 am–11 pm; Apr., May, and Sept., daily 7:30 am–9 pm; Oct.–Mar., daily 7:30–7:30* Ⓜ *Tuileries or Concorde.*

TIPS

■ Garden buffs will enjoy the small bookstore at the entrance to the Tuileries on the Place de la Concorde. Besides books on gardening and plants (including some titles in English), there are also gift items, knickknacks, and toys for the junior gardener. Open from 10 am to 7 pm.

■ The Tuileries is one of the best places in Paris to take your kids if they're itching to run around. There's a carousel (€2) and, in summer, an amusement park.

■ If you're hungry, look for carts serving gelato from Amorino or sandwiches from the chain bakery Paul. Also, there are four cafés with terraces in the center of the garden, all moderately priced. Try Café Renard, which serves French fare, or Café Reale, with an Italian menu, in the center of the garden closer to Place de Concorde.

The Tuileries was once *the* place to see and be seen in Paris. This most French of French gardens, with verdant lawns, manicured rows of trees, and gravel paths, was designed by André Le Nôtre for Louis XIV. After the king moved his court to Versailles, in 1682, the gardens became a popular place for stylish Parisians to stroll. The name is derived from the factories once dotting this area that produced *tuiles*, or roof tiles, fired in kilns called *tuileries*. Monet and Renoir captured the Tuileries with paint and brush, and it's no wonder the Impressionists loved it—the gray, austere light of Paris's famously overcast days make the green trees appear even greener.

HIGHLIGHTS

The garden still serves as a setting for one of Paris's most lovely walks. Laid out before you is a vista of Paris's must-see monuments, with the Louvre at one end and the Place de la Concorde at the other. The Tour Eiffel is on the Seine side, along with the Musée d'Orsay, reachable across a footbridge in the center of the garden. A good place to begin is at the Louvre end, at the Arc du Carrousel, a stone-and-marble arch ordered by Napoléon to showcase the bronze horses he stole from St. Mark's Cathedral in Venice. The horses were eventually returned and replaced here with a statue of a *quadriga*, a four-horse chariot. On the Place de la Concorde end, twin buildings bookend the garden. On the Seine side, the former royal greenhouse is now the exceptional Musée de l'Orangerie, home to the largest display of Monet's lovely *Water Lilies* series, as well as a sizable collection of early-20th-century paintings. On the opposite end is the Musée du Jeu de Paume, which has some of the city's best temporary photography exhibits.

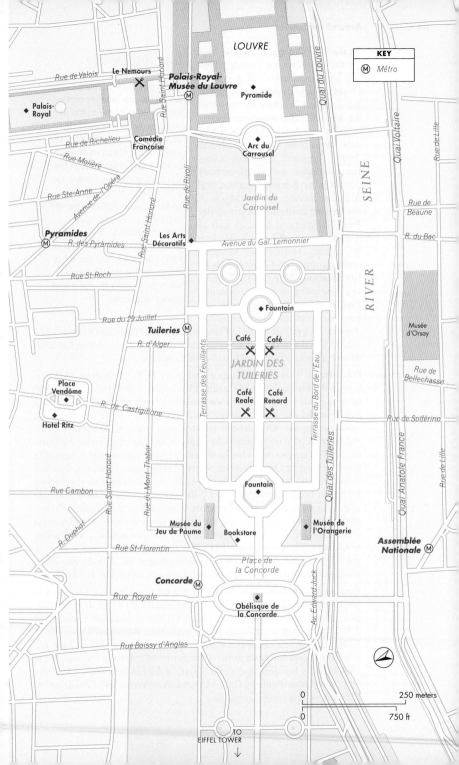

★ **Musée de l'Orangerie.** People line up for hours to see Claude Monet's huge, meditative *Water Lilies* (*Nymphéas*), displayed in galleries designed in 1914 by the master himself. The museum, once a winter greenhouse for the Tuileries' citrus trees, was renovated in 2006. The small, excellent collection includes early-20th-century paintings by Renoir, Cézanne, and Matisse, among others. Much of the private collection of art dealer Paul Guillaume is here, as well as a miniature model of his Parisian apartment. You can see Modigliani's painting of Guillaume with the notation "Novo Pilota," meaning new pilot or leader, signaling Guillaume's status as an important patron of contemporary art. ⊠ *Jardin des Tuileries at Pl. de la Concorde, Louvre/Tuileries* ☎ *01–44–77–80–07* ⊕ *www.musee-orangerie.fr* 💰 *€7.50, or €13 joint ticket with Musée d'Orsay* ⊗ *Wed.–Mon. 9–6* Ⓜ *Concorde.*

> **DID YOU KNOW?**
>
> There was once a palace called the Palais des Tuileries on the eastern edge of the Jardin des Tuileries. Catherine de Medici ordered it built shortly after the death of her husband, Henry II, in 1559. Expanded through the ages, the palace was home to a succession of nobility, from Louis XIV, who bunked here while Versailles was under construction, to Napoléon. It was set afire in 1871 during the tumult of the Paris Commune, and burned to the ground. A private committee is pushing to rebuild it with private donations.

Fodor'sChoice
★ **Palais-Royal.** This most romantic and quiet of Paris gardens, enclosed within the former home of Cardinal Richelieu (1585–1642), is an ideal spot to while away an afternoon, cuddling with your sweetheart on a bench under the trees, soaking up the sunshine beside the fountain, or browsing the 400-year-old arcades, now home to boutiques ranging from quirky (toy soldiers to music boxes) to chic (Stella McCartney and Marc Jacobs). One of the city's oldest restaurants is here, the haute-cuisine Le Grand Véfour, where brass plaques recall regulars like Napoléon and Victor Hugo. Built in 1629, the *palais* became royal when Richelieu bequeathed it to Louis XIII. Other famous residents include Jean Cocteau and Colette, who wrote of her pleasurable "country" view of the *province à Paris*. Today, the garden often plays host to giant-size temporary art installations sponsored by another tenant, the Ministry of Culture. The courtyard off Place Colette is outfitted with a strange collection of black-and-white columns installed in 1986 by the artist Daniel Buren. ⊠ *Pl. du Palais-Royal, Louvre/Tuileries* Ⓜ *Palais-Royal.*

Place de la Concorde. This square at the foot of Champs-Élysées was originally named after Louis XV. It later became the Place de la Révolution, where crowds cheered as Louis XVI, Marie-Antoinette, and some 2,500 others lost their heads to the guillotine. Renamed Concorde in 1836, it got a new centerpiece: the 75-foot granite Obelisk of Luxor, a gift from Egypt quarried in the 8th century BC. Among the handsome 18th-century buildings facing the square is the Hôtel Crillon, originally built as a private home by Gabriel, architect of Versailles's Petit Trianon. ⊠ *Champs-Élysées* Ⓜ *Concorde.*

Place Vendôme. Property laws have kept this refined square spare and pure. The architect Jules-Hardouin Mansart designed the perfectly proportioned plaza in 1702 as an octagon. To maintain a uniform appearance, Mansart built only the facades of the *hôtels particuli-ers* (mansions), and the lots behind were then sold to buyers who customized their palaces. In the square's center, a 144-foot column erected by Napoléon was toppled in 1871 by painter Gustave Courbet and his band of Revolutionaries. The Third Republic stuck the pieces back together again and sent him the bill, though he died before the first payment was due. Chopin lived and died at No. 12, which is also where Napoléon III enjoyed trysts with his mistress; since 1902 it has been home to Chaumet, one of several high-end jewelers in the area. At No. 15, the Hotel Ritz remains a top destination where celebs can often be found quaffing some of the city's best—and priciest—cocktails in the tiny Hemingway Bar. Ⓜ *Opéra.*

WORD OF MOUTH

"If you're not big into museums, stay outside of the Louvre and opt instead for the Orsay and most definitely the Orangerie, where the huge, gorgeous Monet water lily panels are."
—aliced

Fodor'sChoice ★ **Rue Montorgueil.** Lined with food shops and cafés, rue Montorgueil was once the gritty oyster hub when the Les Halles food market fed Paris. It is now the heart of one of the city's most trendy neighborhoods. Rough around the edges (the name means Mount Pride), Honoré de Balzac and his 19th-century band of scribes frequented Au Rocher de Cancale at No. 78, whose famously crumbling facade looks like it hasn't been reno-vated since then. Monet recorded the moment during the 1878 World's Fair when the street was ablaze with tricolor flags (you can see it in the Musée d'Orsay). Other addresses have been around for centuries: Stohrer at No. 58 has been baking elaborate *tartes* since 1730, and L'Escargot Montorgueil at No. 38, a favorite of Charlie Chaplin, is still graced by a giant golden snail. Relative newcomers include the luxury Nuxe spa at Nos. 32 and 34, and Levasseur, a tiny jewel box of a shop selling delicious chocolates in gorgeous boxes at No. 2 rue des Petits Carreaux (the name changes at the top of the street). Wander the streets spiraling off Mon-torgueil and Rue Montmarte, which runs parallel, to find cute boutiques selling clothing and accessories. There's a mini restaurant row along Rue Tiquetonne, and Rue Saint-Sauveur attracts a pretty crowd thanks to Experimental (No. 37), a hip cocktail lounge. Even nearby Rue St-Denis, once a run-down red-light district, is evolving with an injection of new cafés and shops, such as the organic wine bar Ma Cave Fleury at No. 177.

St-Eustache. Built as the market neighborhood's answer to Notre-Dame, this massive church is decidedly squeezed into its surroundings. Con-structed between 1532 and 1640, with foundations dating to 1200, the church mixes a Gothic exterior, complete with impressive flying but-tresses, and a Renaissance interior. On the east end (Rue Montmartre), Dutch master Rubens' *Pilgrims of Emmaus* (1611) hangs in a small chapel. Two chapels to the left is Keith Haring's *The Life of Christ*, a triptych in bronze and white-gold patina: it was given to the church after the artist's death in 1990, in recognition of the parish's efforts to help victims of AIDS. Outside is the gigantic stone head with a hand cupped to its ear: *L'Écoute* by Henri de Miller. On the Rue Montmartre side of the church, look for the small door to Ste-Agnes's crypt, topped with a stone plaque noting the date, 1213, below a curled fish, an indication the patron made his fortune in fish. ⊠ *2 impasse St-Eustache, Beaubourg/Les Halles* ⊕ *www.saint-eustache.org for concert info* ⊙ *Daily 9:30–7* Ⓜ *Les Halles; RER: Châtelet Les Halles.*

WORTH NOTING

Bourse du Commerce. Best approached from the rear, the old Commerce Exchange looks like a giant spaceship. Now home to the Paris Chamber of Commerce, it's worth a stop inside to see the beautifully restored iron-and-glass dome, which Victor Hugo dismissively likened to a jockey's cap. Still, it was the first iron structure built in France, in 1809. Behind it, the 100-foot-tall **Colonne de Ruggieri** is a remnant of a mansion built here in 1572 for Catherine de Medici. The column, which miraculously escaped destruction through the ages, was used as a platform for stargazing by her powerful astrologer, Cosimo Ruggieri. Legend has it that on stormy nights, a silhouetted figure can be seen in the metal cage at the top. ∎ TIP➔ To learn more about the building of the dome, check out the short video of its construction in the Musée des Arts and Métiers. ⊠ *2 rue de Viarmes, Halles* Ⓜ *Métro or RER: Les Halles.*

Comédie Française. Mannered productions of Molière, Racine, and Corneille appear regularly on the bill here, but only in French. Founded in 1680 by Louis XIV, the theater finally opened its doors to the public in 1799. It nearly burned to the ground a hundred years later; what you're looking at dates from 1900. The famed actress Sarah Bernhardt began her career here. ⊠ *1 pl. Colette, Louvre/Tuileries* ☎ *08–25–10–16–80* ⊕ *www.comedie-francaise.fr* Ⓜ *Palais-Royal.*

Église de la Madeleine. With its rows of uncompromising columns, this enormous neoclassical edifice in the center of the Place de la Madeleine was consecrated as a church in 1842, nearly 78 years after construction began. Initially planned as a Baroque building, it was later razed and begun anew by an architect who had the Roman Pantheon in mind. Interrupted by the Revolution, the site was razed yet again when Napoléon decided to make it into a Greek temple dedicated to the glory of his army. Those plans changed when the army was defeated and the emperor deposed. Other ideas for the building included making it into a train station, a market, and a library. Finally, Louis XVIII decided to make it a church, which it still is today. There are also concerts here. ⊠ *Pl. de la Madeleine, Faubourg* ⊕ *www.eglise-lamadeleine.com* ⊙ *Daily 9:30–7* Ⓜ *Madeleine.*

Foyer de la Madeleine. Cheap eats in the Madeleine? Even most Parisians don't know it's possible, but there are a couple of reasonable options in this posh *place.* One is in the basement of the Église: if you're standing in front of the steps to the church, walk to the right, turn the corner, and find a door to the Foyer, where friendly church ladies will serve you lunch for €10.50 (€7.50 plus €3 for a one-year membership card). The fare, if not fancy, is solid, and the wine is a great deal at €4 for a generous carafe. Served weekdays 11:45–2. Come on the early side because the food is not made to order. ⊠ *14 rue de Surène, Madeleine* ☎ *01–47–42–39–84.*

Église St-Germain-l'Auxerrois. Across from the Louvre's Cour Carée, this church, founded in 500 AD, is one of the city's oldest. The current building dates from the 13th century, and the bell, from 1529, still tolls weekly masses. ⊠ *Rue St-Germain-l'Auxerrois, Louvre/Tuileries* ☎ *01–42–60–13–96* ⊕ *www.saintgermainauxerrois.cef.fr* ☉ *Mon.–Sat. 8–7, Sun. 9–8* Ⓜ *Louvre/Rivoli.*

Musée du Jeu de Paume. This 19th-century building at the entrance to the Jardin des Tuileries, on the Rue de Rivoli side, was once used for *jeu de paume* (or "palm game," a forerunner of tennis). It later served as a transfer point for art looted by the Germans in World War II. Today it's been given another lease on life as an ultramodern, white-walled showcase for excellent temporary photography exhibits displaying icons such as Diane Arbus, Richard Avedon, Cindy Sherman, and Robert Frank, as well as up-and-comers. ⊠ *1 pl. de la Concorde, Louvre/Tuileries* ☎ *01–47–03–12–50* ⊕ *www.jeudepaume.org* 💳*€8.50* ☉ *Tues. noon–9, Wed.–Fri. noon–7, weekends 10–7* Ⓜ *Concorde.*

Passage du Grand-Cerf. This pretty glass-roofed arcade was built in 1825 and expertly renovated in 1988. Today it's home to about 20 shops, many of them small designers selling original jewelry or housewares. ⊠ *8 rue Dussoubs, Beaubourg/Les Halles* Ⓜ *Étienne Marcel.*

Angélina. Founded in 1903 and patronized by literary lights like Marcel Proust and Gertrude Stein, Angélina is famous for its (€6.90) *chocolat l'Africain*, ultrarich hot chocolate topped with whipped cream. ⊠ *226 rue de Rivoli, Louvre/Tuileries* ☎ *01–42–60–82–00.*

Ladurée. The frescoes and mirrors are showing the tearoom's age, so finicky Proust might now reserve his affections for a *macaron* at Ladurée, the elegant bakery and tea salon a short walk away. ⊠ *16 rue Royal* ☎ *01–42–60–21–79.*

Pinacothèque de Paris. When this hugely popular picture gallery opened in 2003, skeptics wondered whether Paris needed another museum, particularly one staging only temporary exhibitions. They needn't have worried: the Pinacothèque has been packing them in with shows from Rembrandt to Vermeer to Lichtenstein to Pollock. In fact, the lines in front of this space at the rear of the Èglise de Madeleine are legendary. The privately funded Pinacothèque opened a second space across the street in 2011. Buy your tickets in advance, but prepare to queue up

Continued on page 102

5

MUSÉE DU LOUVRE

Try to wrap your mind around this: The Louvre has about 35,000 pieces of art in its collection, representing nearly every civilization on earth, and more than 675,000 square feet of exhibition space. It's gone through countless cycles of construction and demolition, expansion and renovation, starting as a medieval fortress, then becoming a royal residence before opening its doors as the Museum Central des Arts at the end of the 18th century.

Left: Michelangelo's *Dying Slave*

Below: The Louvre's iconic *Pyramide*, designed by I. M. Pei.

Don't make the mistake of thinking that you'll be able to see the Louvre's entire collection in one visit and still enjoy—or remember—what you've seen. The three most popular arworks here are, of course, the *Mona Lisa,* the *Venus de Milo,* and *Winged Victory.* Beyond these must-sees, your best bet is to focus on highlights that interest you the most—and don't worry about getting lost because you're bound to stumble upon something interesting. Stop by the information desk for a free color-coded map. For help navigating the collection, rent an excellent multimedia guide (€6), or take a guided tour (€9) in English at 11 or 2 daily. The Louvre has three wings—the Richelieu, the Sully, and the Denon—arranged like a horseshoe, with I.M. Pei's striking *Pyramide* nestled outside in the middle.

For more on touring and other general information on the Louvre ⇨ *pg. 100*

HISTORY OF THE LOUVRE

Evolution of the Building

1527. François I (left) expands the palace, demolishing many original buildings and rebuilding in the new Renaissance style.

1655-58. The Queen Mother, Anne of Austria, orders up private apartments and imports Italian artists to decorate it.

1672. Sun King Louis XIV moves the royal court to Versailles and the Louvre is abandoned.

1756. Louis XV (right) resumes construction. After a century, the Cour Carrée finally gets a roof.

12TH C.	13TH C.	14TH C.	15TH C.	16TH CENTURY	17TH CENTURY	18TH CENTURY
FORTRESS		▲		ROYAL PALACE		▲ ROYAL ARTS ACADEMY ▲

1190. Philippe Auguste builds a fortress to protect Paris.

1364. Charles V converts it into a royal palace.

Henry IV adds the Grand Gallery and begins the passage to the adjacent Tuileries Palace. Work halts upon his death in 1610.

1660. Architect **Louis LeVau** is hired to finish the Louvre. Erasing all medieval traces, he adds pavilions, rebuilds facades, and doubles the palace's width.

1699. Royal Academy of Painting and Sculpture stages first exhibition.

1791. Revolutionary government declares the Louvre a national museum.

1793. Doors open to the public. Admission is free.

Acquisition of Art

17TH CENTURY
18TH CENTURY

Mona Lisa
Leonardo da Vinci, 1503-06.

Purchased by Francois I under unknown circumstances. It later adorned Napoléon I's bedroom wall.

The Slaves
Michelangelo 1513-1515.

From François I's collection. **Entered the Louvre in 1794.**

Pilgrimage to Cythera
1717, Watteau.

Acquired in 1793.

Coronation of Napoléon
1806-07, Jacques Louis David.

Commissioned by Napoléon, whose collection fell into state hands after his defeat in 1815.

Venus de Milo (Aphrodite)
Late 2nd century BC.

Found on the Greek island of Milos in 1820 and purchased by the French ambassador to Turkey, who presented it to Louis XVIII. **Placed in the Louvre in 1821.**

The Raft of the Medusa
1819, Géricault.

Purchased after the artist's death, 1824.

18TH CENTURY
19TH CENTURY

1803. Renamed Musée Napoléon and stocked with booty from the emperor's many conquests.

1852. Napoléon III (right) lays the cornerstone of the New Louvre.

1939. Artwork is hidden as World War II erupts.
1940. Near-empty museum reopens.

1989. I.M. Pei's controversial glass *Pyramide* rises over the new entrance in the Cour Napoléon.
1993. Renovated Richelieu Wing reopens.

19TH CENTURY | **20TH CENTURY** | **21ST CENTURY**

NATIONAL MUSEUM

1815. Artworks plundered by **Napoléon** returned to their native countries after his defeat.

1852-1861. Collection expands with works acquired from Egypt, Spain, and Mexico. Cour Napoléon completed.

1871. Mob sets fire to Tuileries Palace. Louvre is damaged.

1945. Asian collection sent to the new Musée Guimet.

1981. President François Mitterrand (above) kicks off Grand Louvre project to expand and modernize the museum.

2000. Non-French works destined for the future Musée de Quai Branly shown at Louvre.

2012. New 30,000-square-foot Islamic art wing opens.

Louis XV's Coronation Crown
1793. Apollo Gallery

Acquired in 1852. Original stones replaced with paste in 1729.

Winged Victory of Samothrace
Around 190 BC.

Discovered on the Greek island of Samothrace in 1863 by a French archaeologist who sent the pieces to be reassembled at the Louvre. Her right hand (in nearby glass case) was discovered in 1950.

Seated Scribe
Around 2500 BC.

Discovered in Saqqara, Egypt in 1850. **Given to France by the Egyptian government in 1854.**

The Lacemaker
Vermeer, 1669-70.

Purchased at auction in Paris, 1870.

The Turkish Bath
Ingres, 1862.

Gift to the Louvre, 1911. Commissioned by Napoléon but deemed too shocking to display. Revealed to the public in 1905.

Gabrielle d'Estrées and One of Her Sisters
Unknown artist, 1594.

Purchased in 1937. This (nipple-pinching) scene could represent sisterly teasing related to the pregnancy of Gabrielle, the favorite mistress of Henri IV.

19TH CENTURY | 20TH CENTURY

21ST CENTURY | 20TH CENTURY

RICHELIEU WING

Below Ground & Ground Floor. Entering from the Pyramide, head upstairs to the sculpture courtyards, Cour Marly and Cour Puget. In Cour Marly you'll find the **Marley Horses** (see right). Salle 2 has fragments from Cluny, the powerful Romanesque abbey in Burgundy that dominated 11th-century French Catholicism. Salles 4–6 follows the evolution of French sculpture, and in Salles 7–10 you'll find funerary art. In Cour Puget, products from the Académie Royale, the art school of 18th-century France, fill Salles 25–33. Behind this is the Near East Antiquities Collection. Salle 3's centerpiece is the Codex of Hammurabi, an 18th-century BC black-diorite stela containing the world's oldest written code of laws. In Salle 4, you'll find **Lamassu** (see right).

First Floor. Head straight through Decorative Arts to see the magnificently restored **Royal Apartments of Napoléon III** (see right).

Second Floor. Much of this floor is dedicated to French and Northern School paintings. At the entrance is a 14th-century painting of John the Good—the oldest-known individual portrait from the north of Italy. In Salle 4 hangs *The Madonna of Chancellor Rolin,* by the 15th-century Early Netherlandish master Jan van Eyck (late 14th century–1441). Peter Paul Rubens's (1577–1640) the *Disembarkation of Marie de' Medici at the Port of Marseille* is in Salle 18. In Salle 31 are several paintings by Rembrandt van Rijn (1606–69), including **Bathsheba**, his largest nude. The masterpiece of the Dutch collection is Vermeer's **The Lacemaker** (see right).

TIPS

■ The 25 paintings by Rubens commisioned by Marie de Medici for the Luxembourg Palace in Salle 18 on the second floor each mark an event in the queen's life.

■ To see what's on the minds of the museum staff, check out the Painting of the Month in Salle 17, French section, on the 2nd floor.

■ Take a hot chocolate break in the newly renovated Café Richelieu on the first floor, run by the upscale *confiseur* Angelina. There is an outdoor terrace in summer and a tempting lunch menu.

DON'T MISS

LAMASSU, 8TH CENTURY   SALLE 4

With their fierce beards and gentle eyes, these massive winged beasts are benevolent guardians straight from the dreamworld. Magical for children and adults, the strangely lifelike sculptures are located in the Near Eastern antiquities collection. The winged bull demigods are part of the Cour Khorsabad, a re-creation of the temple erected by Assyrian king Sargon II. ✦ *Richelieu, ground floor*

Lamassu

THE LACEMAKER, 1669–1671   SALLE 38

This is a small but justifiably famous gem of Dutch optical accuracy (and a must-see for fans of the movie and book, *Girl With a Pearl Earring*, to see how his style evolved over a 5-year period.) Here, Jan Vermeer (1632–75) painted the red thread in the foreground as a slightly blurred jumble, just as one would actually see it if focusing on the girl. The lacemaker's industriousness represents domestic virtue, but the personal focus of the painting is far more engaging than a simple morality tale. ✦ *Richelieu, second floor*

The Lacemaker

MARLY HORSES, 1699–1740   COUR MARLY

During the dramatic 1989 reorganization of the Louvre, two courtyards were elegantly glassed over to match the entrance pyramid. The dramatic glass-roofed Marly sculpture court houses several sculptures from Louis XIV's garden at Marly, including two magnificent winged horses by Antoine Coysevox. Later, the artist's nephew Guillaume Coustou created two accompanying earthbound horse sculptures for Louis XV; their fame was such that, during the Revolution, these sculptures were moved to the Tuileries gardens for public viewing. Now the four original horses greet visitors to the Richelieu Wing, ready to gallop off into the museum; replicas stand guard in the Tuileries. ✦ *Richelieu, lower ground floor*

The Marly Horses

ROYAL APARTMENTS
OF NAPOLÉON III, 1860s   SALLE 87

These dozen reception rooms, hung with crystal chandeliers, elaborate mirrors, and imperial velour, are a gilt-covered reminder that the Louvre was a palace for centuries, regally designed to impress. En route, you'll pass decorative items like the solid-crystal Restoration dressing table (Salle 77) that prepare you for the eye-popping luxury of the Second Empire. ✦ *Richelieu, first floor*

Royal Apartments of Napoléon

5

IN FOCUS THE LOUVRE

SULLY WING

COLLECTIONS
History of the Louvre
Ancient Egypt
Near East Antiquities
Greek, Roman, & Etruscan Antiquities
French Painting
Graphic Arts
Northern Schools
Decorative Arts

Below Ground & Ground Floor. In late 2012 the Louvre introduced its latest architectural wonder: the 30,000-square-foot Galerie Islam. Built into the Cour Visconti and topped with an undulating glass roof evoking a head scarf blowing in the wind, the Islamic arts wing contains Europe's largest collection of art from all corners of the Islamic world, including the former Ottoman Empire.

Upstairs, the north galleries of the Sully continue the ancient Iranian collection begun in the Richelieu Wing. Salle 16 has the 2nd-century BC **Venus de Milo** (see right), anchoring the Greek collection of Salles 7–17.

First Floor. The northern galleries of the first floor continue with the Decorative Arts collection including works from all over Europe, and connect with the Napoléon III apartments. American Cy Twombly's contemporary ceiling in Salle 32 was unveiled in 2010.

Second Floor. Sully picks up French painting in the 17th century where the Richelieu leaves off. The Académiciens are best exemplified by Nicolas Poussin (1594–1665, Salle 19), the first international painting star from France. The antithesis of this style was the candlelit modest work by outsider Georges de La Tour (Salle 28), as in his *Magdalene of Night Light*.

The Académie Royale defined the standards of painting through revolution, republic, and empire. Exoticism wafted in during the Napoleonic empire, as in the **Turkish Bath** (see right) painting of Jean-Auguste-Dominique Ingres (1780–1867). Fresh energy crackled into French painting in the 18th century. Antoine Watteau (1684–1721), was known for his theatrical scenes and *fêtes galantes*, portrayals of well-dressed figures in bucolic settings. In *Pilgrimage to the Island of Cythera* (Salle 36), he used delicate brushstrokes and soft tones to convey the court set, here depicted arriving on (or departing from) Cythera, the mythical isle of love.

TIPS

■ There is a little-known collection with Monet, Renoir, and Cezanne in Salle C on the second floor, the only Impressionist works in the Louvre.

■ There's a surprise in Salle 17 on the ground floor—the *Sleeping Hermaphrodite* by the entrance.

■ Be sure to look up as you make your way up Escalier Henri II. It took four years to complete this 16th-century vaulted ceiling.

■ Need a bathroom? There are some tucked between Salles 22 and 23 on the 1st floor. (And admire the colorful, 4,000-year-old Seated Scribe in Salle 22.)

■ For a breather, duck into this nook off Salle 49 on the 2nd floor, between the two Vernets. Sit on the bench and enjoy a view of the Cour Carrée, one of the oldest parts of the Louvre.

DON'T MISS

RAMSES II, APPROX. 1200 BC   **SALLE 12**

The sphinx-guarded Egyptian Wing is the biggest display of Egyptian antiquities in the world after the Cairo museum—not surprising, considering that Egyptology as a Western concept was invented by a Frenchman, Champollion, founder of the Louvre's Egypt collection and translator of the hieroglyphics on the Rosetta Stone. This statue from the site of Tanis, presumed to be Ramses II, never fails to stop visitors' breath with its gleaming stone, beatific expression, and perfect proportions. ✛ *Sully, ground floor*

Ramses II

VENUS DE MILO, APPROX. 120 BC   **SALLE 16**

After countless photographs and bad reproductions, the original Aphrodite continues to dazzle. The armless statue, one of the most reproduced and recognizable works of art in the world, is actually as beautiful as they say—and even lovelier after a 6-month cleaning and rehab in 2010 that took place afer hours and on Tuesdays, when the museum is closed. She was unearthed on the Greek island of Milos in the 19th century and sold for 6,000 francs to the French ambassador in Constantinople, who presented her to King Louis XVIII. ✛ *Sully, ground floor*

Venus de Milo

MEDIEVAL MOAT, 13TH CENTURY   MEDIEVAL LOUVRE

Wander around the perimeter of the solidly built original moat to reach the remarkable Salle Saint-Louis with its elegant columns and medieval artifacts. Keep an eye out for the parade helmet of Charles VI, which was dug up in 169 fragments and astonishingly reassembled. ✛ *Sully, lower ground floor*

Medieval Moat

THE TURKISH BATH, 1862   **SALLE 60**

Though Jean-August-Dominique Ingres' (1780–1867) long-limbed women hardly look Turkish, they are singularly elegant and his polished immaculate style was imitated by an entire generation of French painters. This painting is a prime example of Orientalism, where Western artists played out fantasies of the Orient in their work. Popular as a society portrait painter, Ingres returned repeatedly to langorous nudes—compare the women of the *Turkish Bath* with the slinky figure in his *La Grande Odalisque*, in the Denon Wing. ✛ *Sully, second floor*

The Turkish Bath

THE DENON WING

Below Ground & Ground Floor. To the south and east of the *Pyramide* entrance are galleries displaying early Renaissance Italian sculpture, including a 15th-century Madonna and Child by the Florentine Donatello (1386–1466). Before going upstairs, it's worth walking through the galleries of Etruscan and Roman works. In Salle 18 you'll find the 6th-century Etruscan Sarcophagus from Cerveteri, showing a married couple pieced together from thousands of clay fragments.

Drift upstairs to Italian sculpture on the ground level, concluding with Salle 4, where you'll find Michelangelo's Slaves (1513–15).

First Floor. Walk up the marble Escalier Daru to discover the sublime **Winged Victory of Samothrace** (see right). Then head to the Gallerie d'Apollon, reopened in 2004 after a stunning renovation. Built in 1661 but not finished until 1851, the hall was a model for Versaille's Hall of Mirrors.

Back out and into Paintings, you'll find four by Leonardo da Vinci (1452–1519). His enigmatic, androgynous St-John the Baptist hangs here, along with more overtly religious works such as the 1483 Virgin of the Rocks. Take a close look at the pretty portrait of La Belle Ferronnière, which Leonardo painted a decade before the **Mona Lisa** (see right); it will give you something to compare with Mona when you finally get to meet her in the Salle des Etats, near Salles 5 and 6. Head across to Salle 75 for an artistic 180°: the gleaming pomp and circumstance of a new empire with the **Coronation of Napoléon** (see right) by French classicist Jacques-Louis David (1748–1825).

In Salle 77 is the graphic 1819 **The Raft of the Medusa,** (see right) by Théodore Géricault (1791–1824).

TIPS

■ Don't skip the coat check on the ground floor tucked behind the stairs. Much of the museum is hot and stuffy.

■ Need a break? Café Mollien on the first floor has a nice view of the pyramid and an outdoor terrace that opens in the summer.

■ For an easy escape, duck out the Porte de Lions at the end of the wing. On your way out, check out the Goyas in Salle 32 on the first floor. (But don't forget your coat!)

■ Don't miss the glass case near *Winged Victory of Samothrace* on the first floor. It contains her two-fingered hand.

DON'T MISS

MONA LISA, 1503   **SALLE 7**

The most famous painting in the world, *La Gioconda* (*La Joconde* in French) is tougher than she looks: the canvas was stolen from the Louvre by an Italian nationalist in 1911, recovered from a Florentine hotel, and survived an acid attack in 1956. She is believed to be the wife of Francesco del Giocondo, a Florentine millionaire, and was probably 24 when she sat for this painting; some historians believe the portrait was actually painted after her death. Either way, she has become immortal through da Vinci's ingenious "sfumato" technique, which combines glowing detail with soft, depth-filled brushwork. ✛ *Denon, first floor*

Mona Lisa

THE RAFT OF THE MEDUSA, 1819   **SALLE 77**

Théodore Géricault was inspired by the grim news report that survivors of a wrecked French merchant ship were left adrift on a raft without supplies. Géricault interviewed survivors, visited the morgue to draw corpses, and turned his painting of the disaster into a strong indictment of authority, the first time an epic historical painting had taken on current events in this way. Note the desperate energy from the pyramid construction of bodies on the raft and the manipulation of greenish light. ✛ *Denon, first floor*

The Raft of the Medusa

WINGED VICTORY OF SAMOTHRACE, 305 BC   STAIRS

Poised for flight at the top of the Escalier Daru, this exhilarating statue was found on a tiny Greek island in the northern Aegean. Depicted in the act of descending from Olympus, *Winged Victory*, or Nike, to the Ancient Greeks, was carved to commemorate the naval victory of Demetrius Poliorcetes over the Persians. ✛ *Denon, first floor*

Winged Victory of Samothrace

CORONATION OF NAPOLÉON, 1805   **SALLE 75**

Classicist Jacques-Louis David (1748–1825) was the ultimate painter-survivor: he began his career under the protection of the King, became official designer of the Revolutionary government, endured two rounds of exile, and became one of the greatest of Napoléon's painters. Here, David avoided the politically fraught moment of December 2, 1804—when Napoléon snatched the crown from the hands of Pope Pius VII to place it upon his own head—choosing instead the romantic moment when the new emperor turned to crown Joséphine. ✛ *Denon, first floor*

Detail from the Coronation of Napoléon

PLANNING YOUR VISIT

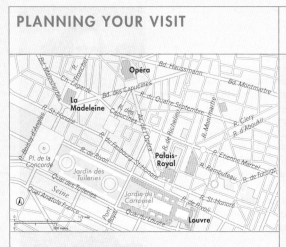

TOURS

Pick up a slick multimedia guide at the entrance to each wing; €6 buys you information on 250 artworks, four self-guided tours, and a "Where Am I?" function you can click to get your bearings.

There are 90-minute guided tours (€9) in English daily at 11 and 2. The meeting point is at "Accueil des Groups" under the pyramid. There are also free thematic leaflets to self-guide through a particular trail—some designed especially for kids. The Louvre has a phenomenal program of courses and workshops (mostly in French); see Web site for details.

ACCESSIBILITY

Wheelchair visitors or those with strollers can skip the long entry line and use the marvelous cylinder lift inside the entrance pyramid.

WITH KIDS

Begin your tour in the Sully Wing at the Medieval moat, which leads enticingly to the sphinx-guarded entrance of the Egyptian Wing, a must for mummy enthusiasts. For a more in-depth visit, you can reserve private kid-centric family tours such as the Paris Muse Clues (www.parismuse.com). Don't forget the Tuileries is right next door (with carnival rides in summer).

ENTRY TIPS

Those in the know head straight for the entrance in the underground mall, Carrousel du Louvre (99 rue de Rivoli), which has automatic ticket machines. There are more machines under the pyramid entrance., or use the Porte de Lions entrance on the southwestern corner (closed Fridays). Be sure to hold onto your ticket. You can come and go as often as you like during one day. The shortest entry lines tend to be around 9:30 AM and 1 PM. Crowds are also thinner on late-night Wednesday and Friday openings. Remember that the Louvre is closed on Tuesday.

A WHIRLWIND TOUR

If you've come to Paris and feel you must go to the Louvre to see the Big Three—**Venus de Milo, Winged Victory,** and **Mona Lisa**—even though you'd rather be strolling along the Champs-Elysees, it can be done in an hour or less if you plan well. Start in Denon and head upstairs through Estruscan and Greek antiquities, walking down the long hall of sculptures until you see the Winged Victory in front of you. Take a right and head up the staircase through French painting to the Mona Lisa. Then go back down under the Pyramide to Sully to see the Venus de Milo.

✉ Palais du Louvre, Louvre/ Tuileries

☎ 01-40-20-53-17 (information)

🌐 www.louvre.fr

🎟 €10 (€10.50 projected). Free 1st Sun. of month, under 18 (anytime); €11 for Napoléon Hall exhibitions

🕐 Mon., Thurs., and weekends 9–6; Wed. and Fri. 9 AM–9:30 PM

Ⓜ Palais-Royal / Musée du Louvre

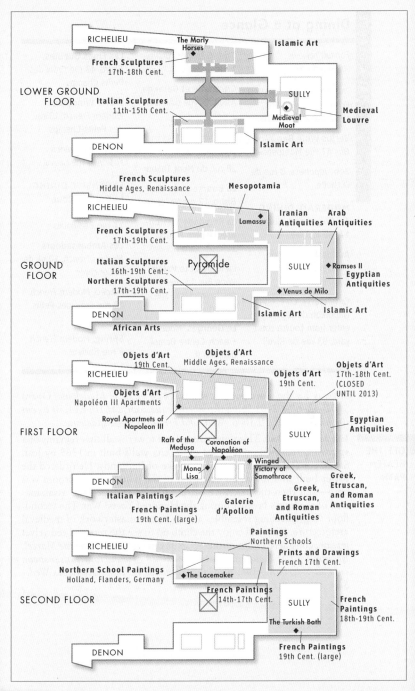

Dining at a Glance

For full reviews
⇨ *Chapter 14.*

INEXPENSIVE DINING
Frenchie Bar à Vins,
Wine Bar, 6 rue du Nil

Verjus Wine Bar, *Wine Bar,* 47 rue Montpensier

Zen, *Japanese,* 8 rue de l'Echelle

MODERATE DINING
Au Gourmand, *Bistro,* 17 rue Molière

Au Pied de Cochon, *Brasserie,* 6 rue Coquillière

Café Marly, *Café,* Cour Napoléon du Louvre, enter from Louvre courtyard, 93 rue de Rivoli

Chez Georges, *Bistro,* 1 rue du Mail

Citronelle et Galanga, *Asian,* 15 rue d'Aboukir

Frenchie, *Bistro,* 5 rue de Nil

L'Ardoise, *Bistro,* 28 rue du Mont Thabor

La Bourse ou la Vie, *Bistro,* 12 rue Vivienne

La Régalade St. Honoré, *Modern French,* 123 rue Saint-Honoré

La Robe et le Palais, *Wine Bar,* 13 rue des Lavandières-Ste-Opportuneen

Le Georges, *Modern French,* Centre Pompidou, 6th fl.

Les Fines Gueules, *Bistro,* 43 rue Croix des Petits Champs

Willi's Wine Bar, *Modern French,* 13 rue des Petits-Champs

Yam'Tcha, *French Fusion,* 4 rue Sauval

EXPENSIVE DINING
Le Grand Véfour, *Modern French,* 17 rue Beaujolais

Les Ambassadeurs, *Modern French,* 10 pl. de la Concorde

Macéo, *Modern French,* 43 rue Crois des Petits Champs

Spring, *Modern French,* 6 rue Bailleul

anyway for the more popular shows. ⊠ *28 pl. de la Madeleine, Opéra* ☎ *01–42–68–02–01* ⊕ *www.pinacotheque.com* 💳 *€10; €11.50 to cut the line* ☉ *Daily 10:30–6, Wed. and Fri. until 9* Ⓜ *Madeleine.*

OFF THE BEATEN PATH

Tour Jean Sans Peur. This unimposing little tower is all that remains of a sprawling mansion on the edge of the city walls built in 1369 by Jean Sans Peur (John the Fearless), the Duke of Burgundy. He ordered the tower built in 1409 as an extension of the house—his bedroom was here—and then the defensive turret after he arranged the assassination of the king's brother during the Hundred Years' War. The second-floor vaulted ceiling resembles a leafy tree, a masterwork of medieval architecture. Kids will enjoy the climb up to see the restored red velvet latrine, considered state-of-the-art in its time. ⊠ *20 rue Étienne Marcel, Beaubourg/Les Halles* ☎ *01–40–26–20–28* ⊕ *www.tourjeansanspeur. com* 💳 *€5* ☉ *Nov.–Apr., Wed. and weekends 1:30–6; May–Sept., Wed.–Sun. 1:30–6* Ⓜ *Étienne Marcel.*

Les Grands Boulevards

WITH THE OPÉRA GARNIER

WORD OF MOUTH

"The [Opéra] Garnier tour is well worth the time. We loved the over-the-top design and the use of so many types of marble. The main stairwell outdoes anything in Versailles . . . the Chagall on the ceiling completely surprised us and must have caused quite a stir at the time."

—Mikenmass

GETTING ORIENTED

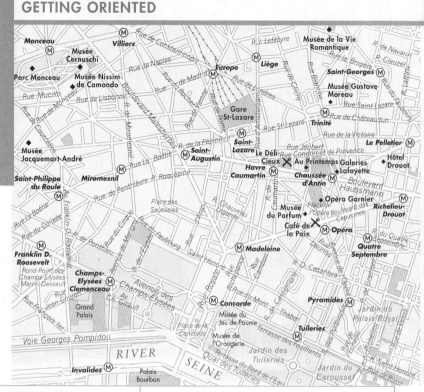

GETTING HERE	TOP REASONS TO GO

This neighborhood covers parts of the 2e, 3e, 8e, and 9e arrondissements. Take the métro to the Opéra station, named for the elegant opera house. Just behind it, you can find the department stores Galeries Lafayette and Au Printemps, each with three buildings (women's, men's, home) along Baron Haussmann's wide avenues known as the Grands Boulevards. If you're planning to visit the numerous small museums, take the métro to Parc Monceau.

Les Grands Magasins. Sample a new perfume under the magnificent dome at Galeries Lafayette; update your look, wander the sumptuous food halls, or gaze at Parisian rooftops from the outdoor café at Au Printemps.

Opéra Garnier. It may not be haunted by the Phantom, but this 19th-century opera house still dazzles. Enjoy a ballet or an opera, take the guided tour, or simply wander the opulent halls bedecked in marble and gold leaf.

Musée Jacquemart-André. Peruse the private collection of Italian Renaissance masterpieces and admire the elegant furnishings in one of the city's grandest mansions.

Parc Monceau. Join the well-dressed children of well-heeled Parisians and frolic on some of the prettiest lawns in the city.

Les Passages Couverts. Stroll the passages Jouffroy, Verdeau, and Panoramas to experience what the original shopping malls were like 200 years ago.

BEST CAFÉS

Café de la Paix. Once described as the "center of the civilized world," this grand café was a meeting place for the glitterati of the Belle Époque. It's still an elegant place to enjoy a drink overlooking the Opéra Garnier. If you're hungry, the terrace serves simpler fare than the restaurant. ✉ *5 pl. de l'Opéra, Opéra/Grands Boulevards* ☎ *01–40–07–36–36* Ⓜ *Havre Caumartin, Opéra.*

Delaville Café. Edgy and cool, this café is a favorite with locals. Open until 2 am, it's best for an evening aperitif and snack. A DJ spins tunes on weekend nights. ✉ *34 bd. de Bonne Nouvelle* ☎ *01–48–24–48–09* Ⓜ *Poissonière.*

Le Déli-Cieux. Perched on the top floor of Printemps Beauté/Maison store, Déli-Cieux serves sandwiches, salads, and burgers. It's not expensive, and the view from the outdoor terrace is priceless. It's open until 10 pm on Thursday. ✉ *Bd. Haussmann and Rue du Havre, 9th fl., Opéra/Grands Boulevards* ☎ *01–42–82–62–76* Ⓜ *Havre-Caumatin, Opéra.*

MAKING THE MOST OF YOUR TIME

If you're a serious shopper, plan on a daylong visit to this neighborhood, beginning with the department stores near the Opéra métro stop. Nearly every French chain has a shop dotting the boulevard, which changes names several times (Boulevard Haussmann, Montmartre, Poissonnière, de Bonne Nouvelle, etc.) as it plods its way from west to east. If shopping isn't your bag, plan on a long afternoon's visit: tour the Opéra Garnier and one or two museums, or bring a picnic lunch to lovely Parc Monceau on the western edge.

6

Sightseeing
★★★
Dining
★★★
Lodging
★★★★★
Shopping
★★★★★
Nightlife
★★★★★

In Belle Époque Paris, the Grands Boulevards were the place to see and be seen: in the cafés, at the opera, or in the ornate *passages couverts*, the glass-roofed arcades that were the world's first shopping malls. If you close your eyes, you can almost imagine the Grands Boulevards immortalized on canvas by the Impressionists: well-dressed Parisians strolling wide avenues dotted with shops, cafés, and horse-drawn carriages—all set against a backdrop of stately Haussmannian buildings. Today, despite the chain stores, sidewalk vendors, and fast-food joints, the Grands Boulevards remain the city's shopping epicenter, home to the most popular department stores, Galeries Lafayette and Au Printemps, near Place de l'Opéra at the heart of the long chain of avenues.

Shopping aside, the Grands Boulevards are a cultural destination anchored by the magnificent **Opéra Garnier,** commissioned by Napoléon III. The neighborhood is also home to some of the city's best small museums, all former private collections housed in 19th-century *hôtels particuliers* (or mansions) that alone are worth the trip. The exquisite **Musée Jacquemart-André** displays an impressive collection of Italian Renaissance art, while the jewel-box **Musée Nissim de Camondo** remembers one family's tragic end. The **Musée Cernuschi** has an impressive collection of Asian art, and the **Musée Gustave Moreau** is a quirky tribute to the Symbolist master.

TOP ATTRACTIONS

Updated by
Bryan Pirolli

Au Printemps. Spread across three buildings, this vast upscale department store has been luring shoppers since 1865. Besides the clothes, shoes, and everything else, there are appealing lunch options here: Admire the Belle Époque green-and-gold dome in Brasserie Printemps on the sixth floor of the main store. Le World Bar on the fifth floor of the men's store is a cozy pub with a cool vibe. And Le Déli-Cieux, the ninth-floor cafeteria-style restaurant at Printemps Beauté/Maison, has a large outdoor terrace with a great view. ⊠ *64 bd. Haussmann, Opéra/Grands Boulevards* ☎ *01–42–82–57–87* ⊕ *www.printemps.com* ⊗ *Mon.–Wed., Fri., and Sat. 9:35–8, Thurs. 9:35 am–10 pm* Ⓜ *Havre Caumartin, Opéra.*

> **SUPER SHOPPING TIP**
>
> Both Galeries Lafayette and Au Printemps offer 10% discount cards to foreign visitors. Some items, usually designer clothing and sale items, are excluded. To get one, go to the welcome desk on the main floor of either store. Remember to bring a passport or driver's license.

☕ **Chocostory: Le Musée Gourmand du Chocolat.** Considering that a daily dose of chocolate is practically obligatory in Paris, it's hard to believe this newcomer (opened in 2010) is the city's first museum dedicated to the sweet stuff. Spread across three floors, exhibits tell the story of chocolate from the earliest traces of the "divine nectar" in Mayan and Aztec cultures, through to its introduction in Europe by the Spanish, who added milk and sugar to the spicy dark brew and launched a continental craze. There are detailed explanations in English, with many for the kids. While the production of chocolate is a major topic, there is a respectable collection of some 1,000 chocolate-related artifacts, such as terra-cotta Mayan sipping vessels (they blew into straws to create foam) and delicate chocolate pots in fine porcelain that were favored by the French royal court. There are frequent chocolate-making demonstrations, which finish with a free tasting. ⊠ *28 bd. de Bonne Nouvelle, Opéra/Grands Boulevards* ☎ *01–42–29–68–60* ⊕ *www.museeduchocolat.fr* 🎫 *€7* ⊗ *Daily 10–5* Ⓜ *Bonne-Nouvelle, Strasbourg, St-Denis.*

Galeries Lafayette. The stunning Byzantine glass *coupole*, or dome of the city's most famous department store, is not to be missed. Wander to the center of the main store, amid the perfumes and cosmetics, and look up. If shopping isn't your thing, enjoy a glass of champagne at the Bar à Bulles at the top of the first-floor escalator. Or have lunch at one of the restaurants, including a new rooftop café in the main store (open in spring and summer). On your way down, the top floor of the main store is a good place to pick up interesting Paris souvenirs. Next door, the excellent Lafayette Gourmet food hall, on the second floor of the men's store, has one of the city's best selections of delicacies. Try a green tea éclair from Japanese–French baker Sadaharu Aoki. ⊠ *40 bd. Haussmann, Opéra/Grands Boulevards* ☎ *01–42–82–34–56* ⊕ *www. galerieslafayette.com* ⊗ *Mon.–Wed., Fri., and Sat. 9:30–9, Thurs. 9:30–10* Ⓜ *Chaussée d'Antin, Opéra; RER: Auber.*

6

Fodor's Choice ★ **Musée Cernuschi.** Wealthy Milanese banker and patriot Enrico (Henri) Cernuschi fled to Paris in 1850 after the new Italian government collapsed, only to be arrested during the 1871 Paris Commune. He subsequently decided to wait out the unrest by traveling and collecting Asian art. Upon his return 18 months later, he had a special mansion built on the edge of Parc Monceau to house his treasures, notably a two-story bronze Buddha from Japan. Today, this well-appointed museum contains Paris's second-most important collection of Asian art, after the Musée Guimet. Cernuschi had a stunning eye not only for the bronze pieces he adored but also for Neolithic pottery (8,000 BC), *mingqi* tomb figures (300–900 AD), and an impressive array of terra-cotta figures from various dynasties. A collection highlight is *La Tigresse*, a bronze wine vessel in the shape of a roaring feline (11th century BC) purchased after Cernuschi's death. The museum is free but there is a charge for temporary exhibitions; previous shows have featured Japanese drawings, Iranian sculpture, and vintage photographs of Cambodia's temples. ⊠ *7 av. Velasquez, Parc Monceau* ☎ *01–53–96–21–50* ⊕ *www.paris.fr/musees* ⊠ *Free; temporary exhibitions about €7* ⊗ *Tues.–Sun. 10–6* Ⓜ *Monceau.*

> ### DID YOU KNOW?
>
> The inspiration for the mysterious lake underneath the Opéra Garnier in *The Phantom of the Opera* occurred when construction of the building was delayed while the marshy site was drained. Rumors of an underground river began to circulate, and from there it was a small leap for Gaston Leroux to invent the Phantom sailing on an underground waterway. In the movie version, a vengeful Phantom sent the opera's chandelier crashing into the audience, an idea also inspired by real life: in 1896 one of the counterweights of the 8-ton crystal chandelier fell, crushing a woman in her red velvet seat.

OFF THE BEATEN PATH

Musée Gustave Moreau. A visit to the quirky town house and studio of painter Gustave Moreau (1826–98), a high priest of the Symbolist movement, is well worth your time. With an eye on his legacy, Moreau created a light-flooded gallery on the two top floors of his four-story home that would best show off his dark paintings after his death. Some of the works appear unfinished, such as the *Unicorns (No. 213)* inspired by the medieval tapestries in the Musée Cluny: Moreau refused to work on it further, spurning the wishes of a wealthy would-be patron. His interpretation of Biblical scenes and Greek mythology combine flights of fantasy with a keen use of color, shadow, and tracings influenced by Persian and Indian miniatures. There are wax sculptures and cupboards with sliding vertical doors containing small-format paintings. The Symbolists loved objects, and Moreau was no different. His cramped private apartment on the second floor is jam-packed with bric-a-brac, and artworks cover every inch of the walls. ⊠ *14 rue de la Rochefoucauld, Opéra/Grands Boulevards* ☎ *01–48–74–38–50* ⊕ *www.musee-moreau.fr* ⊠ *€5* ⊗ *Wed.–Mon. 10–12:45 and 2–5:15* Ⓜ *Trinité.*

Fodor's Choice ★ **Musée Jacquemart-André.** Perhaps the city's best small museum, the opulent Musée Jacquemart-André is home to a vast collection of art and furnishings lovingly assembled in the late 19th century by banking heir

Edouard André and his artist wife, Nélie Jacquemart. Their midlife marriage in 1881 raised eyebrows—he was a dashing bachelor and a Protestant, and she, no great beauty, hailed from a modest Catholic family. Still, theirs was a happy union fused by a common passion for art. For six months every year, the couple traveled, most often to Italy, where they hunted works from the Renaissance, their preferred period. Their collection also includes French painters Fragonard, Jacques-Louis David, and François Boucher, and Dutch masters Van Dyke and Rembrandt. The Belle Époque mansion itself is a star attraction. The elegant ballroom, equipped with collapsible walls operated by then-state-of-the-art hydraulics, could hold 1,000 guests. The winter garden was a wonder of its day, spilling into the *fumoir*, where the dashing André would share cigars with the *grands hommes* (important men) of the day. You can tour the separate bedrooms—his in dusty pink, hers in pale yellow. The former dining room, now an elegant café features a ceiling by Tiepolo. Don't forget to pick up the free audioguide in English, and do inquire about the current temporary exhibition (two per year), which is usually top-notch. ■ TIP➜ Plan on a Sunday visit and enjoy the popular brunch (€28) in the café from 11 to 3. Reservations are not accepted, so come early or late to avoid waiting in line. ⊠ *158 bd. Haussmann, Parc Monceau* ☎ *01–45–62–11–59* ⊕ *www.musee-jacquemart-andre.com* 🎟 *€10* ⏱ *Daily 10–6; Mon. and Sat. until 9:30 during exhibitions* Ⓜ *St-Philippe-du-Roule, Miromesnil.*

6

Fodor's Choice
★

Opéra Garnier. Haunt of the Phantom of the Opera and the real-life inspiration for Edgar Degas's dancer paintings, the opulent Opéra Garnier is one of two homes of the National Opera of Paris. The building, the Palais Garnier, was begun in 1860 by then-unknown architect Charles Garnier, who finished his masterwork 15 long years later, way over budget. Festooned with (real) gold leaf, colored marble, paintings, and sculpture from the top artists of the day, the opera house was about as subtle as Versailles and sparked controversy in post-Revolutionary France. The sweeping marble staircase, in particular, drew criticism from a public skeptical of its extravagance. But Garnier, determined to make a landmark that would last forever, spared no expense. The magnificent grand foyer, restored in 2004, is one of the most exquisite salons in France. In its heyday, the cream of Paris society strolled all 59 yards of the vast hall at intermission, admiring themselves in the towering mirrors. To see the opera house, buy a ticket for an unguided visit, which allows access to most parts of the building, including a peek into the auditorium. There is also a small ballet museum with a few works by Degas and the tutu worn by prima ballerina Anna Pavlova when she danced her epic Dying Swan in 1905. To get to it, pass through the unfinished entrance built for Napoléon III and his carriage (construction was abruptly halted when the emperor abdicated in 1870). On the upper level, you can see a sample of the auditorium's original classical ceiling, which was later replaced with a modern version by an octagenarian Mark Chagall. His trademark willowy figures encircling the dazzling crystal chandelier—today the world's third largest—shocked an unappreciative public upon its debut in 1964. Critics who fret that Chagall's masterpiece clashes with the fussy crimson-and-gilt decor can take some comfort in knowing that the original ceiling is preserved underneath, encased in a plastic dome.

Continued on page 115

C'EST *SUPER* CHIC:
HOW NOT TO LOOK LIKE AN AMERICAN IN PARIS

It's hard to imagine a trip to Paris that doesn't include, at the very least, an afternoon of shopping. But the question is what to wear *while* you're shopping—and sightseeing, and eating at a café—since fashion will always reign supreme in the City of Light.

No matter where you live or what your style, from the moment you step off the plane you'll obsess over how to achieve the relaxed, elegant way Parisian women dress. You'll marvel at how they casually toss a scarf around their neck and have it look amazing, or how they can make a 15-year-old cashmere cardigan look fresh with a skinny belt. Suddenly, virtually all the clothes in your suitcase may feel outdated, frumpy, and wrong.

But fret not, *ma chère amie*. You're not destined to walk around Paris feeling less-than. We've given you a fail-safe guide that promises to keep you looking fabulous as you stroll down the Champs-Elysées or around the Marais. But we can't promise that once you hit the streets of this fashion-obsessed city, that your credit card won't max out faster than you can say *oh la la*.

LA JEUNE FEMME

She's that young wisp of a thing standing on rue Oberkampf, chatting with her friends, cigarette in hand, looking as if she's had less than her eight hours—and whatever she has on, she wears it well.

Denim mini

Antoine & Lili

Vanessa Bruno tote

Repetto ballet flats

L'Autre Cafe, Oberkampf

Converse high top

INSPIRATION: Audrey Tautou

BEST ACCESSORY: The huge, costume cocktail ring you found at the bar last night.

FAVORITE PARTS OF TOWN: Canal St-Martin, Oberkampf, the Bastille.

BIGGEST SPLURGE: Are those 200 euro jeans from Colette really considered a splurge when you wear them every day?

CHIC BOUTIQUE: Thank goodness the designers have secondary lines! Now you'll only spend one paycheck at Antoine & Lili.

CHAIN STORE KNOCKOFF: Never underestimate the genius that is H&M.

FAVORITE PICK—ME—UP: A croque madame and side of *frites*.

MODE OF TRANSPORT: Get thee a boyfriend with a Vespa! Otherwise, it's the métro for you.

WON'T LEAVE THE HOUSE WITHOUT: Your trendy new cell phone.

MUST-HAVE ITEM: Nearly-destroyed high-top Converse. Hands down.

LA DAME ELEGANTE

How's she so stunning at the Sunday market, children in tow, no make-up, hair up in a knot? Easy—she's meticulous about skincare, has in-laws with a house in the south, and is carrying the latest bag from Longchamps.

Cartier necklace

agnès b.

Longines watch

Lamarthe bag

Café L'Etoile Manquante

Cacharel perfume

INSPIRATION: Juliette Binoche

BEST ACCESSORY: The 400 euro cashmere Chanel sweater you just scored from that fabulous consignment shop on rue St-Honoré. It retailed for more than double the price!

FAVORITE PARTS OF TOWN: The Marais, Rive Gauche.

BIGGEST SPLURGE: It's hard to resist those new platform sandals from Dior.

CHIC BOUTIQUE: You can't get enough of Chloé, but you'll settle for anything from Vanessa Bruno.

CHAIN STORE KNOCKOFF: How is it that you ever survived without agnès b.?

FAVORITE PICK—ME—UP: Lentil and poached egg salad and sparkling water.

MODE OF TRANSPORT: You take the métro, but chances are you have an Audi that'll get you and the kids out of town.

WON'T LEAVE THE HOUSE WITHOUT: The scarf your grandmother bought you for Christmas.

MUST-HAVE ITEM: Every elegant woman needs a trench coat.

LA GRANDE DAME

You can't miss her walking down the Champs-Elysées—she's still turning heads, with her Chanel suit, Hermès scarf, and her near-perfect posture. Something to aspire to...

Cartier earrings

Les Ambassadeurs, Place de la Concorde

Place Vendome Square

Roger Vivier flats

Cartier tank watch

IN FOCUS 6 C'EST SUPER CHIC: HOW NOT TO LOOK LIKE AN AMERICAN IN PARIS

INSPIRATION: Catherine Deneuve

BEST ACCESSORY: Your favorite companions: your two French poodles.

FAVORITE PARTS OF TOWN: The Faubourg St-Honoré and the Grand Boulevards to name a few...but definitely not the Rive Gauche.

BIGGEST SPLURGE: Does it really have to be just one? If so, a private jet will do.

CHIC BOUTIQUE: Only the standards—that's Chanel and Hermès, darling...

CHAIN STORE KNOCKOFF: What's a knockoff?

FAVORITE PICK—ME—UP: Foie gras or steak tartare...plus champagne.

MODE OF TRANSPORT: Having a driver is really the only way to get around with all those shopping bags.

WON'T LEAVE THE HOUSE WITHOUT: Your Chanel No. 5.

MUST-HAVE ITEM: A Kelly bag, of course!

SCARF–TYING 101

THE FRENCH KNOT

Wrap around once so both ends are behind your neck; bring ends forward and tie double-knot to the side, under chin.

THE NECK WRAP

With a square scarf, make a triangle. Bring to neck with point facing downward; wrap long ends around back and bring forward; tie loose double-knot, just off-center.

THE SQUARE KNOT

Tie around neck with ends in front. Alternate wrapping ends up and through neck loop until they reach the back. Tie end tips and tuck in knot.

DO'S & DON'TS OF DRESSING IN PARIS

- When in doubt, DO wear black.

- DON'T overdo jewelry. A minimalist look is better.

- For those on the smaller side, DO go braless—they're decidedly optional.

- DON'T get a french manicure (the French don't!). Your best bet is to keep nails short with clear polish.

- DO wear your glasses if they're funky and colorful. Bonus for not having to schlep solution on the plane!

- If you visit in summer, DON'T dress like you're going to camp.

- DO bring a scarf or two. You'll look instantly chic with one wrapped loosely around your neck.

- DON'T match your shoes to your bag—or spend time worrying about matching too much at all.

- DO carry a backpack— but only if it's small, sleek, and doesn't say college student.

- DO rock your best t-shirt and a pair of Chucks with just about anything—even a skirt!

Paris's Covered Arcades

Before there were the *grands magasins,* there were the *passages couverts,* covered arcades that offered the early-19th-century Parisian shopper a hodgepodge of shops under one roof, and a respite from the mud and grit of streets that did not have sidewalks. Until the rise of the department stores in the latter part of the century, they would rule as the top places to wander, as well as shop. Technical and architectural wonders of the time, the vaulting structures of iron and frosted glass inspired artists and writers such as Émile Zola.

Of the 150 arcades built around Paris in the early 1800s, only about a dozen are still in business today, mostly in the 2e and 9e arrondissements. Two arcades still going strong are the fabulously restored Galerie Vivienne (⊠ 4 rue Petits Champs, 2e) and the Galerie Véro-Dodat (⊠ 19 rue Jean-Jacques Rousseau, 1er), both lined with glamorous boutiques such as Jean-Paul Gaultier and shoemaker-to-the-stars Christian Louboutin *(see Chapter 5: The Faubourg St-Honoré).*

Three other modest passages enjoying a renaissance can be found end to

end off the Grands Boulevards, east of Place de l'Opéra. Begin with the most refined, the **Passage Jouffroy** (⊠ 10 bd. Montmartre, 9e), which is home to the Musée Grevin and the well-regarded budget Hotel Chopin. There's a quirky array of shops such as M.G.W. Segas at No. 34, where the three Segas brothers sell a wildly eccentric collection of furnishings and canes capped with animal heads and whatnot. Or outfit your dollhouse at Pain d'épices (No. 29), which stocks thousands of miniatures. Pop out at the northern end of Passage Jouffroy and cross the Rue de la Grange-Batelière into the **Passage Verdeau** (9e), where you can pick up some antique candlesticks—or a cow skull—at the quirky red-walled Valence gallery at No. 22. On the southern end of the Passage Jouffroy, across Boulevard Montmartre, is the **Passage des Panoramas** (2e). The granddaddy of the arcades, built in 1800, became the first public space in Paris equipped with gaslights in 1817. A few philatelist shops remain, though the arcade is now dominated by restaurants, including two popular wine bar/bistros, Racines at No. 8 and Coinstot at No. 26 bis.

6

The Opéra Garnier plays host to the Paris Ballet as well as a few operas each season (most are performed at the Opéra Bastille). If you're planning to see a performance, reserve two months in advance, when tickets go on sale (€5–€180), or try your luck at the last minute at the box office. At this writing, long-delayed renovations were set to begin on parts of the building in late 2011 or 2012; plans include space for the first restaurant on the premises, run by Michelin-starred chef Nicolas Le Bec. ■ TIP➔ To learn about the building's history, and get a taste of aristocratic life during the Second Empire, take the entertaining guided tour in English. The ticket also allows entry to the auditorium. ⊠ *Pl. de l'Opéra, Opéra/Grands Boulevards* ☎ *08–92–89–90–90* ⊕ *www.operadeparis. fr* ☛ €9; €12.50 for guided visit Wed. and weekends at 11:30 and 2:30 ☉ *Daily 10–4:30* Ⓜ *Opéra.*

🕈 **Parc Monceau.** This exquisitely landscaped park began in 1778 as the
★ Duc de Chartres's private garden. Though some of the parkland was
sold off under the Second Empire (creating the exclusive real estate that
now borders the park), the refined atmosphere and some of the fanciful
faux-ruins have survived. Immaculately dressed children play under the
watchful eye of their nannies, while lovers cuddle on the benches. In
1797 André Garnerin, the world's first-recorded parachutist, staged a
landing in the park. The rotunda—known as the Chartres Pavilion—is
surely the city's grandest public restroom; it started life as a tollhouse.
✉ *Entrances on Bd. de Courcelles, Av. Velasquez, Av. Ruysdaël, Av. van
Dyck, Parc Monceau* Ⓜ *Monceau.*

WORTH NOTING

Hôtel Drouot. Hidden away in a small antiques district not far from the
opera house is Paris's central auction house. With everything from old
clothes to *haute couture* gowns and from bric-a-brac to ornate Chinese
lacquered boxes and rare books, Drouot sells it all. Anyone can attend
the sales and viewings, which draw a mix of art dealers, ladies who
lunch, and art amateurs hoping to discover an unknown masterpiece.
Check the website to see what's on the block. ■**TIP**➜ Don't miss the
small galleries and antiques dealers in the Quartier Drouot, a warren of
small streets around the auction house, notably on rues Rossini and de la
Grange-Batelière. ✉ *9 rue Drouot, Opéra/Grands Boulevards* ☎ *01–48–
00–20–00* ⊕ *www.drouot.com* ⊙ *Viewings of merchandise Mon.–Sat.
11–6. Auctions begin at 2* Ⓜ *Richelieu Drouot.*

**NEED A
BREAK?**

J'go. Steps from the Drouot auction house, J'go, one of two Paris outposts
of the Toulouse wine bar/restaurant, is perfect for an apéritif or light
dinner. The cozy bar serves impressive *grignotages* (tapas) from France's
southwest. ✉ *4 rue Drouot, Grands Boulevards* ☎ *01–40–22–09–09*
⊕ *www.lejgo.com.*

🕈 **Musée Grévin.** If you like wax museums, this one founded in 1882 ranks
with the best. Pay the steep entry price and ascend a grand Phantom-of-
the-Opera–like staircase into the Palais des Mirages, a mirrored salon
from the 1900 Paris Exposition that transforms into a hokey light-and-
sound show the kids will love (it was a childhood favorite of designer
Jean-Paul Gaultier). From there, get set for a cavalcade of nearly 300
statues, from Elvis to Ernest Hemingway, Picasso to Barak Obama.
Every king of France is here, along with Michael Jackson and George
Clooney, plus scores of French singers and celebrities. ✉ *10 bd. Montmartre, Opéra/Grands Boulevards* ☎ *01–47–70–85–05* ⊕ *www.grevin.
com* 🎟 *€21.50 adults; €14 kids 6–14 (check website for discounts)*
⊙ *Weekdays 10–6:30, weekends until 7* Ⓜ *Grands Boulevards.*

Musée Nissim de Camondo. The story of the Camondo family is steeped
in tragedy, and it's all recorded within the walls of this superb museum.
Patriarch Moïse de Camondo, born in Istanbul to a successful banking
family, built his showpiece mansion in 1911 in the style of the Petit
Trianon at Versailles, and stocked it with some of the most exquisite
furniture, wainscoting, and bibelots of the mid- to late 18th century.

CLOSE UP

Spas for Paris Pampering

After a long day of shopping, nothing beats a retreat to a Parisian spa. They're easy to find, with one or two in the department stores and an *institut de beauté* on practically every corner. The French consider a *soin* (treatment) and a spell in a *hammam* (steam room) essential to ensuring *bien-être* (well-being), and Parisiennes have been waxing and plucking since Marie-Antoinette soaked in tubs of milk. Reserve one to two months ahead for a weekend appointment. Tax and service charges are included in the prices, but a tip (€5–€10) is customary for good service. Here are some top-rated spas:

Harnn & Thann. Harnn & Thann specializes in Thai treatments. If time is limited, try the "express Paris-Bangkok," a 30-minute all-body massage for €40. ☒ *11 rue Molière, 1er, Opéra/Grands Boulevards* ☎ *01–40–15–02–20* ⊕ *www.harnn.fr* Ⓜ *Pyramides.*

Joïya. At Joïya rejuvenate head-to-toe with the Russie Blanche (White Russia) treatment (€95 for one hour). ☒ *6 rue de la Renaissance, 8e, Champs-Élysées* ☎ *01–40–70–16–49* ⊕ *www.joiya.fr* Ⓜ *Alma Marceau, Franklin D. Roosevelt.*

Nickel. Nickel is the place for him, specializing in men's products and body treatments. Attack *poignées d'amour* (love handles) with a one-hour massage (€69), or try the express 30-minute back massage (€42). ☒ *48 rue des Francs-Bourgeois, 4e, Marais* ☎ *01–42–77–41–10* ⊕ *www.nickel.fr* Ⓜ *St-Paul.*

Spa Anne Fontaine. Anne Fontaine, doyenne of the fine cotton blouse, spared no expense when she opened her luxurious Spa Anne Fontaine, where the specialty is a relaxing massage with—what else?—cotton oil (€145 for 50 minutes). ☒ *370 rue St-Honoré, 1er, Louvre/Tuileries* ☎ *01–42–61–03–70* ⊕ *www.annefontaine.com* Ⓜ *Tuileries.*

Spa Nuxe. Spa Nuxe is a hip spa by the creators of Nuxe skin-care products. The ancient cellar with arched corridors has cozy treatment rooms. Try the *rêverie orientale*, a two-hour *hammam*, body scrub, and detoxifying wrap, plus massage (€155). There is a second branch right next door, and a third one in Au Printemps. ☒ *32 rue Montorgueil, 1er, Beaubourg/Les Halles* ☎ *01–55–80–71–40* ⊕ *www.nuxe.com* Ⓜ *Les Halles.*

Villa Thalgo. Dip into the pools at Villa Thalgo to experience the benefits of a *spa marin* (literally, sea spa) in the heart of Paris. There is an aqua-gym, fitness room, and *hammams* (€100, half-day pass), which you can follow with an Aquazen massage with warm water balloons to de-stress your sore spots (€105, one hour). ☒ *8 av. Raymond Poincaré, 16e, Trocadéro* ☎ *01–45–62–00–20* ⊕ *www.villathalgo.com.*

6

Despite his vast wealth and purported charm, his wife left him five years after their marriage. Then his son, Nissim, was killed in World War I. Upon Moïse's death in 1935, the house and its contents were left to the state as a museum named for his lost son. A few years later, daughter Irène, her husband, and two children were murdered at Auschwitz. No heirs remained and the Camondo name died out. Today, the house remains an impeccable tribute to Moïse's life, from the gleaming salons to the refined private rooms. You can even see the condolence letter written by Marcel Proust, a family friend, after Nissim's death. There are background materials and an excellent free audioguide in English. ⊠ *63 rue de Monceau, Parc Monceau* ☎ *01–53–89–06–50* ⊕ *www.lesartsdecoratifs.fr* ⊠ *€7, €11.50 joint ticket with Musée des Arts Décoratifs* ☉ *Tues.–Sun. 10–6, Thurs. 10–9* Ⓜ *Villiers.*

Musée de la Vie Romantique. A visit to the charming Museum of the Romantic Life, dedicated to novelist George Sand (1804–76), will transport you to the countryside. In a pretty 1830s mansion in a tree-lined courtyard, the small permanent collection includes drawings by Delacroix and Ingrès, among others, though Sand is the star. There are glass cases stuffed with her jewelry and snuff boxes, and even a mold of the hand of composer Frederic Chopin, one of her many lovers. The museum, about a five-minute walk from the Musée Gustave Moreau, is in a picturesque neighborhood once called New Athens, a reflection of the architectural tastes of the writers and artists who lived there. There is usually an interesting temporary exhibit. ■TIP➜ The garden café is a nice for lunch or afternoon tea (open from Easter to October). ⊠ *16 rue Chaptal, Opéra/Grands Boulevards* ☎ *01–55–31–95–67* ⊕ *www. vie-romantique.paris.fr* ⊠ *Free (€7 temporary exhibits)* ☉ *Tues.–Sun. 10–6* Ⓜ *Blanche, Pigalle, St-Georges.*

Musée du Parfum. More of a showroom than a museum, the small exhibit run by *parfumier* Fragonard above its boutique on Rue Scribe is heavy on decorative objects associated with perfume, including crystal bottles, gloves, and assorted bibelots. The shop is a good place to find gifts, like the €12 honey body lotion, myriad soaps, and, of course, perfume. There's another mini-museum in the Fragonard shop nearby at 39 boulevard des Capucines. ⊠ *9 rue Scribe, Opéra* ☎ *01–47–42–04–56* ⊕ *www.fragonard.com* ⊠ *Free* ☉ *Mon.–Sat. 9–6, Sun. 9–5* Ⓜ *Opéra.*

Montmartre

WORD OF MOUTH

"There is always considerable debate about the merits of Montmartre. Frankly, I think that the Sacré-Coeur is spectacular, both the
basilica and the view in front, and old Montmartre (Place du Tertre
and the surrounding streets—and also rue des Abbesses) need to
be seen—if possible when they are not jammed with tourists."
—kerouac

GETTING ORIENTED

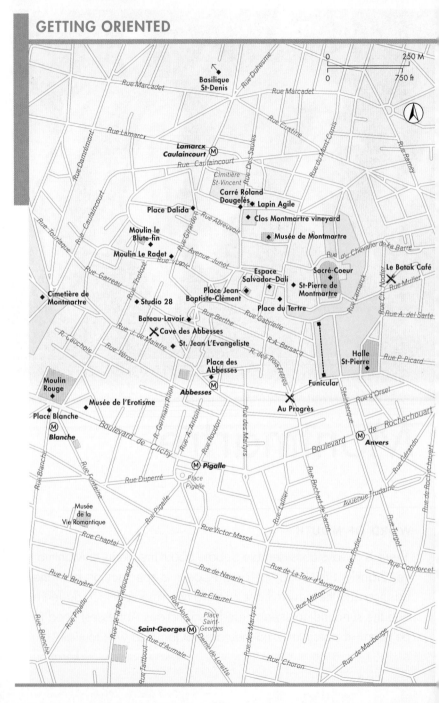

Rue Marcadet

Basilique
St-Denis

Rue Marcadet

Rue Custine

Rue Duhesme

0 _____ 250 M
0 _____ 750 ft

Rue Lamarcx

Rue Dancremont

Rue Mont-Cenis

Rue Ramey

**Lamarcx
Caulaincourt** Ⓜ

Rue Caulaincourt

Cimitière
St-Vincent

Rue Des Saules

**Carré Roland
Dougelès ◆ ◆ Lapin Agile**

Rue Tourlaque

Rue Caulaincourt

Place Dalida ◆

Rue Girardon

Rue Abreuvoir

◆ **Clos Montmartre vineyard**

**Moulin le
Blute-fin** ◆

Avenue Junot

◆ **Musée de Montmartre**

Rue du Chevalier de ka Barre

Moulin Le Radet ◆

Rue V Lenic

Rue Garreau

Rue Tholozé

**Espace
Salvador–Dali**
◆

Sacré-Coeur
◆

Rue Lamarck

Rue Ch. Nodier

Le Botak Café
✕

Rue Muller

**Cimetière de
Montmartre** ◆

◆ **Studio 28**

**Place Jean-
Baptiste-Clément** ◆

◆ **St-Pierre de
Montmartre**

Rue A. del Sarte

Bateau-Lavoir ◆
✕ **Cave des Abbesses**

Rue Berthe

Place du Tertre

R. Cauchois

R. J. de Maistre

Rue Véron

◆ **St. Jean L'Evangeliste**

Rue Gabrielle

R.A. Barsacq

R. des Trois Frères

**Halle
St-Pierre** ◆

Rue P. Picard

**Place des
Abbesses**
◆

**Moulin
Rouge**
◆

◆ **Musée de l'Erotisme**

Ⓜ **Abbesses**

Rue Germain Pilon

Rue A. Antoine

Rue Roudon

Rue des Martyrs

Funicular

Steinberque

Rue d'Orsel

de Rochechouart

Place Blanche
Ⓜ

Blanche

Boulevard de Clichy

✕ **Au Progrès**

Boulevard Ⓜ **Anvers**

Rue Géranto

Rue de Rochechouart

Rue Blanche

Rue Fontaine

Ⓜ **Pigalle**

Rue Duperré

Place
Pigalle

Rue Pigalle

Avenue Trudaine

Rue Lallier

Rue Bochart de Saron

Rue Rodier

Rue Turgot

**Musée
de la
Vie Romantique**

Rue Chaptal

Rue Victor Massé

Rue la Bruyère

Rue Pigalle

Rue de Navarin

Rue de La Tour d'Auvergne

Rue Milton

Rue Condorcet

Rue Clauzel

Rue Notre

Rue Blanche

Rue de la Rochefoucauld

Saint-Georges Ⓜ

Place
Saint-
Georges

Dame de Lorette

Rue des Martyrs

Rue Maubeuge

Rue Taittout

Rue d'Aumale

Rue Choran

TOP REASONS TO GO

Sacré-Coeur. The best view of Paris is worth the climb—or the funicular ride—especially at twilight when the city lights create a magnificent panorama below the hill of Montmartre.

Place du Tertre. This bustling square behind Sacré-Coeur teems with crowds of tourists and hordes of street artists clamoring to paint them.

Place des Abbesses. Capture the village ambience that makes Montmartre special by exploring the tiny streets branching out from this picturesque square.

Carré Roland Dorgelès. Bring your camera and head to this little square overlooking two special Montmartre sights: the city's only vineyard, and the famous pink-and-green cabaret Lapin Agile.

MAKING THE MOST OF YOUR TIME

Devote a day to this neighborhood if you want to see more than the obligatory Sacré-Coeur basilica. If possible, avoid weekends, when the narrow—and extremely hilly—streets are jam-packed.

GETTING HERE

Montmartre is in the 18ᵉ arrondissement. Take Line 2 to Anvers métro station, and then take the funicular (costs one métro ticket) up to Sacré-Coeur. Or take Line 12 to Abbesses station and take your time wandering the cobbled streets and staircases that lead up to the basilica. For a scenic tour, hop the public bus, Montmartrobus (costs one métro ticket). An easy starting point is the métro station Jules-Joffrin (Line 12): the bus winds up the hilly streets, with a convenient stop at Sacré-Coeur. Or pile the kids onto Le Petit Train de Montmartre, a bus disguised as a minitrain that runs a circuit every 30 minutes from Place Blanche (€3–€6).

BEST CAFÉS

Cave des Abbesses. Locals head to this charming retro-looking *caviste* (wine shop) and wine bar for a glass of something special with a side of oysters, or perhaps La Grande Mixte, a platter of charcuterie, terrine, and cheese (€12). ✉ *43 rue des Abbesses, Montmartre* ☎ *01–42–52–81–54* Ⓜ *Abbesses.*

Le Botak Café. On the eastern side of Sacré-Coeur, at the bottom of the stairs, you'll find the leafy Square Louise Marie and this little café, which serves a small, ever-changing menu of French home cooking like *saumon au pistou* (salmon in pesto) and *poulet botak* (roasted chicken with garlic and mashed potatoes). The daily lunch specials (about €12) are a great deal. ✉ *1 rue Paul Albert, Montmartre* ☎ *01–46–06–98–30* Ⓜ *Anvers.*

Au Progrès. This photo op-ready corner café draws a quirky mix of hipsters, artists, and discriminating tourists. The food is good, with classics like steak tartare. Try the menu du jour (about €15 for two courses). If you're craving the tastes of home, the excellent cheeseburger (€16) comes with a heap of crispy fries. ✉ *7 rue Trois Frères, Montmartre* ☎ *01–42–64–07–37* Ⓜ *Abbesses.*

Sightseeing
★★★★
Dining
★★★
Lodging
★★
Shopping
★★★
Nightlife
★

Montmartre has become almost too charming for its own good. Yes, it feels like a village (if you wander off the beaten path); yes, there are working artists here (though far fewer than there used to be); and yes, the best view of Paris is yours for free from the top of the hill (if there's no haze). That's why on any weekend day, year-round, you can find hordes of visitors crowding these cobbled alleys, scaling the staircases that pass for streets, and queuing to see Sacré-Coeur, the "sculpted cloud," at the summit.

If you're lucky enough to have a little corner of Montmartre to yourself, you'll understand why locals love it so. Come at nonpeak times, on a weekday, or in the morning or later in the evening. Stroll around **Place des Abbesses,** where the rustic houses and narrow streets escaped the heavy hand of urban planner Baron Haussmann. Until 1860 the area was in fact a separate village, dotted with windmills. Always a draw for bohemians and artists, many of whom had studios at what is now the **Musée de Montmartre** and **Bateau-Lavoir,** Montmartre has been home to such painters as Suzanne Valadon and her son Maurice Utrillo, Picasso, van Gogh, Géricault, Renoir, and of course Henri de Toulouse-Lautrec, whose iconic paintings of the cancan dancers at the **Moulin Rouge** are now souvenir-shop fixtures. You can still see shows at the Moulin Rouge in the **Place Blanche** and the pocket-size cabaret **Lapin Agile** *(see the Nightlife chapter),* though much of the entertainment here is on the seedier side—the area around Pigalle is the city's largest red-light district, though it's far tamer than it used to be. The **Boulevard de Clichy** was virtually an artists' highway at the turn of the 20th century: Degas lived and died at No. 6, and Picasso lived at No. 11. The *quartier* is a favorite of filmmakers; the blockbuster *Moulin Rouge* was inspired here, and visitors still seek out Café des Deux Moulins (15 rue Lepic), the real-life café (unfortunately with a remodeled look) where Audrey Tautou waited tables in 2001's *Amélie.* In 1928 **Studio 28** opened as the world's first cinema for experimental films.

DID YOU KNOW?

Like many of the "streets" in Montmartre, the Rue du Calvaire, off the Place du Terte, is actually a staircase, and a scenic way down from the top of the hill.

TOP ATTRACTIONS

Updated by
Bryan Pirolli

Bateau-Lavoir (*Wash-barge*). The birthplace of Cubism isn't open to the public, but a display in the front window details this unimposing building's rich history. Montmartre poet Max Jacob coined the name for the original building here, which reminded him of the laundry boats that used to float in the Seine, and he joked that the warren of paint-splattered artists' studios needed a good hosing down (wishful thinking, since the building had only one water tap). It was in the original Bateau-Lavoir that, early in the 20th century, Pablo Picasso, Georges Braque, and Juan Gris made their first bold stabs at Cubism, and Picasso painted the groundbreaking *Les Demoiselles d'Avignon* in 1906–07. The experimental works of the artists weren't met with open arms, even in liberal Montmartre. All but the facade was rebuilt after a fire in 1970. Like the original building, the Bateau houses artists and their studios. ✉ *13 pl. Émile-Goudeau, Montmartre* Ⓜ *Abbesses.*

Carré Roland Dougelès. This unassuming square is a perfect place to take in two of Montmartre's most photographed sites: the pink-and-green cabaret **Lapin Agile** and **Clos Montmartre,** Paris's only working vineyard. While Lapin Agile, famously painted by Camille Pissarro, still welcomes revelers after 150 years, the vineyard is closed to visits except during the annual Fête de Jardins (Garden Festival) weekend in September. The stone wall on the northwestern edge of the square borders the peaceful Cimitière Saint-Vincent, one of the neighborhood's three atmospheric cemeteries. ✉ *Corner of Rue des Saulnes and Rue St-Vincent, Montmartre.*

Halle St-Pierre. This elegant iron-and-glass 19th-century market hall at the foot of Sacré-Coeur stages dynamic exhibitions of *art brut* (raw art), or outsider and folk art. The international artists featured are contemporary in style and out of the mainstream. There's also a good bookstore and a café serving light, well-prepared food such as savory tarts and quiches served with salad and homemade desserts. ✉ *2 rue Ronsard, Montmartre* ☎ *01–42–58–72–89* ⊕ *www.hallesaintpierre.org* 🎫 *Museum €8* ⊗ *Mon.–Fri. 10–6, Sat. 10–7, Sun. 11–6. Closed weekends in Aug.* Ⓜ *Anvers.*

Moulin de la Galette. Of the 14 windmills (*moulins*) that used to sit atop this hill, only two remain, known collectively as Moulin de la Galette—the name is taken from the bread that the owners used to produce. The more storied of the two is known as Le Blute-fin. In the late 1800s there was a dance hall on the site, famously painted by Renoir (you can see the painting in the Musée d'Orsay). Unfortunately, the windmill is on private land and can't be visited. Down the street is the other moulin, Le Radet. ✉ *Le Blute-fin, corner of Rue Lepic and Rue Tholozé, Montmartre* Ⓜ *Abbesses.*

Place des Abbesses. This triangular square is typical of the countrified style that has made Montmartre famous. Now a hub for shopping and people-watching, the *place* is surrounded by hip boutiques, sidewalk cafés, and shabby-chic restaurants—a prime habitat for the young, neo-bohemian crowd and a sprinkling of expats. Trendy streets like Rue

CLOSE UP

A Scenic Walk in Montmartre

One of the Paris's most charming walks begins at the Abbesses métro station (Line 12), which has one of only two remaining iron-and-glass Art Nouveau canopies designed by famed architect Hector Guimard. Explore the streets ringing **Place des Abbesses,** or begin the walk immediately by heading west along Rue des Abbesses. Turn right on Rue Tholozé and note the historic movie house, **Studio 28,** at No. 10. At the top of the street is the windmill **Le Blute-fin,** famously painted by Renoir. A right on Rue Lepic takes you past the only other windmill still standing, **Le Radet.** Take a left here onto Rue Girardon, to **Place Dalida,** marked with a voluptuous bust of the beloved French singer who popularized disco. (Yolanda Gigliotti, aka Dalida, lived until her death in 1987 at 11 bis, rue d'Orchampt, one of the city's narrowest streets, opposite Le Radet.)

The stone house behind Dalida's bust is the 18th-century **Château des Brouillards,** whose name, Castle of the Mists, is taken from the light fog that used to cloak this former farmland. Detour down the romantic alley of the same name. Renoir is said to have lived in the château before moving to the small house across the way at No. 8. From Place Dalida, head down the winding Rue Abreuvoir, one of the most-photographed streets in Paris. Residents used to walk their horses to the *abreuvoir,* or watering trough, at No. 15. Pissarro kept a pied-à-terre at No. 12. The stone-and-wood-beamed house at No. 4 was once home to a historian of the Napoleonic wars whose family symbol was an eagle. Notice the wooden sundial with a rooster and the inscription: "When you chime, I'll sing." At

the pink-and-green **Maison Rose** restaurant, committed to canvas by resident artist Maurice Utrillo, turn left on Rue des Saules where you'll find Paris's only working vineyard, **Clos de Montmartre.** The vineyard is open to visits one weekend a year during the Fête des Jardins in September.

Across the street is the famous cabaret **Lapin Agile,** still going strong. On the opposite corner, the stone wall rings the **Cimetière Saint-Vincent,** one of the city's smallest cemeteries, where Utrillo is buried (to see it, walk west along rue St-Vincent, take a right, then another quick right). Backtrack up the Rue des Saules and take the first left onto Rue Cortot to the **Musée de Montmartre,** once home to a bevy of artists. Renoir rented a studio here to store his painting of Le Blute-fin. A few doors down, at No. 6, the composer Erik Satie, piano player at Le Chat Noir nightclub, lived during a penniless period in a 6-by-4-foot flat with a 9-foot ceiling (plus skylight). At the corner of Rue Mont-Cenis, the white water tower Château d'Eau still services the neighborhood. Turn right to reach the **Place du Tertre,** a lively square packed with tourists and street artists. Easily overlooked is **St-Pierre de Montmartre,** one of the city's oldest churches, founded in 1147. End your walk at the basilica **Sacré-Coeur,** and enjoy one of the best views of Paris from the city's highest point. This *butte,* or hilltop, has been famous since the 3rd century, when St-Denis, the first bishop of Paris, was martyred here, and after his beheading was said to have walked for miles while holding his own head. For an easy descent, take the funicular, which has been ferrying people up and down since 1900.

7

DID YOU KNOW?

The views *of* majestic Sacré-Coeur might be as lovely as the views *from* Sacré-Coeur, especially as the sun is setting or rising.

SACRÉ-COEUR

✉ *Pl. du Parvis-du-Sacré-Coeur, Montmartre*
☎ *01–53–41–89–00*
⊕ *www.sacre-coeur-montmartre.com* ✉ *Free; dome €6* ⊗ *Basilica daily 6 am–11 pm; dome and crypt Oct.–Mar., daily 9–6; Apr.–Sept., daily 9–7* Ⓜ *Anvers, plus funicular; Jules Joffrin plus Montmartrobus.*

TIPS

■ The best time to visit Sacré-Coeur is early morning or early evening, and preferably not on a Sunday, when the crowds are thick. If you're coming to worship, there are daily masses.

■ Photographers angling for the perfect shot of the church should aim for a clear blue-sky day or come at dusk, when the pink sky plays nicely with the lights of the basilica.

■ To avoid the steps, take the funicular, which costs one métro ticket each way.

It's hard to not feel as though you're climbing up to heaven when you visit Sacré-Coeur, the white castle in the sky, perched atop Montmartre. The French government built Sacred Heart Basilica in 1873 to symbolize the return of self-confidence after the devastating years of the Commune and Franco-Prussian War. It was designed by architect Paul Abadie, using elements from Romanesque and Byzantine architectural styles—a mélange many critics dismissed as gaudy. Construction lasted until World War I, and the church was consecrated in 1919.

HIGHLIGHTS

Many people come to Sacré-Coeur to admire the superlative view from the top of the 271-foot-high dome, the second-highest point in Paris after the Eiffel Tower. If you opt to skip the climb up the spiral staircase, the view from the front steps is still well worth the trip.

Don't miss spending some time inside the basilica gazing at the massive golden mosaic set high above the choir. Created in 1922 by Luc-Olivier Merson, *Christ in Majesty* depicts Christ with a golden heart and outstretched arms, surrounded by various figures, including the Virgin Mary and Joan of Arc. It remains one of the largest mosaics of its kind. There are also the seemingly endless vaulted arches in the basilica's crypt, the portico's bronze doors—decorated with biblical scenes, including the Last Supper—and the stained-glass windows, which were installed in 1922, destroyed by a bombing during World War II (there were miraculously no deaths), and later rebuilt in 1946. In the basilica's 262 foot-high campanile hangs La Savoyarde, one of the world's heaviest bells, weighing about 19 tons.

7

Houdon and Rue des Martyrs have attracted small designers, and some shops are open on Sunday afternoon. Ⓜ *Abbesses.*

Place du Tertre. Artists have peddled their wares in this squafe for centuries (*tertre* means "hillock"). Though busloads of tourists have changed the atmosphere, if you come off-season, when the air is chilly and the streets are bare, you can almost feel what is was like when up-and-coming Picassos lived in the houses, which today are given over to souvenir shops and cafés. Ⓜ *Abbesses.*

Fodor'sChoice
★

Sacré-Coeur. *See the highlighted listing in this chapter.*

WORTH NOTING

**OFF THE
BEATEN
PATH**

Basilique de St-Denis. Built between 1136 and 1286, the St-Denis basilica is one of the most important Gothic churches in France. It was here, under dynamic prelate Abbé Suger, that Gothic architecture (typified by pointed arches and rib vaults) was said to have made its first appearance. The kings of France soon chose St-Denis as their final resting place, and their richly sculpted tombs—along with what remains of Suger's church—can be seen in the choir area at the east end of the church. The basilica was battered during the Revolution; afterward, Louis XVIII reestablished it as the royal burial site by moving the remains of Louis XVI and Marie-Antoinette here to join centuries' worth of monarchial bones. The vast 13th-century nave is a brilliant example of structural logic; its columns, capitals, and vault are a model of architectural harmony. The facade, retaining the rounded arches of the Romanesque that preceded the Gothic period, is set off by a small rose window, reputedly the oldest in France. Check out the extensive archaeological finds, such as a Merovingian queen's grave goods; there's information in English. ✉ *1 rue de la Légion d'Honneur, St-Denis* ☎ *01–48–09–83–54* ⊕ *www.saint-denis.monuments-nationaux.fr* 🎫 *Choir and tombs €7* 🕙 *Apr.–Sept., Mon.–Sat. 10–6:15, Sun. noon–6:15; Oct.–Mar., Mon.–Sat. 10–5, Sun. noon–5:15. Guided tours in English by reservation* Ⓜ *St-Denis Basilique.*

Cimetière de Montmartre. Overshadowed by better-known Père-Lachaise, this cemetery is just as picturesque. It's the final resting place of a host of luminaries, including painters Degas and Fragonard; Adolphe Sax, inventor of the saxophone; dancer Vaslav Nijinsky; and composers Hector Berlioz and Jacques Offenbach. The Art Nouveau tomb of novelist Émile Zola (1840–1902) lords over a lawn near the entrance—though Zola's remains were removed to the Panthéon in 1908. ✉ *20 av. Rachel, Montmartre* 🕙 *Mar. 16–Nov. 5, weekdays 8–6, Sat. 8:30–6, Sun. 9–6; Nov. 6–Mar. 15, weekdays 8–5:30, Sat. 8:30–5:30, Sun. 9–5:30* Ⓜ *Blanche.*

Espace Salvador-Dalí (*Dalí Center*). One of several museums dedicated to the Surrealist master, the collection in this black-walled exhibition space includes about 300 works, mostly etchings and lithographs. The two-dozen sculptures include several versions of Dalí's melting bronze clock and variations on the Venus de Milo. A multimedia pioneer ahead of his time, there are videos with Dalí's voice, and temporary exhibits have included the mustached man's foray into holograms. There's plenty of information in English. ⊠ *11 rue Poulbot, Montmartre* ☎ *01–42–64–40–10* ⊕ *www.daliparis.com* ⊠ *€10* ⊗ *Daily 10–6* Ⓜ *Abbesses.*

Moulin Rouge. When the world-famous cabaret opened in 1889, aristocrats, professionals, and the working classes all flocked to see the scandalous performers. The can-can was considerably more kinky in Toulouse-Lautrec's day, when girls kicked off their knickers. There's not much to see from the outside except for tourist buses and sex shops, but this square, called Place Blanche, takes its name from the chalky haze once churned up by carts carrying plaster of Paris down from the quarries. ■TIP→ Souvenir seekers should check out the Moulin Rouge gift shop (around the corner at 11 rue Lepic), which sells better-quality official merchandise, from jewelry to sculpture, by reputable French makers. *(See the Nightlife chapter.)* ⊠ *82 bd. de Clichy, Montmartre* ☎ *01–53–09–82–82* ⊕ *www.moulinrouge. fr* Ⓜ *Blanche.*

Musée de l'Érotisme. What better place for the Museum of Erotic Art than smack in the heart of the city's red-light district? Though the subject matter is rather limited, the collection is a respectable mix of world art, such as carvings from Africa, Indonesia, and Peru; Chinese ivories; and Japanese prints. There are racy cartoons by Robert Crumb and photographs of Pigalle prostitutes and bordellos, some quite chic, from the 1930s and 1940s. Three floors are dedicated to temporary exhibitions by contemporary artists and photographers. ⊠ *72 bd. de Clichy, Montmartre* ☎ *01–42–58–28–73* ⊕ *www.musee-erotisme.com* ⊠ *€9, €6 if purchased online* ⊗ *Daily 10 am–2 am* Ⓜ *Blanche.*

Musée de Montmartre. In its turn-of-the-20th-century heyday, the building—now home to Montmartre's historical museum—was a studio block for painters, writers, and cabaret artists. Foremost among them were Renoir—he painted the *Moulin de la Galette,* an archetypal scene of sun-drenched revelers, while he lived here—and Maurice Utrillo. The museum, with a lovely garden, has a charming permanent collection recapping the area's history, notably the many Toulouse-Lautrec posters and original Eric Satie scores. An ambitious renovation that will double the current museum's space is due to be completed by 2014; the museum will remain open in the meantime. ⊠ *12 rue Cortot, Montmartre* ☎ *01–49–25–89–37* ⊕ *www.museedemontmartre.fr* ⊠ *€8* ⊗ *Daily 10–6* Ⓜ *Lamarck Caulaincourt.*

Place Jean-Baptiste-Clément. Monsieur Clément, a singer, was "Mayor of Montmartre" during the heady 70 days of the 1871 Commune, when this area actually seceded from Paris. Painter Amedeo Modigliani (1884–1920) had a studio at No. 7, and Picasso lived around the corner at 49 rue Gabrielle. Look for the octagonal tower at the north end of the square; it's all that's left of Montmartre's first water tower, built around 1840 to boost the area's feeble water supply. ✉ *Pl. Jean-Baptiste-Clément, Montmartre* Ⓜ *Abbesses.*

Saint Jean L'Evangéliste de Montmartre. This eye-catching church was the first modern house of worship built in Paris (1897–1904) and the first to be constructed of reinforced cement. Architect Anatole de Baudot's revolutionary technique defied the accepted rules at the time with its use of unsupported masonry. Critics, who failed to stop construction, feared the building would crumble under its own weight. Today the church attracts

DINING AT A GLANCE

For full reviews ⇨ Chapter 14.

MODERATE DINING
Bistrot des Deux Théâtres, *Bistro,* 18 rue Blanche

Guilo Guilo, *Japanese,* 8 rue Garreau

La Mascotte, *Brasserie,* 52 rue des Abbesses

Le Miroir, *Bistro,* 94 rue des Martyrs

Rose Bakery, *British,* 46 rue des Martyrs

a steady flow of visitors curious about its unusual Moorish-inspired facade of redbrick and curved arches. Note the tiny clock at the top left of the bell tower. The compact Art Nouveau interior features impressive stained-glass windows. There are free concerts from time to time. ✉ *19 rue des Abbesses, Montmartre* ☎ *01–46–06–43–96* ⊕ *www. saintjeandemontmartre.com* ◷ *Mon.–Sat. 9–7, Sun. 9:30–6.*

St-Pierre de Montmartre. Tucked in the shadow of mighty Sacré-Coeur is one of the oldest churches in Paris. Built in 1147 on the site of a 5th-century temple to the god Mars, this small church with impressive sculpted metal doors was once part of a substantial Benedictine abbey. Besides the church, all that remains is a small cemetery, now closed (you can see it through the ornate metal door on the left as you enter the courtyard). Renovated multiple times through the ages, the church mixes various styles: interior elements such as the columns in the nave are medieval, the facade dates to the 18th century, with renovations in the 19th century; the impressive stained-glass windows are 20th century. Maurice Utrillo's 1914 painting of St-Pierre hangs in the Musée de l'Orangerie. ✉ *2 rue du Mont Cenis, off Pl. du Tertre, Montmartre* ☎ *01–46–06–57–63* Ⓜ *Anvers.*

Studio 28. This little movie house has a distinguished history: when it opened in 1928, it was the first theater in the world purposely built for *art et essai,* or experimental film. Through the years artists and writers flocked here to see the "seventh art" creations by directors such as Jean Cocteau, Luis Buñuel, François Truffaut, and Orson Welles. Today it's a repertory cinema, showing first-runs, just-runs, and previews, usually in their original language. In the back of the movie house is a cozy bar and café with a quiet outdoor terrace decorated with murals of film stars. ✉ *10 rue Tholozé, Montmartre* ☎ *01–46–06–36–07* ⊕ *www. cinemastudio28.com* Ⓜ *Abbesses.*

The Marais

WORD OF MOUTH

"If you haven't been to the Marais, I would highly recommend it. Lots of small boutiques on rue des Francs Bourgeois, the magnificent Place des Vosges is a wonderful plaza . . . and rue des Rosiers is the heart of the old Jewish quarter and a great place to wander with a falafel in hand."

—macdogmom

GETTING ORIENTED

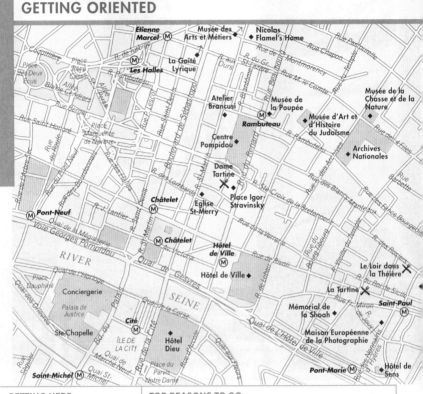

GETTING HERE	TOP REASONS TO GO
The Marais includes the 3e and 4e arrondissements. It's a pleasant walk from the Beaubourg—the area around Centre Pompidou— into the heart of the Marais. Rue Rambuteau turns into Rue des Francs Bourgeois, which runs right past the Place des Vosges. If you're going by métro, the most central stop is St-Paul on the 1 line. If you're going to the Pompidou, take the 11 line to Rambuteau. For the Musée Picasso, the closest stop is St-Sébastien Froissart on the 8 line. For the 3e arrondissement, get off at Arts et Métiers on the 3 or 11 line, or Filles du Calvaire on Line 8.	**Centre Pompidou.** The city's leading modern art museum is also a vast arts center presenting films, theater, and dance performances.
	Place des Vosges. Paris's prettiest square surrounds a manicured park whose inviting patches of grass are—unusual for Paris—accessible to those needing a siesta.
	Musée Picasso. This is a must-stop for fans of the master, who painted some of his best work in Paris.
	Jewish history tour. The historic Jewish quarter has two world-class sites: Mémorial de la Shoah (the Holocaust Memorial) and the Musée d'Art et d'Histoire du Judaïsme, with fascinating artwork and cultural artifacts.
	No reason at all. Lose yourself in this neighborhood. Explore the tiny streets near the Centre Pompidou, grab a falafel sandwich on the Rue des Rosiers, or people-watch in a café on the Rue Vieille du Temple.

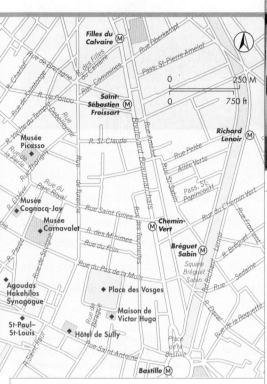

BEST CAFÉS

Dame Tartine. There are many cafés around the Centre Pompidou, but this one overlooking the Stravinsky fountain, with its colorful sculptures, is a good choice. You won't go wrong with one of their many *tartines*, toasts topped with delicious ingredients. ✉ *2 rue Brisemiche, Marais* ☎ *01–42–77–32–22* Ⓜ *Rambuteau.*

La Tartine. This calm café on busy Rue de Rivoli is a local favorite with an impressive wine list. Try the €8 French onion soup or indulge in classic French dishes like *steak frites* or even escargots. ✉ *24 rue de Rivoli, Marais* ☎ *01–42–72–76–85* Ⓜ *St-Paul.*

Le Loir dans la Théière. Sink into one of the comfortable shabby armchairs at this popular tearoom, whose name translates to the Dormouse in the Teapot (from *Alice in Wonderland*). The sweet and savory tarts are stellar, but the real stars are desserts like the decadent chocolate crumble tart. ✉ *3 rue des Rosiers, Marais* ☎ *01–42–72–90–61* Ⓜ *St-Paul.*

MAKING THE MOST OF YOUR TIME

The Marais has something for everyone, and how much time you spend here depends on how much time you have in Paris. One day seems painfully short, but it would afford you a walking tour. Leave at least two days if your itinerary includes the Centre Pompidou and the Musée Picasso. In three days you could cover some of the smaller museums, well worth the time as many of them are housed in exquisite mansions. If time permits, wander to the 3e arrondissement to see the charming streets, away from the crowds, or visit the quirky science-centric Musée des Arts et Métiers. Leave time to peek into private courtyards, and picnic in the Place des Vosges. Sunday afternoon is a lively time to come, when many shops are open, notably on the Rue des Francs-Bourgeois. Nightlife is tops as well, with a lively café and bar scene, particularly those aimed at the gay community.

8

Sightseeing
★★★★★

Dining
★★★★

Lodging
★★★★

Shopping
★★★★★

Nightlife
★★★★

From swampy to swanky, the Marais has a fascinating history. Like an aging pop star, the *quartier* has remade itself many times, and today retains several identities: the city's epicenter of cool with hip boutiques, designer hotels, and art galleries galore; the hub of Paris's gay community; and, though fading, the nucleus of Jewish life. You could easily spend your entire visit to Paris in this neighborhood, there is that much to do.

"Marais" means marsh, and that is exactly what this area was until the 12th century, when it was converted to farmland. In 1605 Henri IV began building the Place Royale (today's Place des Vosges, the oldest square in Paris), which touched off a building boom, and the wealthy and fabulous moved in. Despite the odors—the area was one of the city's smelliest—it remained the chic quarter until Louis XIV moved his court to Versailles, trailed by dispirited aristocrats unhappy to decamp to the country. Merchants moved into their exquisite *hôtels particuliers* (private mansions), which are some of the city's best surviving examples of Baroque architecture. Here you can see the hodgepodge of narrow streets that so vexed Louis Napoléon and his sidekick, Baron Haussmann, who feared a redux of the famous *barricades* that revolutionaries threw up to thwart the monarchy. Haussmann leveled scores of blocks like these, creating the wide, arrow-straight avenues that are a hallmark of modern Paris. Miraculously, the Marais escaped destruction, though much of it fell victim to neglect and ruin. Thanks to restoration efforts over the past half-century, the district is enjoying its latest era of greatness, and the apartments here—among the city's oldest—are also the most in demand, with *beaucoup* charm, exposed beams, and steep crooked staircases barely wide enough to fit a supermodel. (Should you be lucky enough to find an elevator, don't expect it to fit your suitcase.) Notice the impressive *portes cochères*, the huge doors built to accommodate aristocratic carriages that today open into many sublime courtyards and hidden gardens.

The 4e arrondissement, the Marais's glitzier half, is sandwiched between two opposite poles—the regal **Place des Vosges** in the east and the eye-teasing modern masterpiece **Centre Pompidou** in the west. Between these points you'll find most of the main sites, including the **Musée Picasso,** the **Maison Européenne de la Photographie,** and the **Musée Carnavalet,** which is the best place to see how the city evolved through the ages. To tour an exquisitely restored 17th-century hôtel particulier, visit the excellent **Musée Cognacq-Jay** (like the Carnavalet, admission is free) or wander into the manicured back garden of the magnificent **Hôtel de Sully.** To the north, the quieter 3e arrondissement is a lovely neighborhood to explore. Techies will appreciate a stop at the **Musée des Arts and Métiers,** Europe's oldest science museum.

Paris's **Jewish quarter** has existed here in some form since the 13th century, and still thrives around the Rue des Rosiers, even as hip boutiques encroach on the traditional bakeries, delis, and falafel shops. Not far away is the beating heart of the gay Marais, radiating out from Rue Vieille du Temple, along the Rue St-Croix de la Bretonnerie to Rue du Temple, where you can find trendy cafés and shops and cool nightspots aimed at gays but welcoming to all.

The 3e arrondissement half of the Marais, around the Rue de Bretagne, has evolved into one of Paris's most in-demand areas to live—and one of the most interesting areas to explore. Here you can find art galleries, trendy boutiques, and funky cafés and bars off the tourist track.

TOP ATTRACTIONS

Updated by
Bryan Pirolli

3e arrondissement. The thick crowds that flock to the Place des Vosges rarely venture to the other side of the Marais: the 3e arrondissement, which has morphed into one of the hottest neighborhoods in Paris. Good luck finding an apartment to rent here—most of them are small walk-ups with exposed wooden beams and lots of charm. But even if you can't move in, you can enjoy this trendy *quartier* like a local. First, head to the Rue de Bretagne, the main drag, with its newly widened sidewalks. Stop for lunch at one of the food stalls in the Marché des Enfants Rouges (No. 39), the oldest covered market in Paris (open Tuesday through Sunday). Explore the narrow side streets, like rues Charlot, Debelleyme, and Poitou, lined with art galleries and small boutiques. Stop for a real English scone at the latest outpost of the popular Rose Bakery, at 30 rue Debelleyme, or a cup of Joe to go at the New

York–style coffeehouse Merce and the Muse, at 1 bis, rue Dupuis. Just next store is Mary's, at 1 rue Dupuis, serving up some of the best Italian gelato. Across the street is the 19th-century iron-and-glass Carreau du Temple, which, after a long overdue renovation, is now a locally-driven arts and sports community center. This is the site of the former Templar Tower, where Louis XIV and Marie Antoinette were imprisoned before the king's date with the guillotine (Napoléon later razed it). For your evening *aperitif,* make a beeline for the buzzy Café Charlot, at 38 rue de Bretagne. If you're in the mood for couscous, try Chez Omar, a neighborhood institution at No. 27.

Ⓒ **Centre Pompidou**

Fodor'sChoice *See highlighted listing in this chapter.*
★

Église St-Merry. This impressive Gothic church, in the shadow of the Centre Pompidou, was completed in 1550 and has a turret containing the oldest bell in Paris (cast in 1331) and an 18th-century pulpit supported on carved palm trees. There are free concerts Saturday at 8 pm and Sunday at 4 pm. See the website for more information. ⊠ *76 rue de la Verrerie, Beaubourg/Les Halles* ☏ *01–42–71–93–93* ⊕ *www. accueilmusical.fr* Ⓜ *Hôtel de Ville.*

Hôtel de Sully. This early Baroque gem, built in 1624, is one of the city's loveliest hôtels particuliers, with an equally lovely garden. Like much of the area, it fell into ruin until the 1950s, when it was rescued by the administration of French historic monuments, Centre des Monuments Nationaux, which is headquartered here. This is also one of two homes of the Jeu de Paume (the other is in the Tuileries), which stages regular photography exhibitions. The garden is open to the public. Now that an extensive and much-delayed renovation has been completed, the private apartment of the Duchesse de Sully—four rooms furnished with period pieces—is open for visits for the first time, by reservation only, for a small charge. The Orangerie in the garden has also reopened with a branch of the tea salon Angelina. The bookstore (with a 17th-century ceiling of exposed wooden beams) stocks specialized Paris guides in English. ⊠ *62 rue St-Antoine, Marais* ☏ *01–44–61–21–50 Hotel de Sully, 01–42–74–47–75 Jeu de Paume* ☉ *Tues.–Sun. 10–7 Hotel de Sully; Tues.–Fri. noon–7, weekends 10–7 Jeu de Paume* Ⓜ *St-Paul.*

Hôtel de Ville. Overlooking the Seine, City Hall is the residence and offices of the popular Mayor Bertrand Delanoë. The building, rebuilt in 1873 after an attack by rioting crowds, is one of the city's most stunning, made all the more dramatic by elaborate nighttime lighting. There are frequent free photography exhibits celebrating famous photographers like Doisneau or Atget and their notable subjects, often the city of Paris herself—the entrance is on the side across from the department store BHV. Alas, the impressive interior, with lavish reception halls, are open only for public visits during Patrimony Weekend in September, but the grand public square out front is always lively, playing host to events and temporary exhibitions. There's a carrousel and a beach volleyball court (or similar) in summer, and an ice-skating rink (with skate rental) in winter. ⊠ *Pl. de l'Hôtel-de-Ville, Marais* Ⓜ *Hôtel de Ville.*

La Gaîté Lyrique. La Gaîté Lyrique, one of Paris's newest contemporary art spaces, brings together innovative exhibits with live music performances and a multimedia space that features a library, movies, and free video games. Think of it as a smaller, more interactive Centre Pompidou. Housed in a 19th-century theatre—remnants of which are visible in the café upstairs—La Gaîté Lyrique offers three floors of innovative exhibitions and interaction. If you have a question or need some more light, the gallery's curators can fix it via their iPads which control the building's utilities. That's cutting edge, for Paris. ⊠ *3 bis rue Papin, Marais* ☎ *33/01-53-01-51-70* ⊕ *www.gaite-lyrique.net/* ☾ *Closed Mon.*

★ **Maison Européenne de la Photographie** (*Center for European Photography*). Much of the credit for the city's ascendancy as a hub of international photography goes to MEP and its director, Jean-Luc Monterosso, who also founded Paris's hugely successful Mois de la Photographie festival in November. The MEP hosts up to four simultaneous exhibitions, changing about every three months. Shows feature the work of an international crop of photographers and video artists. Works by superstar Annie Leibovitz or designer-photographer Karl Lagerfeld may overlap with a collection of self-portraits by an up-and-coming Japanese artist. MEP often stages retrospectives of the classics (by Doisneau, Cartier-Bresson, Man Ray, and others) from its vast private collection. Programs are available in English and guided tours are sometimes given in English (call ahead to find out). ⊠ *5 rue de Fourcy, Marais* ☎ *01-44-78-75-00* ⊕ *www.mep-fr.org* ⊠ *€7, free Wed. after 5 pm* ☾ *Wed.–Sun. 11–8* Ⓜ *St-Paul.*

Maison de Victor Hugo. France's most famous scribe lived in this house on the northeast corner of Place des Vosges between 1832 and 1848. It's now a museum dedicated to the multitalented author of *Les Misérables*. In Hugo's apartment on the second floor, you can see the tall desk, next to the short bed, where he began writing his masterwork *Les Miz* (as always, standing up). There are manuscripts and early editions of that famous work on display, as well as others such as *The Hunchback of Notre Dame*. You can see illustrations of Hugo's writings by other artists, including Bayard's rendition of the impish Cosette holding her giant broom (which has graced countless *Les Miz* T-shirts). The collection includes many of Hugo's own, sometimes macabre, ink drawings (he was a fine artist) and furniture from several of his homes. Particularly impressive is the room of carved and painted Chinese-style wooden panels that Hugo designed for the house of his mistress, Juliet Drouet, on the island of Guernsey, during the writer's exile there (for agitating against Napoléon III). Try to spot the intertwined Vs and Js. (Hint: Look for the angel's trumpet in the left corner.) The first floor is dedicated to temporary exhibitions that often have modern ties to Hugo's work. ⊠ *6 pl. des Vosges, Marais* ☎ *01-42-72-10-16* ⊕ *www.musee-hugo.paris.fr* ⊠ *Free; temporary exhibitions €7* ☾ *Tues.–Sun. 10–6* Ⓜ *St-Paul.*

Mémorial de la Shoah (*Memorial to the Holocaust*). The first installation of this stunning memorial and museum is the deeply moving Wall of Names, tall plinths honoring the 76,000 French Jews deported from

CENTRE POMPIDOU

✉ *Pl. Georges-Pompidou, Beaubourg/Les Halles*
☎ *01–44–78–12–33*
⊕ *www.centrepompidou.fr*
💳 *€10; €12 during temporary exhibitions* ⊙ *Wed.–Mon. 11–9, Thurs. 11–11 during temporary exhibitions, Atelier Brancusi Wed.–Mon. 2–6*
Ⓜ *Rambuteau.*

TIPS

■ The Pompidou's permanent collection takes up a relatively small amount of the space when you consider this massive building's other features: temporary exhibition galleries, with a special wing for design and architecture; a highly regarded free reference library (there's often a queue of university students on Rue Renard waiting to get in); and the basement, which includes two cinemas, a theater, a dance space, and a small, free exhibition space.

■ On your way up the escalator, you'll have spectacular views of Paris, ranging from the Tour Montparnasse, to the left, around to the hilltop Sacré-Coeur on the right.

■ The trendy rooftop restaurant, Georges (01–44–78–47–99), is a romantic spot for dinner. Be sure to reserve a table near the window.

■ There are public toilets on the lower level without the long lines of those on the ground floor.

Love it or hate it, the Pompidou is certainly the city's most unique-looking building. Most Parisians have warmed to the industrial, Lego-like exterior that caused a scandal when it opened in 1977. Named after French president Georges Pompidou (1911–74), it was designed by then-unknowns Renzo Piano and Richard Rogers. The architects' claim to fame was putting the building's guts on the outside and color-coding them: water pipes are green, air ducts are blue, electrics are yellow, and things like elevators and escalators are red. Art from the 20th century to the present day is what you can find inside.

HIGHLIGHTS

The Musée National d'Art Moderne (Modern Art Museum, entrance on Level 4) occupies the top two levels. Level 5 is devoted to modern art, 1905–60 including major works by Matisse, Modigliani, Marcel Duchamp, and Picasso; Level 4 is dedicated to contemporary art from the '60s on, including video installations. The Galerie d'Enfants (Children's Gallery) on the mezzanine level has interactive exhibits designed to keep the kids busy. Outside, next to the museum's sloping plaza—where throngs of teenagers hang out (and where there's free Wi-Fi)—is the Atelier Brancusi. This small, airy museum contains four rooms reconstituting Brancusi's Montparnasse studios with works from all periods of his career. On the opposite side, in the Place Igor-Stravinsky, is the Stravinsky fountain, which has 16 gyrating mechanical figures in primary colors, including a giant pair of ruby red lips. On the opposite side of Rue Rambuteau, on the wall at the corner of Rue Clairvaux and Passage Brantôme, is the appealingly bizarre mechanical brass-and-steel clock, Le Défenseur de Temps.

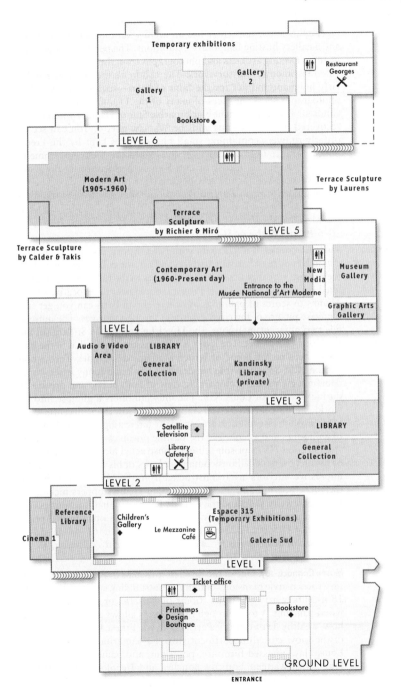

Temporary exhibitions

Gallery
1

Gallery
2

🚻 Restaurant
Georges ✗

Bookstore ◆

LEVEL 6

🚻

Modern Art
(1905-1960)

Terrace Sculpture
by Laurens

Terrace
Sculpture
by Richier & Miró

LEVEL 5

Terrace Sculpture
by Calder & Takis

Contemporary Art
(1960-Present day)

New
Media

Museum
Gallery

Entrance to the
Musée National d'Art Moderne

Graphic Arts
Gallery

🚻

LEVEL 4

Audio & Video
Area

LIBRARY

General
Collection

Kandinsky
Library
(private)

LEVEL 3

8

Satellite
Television ◆

LIBRARY

Library
Cafeteria ✗

General
Collection

🚻

LEVEL 2

Reference
Library

Children's
Gallery ◆

Le Mezzanine
Café ☕

Espace 315
(Temporary Exhibitions)

Cinema 1

Galerie Sud

LEVEL 1

Ticket office ◆

🚻

Printemps
Design
Boutique ◆

Bookstore
◆

GROUND LEVEL

ENTRANCE

France to Nazi concentration camps, of whom only 2,500 survived. Opened in 2005, the center has an archive on the victims, a library, and a gallery hosting temporary exhibitions. The permanent collection includes riveting artifacts and photographs from the camps, along with video testimony from survivors. The children's memorial is particularly poignant and not for the faint of heart—scores of back-lighted photographs show the faces of many of the 11,000 murdered French children. The crypt, a giant black marble Star of David, contains ashes recovered from the camps and the Warsaw ghetto. You can see the orderly drawers containing small files on Jews kept by the French police. (France only officially acknowledged the Vichy government's role in 1995.) The history of anti-Semitic persecution in the world is revisited as well as the rebounding state of Jewry today. There is a free guided tour in English the second Sunday of every month at 3 pm. ⊠ *17 rue Geoffroy-l'Asnier, Marais* ☎ *01–42–77–44–72* ⊕ *www.memorialdelashoah.org* ✉ *Free* ☉ *Sun.–Wed. 10–6, Thurs. 10–10, Fri. 10–6* Ⓜ *Pont Marie or St-Paul.*

Fodor'sChoice
★

Musée Carnavalet. If it has to do with Paris history, it's here. A fascinating hodgepodge of Parisian artifacts and art, the collection ranges from the prehistoric canoes used by Parisii tribes to the furniture of the cork-lined bedroom where Marcel Proust labored over his evocative novels. Thanks to scores of paintings, nowhere else in Paris can you get such a precise picture of the city's evolution through the ages. The museum fills two adjacent mansions, the Hôtel Le Peletier de St-Fargeau and the Hôtel Carnavalet. The latter is a Renaissance jewel that in the mid-1600s became the home of writer Madame de Sévigné. Throughout her long life, Sévigné wrote hundreds of frank and funny letters to her daughter, giving an incomparable view of both public and private life during the time of Louis XIV. The museum offers a glimpse into her world, but the collection covers far more than just the 17th century. The exhibits on the Revolution are especially interesting, with scale models of guillotines and a replica of the Bastille prison carved from one of its stones. Louis XVI's prison cell is reconstructed along with mementos of his life, even medallions containing locks of his family's hair. Other impressive interiors are reconstructed from the Middle Ages through the rococo period and into Art Nouveau—showstoppers include the Fouquet jewelry shop and the Café de Paris's original furnishings. The sculpted garden at 36 rue des Francs Bourgeois is open from April to the end of October. ⊠ *23 rue de Sévigné, Marais* ☎ *01–44–59–58–58* ⊕ *www.carnavalet.paris.fr* ✉ *Free for permanent collection, €7 for exhibits* ☉ *Tues.–Sun. 10–6* Ⓜ *St-Paul.*

Musée Cognacq-Jay. One of the loveliest museums in Paris, this 16th-century rococo-style mansion contains an outstanding collection of mostly 18th-century artwork in its rooms of *boiserie*, or intricately carved wood paneling. A tour through these rooms allows a rare glimpse into how wealthy 19th-century Parisians lived. Ernest Cognacq, founder of the (now closed) department store La Samaritaine, and his wife, Louise Jay, amassed furniture, porcelain, and paintings—notably by Fragonard, Watteau, François Boucher, and Tiepolo—to create one of the world's finest private collections of this period. Some of the best displays are also the smallest, like the tiny enamel medallion portraits showcased on the second floor; or on the third floor, the glass cases filled with exquisite inlaid snuff boxes, sewing cases, pocket watches, perfume bottles, and cigar cutters. There are no exhibit descriptions in English, but pamphlets and museum guides are sold in English. ⊠ *8 rue Elzévir, Marais* ☎ *01–40–27–07–21* ⊕ *www.cognacq-jay.paris.fr* 🎫 *Free for permanent collection, €5 for temporary exhibits* ⊙ *Tues.– Sun. 10–6* Ⓜ *St-Paul.*

Musée d'Art et d'Histoire du Judaïsme. This excellent museum traces the tempestuous history of French and European Jews through art and history. Opened in 1998 in the refined 17th-century Hôtel St-Aignan, exhibits have good explanatory texts in English, and the free English audioguide is a must; guided tours in English are also available on request. Highlights include 13th-century tombstones excavated in Paris; a wooden model of a destroyed Eastern European synagogue; a roomful of early paintings by Marc Chagall; and Christian Boltanski's stark, two-part tribute to Shoah (Holocaust) victims in the form of plaques on an outer wall naming the (mainly Jewish) inhabitants of the Hôtel St-Aignan in 1939, and canvas hangings with the personal data of the 13 residents who were deported and died in concentration camps. ■TIP➜ The rear-facing windows offer a view of the Jardin Anne Frank. To visit it, use the entrance on the Impasse Berthaud, off Rue Beaubourg, just north of Rue Rambuteau. ⊠ *71 rue du Temple, Marais* ☎ *01–53–01–86– 60* ⊕ *www.mahj.org* 🎫 *€6.80* ⊙ *Weekdays 11–6, Sun. 10–6* Ⓜ *Rambuteau or Hôtel de Ville.*

☺ **Musée des Arts et Métiers** (*Museum of Arts and Crafts*). Science buffs should not miss this cavernous museum, Europe's oldest dedicated to invention and technology. It's a treasure trove of wonkiness with 80,000 instruments, machines, and gadgets from 16th-century astrolabes to Edison's phonographs to film-camera prototypes by the Frères Lumière. You can see video simulations of groundbreaking architectural feats, like the cast-iron dome, or see how Jacquard's machine revolutionized cloth-making. Kids will love the flying machines, including the first plane to cross the English Channel, and the impressive display of old automobiles in the high-ceilinged chapel of St-Martin-des-Champs. Also in the chapel is a copy of Foucault's Pendulum, which proved to the world in 1851 that the Earth rotated. Demonstrations are staged daily at noon and 5 pm. (The original pendulum fell and is on display elsewhere.) The building, built between the 11th and 13th centuries, was a church and priory. It was confiscated during the Revolution, and after incarnations as a school and a weapons factory, it became a museum in 1799. Most displays have information in English. There is a quiet café on the first floor. ■TIP➜ If you're taking the subway here, check out the platform of métro Line 11 in the Arts and Métiers station—one of the city's most elaborate—made to look like the inside of a machine, complete with rust-color metal walls, giant bolts, and faux gears. ⊠ *60 rue Réaumur, Opéra/Grands Boulevards* ☎ *01–53–01–82–00* ⊕ *www.arts-et-metiers. net* 🎫 *€6.50, €7.50 with temporary exhibit; €5 English audioguide (recommended)* ⊙ *Tues., Wed., and Fri.–Sun. 10–6, Thurs. 10–9:30* Ⓜ *Arts et Métiers.*

8

★ **Musée Picasso**
See highlighted listing in this chapter.

NEED A BREAK?
Jardin Francs-Bourgeois-Rosier. The Jardin Francs-Bourgeois-Rosier, a quiet garden tucked behind the Maison de l'Europe, is a hidden gem. Bring a snack to enjoy in this quiet patch of green amid the roses and little trees—a Zen oasis in the heart of the bustling Marais. (The garden opens at 1:30 daily.) ✉ *5–37 rue des Francs Bourgeois.*

↺ **Place des Vosges**
Fodor's Choice *See highlighted listing in this chapter.*
★

WORTH NOTING

Agoudas Hakehilos Synagogue. Art Nouveau genius Hector Guimard built this unique synagogue (also called Synagogue de la Rue Pavée) in 1913 for a Polish-Russian Orthodox association. The facade resembles an open book: Guimard used the motif of the Ten Commandments to inspire the building's shape and its interior, which can only rarely be visited. Knock on the door and see if the caretaker will let you upstairs to the balcony, where you can admire Guimard's well-preserved interior decor. Like other Parisian synagogues, the front door of this address was dynamited by the Nazis on Yom Kippur 1940. The Star of David over the door was added after the building was restored. ✉ *10 rue Pavé, Marais* ☎ *01–48–87–21–54* Ⓜ *St-Paul.*

NEED A BREAK?
L'As du Falafel. Jewish food is tops in the Marais, where you can get a falafel (fried chickpeas) sandwich to go, loaded with salad and sauce, for €5. You'll find one of the best versions here. ✉ *34 rue des Rosiers, Marais* ☎ *01–48–87–63–60* ↺ *Closed Fri. at sundown and Sat.*

Sacha Finkelsztajn. Order a Yiddish sandwich (a poppy seed roll piled high with meats) or baba ghanoush (eggplant puree) at Sacha Finkelsztajn, which has two delis at No. 27 and No. 19. Don't forget dessert; Finkelsztajn makes yummy cookies and pastries like apple strudel. ✉ *Rue des Rosiers, Marais* ☎ *01–42–72–78–91* ↺ *Closed Tues. and mid-July–mid-Aug.*

Schwartz's Deli. Schwartz's Deli is a taste of New York's Lower East Side, with hefty pastrami and club sanwiches. The cheesecake isn't bad either. ✉ *16 Rue des Ecouffes, Marais* ☎ *01–48–87–31–29.*

Archives Nationales. Thousands of important historical documents are housed in these two spectacular buildings, built in 1705 as private homes. Fans of the decorative arts will appreciate a visit to the Hôtel de Soubise, where the well-preserved private apartments of the Prince and Princess de Soubise are among the first examples of the rococo style, which preceded the more somber Baroque opulence of Louis XIV. Many important architects left their mark here. The Hôtel de Rohan, open to the public only during Patrimony weekend in September, was built for Soubise's son, Cardinal Rohan. On display are documents dating from 625 to the 20th century. Highlights are

MUSÉE PICASSO

✉ *5 rue de Thorigny, Marais*
☎ *01–42–71–25–21*
🌐 *www.musee-picasso.fr*
💳 *Admission to be determined* 🕐 *Closed Tues.; hrs to be determined* Ⓜ *St-Sébastien.*

TIPS

■ While the museum plans to reopen in summer 2013, delays are likely. Check the website for updates or call before you go.

To the chagrin of Picasso fans everywhere, this immensely popular museum closed in August 2009 for a top-to-bottom overhaul. It is set to reopen in summer 2013. (About 200 works from the permanent collection have been on the road in the United States and elsewhere during the renovation.) The $62 million face-lift will thoroughly transform the Picasso, more than quadrupling the museum's size to 75,000 square feet with new galleries and a performance space. A new 4,800-square-foot building in the back garden, dedicated to temporary exhibitions and other programs, will open when the final stage is completed in spring 2014.

HIGHLIGHTS

The collection of more than 100,000 paintings, sculptures, drawings, and documents (much of it previously in storage for lack of space) spans Picasso's entire life's work, from the Blue Period to Surrealism, when he painted perhaps his most renowned work, the mammoth *Guernica*, which hangs in the Museo Reina Sofia in Madrid. The Paris collection does not comprise the master's most famous works, but rather "Picasso's Picassos," many of the paintings and sculptures treasured most by the artist, including his personal collection of works by friends and influences such as Matisse, Braque, Cézanne, and Rousseau. There is a detailed overview of Picasso's life and loves, with information in English. The museum opened in 1985 in the regal 17th-century Hôtel Salé as a permanent home for the collection, after much of it was given to the government by the artist's heirs to settle a hefty tax bill after the painter's death in 1973.

8

the Edict of Nantes (1598), the Treaty of Westphalia (1648), the wills of Louis XIV and Napoléon, and the Declaration of Human Rights (1789). Louis XVI's diary is also here, containing his sadly clueless entry for July 14, 1789, the day the Bastille was stormed and the French Revolution was launched. Before you leave, notice the medieval turrets to the right in the courtyard: this is the Porte de Clisson, all that remains of a stately 14th-century mansion. At this writing, plans were underway to transform a portion of the Archives into a museum devoted to the history of France. The Maison de l'Histoire de la France, set to open in 2015, will consolidate the collections of several smaller museums around the country. ⊠ *60 rue des Francs-Bourgeois, Marais* ☎ *01–40–27–60–96* ⊕ *www.archivesnationales. culture.gouv.fr/chan* ✉ *Free; €6 temporary exhibitions* ⊙ *Mon. and Wed.– Fri. 10–12:20 and 2–5:30, weekends 2–5:30* Ⓜ *Rambuteau.*

Hôtel de Sens. One of the few remaining structures in Paris from the Middles Ages, this little castle was most famously the home of Queen Margot, who took up residence here in 1605 after her marriage to Henry IV was annulled. Margot was known for her many lovers (she supposedly wore wigs made from locks of their hair) and reputedly ordered a servant beheaded in the courtyard after he ridiculed one of her companions. The street is said to be named after a fig tree she ordered cut down because it was inconveniencing her carriage. Perhaps for that reason there's a fig tree planted in the elegant rear garden, which is open to the public. Notice the cannonball lodged in the front facade commemorating a battle here during the three-day revolution in July 1830. Built for Archbishop of Sens in 1475, the castle was extensively renovated in the 20th century and is today home to the **Bibliothèque Forney,** a library that also stages temporary exhibitions drawn from its extensive collection of fine and graphic arts. ⊠ *1 rue du Figuier, Marais* ☎ *01–42–78–14–60* ✉ *Exhibitions €4* ⊙ *Tues., Fri., Sat. 1–7:30, Wed., Thurs. 10–7:30* Ⓜ *Pont Marie.*

☪ **Musée de la Chasse et de la Nature.** Mark this down as one of Paris's most bizarre—and fascinating—collections. The museum, which opened in 2007 in the gorgeous 17th-century Hôtel de Guénégaud, features lavishly appointed rooms stocked with animal- and hunt-theme art by the likes of Rubens and Gentileschi, plus antique weaponry and taxidermy animals. In a tribute to Art Nouveau, the decor includes chandeliers curled like antlers and matching railings. Older kids will appreciate the jaw-dropping Trophy Room with an impressive menagerie of beasts, not to mention the huge polar bear stationed outside. There is a lovely multimedia exhibit on the myth of the unicorn; as well as an interactive display of bird calls. Temporary exhibits and silent auctions take place on the first floor. It's worth a quick visit for the elegant rooms alone. ⊠ *62 rue des Archives, Marais* ☎ *01–53–01–92–40* ⊕ *www. chassenature.org* ✉ *€6* ⊙ *Tues.–Sun. 11–6* Ⓜ *Rambuteau.*

☪ **Musée de la Poupée** (*Doll Museum*). Home to an impressive collection of dolls through the centuries, this charming museum is a little girl's dream. There are dolls of 18th-century Bisque porcelain, sturdy wood, soft cotton, delicate papier mâché, and the first plastic baby dolls from the early 20th century. Some dolls play music, others make tea. Cases lining the walls are stocked with newborn dolls, minidolls (*mignonettes*), and grown-up lady dolls in satin dresses—the foremothers of

PLACE DES VOSGES

✉ *Off Rue des Francs Bourgeois, near Rue de Turenne*
🎫 *Free* ⊙ *Open year-round*
Ⓜ *Bastille or St-Paul.*

TIPS

■ Unlike so many parks in Paris, one of the best things about the Place des Vosges is that you're allowed to sit—or snooze or snack—on the grass during the spring and summer.

■ There is no better spot in the Marais for a picnic. Drop by the street market on nearby Boulevard Richard Lenoir on Thursday and Saturday mornings to pick up lunch fixings. (It's on Boulevard Richard Lenoir between Rues Amelot and St-Sabin.)

■ The most likely approach to the Place des Vosges is from Rue de Francs Bourgeois, the main shopping street. However, for a grander entrance walk along Rue St-Antoine until you get to Rue de Birague, which leads directly into the square.

The oldest square in Paris and—dare we say it?—the most beautiful, the Place des Vosges is one of Europe's oldest stabs at urban planning. The precise proportions offer a placid symmetry, but things weren't always so calm. Four centuries ago this was the site of the Palais des Tournelles, home to King Henri II and Queen Catherine de Medici. The couple staged regular jousting tournaments, and during one of them, in 1559, Henry was fatally lanced in the eye. Catherine fled for the Louvre, abandoning her palace and ordering it destroyed. In 1612 it became the Place Royal on the occasion of Louis XIII's engagement to Anne of Austria. Napoléon renamed it Place des Vosges to honor the northeast region of Vosges, the first in the country to pony up taxes to the Revolutionary government.

HIGHLIGHTS

At the base of the 36 redbrick-and-stone houses—nine on each side of the square—is an arcaded, covered walkway lined with art galleries, shops, and cafés. There's also an elementary school, a synagogue (whose barrel roof was designed by Gustav Eiffel), and several chic hotels. The formal, gated garden's perimeter is lined with chestnut trees; inside are a children's play area and a fountain.

Aside from hanging out in the park, people come here to see the house of the man who once lived at No. 6—Victor Hugo, the author of *Les Misérables* and *Notre-Dame de Paris (The Hunchback of Notre-Dame).*

8

Dining at a Glance

For full reviews
⇨ Chapter 14.

INEXPENSIVE DINING
Breizh Café, *French,* 109 rue Vieille du Temple

Bubar, *Wine Bar,* 3 rue des Tournelles

Café des Musées, *Bistro,* 49 rue de Turenne

Cantine Merci, *Modern French,* 111 bd. Beaumarchais

L'As du Falafel, *Israeli,* 34 rue des Rosiers

MODERATE DINING
Au Bourguignon du Marais, *Bistro,* 52 rue François-Miron

L'Ambassade d'Auvergne, *Bistro,* 22 rue du Grenier St-Lazare

Le Georges, *Modern French,* Centre Pompidou, 6th fl.

Le Rouge Gorge, *Bistro,* 12 rue Pecquay

Restaurant le Gaigne, *Wine Bar,* 8 rue St-Paul

EXPENSIVE DINING
Benoît, *Bistro,* 20 rue St-Martin

Chez Julien, *Bistro,* 1 rue du Pont Louis-Philippe

Le Murano, *Modern French,* 13 bd. du Temple

Barbie. There are antique doll prams, high chairs, and tattered teddy bears in need of a hug. Too extensive to show at one time, the permanent collection changes frequently and can be arranged by period or theme. Temporary exhibitions may feature modern themes like Barbie's evolution, or a classic look at postwar French dolls. Workshops allow kids to make a doll to take home (they're in French but the mostly bilingual staff is happy to speak English; call ahead to confirm). There's also a doll hospital and a well-stocked gift shop. ⊠ *Impasse Berthaud, Marais* ☎ *01–42–72–73–11* ⊕ *www.museedelapoupeeparis.com* ⊡ *€8; €4 ages 3–11 or €14 with workshop* ⊘ *Tues.–Sun. 10–6* Ⓜ *Rambuteau.*

OFF THE BEATEN PATH

Nicolas Flamel's Home. Built in 1407 and reputed to be the oldest house in Paris (though other buildings claim that title), this abode has a mystical history. Harry Potter fans should take note: this was the real-life home of Nicolas Flamel, the alchemist whose sorcerer's stone is the source of immortality in the popular book series. A wealthy scribe, merchant, and dabbler in the mystical arts, Flamel willed his home to the city as a dormitory for the poor, on the condition that boarders pray daily for his soul. Today, the building is home to apartments and a restaurant. ⊠ *51 rue Montmorency, Marais* Ⓜ *Rambuteau.*

St-Paul–St-Louis. The leading Baroque church in the Marais, its dome rising 180 feet above the crossing, was begun in 1627 by the Jesuits, who modeled it after their Gesù church in Rome. Dark and brooding, the church contains Delacroix's *Christ on the Mount of Olives* in the transept and a shell-shaped holy-water font at the entrance, which was donated by Victor Hugo, who lived in nearby Place des Vosges. Hugo's beloved daughter, Léopoldine, was married here in 1843—though only to meet a tragic end less than seven months later, when she fell into the Seine and drowned, along with her husband Charles, who tried to save her. ■TIP➜ Compare the church's soot-stained exterior with the squeaky-clean Hôtel de Sully (No. 62) to see what Paris's buildings would look like without regular cleanings. ⊠ *99 rue St-Antoine, Marais* Ⓜ *St-Paul.*

Eastern Paris

WITH BASTILLE, CANAL ST-MARTIN, RÉPUBLIQUE, OBERKAMPF, AND BELLEVILLE

WORD OF MOUTH

"The Canal St-Martin area is very interesting for walking around on Sunday because both sides of the canal are closed to traffic for most of the day . . . consider taking the Canauxrama canal boat from Bastille to La Villette, which would give you an overview of the entire length of the canal."

—kerouac

GETTING ORIENTED

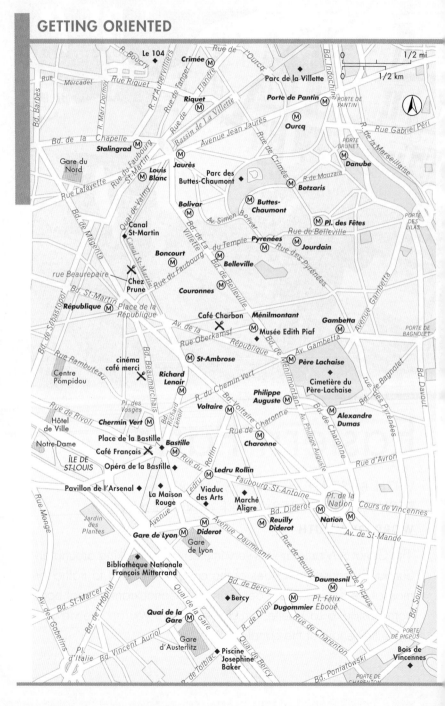

TOP REASONS TO GO

Canal St-Martin. The scenic canal has evolved into one of the city's top hangouts—it's great for strolling, and galleries, shops, and cafés abound.

Place de la Bastille. The flashpoint of the French Revolution still draws modern-day agitators and their frequent noisy demonstrations. It's also a nightlife destination for all ages and home to the Opéra Bastille.

Cimetière du Père Lachaise. The final address of dozens of celebrities, from Chopin to Oscar Wilde to Jim Morrison, whose elaborate tombs are laid out along twisting, tree-shaded paths.

Parc de la Villette. Home to the city's well-regarded science museum and planetarium, this is a good place to take the kids or grown-up science buffs.

Viaduc des Arts/Promenade Plantée. An abandoned rail line serves as the setting for this lovely garden and 2.7-mile walkway perched atop the **Viaduc des Arts,** a collection of artisan shops focused on design.

MAKING THE MOST OF YOUR TIME

The Canal St-Martin is one of the city's most popular destinations, particularly on Sunday afternoon, when the streets are closed to cars. Have lunch in one of the cafés, grab a Vélib' rental bike *(see "Bicycling in Paris" Close-Up, Chapter 3)* and head to Parc de la Villette, or take a canal boat tour. A Sunday-morning stop at the picturesque Marché Aligre is also recommended, even if you're not buying. The heaps of fresh produce and colorful flowers hawked by excited vendors are worth seeing. On any day the Place de la Bastille is a lively place to stop for drinks or lunch; if time is limited, reserve this neighborhood for after dark, when the streets around Place de la Bastille and Oberkampf really come to life.

GETTING HERE

Canal St-Martin, Bastille, and Oberkampf include the 10ᵉ, 11ᵉ, 12ᵉ, 19ᵉ, and 20ᵉ arrondissements. The Bastille métro stop, on the 1, 5, and 8 lines, is a good place to start. For Canal St-Martin, use the Place de la République stop (lines 3, 5, 8, 9, 11) and walk along Rue Faubourg du Temple, or go to Gare de l'Est stop (lines 4, 5, 7) and walk along Rue des Récollets to the canal. For Oberkampf, go to the Parmentier stop on the 3 line or the Oberkampf stop on the 9. For the Cimetière Père Lachaise, take the 3 to the eponymous stop.

BEST CAFÉS

Café Charbon. This ultracool café, with a restored zinc bar, mirrored walls, and mismatched chandeliers, is a neighborhood institution. ⊠ *109 rue Oberkampf, Oberkampf* ☎ *01–43–57–55–13* Ⓜ *Parmentier.*

Chez Prune. Grab an outdoor table at this neighborhood hot spot on the Canal St-Martin and watch the world go by. ⊠ *36 rue Beaurepaire* ☎ *01–42–41–30–47* Ⓜ *Jacques Beaurepaire, République.*

cinéma café merci. This sweet little café works wonders with a small menu of mostly organic, high-quality ingredients. Come for lunch, tea, or a freshly squeezed juice. ⊠ *111 bd. Beaumarchais* ☎ *01–42–77–00–33* Ⓜ *St-Sébastien Froissart.*

9

Sightseeing
★★
Dining
★★★★
Lodging
★★
Shopping
★★★★
Nightlife
★★★★★

The Bastille used to be the star of this area, and a stop here—home turf of the French Revolution—was a must. The small streets forking off the Place de la Bastille still buzz at night, with bars and music clubs and the top-flight Opéra Bastille, but today the neighborhoods farther afield are the real draw, having evolved into some of Paris's hottest and hippest destinations. The Canal St-Martin, once the down-and-out cousin on the northeastern border, is now trend-spotting central, brimming with funky bars, cafés, art galleries, and boutiques. The scene is similar to the south, on rues Oberkampf, St-Maur, and Jean-Pierre-Timbaud, where artists and small designers have set up shop, and where a substantial slice of the city's *bobo* (bourgeois-bohemian) set is buying up the (momentarily) still-affordable apartments.

The areas to the north and east of the canal are also flourishing, around the rougher streets near **Ménilmontant** and **Belleville,** home to a small Chinatown (watch your purse and avoid wearing attention-getting jewelry). The city's largest cemetery, **Père Lachaise,** is here, with a roster of famous tenants including Proust, Oscar Wilde, and Jim Morrison. Not far away is the impressively wild **Parc Buttes-Chaumont,** with grassy fields, a small Greek-style temple, and sweeping hilltop views of Paris. It's a perfect place for a picnic lunch and to let museum-weary kids work off some steam. There are two other notable parks to the east: **Parc de la Villette,** which is also home to the city's well-regarded science museum, and the **Bois de Vincennes.**

Not far from the Bastille opera house, the **Viaduc des Arts** is a much-admired urban-renewal project that turned an old elevated rail line into arcaded design-focused studios and shops. Along the top, the

Promenade Plantée makes for a lovely stroll through the 12e arrondissement, a nice middle-class neighborhood with stately apartment buildings and the pretty **Square Trousseau**, gateway to the **Marché d'Aligre**, one of the city's best covered markets. Come on Sunday morning with a shopping basket—or just your camera—when the vendors spill over into neighboring streets.

To the south of **Bastille**, the old wine warehouses at **Bercy** have been transformed into a veritable village of shops and restaurants bordering Park de Bercy. Directly across the Seine is the **Bibliothéque National François Mitterand**, the National Library of France, a sprawling complex of modern glass towers heralded as the world's most modern library when it opened in 1998.

TOP ATTRACTIONS

Updated by
Linda Hervieux

Bercy. Tucked away south of the Gare de Lyon in the 12e arrondissement, blocks of stone warehouses that once stored wine are now home to Bercy Village, a collection of shops and restaurants that stay open unusually late for Paris (until 9 pm, even on Sundays). You can still see the old train tracks used to transport the wine barrels from the provinces. Adjacent to the shops is the tranquil Parc de Bercy, with lawns, ponds and flower beds crisscrossed by gravel paths, and the Jardin Yitzhak Rabin, a garden named for the late Nobel Peace Prize winner. On the western edge of the park, near the Bercy métro stop, is the Palais Omnisports, a venue for concerts and sports. Nearby, at 51 rue de Bercy, is a quirky cubist Frank Gehry building now home to the Cinémathèque Française, a film buff's paradise showing classic films, many in English. There are frequent homages to directors and actors, plus a cinema library and museum (see the listing in Chapter 15, Performing Arts). ⊠ *Bercy Village, 28 rue François Truffaut, Bercy/Tolbiac* ☎ *08–25–16–60–75* ⊕ *www.bercyvillage.com* ⊙ *Daily 11–9* Ⓜ *Cour St-Emilion, Bercy.*

9

NEED A BREAK?

Pink Flamingo. Pink Flamingo is an American-owned pizzeria that will deliver your pie directly to the banks of the canal—they spot you thanks to the pink balloon you're holding. ⊠ *67 rue Bichat, Canal St-Martin* ☎ *01–42–02–31–70.*

Fodor'sChoice
★

Canal St-Martin. The once-forgotten canal has morphed into one of the city's trendiest places to wander. A good time to come is Sunday afternoon, when the Quai de Valmy is closed to cars and some of the shops are open. Rent a bike at one of the many Vélib' stations, stroll along the banks, or go native and cuddle quai-side in the sunshine with someone special.

In 1802 Napoléon ordered the 2.7-mile canal dug as a source of clean drinking water after cholera and other epidemics swept the city. When it finally opened 23 years later, it stretched north from the Seine at Place de la Bastille to the Canal de l'Ourcq, near La Villette. Baron Haussmann later covered a mile-long stretch of it, along today's Boulevard Richard Lenoir. It nearly became a highway in the 1970s, before the city's urban planners regained their senses. These days you can take a boat tour from end to end through the canal's nine locks: along the way, the bridges swing or lift open. The drawbridge with four giant pulleys at Rue de Cri-mée, near La Villette, was a technological marvel when it opened in 1885.

In recent years gentrification has swept the once-dodgy canal, with artists taking over former industrial spaces and creating studios and galleries. The bar and restaurant scene is hipster central, and small designers have arrived, fleeing expensive rents in Le Marais. To explore this evolving *quartier,* set out on foot: Start on the Quai de Valmy at Rue Faubourg du Temple (use the République métro stop). Here, at Square Frédéric Lemaître facing north, there is a good view of one of the locks (behind you the canal disappears underground). As you head north, detour onto side streets like Rue Beaurepaire, a fashionista destination with several "stock" (or surplus) shops for popular brands like Maje, some open on Sunday *(⇨ see Chapter 16, Shopping, for details).* The rues Lancry and Vinaigriers are lined with bars, restaurants, and small shops.

A swing bridge across the canal connects Lancry to the Rue de la Grange aux Belles, where you'll find the entrance to massive Hôpital Saint-Louis, built in 1607 to house plague victims and still a working hospital today. In front of you is the entrance to the chapel, which held its first Mass in July 1610, two months after the assassination of the hospital's patron, Henry IV. Stroll the grounds, flanked by the original brick-and-stone buildings with steeply sloping roofs. The peaceful courtyard garden is a neighborhood secret.

Back on Quai Valmy, browse more shops near the Rue des Récollets. Nearby is the Jardin Villemin, the 10e arrondissement's largest park (4½ acres) on the former site of another hospital. The nighttime scene, especially in summer, is hopping with twenty-somethings spilling out of cafés and bars and onto the canal banks. You can catch a live music show at the mostly soul Bizz'Art club-restaurant at No. 167 Quai Valmy (⇨ *see Chapter 14, Nightlife, for more details).* If you've made it this far, reward yourself with a fresh taco or burrito at the tiny and authen-tically Mexican El Nopal taqueria at 3 rue Eugène Varlin. Farther up, just past Place Stalingrad, is the Rotonde de la Villette, a lively square with restaurants and twin MK2 cinemas on either side of the canal, with a boat to ferry ticket-holders across. On the approach to Parc de la Villette there are antiques shops along the quai and a few float-ing restaurants and theaters. **Canauxrama** offers 2½-hour boat cruises through the locks (€16 adults). Check the website for times (⊕ *www. canauxrama.com).* Embarkation is at each end of canal: at Bassin de la Villette *(13 quai de la Loire, La Villette)* or Marina Arsenal *(50 bd. de la Bastille, Bastille).* Ⓜ *Jaurès (northern end) or Bastille (southern end).*

NEED A BREAK? **Hôtel du Nord.** With a retro white facade, the Hôtel du Nord looks like a movie set, and, in fact, it was famously used by Marcel Carné in his 1938 namesake movie. The film's star, actress-icon Arletty, claimed to be unmoved by the romantic canal-side setting, uttering the memorable line "Atmosphere, atmosphere, I've had it with atmosphere!" Today the restaurant, beautifully restored, is a hipster favorite, though the food is not as fabulous as the ambience. ⊠ *102 quai de Jemmappes, République* ☏ *01-40-40-78-78* Ⓜ *Jacques Bonsergent.*

CANAUXRAMA

★ **Cimetière du Père Lachaise**

See highlighted listing in this chapter.

★ **La Maison Rouge.** One of the city's premier spaces for contemporary art, La Maison Rouge art foundation was established by former gallery owner Antoine de Galbert to fill a hole in the Parisian art world. Always edgy, often provocative, the foundation stages several temporary exhibitions each year in cleverly renovated industrial space anchored around a central courtyard building painted bright red on the outside (hence the name). Past shows include 2011's "Tous Cannibales"—a mix of art with a cannibalism theme—and "Memories of the Future," from a death-obsessed private collection with works from Bosch to Damien Hirst to photographer Cindy Sherman. Check the website to see what's on. ■TIP→ Stop by the Rose Bakery near the entrance, the latest Parisian outpost of the popular English café. ✉ *10 bd. de la Bastille, Bastille* 📞 *01–40–01–08–81* ⊕ *www.lamaisonrouge.org* 💶 *€7* ☉ *Wed.–Sun. 11–7, Thurs. 11–9* Ⓜ *Quai de la Rapée/Bastille.*

Marché Aligre. Place d'Aligre is home to two of Paris's best markets: the lively outdoor Marché Aligre and the covered Marché Beauvau. Open at 8 am every day but Monday, both are great places to pick up the essentials for a picnic lunch, which you can enjoy in the small park nearby at Square Trousseau or on the nearby Promenade Plantée. The picturesque outdoor market has dozens of excitable vendors, their stands spilling over with fresh fruits and vegetables, flower bouquets, and regional products such as jam, honey, and dried sausage. The best bargains are had just before the closing time at 1 pm, and many vendors are happy to give you a taste of whatever they're selling. The covered market, which closes in the afternoon and reopens from 4 to 7:30 pm, stocks everything from meats and cheeses to Belgian beer. Sunday morning is the liveliest time to visit. Don't forget your camera. ■TIP→ Stop for a plate of saucisse and a glass of rouge (even Sunday morning) at one of the city's quirkiest wine bars, Le Baron Bouge, 1 rue Théophile Roussel. ✉ *Pl. d'Aligre, Bastille* Ⓜ *Ledru-Rollin/Bastille.*

Opéra de la Bastille. Paris's main opera house opened its doors on July 14, 1989, to mark the bicentennial of the French Revolution. The fabulous acoustics of the steeply sloping, stylish auditorium have earned more plaudits than the modern facade designed by Uruguay-born architect Carlos Ott. If you want to see a show, reserve your seat well in advance, or take your chances on the same day, when any unclaimed seats (at all price levels) are released 45 minutes before showtime. There are also 32 standing-room-only tickets available before each show for €5. Same-day seats are much in demand, so be sure to line up two hours or more before the curtain. ✉ *Pl. de la Bastille, Bastille/Nation* 📞 *08–92–89–90–90 tickets (€0.34 minute), 01–71–25–24–23 from outside of France* ⊕ *www.operadeparis.fr* Ⓜ *Bastille.*

☿ **Parc de la Villette.** This former abattoir is now a 130-acre ultramodern park and the perfect place to entertain sightseeing-weary kids, with lawns and play spaces, an excellent science museum, a music complex, and a cinema. You could easily spend a whole day here.

The park itself was designed in the 1980s by postmodern architecture star Bernard Tschumi, who teamed industrial elements, children's games (don't miss the dragon slide), ample green space, and funky sculptures along the canal into one vast yet unified playground. A great place for a picnic, the lawns attract rehearsing samba bands and pickup soccer games. In summer there are outdoor festivals and a free outdoor cinema festival—people gather at dusk to picnic and watch movies on a huge inflatable screen.

In cold weather you can visit the museums, the submarine, the Espace Chapiteaux (a circus tent featuring contemporary acrobatic theater performances), and **La Géode**— an Omnimax cinema housed in a giant silver ball. The postmodern **Cité de la Musique** is a music academy designed by noted urban architect Christian de Portzamparc. It has a state-of-the-art concert hall and houses the excellent **Musée de la Musique** (⇨ *below*). All that's left of the slaughterhouse is La Grande Halle, a magnificent iron-and-glass building now used for exhibitions, performances, and trade shows.

Cité des Sciences et de l'Industrie. This ambitious science museum, in a colorful three-story industrial space that recalls the Pompidou Center, is packed with things to do, all accessible to English speakers. There are scores of exhibits, from space and the universe to transportation and technology. Hands-on workshops keep the kids entertained and the planetarium is always a hit. Temporary shows, like 2011's history of the Gauls, are always multi-lingual and usually interactive. ⊠ *30 av. Corentin-Cariou, La Villette* ☎ *01–40–05–70–00* ⊕ *www.cite-sciences. fr* ⊡ *€8; €11 with planetarium or temporary exhibits* ☉ *Tues.–Sat. 9:30–6, Sun. 9:30–7* Ⓜ *Porte de la Villette.*

Musée de la Musique. This recently renovated music museum contains some 1,000 instruments from around the world over four centuries, many of them exquisite works of art. Their sounds and story are evoked on numerous video screens and via commentary you can follow on headphones (ask for a free audioguide in English). Temporary exhibitions such as 2011's Paul Klee Polyphonies are usually excellent and bilingual. ⊠ *221 av. Jean-Jaurès, La Villette* ☎ *01–44– 84–44–84* ⊕ *www.cite-musique.fr* ⊡ *€8* ☉ *Tues.–Sat. noon–6, Sun. 10–6* Ⓜ *Porte de Pantin.*

Café de la Musique. Across the plaza, the outdoor terrace at Café de la Musique is an inviting place to have a drink on a sunny day. ⊠ *213 av. Jean-Jaurès, La Villette* ☎ *01–48–03–15–91* Ⓜ *Porte de Pantin* ⊠ *30 av. Corentin-Cariou* ☎ *01–44–84–44–84* ⊕ *www.cite-sciences.fr.*

☽ **Parc des Buttes-Chaumont.** If you're tired of perfectly manicured Parisian parks with lawns that are off-limits to your weary feet, this is the place for you. This lovely 61-acre hilltop park in the untouristy 19e arrondissement has grassy fields, leafy walkways, waterfalls, and a picturesque lake dotted with swans. Rising from the lake is a rocky cliff you can climb to find a mini Greek-style temple and a commanding view of Sacré-Coeur Basilica. Built in 1863 on abandoned gypsum quarries and a former gallows, this was northern Paris's first park, part of Napoléon III's planned greening of Paris (the emperor had

CIMITÈRE DU PÈRE-LACHAISE

✉ *Entrances on Rue des Rondeaux, Bd. de Ménilmontant, and Rue de la Réunion, Père Lachaise* ☎ *01–55–25–82–10* ⊕ *www.pere-lachaise.com* ⊙ *Daily 8–6* Ⓜ *Gambetta, Philippe-Auguste, Père-Lachaise.*

TIPS

■ Pinpoint grave sites on the website before you come, but buy a map anyway outside the entrances—you'll still get lost, but that's part of the fun.

■ One of the best days to visit is on All Saints' Day (November 1), when Parisians bring flowers to adorn the graves of loved ones or favorite celebrities.

Bring a red rose for "the little sparrow" Edith Piaf when you visit the cobblestone avenues and towering trees that make this 118-acre oasis of green perhaps the world's most famous cemetery. Named for Père François de la Chaise, Louis XIV's confessor, Père-Lachaise is more than just a who's who of celebrities. The Paris Commune's final battle took place here on May 28, 1871, when 147 rebels were lined up and shot against the Mur des Fédérés (Federalists' Wall) in the southeast corner.

HIGHLIGHTS

Aside from the sheer aesthetic beauty of the cemetery, the main attraction is what (or who, more accurately) is belowground.

Two of the biggest draws are Jim Morrison's grave (with its own guard to keep Doors fans under control) and the life-size bronze figure of French journalist Victor Noir, whose alleged fertility-enhancing power accounts for the patches rubbed smooth by hopeful hands. Other significant grave sites include those of 12th century French philosopher Pierre Abélard and his lover Heloïse; French writers Colette, Honoré de Balzac, and Marcel Proust; American writers Richard Wright, Gertrude Stein, and Alice B. Toklas; Irish writer Oscar Wilde; French actress Sarah Bernhardt; French composer Georges Bizet; the Greek-American opera singer Maria Callas; Franco-Polish composer Frédéric Chopin; painters of various nationalities including Georges-Pierre Seurat, Camille Pissaro, Jean Auguste Dominique Ingres, Jacques-Louis David, Eugène Delacroix, Théodore Géricault, Amedeo Clemente Modigliani, and Max Ernst; French jazz violinist Stephane Grappelli; French civic planer Baron Haussmann; the French playwright and actor Molière; and French singer Edith Piaf.

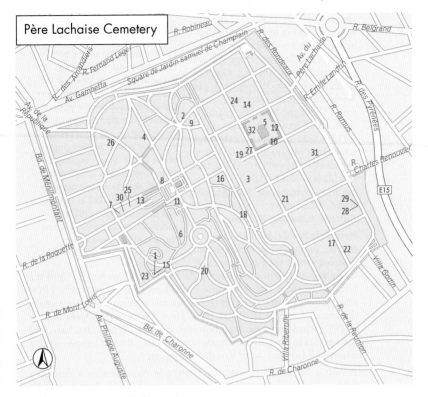

Père Lachaise Cemetery

Pierre Abélard **1**

Honoré de Balzac **2**

Sarah Bernhardt **3**

Georges Bizet **4**

Maria Callas **5**

Frédéric Chopin **6**

Sidonie-Gabrielle Colette .. **7**

Jacques-Louis David **8**

Eugène Delacroix **9**

Max Ernst **10**

Théodore Géricault **11**

Stéphane Grappelli **12**

Baron Haussmann **13**

Sedegh Hedayat **14**

Héloïse **15**

Jean-Auguste-
Dominique Ingres **16**

Amedeo Clemente
Modigliani **17**

Molière (Jean-Baptiste
Poquelina) **18**

Yves Montand **19**

Jim Morrison **20**

Victor Noir **21**

Edith Piaf **22**

Camille Pissarro **23**

Marcel Proust **24**

Giaocchino Rossini **25**

Georges-Pierre Seurat **26**

Simone Signoret **27**

Gertrude Stein **28**

Alice B. Toklas **29**

Louis Visconti **30**

Oscar Wilde **31**

Richard Wright **32**

9

spent years in exile in London, where he fel l in love with the public parks). It's a good place to take the kids, with pony rides and an open-air puppet theater, Guignol de Paris (€3.50; shows at 4 pm Wednesday and weekends year-round), not far from the entrance at Buttes-Chaumont métro stop. ■TIP➔ Grab a snack at café Rosa Bonheur or reserve a table for weekend lunch at Le Pavillon du Lac restaurant (01-42-00-07-21). ⊠ *Entrances on Rue Botzaris or Rue Manin, Buttes-Chaumont* Ⓜ *Laumière, Buttes-Chaumont, Botzaris.*

Place de la Bastille. Nothing remains of the infamous Bastille prison, destroyed more than 200 years ago,

> **DID YOU KNOW?**
>
> The Bastille prison is long gone, but you can still see remnants of it. The best place to look is in the Bastille métro station, where large stones are visible on the platform of Line 5 (direction Bobigny), with an explanation and artist's rendering of the prison. Another chunk of one of the towers, excavated during construction of the métro in 1898, sits nearby, unmarked, in the Square Henri-Galli at the edge of a small park: go to the intersection of Boulevard Henri IV and the quai of the same name.

though tourists still ask bemused Parisians where to find it. Until the late 1980s, there was little more to see here than a busy traffic circle ringing the Colonne de Juillet (July Column), a memorial to the victims of later uprisings in 1830 and 1848. The opening of the Opéra Bastille in 1989 rejuvenated the area, however, drawing art galleries, bars, and restaurants to the narrow streets, notably along Rue de Lappe—once a haunt of Edith Piaf—and Rue de la Roquette.

Before it became a prison, the Bastille St-Antoine was a defensive fortress with eight immense towers and a wide moat. It was built by Charles V in the late 14th century and transformed into a prison during the reign of Louis XIII (1610–43). Famous occupants included Voltaire, the Marquis de Sade, and the Man in the Iron Mask. On July 14, 1789, it was stormed by an angry mob that dramatically freed all of the remaining prisoners (there were only seven, including one lunatic), launching the French Revolution. The roots of the revolt ran deep. Resentment toward Louis XVI and Marie-Antoinette had been building amid a severe financial crisis. There was a crippling bread shortage, and the free-spending monarch was blamed. When the king dismissed the popular finance minister, Jacques Necker, enraged Parisians took to the streets. They marched to Les Invalides, helping themselves to stocks of arms, then continued on to the Bastille. A few months later, what was left of the prison was razed—and 83 of its stones were carved into miniature Bastilles and sent to the provinces as a memento (you can see one of them in the Musée Carnavalet). The key to the prison was given to George Washington by Lafayette, and has remained at Mount Vernon ever since. Today, nearly every major street demonstration in Paris—and there are many—passes through this square. Ⓜ *Bastille.*

★ **Viaduc des Arts/Promenade Plantée.** Once a train line from the Paris suburbs to Bastille, this redbrick viaduct is now a leafy oasis in the heart of the unpretentious 12e arrondissement. The rails have been transformed into a 2.8-mile walkway lined with trees, bamboo, and flowers, offering

Bastille at Night

From Place de la Bastille, take Rue de la Roquette and turn right onto Rue de Lappe, Paris's answer to Bourbon Street, once a haunt of artists and writers like Henry Miller. Today it draws a mostly young crowd to its many bars and restaurants, though there's something for everyone. Detour down the tiny Passage Louis Philippe to find Café de la Danse, one of the city's best venues to see all sorts of live music. In the early 1900s, Auvergne immigrants brought *bal musette*—accordion-driven popular music—with them, and many later collaborated with gypsy jazzman Django Reinhardt. One of its anchors is the Balajo dance club at No. 9 rue de Lappe *(see Chapter 14, Nightlife)*, established in 1936 and still going strong. In recent years these tangled streets have added shops, theaters, and galleries to the constantly evolving bar lineup.

a bird's-eye view of the stately Haussmanian buildings along Avenue Daumesnil. Below, the *voûtes*, or arcades, have been transformed by the city into artisan boutiques, many focused on decor and design. All of the tenants are hand-picked. There are also temporary galleries showcasing art and photography. The Promenade, which gained fame as a setting in the 2004 film *Before Sunset*, was the inspiration for New York's High Line. It ends at the Jardin de Reuilly. From here you can continue your walk to the Bois de Vincennes. ■TIP➜ If you're hungry, grab a bite at L'Arrosoir, a cozy café under the viaduct at 75 Avenue Daumesnil. ⊠ *Av. Daumesnil, Bastille* Ⓜ *Bastille, Gare de Lyon.*

WORTH NOTING

Bibliothèque National François Mitterand. The National Library of France, across the sleek Simone de Beauvoir footbridge from Bercy Park, is a stark modern complex of four 22-story L-shaped buildings representing open books. Commissioned by President Mitterrand before his death, the $1.5 billion library was said to be the world's most modern when it opened in 1998—a reputation quickly sullied when it was discovered that miles of books and rare documents were baking in the glass towers, unprotected from the sun (movable shutters were eventually installed). Some of the most important printed treasures of France are stored here, though most are available only to researchers. Visitors can see the impressive 17th-century Globes of Coronelli, a pair of 2-ton orbs made for Louis XIV. There's a sunken center garden with tall trees (open to the public the first weekend in June) ringed by low-ceilinged reading rooms, which are nothing special. A first-floor gallery hosts popular temporary exhibitions on subjects such as the life of Casanova and the adults-only erotica show—telegraphed across Paris thanks to a giant X written in lights on one of the towers. Enter through the easternmost tower. ⊠ *Quai François Mauriac, Bibliothèque* ☎ *01–53–79–59–59* ⊕ *www.bnf.fr* ⌁ *Globes gallery free; reading rooms €3.50; exhibitions €7* ☯ *Tues.–Sat. 10–8, Sun. 1–7* Ⓜ *Bibliothèque, Quai de la Gare.*

9

♻ **Bois de Vincennes.** Like the Bois de Boulogne to the west, the lovely Vincennes Woods was landscaped by Napoléon III, and it is a much-loved retreat on the city's eastern border. The bois, or wood, traces its roots back to the 13th century, when Philippe Auguste created a hunting preserve in the shadow of the royal **Château de Vincennes.** In 1731 Louis XV created a public park. Today the bois features lush lawns, a flower garden, and summertime jazz concerts. Rowboats are for hire at the two lakes, Lac Daumesnil, which has two islands, and Lac des Minimes, which has three. There's also a zoo (closed until 2014) and a racetrack, the **Hippodrome de Vincennes,** two cafés, and an amusement park in the spring. You can rent a bike at the Château de Vincennes métro stop. To reach the park, use the Château de Vincennes stop (Line 1) or Porte Dorée (Line 8).

The imposing high-walled castle was France's medieval Versailles. Today it is surrounded by a dry moat and dominated by a 170-foot keep, the last of nine original towers. The royal residence eventually became a prison holding convicts, notably of both sexes—and "the doors did not always remain closed between them," as one tour guide coyly put it. Inmates included the philosopher Diderot and the Marquis de Sade. The château and its cathedral, **Sainte-Chapelle** (designed in the style of the Paris church of the same name) have undergone a spectacular restoration, yet some renovation is ongoing. If you speak French, the free 90-minute tour is worthwhile (call before you go to check when the tours are offered that day).

Château de Vincennes. The impressive Château de Vincennes was once the largest château in Europe. On the northern edge of the Bois, it was built and expanded by various kings between the 12th and 14th centuries. ⊠ *Av. de Paris, Bois de Vincennes* ☎ *01–48–08–31–20* ⊕ *www. chateau-vincennes.fr* 🎫 *€8* ☉ *May–Aug., daily 10–6; Sept.–Apr., daily 10–5* Ⓜ *Château de Vincennes.*

Parc Floral de Paris. The Parc Floral de Paris is the Bois de Vincennes's 70-acre park and flower garden. There is a lake, a butterfly garden, a biodiversity hothouse, and seasonal displays of blooms. Kids will enjoy the miniature train, paddleboats, mini-golf, ponies, pool and game area, among other attractions (most of which cost extra). The park is a lovely place to spend an afternoon in the summer, and there are jazz concerts most weekends from April to October; from late October to early April, many attractions are closed. ⊠ *Rte. de la Pyramide, Bois de Vincennes* 🎫 *€5 Wednesday and weekends from May to October; free other days in season and free every day off-season* ☉ *Open daily 9:30–5 in winter and 9:30–8 in summer* Ⓜ *Château de Vincennes.*

Parc Zoologique. The 35-acre Parc Zoologique, the largest zoo in France, is closed for renovations until 2014. ⊠ *53 av. de St-Maurice, Bois de Vincennes* ☎ *01–44–75–20–00* Ⓜ *Porte Dorée.*

Palais de la Porte Dorée & Tropical Aquarium. One of the best examples of Art Deco architecture in Paris, this stunning building is home to a tropical aquarium and an immigration museum. It's worth a visit just to see the Palais, built for the 1931 Colonial Exhibition. (Entry to the ground floor is free.) The ornate facade features bas-relief sculptures

AT A GLANCE

Dining at a Glance

For full reviews
⇨ *Chapter 14.*

INEXPENSIVE DINING
Au Passage, *Wine Bar,* 1 bis passage St-Sébastien

Chez Omar, *Moroccan,* 47 rue de Bretagne

Dong Huong, *Vietnamese,* 14 rue Louis-Bonnet

Jacques Genin, *French,* 133 rue de Turenne

Jacques Mélac, *Wine Bar,* 42 rue Léon-Frot

Jeanne A, *Wine Bar,* 42 rue Jean-Pierre-Timbaud

La Boulangerie, *Bistro,* 15 rue des Panoyaux

Le Baron Bouge, *Wine Bar,* 1 rue Théophile Roussel

Le Dauphin, *Wine Bar,* 131 av. Parmentier

Le Martel, *Moroccan,* 3 rue Martel

Le Verre Volé, *Wine Bar,* 67 rue de Lancry

Véronique Mauclerc, *Bakery,* rue de Crimée

MODERATE DINING
Astier, *Bistro,* 44 rue Jean-Pierre Timbaud

Bofinger, *Brasserie,* 5–7 rue de la Bastille

La Gazzetta, *Bistro,* 29 rue de Cotte

La Table de Claire, *Bistro,* 30 rue Emile Lepeu

Le Baratin, *Bistro,* 3 rue Jouye Rouve

Le Bistro Paul Bert, *Bistro,* 18 rue Paul Bertc

Le Repaire de Cartouche, *Bistro,* 8 bd. des Filles du Calvaire

Philou, *Bistro,* 10 av. Richarand

Rino, *Bistro,* 46 rue Trousseau

Septime, *Bistro,* 80 rue de Charonne

Unico, *Modern Argentine,* 15 rue Paul-Bert

EXPENSIVE DINING
Au Trou Gascon, *Bistro,* 40 rue Taine

Le Chateaubriand, *Modern French,* 44 rue du Bac

Sardegna a Tavola, *Italian,* 1 rue de Cotte

9

representing France's erstwhile empire. Inside, the elaborate marble, ornate metal work, and original lighting are all beautifully maintained. On either end of the ground floor are furnished salons, one representing Asia, the other Africa (a Gucci commercial was filmed in the latter one). Peek into the central room, called the Forum, to see the Africa-inspired mosaics, all restored, lining the walls. The upper floors are home to the **Cité Nationale de l'Historie de l'Immigration,** a well-executed modern museum tracing the history of immigration in France. There are usually similarly themed temporary exhibitions. The basement is home to **L'Aquarium Tropical,** an aquarium with a pair of alligators from Mississippi. There is little information available in English. ⊠ *293 av. Daumesnil, Bois de Vincennes* ☎ *01–53–59–58–60* ⊕ *www.aquarium-portedoree.fr* 🖃 *€3 for the musuem; €4.50 for the aquarium, prices vary during special exhibitions* ⊙ *Tues.–Sun. 10–5:30, palace open until 7 weekends* Ⓜ *Porte Dorée.*

OFF THE BEATEN PATH

Le 104. Le Cent Quatre takes its name from its address in this rough-around-the-edges corner of the 19e arrondissement, not far from the top of the Canal St-Martin. The former site of the city morgue, this cavernous offbeat art hub is home to an eclectic collection of performance space, shops, and studios where artists of all genres compete for free studio space. Sometimes you can get a sneak peak of them at work. Contemporary art exhibits, some of which charge admission fees, are staged here, as well as concerts. Also here are a restaurant, a café, a bookstore, a natural clothing boutique, a secondhand shop, and a play area for children. Check the schedule on the website before you go to see what's on. ⊠ *104 rue d'Aubervilliers, or 5 rue Curial, Stalingrad* ☎ *01–53–35–50–01* ⊕ *www.104.fr* 🖾 *Free; prices for exhibits and concerts vary* ☉ *Tues.–Fri. 12–8, Sat. 11–8, Sun. 11–7* Ⓜ *Stalingrad.*

OFF THE
BEATEN
PATH

Musée Edith Piaf. True fans will appreciate the tiny two-room apartment where the "little sparrow" lived for a year, when she was 28 years old and sang in the working-class cafés on Rue Oberkampf. The flat was obtained by Les Amis d'Edith Piaf in 1978 and is now a shrine to the pint-size crooner, whose life-size photo (she was 4 feet, 9 inches) greets visitors at the door. The red walls are covered with portraits of Piaf done by her many artist friends, and her personal letters are framed. Her books and handbags are displayed, as well as a few dresses and her size 4 shoes. ⊠ *5 rue Crespin du Gast, Oberkampf* ☎ *01–43–55–52–72* 🖾 *Free, donations encouraged* ☉ *By reservation only; no English spoken; Mon.–Wed. 1–6 pm* Ⓜ *Ménilmontant.*

🕑 **Pavillon de l'Arsenal.** If your knowledge of Paris history is *nul* (nil), stop here for an entertaining (and free) explainer. Built in 1879 as a private museum, the Pavillion today is a restored structure of glass-and-iron that showcases the city's urban development through the ages. A giant model of Paris traces the city's development (with information in English). There are photos, maps, and videos, plus a giant digital interactive model detailing what Paris is predicted to look like in 2020. There are frequent architecture-theme temporary exhibits, plus a café and bookstore. ⊠ *21 bd. Morland, Bastille* ☎ *01–42–76–33–97* ⊕ *www.pavillon-arsenal.com* 🖾 *Free* ☉ *Tues.–Sat. 10:30–6:30, Sun. 11–9* Ⓜ *Sully-Morland, Bastille.*

🕑 **Piscine Josephine Baker.** This modern floating aquatic center, named after the much-beloved American entertainer, features a pool with a retractable glass roof, two solariums, a steam room, Jacuzzis, and a gym. Entry is a bargain €6 (or €3 for the pool only). Check the opening hours and schedule of classes online. ⊠ *21 Quai François Mauriac, Bibliothèque* ☎ *01–56–61–96–50* ⊕ *www.paris.fr/portail/ Sport/Portal.lut?page_id=6085* ☉ *Mon., Wed., Fri. 7–8.30 and 1–9, Tues. and Thurs. 1–11, Sat. 11–8, Sun. 10–8* Ⓜ *Quai de la Gare, Bibliothèque François Mitterrand.*

The Latin Quarter

WORD OF MOUTH

"We decided to see the Paris Mosque. It was on our way (kind of) to Rue Mouffetard . . . the mosque is lovely, built similarly to Moorish architecture. We LOVED the Latin Quarter. It's filled with cafes, bakeries, bookstores . . . and has a certain energy and atmosphere that I associate with Paris.

— layanluvstotravel

GETTING ORIENTED

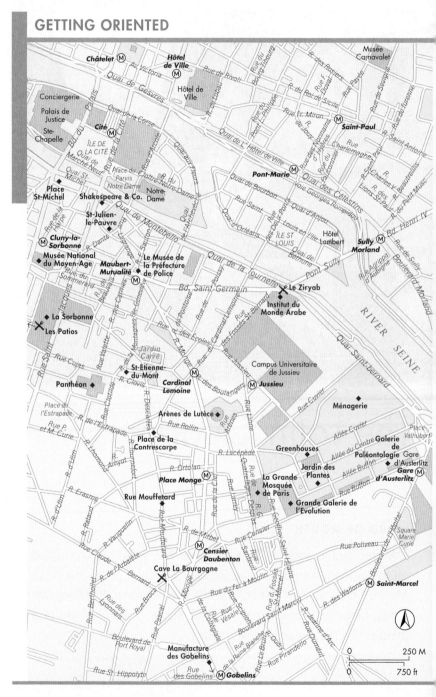

TOP REASONS TO GO

Musée National du Moyen-Age. On the site of an ancient Roman bath, this former abbey is home to the famous *Lady and the Unicorn* tapestries; the building, tranquil garden, and extensive collection have the hush of a medieval monastery.

Shakespeare & Co. This legendary English-language bookstore is more than a shopping destination; it's a meeting place for young expats and curious travelers alike.

Rue Mouffetard. Stroll down this winding market street to collect fixings for a picnic à la française with warm bread, delicious cheese, and fresh oysters.

Jardin des Plantes. This is a great spot to picnic or to rest your tired feet on one of the many shaded benches.

La Grande Mosquée de Paris. Enjoy a mint tea in the leafy courtyard café at Paris's most beautiful mosque.

MAKING THE MOST OF YOUR TIME

The Quartier Latin is the perfect place to wander sans itinerary, though there is no shortage of sites worth seeing. Shopping here is generally more affordable, though less original, than in other neighborhoods, and there are lots of new- and used-book stores, many of which stock English-language titles. Pick up a picnic at the many food shops along Rue Mouffetard (closed Monday), or head to the open-air market at Place Monge (Wednesday, Friday, and Sunday mornings), then savor your booty on a bench at the Jardin des Plantes. Sip mint tea in the courtyard café at the lovely Grande Mosquée (Mosque) de Paris or take in a terrific view on the roof of the Institut du Monde Arabe (closed Monday). Stroll the hilly streets around the Panthéon on your way to see the treasures at the Musée National du Moyen-Age (closed Tuesday). Finish with a sunset apéritif on one of the barge cafés (open spring to fall) along the Seine, across from Notre-Dame.

GETTING HERE

The Quartier Latin is the 5ᵉ arrondissement. Take métro Line 4 to St-Michel to start exploring at the Lucifer-slaying fountain near Shakespeare & Co., across the Seine from Notre-Dame. Go to the Cluny stop on Line 10 if you're heading to the Musée du Moyen-Age. The Place Monge stop on Line 7 puts you near the Panthéon and Rue Mouffetard, the Mosquée de Paris, and the Jardin des Plantes. Les Gobelins neighborhood straddles the 5e, 13e, and 14e arrondissements, but is considered part of the 5e because of the Manufacture des Gobelins.

BEST CAFÉS

Cave La Bourgogne. Settle in on the terrace of this old-school bistro for lunch, or join the locals at the zinc bar for a coffee or glass of wine. ⊠ *144 rue Mouffetard, Latin Quarter* ☎ *01–47–07–82–80.*

Les Patios. If you're young—or young at heart—come here to hang with the Sorbonne crowd. It's in the square across from the university. ⊠ *5 pl. de la Sorbonne, Latin Quarter* ☎ *01–43–54–34–43.*

Le Ziryab. This café–outdoor terrace on the top floor of the Institut du Monde Arabe is great for a Lebanese lunch or dinner with a fantastic view. Closed Monday. ⊠ *Institut du Monde Arabe, 1 rue des Fossés-St-Bernard, Latin Quarter* ☎ *01–55–42–55–42.*

10

Sightseeing
★★★★
Dining
★★★
Lodging
★★★★
Shopping
★★★
Nightlife
★★★

The Quartier Latin is the heart of student Paris—and has been for more than 800 years. France's oldest university, *La Sorbonne,* was founded here in 1257, and the neighborhood takes its name from the fact that Latin was the common language of the students, who came from all over Europe. Today the area is full of cheap and cheerful cafés, bars, and shops.

The main drag, **Boulevard St-Michel,** is a bustling street where bookshops have given way to chain clothing stores and fast-food joints—but don't let that stop you! There are (almost) as many French people wandering the streets here as there are tourists. At **Place St-Michel,** the symbolic gateway to the *quartier,* notice the 19th-century fountain depicting Saint Michael slaying the "great dragon," Satan, a symbolic warning to rebellious locals from Napoléon III. Today the fountain serves as a meeting spot and makes a rather fine metaphor for the boulevard it anchors: a bit grimy but extremely popular.

When you've had enough of the crowds, turn off the boulevard and explore the side streets, where you can find quirky boutiques and intimate bistros. Or stop for a demi (a half pint of draft beer) at one of the cafés on the **Place de la Sorbonne,** ground zero for students (and their many noisy demonstrations). Around the winding streets behind the **Panthéon,** where French luminaries are laid to rest, you can still find plenty of academics arguing philosophy while sipping espresso, but today the 5e arrondissement is also one of Paris's most charming and sought-after (read: expensive) places to live.

Shop along **Rue Mouffetard** as Parisians do—all the while complaining about the high prices—for one of the best selections of runny cheeses, fresh breads, and charcuterie. Grab a seat in a bustling café—or do as the locals do and stand at the bar, where drinks are always cheaper. Film buffs won't have to look far to find one of the small cinema revival houses showing old American films in English (look for v.o., for version originale). Not far from "*le Mouffe*" is the gorgeous white **Grande Mosquée**

de Paris with its impressive minaret. Just beyond the mosque is the **Jardin des Plantes**—a large, if somewhat bland, botanical garden that is home to three natural-history museums, most notably the **Grande Galerie de l'Évolution**. Inside, kids can marvel at enormous whale skeletons, along with all sorts of taxidermy. Some of Paris's most intriguing sites are in this neighborhood, including the **Musée National du Moyen-Age** and the innovative **Institut du Monde Arabe**. See ancient history mingle with modern life at the **Arènes de Lutèce,** a Roman amphitheater and favorite soccer pitch for neighborhood kids.

> **DID YOU KNOW?**
>
> French architect Jean Nouvel made news when the Quai Branly museum opened in 2006, but in 1987 he was already wowing Parisians with the Institut du Monde Arabe, an intriguing fusion of Arabian and French styles. His new Orchestra Hall, slated to open in 2014, is sure to get attention, too. He was awarded the Pritzker Architecture Prize in 2008.

TOP ATTRACTIONS

Updated by Bryan Pirolli

Grande Galerie de l'Évolution (*Great Hall of Evolution*). With a parade of taxidermied animals ranging from the tiniest dung beetle to the tallest giraffe, this four-story natural history museum in the Jardin des Plantes is an excellent break for museum-weary kids. The flagship of the three natural-history museums in the Jardin des Plantes, the restored 1889 building has a ceiling that changes color to suggest storms, twilight, or the hot savanna sun. Don't miss the gigantic skeleton of a blue whale, and the stuffed royal rhino—he came from the menagerie at Versailles, where he was a pet of Louis XV. Kids 6 to 12 years old will enjoy La Galerie d'Enfants (Children's Gallery), which opened in 2010 and has interactive exhibits on the natural world, in French and English. A lab stocked with microscopes often offers free workshops, and most of the staff speaks some English. ■TIP➔ Hang on to your ticket; it'll get you a discount at the other museums within the Jardin des Plantes. ⊠ *36 rue Geoffroy-St-Hilaire, Latin Quarter* ☎ *01-40-79-54-79* ⊕ *www.mnhn. fr* ⊴ *€7* ☉ *Wed.–Mon. 10–6* Ⓜ *Pl. Monge or Jussieu.*

★ **Institut du Monde Arabe.** This eye-catching metal-and-glass tower by Architect Jean Nouvel cleverly uses metal diaphragms in the shape of square Arabic-style screens to work like a camera lens, opening and closing to control the flow of sunlight. The layout of this vast cultural center is intended to reinterpret the traditional enclosed Arab courtyard. Inside, there are various spaces, including a museum dedicated to Arab and Islamic civilizations set to reopen in late 2011 after a sweeping renovation. With the addition of elements from the Musée du Louvre's holdings, the impressive collection will include Islamic art, artifacts, ceramics, and textiles from across some 20 countries. There is also a performance space, a sound-and-image center, a library, and a bookstore. Temporary exhibitions usually have information and an audioguide in English. ■TIP➔ Glass elevators whisk you to the ninth floor, where you can sip mint tea in the rooftop café, Le Ziryab, while feasting on one of the best views in Paris. ⊠ *1 rue des Fossés-St-Bernard, Latin*

CLOSE UP

Shakespeare & Company

This English-language bookstore is one of Paris's most eccentric and lovable literary institutions. Founded by George Whitman, the maze of new and used books has offered a sense of community (and often a bed) to wandering writers since the 1950s. The store takes its name from Sylvia Beach's original Shakespeare & Co., which opened in 1919 at 12 rue d'Odeon, welcoming the likes of Ernest Hemingway, James Baldwin, and James Joyce. Beach famously bucked the system when she published Joyce's *Ulysses* in 1922, but her original store closed in 1941. After the war Whitman picked up the gauntlet, naming his own bookstore after its famous predecessor.

When Whitman passed away in December 2011, heavy-hearted locals left candles and flowers in front of his iconic storefront. He is buried in the literati-laden Père Lachaise cemetery.

His legacy lives on through his daughter Sylvia who runs the shop and welcomes a new generation of Paris dreamers. Walk up the almost impossibly narrow stairs to the second floor and you'll still see laptop computers and sleeping bags tucked between the aging volumes and under dusty daybeds; it's sort of like a hippie commune. A revolving cast of characters helps out in the shop or cooks meals for fellow residents. They're in good company; Henry Miller, Samuel Beckett, and William Burroughs are among the famous writers to benefit from the Whitman family hospitality.

Shakespeare & Company (✉ *37 rue de la Bûcherie* ☎ *01–43–25–40–93*) is open weekdays 10 am to 11 pm (weekends 11 am to 11 pm) and has readings most Monday evenings. Check the website (⊕ *www. shakespeareandcompany.com*) for a schedule of events.

Quarter ☎ *01–40–51–38–38* ⊕ *www.imarabe.org* 🎟 *€6* ☾ *Tues.–Sun. 10–6* Ⓜ *Cardinal Lemoine.*

☾ **Jardin des Plantes** (*Botanical Gardens*). Once known as the Jardin du Roi, or King's Garden, this vast patch of greenery, which opened in 1640, is a neighborhood gem. It is home to several gardens and various museums, all housed in 19th-century buildings whose original architecture blends glass with ornate ironwork. Come to picnic, or if you have kids, take them to the excellent Grande Galerie de l'Évolution (*see entry above*), or one of the other natural-history museums here: the Galerie de Paléontologie, stocked with dinosaur and other skeletons, and the Galerie de Minéralogie, with rocks and minerals. The botanical and rose gardens are impressive, and plant lovers won't want to miss the towering greenhouses (*serre* in French), reopened in 2010 after a five-year renovation, filled with one of the world's most extensive collections of tropical and desert flora. If the kids prefer fauna, visit the Ménagerie, a small zoo founded in 1795 whose animals once fed Parisians during the 1870 Prussian siege. The star attractions are Nénette, the grande-dame orangutan from Borneo, her son Tübo, and their swinging friends in the monkey and ape house. If you need a break, there are three kiosk cafés in the Jardin. ■**TIP→** Keep your ticket: Entrance to any of these sites will get you a discount to other museums within the gardens. ✉ *Entrances*

10

on Rue Geoffroy-St-Hilaire, Rue Cuvier, Rue de Buffon, and Quai St-Bernard, Latin Quarter ☎ 01–40–79–54–79 ⊕ www.mnhn.fr ⊠ Museums and zoo €4–€9 (free, 4 and under), greenhouses €5 ⊙ Museums Wed.–Mon. 10–5 or 6. Zoo daily 9–6. Garden daily 8–7 (hours vary by season) Ⓜ Gare d'Austerlitz, Jussieu.

Fodor's Choice
★

Musée National du Moyen-Age (*National Museum of the Middle Ages, also called the Musée Cluny*). Built on the ruins of Lutecia's Roman Baths, the **Hôtel de Cluny** has been a museum since medievalist Alexandre Du Sommerard established his collection here in 1844. The ornate 15th-century mansion was created for the abbot of Cluny, leader of the most powerful monastery in France. Symbols of the abbot's power literally surround the building, from the crenellated walls that proclaimed his independence from the king, to the carved Burgundian grapes, symbolizing his valuable vineyards, twining up the entrance. The scallop shells (*coquilles St-Jacques*) covering the facade are a symbol of religious pilgrimage, another important source of income for the abbot; the well-traveled pilgrimage route to Spain once ran around the corner along the rue St-Jacques. The highlight of the collection is the world-famous *Dame à la Licorne* (*Lady and the Unicorn*) tapestry series, woven in the 16th century, probably in Belgium. The vermillion tapestries (Room 13) are an allegorical representation of the five senses. In each, a unicorn and a lion surround an elegant young woman against an elaborate *mille-fleur* (literally, 1,000 flowers) background. The enigmatic sixth tapestry is thought to be either a tribute to a sixth sense, perhaps intelligence, or a renouncement of the other senses. "To my only desire" is inscribed at the top. The collection also includes the original sculpted heads of the *Kings of Israel and Judah* from Notre-Dame, decapitated during the Revolution, and discovered in 1977 in the basement of a French bank. The *frigidarium* (Room 9) is a stunning ruin of the city's cold-water Roman baths. The soaring space, painstakingly renovated in 2009, houses temporary exhibits. Don't miss the pocket-size chapel (Room 20) with its elaborate Gothic ceiling. Outside, in the Place Paul Painlevé, is a charming medieval-style garden with flora depicted in the unicorn tapestries. The free audioguide in English is highly recommended. ⊠ 6 pl. Paul-Painlevé, Latin Quarter ☎ 01–53–73–78–00 ⊕ www.musee-moyenage.fr ⊠ €8.50 (includes English audioguide), free 1st Sun. of month ⊙ Wed.–Mon. 9:15–5:45 Ⓜ Cluny–La Sorbonne.

10

NEED A
BREAK?

Place de la Contrescarpe. Place de la Contrescarpe is a popular square behind the Panthéon, with a small-town feel during the day and a lively atmosphere after dusk. Café Delmas (*2 pl. de la Contrescarpe* ☎ *01–43–26–51–26*) has a large terrace and serves food every day until 2 am. During the day people haggle over produce at the daily market at the bottom of Rue Mouffetard. ⊠ *Latin Quarter* Ⓜ *Pl. Monge.*

Panthéon. Rome has St. Peter's, London has St. Paul's, and Paris has the Panthéon, whose enormous dome dominates the Left Bank. Built as the church of Ste-Geneviève, the patron saint of Paris, it was later converted to an all-star mausoleum with some of France's biggest names, including Voltaire, Zola, Dumas, Rousseau, and Victor Hugo. Pierre and Marie

Curie were reinterred here together in 1995. Begun in 1764, the building was almost complete when the French Revolution erupted. By then, architect Jacques-German Soufflot had died, supposedly from worrying that the 220-foot-high dome would collapse. He needn't have fretted: the dome is so perfect that Foucault used it to test his famous pendulum to prove the Earth rotates on its axis. A model of the pendulum still hangs from the dome and the staff offer demonstrations (there's also a video in English that explains the theory). To access the upper level, take a free guided tour (offered several times a day, in French only). There is information in English at the entrance and on boards in the crypt. ✉ *Pl. du Panthéon, Latin Quarter* ☎ *01–44–32–18–00* 🌐 *www.pantheon.monuments-nationaux.fr/en/* 🎫 *€8* ⏲ *Apr.–Sept., daily 10–6:30; Oct.–Mar., daily 10–6* Ⓜ *Cardinal Lemoine; RER: Luxembourg.*

THE 13E ARRONDISSEMENT

The village-like neighborhood of La Butte aux Cailles, in the 13e arrondissement, south of the Place d'Italie, is a fun destination with a hip crowd, not far from the Quartier Latin if you want a break from the tourists. The many bars and cafés buzz until well after the last métro stops running.

Le Temps des Cerises. Settle in for bistro fare at the crowded, fun, and cooperatively run Le Temps des Cerises, whose name recalls a song made famous by the Paris Commune. ✉ *18–20 rue de la Butte aux Cailles, La Butte aux Cailles* ☎ *01–45–89–69–48.*

Fodor's Choice ★ **Rue Mouffetard.** This winding cobblestone street is one of Paris's oldest and was once a Roman road leading south from Lutetia (the Roman name for Paris) to Italy. The upper half of the street is dotted with restaurants and bars that cater to tourists and students; the lower half is the setting of a lively market, Tuesday through Sunday. The highlight of *le Mouffe* is the stretch in between where the shops are literally spilling into the street with luscious offerings such as roasting chickens and potatoes, rustic *saucisson,* pâtés, and pungent cheeses, especially at Androuët (No. 134). You can find everything you'll need for a picnic. Sample the chocolates at de Neuville (No. 108) and Mococha (No. 89). If you're here in the morning, Le Mouffetard Café (No. 116) is a good place to stop for a continental breakfast (about €10). If it's *apéritif* time, head to Place des Contrescarpe for a cocktail (⇨ *Need a Break entry)*, or enjoy a glass of wine at Cave La Bourgogne (No. 144). For one of the best baguettes in Paris and other delicious organic offerings, detour to nearby Boulanger de Monge, at 123 rue Monge. Note that most shops are closed Monday.

WORTH NOTING

Arènes de Lutèce (*Lutetia Amphitheater*). This Roman amphitheater, designed as a theater and circus, was almost completely destroyed by barbarians in AD 280. The site was rediscovered in 1869, and you can still see part of the stage and tiered seating. Along with the remains of the baths at Cluny, the arena constitutes rare evidence of the powerful

Roman city of Lutetia that flourished on the Rive Gauche in the 3rd century. It's a favorite spot for picnicking, pickup soccer or *boules*. ⊠ *47 rue Monge, or Rue de Navarre, Latin Quarter* 🎟 *Free* 🕙 *Daily 8–dusk* Ⓜ *Pl. Monge, Cardinal Lemoine.*

★ **La Grande Mosquée de Paris.** This awe-inspiring white mosque was built between 1922 and 1926 and has tranquil arcades and a minaret decorated in the style of Moorish Spain. Enjoy a sweet mint tea and an exotic pastry in the charming courtyard tea salon or tuck into some couscous in the restaurant. Prayer rooms are not open to the public. There are inexpensive—and quite rustic—*hammams,* or Turkish steam baths, with scrubs and massages on offer (check website for prices). ⊠ *2 bis pl. du Puits de l'Ermite; entrance to tea salon and restaurant at 39 rue Geoffroy Saint-Hillaire, Latin Quarter* 🕾 *01–43–31–38–20, 01–45–33–97–33 for guided tours* ⊕ *www.la-mosquee.com* 🎟 *Guided tour €3* 🕙 *Guided tours in French daily at 9, noon, 2, and 6; call to reserve* Ⓜ *Pl. Monge.*

La Sorbonne. You can't get into Paris's most famous university without a student ID, but it's fun to hang out in the area with all the students. La Sorbonne remains the heart and soul of the Quartier Latin, though it is also known as Paris IV, one of several campuses that make up the public Université de Paris. ⊠ *1 rue Victor Cousin, Latin Quarter* Ⓜ *Cluny-La Sorbonne.*

Manufacture des Gobelins. Tapestries have been woven on this spot in southeastern Paris, on the banks of the long-covered Bièvre River, since 1662. The newly renovated Galerie des Gobelins stages exhibitions on two light-flooded floors of tapestries, furnishings, timepieces, and other treasures mostly drawn from the state collection. Guided visits to the Manufacture (in French only) allow a fascinating look at weavers—from students to accomplished veterans—at work making tapestries and rugs, which take years to create. Also on the site is a highly selective school that teaches weaving, and a workshop charged with repairing and restoring furnishings belonging to the French government, which are also stored here in a vast concrete warehouse. ⊠ *42 av. des Gobelins, Les Gobelins* 🕾 *01–44–08–53–49* ⊕ *www.mobiliernational. fr* 🎟 *€6 temporary exhibitions; €11 workshop visit* 🕙 *Galerie, Tues.– Sat. 11–6; guided tours in French by reservation only, Tues.–Thurs. at 1:15, 2:45, and 3* Ⓜ *Gobelins.*

10

Place St-Michel. This square was named for Gabriel Davioud's grandiose 1860 fountain sculpture of St. Michael vanquishing Satan—a loaded political gesture from Napoléon III's go-to guy, Baron Haussmann, who hoped St-Michel would quell the Revolutionary fervor of the neighborhood. The fountain is often used as a meeting point. ⊠ *Latin Quarter* Ⓜ *Métro or RER: St-Michel.*

St-Étienne-du-Mont. This jewel box of a church has been visited by several popes, owing to the fact that Ste-Geneviève, the patron saint of Paris, was buried here before Revolutionaries burned her remains. It was built on the ruins of a first-century abbey founded by Clovis, the first King of the Franks. The church's unique combination of Gothic, Renaissance, and early Baroque styles adds a certain warmth that is lacking in other Parisian churches of pure Gothic style. Here you'll find the only rood

Dining at a Glance

For full reviews
⇨ Chapter 14.

INEXPENSIVE DINING
L'Avant-Goût, *Bistro*,
26 rue Bobillot

La Chine Massena,
Chinese, Centre
Commercial Massena,
13 pl. de Venetie

Le Bambou, *Vietnamese*,
70 rue Baudincourt

MODERATE DINING
L'Avant-Goût, *Modern French*, 26 rue Bobillot

L'Ourcine, *Bistro*,
92 rue Broca

Le Balzar, *Brasserie*,
49 rue des Écoles

Le Buisson Ardent,
Bistro, 25 rue Jussieu

Le Pré Verre, *Modern French*, 8 rue Thénard

Les Papilles, *Wine Bar*,
30 rue Gay-Lussac

Ribouldingue, *Bistro*, 10
rue St-Julien-le-Pauvre

EXPENSIVE DINING
Fògon St-Julien,
Spanish, 45 quai des
Grands-Augustins

Itinéraires, *Bistro*,
5 rue de Pontoise

Lapérouse, *Bistro*,
51 quai des Grands
Augustins

La Tour d'Argent, *Modern French*, 15–17 quai
de la Tournelle

Sola, *Eclectic*, 12 rue de
l'Hôtel Colbert

Ze Kitchen Galerie,
Modern French, 4 rue
des Grands-Augustins

---

screen left in Paris—an ornate 16th-century masterwork of carved wood spanning the nave like a bridge, with a spiral staircase on either side. The organ is the oldest in the city, from 1631. An archbishop of Paris was stabbed to death here in 1857 by a defrocked priest. Look for the marker in the floor near the entrance. ⊠ *30 rue Descartes, Latin Quarter* ☏ *01–43–54–11–79* ⊕ *www.saintetiennedumont.fr* Ⓜ *Cardinal Lemoine.*

St-Julien-le-Pauvre. This tiny shrine in the shadow of Notre-Dame is one of the three oldest churches in Paris. Founded in 1045, it became a meeting place for university students in the 12th century. This was Dante's church when he was in Paris writing his *Divine Comedy* in 1300. Today's structure dates mostly from the 1600s, but keep an eye out for older pillars, which crawl with carvings of demons. The church holds classical and gospel concerts, or you can simply perch on a bench in the garden to enjoy the view of Notre-Dame. ⊠ *1 rue St-Julien-le-Pauvre, Latin Quarter* ☏ *01–43–54–52–16* ⊕ *www.sjlpmelkites.org, for concert schedule; www.concertinparis.com* Ⓜ *St-Michel.*

OFF THE BEATEN PATH

Le Musée de la Préfecture de Police. Crime buffs will enjoy this museum hidden on the second floor of the 5e arrondissement's police station. Although the exhibits are in French only, the photographs, letters, drawings, and memorabilia of some of the city's most sensational crimes are easy enough to follow. The 2,000 relics include a guillotine, old uniforms, and remnants of the World War II occupation, including what's left of a firing post, German machine guns, and the star insignias worn by Jews. ⊠ *4 rue de la Montagne Ste-Geneviève, Latin Quarter* ☏ *01–44–41–52–50* 🖾 *Free* ☉ *Mon.–Fri. 9–5:30, Sat. 10:30–5:30* Ⓜ *Maubert-Mutualité.*

St-Germain-des-Prés

WORD OF MOUTH

"We started with a tour of Musée d'Orsay. Here we saw "Whistler's Mother," the Degas dancers, works by Manet, Monet, Renoir, Pissarro, van Gogh, Cézanne, Gauguin, Vuillard, Rodin, Matisse, and wonderful period rooms and furniture. I was very impressed with the building itself, however. It took a true artist to turn the former train station into the current showcase."

—TC

GETTING ORIENTED

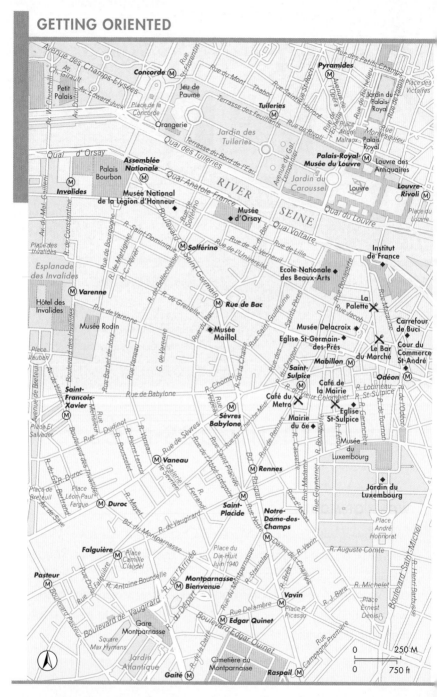

TOP REASONS TO GO

Musée d'Orsay. The graceful vaulted ceiling and abundance of natural light in this train station–turned-museum are reminders of why the Impressionist painters thought that train stations were the cathedrals of the 19th century.

Jardin du Luxembourg. Take in a puppet show, wander the tree-lined gravel paths, or just laze by the fountain at this most elegant of Parisian gardens.

Boulevard St-Germain. The main artery of this chic neighborhood is lined with shops, art galleries, and cafés. The top boutiques are clustered around Rue de Rennes, off the main stretch; for more art galleries, head north to Rue de Seine.

Cafés, cafés, cafés. This is excellent people-watching territory. Take a seat at one of the many cafés, hang out, and watch the world go by.

MAKING THE MOST OF YOUR TIME

Aim for an early start—have a *café crème* at a café along the river and get to the Musée d'Orsay early, when crowds are thinner. Leave some time for window-shopping around the Boulevard St-Germain and Rue de Rennes on your way to the Jardin du Luxembourg. You might want to plan your visit on a day other than Monday, when the Orsay, many of the art galleries, and even some shops are closed. The Maillol museum is open every day and late on Friday while the Delacroix is closed on Wednesday.

GETTING HERE

The St-Germain neighborhood is the 6e arrondissement and a bit of 7e. To get to the heart of this area, take the Line 4 métro to St-Germain-des-Prés. For shopping, use this station or St-Sulpice. It's a short walk to the Jardin du Luxembourg, or take the RER B line to the Luxembourg station. For the Musée d'Orsay, take the Line 12 métro to Solferino or the RER C line to the Musée d'Orsay.

BEST CAFÉS

Café de la Mairie. This slightly shabby café, once the haunt of existentialist author Albert Camus, is a good place to spy celebrities like actress Catherine Deneuve, who lives nearby. ✉ *8 pl. St-Sulpice, St-Germain-des-Prés* ☎ *01–43–26–67–82.*

Café du Métro. Settle in at this friendly café-brasserie for hot chocolate or French onion soup after an exhausting round of shoe shopping around the Rue de Rennes. Closed Sunday. ✉ *67 rue de Rennes, St-Germain-des-Prés* ☎ *01–45–48–58–56.*

La Palette. The terrace of this corner café, opened in 1902, is a favorite haunt of local gallery owners and Beaux Arts students. Meals are served at lunch, and sandwiches and lighter fare are available at other times of day. Come at sunset—or later—when the scene gets lively. ✉ *43 rue de Seine, St-Germain-des-Prés* ☎ *01–43–26–68–15.*

Le Bar du Marché. Grab a sidewalk table—if you're lucky—or stand at the bar, skip the food, and order an apéritif at this constantly packed little place. The feel is classic French with a splash of kitsch, right down to the waiters in overalls and berets. ✉ *75 rue de Seine, St-Germain-des-Prés* ☎ *01–43–26–55–15.*

Sightseeing
★★★★★
Dining
★★★
Lodging
★★★★★
Shopping
★★★★★
Nightlife
★★

If you had to choose the most classically Parisian neighborhood in Paris, this would be it. St-Germain-des-Prés has it all: genteel blocks lined with upscale art galleries, storied cafés, designer boutiques, and a fine selection of museums. Cast your eyes upward after dark and you may spy a frescoed ceiling in a tony apartment. These historic streets can get quite crowded, so mind your elbows and plunge in.

This *quartier* is named for the oldest church in Paris, **St-Germain-des-Prés,** and it's become a prized address for Parisians and expats alike. Despite its pristine facade, though, this wasn't always silver-spoon territory. Claude Monet and Auguste Renoir shared a cramped studio at 20 rue Visconti, and the young Picasso barely eked out an existence in a room on the Rue de Seine. By the 1950s St-Germain bars bopped with jazz, and the likes of Albert Camus, Jean-Paul Sartre, and Simone de Beauvoir puffed away on Gauloises while discussing the meaninglessness of existence at Café Flore. Nearby in the 7e arrondissement, the star attraction is the **Musée d'Orsay,** home to a world-class collection of Impressionist paintings in a converted Belle Époque rail station on the Seine. It's famous for having some of Paris's longest lines, so a visit to the Orsay should be planned with care. There are also several smaller museums worth a stop, including the impressive **Musée Maillol,** a private collection in an elegant mansion dedicated to the work of sculptor Aristide Maillol. The **Musée Delacroix,** in lovely Place Furstenburg, is home to a small collection of the Romantic master's works. Not far away is the stately **Église St-Sulpice,** where you can see two impressive Delacroix frescoes.

Paris is a city for walking, and St-Germain is one of the most enjoyable places to practice the art of the *flâneur,* or stroller. Make your way to the busy crossroads of **Carrefour de Buci,** dotted with cafés, flower markets, and shops. Rue de l'Ancienne Comédie is so named because it was the first home of the legendary Comédie Française; it cuts through to busy Place de l'Odéon and Rue St-André des Arts. Along the latter you can find the historic **Cour du Commerce St-André** (opposite No. 66),

The cafés in St-Germain-des-Prés are perfect for people-watching along with coffee, dinner, or a cocktail.

a charming cobbled passageway lined with cafés, including, halfway down on the left, Paris's oldest, Le Procope.

Make sure you save some energy for the exquisite **Jardin du Luxembourg,** a classic French garden whose tree-lined paths have attracted fashionable wanderers through the ages, though the swish of crinolines has given way to the crunch of designer tracksuits sported by Parisians on their morning constitutional. Fortunately, there are lots of chairs for resting those weary feet.

TOP ATTRACTIONS

Updated by
Bryan Pirolli

Fodor's Choice
★

Carrefour de Buci. This colorful crossroads (carrefour is French for "intersection") was once a notorious Rive Gauche landmark: during the 18th century it contained a gallows, and during the French Revolution the army used the site to enroll its first volunteers. Many royalists and priests lost their heads here during the bloody course of the Terror. There's certainly nothing sinister about the carrefour today; brightly colored flowers are for sale alongside take-out ice-cream and snack kiosks. Devotees of the superb, traditional bakery Carton (at No. 6) line up for pastries (try their *tuiles* cookies). Ⓜ *Mabillon.*

Église St-Germain-des-Prés. Paris's oldest church was built to shelter a simple shard of wood, said to be a relic of Jesus's cross brought back from Spain in AD 542. Vikings came down the Seine and sacked the church, and Revolutionaries used it to store gunpowder, yet the elegant building has defied history's abuses: its 11th-century Romanesque tower continues to be the central symbol of the neighborhood. The colorful

19th-century frescoes in the nave are by Hippolyte Flandrin, a pupil of the classical master Ingres. The church stages superb organ concerts and recitals. Step inside for spiritual nourishment, or pause in the square to people-watch—there's usually a street musician tucked against the church wall, out of the wind. ⊠ *Pl. St-Germain-des-Prés, St-Germain-des-Prés* ☉ *Daily 8–7:30* Ⓜ *St-Germain-des-Prés.*

DID YOU KNOW?

Ste-Catherine Labouré was famed for having been visited twice by the Virgin Mary, who told her to create the "miraculous medal" worn by millions of Catholics. When her body was exhumed in 1933, her eyes were said to be as blue as the day this humble nun died 57 years earlier. You can see her perfectly preserved body in a glass case at Chapelle Notre Dame de la Médaille Miraculeuse, 140 rue du Bac, just steps from Le Bon Marché.

Fodor's Choice ★ **Église St-Sulpice.** Dubbed the Cathedral of the Rive Gauche, this enormous 17th-century Baroque church has entertained some unlikely christenings—among them those of the Marquis de Sade and Charles Baudelaire—as well as the nuptials of novelist Victor Hugo. The church's most recent appearance was a supporting role in the best-selling novel *The Da Vinci Code,* and it now draws scores of tourists to its obelisk, part of a *gnomon,* a device used to determine exact time and the equinoxes, built in the 1730s. The 18th-century facade was never finished, and its unequal towers add a playful touch to an otherwise sober design. There are two magnificent Delacroix frescoes in a chapel to the right of the entrance. ⊠ *Place St-Sulpice, St-Germain-des-Prés* Ⓜ *St-Sulpice.*

QUICK BITES

les éditeurs. A trendy café favored by the Parisian publishing set, les éditeurs is a perfect place to sip a kir (white wine with black currant syrup) from a perch on the skinny sidewalk or at an inside table shadowed by book-lined walls. The menu offers a modern twist on French classics, like scallops with creamy nutmeg lentils or confit of lamb with eggplant and cilantro purée. ⊠ *4 carrefour de l'Odéon, St-Germain-des-Prés* ☎ *01–43–26–67–76* ⊕ *www.lesediteurs.fr.*

Fodor's Choice ★ **Jardin du Luxembourg**
See the highlighted listing in this chapter.

Fodor's Choice ★ **Musée d'Orsay**
See the highlighted listing in this chapter.

NEED A BREAK?

Shanghai Café. Secreted away in the Maison de la Chine (China House), Shanghai Café is a little-known oasis of calm in this bustling 'hood. Come for lunch (best to reserve) or a lovely afternoon tea, and try a green-tea éclair or another of the exotic pastries. To find it, head to the back of the Maison de la Chine and pass through a small outpost of the upscale Hong Kong boutique Shanghai Tang. Open 10–7 for tea; lunch is served 12:30–2:30. Closed Sunday. ⊠ *76 rue Bonaparte, St-Germain-des-Prés* ☎ *01–40–51–95–17* ⊕ *www.maisondelachine.fr.*

11

Dueling Cafés

Les Deux Magots (⊠ 6 pl. St-Germain-des-Prés) and the neighboring **Café de Flore** (⊠ 172 bd. St-Germain) have been duking it out on this bustling corner in St-Germain for more than a century. Les Deux Magots, the snootier of the two, is named for the two Chinese figurines, or *magots,* inside, and has hosted the likes of Oscar Wilde, Hemingway, James Joyce, and Richard Wright. Jean-Paul Sartre and Simone du Beauvoir frequented both establishments, though they are claimed by the Flore. The two cafés remain packed, though these days you're more likely to rub shoulders with tourists than with philosophers. Still, if you're in search of that certain *je ne sais quoi* of the Rive Gauche, you can do no better than to station yourself at one of the sidewalk tables—or at a window table on a wintry day—to watch the passing parade. Stick to a croissant and an overpriced coffee or an early-evening apéritif; the food is expensive and nothing special.

WORTH NOTING

Fodor's Choice
★

Cour du Commerce St-André. Like an 18th-century engraving come to life, this charming street arcade is a remnant of *ancien* Paris with its enormous uneven cobblestones. Famed for its rabble-rousing inhabitants—journalist Jean-Paul Marat ran the Revolutionary newspaper *L'Ami du Peuple,* at No. 8, and the agitator Georges Danton lived at No. 20—it's also home to Le Procope, Paris's oldest café. This passageway also contains a turret from the 12th-century wall of Philippe-Auguste (visible through the windows at No. 4). ⊠ *Linking Bd. St-Germain and Rue St-André-des-Arts, St-Germain-des-Prés* Ⓜ *Odéon.*

École Nationale des Beaux-Arts. Occupying three large mansions near the Seine, the national fine-arts school—today the breeding ground for painters, sculptors, and architects—was once the site of a convent founded in 1608 by Marguerite de Valois, the first wife of Henri IV. After the Revolution the convent was turned into a museum for works of art salvaged from buildings attacked by the rampaging French mobs. In 1816 the museum was turned into a school. Today its peaceful courtyards harbor some contemporary installations and exhibits. The courtyard and galleries of the school are accessible by guided tour, which can be arranged through Cultivale (☎ *01–42–46–74–62*). ⊠ *14 rue Bonaparte, St-Germain-des-Prés* ☉ *Daily 1–7* Ⓜ *St-Germain-des-Prés.*

Institut de France. The *Institut* is one of France's most revered cultural institutions, and its golden dome is one of the Rive Gauche's most impressive landmarks. The site once held the Tour de Nesle, which formed part of Philippe-Auguste's medieval fortification wall along the Seine; the tower had many royal occupants, including Henry V of England. In 1661 the wealthy Cardinal Mazarin willed 2 million French *livres* (pounds) for the construction of a college. It's also home to the Académie Française: protectors of the French language. The edicts issued by this fusty group of 40 "perpétual" (lifelong) members are happily ignored by the French public, who prefer to send an e-mail

JARDIN DU LUXEMBOURG

✉ *Bordered by Bd. St-Michel and Rues de Vaugirard, de Medicis, Guynemer, and Auguste-Comte, St-Germain-des-Prés* 🎫 *Free* 🕙 *Daily 7:30–dusk (hrs may vary depending on season)* Ⓜ *Odéon; RER: B Luxembourg.*

TIPS

■ If the grass is en repos, a nice way of saying "stay off," feel free to move the green chairs around to create an ideal picnic spot or people-watching perch.

■ If you're eager to burn off that breakfast pain au choco-lat, the Jardin du Luxembourg has a well-maintained trail around the perimeter fre-quented by a surprising (for France) number of joggers—mostly groups of buff cops. It is one of the few public places where you can spy the French clad in (perfectly matching) athletic wear.

■ If you're looking for a famil-iar face, one of the original (miniature) casts of the Statue of Liberty was installed in the gardens in 1906.

The Luxembourg Gardens has all that is charming, unique, and befuddling about Parisian parks: cookie-cutter trees, ironed-and-pressed walkways, sculpted flower beds, and immaculate emerald lawns meant for admiring, not for lounging. The tree- and bench-lined paths are, however, a marvelous reprieve from the bus-tle of the two neighborhoods it borders: the Quartier Latin and St-Germain-des-Prés. Beautifully austere during the winter months, the garden grows intoxicat-ing as spring brings blooming beds of daffodils, tulips, and hyacinths, and the circular pools teem with boats nudged along by children. The park's northern bound-ary is dominated by the Palais du Luxembourg and the Sénat (Senate), which is one of two chambers that make up the Parliament.

HIGHLIGHTS

The original inspiration for the gardens came from Marie de Medici, nostalgic for the Boboli Gardens of her native Florence. She is commemorated by the Fon-taine de Medicis.

A sweet attraction is Les Marionettes du Théâtre du Luxembourg, where, on weekends at 11, 3, and 4 and Monday through Wednesday at 10:30, 3, and 4 (though hours may vary), you can catch classic *guignols* (marionette shows) for a €4.50 *guignolduluxembourg. monsite-orange.fr*. The wide-eyed kids might be the real attraction; their expressions of utter surprise, despair, and glee have fascinated the likes of Henri Cartier-Bresson and François Truffaut. The park also has a merry-go-round, swings, and pony rides; the bandstand hosts free concerts on summer afternoons.

Check out the rotating photography exhibits hanging on the perimeter fence near the entrance on the Boule-vard St-Michel and Rue Vaugirard.

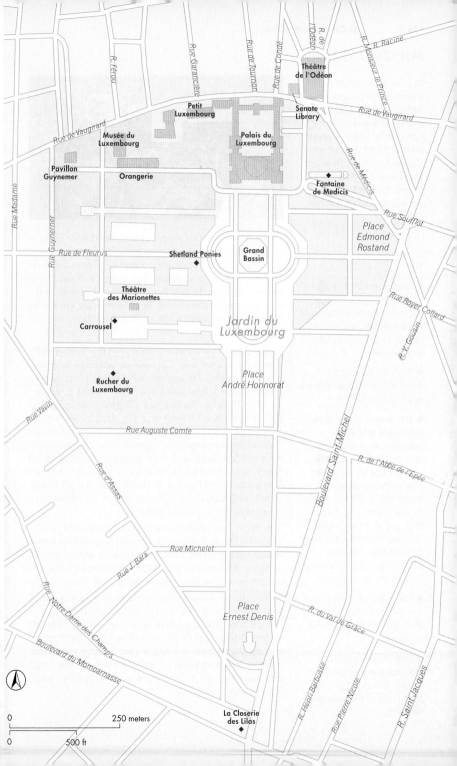

MUSÉE D'ORSAY

✉ *1 rue de la Légion d'Honneur, St-Germain-des-Prés* ☎ *01–40–49–48–14*
🌐 *www.musee-orsay.fr*
🎟 *€9.50 (€8 without special exhibit); €7 (€5 without special exhibit) after 4:15 except Thurs. after 6* 🕐 *Tues.–Sun. 9:30–6, Thurs. 9:30 am–9:45 pm* Ⓜ *Solférino; RER: Musée d'Orsay.*

TIPS

■ Lines at the d'Orsay are some of the worst in Paris. Book ahead on the Internet or buy a Museum Pass; then go directly to entrance C. Otherwise, go early.

■ Thursday evening the museum is open until 9:45 pm and less crowded.

■ The elegant Musée d'Orsay Restaurant once served patrons of the 1900 World's Fair; the Café du Lion serves up quick fare on the ground floor by the entrance, and there's also a café and a self-service cafeteria on the top floor just after the Cézanne galleries. Don't miss the views of Sacré-Coeur from the balcony—this is the Paris that inspired the Impressionists.

■ The d'Orsay is closed Monday, unlike the Pompidou and the Louvre, which are closed on Tuesday.

■ English audioguides are available just past the ticket booths; pick up a free color-coded map of the museum here, too.

Opened in 1986, this gorgeous renovated Belle Époque train station has a world-famous collection of Impressionist and Postimpressionist paintings. There are three floors; to visit the exhibits in a roughly chronologic manner, start on the first floor, take the escalators to the top, and end on the second. Renovations are underway until 2015, so expect some gallery closings.

HIGHLIGHTS

Ground floor: Galleries off the main alley feature early works by Manet and Cézanne in addition to pieces by masters like Delacroix and Ingres. Later works by the likes of Toulouse-Lautrec are found in gallery 10. The Pavillon Amont has Courbet's masterpieces *L'Enterrement à Ornans* and *Un Atelier du Peintre.* More experimental visions, including Gustave Moreau's myth-laden decadence and Puvis de Chavanne's surprisingly modern lines, make the leap into Impressionism easier to understand. In Salle 14 is Manet's *Olympia.* The artist is poking fun at the fashion for all things Greek and Roman; this young lady is a 19th-century courtesan, not a classical goddess.

Top floor: Impressionism gets going here, with iconic works by Degas, Pissarro, Sisley, and Renoir. Don't miss Monet's series on the cathedral at Rouen and, of course, samples of his waterlilies. Other selections by these artists are housed in galleries on the ground floor.

Second floor: An exquisite collection of sculpture as well as Art Nouveau furniture and decorative objects is housed here. There are rare surviving works by Hector Guimard (designer of the swooping green Paris métro entrances), as well as Lalique and Tiffany glassware. Postimpressionist galleries include work by van Gogh and Gauguin, while Neo-impressionist galleries highlight Seurat and Signac.

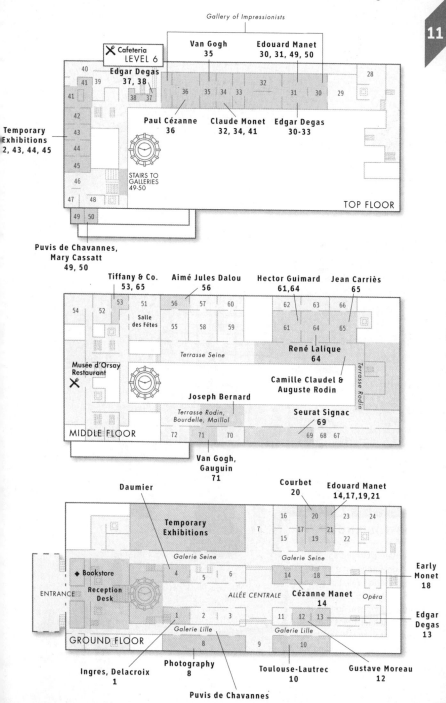

Gallery of Impressionists

Cafeteria
LEVEL 6

Van Gogh
35

Edouard Manet
30, 31, 49, 50

Edgar Degas
37, 38

40

41 39

41

38 37

36 35 34 33   32   31 30 29   28

Paul Cézanne
36

Claude Monet
32, 34, 41

Edgar Degas
30-33

Temporary
Exhibitions
2, 43, 44, 45

42

43

44

45

46

47 48

STAIRS TO
GALLERIES
49-50

TOP FLOOR

49 50

Puvis de Chavannes,
Mary Cassatt
49, 50

Tiffany & Co.
53, 65

Aimé Jules Dalou
56

Hector Guimard
61,64

Jean Carriès
65

54 52

53 51

Salle
des Fêtes

56 57 60

55 58 59

62 63 66

61 64 65

Musée d'Orsay
Restaurant

Terrasse Seine

René Lalique
64

Terrasse Rodin

Camille Claudel &
Auguste Rodin

Joseph Bernard

MIDDLE FLOOR

Terrasse Rodin,
Bourdelle, Maillol

72 71 70

Seurat Signac
69

69 68 67

Van Gogh,
Gauguin
71

Daumier

Courbet
20

Edouard Manet
14,17,19,21

16   20 23 24

15 17 19 21 22

7

Temporary
Exhibitions

Galerie Seine

Galerie Seine

Early
Monet
18

Bookstore

4   5 6

14 18

ENTRANCE

Reception
Desk

ALLÉE CENTRALE

Cézanne Manet
14

Opéra

Edgar
Degas
13

1 2 3

11 12 13

GROUND FLOOR

Galerie Lille

8   9

Galerie Lille

10

Gustave Moreau
12

Ingres, Delacroix
1

Photography
8

Toulouse-Lautrec
10

Puvis de Chavannes

DID YOU KNOW?

The Gare d'Orsay train station opened in time for the 1900 World's Fair, but was obsolete by 1939 because the platform was too short for the longer trains that had come into use. After several incarnations, the building was converted into the Musée d'Orsay and opened in 1986.

Montparnasse

WORD OF MOUTH

"Montparnasse was the center of art and free thinkers during the 'Crazy Years'—les Années Folles in the 30s. Famous from that time, the cafés La Coupole and La Rotonde are still there . . . It is a lively area, not that touristy and quite pleasant. There are some great open-air restaurants on Boulevard du Montparnasse."

—nikt32

GETTING ORIENTED

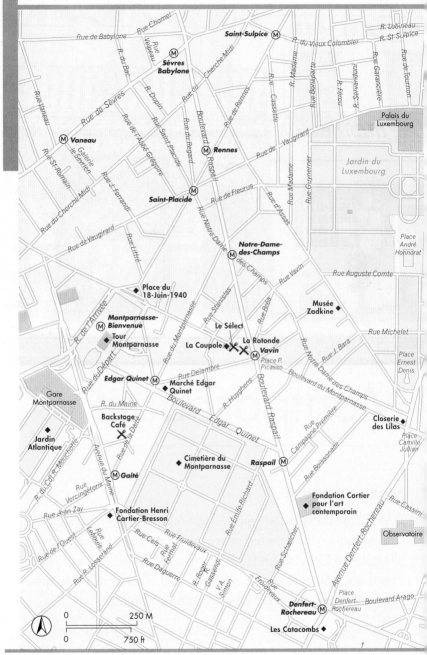

Rue de Babylone
Rue Chomel
Saint-Sulpice Ⓜ
R. du Vieux Colombier
R. Lobineau
R. St Sulpice
R. du Bac
Rue Verbeau
Rue de Grenelle
Ⓜ Sèvres
Babylone
Rue du Cherche-Midi
Rue Cassette
Rue Madame
Rue Bonaparte
R. Férou
R. Servandoni
Rue Garancière
Rue de Tournon
Rue Vaneau
Rue de Sèvres
R. Dupin
Boulevard Raspail
Rue du Regard
Rue de Rennes
Palais du
Luxembourg
Ⓜ Vaneau
Galerie
le Sentier
Rue de l'Abbé Grégoire
Rue St-Romain
Rue Saint-Placide
Ⓜ Rennes
Rue de Vaugirard
Jardin du
Luxembourg
Rue du Cherche-Midi
Rue Férrandi
Saint-Placide Ⓜ
Rue de Fleurus
Rue d'Assas
Rue Guynemer
Rue Madame
Rue de Vaugirard
Rue Notre-Dame
Rue Littré
Place
André
Honnorat
Notre-Dame-
des-Champs Ⓜ
Rue Vavin
Rue Auguste Comte
Place du
18-Juin-1940
Rue des Champs
Rue Bréa
Rue Stanislas
Musée
Zadkine ◆
Montparnasse-
Bienvenüe Ⓜ
Rue de l'Arrivée
Tour
Montparnasse
Le Sélect
La Rotonde
Rue Michelet
Place
Ernest
Denis
R. du Départ
Rue du Montparnasse
La Coupole ✗ ✗ Vavin Ⓜ
Place P.
Picasso
Rue Notre-Dame-des-Champs
Rue J. Bara
Edgar Quinet Ⓜ
Rue Delambre
Boulevard du Montparnasse
Gare
Montparnasse
Marché Edgar
Quinet
R. du Maine
Boulevard Edgar Quinet
R. Huyghens
Boulevard Raspail
Rue Campagne-Première
Closerie
des Lilas ◆
Backstage
Café ✗
Rue de la Gaîté
Place
Camille
Jullian
Jardin
Atlantique ◆
Cimetière du
Montparnasse ◆
Raspail Ⓜ
Rue Boissonade
Ⓜ Gaîté
Avenue du Maine
R. du Cdt. R. Mouchotte
Rue
Vercingétorix
Fondation Cartier
pour l'art
contemporain ◆
Rue Cassini
Rue Jean Zay
Fondation Henri
Cartier-Bresson ◆
Rue Émile-Richard
Avenue Denfert-Rochereau
Observatoire
Rue de l'Ouest
Rue Lebouis
Rue Cels
Rue Lernat
Rue Fruidevaux
Rue R. Losserand
Rue Daguerre
R. Roger-Gassendi
V.A. Simon
Rue Froidevaux
Rue Schœlcher
Place
Denfert-
Rochereau
Boulevard Arago
Denfert-
Rochereau Ⓜ
Les Catacombs ◆

0 ___ 250 M
0 ___ 750 ft

OSSEMENT.DU CIMETIERE DEs INNOCENTS DÉ POSÉS.EN 8ÈRE 1787

TOP REASONS TO GO

Catacombs. It's not a great place to visit if you're claustrophobic or uncomfortable about the macabre, but if you're into the history of Paris, you won't want to miss this underground mecca of bones.

Fondation Cartier pour l'art contemporain. If cutting-edge art is what you're after, don't miss what's on view at this exhibition space. The building was designed by internationally acclaimed Jean Nouvel, the darling of Paris architecture.

Fondation Henri Cartier-Bresson. No photography fan should pass up the chance to see Cartier-Bresson's restored atelier, which features a small collection of his work as well as photographs from young, contemporary artists.

The Tour Montparnasse. Even though this 680-foot black behemoth of a skyscraper is one of the most hated buildings in Paris, the open-air roof terrace is one of the best spots to see the City of Light.

MAKING THE MOST OF YOUR TIME

If you can get to the top of the Tour Montparnasse on a clear day, you'll be rewarded with the best view in all of Paris. The viewing deck is open until 10:30 pm, so you can watch the lights sparkle on the Eiffel Tower at the top of the hour. The Catacombs and the Fondation Henri Cartier-Bresson are closed on Monday. The Cimetière du Montparnasse is open daily. La Coupole is perfect for a celebratory evening, but make reservations for this famous brasserie well in advance.

GETTING HERE

Montparnasse includes the 14e and 15e arrondissements. Take Line 4, 6, 12, or 13 to Montparnasse-Bienvenue for the Tour Montparnasse; walk along the Boulevard du Montparnasse to hit the cafés. Or take Line 4 or 6 to the Raspail métro stop for the Cimetière du Montparnasse or the Fondation Henri Cartier-Bresson. To visit the Catacombs, take the 4 or 6 to Denfert-Rochereau. Other nearby métro stops include the Edgar Quinet stop on the 6 line and the Gaîté stop on the 13 line.

12

BEST CAFÉS

Backstage Café. Settle into a comfy chair and order a creation from the extensive cocktail list; this hot spot is on one of Montparnasse's most lively streets, aptly named Rue de la Gaîté (or "Cheerful Street"). ⊠ *31 bis, rue de la Gaîté, Montparnasse* ☎ *01–43–20–68–59* Ⓜ *Edgar Quinet.*

La Rotonde. This café, a second home to foreign artists and political exiles in the 1920s and '30s, has a less exotic clientele today, but it's still very pleasant to have coffee on the sunny terrace. ⊠ *105 bd. Montparnasse, Montparnasse* ☎ *01–43–26–48–26* Ⓜ *Vavin.*

Le Sélect. Isadora Duncan and Hart Crane used to hang out here; now it's a popular spot for a postcinema beer or a well-made cocktail. ⊠ *99 bd. Montparnasse, Montparnasse* ☎ *01–45–48–38–24* Ⓜ *Vavin.*

Sightseeing
★★★
Dining
★★★
Lodging
★★
Shopping
★
Nightlife
★★

Once a warren of artists' studios and swinging cafés, much of Montparnasse was leveled in the 1960s to make way for a gritty train station and Paris's only—and much maligned—skyscraper, Tour Montparnasse. Over the years, this neighborhood has evolved into a place where Parisians can find more reasonable rents, well-priced cafés, and the kind of real-life vibe lost in some of the trendier parts of the city.

Despite the soulless architecture, the modernity of **Tour Montparnasse** has its advantage: the rooftop terrace has the best panoramic view of Paris. It's okay to feel smug during your ascent, as you consider yourself savvy for avoiding long lines at Tour Eiffel. And you can reward yourself with a fancy cocktail at Le Bar Américain on the 56th floor.

The other star attraction of Montparnasse is belowground. The maze-like tunnels of the Paris **Catacombs** contain the bones of centuries' worth of Parisians, moved here when disease, spread by rotting corpses, threatened the city center.

The café society that flourished in the early 20th century—Picasso, Modigliani, Hemingway (where *didn't* he drink?), Man Ray, and even Trotsky raised a glass here—is still evident along the Boulevard du Montparnasse. The Art Deco interior of **La Coupole** attracts diners seeking piles of golden *choucroute*.

Along the Boulevard Raspail you can see today's cutting-edge art stars at the **Fondation Henri Cartier-Bresson** or the **Fondation Cartier pour l'art contemporain,** or pay your respects to Baudelaire, Alfred Dreyfus, or Simone de Beauvoir in the **Cimetière du Montparnasse.**

TOP ATTRACTIONS

Updated by
Bryan Pirolli

Cimetière du Montparnasse. Many of the neighborhood's most illustrious residents are buried here, a stone's throw from where they lived and loved: Charles Baudelaire, Frédéric Bartholdi (who designed the Statue of Liberty), Alfred Dreyfus, Guy de Maupassant, and, more recently, photographer Man Ray, playwright Samuel Beckett, writers Marguerite Duras, Jean-Paul Sartre, and Simone de Beauvoir, actress Jean Seberg, and singer-songwriter Serge Gainsbourg. ⊠ *Entrances on Rue Froidevaux, Bd. Edgar Quinet, Montparnasse* ⊗ *Mar. 16–Nov. 5, weekdays 8–6, Sat. 8:30–6, Sun. 9–6; Nov. 6–Mar. 15, weekdays 8–5:30, Sat. 8:30–5:30, Sun. 9–5:30* Ⓜ *Raspail, Gaîté.*

12

★ **Fondation Cartier pour l'art contemporain.** There's no shortage of museums in Paris, but this eye-catching contemporary-art gallery may be the city's best place to view cutting-edge art. Funded by luxury giant Cartier, the foundation is at once an architectural landmark, a corporate collection, and an exhibition space. Architect Jean Nouvel's 1993 building is a glass house of cards layered seamlessly between the boulevard and the garden. Along with high-quality exhibitions of contemporary art, the foundation hosts Soirées Nomades, or performance nights (contemporary dance, music, film, fashion), on Thursday evenings, some in English. Check the website for times and details. ⊠ *261 bd. Raspail, Montparnasse* ☎ *01–42–18–56–50* ⊕ *www.fondation.cartier.com* ⊠ *€9.50* ⊗ *Tues. 11–10, Wed.–Sun. 11–8* Ⓜ *Raspail.*

★ **Fondation Henri Cartier-Bresson.** Photography has deep roots in Montparnasse, as great experimenters like Louis Daguerre and Man Ray lived and worked here. In keeping with this spirit of innovation, Henri Cartier-Bresson, legendary photographer and creator of the Magnum photo agency, opened this foundation supporting contemporary photography in 2003. The restored 1913 artists' atelier holds three temporary exhibitions each year. Be sure to go to the top floor to see a small gallery of Cartier-Bresson's own work. ⊠ *2 impasse Lebouis, Montparnasse* ☎ *01–56–80–27–00* ⊕ *www.henricartierbresson.org* ⊠ *€6, free on Wed. 6:30 pm–8:30 pm* ⊗ *Tues.–Sun. 1–6:30, Wed. 1–8:30, Sat. 11–6:45* Ⓜ *Gaîté, Edgar Quinet.*

★ **Les Catacombes.** This is just the thing for anyone with morbid interests: what you'll see after a descent through dark, clammy passages is Paris's principal ossuary, which also once served as a hideout maze for the French Resistance. Bones from the defunct Cimetière des Innocents were the first to arrive in 1786, when decomposing bodies started seeping into the cellars of the market at Les Halles, drawing swarms of ravenous rats. The legions of bones dumped here are stacked not by owner but by type—rows of skulls, packs of tibias, and piles of spinal disks, often rather artfully arranged. Be prepared for stairs and a long underground walk; the floor can be damp, so wear appropriate shoes. Note that you won't be shrouded in tomblike darkness: the tunnels are well lighted. Among the nameless 6 million or so are the bones of Madame de Pompadour (1721–64), laid to rest with the riffraff after a lifetime spent as the mistress of Louis XV. Unfortunately, one of the most interesting aspects of the catacombs is one you probably won't see: *cataphiles*, mostly art students, have found alternate entrances into the 300 km

(186 miles) of tunnels and here they make art, party, and raise hell. ☒ *1 Ave. du Colonel Henry Roi-Tanguy, Montparnasse* ☎ *01–43–22–47–63* ⊕ *www.catacombes-de-paris.fr* ✉ *€8* ☉ *Tues.–Sun. 10–5 (last entry at 4)* Ⓜ *Métro or RER: Denfert-Rochereau.*

★ **Musée Zadkine.** The sculptor Ossip Zadkine spent nearly four decades living in this bucolic retreat near the Jardin du Luxembourg, creating graceful, elongated figures known for their clean lines and simplified features. Zadkine, a Russian-Jewish émigré, moved to Paris in 1910 and fell into a circle of avant-garde artists. His early works, influenced by African, Greek, and Roman art, later took a Cubist turn, no doubt under the influence of his friend, the founder of the Cubist movement: Pablo Picasso. The museum displays a substantial portion of the 400 sculptures and 300 drawings bequeathed to the city by his wife, the artist Valentine Prax. It was recently renovated in 2012 to celebrate its 30th anniversary. There are busts in bronze and stone reflecting the range of Zadkine's style, and an airy back room filled with lithe female nudes in polished wood. The leafy garden is worth the trip alone, containing a dozen statues nestled in the trees, including "The Destroyed City," a memorial to the Dutch city of Rotterdam, destroyed by the Germans in 1940. ☒ *100 bis, rue d'Assas, Montparnasse* ☎ *01–55–42–77–20* ⊕ *www.zadkine.paris.fr* ✉ *Free; fee (varies) for temporary exhibitions only* ☉ *Tues.–Sun. 10–6* Ⓜ *Vavin, Notre-Dame-des-Champs.*

Tour Montparnasse. One of continental Europe's tallest skyscrapers offers visitors a stupendous view of Paris from its 56th-floor observation deck, or you can climb another three flights to the open-air roof terrace. Completed in 1973, the 680-foot building attracts 800,000 gawkers each year; on a clear day you can see for 40 km (25 miles). A glossy brochure, "Paris Vu d'en Haut" ("Paris from on High"), explains what to look for. Have a cocktail with your view at **Le Bar Américain** on the 56th floor, which also serves light food, or splurge on dinner in **Le Ciel de Paris** restaurant. The tower sparkles to life every evening thanks to new pulsating lights installed in 2011. ☒ *Rue de l'Arrivée, Montparnasse* ☎ *01–45–38–52–56, 01–40–64–77–64 Le Ciel de Paris* ⊕ *www.tourmontparnasse56. com* ✉ *€11.50* ☉ *Apr.–Sept., daily 9:30 am–11:30 pm; Oct.–Mar., Sun.–Thurs. 9:30 am–10:30 pm, Fri. and Sat. 9:30 am–11 pm; last elevator 30 min before closing* Ⓜ *Montparnasse Bienvenüe.*

WORTH NOTING

Closerie des Lilas. Now a pricey bar-restaurant, the Closerie remains a staple of all literary tours of Paris. Commemorative plaques are bolted to the bar as if they were still saving seats for their former clientele—an impressive list of literati including Zola, Baudelaire, Rimbaud, Apollinaire, Beckett, and, of course, Hemingway. (Hemingway wrote pages of *The Sun Also Rises* here; he lived around the corner at 115 rue Notre-Dame-des-Champs.) Although the lilacs that graced the garden are gone—they once shaded such habitués as Ingres, Whistler, and Cézanne—the terrace still opens onto a garden wall of luxuriant foliage. There is live music in the piano bar. ☒ *171 bd. du Montparnasse, Montparnasse* ☎ *01–40–51–34–50* Ⓜ *Vavin; RER: Port Royal.*

Artists, Writers, and Exiles

12

Paris became a magnet for the international avant-garde in the mid-1800s and remained Europe's creative capital until the 1950s. It all began south of **Montmartre**, when Romantics, including writers Charles Baudelaire and George Sand (with her lover, Polish composer Frédéric Chopin), moved into the streets below Boulevard de Clichy. Impressionist painters Claude Monet, Edouard Manet, and Mary Cassatt had studios here, near Gare St-Lazare, so they could commute to the countryside. In the 1880s the neighborhood dance halls had a new attraction: the cancan, and in 1889 the **Moulin Rouge** cabaret was opened. Toulouse-Lautrec designed posters advertising the neighborhood stars and sketched prostitutes in his spare time.

The artistic maelstrom continued through the Belle Époque and beyond. In the early 1900s Picasso and Braque launched Cubism from a ramshackle hillside studio, the **Bateau-Lavoir**, and a similar beehive of activity was established at the south end of the city in a curious studio building called La Ruche (the beehive, at the Convention métro stop). Artists from different disciplines worked together on experimental productions. In 1917 the modernist ballet *Parade* hit the stage, danced by impresario Sergei Diaghilev's Ballets Russes, with music by Erik Satie and costumes by Picasso—and everyone involved

was hauled off to court, accused of being cultural anarchists.

World War I shattered this creative frenzy, and when peace returned, the artists had moved. The narrow streets of **Montparnasse** had old buildings suitable for studios, and the area hummed with a wide, new, café-filled boulevard. At No. 27 rue Fleurus, Gertrude Stein held court with her partner, Alice B. Toklas. Picasso drew admirers to **La Rotonde**, and F. Scott Fitzgerald drank at the now-defunct Dingo. In the '30s **La Coupole** became a favorite brasserie of Henry Miller, Anaïs Nin, and Lawrence Durrell.

The Spanish Civil War and World War II brought an end to carefree Montparnasse. But the literati reconvened in **St-Germain-des-Prés. Café de Flore** and **Deux Magots** had long been popular with an alternative crowd. Expat writers Samuel Beckett and Richard Wright joined existentialists Jean-Paul Sartre, Simone de Beauvoir, and Albert Camus in the neighborhood, drawn into the orbit of literary magazines and publishing houses.

Although Paris can no longer claim to be the epicenter of Western artistic innovation, pockets of outrageous creativity still bubble up. The galleries on Rue Louise Weiss in **Tolbiac** and open-studio weekends in **Belleville** and **Oberkampf** reveal the city's continuing artistic spirit.

Jardin Atlantique. Built above the tracks of Gare Montparnasse, this park nestled among tall modern buildings is named for its assortment of trees and plants found in coastal regions near the Atlantic Ocean. At the far end of the garden are twin small museums devoted to World War II: the **Mémorial du Maréchal-Leclerc,** named for the liberator of Paris, and the adjacent **Musée Jean-Moulin,** devoted to the leader of the French Resistance. Both feature memorabilia and share a common second floor showing photo and video footage (with English subtitles)

Dining at a Glance

For full reviews
⇨ Chapter 14.

INEXPENSIVE DINING
La Crêperie Josselin, *Modern French*, 67 rue du Montparnasse

MODERATE DINING
La Coupole, *Brasserie*, 102 bd. du Montparnasse

La Cerisaie, *Bistro*, 70 bd. Edgar Quinet

Le Timbre, *Bistro*, 3 rue Ste-Beuve

EXPENSIVE DINING
L'Assiette, *Bistro*, 181 rue du Château

Le Dôme, *Brasserie*, 108 bd. Montparnasse

---

of the final days of the war and the liberation of Paris. Entrance is free; temporary exhibitions cost a few euros. In the center of the park, what looks like a quirky piece of metallic sculpture is actually a meteorological center, with a battery of flickering lights reflecting temperature, wind speed, and monthly rainfall. ⊠ *1 pl. des Cinq-Martyrs-du-Lycée-Buffon, Montparnasse* ☎ *01–40–64–39–44* ⊕ *www.ml-leclerc-moulin.paris.fr* ⊙ *Jardin weekdays 8–dusk, weekends 9–dusk (hrs vary depending on season); musée Tues.–Sun. 10–6* Ⓜ *Montparnasse Bienvenüe.*

La Coupole. One of Montparnasse's most famous brasseries, La Coupole, opened in 1927 and soon became a home-away-from-home for Apollinaire, Cocteau, Satie, Stravinsky, and (again) Hemingway. In the 1980s the brasserie was bought by the Flo chain, which preserved the superb Art Deco interior, including pillars by Chagall and Brancusi. The place retains its hustle and bustle—with scurrying waiters and the overwhelming noise of clinking glasses and clattering silverware. ⊠ *102 bd. du Montparnasse, Montparnasse* ☎ *01–43–20–14–20* ⊙ *Weekdays 8 am–midnight, weekends 8:30 am–1 am* Ⓜ *Vavin.*

Marché Edgar Quinet. This excellent street market sells everything from fresh fruit to hot crêpes to wool shawls on Wednesday and Saturday. It's a good place to pick up lunch to go before strolling through Cimetière du Montparnasse across the street. ⊠ *Bd. du Edgar Quinet at métro Edgar Quinet* Ⓜ *Edgar Quinet*

Place du 18-Juin-1940. Next to Tour Montparnasse, this square commemorates Charles de Gaulle's famous radio broadcast from London urging the French to resist the Germans after the Nazi invasion of May 1940. It was here that German military governor Dietrich von Choltitz surrendered to the Allies in August 1944, ignoring Hitler's orders to destroy the city as he withdrew. Ⓜ *Montparnasse Bienvenüe.*

Western Paris

WITH THE BOIS DE BOULOGNE

WORD OF MOUTH

"[Musée] Marmottan is a very special place if you like the art, and for me it is in my must-see triad with the Louvre and Orsay. I walk into the Marmottan and I immediately start to smile."

—elaine

GETTING ORIENTED

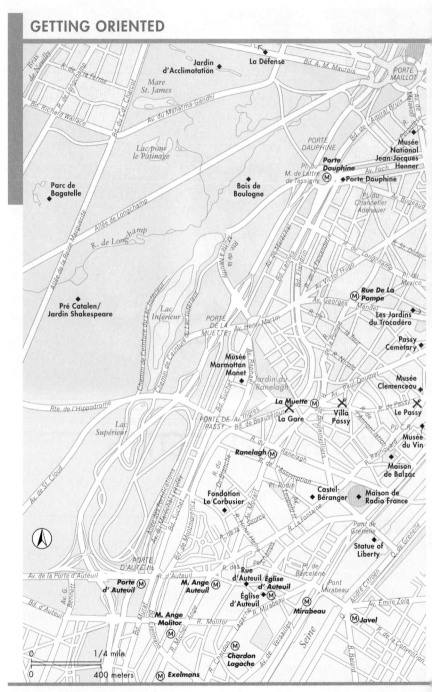

La Défense

Jardin
d'Acclimatation

Bd. A. M. Maurois

PORTE
MAILLOT

Mare
St. James

Lac pour
le Pátinage

PORTE
DAUPHINE

Musée
National
Jean-Jacques
Henner

Porte
Dauphine

Av. Foch

Pl. du
M. de Lattre
de Tassigny

Porte Dauphine

Parc de
Bagatelle

Bois de
Boulogne

Pl. du
Chancelier
Adenauer

Pl. du
Mexico

Rue De La
Pompe

Les Jardins
du Trocadéro

Pré Catalen/
Jardin Shakespeare

Lac
Inférieur

PORTE
DE LA
MUETTE

Av. Henri Martin

Passy
Cemetary

Musée
Marmottan
Monet

Jardin du
Ranelagh

Musée
Clemenceau

Rte. de l'Hippodrome

La Muette

Le Passy

PORTE DE LA
PASSY

Av. Ingres

Bd. de Beauséjour

La Gare

Villa
Passy

Lac
Supérieur

Av. de St. Cloud

Ranelagh

Musée
du Vin

Maison
de Balzac

Fondation
Le Corbusier

Pl. Robin

Castel-
Béranger

Maison de
Radio France

Pont de
Grenelle

PORTE
D'AUTEUIL

Statue of
Liberty

Av. de la Porte d'Auteuil

Porte
d'Auteuil

R. d'Auteuil

Rue
d'Auteuil

M. Ange
Auteuil

Église
d' Auteuil

Pl. de
Barcelone

Pont
Mirabeau

Église
d'Auteuil

Mirabeau

Javel

M. Ange
Molitor

R. Molitor

Chardon
Lagache

0   1/4 mile

0   400 meters

Exelmans

TOP REASONS TO GO

Musée Marmottan Monet. If you're a fan of Monet, don't miss this gem of a museum tucked away deep in the 16e.

Bois de Boulogne. Whether you spend your afternoon in a rowboat or wandering gardens filled with foliage, the Bois is the perfect escape from the city.

Jardin d'Acclimatation. There's not a child under the age of five who won't love this amusement park on the northern edge of the Bois de Boulogne.

Fondation Le Corbusier. The iconic Modernist designs of Swiss-born pioneering architect Le Corbusier fill this compelling museum, which was built as a private house—one of the first Corbusier was commissioned to do in Paris.

MAKING THE MOST OF YOUR TIME

If this isn't your first time in Paris, or even if it is and you've had enough of the touristy central part of the city, this neighborhood is a great choice and can be treated like a day trip. Spend the morning admiring the Monets at the uncrowded Musée Marmottan Monet (closed Monday), then take in the Art Nouveau architecture on Rue la Fontaine. If your goal is to leave the city lights behind altogether, pack a picnic and spend the day in the Bois de Boulogne.

GETTING HERE

Western Paris includes the 16e and 17e arrondissements. Take Line 9 to La Muette métro stop for the Musée Marmottan Monet, or to the Jasmin stop (also Line 9) to explore Rue la Fontaine. Take Line 6 to the Passy stop for the Musée du Vin or to reach the main drag, Rue de Passy. Or take bus 72 from the Hôtel de Ville or 63 from St. Sulpice. For the Bois de Boulogne, take Line 2 to the Porte Dauphine stop or RER C to Avenue Foch. For the Jardin d'Acclimatation, enter the park from the Les Sablons or Port Maillot métro stops on Line 1. If you're heading out to La Défense, it's the end of Line 1.

BEST CAFÉS

Carette. Tucked into Place du Trocadéro, this grande dame of tea salons has been offering light lunches and sweet treats since 1927. Dive into a *salade composée* or enjoy a cup of tea and a slice of raspberry charlotte. ⌧ *4 pl. du Trocadero, Trocadéro/Tour Eiffel* ☎ *01–47–27–98–85* Ⓜ *Trocadéro.*

La Gare. For good food in a trendy atmosphere, try this bar/restaurant housed in a former train station. In nice weather, enjoy the large outdoor terrace. ⌧ *19 chausée de la Muette, Passy, Western Paris* ☎ *01–42–15–15–31* Ⓜ *La Muette.*

Le Passy. The plush chestnut-and-cream decor of this café is the work of one of Givenchy's nephews. Cocktails are classy, there's a good variety of beer on tap, the food—bistro fare such as steaks, fish, and frites—is yummy, and candlelight makes everyone look that much more glamorous. ⌧ *2 rue de Passy, Passy, Western Paris* ☎ *01–42–88–31–02* Ⓜ *Passy or Trocadéro.*

Villa Passy. The leafy, tucked-away courtyard of this café just off Rue de Passy may make you think you've stumbled into a small village. Sit outside on a cushioned banquette shaded by ivy and order the plat du jour, prepared with fresh market ingredients. Try the €23 Sunday brunch. ⌧ *4 impasse des Carrières (opposite 31 rue de Passy), Passy, Western Paris* ☎ *01–45–27–68–76* Ⓜ *Passy.*

13

Sightseeing
★★
Dining
★
Lodging
★
Shopping
★

Welcome to Paris at its most prim and proper—but hardly stodgy. This genteel area is a study in smart urban planning, with classical architecture and newer construction commingling as easily as the haute bourgeoisie inhabitants mix with their American expat neighbors. There's no shortage of celebrities seeking some peace and quiet here, but you're just as likely to find well-heeled families who decamped from the center of the city in search of a spacious apartment. Passy, once a separate village and home to American ambassadors Benjamin Franklin and Thomas Jefferson, was incorporated into the city in 1860 under Napoleon III.

A walk along the main avenues gives you a sense of Paris's finest Art Nouveau and Modernist buildings, including **Castel-Béranger,** by Hector Guimard, and the **Fondation Le Corbusier** museum, a prime example of the Swiss architect's Modernist style. This neighborhood is also home to one of the city's best and most overlooked museums—the **Musée Marmottan Monet**—which has an astonishing collection of Impressionist art. Enjoy a *dégustation* (tasting) at the **Musée du Vin** or simply find a café on Rue de Passy and savor a moment in one of the city's most exclusive enclaves. If it's a leafy landscape you're after, spend an afternoon at the **Bois de Boulogne,** especially if you have kids. At *Le Bois,* you can explore the Pré Catelan and Bagatelle gardens, both meticulously landscaped and surrounded by woods. Head to the old-fashioned amusement park at the Jardin d'Acclimatation or take a rowboat out on one of the park's two bucolic lakes. You can also rent a bike and hit the 14 km (9 miles) of marked trails.

TOP ATTRACTIONS

🐾 **Bois de Boulogne**

Fodor's Choice
★

See highlighted listing in this chapter.

Fodor's Choice
★

Updated by
Paige Donner

13

Castel-Béranger. It's a shame you can't go inside this house, considered the city's first Art Nouveau structure, dreamed up in 1898 by Hector Guimard. The wild combination of materials and the grimacing grill-work led neighbors to call this the Castle *Dérangé* (Deranged), but this private commission catapulted the 27-year-old Guimard into the public eye, leading to his famous métro commission. After admiring the sea-inspired front entrance, go partway down the alley to admire the inventive treatment of the traditional Parisian courtyard, complete with a melting water fountain. Just up the road at No. 60 is the **Hotel Mezzara,** designed by Guimard in 1911 for textile designer Paul Mezzara. You can trace Guimard's evolution by walking to the subtler Agar complex at the end of the block (at the corner of Rue la Fontaine and Rue Gros). Tucked beside the stone entrance at the corner of Rue Gros is a tiny café-bar with an Art Nouveau glass front and furnishings. ✉ *14 rue la Fontaine, Passy-Auteuil* Ⓜ *Ranelagh; RER: Maison de Radio France.*

QUICK
BITES

Café Antoine. It seats just 15, but charming Café Antoine warrants a visit for its Art Nouveau facade, floor tiles, and carved wooden bar. Count on €35 for a meal, or share a charcuterie plate (about €17) and wine. ✉ *17 rue la Fontaine, Passy-Auteuil* ☎ *01–40–50–14–30.*

Fondation Le Corbusier (*Le Corbusier Foundation*). Fresh from a major renovation, the 1923 Maison La Roche is a stellar example of Swiss architect Le Corbusier's innovative construction techniques based on geometric forms, recherché color schemes, and an unblushing use of iron and concrete. The sloping ramp that replaces the traditional staircase is one of the most eye-catching features. ✉ *8–10 sq. du Docteur Blanche, Passy-Auteuil* ☎ *01–42–88–41–53* ⊕ *www. fondationlecorbusier.fr* 🎫 *€5* ⊗ *Mon. 1:30–6, Tues.–Thurs. 10–6, Fri. and Sat. 10–5. Closed Sun.* Ⓜ *Jasmin; Michel Ange Auteuil.*

Fodor's Choice
★

Musée Marmottan Monet. A few years ago the underrated Marmottan tacked "Monet" onto its official name—and justly so, as this is the largest collection of the artist's works anywhere. Monet's works, donated by his son Michel, occupy a specially built basement gallery in this elegant 19th-century mansion, once the hunting lodge of the Duke de Valmy, where you can find such captivating works as the *Cathédrale de Rouen* series (1892–96) and *Impression: Soleil Levant* (*Impression: Sunrise*, 1872), the work that helped give the Impressionist movement its name. Other exhibits include letters exchanged by Impressionist painters Berthe Morisot and Mary Cassatt. Upstairs, the mansion still feels like a graciously decorated private home. Empire furnishings fill the salons overlooking the Jardin de Ranelagh on one side and the private yard on the other. There's also a captivating room of illuminated medieval manuscripts. To best understand the collection's context, buy an English-language catalog in the museum shop on your way in. ✉ *2 rue Louis-Boilly, Passy-Auteuil* ☎ *01–44–96–50–33*

BOIS DE BOULOGNE

⊠ *Porte Dauphine for main entrance; Porte Maillot or Les Sablons for northern end; Porte d'Auteuil for southern end* ☎ *01–40–71–75–60 Parc de Bagatelle, 01–40–67–90–82 Jardin d'Acclimatation* ⊕ *www.jardindacclimatation. fr* ⊠ *Parc de Bagatelle free except during exhibitions; otherwise €5; Jardin Shakespeare: €1; Jardin d'Acclimatation: €2.90, does not include individual ride tickets.* ⊙ *Daily; hrs vary according to time of yr but are generally around 10 am to dusk* Ⓜ *Porte Dauphine for main entrance; Porte Maillot for norther entrance; Porte d'Auteuil for southern end.*

TIPS

■ The main entrance to the Bois de Boulogne is off Avenue Foch near the Porte Dauphine métro stop on the 2 line, best for accessing Pré Catelan and Jardin Shakespeare off Route de la Grande-Cascade. For the Jardin d'Acclimatation, off Boulevard Des Sablons, take the 1 line to Les Sablons or Porte Maillot, where you can ride the petit train to the amusement park. The Parc de Bagatelle, off Route de Sèvres-à-Neuilly, can be accessed from either Porte Dauphine or Porte Maillot, though it's a bit of a hike.

■ You'll want to leave the park by dusk, as the Bois becomes a distinctly adult playground after dark.

When Parisians need a day in the great outdoors close to home, they head to the Bois de Boulogne. The Bois is not a park in the traditional sense—more like a tamed forest, as it was once a royal hunting ground. On nice days the park is filled with cyclists, rowers, joggers, *pétanque* players, and picnickers enjoying the formal gardens, romantic lakes, and wooded paths.

HIGHLIGHTS

The Parc de Bagatelle is a floral garden of irises, roses, tulips, and water lilies, at its most colorful between April and June. Pré Catelan contains one of Paris's largest trees: a copper beech more than 200 years old. The romantic Le Pré Catelan restaurant, where *le tout Paris* of the Belle Époque used to dine on the elegant terrace, still lures diners and wedding parties, especially on weekends. The Jardin Shakespeare inside the Pré Catelan has a sampling of the flowers, herbs, and trees mentioned in Shakespeare's plays, and becomes an open-air theater for the Bard's works in spring. The Jardin d'Acclimatation, on the northern edge of the park, is a fabulous amusement park where it seems that every child under the age of five in Paris spends his or her summer Sunday afternoons. Highlights include boat trips along an "enchanted river" and an aviary. A miniature railway shuttle runs from Porte Maillot on Wednesday and weekends beginning at 1:30; tickets cost €2.70 (round-trip). Rent boats or bikes for a few euros at Lac Inférieur. You can row or take a quick ferry to the island restaurant Chalet des Iles. Two popular horse-racing tracks are in the park, the Hippodrome de Longchamp and the Hippodrome d'Auteuil. Fans of the French Open can visit its home base, Stade Roland-Garros (tours in English Wednesday to Sunday at 11 am and 3 pm, €10), and true devotees can check out the Tenniseum (tennis museum, €15 with stadium entry).

⊕ *www.marmottan.com* ⊠ *€10*
⊙ *Thurs. 10–8, Wed.–Sun. 11–6*
Ⓜ *La Muette.*

★ **Musée National Jean-Jacques Henner.**
French artist Jean-Jacques Henner
(1829–1905) was a star in his day,
though his luminous nudes and
clear-eyed portraits are largely for-
gotten today. This elegant museum
stocked with his works reopened in
late 2009 after a two-year renovation that restored the *maison par-
ticulière* (private mansion) to its
19th-century glory. Henner's style is
hard to categorize: he painted more

13

than 400 portraits, including a substantial number sold in America, with
a Realist's eye—red nose, mottled skin, and all. But there is much beauty
as well, as in *Lady with Umbrella,* a portrait of a fur-clad aristocrat with
glistening blue eyes. Yet many of his soft-featured nudes betray other
influences. Don't miss them in the light-filled atelier on the museum's
third floor, where they share space with a series of religious paintings,
notably the haunting *Saint Sebastian,* and a stark portrayal of a lifeless
Christ, whose luminescent white skin is offset by a shock of flaming red
hair. Henner never lived here; his heirs bought the home from the family
of painter Guillaume Dubufe, and it opened as a museum in 1924. There
is some information in English. ⊠ *43 av. de Villiers* ☎ *01–47–63–42–73*
⊕ *www.musee-henner.fr* ⊠ *€5* ⊙ *Wed.–Mon. 11–6; 1st Thurs. of month
11–9* Ⓜ *Malesherbes.*

WORTH NOTING

**OFF THE
BEATEN
PATH**

La Défense. First conceived in 1958, this Modernist suburb just west of
Paris was inspired by Le Corbusier's dream of high-rise buildings, pedestrian walkways, and sunken vehicle circulation. Built as an experiment
to keep high-rises out of the historic downtown, the Parisian business
hub has survived economic uncertainty to become a surprising success.
Visiting La Défense gives you a crash course in contemporary skyscraper
evolution, from the solid blocks of the 1960s and '70s to the curvy fins
of the '90s and beyond. Today 20,000 people live in the suburb, but
150,000 people work here, and many more come to shop in its enormous
mall. While riding the métro Line 1 here, you'll get a view of the Seine,
then emerge at a pedestrian plaza studded with some great public art,
including César's giant thumb and one of Calder's great red "stabiles."
The Grande Arche de La Défense dominates the area; it was designed
as a controversial closure to the historic axis of Paris (an imaginary line
that runs through the Arc de Triomphe, the Arc du Carrousel, and the
Louvre glass pyramid). Glass bubble elevators in a metal-frame tower
whisk you a heart-jolting 360 feet to the viewing platform. ⊠ *Parvis de
La Défense, La Défense* ☎ *01–49–07–27–27* ⊕ *www.grandearche.com*

✉ *Grande Arche €10* ☉ *Apr.–Aug., daily 10–8; Sept.–Mar., daily 10–7* Ⓜ *Métro or RER: Grande Arche de La Défense.*

Maison de Balzac. The modest Paris home of the great French 19th-century novelist Honoré de Balzac (1799–1850) contains exhibits charting his tempestuous yet prolific career. Balzac penned the nearly 100 novels and stories known collectively as *The Human Comedy*, many of them set in Paris. You can still feel his presence in his study and pay homage to his favorite coffeepot—his working hours were fueled by his tremendous consumption of the "black ink." He would escape his creditors by exiting the flat through a secret passage that led down to what is now the Musée du Vin. ✉ *47 rue Raynouard, Passy-Auteuil* ☎ *01–55–74–41–80* ⊕ *www.balzac.paris.fr* ✍ *Free; temporary exhibitions €4* ☉ *Tues.–Sun. 10–6* Ⓜ *Passy; La Muette.*

Maison de Radio France. Headquarters to France's state radio, this imposing 1962 circular building is more than 500 yards in circumference. It's said to have more floor space than any other building in France and features a 200-foot tower that overlooks the Seine. Radio France sponsors more than 100 concerts a year, including performances by its own Orchestre Philharmonique de Radio France and the Orchestre National de France. Though these concerts take place at venues throughout the city, a number are held here, and these are generally either free of charge or inexpensive. ✉ *116 av. du Président-Kennedy, Passy-Auteuil* ☎ *01–56–40–15–16* ⊕ *www.francemusique.fr* Ⓜ *Ranelagh; RER: Maison de Radio France, Bus 22, 52, 72.*

Musée du Vin. Fans of wine making will enjoy this quirky museum housed in a 15th-century abbey, a reminder of Passy's roots as a pastoral village. Though hardly exhaustive, the collection includes old wine bottles, glassware, and ancient wine-related pottery excavated in Paris. Wine-making paraphernalia shares the grottolike space with hokey figures retired from the city's wax museum, including Napoléon appraising a glass of Burgundy, but you can partake in a thoroughly nonhokey wine tasting, or bring home one of the 200-plus bottles for sale in the tiny gift shop. There's a free English audioguide. Check online for a calendar of wine tastings and classes offered in English. You can book ahead for lunch, too. (Restaurant open Tuesday through Saturday, noon–3). ■ TIP➜ This is one of the only places in Paris where you'll find a non-dosage (no sugar added) champagne. ✉ *Rue des Eaux/5 sq. Charles Dickens, Passy-Auteil* ☎ *01–45–25–63–26* ⊕ *www.museeduvinparis. com* ✍ *€11.90 with glass of wine; wine tastings €27, admission included* ☉ *Tues.–Sun. 10–6* Ⓜ *Passy.*

Porte Dauphine métro entrance. Visitors come here to snap pictures of the queen of subway entrances, one of the city's two remaining Art Nouveau canopied originals designed by Hector Guimard (the other is at the Abbesses stop on Line 12). The flamboyant "crown" of amber-painted panels and runaway metal struts adorns this whimsical 1900 creation. The entrance is on the Bois de Boulogne side of Avenue Foch, so take the Boulevard de l'Amiral Bruix exit from the Line 2 station.

Rue d'Auteuil. This narrow, crooked shopping street escaped Haussmann's urban renovations and today still retains the country feel of old Auteuil. Molière once lived on the site of No. 2; Racine was on nearby Rue du Buis; the pair met up to clink glasses and exchange drama notes at the Mouton Blanc

DINING AT A GLANCE

For full reviews ⇨ Chapter 14.

EXPENSIVE DINING
Le Pré Catelan, *Modern French,*
Rte. de Surèsnes

13

Inn, now a brasserie, at No. 40. Numbers 19–25 and 29 are an interesting combination of 17th- and 18th-century buildings. At the foot of the street, the scaly dome of the **Église d'Auteuil** (built in the 1880s) is an unmistakable small-time cousin of the Sacré-Coeur. Rue d'Auteuil is at its liveliest on Wednesday and Saturday mornings, when a much-loved street market crams onto Place Jean-Barraud. Ⓜ *MichelAnge Auteuil, Église d'Auteuil.*

Les Jardins du Trocadéro. Nestled just behind the bronze Benjamin Franklin statue where Place Trocadéro turns into rue Benjamin Franklin, this cafe/bar/tearoom has just been magnificently renovated with no spared expense. The pewter countertop, the white custom-made furniture with ginger and tourquoise velvet accent chairs offers the only chic and loungey venue on Place Trocadéro where you can sip a flute of (organic) champagne—and even sign yourself up for a guided champagne tasting tour to Reims or Epernay. It is located on the first floor of the Hotel Eiffel Trocadéro, itself just recently completely renovated top to bottom. Benjamin Franklin, America's first ambassador to France, was a resident of Passy during most of the 9 years he lived in Paris, 1776 to 1785, as was future U.S. President Thomas Jefferson when he arrived in France in 1784 to replace Franklin. ■TIP➔ As you walk down rue Benjamin Franklin towards rue Passy, be sure to notice #25, the celebrated Art Deco building by architect Auguste Perret. ✉ *35 rue Benjamin Franklin, Trocadéro* ☎ *01–53–70–17–70* ⊕ *www.hoteleiffeltrocadero. com* Ⓜ *Trocadéro or Passy.*

Passy Cemetery. Visiting cemeteries in Paris can become addictive. The Passy Cemetery dates to 1821 and sits in the shadows of Trocadéro. Here you'll find the tombstones of famous aristocrats and artists such as composer Claude Debussy and impressionist painters Édouard Manet and Berthe Morisot. ✉ *2 rue du Commandant Schlœsing, Passy* Ⓜ *Trocadéro (lines 6, 9).*

Tenniseum. This sprawling museum hidden underneath the Stade Roland Garros, home to the French Open, claims to house the world's largest collection of tennis memorabilia and historical archives relating to tennis. It also showcases fantastic art and photo exhibits. Even if you aren't a serious tennis buff, the museum is worth the short walk from the metro station. After all, haven't you always wanted to know where that little alligator emblem got its illustrious start? ✉ *2 avenue Gordon-Bennett, Auteil* ☎ *33/01–47–43–48–48* ⊕ *www.fft.fr/site-tenniseum/en/* ✍ *€7.50* ✆ *Wed. and Fri.–Sun. 10–6* Ⓜ *Porte d'Auteil.*

Where to Eat

Updated
by Jennifer
Ditsler-Ladonne

A new wave of culinary confidence has been running through one of the world's great food cities and spilling over both banks of the Seine. Whether cooking up *grand-mère*'s roast chicken and *riz au lait* or placing a whimsical hat of cotton candy atop wild-strawberry-and-rose ice cream, Paris chefs have been breaking free from the tyranny of tradition and following their passions.

Emblematic of this movement is the proliferation of haute cuisine—trained bistro chefs who have opened their own restaurants. Among the newcomers to the bistronomique scene are David Rathgeber, who left Benoît to take over the chic Montparnasse bistro L'Assiette; Mickaël Gaignon, a veteran of Pierre Gagnaire and Le Pré Catelan who now runs the Marais bistro Le Gaigne; and Stéphane Marcouzzi, who was maître d'hôtel at Guy Savoy's Le Cap Vernet before opening L'Epigramme in St-Germain with chef Aymeric Kräml, and now L'Epicuriste, in the 15th arrondissement. But self-expression is not the only driving force behind the current changes. A traditional high-end restaurant can be prohibitively expensive to operate. As a result, more casual bistros and cafés, which often have lower operating costs and higher profit margins, have become attractive businesses for even top chefs.

For tourists, this development can only be good news, because it makes the cooking of geniuses such as Joël Robuchon, Guy Savoy, Alain Senderens, and Pierre Gagnaire more accessible (even if these star chefs rarely cook in their lower-price restaurants).

Like the chefs themselves, Paris diners are breaking away—albeit cautiously—from tradition. New restaurants, wine bars, and rapidly multiplying sandwich shops recognize that not everyone wants a three-course blowout every time they dine out. And because Parisians are more widely traveled than in the past, many ethnic restaurants—notably the best North African, Vietnamese/Laotian, Chinese, Spanish, and Japanese spots—are making fewer concessions to French tastes, resulting in far better food.

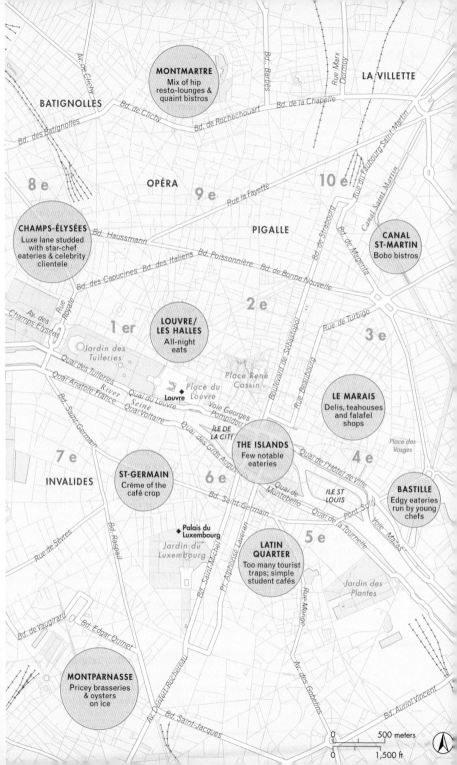

MONTMARTRE
Mix of hip resto-lounges & quaint bistros

LA VILLETTE

BATIGNOLLES

Av. de Clichy

Bd. de Clichy

Bd. des Batignolles

Bd. de la Chapelle

Rue Marx Dormoy

Rue Barbès

Bd. de Rochechouart

8 e

OPÉRA

9 e

Rue la Fayette

10 e

Rue du Faubourg Saint-Martin

Canal Saint-Martin

Bd. Haussmann

PIGALLE

CHAMPS-ÉLYSÉES
Luxe lane studded with star-chef eateries & celebrity clientele

Bd. des Capucines   Bd. des Italiens   Bd. Poissonnière   Bd. de Bonne Nouvelle

Av. des Champs-Élysées

Rue Royale

1 er

2 e

Bd. de Strasbourg

Bd. de Magenta

CANAL ST-MARTIN
Bobo bistros

LOUVRE/ LES HALLES
All-night eats

Rue de Turbigo

3 e

Jardin des Tuileries

Quai des Tuileries

Quai Anatole France

River Seine

Quai du Louvre

Place René Cassin

Boulevard de Sébastopol

Rue Beaubourg

LE MARAIS
Delis, teahouses and falafel shops

Bd. Saint-Germain

Quai Voltaire

Place du Louvre

Louvre

Voie Georges Pompidou

ÎLE DE LA CITÉ

Quai des Grands Augustins

Place des Vosges

7 e

INVALIDES

ST-GERMAIN
Créme of the café crop

6 e

Bd. Saint-Germain

THE ISLANDS
Few notable eateries

Quai de l'Hôtel de Ville

4 e

Quai de Montebello

ÎLE ST LOUIS

BASTILLE
Edgy eateries run by young chefs

Rue de Sèvres

Bd. Raspail

Palais du Luxembourg

Pt. Alphonse Laveran

Rue St-Michel

Quai de la Tournelle

Pont Sully

Voie Mazas

Jardin du Luxembourg

LATIN QUARTER
Too many tourist traps; simple student cafés

5 e

Rue Monge

Jardin des Plantes

Bd. de Vaugirard

Bd. Edgar Quinet

MONTPARNASSE
Pricey brasseries & oysters on ice

Av. Denfert-Rochereau

Bd. Saint-Jacques

Av. des Gobelins

Bd. Auriol Vincent

0   500 meters
0   1,500 ft

PLANNING

WINE BARS

For tantalizing wines, good food, and great value, look no further than one of Paris's many wine bars. The past 10 years have seen an explosion of a new kind of *bar à vins,* or, more accurately, *cave à manger*—essentially amplified wine shops with a few tables, which serve a plate or two of regional cheeses or artisanal charcuterie to complement the wines. The new generation of *cavists* stood apart as champions of natural wines, which are unfiltered, contain minimal or no added sulphites, and are often *bio* (organic) or grown biodynamically: according to a specific set of agricultural guidelines. As the natural wine movement dovetailed with the crusade toward simply prepared foods made from quality seasonal ingredients, the contemporary wine bar was born. Indeed, the food in a handful of wine bars now rivals that in the best Paris bistros—and can be a lot more affordable. Whatever the emphasis, the upward trajectory of the wine bar has had a major hand in reinvigorating Paris's wine and food scene.

Wine bars usually keep restaurant hours (12–2 pm and 7:30–11 pm); some combine with an *épicerie* (gourmet grocer), stay open all day, and close earlier in the evening; others offer a late-night scene. Although casual, most wine bars nowadays require reservations, so call in advance, especially if Sunday brunch is available—still a rarity in Paris. Look for the "wine bar" designation in our restaurant listings.

CHILDREN

Some restaurants provide booster seats, but don't count on them: be sure to ask when you confirm your reservation.

DINING STRATEGY

Where should we eat? With thousands of Paris eateries competing for your attention, it may seem like a daunting question. But fret not—our expert writers and editors have done the legwork. The 120-plus selections here represent the best this city has to offer. Search our "Best Bets" for top recommendations by price, cuisine, and experience; read about local flavors in the neighborhood features; or find a review in the listings, arranged by neighborhood. Delve in, and enjoy!

HOURS

Paris restaurants generally serve food from noon to 2 pm and from 7:30 or 8 pm to about 11 pm. Brasseries have longer hours and often serve all day and late into the evening; some are open 24 hours. Surprisingly, many restaurants close on Saturday as well as Sunday, and Monday closings are also not uncommon. July and August are common months for annual closings, but restaurants may also close for a week in February, around Easter, or at Christmas.

MENUS

All establishments must post menus outside so they're available to look over before you enter. Most have two basic types of menu: à la carte and fixed price (*prix fixe, le menu,* or *la formule*). Although it limits your choices, the prix fixe is usually the best value. If you feel like indulging, the *menu dégustation* (tasting menu), consisting of numerous small courses, lets you sample the chef's offerings. *See the Menu Guide at the back of this book for guidance with common French menu items.*

RESERVATIONS

Restaurant staff will nearly always greet you with the phrase *"Avez-vous réservé?"* (Have you reserved?) and a confident *"Oui"* is the best answer, even in a neighborhood bistro. Although some wine bars do not take reservations, many do, so call and check.

SMOKING

Many Parisians are accustomed to smoking before, during, and after meals, but in January 2008 the national smoking ban was extended to restaurants, bars, and cafés. Many establishments have compensated by adding covered terraces for smokers, but you'll be happy to know that inside, the air is much clearer.

14

TIPPING AND TAXES

According to French law, prices must include tax and tip (*service compris or prix nets*), but pocket change left on the table in cafés, or an additional 5% in better restaurants, is always appreciated. Beware of bills stamped "Service Not Included" in English or restaurants slyly using American-style credit-card slips, hoping that you'll be confused and add the habitual 15% tip.

WHAT IT COSTS

You'll be lucky to find a good bistro meal for €25 or less, even at lunch, so consider economizing on some meals to have more to spend on the others. Slurping inexpensive Japanese noodles on Rue Ste-Anne or having a picnic in a park at lunch will save euros for dinner. And, of course, if you've rented an apartment, you can shop at the city's wonderful markets and cook a few meals at "home." *Prices in the reviews are the average cost of a main course at dinner or, if dinner is not served, at lunch.*

WHAT TO WEAR

Casual dress is acceptable at all but the fanciest restaurants—this usually means stylish sportswear, which might be a bit dressier than in the U.S. When in doubt, leave the T-shirts and sneakers behind. If an establishment requires jacket and tie, it's noted in the review.

WINE

Most sommeliers are knowledgeable about their lists and can make appropriate suggestions after you've made your tastes and budget known. Simpler spots serve wine in carafes (*en carafe,* or *en pichet*). Many restaurants now sell wine by the glass, but prices can be steep; be sure to do the math.

BEST BETS FOR PARIS DINING

With thousands of restaurants to choose from, how will you decide where to eat? Fodor's writers and editors have selected their favorite restaurants by price, cuisine, and experience below. You can also search by neighborhood for excellent eating experiences—peruse the following pages for spotlights on specific neighborhoods.

Fodor'sChoice ★

Guy Savoy, $$$$, p. 244

Hiramatsu, $$$$, p. 234

Il Vino, $$$, p. 232

L'Arpège, $$$$, p. 233

L'Astrance, $$$$, p. 235

Le Baratin, $$, p. 252

Le Bistrot Paul Bert, $$, p. 250

Le Cinq, $$$$, p. 245

Mon Vieil Ami, $$, p. 274

Pierre Gagnaire, $$$$ p. 247

Rech, $$$, p. 247

Spring, $$$$, p. 242

Zen, $, p. 243

By Price

$

Au Passage, p. 254

Breizh Cafe, p. 260

Café des Musées, p. 261

Cantine Merci, p. 261

Dong Huong, p. 254

Higuma, p. 267

L'As du Fallafel, p. 262

La Crêperie Josselin, p. 265

Le Café Constant, p. 231

$$

Aux Lyonnais, p. 266

Drouant, p. 266

Frenchie, p. 238

L'Ardoise, p. 240

La Bourse ou la Vie, p. 240

Les Papilles, p. 258

Mon Vieil Ami, p. 274

Ribouldingue, p. 258

Rose Bakery, p. 264

$$$

Guilo Guilo, p. 263

L'Atelier de Joël Robuchon, p. 271

Rech, p. 247

Saturne, p. 268

$$$$

Guy Savoy, p. 244

L'Abeille, p. 235

L'Arpège, p. 233

L'Astrance, p. 235

Pierre Gagnaire, p. 247

Spring, p. 242

By Type

BISTRO

Philou, $$, p. 253

Benoît, $$$, p. 260

Frenchie, $$, p. 238

Jadis, $$, p. 230

Josephine Chez Dumonet, $$, p. 271

La Table Lauriston, $$, p. 235

Le Café Constant, $, p. 231

BRASSERIE

La Coupole, $$, p. 265

Le Dôme, $$$, p. 265

CAFÉ

Café de Flore, $$, p. 269

CHINESE

La Chine Massena, $, p. 259

FRENCH FUSION

Hiramatsu, $$$$, p. 234

Il Vino, $$$, p. 232

Stella Maris, $$$, p. 248

Yam'Tcha, $$$, p. 239

Sola, $$$, p. 259

JAPANESE

Guilo Guilo, $$$, p. 263

Higuma, $, p. 267

Kifune, $$$, p. 244

Yen, $$$, p. 273

Zen, $, p. 243

LATIN AMERICAN

Unico, $$, p. 251

MIDDLE EASTERN

L'As du Fallafel, $, p. 262

MODERN

Drouant, $$, p. 266
KGB, $$$, p. 271
L'Atelier de Joël Robuchon, $$$, p. 271
Ze Kitchen Galerie, $$$, p. 259

NORTH AFRICAN

Chez Omar, $, p. 255
Le Martel, $, p. 255

SEAFOOD

Huîtrerie Régis, $$, p. 270
L'Huîtrier, $$, p. 244
Le Dôme, $$$, p. 265
Rech, $$$, p. 247

SPANISH

Fogón St-Julien, $$$, p. 255

VEGETARIAN

Cantine Merci, $, p. 261
L'Arpège, $$$$, p. 233
L'As du Fallafel, $, p. 262
La Bastide Odéon, $$, p. 272
Macéo, $$$, p. 241
Rose Bakery, $$, p. 264

SOUTHEAST ASIAN

Citronelle et Galanga, $, p. 238
Dong Huong, $, p. 254

By Experience

CHILD-FRIENDLY

Bofinger, $$, p. 249
Breizh Café, $, p. 260
La Coupole, $$, p. 265
La Crêperie Josselin, $, p. 265
Le Troquet, $$, p. 231
Rose Bakery, $$, p. 264

DESSERT

Alain Ducasse au Plaza Athénée, $$$$, p. 243
Josephine Chez Dumonet, $$, p. 271
Pierre Gagnaire, $$$$, p. 247
Taillevent, $$$$, p. 248

DINING ALONE

Breizh Café, $, p. 260
Cantine Merci, $, p. 261
L'Ambassade d'Auvergne, $$, p. 262
Rose Bakery, $$, p. 264

DINNER PRIX FIXE

Spring, $$$$, p. 242
Philou, $$, p. 253
Le Troquet, $$, p. 231
Le Vaudeville, $$, p. 268
Ribouldingue, $$, p. 258

EXPENSE ACCOUNT

Alain Ducasse au Plaza Athénée, $$$$, p. 243
L'Abeille, $$$$, p. 235
L'Arôme, $$$, p. 244
La Fermette Marbeuf, $$, p. 245
Pierre Gagnaire, $$$$, p. 247

GREAT VIEW

Lapérouse, $$$, p. 257
La Tour d'Argent, $$$$, p. 256
Le Georges, $$, p. 239
Le Jules Verne, $$$$, p. 231

HOT SPOT

L'Atelier de Joël Robuchon, $$$, p. 271
Le Dauphin, $, p. 252
Le Murano, $$$, p. 262
Mini Palais, $$, p. 247
Thoumieux, $$$, p. 233

LATE-NIGHT

Au Pied de Cochon, $$, p. 238
Bofinger, $$, p. 249
Julien, $$, p. 267
La Coupole, $$, p. 265
Le Vaudeville, $$, p. 268

LOTS OF LOCALS

Josephine Chez Dumonet, $$, p. 271
La Ferrandaise, $$, p. 272

Le Petit Rétro, $$, p. 237
Unico, $$, p. 251

LUNCH PRIX FIXE

Au Passage, $, p. 254
Café des Musées, $, p. 261
La Boulangerie, $, p. 254
Le Pré Verre, $$, p. 257
Le Repaire de Cartouche, $$, p. 250
Taillevent, $$$$, p. 248
Willi's Wine Bar, $, p. 242

MOST ROMANTIC

Lapérouse, $$$, p. 257
La Tour d'Argent, $$$$, p. 256
Le Pré Catelan, $$$$, p. 274

NEWCOMERS

Au Passage, $ p. 254
Jeanne A, $ p. 252
Le Dauphin, $, p. 252
Saturne, $$$ p. 268
Septime, $$, p. 251
Verjus Bar à Vins, $, p. 242

OUTDOOR DINING

Au Bourguignon du Marais, $$, p. 260
Le Georges, $$, p. 239
Le Pré Catelan, $$$$, p. 274
Mini Palais, $$, p. 247

14

ST-GERMAIN AND MONTPARNASSE
6E, 14E ARRONDISSEMENTS

Small bistros are moving into the spotlight in St-Germain, and crêpe stands, fish restaurants, and oyster bars attest to the Breton influence around Montparnasse.

Whether you're sipping rich hot chocolate at Les Deux Magots, diving into a platter of *choucroute garnie* at La Coupole, or slurping *fines de claires* at the pristine oyster bar Régis, it's hard not to feel part of the café culture in St-Germain and Montparnasse. Along the broad boulevards you can find some of the city's classic brasseries. But as much fun as these are for their storied settings and buzzy atmospheres, some of the area's best food is found at small bistros on narrow side streets. St-Germain is enjoying a revival as a foodie haunt, with Yves Camdeborde's Le Comptoir du Relais Saint-Germain the perfect example of the kind of market-inspired bistro that Parisians (and foreigners) adore. For a change of pace, try freshly made *galettes* (buckwheat crêpes) washed down with dry cider at La Crêperie Josselin or another of Boulevard du Montparnasse's many crêperies.

BRINY BLISS

Ever since the first trains from Brittany brought oyster-loving settlers to Montparnasse, the neighborhood has had a proud seafood tradition. The best oysters come from Normandy, Brittany, or Marennes-Oléron on the Atlantic coast. The knobbly shelled *creuses* are more common than the rounder *plates*, which are beloved by connoisseurs. Oysters can be dressed with vinegar and shallots, but a squeeze of lemon—or nothing at all—is probably the best accompaniment. Scoop the raw oyster from its shell with a small fork, slurp the juice, and chew a little before swallowing the taste of the sea.

CLASSIC CAFÉ ITEMS

THE ITEM	WHERE TO GET IT	WHY THERE?
Omelet	The Café de Flore (✉ 172 bd. St-Germain, 6e ☎ 01-45-48-55-26), the last classic café that attracts genuine Left Bank intellectuals.	The omelet arrives pale on the outside and slightly runny within—that is, perfect. Try ham and cheese or, for a splurge, crabmeat.
Chocolat chaud	Ladurée (✉ 6 rue Royale, 8e ☎ 01-42-60-21-79), one of the oldest and prettiest tea salons in Paris.	Thick, rich, and served in a lovely silver pitcher. Alongside a raspberry mille-feuille or an airy, salted caramel macaron, it's pure bliss.
Choucroute garnie	La Coupole (✉ 102 bd. du Montparnasse, 14e ☎ 01-43-20-14-20), the Art Deco brasserie that never fails to entertain.	The choucroute garnie brings you heaps of sauerkraut topped with chunks of pork and sausages.

SWEETS

What does St-Germain have over the rest of Paris? In a word: chocolate, with seven world-class chocolatiers in a single square mile. But choosing between **Christian Constant's** (✉ 37 rue d'Assas, 6e ☎ 01-53-63-15-15 Ⓜ Saint-Placide) famously perfumed ganaches, **Pierre Marcolini's** (✉ 89 rue de Seine, 6e ☎ 01-44-07-39-07 Ⓜ Mabillon, Odéon) bittersweet truffles, or **Jean-Paul Hévin's** (✉ 3 rue Vavin, 6e ☎ 01-43-54-09-85 Ⓜ Vavin) hazelnut-studded *rochers* ("rocks") is another matter. Also worth checking out are **Patrick Roger** (✉ 108 bd. St-Germain, 6e ☎ 01-43-29-38-42 Ⓜ Odéon) and **Jean-Charles Rochoux** (✉ 16 rue d'Assas, 6e ☎ 01-42-84-29-45 Ⓜ Rennes), as well as household names, like legendary **Maison du Chocolat** (✉ 19 rue de Sèvres, 6e ☎ 01-45-44-20-40 Ⓜ Sevres-Babylone) or rock-star pâtissier **Pierre Hermé** (✉ 72 rue Bonaparte, 6e ☎ 01-43-54-47-77 Ⓜ St-Sulpice).

PIQUE-NIQUE IN THE PARC

Everything you need for the perfect Luxembourg Gardens picnic is just minutes away from the park. For cheese, **Fromagerie Quatrehomme** (✉ 62 rue de Sèvres ☎ 01-47-34-33-45). For cured meats and sparkling water, **Bon Marché's Grande Epicerie** (✉ 38 rue de Sèvres ☎ 01-44-39-81-00). For sourdough bread, **Boulangerie Poilâne** (✉ 8 rue du Cherche-Midi ☎ 01-45-48-42-59). For something sinfully sweet, **Pâtissiere Pierre Hermé** (✉ 72 rue Bonaparte ☎ 01-43-54-47-77).

THE LATIN QUARTER AND THE ISLANDS
5E, 13E ARRONDISSEMENTS

Whether you're seeking a cheap Chinese eatery or a table for two at La Tour d'Argent, the Latin Quarter dishes up something for every taste and budget.

Thanks to its student population, the Latin Quarter caters to those on a budget with kebab shops, crêpe stands, Asian fast-food joints, and no-nonsense bistros. Look beyond the pedestrian streets such as Rue de la Huchette and Rue Mouffetard for less touristy eateries preferred by locals. As you might expect in an area known for its *gauche caviar* (wealthy intellectuals who vote Socialist), the Latin Quarter brims with atmospheric places to linger over a tiny cup of black coffee. Top-notch bistros lurk in the nearby but off-the-beaten-track 13^e arrondissement, which is also home to the city's most authentic Chinese, Vietnamese, and Laotian restaurants along Avenue d'Ivry. Wander across the Seine to the Ile St-Louis for a meal in a long-established brasserie or classy bistro.

SECRET CELLAR

Few restaurants in Paris have a more storied history than the Seine-side **Tour d'Argent** (⊠ *15 quai de la Tournelle* ☎ *01–43–54–23–31*). It opened in 1780, only to be burned down nine years later by the same Revolutionaries who set the Bastille ablaze. When Paris was occupied by the Germans during World War II, La Tour was plundered by Nazi officers who helped themselves to 80,000 bottles of wine. Little did they know that most of the restaurant's laughably large stock of wine was safely hidden behind a brick wall. Today the wine cellar contains almost 400,000 bottles of the world's finest wines.

UNCOVERING THE QUARTIER

DODGING THE "FAUX BISTRO"

Is it a genuine bistro? It's often hard to tell. Tourist traps can seem thoroughly charming until the food arrives. The Quartier Latin is dangerous rip-off territory, but there are some sure bets: around Notre-Dame, try **Le Pré Verre** (✉ *8 rue Thénard* ☎ *01–43–54–59–47*), where Philippe Delacourcelle tinkers successfully with Asian spices, and the Lyonnais-style bistro **Ribouldingue** (✉ *10 rue St-Julien Le Pauvre* ☎ *01–46–33–98–80*), where the €28 prix fixe is one of the area's best bargains. You'll also find a few honest, old-fashioned bistros like **Au Moulin à Vent ("Chez Henri")** (✉ *20 rue des Fossés St-Bernard* ☎ *01–43–54–99–37*) and **La Rôtisserie du Beaujolais** (✉ *19 quai de la Tournelle* ☎ *01–43–54–17–47*), an annex of La Tour d'Argent. Tread carefully on the Ile St-Louis: star Alsatian chef Antoine Westermann's **Mon Vieil Ami** (✉ *69 rue St-Louis-en-l'Ile* ☎ *01–40–46–01–35*) is the most reliable choice.

THE ANATOMY OF A TABAC

In their primary function, selling cigarettes, *tabacs* play an essential role in the lives of many Parisians, but they're indispensable to those who don't smoke, too. At the small counter where customers pick up Gitanes or Marlboros, you also can buy métro or lottery tickets, phone cards, batteries, and chewing gum. Next to this counter is a bar perfect for a quick drink, like the one Audrey Tautou imbibed at the **Le Verre à Pied** (✉ *118 bis, rue Mouffetard*) in the film *Amélie*. *Tabacs* often sell newspapers, which you can read while perched at the bar sipping an *express* (strong black coffee). Food can be surprisingly palatable in *tabacs*—expect anything from a *jambon-beurre* (a ham sandwich) to hearty dishes such as boeuf Bourguignon. Many *tabacs*, like **Romieu Alban** (✉ *45 rue Bonaparte* ☎ *01–43–26–00–11*), attract a variety of regulars, from moneyed businessmen to *les sans-abri* (the homeless), who joke and drink together.

14

SWEETS

The moss wall murals are the first clue that this is not your everyday pastry shop. **Sadaharu Aoki** (✉ *56 bd. de Port-Royal, 5e* ☎ *01–45–35–36–80* Ⓜ *Gobelins*; also ✉ *35 rue de Vaugirard, 6e* ☎ *01–45–44–48–90* and ✉ *25 rue Pérignon, 15e* ☎ *01–42–53–05–91*) earned his reputation in the rarified world of top *pâtissiers* by combining a pared-down aesthetic with rigorous French technique and using traditional Japanese ingredients like *yuzu*—a tart citrus fruit—red bean, black sesame, and *matcha* (powdered green tea), which work exceptionally well with rich French-style ganaches and chocolate. For the *duomo mâcha azuki*, grass-green matcha's pleasant bitterness pairs beautifully with mellow white chocolate cream and a just-sweet red-bean center. Take home a sachet of tart, bite-size, yuzu-flavor pound cakes, some green tea–enhanced chocolate tablettes, or any of a dozen small pastries individually wrapped for snacking on the go.

THE MARAIS, BASTILLE, NATION
3E, 4E, 11E, 12E, 20E ARRONDISSEMENTS

The center of Jewish and gay life in Paris, the Marais is the place to find the best falafel in town and some great bistro fare, too. Farther east, the Bastille area has attracted more than its share of gifted young chefs.

The once run-down Marais is now the epitome of chic, but you can still find reminders of its down-to-earth past along Rue des Rosiers, where falafel shops and Eastern European delis jostle with designer boutiques. Ambitious restaurants are few and far between in the Marais, but the popular Breizh Café attracts many with its inexpensive and authentic *galettes* (buckwheat crêpes) made with quality ingredients. The bistro scene gets interesting east of the Bastille, where lower rents have encouraged young chefs to set up shop. Around Père Lachaise the selection thins, but wander a little farther to multicultural Belleville to find an intriguing mix of Chinese and North African eateries.

TARTE TATIN

For the perfect *tarte tatin*, which is like an upside-down apple pie, take a seat at the horseshoe-shaped bar of **Le Petit Fer à Cheval** (✉ *30 rue Vieille-du-Temple* ☎ *01–42–72–47–47*). The restaurant's recipe calls for juicy Gala apples, which produce a buttery, cara-melized tarte that is served warm and pairs perfectly with a glass of hot wine. The *tarte* was first dis-covered by mistake in the 19th century at the Hôtel Tatin in Lamotte-Beuvron—the product of a botched apple pie recipe. It can be made with other fruit—like pineapple or pears—but nothing beats the classic, faithfully reproduced at this Marais café.

MARAIS NOSHES

	THE OBVIOUS CHOICE	DON'T FORGET
L'As du Fallafel 34 rue de Rosiers	The falafel special, a packed pita with chickpea and herb balls, eggplant, harissa, hummus, and tahini.	Napkins and a glass of fresh-squeezed lemonade help tame this greasy feast.
Chez Marianne 2 rue Hospitalières St-Gervais	Chopped liver. Who'd have thought that chicken livers and onion fried in melted goose fat could ever taste this good?	A more genteel version of pastrami than the slabs of fatty meat you'll find back home, it'll satisfy any deli devotee.
Korcarz 29 rue de Rosiers	A loaf of shiny, sweet, and delicious challah. For best results, take the bread back to your hotel room and dip in salt and honey.	A pletzl, a small onion roll that—surprisingly—tastes great with jam for breakfast.

SWEETS

Master *chocolatier-pâtissièr* **Jacques Genin** (✉ *133 rue de Turenne, Marais* ☎ *01-45-77-29-01* M *Filles du Calvaire*) deserves the *legion d'honneur* for his efforts to restore great traditional French pastries to their classic form, particularly the august mille-feuille. Genin's stripped-down version disposes with the usual bells and whistles—fresh fruit, custard, chocolate—to achieve a scintillating clarity: layers of lightly caramelized *pâte feuilletée*, a buttery puff pastry, and an ethereal, barely sweet pastry cream in either vanilla, caramel, or praline. All of the glorious pastries in this tearoom-chocolate-boutique-pastry shop (probably the most beautiful in Paris, by the way) are available for takeaway, but this one is assembled to order and is best eaten fresh on the premises. Along with a cup of Genin's bittersweet hot chocolate, well, you get the picture. Oh, yes, and then there are the chocolates, some of Paris's finest.

FANTASTIQUE THREE: THE RUE PAUL BERT

This side street between Bastille and Nation is home to three local favorites. **Bistrot Paul Bert** (✉ *18 rue Paul Bert* ☎ *01-43-72-24-01*) boasts bistro classics, and its seafood annex, **L'Ecailler du Bistrot** (✉ *22 rue Paul Bert* ☎ *01-43-72-76-77*), serves exemplary oysters. And the Argentinian **Unico** (✉ *15 rue Paul Bert* ☎ *01-43-67-68-08*) draws hungry hordes for its charcoal-grilled steaks.

14

MONTMARTRE, CANAL ST-MARTIN, NORTHEAST PARIS
10E, 18E, 19E ARRONDISSEMENTS

Perched above central Paris, Montmartre is buzzing with a hip vibe, and cutting-edge cafés are springing up along the banks of the Canal St-Martin.

Idyllic as the portrayal of Montmartre might seem in Jean-Pierre Jeunet's film *Amélie*, it's surprisingly close to reality. One of the most desirable areas in Paris, Montmartre seamlessly blends the trendy and the traditional. Less picturesque is the neighborhood around Gare du Nord and Gare de l'Est, but you can still find classic brasseries and tucked-away bistros, as well as the city's most authentic Indian restaurants. Head over to the up-and-coming Canal St-Martin to watch Parisian *bobos*, or bohemian bourgeois, in action. The area is home to fashion designers, artists, and media folk who make the most of the waterside cafés on sunny days. Restaurants are sparse in the undiscovered Buttes Chaumont area, but you won't have to worry about stumbling onto a tourist rip-off.

GARE GRUB

If you're catching the Eurostar at Gare du Nord, it's worth planning ahead to fit in one last feast. Across the street from the train station, **Terminus Nord** (⌧ *23 rue de Dunkerque* ☎ *01–42–85–05–15*) is a classic Art Deco brasserie where you can treat yourself to a seafood platter, bouillabaisse, or *sole meunière* before indulging in another house specialty, crêpes Suzette (flambéed in Grand Marnier). Just a few blocks farther, try the acclaimed **Chez Casimir** (⌧ 6 rue Belzunce ☎ *01–48–78–28–80*), run by the Breton chef Thierry Breton *(above)*.

CANAL-SIDE CAFÉS

More laid-back than the Seine with its vehicle-clogged *quais*, the Canal St-Martin attracts artsy young professionals who scorn the self-consciously elegant Rive Gauche. Its once-vibrant live music scene has been quelled somewhat in the last few years by the city's noise restrictions, but that hasn't made the cafés any less entertaining. At the scruffy, long-established **La Patache** (✉ *60 rue de Lancry* ☎ *01–42–08–14–35*), the owner provides scraps of paper at each table for note writing, in case customers feel too coy to speak to each other. Bohemian institution **Chez Adel** (✉ *10 rue de la Grange aux Belles* ☎ *01–42–08–24–61*) holds live concerts Tuesday to Saturday and avant-garde theater on Sunday. The café of choice on the water is **Chez Prune** (✉ *36 rue Beaurepaire, 10e* ☎ *01–42–41–30–47*), whose terrace is overrun with locals as soon as a ray of sunshine emerges.

THE "NEW MONTMARTRE"

At the Montmartre restaurant **Guilo Guilo** (✉ *8 rue Garreau* ☎ *01–42–54–23–92*), a handful of diners perch around the counter while a Japanese chef who made his name in Kyoto turns out plate after perfect plate of inventive food (a signature dish is his foie gras sushi). Guilo Guilo is typical of the "new Montmartre," which stands in stark contrast to the area's ancient cobbled streets. The district's hip young population occupies the area, perfectly representing 21st-century Paris: nostalgic yet forward-thinking. **Café Burq** (✉ *6 rue Burq* ☎ *01–42–52–81–27*) is a popular, slightly less ambitious Montmartre hangout. Owned by an architect and an actor, it buzzes with a fashionable crowd that comes for the 1970s decor but also for the satisfying bistro fare. On the other side of the *Butte Montmartre*, the friendly **Café Arrosé** (✉ *123 rue Caulaincourt* ☎ *01–42–57–14–30*) proves that even this once-sleepy part of Montmartre is coming to life.

SWEETS

To really know Paris is to know her great *boulangeries*, a tradition in free fall since the advent of that notorious cricket bat, the industrial baguette. Thankfully there's an ever-growing group of bakers carrying the flame, literally, as **Véronique Mauclerc** (✉ *83 rue de Crimée, Eastern Paris/Canal St-Martin* ☎ *01–42–40–64–55* Ⓜ *Botzaris*; Patisserie Véronique Mauclerc: ✉ *11 rue Poncelet, 17e* ☎ *01–42–27–81–83*), one of the very best, makes her breads, classic *viennoiserie* (croissants, turnovers, pain au chocolat), and savory tarts on the premises in a traditional wood-fired oven using only organic flour and natural ferments for leavening. As if this weren't enough, her pastries are a triumph. The fine traditional Paris Brest—a slightly sweet, hazelnut cream-filled *pâte à choux* sprinkled with slivered almonds—sells out quickly, as do the excellent mini chocolate cakes and fruit strudels. Although out of the way, being two steps from the lovely Buttes Chaumont makes it picnic perfect.

14

CHAMPS-ÉLYSÉES AND WESTERN PARIS

8E, 16E, 17E ARRONDISSEMENTS

Style often wins out over substance around the Champs-Élysées, but a handful of luxury restaurants continue to defy fashion.

Perma-tans and Botox are de rigueur at fashionable restaurants near the Champs-Élysées, where the St-Tropez set picks at dishes with names like "le tigre qui pleure," the weeping tiger, a Thai-style beef dish. Yet this part of Paris is also home to many of the city's most ambitious chefs, whose restaurants are surrounded by palatial hotels, bourgeois apartments, embassies, and luxury boutiques. Some, such as Eric Frechon at Le Bristol, offer sophisticated updates of French classics, whereas others, like Pierre Gagnaire, constantly push culinary boundaries in the manner of a mad scientist. A few solid bistros survive here, notably the Art Deco Savy. Unlike the uniformly chic 16^e, the 17^e arrondissement has its bourgeois and its bohemian sides. Head over to Batignolles, where an organic market takes place on Saturday, to discover up-and-coming neighborhood bistros.

FIT FOR A KING

In a neighborhood rich in landmarks yet lacking in casual, affordable eateries, Mini Palais graciously fills in all the blanks. After a complete makeover in 2010, the restaurant reopened with the imprimatur of superstar chef Eric Fréchon (notably of Le Bristol), who designed the menu. It's a lively spot for a fashionable crowd at dinnertime, but the real draw is nonstop service 7 days a week from 10 am to 2 am, when good food in Paris is nearly impossible to find. In warm weather, the restaurant's soaring balcony is a destination unto itself.

MUSEUM DINING

Most Paris museums offer a passable café, but sometimes a top-notch lunch, teatime or even dinner is just the thing after a few hours of museum going. For a good meal in a superb environment, these spots can't be beat, even if you don't buy a ticket.

Musée Jacquemart-André Café: Housed in the mansion's original dining room—with marble-topped tables, painted ceilings and murals—the excellent salads and daily plat du jour make this lovely café a favorite with Parisian ladies who lunch, whether or not they've seen the show. Wonderful for teatime or a copious prix-fixe brunch on Saturday and Sunday. ⊠ *158 boulevard Haussmann, 8e* ☎ *01–45–62–11–59* Ⓜ *Miromesnil* ⊕ *musee-jacquemart-andre.com.*

Les Arts Décoratifs, Le Saut Loup: The menu here reflects the décor—elegant and contemporary. A sleek upstairs lounge has great views of the Eiffel Tower and the Louvre, and the outdoor terrace, part of the Tuilerie gardens, is one of the nicest in Paris. Afternoon tea is served, too. Museum entrance not necessary, but a slight discount is offered on prix-fixe menus with a ticket. ⊠ *107 Rue de Rivoli, 1e* ☎ *01–42–25–49–55* Ⓜ *Palais Royal* ⊕ *lesautduloup.com.*

Musée du Quai Branly, Les Ombres: The magnificent glass-ceilinged dining room, designed by museum architect Jean Nouvel, is perched atop the museum and boasts a gastronomic restaurant with some of the best views of Paris and the Eiffel Tower. Good prix-fixe deals on lunch, dinner, and teatime and a roomy outdoor terrace. ⊠ *27 Quai Branly, 7e* ☎ *01–47–53–68–00* Ⓜ *Alma-Marceau* ⊕ *lesombres-restaurant.com.*

Musee d'Orsay: A classified historic monument, the soaring ceilings, chandeliers, gilding, and murals are part of the original train station's dining room. Open for lunch every day, and dinner on Thursday, the classic French fare is punctuated by a special dish inspired by the museum program. ⊠ *1 rue de la Légion d'Honneur, 7e* ☎ *01–45–49–47–03* Ⓜ *Solférino* ⊕ *musee-orsay.fr.*

14

SWEETS

It's no accident that **Ladurée** (⊠ *75 av. des Champs-Élysées, 8e* ☎ *01–40–75–08–75* Ⓜ *Georges V,* or ⊠ *16 rue Royale, 8e* ☎ *01–42–60–21–79 RER: Louvre-Tuileries; Madeleine, Concord,* or ⊠ *21 rue Bonaparte, 6e* ☎ *01–44–07–64–93)* is almost as well known overseas as it is in Paris. Having nearly 150 years to foster brand recognition helps, but the top-notch confections, and three of Paris's loveliest tearooms, clinch it. And Ladurée has deftly moved with the times, hiring fashion superstars like Lacroix, Galliano, and Louboutin to design eye-popping packaging for their superb *macarons*. Try the Isphahan, a rose-scented *macaron* filled with rose cream and fresh raspberries, or the excellent mille-feuilles, one with raspberry and vanilla cream, the other a classic *caramel au beurre salé.* To enjoy a *carré chocolat* (chocolate cake, chocolate ganache, and chocolate cream) over a cup of the famously rich hot chocolate or a raspberry-passion fruit tart and a glass of champagne? That's Paris.

THE EIFFEL TOWER AND LES INVALIDES

7E, 15E ARRONDISSEMENTS

Lively bistros and daring contemporary restaurants bring unexpected exuberance to the otherwise sedate streets around the Eiffel Tower and in the sprawling, residential 15e.

Eerily quiet as it might sometimes seem, the 7e arrondissement has a food-loving population of locals and tourists who pack its best restaurants nightly. Since money is rarely an object in this area, you can find everything from top-notch contemporary restaurants—L'Arpège, 144 Petrossian, Gaya Rive Gauche, and L'Atelier de Joël Robuchon—to nostalgic bistros like Thoumieux and Le Café Constant, which appeal to aristocratic residents with comfort-food cravings. The 15e arrondissement is known for quaint eateries that provide great value for the money. Even its unlovely outer reaches are filled with warm bistros like Jadis and Afaria. Explore the little-known area around Avenue Émile Zola to find the city's best Middle Eastern restaurants.

JOYEUX JOËL

Tomato jelly topped with avocado puree? Thin-crusted mackerel tart? One of the best things about eating at **L'Atelier de Joël Robuchon** (✉ *5 rue Montalembert* ☎ *01–42–22–56–56*) is your position on the U-shaped bar, which encourages you to share opinions—or even a bite—of this cutting-edge fare with your neighbor. Creative small plates, like a flavor-packed little tower of roasted eggplant, zucchini, and tomato layered with buffalo mozzarella, or smoked foie gras and caramelized eel, make it clear that L'Atelier really is an artist's workshop.

CULINARY TRENDSETTERS

THE LEEK—C'EST CHIC

Vegetarianism was so uncommon in Paris that star chef Alain Passard caused a sensation when he declared a few years ago that he was bored with red meat and would be focusing on vegetables and fish. True to his word, Passard established a small farm outside Paris where he grows heirloom vegetables that are whizzed to his restaurant **L'Arpège** (⊠ *84 rue Varenne* ☎ *01–45–51–47–33*) by high-speed train. Customers pay the price; a simple yet sensational beet dish costs €45. Though Paris is hardly a vegetarian paradise, Passard's initiative seems to have rubbed off on other chefs in the 7ᵉ. **Le Violon d'Ingres** (⊠ *135 rue St-Dominique* ☎ *01–45–55–15–05*) and **L'Atelier de Joël Robuchon** (⊠ *5 rue Montalembert* ☎ *01–42–22–56–56*) both cater, with imagination, to vegetarians.

A CONSTANT CONNECTION

During the 1980s Christian Constant trained a group of young chefs at the Hôtel Crillon who would go on to open their own trendsetting bistros, among them Yves Camdeborde (Le Comptoir), Christian Etchebest (Le Troquet), and Rodolphe Paquin (Le Repaire de Cartouche). Despite cherishing his mentor role, Constant still has a thriving career of his own. In 2006 he did away with the lobster dishes and wall-to-wall carpeting at his **Le Violon d'Ingres** (⊠ *135 rue St-Dominique* ☎ *01–45–55–15–05*), transforming it into a happening bistro with a single €45 set menu that doesn't skimp on high-quality ingredients. He also runs three other successful restaurants in the same street: the no-reservations **Café Constant** (⊠ *139 rue St-Dominique* ☎ *01–47–53–73–34*), specializing in fabulous, unfussy French food, where Constant himself likes to chat with customers in the relaxed atmosphere, and **Les Cocottes** (⊠ *135 rue St-Dominique [note this is the same building as Le Violon d'Ingres]* ☎ *01–45–50–10–31*), which serves nonstop all day, at a long counter.

SWEETS

Hugo & Victor (⊠ *40 bd. Raspail, 7e, St-Germain-des-Prés* ☎ *01–44–39–97–73* Ⓜ *St. Placide;* also ⊠ *7 rue Gomboust, 1er* ☎ *01–42–96–10–20* Ⓜ *Louvre/Tuileries*), a newcomer on the scene, is clearly aiming for the bling factor in this chic, black-lacquered boutique modeled after a jewel box or jewelry store. Pastries are displayed individually in small glass vitrines in the wall like, you know, jewels. Although this may sound a tad precious, hang on a minute, because the pastries, chocolates, and other sweets not only look gorgeous, they're good! Pâtissier Hugues Pouget has a storied pedigree, most lately from Guy Savoy, and the pastries—which change with the seasons according to available ingredients—are elegant and sculptural. Some, like the Hugo caramel, a glittering chocolate ball filled with luscious caramel pudding, are both innovative and scrumptious. If you hadn't already gathered that this is a gourmet pâtisserie, the wine pairings for each pastry should clue you in.

14

LOUVRE, LES HALLES, AND THE OPÉRA
1ER, 2E, 9E ARRONDISSEMENTS

All-night restaurants and hearty bistros continue to thrive around Paris's former wholesale market, creating a boisterous contrast with the elegant streets around the Louvre and Opéra.

Home to the city's wholesale food market until the 1960s, Les Halles is still the place to go for late-night onion soup or steak frites, washed back with gulps of cheap and tasty red wine. The streets grow more subdued around the Louvre and Palais Royal, where you can relax in elegant cafés, slurp oysters at a classic brasserie like Le Vaudeville, or treat yourself to a meal of a lifetime at Le Grand Véfour or indulge in the more experimental haute cuisine at Spring. Though Madeleine is a food hub, thanks to the gourmet emporiums Fauchon and Hédiard, good restaurants are scarce between here and Opéra. For a quick bite, wander over to Rue Ste-Anne for a cheap and satisfying bowl of Japanese noodles. Quick lunch options are plentiful in this area, because it's crawling with office workers who pack the British-inspired sandwich shop Cojean.

ESCAPE TO ASIA

If you can't face another slab of panfried foie gras, take a stroll down Rue Ste-Anne. The hub of the Japanese community in Paris is lined with noodle shops offering unparalleled value. At the ever-popular, cafeteria-style **Higuma** (⊠ 32 rue Ste-Anne ☎ 01–47–03–38–59), €10 will buy not just a sink-size bowl of ramen but a plate of six gyoza (pork-filled dumplings). For udon, squeeze into **Kunitoraya** (⊠ 39 rue Ste-Anne ☎ 01–47–03–33–65), where these thick wheat noodles are a specialty. Unique in Paris is **Zenzoo** (⊠ 2 rue Cherubini ☎ 01–42–96–27–28), which serves bubble tea made with tapioca, and dim sum–style Taiwanese food.

INSIDE LES HALLES

Faced with the unsightly 1970s shopping mall known as the Forum des Halles undergoing yet another facelift, it's hard to conjure up the colors, sounds, and smells of the wholesale market that took place here until the late 1960s. Émile Zola dubbed Les Halles "the belly of Paris," and although the belly has shrunk significantly since the market moved to the suburb of Rungis in 1971, it's not completely empty. The cobblestone street market on Rue Montorgueil (open daily except Sunday afternoons and Monday) is still a feast for the senses. And some area restaurants continue to offer savory, market-inspired fare. Newcomers to Les Halles should tread carefully. A hub for 800,000 daily commuters, the area attracts chain restaurants and street hawkers. With all of the commotion, it's easy to overlook worthy shops and eateries.

FOR SOMETHING SWEET

The scent of butter and almonds has been known to stop traffic outside the bakery and restaurant **Stohrer** (✉ *51 rue Montorgueil* ☎ *01-42-33-38-20*), founded in 1730. At the warehouse-style **Dehillerin** (✉ *18 rue Coquillière* ☎ *01-42-36-53-13*) nearby, cooks from around the world come searching for gleaming copper pots or silicone madeleine molds. Amateur and professional pastry chefs indulge their fantasies at **Detou** (✉ *58 rue Tiquetonne, 1er* ☎ *01-42-36-54-67*), the grocer for pastry chefs, which sells 3-kilogram hunks of Valrhona chocolate.

FOR SOMETHING SAVORY

Hidden in an inconspicuous street, **Chez La Vieille** (✉ *1 rue Bailleul* ☎ *01-42-60-15-78*) serves uncompromising French country fare at lunchtime and on Thursday nights. If you're still not convinced that the spirit of Les Halles lives on, visit the brasserie **Au Pied de Cochon** (*see photo below* ✉ *6 rue Coquillière* ☎ *01-40-13-77-00*) or the boisterous bistro **La Tour de Montlhéry–Chez Denise** (✉ *5 rue des Prouvaires, 1er* ☎ *01-42-36-21-82*) and enjoy restorative food in the wee hours, just like the market vendors used to do.

SWEETS

When sampling the rarified wares of Paris's master *chocolatier-pâtissiers*, the distinctions become less about merit than about nuance. Yet there are three or four pastries at **Jean-Paul Hévin** (✉ *231 rue Saint-Honoré, 1er* ☎ *01-55-35-35-96* Ⓜ *Tuileries*; also ✉ *3 Rue Vavin, 6e* ☎ *01-43-54-09-85* and ✉ *23 bis, av. la Motte-Picquet, 7e* ☎ *01-45-51-77-48*) that leave his toughest rivals in the dust. Hévin isn't a household name, and unlike some of his competitors, his output is relatively understated. As they say, though, the proof is in the pudding. Take the Longchamp: lightness incarnate with a *crème praliné* center surrounded by a delicate meringue enrobed in almond-studded chocolate. The simple *tarte à l'orange*, all ambrosial orange cream and melting crust, is nothing short of miraculous, and the *pomme de terre*, a little marzipan-coated dumpling filled with silky dark-chocolate ganache, candied orange peel, and rum-macerated raisins, is heaven.

14

RESTAURANT REVIEWS

In alphabetical order by neighborhood. Use the coordinate (⊕ 1:B2) at the end of each review to locate a property on the corresponding map at the end of the chapter.

AROUND THE EIFFEL TOWER

AROUND THE EIFFEL TOWER

$$ BISTRO 🍴 **Afaria.** This otherwise unexciting arrondissement has become home to yet another promising young chef: Julien Duboué, who worked with fellow Basque Alain Dutournier at Le Carré des Feuillants and Daniel Boulud in New York before settling into this high-ceiling space near Porte de Versailles. Basque cooking is known for its bold flavors and generosity, and the choices at Afaria are no exception: crisp-skinned duck breast with balsamic-fig vinegar (for two) is served dramatically, inside a roof tile, with the accompanying potato gratin perched on a bed of twigs; and big chunks of spoon-tender slow-cooked pork from Gascony come in an earthenware dish with cubes of roasted celery root. Another signature dish consists of slices of blood sausage layered with apple and topped with grainy mustard. Tapas are served at a high table near the entrance, and there's a large-screen TV for rugby matches. [$] *Average main: €21* ✉ *15 rue Desnouettes, 15e, Around the Eiffel Tower* ☎ *01–48–56–15–36* 🕓 *Closed Sun., Mon., 3 wks in Aug., and 2 wks in Feb.* [M] *Convention* ⊕ *3:C6.*

$$$ BISTRO 🍴 **Au Bon Accueil.** To see what well-heeled Parisians like to eat these days, book a table at this chic little bistro run by Jacques Lacipière as soon as you get to town. The contemporary dining room is unusually comfortable, and the sidewalk tables have an Eiffel Tower view; the excellent, well-priced *cuisine du marché* has made this spot a hit. Typical of the sophisticated fare from chef Keita Kitamura, who trained at Le Bristol, are Salers beef and green asparagus, roast lobster with mushroom risotto, and game in season. Homemade desserts could include citrus terrine with passion-fruit sorbet or caramelized apple mille-feuille with hazelnut ice cream. The €32 lunch menu, featuring dishes with a distinct haute-cuisine touch, is one of the city's great bargains. [$] *Average main: €34* ✉ *14 rue de Monttessuy, 7e, Around the Eiffel Tower* ☎ *01–47–05–46–11* 🌐 *www.aubonaccueilparis.com* ✍ *Reservations essential* 🕓 *Closed weekends and 2 wks in Aug.* [M] *Métro or RER: Pont de l'Alma* ⊕ *3:D1.*

$$ BISTRO 🍴 **Jadis.** There's something very grown-up about the cooking of young chef Guillaume Delage, which isn't so much of a surprise when you learn that he trained with the likes of Michel Bras, Frédéric Anton (of Le Pré Catelan), and Pierre Gagnaire. It's worth making your way to what seems like the middle of nowhere to taste his nostalgic bistro cooking with a modern touch: you might find pâté en croûte among the chef's suggestions, but there are also dishes like the shrimp with saté spices, creamed black rice, and spinach. The best value is the €34 set menu (€29 for two courses), with several choices for each course; tasting menus are €48 and €65. Though simple, the gray-and-burgundy dining room decorated with mirrors and vintage posters has charm. [$] *Average*

main: €20 ✉ *208 rue de la Croix-Nivert, 15e, Around the Eiffel Tower* ☎ *01–45–57–73–20* 🌐 *www.bistrot-jadis.com* ✍ *Reservations essential* ⏲ *Closed weekends, 1 wk in May, 3 wks in Aug., 1 wk at Christmas* [M] *Convention or Porte de Versailles* ✥ *3:B6.*

$ BISTRO

🍴 **Le Café Constant.** Parisians are a nostalgic bunch, which explains the popularity of this down-to-earth venue from esteemed chef Christian Constant. This is a relatively humble bistro with cream-color walls, red banquettes, and wooden tables, and you'll often see Constant himself perched at the bar at the end of lunch service. The menu reads like a French cookbook from the 1970s—who cooks veal *cordon bleu* these days?—but with Constant overseeing the kitchen, the dishes taste even better than you remember. There's delicious and creamy lentil soup with morsels of foie gras, and the artichoke salad comes with fresh—not bottled or frozen—hearts. A towering *vacherin* (meringue layered with ice cream) might bring this delightfully retro meal to a close. On weekdays there is a bargain lunch menu for €16 (two courses) or €23 (three courses). [$] *Average main: €16* ✉ *139 rue St-Dominique, 7e, Around the Eiffel Tower* ☎ *01–47–53–73–34* 🌐 *www.cafeconstant.com* ✍ *Reservations not accepted* [M] *Métro École Militaire, Métro or RER: Pont de l'Alma* ✥ *3:D2.*

$$$$ MODERN FRENCH

🍴 **Le Jules Verne.** Alain Ducasse doesn't set his sights low, so it was no real surprise when he took over this prestigious dining room on the second floor of the Eiffel Tower and had designer Patrick Jouin give the room a neo-futuristic look in shades of brown. Sauces and pastries are prepared in a kitchen below the Champ de Mars before being whisked up the elevator to the kitchen, which is overseen by young chef Pascal Féraud. Most accessible is the €88 lunch menu (weekdays only), which brings you à la carte dishes in slightly smaller portions. Spend more (about €175–€210 per person without drinks) and you'll be entitled to more lavish dishes such as lobster with celery root and black truffle, and fricassee of Bresse chicken with crayfish. For dessert the kitchen reinterprets French classics, as in an unsinkable pink grapefruit soufflé with grapefruit sorbet. Book months ahead or try your luck at the last minute. [$] *Average main: €75* ✉ *Tour Eiffel, south pillar, Av. Gustave Eiffel, 7e, Around the Eiffel Tower* ☎ *01–45–55–61–44* 🌐 *www.lejulesverne-paris.com* ✍ *Reservations essential* 👔 *Jacket and tie* [M] *Bir-Hakeim* ✥ *3:C2.*

$$ MODERN FRENCH

🍴 **Le Troquet.** A quiet residential street shelters one of the best-value bistros around: prix-fixe menus start at €30 at lunch and rise to €45.50 for a six-course tasting menu (there is no à la carte), but it's the quality, not quantity, that counts. Chef Marc Mouton sends out a changing roster of dishes from the Basque and Béarn regions of southwestern France, and a typical meal might include vegetable soup with foie gras and cream, panfried scallops in crab sauce or *axoa de veau* (a Basque veal sauté), and a vanilla soufflé with cherry jam. Béarn red wine fills the glasses and happy regulars fill the dining room. [$] *Average main: €22* ✉ *21 rue François-Bonvin, 15e, Around the Eiffel Tower* ☎ *01–45–66–89–00* ⏲ *Closed Sun., Mon., 3 wks in Aug., 1 wk in May, and 1 wk at Christmas* [M] *Ségur* ✥ *3:E5.*

$$
MODERN FRENCH
✗ **Le Violon d'Ingres.** Following in the footsteps of Joël Robuchon and Alain Senderens, Christian Constant gave up the Michelin star chase in favor of more accessible prices and a packed dining room (book at least a week ahead). And with Jérémie Tourdjman in charge of the kitchen here, Constant can dash between his four restaurants on this street, making sure the hordes are happy. And why wouldn't they be? The food is sophisticated and the atmosphere is lively; you can even find signature dishes like the almond-crusted sea bass with rémoulade sauce (a buttery caper sauce), alongside game and scallops (in season), and comforting desserts like *pots de crème* and chocolate tart. The food is still heavy on the butter, but with wines starting at around €20 (and a €31 lunch menu) this is a wonderful place for a classic yet informal French meal. $ *Average main: €26* ⊠ *135 rue St-Dominique, 7e, Around the Eiffel Tower* ☏ *01–45–55–15–05* ⊕ *www.leviolondingres. com* ⌂ *Reservations essential* Ⓜ *École Militaire* ✛ *3:D2.*

$
MODERN FRENCH
✗ **Les Cocottes de Christian Constant.** Chef Christian Constant has an unfailing sense of how Parisians want to eat these days, as proved by his third addition to his mini restaurant empire near the Eiffel Tower. At Les Cocottes he's shifted the normally leisurely bistro experience into high gear, which allows him to keep prices moderate. Seated at a long counter on slightly uncomfortable stools that discourage lingering, diners can mix and match from a menu of soups, salads, *cocottes* (dishes served in cast-iron pots), *verrines* (starters presented in tapas-style glasses), and comforting desserts, all made from fresh, seasonal ingredients. Bonus: lunch and dinner are served seven days a week. $ *Average main: €17* ⊠ *135 rue St-Dominique, 7e, Around the Eiffel Tower* ☏ *01–45–50–10–31* ⊕ *www.maisonconstant.com/fr_cocottes. htm* ⊙ *Open 7 days a week, lunch and dinner* Ⓜ *École Militaire, Métro or RER: Pont de l'Alma* ✛ *3:D2.*

INVALIDES

$$
BISTRO
✗ **D'Chez Eux.** The red-checked tablecloths and jovial maître d'hôtel at this authentic southwestern French bistro near the École Militaire might seem like a tourist cliché—until you realize that the boisterous dining room is just as popular with food-loving locals and French politicians as it is with foreigners. The best way to start a meal here is with the "chariot" of starters, everything from lentil salad to ratatouille; just point to the ones you want. Classics among the main courses are duck confit with sautéed garlic potatoes, cassoulet, and game dishes in winter. Everything is hearty and delicious, if not especially refined—don't miss the gooey help-yourself chocolate mousse. Best value is the *tradition gourmande* set menu for €34, which brings you the hors d'oeuvres spread, a main course, three desserts (you can try them all), and coffee. $ *Average main: €28* ⊠ *2 av. de Lowendal, 7e, Invalides* ☏ *01–47–05–52–55* ⊕ *www.chezeux.com* ⊙ *Closed in Aug.* Ⓜ *Varenne, École Militaire* ✛ *3:E3.*

$$$
FRENCH FUSION
✗ **Il Vino.** It might seem audacious to present hungry diners with nothing more than a wine list, but the gamble is paying off for Enrico Bernardo at his wine-centric restaurant with a branch in Courchevel, in the French Alps. This charismatic Italian left the George V to oversee a dining room where food plays second fiddle (in status, not quality).

The hip decor—plum-color banquettes, body-hugging white chairs, a few high tables—attracts a mostly young clientele that's happy to play the game by ordering one of the blind, multicourse tasting menus. The €98 menu, with four dishes and four wines, is a good compromise that might bring you a white Mâcon with saffron risotto, crisp Malvasia with crabmeat and black radish, a full-bodied red from Puglia with Provençal-style lamb, sherrylike *vin jaune* d'Arbois with aged Comté cheese, and sweet Jurançon with berry crumble. You can also order individual wine-food combinations à la carte or pick a bottle straight from the cellar and ask for a meal to match. $ *Average main: €40* ⌂ *13 bd. de la Tour-Maubourg, 7e, Invalides* ☎ *01–44–11–72–00* ⊕ *www. ilvinobyenricobernardo.com* ⊘ *Closed Sun. No lunch Sat. and Mon.* Ⓜ *Invalides* ✚ *3:F1.*

$$ ✗ **L'Ami Jean.** If you love Yves Camdeborde's southwestern France–
SPANISH   inflected cooking at Le Comptoir but can't get a table for dinner, head to this tavernlike Basque restaurant run by his longtime second-in-command, Stéphane Jégo. Jego's style is remarkably similar to Camdeborde's because he uses the same suppliers and shares his knack for injecting basic ingredients with sophistication reminiscent of haute cuisine. You can go hearty with Spanish *piquillo* peppers stuffed with salt-cod paste or *poulet basquaise* (chicken stewed with peppers), or lighter with seasonal dishes that change weekly. The restaurant is popular with rugby fans (a sport beloved of Basques), who create a festive mood. Reserve at least a week ahead for dinner. $ *Average main: €28* ⌂ *27 rue Malar, 7e, Invalides* ☎ *01–47–05–86–89* ⊕ *www.amijean.eu* ⌖ *Reservations essential* ⊘ *Closed Sun., Mon., and Aug.* Ⓜ *Invalides* ✚ *3:E1.*

$$$$ ✗ **L'Arpège.** Breton-born Alain Passard, one of the most respected chefs
MODERN FRENCH   in Paris, famously shocked the French culinary world by declaring that
Fodor's Choice   he was bored with meat. Though his vegetarianism is more theoretical
★   than practical—L'Arpège still caters to fish and poultry eaters—he does cultivate his own vegetables outside Paris, which are then zipped into the city by high-speed train. His dishes elevate the humblest vegetables to sublime heights: salt-roasted beets with aged balsamic vinegar, leeks with black truffles, black radishes, and *cardon,* a kind of thistle related to the artichoke, with parmigiano-reggiano. Seafood dishes such as turbot cooked at a low temperature for three hours or lobster braised in vin *jaune* from the Jura are also extraordinary—as are the prices. A €130 lunch menu, while still pricey, gives access to this revered cuisine. The understated decor places the emphasis firmly on the food, but try to avoid the gloomy cellar room. $ *Average main: €100* ⌂ *84 rue de Varenne, 7e, Invalides* ☎ *01–47–05–09–06* ⊕ *www.alain-passard.com* ⊘ *Closed weekends* Ⓜ *Varenne* ✚ *3:G2.*

$$$ ✗ **Thoumieux.** Former Crillon chef Jean-François Piège and Thierry
BRASSERIE   Costes of the fashionable brasserie clan that created Café Marly and Le Georges are behind the revival of this old-world bistro. The space has been opened up to eliminate the private booths while thankfully preserving much of its vintage character with globe lights and etched mirrors. Despite its location in the sedate 7e arrondissement, this has quickly become the place to be seen, with food that's a good notch above brasserie fare. A juicy Angus beef hamburger comes with a

14

CLOSE UP

French Restaurant Types

Bistro: The broadest category, a bistro can be a simple, relaxed restaurant serving traditional fare or a chic hot spot where dinner costs more than €50 per person. The bistro menu is fairly limited and usually changes with the season.

Brasserie: More informal than a bistro, the brasserie is large, lively, and almost always has a bar. Ideal for relatively quick meals, it often specializes in Alsatian fare, like *choucroute garnie* (a mixed meat dish with sauerkraut and potatoes) or seafood platters. With flexible hours and diverse menus, brasseries are an excellent choice if you're traveling with kids.

Café: Often an informal neighborhood hangout, the café may also be a showplace attracting a well-heeled crowd. A limited menu of sandwiches and simple dishes is usually available throughout the day. Beware of the prices: a half bottle of mineral water can cost €4 or more.

French Fusion: The French Fusion restaurant has discernable influences of French cuisine and the cuisine of one other region or country.

Haute French: Ambitious and expensive, the Haute French restaurant is helmed by a pedigreed chef who prepares multicourse meals to be remembered.

Modern French: Although not necessarily superexpensive or pretentious, the Modern French restaurant boasts a creative menu showcasing a variety of culinary influences.

Wine Bar: A fairly recent phenomenon, the wine bar serves more than the usual three or four wines by the glass—often with an emphasis on natural wines—along with traditional charcuterie or cheese, small dishes, or, more often nowadays, a full gourmet meal.

superfluous shower of Parmesan and fries whose skinniness mirrors the waitresses' legs, while the more sophisticated slow-cooked salmon is accompanied by vegetables from star market gardener Joël Thiébault. For dessert, try the piping-hot churros with chocolate sauce. The new *restaurant gastronomique* upstairs is ever so chic and a good bit pricier, yet proffers an experience commensurate with the top bistros in town (€95, €115 set menus at lunch and dinner and a €85 three-course menu at lunch that includes two glasses of wine, closed weekends). Reservations are taken exactly six days ahead. [$] *Average main: €28* ✉ *79 rue St-Dominique, 7e, Invalides* ☎ *01–47–05–49–75* 🌐 *www.thoumieux.fr* ✍ *Reservations essential* [M] *La Tour-Maubourg* ✥ *3:E1.*

TROCADÉRO

$$$$ FRENCH FUSION Fodor's Choice ★

🍴 **Hiramatsu.** In this Art Deco dining room near Trocadéro, Hajime Nakagawa continues his variations on the subtly Japanese-inspired French cuisine of restaurant namesake Hiroyuki Hiramatsu, who still sometimes works the kitchen. Luxury ingredients feature prominently in dishes such as thin slices of lamb with onion jam and thyme-and-truffle-spiked jus, or an unusual pot-au-feu of oysters with foie gras and black truffle. For dessert, a mille-feuille of caramelized apples comes with rosemary sorbet. Helpful sommeliers will guide you through the staggering wine list, with more than 1,000 different bottles to choose from. There's no way to get away cheaply, so save this for a special occasion, when you might be tempted to order a carte blanche menu for €115 (lunch menus at €48). [$] *Average main: €50* ✉ *52 rue de Longchamp, 16e, Trocadéro* ☎ *01–56–81–08–80* 🌐 *www.hiramatsu.co.jp/fr* ✍ *Reservations essential* ⏲ *Closed weekends, Aug., and 1 wk at Christmas* [M] *Trocadéro* ✣ *1:B6.*

$$$$ MODERN FRENCH 🍴 **L'Abeille.** The name of the palatial new Paris Shangri-La Hotel's premier restaurant refers to Napoléon's imperial emblem, the bee (the building once housed his grand-nephew), but also pays homage to Philippe Labbé, one of France's distinguished chefs. Everything, from the dove-gray decor to the sparkling silver, speaks of quiet elegance—all the better to highlight a masterful cuisine: "harlequin" of yellow, red, and white beets with a ginger-tinged yogurt and aloe vera emulsion; Breton langoustine in a cinnamon-perfumed gelée, with grapefruit pulp and a ginger- and Tahitian vanilla–infused mayonnaise; lightly caramelized scallops in an ethereal cloud of white-chocolate foam; tender fillet of wild duck with a tart-sweet apricot reduction. Desserts are subtle and surprising, like the apple Reinette, paired with fennel and candied lemon zest. For cuisine of this quality, the €195, seven-course tasting menu at dinner is not outlandish. Service is friendly, discrete, and devoid of snobbery, and includes all the flourishes that make a dining experience unforgettable—from the first flute of champagne to the parting gift of, what else? a jar of honey. [$] *Average main: €100* ✉ *10 av. d'Iéna, 16e, Trocadéro* ☎ *01–53–67–19–90* 🌐 *www.shangri-la.com* ✍ *Reservations essential* ⏲ *Closed Mon.* [M] *Iéna* ✣ *1:C6.*

$$$$ MODERN FRENCH Fodor's Choice ★ 🍴 **L'Astrance.** Granted, Pascal Barbot rose to fame thanks to his restaurant's amazing-value food and casual atmosphere, but after the passage of several years, Astrance has become resolutely haute, with prices to match. There's no à la carte; you can choose from a lunch menu for €70, a seasonal menu for €120, or the full tasting menu for €210 (this is what most people come for)—the latter two are available at lunch and dinner. Barbot's cooking has such an ethereal quality that it's worth the considerable effort of booking a table—you should start trying at least two months in advance. His dishes often draw on Asian ingredients, as in grilled lamb with miso-lacquered eggplant and a palate-cleansing white sorbet spiked with chili pepper and lemongrass. Each menu also comes at a (considerably) higher price with wines to match each course. [$] *Average main: €120* ✉ *4 rue Beethoven, 16e, Trocadéro* ☎ *01–40–50–84–40* ✍ *Reservations essential* ⏲ *Closed Sat.–Mon., 1 wk in Feb., Aug., and 1 wk in late Oct.–early Nov.* [M] *Passy* ✣ *1:B6.*

$$ BISTRO 🍴 **La Table Lauriston.** Serge Barbey has developed a winning formula in his chic bistro near the Trocadéro: top-notch ingredients, simply prepared and generously served. To start, you can't go wrong with his silky foie gras *au torchon*—the liver is poached in a flavorful bouillon—or one of the seasonal salads, such as white asparagus in herb vinaigrette; his trademark dish, a gargantuan rib steak, is big enough to silence even the hungriest Texan. Given the neighborhood you might expect a businesslike setting, but the dining room feels cheerful, with vividly colored

CLOSE UP

A Cheese Primer

Their cuisine might be getting lighter, but the French aren't ready to relinquish their cheese. Some restaurants present a single, lovingly selected slice, whereas the more prestigious restaurants wheel in a trolley of specimens aged on the premises. Cheese always comes after the main course and before—or instead of—dessert.

Among the best bistros for cheese are **Astier,** where a giant basket of oozy wonders is brought to the table, and **Le Comptoir,** where a dazzling cheese platter is part of the five-course prix-fixe dinner, or Bistro Paul Bert, where an overflowing cheese board is left on your table for you to help yourself. A few *bars à fromages* are springing up, too: devoted to cheese the way *bars à vins* are dedicated to wine. **Fromagerie Cantin** (⊠ *12 rue du Champ de Mars* 🕾 *01–45–50–43–94* ⊕ *www.cantin.fr*) is a terrific example.

Armed with these phrases, you can wow the waiter and work your way through the most generous platter.

Avez-vous le Beaufort d'été? Do you have summer Beaufort?

Beaufort is similar to Gruyère, and the best Beaufort is made with milk produced in summer, when cows eat fresh grass. Aged Beaufort is even more reminiscent of a mountain hike.

Je voudrais un chèvre bien frais/bien sec. I'd like a goat cheese that's nice and fresh/nice and dry.

France produces many goat cheeses, some so fresh they can be scooped with a spoon, some tough enough to use as doorstops. It's a matter of taste, but hard-core cheese eaters favor drier specimens, which stick to the roof of the mouth and have a frankly goaty aroma.

C'est un St-Marcellin de vache ou de chèvre? Is this St-Marcellin made with cow's or goat's milk?

St-Marcellin is a more original choice than ubiquitous *crottin de chèvre* (poetically named after goats' turds). Originally a goat cheese, today it's more often made with cow's milk. The best have an oozy center, though some like it dry as a hockey puck.

C'est un Brie de Meaux ou de Melun? Is this Brie from Meaux or Melun?

There are many kinds of Brie. Brie de Meaux is the best known, with a smooth flavor and runny center; the much rarer Brie de Melun is more pungent and saltier.

Je n'aime pas le Camembert industriel! I don't like industrial Camembert!

Camembert might be a national treasure, but most of it is industrial. Real Camembert has a white rind with rust-color streaks and a yellow center.

Avez-vous de la confiture pour accompagner ce brebis? Do you have any jam to go with this sheep's cheese?

In the Basque region berry jam is the traditional accompaniment for sharp sheep's-milk cheeses like Ossau-Iraty.

C'est la saison du Mont d'Or. It's Mont d'Or season.

This potent mountain cheese, also known as Vacherin, is produced only from September to March. It's so runny it's eaten with a spoon.

—Rosa Jackson

walls and velvet-upholstered chairs, and there is a 16-seat terrace. Don't miss the giant baba au rhum, which the waiters will douse with a choice of three rums. $ *Average main: €28* ✉ *129 rue de Lauriston, Trocadéro* ☎ *01–47–27–00–07* ⊕ *www.restaurantlatablelauriston.com* ⌂ *Reservations essential* ⊙ *Closed Sun., 3 wks in Aug., and 1 wk at Christmas. No lunch Sat.* Ⓜ *Trocadéro* ✛ *3:B6.*

$$
BISTRO
✕ **Le Petit Rétro.** A diverse clientele (men in expensive suits at noon, well-dressed locals in the evening) frequents this little bistro with Art Nouveau tiles and bentwood furniture. You can't go wrong with the daily specials, which are written on a chalkboard presented by one of the friendly servers: perhaps crisp-skinned blood sausage with apple-and-honey sauce, *blanquette de veau,* and a crêpe mille-feuille with orange and Grand Marnier. Arrive with an appetite because the food is hearty. There are several prix-fixe menus to choose from, starting at €25 at lunch (two courses). $ *Average main: €23* ✉ *5 rue Mesnil, 16e, Trocadéro* ☎ *01–44–05–06–05* ⊕ *www.petitretro.fr* ⊙ *Closed weekends and 3 wks in Aug.* Ⓜ *Victor-Hugo* ✛ *1:A5.*

AROUND THE LOUVRE

FAUBOURG ST-HONORÉ

$$
BISTRO
✕ **Au Gourmand.** In a city where many restaurants seem to take customers for granted, it's refreshing to come across someone who sounds delighted when you call to make a reservation. And the staff is just as eager to please once you're seated in the dining room, whose traditional theater-theme decor belies the kitchen's modern spirit. The cooking highlights vegetables from famed market gardener Joël Thiébault: his multicolor tomatoes, for instance, might be displayed on a puff pastry base with the tiniest salad leaves, or a medley of sautéed spring vegetables accompany spoon-tender pork cheek—there's also a €31, three-course vegetarian menu. The best desserts are the least adventurous: try a variation on *pain perdu* (French toast), perhaps with figs, nuts, and almond ice cream. $ *Average main: €30* ✉ *17 rue Molière, 1er, Faubourg St-Honoré* ☎ *01–42–96–22–19* ⊕ *www.restaurantaugourmandparis.com* ⊙ *Closed Sun. No lunch Mon. and Sat.* Ⓜ *Palais Royal, Pyramides* ✛ *2:B6.*

$$
MODERN FRENCH
Fodor's Choice
★
✕ **La Régalade St. Honoré.** When Bruno Doucet bought the original La Régalade from bistro-wizard Yves Camdeborde, some feared the end of an era. How wrong they were. While Doucet kept some of what made the old dining room so popular (country terrine, wine values, convivial atmosphere), he had a few tricks under his toque, creating a brilliantly successful haute-cuisine-meets-comfort-food destination with dishes like earthy morel mushrooms in a frothy cream for a starter, followed by the chef's signature succulent caramelized pork belly over tender Puy lentils, and a perfectly cooked fillet of cod, crispy on the outside and buttery within, served in a rich shrimp bouillon. For dessert, don't skip the updated take on *grand-mère's* creamy rice pudding or the house Grand Marnier soufflé. With an excellent price-to-value ratio (€35 for the prix-fixe menu at lunch and dinner), this chic bistro and its elder sister in the 14th have evolved into staples for Paris gastronomes. $ *Average main: €24* ✉ *123 rue Saint-Honoré, 1er, Faubourg St-Honoré*

14

☎ *01–42–21–92–40* ☝ *Reservations essential* ⊘ *Closed weekends, Aug., 1 wk at Christmas* Ⓜ *Louvre-Rivoli* ✛ *2:C1* ✉ *49 av. Jean Moulin, 14e, Montparnasse* ☎ *01–45–45–68–58* ☝ *Reservations essential* ⊘ *Closed weekends, Aug., 1 wk at Christmas. No lunch Mon.* Ⓜ *Alesia, Porte d'Orleans* ✛ *4:C1.*

LES HALLES

$$
BRASSERIE

✕ **Au Pied de Cochon.** One of the few remnants of Les Halles's raucous all-night past is this brasserie, which has been open every day since 1946. Now run by the Frères Blanc group, it still draws both a French and a foreign crowd with round-the-clock hours and trademark traditional fare such as seafood platters, breaded pigs' trotters, beer-braised pork knuckle with sauerkraut, and cheese-crusted onion soup. It's perfect rib-sticking fare for a winter's day or to finish off a bar crawl. The dining room, with its white tablecloths and little piggy details, feels resolutely cheerful, and it's open 24/7. Ⓢ *Average main: €21* ✉ *6 rue Coquillière, 1er, Les Halles* ☎ *01–40–13–77–00* ⊕ *www.pieddecochon. com* Ⓜ *Les Halles* ✛ *2:C6.*

$
ASIAN

✕ **Citronnelle et Galanga.** For 20 years the Ta family has served up the enticing cuisine of French Indochina (Laos, Cambodia, Vietnam) much to Parisians' delight. Their newest and sleekest outpost near the elegant Place des Victoires has creamy banquettes, black lacquered chairs, and exotic travel posters to set the mood for dishes like plump raviolis with minced vegetables and pork, spicy marinated whole fish wrapped in banana leaves and poached in coconut milk, or minty vegetable spring rolls. Desserts are light and refreshing, like green-tea flan or roasted mango with black-sesame tuilles. Wines by the bottle or glass pair well with unusual spices. At €15 for the 2-course lunch menu and €28 for three courses at dinner, it's also an excellent bargain. Ⓢ *Average main: €17* ✉ *15 rue d'Aboukir, 2e, Bourse* ☎ *01–42–21–05–62* Ⓜ *Sentier* ✛ *2:C5.*

$$
BISTRO

✕ **Frenchie.** Grégory Marchand worked in New York and with Jamie Oliver in London before opening this brick-and-stone-walled bistro on a pedestrian street near Rue Montorgueil, which explains the tongue-in-cheek name. Word of mouth, and bloggers, quickly made this one of the most packed bistros in town, with tables booked two months in advance. Marchand owes a large part of his success to the great-value €38 three-course menu at dinner—boldly flavored dishes such as calamari gazpacho with squash blossoms, and melt-in-the-mouth braised lamb with roasted eggplant and spinach are excellent options. Service can be, shall we say, a tad brusque, but for some that's a small price to pay for food this good. It's prix fixe only. Ⓢ *Average main: €34* ✉ *5 rue de Nil, 2e, Les Halles* ☎ *01–40–39–96–19* ⊕ *www.frenchie-restaurant. com* ⊘ *Closed weekends, 2 wks in Aug., 10 days at Christmas. No lunch* Ⓜ *Sentier* ✛ *2:D5.*

$
WINE BAR

✕ **Frenchie Bar à Vins.** If this weren't one of Paris's outstanding wine bars, the wait, attitude, and metal tractor seats might be a deterrent. Yet wine lovers would be hard pressed to find a better venue for sampling a great list of French wines, many natural, and inspired selections from Italy and Spain—all sold by the bottle or glass, with superb cuisine to match. Feast on masterful small dishes like the "coleslaw" of citrusy calimari and carrot, black-olive coulis and sprinkling of pine nuts; bresaola with apple, spicy mizuna leaves, and dollops of creamy horseradish; a wedge of Stilton served atop a paste of speculoos biscuits, with poached pear and smoked walnuts. Since getting a reservation at the restaurant across the street is nearly impossible, this is an excellent alternative. Hint: get there five minutes before opening time. $ *Average main: €16* ⊠ *6 rue du Nil, 2e, Les Halles* ☎ *No phone* ⌗ *Reservations not accepted* ☾ *Weekdays 7–11 pm* Ⓜ *Sentier* ✛ *2:D5.*

$$ ✕ **La Robe et le Palais.** Come here for the more than 120 French wines
WINE BAR served *au compteur* (according to the amount consumed), and a good selection of bistro-style food in a congenial atmosphere for lunch or dinner. Although a tad pricier than other *bistrot à vins*, the food is reliably good. $ *Average main: €20* ⊠ *13 rue des Lavandières-Ste-Opportune, 1er, Beaubourg/Les Halles* ☎ *01–45–08–07–41* ⊕ *www.robe-et-palais. com* ☾ *Closed Sun.* Ⓜ *Châtelet Les Halles* ✛ *4:D1.*

$$ ✕ **Le Georges.** One of those rooftop show-stopping venues so popu-
MODERN FRENCH lar in Paris, Le Georges preens atop the Centre Georges Pompidou, accessed by its own entrance to the left of the main doors. The staff is as streamlined and angular as the furniture, and about as responsive. Come snappily dressed or you may be relegated to something resembling a dentist's waiting room. Part of the Costes brothers' empire, the establishment trots out fashionable dishes such as sesame-crusted tuna and coriander-spiced beef fillet flambéed with cognac. It's all considerably less dazzling than the view, except for the suitably decadent desserts (indulge in the Cracker's cheesecake with yogurt sorbet). $ *Average main: €28* ⊠ *Centre Pompidou, 6th fl., 19 rue Beaubourg, 4e, Les Halles* ☎ *01–44–78–47–99* ⌗ *Reservations essential* ☾ *Closed Tues.* Ⓜ *Rambuteau* ✛ *4:E1.*

$$$ ✕ **Yam'Tcha.** Adeline Grattard's little bistro has become so popular that
FRENCH FUSION tables are snapped up several weeks ahead, which is no surprise when
Fodor'sChoice you learn that she worked in the kitchens of L'Astrance before spend-
★ ing time in Hong Kong, where she picked up many of her techniques and ingredients. Inspired by Chinese cooking, many of her dishes rely on brilliant flavor combinations and very precise cooking. A signature dish is the roasted Challans duck (a cross between wild and domestic) with Sichuan-style eggplant: two elements that create magic together. Adeline's husband Chi Wa acts as a tea sommelier, introducing diners to earthy or grassy flavors that complement the food (Yam'Tcha means "to eat small steamed dishes while sipping tea"), though alcohol is also available. It's prix fixe only. $ *Average main: €38* ⊠ *4 rue Sauval, 1er, Les Halles* ☎ *01–40–26–08–07* ⌗ *Reservations essential* ☾ *Closed Mon. and Tues., Sun. lunch only; closed Aug. and Christmas holidays* Ⓜ *Louvre-Rivoli or Les Halles* ✛ *2:C6.*

LOUVRE/TUILERIES

$$$ ✕ **Café Marly.** Run by the Costes brothers, this café overlooking the main
CAFÉ courtyard of the Louvre and I.M. Pei's glass pyramid is one of the more stylish places in Paris to meet for a drink or a coffee, whether in the stunning jewel-toned dining rooms with their molded ceilings or on the Louvre's long, sheltered terrace. Regular café service shuts down during meal hours, when fashion-conscious folks dig into Asian-inspired

14

salads and pseudo-Italian pasta dishes. $ *Average main: €34* ✉ *Cour Napoléon du Louvre, enter from Louvre courtyard, 93 rue de Rivoli, 1er, Louvre/Tuileries* ☎ *01–49–26–06–60* Ⓜ *Palais-Royal* ✛ *4:B1.*

$$
BISTRO

✕**Chez Georges.** If you were to ask Parisian bankers, aristocrats, or antiques dealers to name their favorite bistro for a three-hour weekday lunch, many would choose Georges. The traditional fare, described in authentically indecipherable handwriting, is very good—chicken-liver terrine, curly endive salad with bacon and a poached egg, steak with béarnaise—and the atmosphere is better, compensating for the steep prices. In the dining room, a white-clothed stretch of tables lines the mirrored walls, and attentive waiters sweep efficiently up and down. Order one of the wines indicated in colored ink on the menu and you can drink as much or as little of it as you want (and be charged accordingly); there's also another wine list with grander bottles. $ *Average main: €29* ✉ *1 rue du Mail, 2e, Louvre/Tuileries* ☎ *01–42–60–07–11* ☾ *Closed weekends, Aug., 1 wk at Christmas* Ⓜ *Sentier* ✛ *2:C5.*

$$
BISTRO
Fodor's Choice
★

✕**L'Ardoise.** This minuscule storefront, decorated with enlargements of old sepia postcards of Paris, is a model of the kind of contemporary bistros making waves in Paris. Chef Pierre Jay's first-rate three-course dinner menu for €35 tempts with such original dishes as mushroom and foie gras ravioli with smoked duck; farmer's pork with porcini mushrooms; and red mullet with creole sauce (you can also order à la carte, but it's less of a bargain). Just as enticing are the desserts, such as a superb *feuillantine au citron*—caramelized pastry leaves filled with lemon cream and lemon slices—and a boozy baba au rhum. With friendly waiters and a small but well-chosen wine list, L'Ardoise would be perfect if it weren't so popular (meaning noisy and crowded). $ *Average main: €26* ✉ *28 rue du Mont Thabor, 1er, Louvre/Tuileries* ☎ *01–42–96–28–18* ⊕ *www.lardoise-paris.com* ☾ *Closed Mon., 1 wk in Jan. and late July–late Aug. Sun. dinner only* Ⓜ *Concorde* ✛ *1:H6.*

$$
BISTRO

✕**La Bourse ou La Vie.** If you've been dreaming of the perfect steak frites in Paris, head for this eccentric little place run by a former architect in partnership with two loyal clients. The chairs in this cheery yellow-and-red dining room appear to have been salvaged from a theater, but they pair nicely with founder Patrice Tatard's theatrical streak. There's no questioning the threesome's enthusiasm for their new vocation when you taste the steak in its trademark creamy, peppercorn-studded sauce, accompanied by hand-cut french fries cooked to crisp perfection. Aside from a whole veal kidney with mustard sauce, there's little else on the menu. $ *Average main: €19* ✉ *12 rue Vivienne, 2e, Louvre/Tuileries* ☎ *01–42–60–08–83* ☾ *Closed Fri. and Aug. No dinner Sat., Sun.* Ⓜ *Bourse* ✛ *2:C5.*

$$$$
MODERN FRENCH

✕**Le Grand Véfour.** Victor Hugo could stride in and still recognize this restaurant, which was in his day, as now, a contender for the title of most beautiful restaurant in Paris. Originally built in 1784, it has welcomed everyone from Napoléon to Colette to Jean Cocteau under its mirrored ceiling, and amid the early-19th-century glass paintings of goddesses and muses that create an air of restrained seduction. The rich and fashionable gather here to enjoy chef Guy Martin's unique blend of sophistication and rusticity, as seen in dishes such as frogs' legs with sorrel sauce, and oxtail *parmentier* (a kind of shepherd's pie) with truffles. There's an outstanding cheese trolley, and for dessert try the house specialty, *palet aux noisettes* (meringue cake with chocolate mousse, hazelnuts, and salted caramel ice cream). Prices are as extravagant as the decor, but there's an €96 lunch menu. Ⓢ *Average main: €120* ✉ *17 rue de Beaujolais, 1er, Louvre/Tuileries* ☎ *01–42–96–56–27* ⊕ *www. grand-vefour.com* ⚑ *Reservations essential* ⊗ *Closed weekends, Aug., and Christmas holidays. No dinner Fri.* Ⓜ *Palais-Royal* ✛ *2:B5.*

$$$$
MODERN FRENCH
✕**Les Ambassadeurs.** Following a roster of superstar chefs in one of Paris's most spectacular dining rooms is no small feat, yet 31-year-old Christopher Hache steps up to the task with confidence and maturity, earning a Michelin star after less than a year at the helm. Hache's cooking is squarely haute cuisine, though he avoids preciousness in favor of more hearty dishes like Volaille "Galouise Blanche," a golden-hued filet of Landes hen, extravagantly laden with shaved white truffles alongside fluffy tiny pasta in a white-truffle sauce, or a dish of succulent Breton langoustine with lightly caramelized fennel and a sauce laced with tart Japanese yuzu. Desserts are both luxe and homey, like Riz à l'Imperatrice, an exalted rice pudding with raspberry confit and star-anise ice cream, and his luscious take on the humble tarte tatin. Another good reason to indulge yourself with a visit here: the service is graciousness itself. Les Ambassadeurs will remain open while the Hôtel de Crillon undergoes renovations. Ⓢ *Average main: €80* ✉ *10 pl. de la Concorde, 11e, Louvre/Tuileries* ☎ *01–44–71–16–16* ⊕ *www.crillon. com* ⚑ *Reservations essential* ⊗ *Closed Sun., Mon. 1 wk in Feb. and Aug.* Ⓜ *Concord* ✛ *1:G6.*

$$
BISTRO
✕**Les Fines Gueules.** Invest in good ingredients and most of the work is done: that's the principle of this wine bar–bistro that's developed a loyal following since opening in 2007. If you're not on first-name terms with food personalities like butcher Hugo Desnoyer, market gardener Joël Thiébault, and sausage-maker Thierry Daniel, you need only know that these are the crème de la crème of suppliers. Owner Arnaud Bradol wisely treats their products simply, often serving them raw alongside a salad or sautéed potatoes: the steak tartare with mesclun salad dressed in truffle oil is unparalleled. Beyond the tiny cafélike area downstairs is a staircase leading to a cozy upstairs dining room, which is invariably lively. In keeping with the theme, wines are organic or natural and many are available by the glass. There's live jazz two Sundays a month and classical recitals, too. Ⓢ *Average main: €19* ✉ *43 rue Croix des Petits Champs, 1er, Louvre/Tuileries* ☎ *01–42–61–35–41* ⊕ *www. lesfinesgueules.fr* ⚑ *Reservations essential* Ⓜ *Palais Royal* ✛ *2:C6.*

$$$
MODERN FRENCH
✕**Macéo.** Natural light streams through the restaurant, and a broad, curved staircase leads to a spacious upstairs salon. With reasonably priced set menus ranging from €35 (for the vegetarian menu) to €39 (for three courses at lunch or dinner), this is an ideal spot for a relaxed meal after the Louvre. It's also a hit with vegetarians: chef Maître Park whips up a meatless set menu with two starter and two main course options—perhaps summer vegetables with mimolette cheese, followed by mini-pasta with wild mushrooms, herbs, and artichoke (though his efforts can be hit-or-miss). Meat lovers might sink their teeth into

14

farmer's lamb with confit vegetables and mousseline potatoes. The wine list spotlights little-known producers alongside the big names—as befits this sister restaurant to Willi's Wine Bar. [$] *Average main: €30* ✉ *15 rue des Petits-Champs, 1er, Louvre/Tuileries* ☎ *01–42–97–53–85* 🌐 *www.maceorestaurant.com* 🕒 *Closed Sun. and 3 wks in Aug. No lunch Sat.* [M] *Palais-Royal* ✥ *2:B5.*

$$$$ MODERN FRENCH Fodor's Choice ★

🍴 **Spring.** The private party atmosphere in this intimate, elegantly modern space may be exuberance at having finally snagged a table, but most likely it's chef Daniel Rose's inspired—often resplendent—cuisine. Though firmly rooted in technique, Rose sets himself the task of improvising two different menus each day, one for lunch and one for dinner, from whatever strikes his fancy that morning. His insistence on fresh, top-quality ingredients is evident in dishes that are both refined and deeply satisfying: you might have an updated *parmentier* with a velvety layer of deboned pig's foot topped with lemon-infused whipped potatoes or buttery venison with tart-sweet candied kumquat; for dessert, a sublime combo of whiskey-and-vanilla-infused pineapple, crunchy toasted coconut biscuits, and lime-zest-sprinkled vanilla ice cream. The 17th-century vaulted dining room is an intimate spot yet can accommodate larger groups. It's prix fixe only. [$] *Average main: €45* ✉ *6 rue Bailleul, 1er, Louvre/Tuileries* ☎ *01–45–96–05–72* ✍ *Reservations essential* 🕒 *Dinner Tues.–Sat.; lunch, Wed.–Fri.* [M] *Louvre-Rivoli* ✥ *4:C1.*

$ WINE BAR

🍴 **Verjus Bar à Vins.** On an atmospheric street behind the Palais Royal gardens, this tiny wine bar is the latest endeavor of the American couple behind the wildly popular (and now defunct) Hidden Kitchen. A dozen customers perch on metal stools at a narrow bar to enjoy a small but choice selection of wines by the glass and some very good nibbles, like crisp buttermilk chicken, succulent Basque pork belly, or the excellent house-smoked salmon. Although not a substitute for dinner—portions are miniscule, with three to five bite-size morsels—for a drink and a nosh on your way to or from somewhere else it's ideal. The most plentiful dish is an assortment of artisanal cheeses, and the scrumptious butterscotch pudding flecked with toffee and topped with crème Chantilly is a toothsome finale. Open weeknights only. [$] *Average main: €7* ✉ *47 rue Montpensier, 1e, Louvre/Tuileries* ☎ *01–42–97–54–40* 🌐 *verjusparis.com* ✍ *Reservations not accepted* 🕒 *Closed Sat., Sun.* [M] *Palais Royal–Musée du Louvre* ✥ *2:B6.*

$$ MODERN FRENCH

🍴 **Willi's Wine Bar.** More a restaurant than a wine bar, this British-owned spot is a stylish haunt for Parisian and visiting gourmands who might stop in for a glass of wine at the oak bar or settle into the wood-beamed dining room. The selection of reinvented classic dishes changes daily and might include roast cod with artichokes and asparagus in spring, venison in wine sauce with roast pears and celery-root chips in fall, and mango candied with orange and served with vanilla cream in winter. Chef François Yon has been in the kitchen for 18 years, ensuring a consistency that isn't always reflected in the service. The restaurant is prix-fixe only, but you can order appetizers at the bar. The list of about 250 wines reflects co-owner Mark Williamson's passion for the Rhône Valley and Spanish sherries. [$] *Average main: €20* ✉ *13 rue* *des Petits-Champs, 1er, Louvre/Tuileries* ☎ *01–42–61–05–09* 🌐 *www.williswinebar.com* 🕓 *Closed Sun. and 2 wks in Aug.* [M] *Bourse* ✣ *2:B5.*

$ JAPANESE 🍴 **Zen.** There's no shortage of Japanese restaurants around the Louvre, but this one is a cut above much of the competition. The white-and-lime-green space feels refreshingly bright and modern, and you can perch at one of the curvy counters for quick bite or settle in at a table. The menu has something for every taste, from warming ramen soups (part of a €9.90 lunch menu that includes five pork dumplings) to sushi and sashimi prepared with particular care. The donburi—rice topped with meat or fish—and the Japanese curry with breaded pork or shrimp are also very good. A sign of the chef's pride in his food is that he offers cooking classes some Sundays (in French). [$] *Average main: €17* ✉ *8 rue de l'Echelle, 1er, Louvre/Tuileries* ☎ *01–42–61–93–99* 🕓 *Closed 10 days in mid-Aug.* [M] *Pyramides or Palais Royal* ✣ *2:B6.*

14

CHAMPS-ÉLYSÉES

$$$$ MODERN FRENCH 🍴 **Alain Ducasse au Plaza Athénée.** The dining room at Alain Ducasse's flagship Paris restaurant gleams with 10,000 crystals, confirming that this is the flashiest place in town for a blowout meal. Clementine-color tablecloths and space-age cream-and-orange chairs with pullout plastic trays for business meetings provide an upbeat setting for the cooking of young Ducasse protégé chef Christophe Saintagne. Some dishes are subtle, whereas in others strong flavors overwhelm delicate ingredients; service is also a little inconsistent, with occasional long waits between courses. Even so, a meal here is delightfully luxe, starting with a heavenly *amuse-bouche* of perhaps langoustine with caviar and a tangy lemon cream. You can continue with a truffle-and-caviar fest, or opt for more down-to-earth dishes like lobster in spiced wine with quince or saddle of lamb with sautéed artichokes. [$] *Average main: €120* ✉ *Hôtel Plaza Athénée, 25 av. Montaigne, 8e, Champs-Élysées* ☎ *01–53–67–65–00* 🌐 *www.alain-ducasse.com* ✍ *Reservations essential* 👔 *Jacket required* 🕓 *Closed weekends, 2 wks in late Dec., and mid-July–mid-Aug. No lunch Mon.–Wed.* [M] *Alma-Marceau* ✣ *1:D6.*

$ BISTRO 🍴 **Au Petit Verdot du 17e.** Sandwich bars might be threatening the traditional two-hour lunch, but that doesn't stop this old-fashioned neighborhood bistro with its painted facade and wine-themed dining room from flourishing—even though it's open only at lunch, except Thursday. Businessmen loosen their neckties to feast on homemade pâté, plate-engulfing steak for two, or guinea hen with cabbage, along with one of 40 or so small-producer wines. [$] *Average main: €17* ✉ *9 rue Fourcroy, 17e, Champs-Élysées* ☎ *01–42–27–47–42* 🕓 *Closed weekends. No dinner except Thurs.* [M] *Charles-de-Gaulle–Étoile* ✣ *1:C2.*

$$ BISTRO 🍴 **Chez Savy.** Just off the glitzy Avenue Montaigne, Chez Savy occupies its own circa-1930s dimension, oblivious to the area's fashionization. The Art Deco cream-and-burgundy interior is blissfully intact (avoid the back room unless you're in a large group), and the waiters show not a trace of attitude. Fill up on rib-sticking specialties from the Aveyron region of central France—lentil salad with bacon, foie gras (prepared on the premises), perfectly charred lamb with feather-light shoestring frites, and pedigreed Charolais beef. Order a celebratory bottle of Mercurey

with your meal and feel smug that you've found this place. À la carte prices are high, but there is a set menu for €31.60. $ *Average main: €29* ✉ *23 rue Bayard, 8e, Champs-Élysées* ☎ *01–47–23–46–98* ☉ *Closed weekends and Aug.* Ⓜ *Franklin-D.-Roosevelt* ✛ *1:E5.*

$$$$
MODERN FRENCH
Fodor's Choice
★

✕ **Guy Savoy.** Revamped with dark African wood, rich leather, cream-color marble, and the chef's own art collection, Guy Savoy's luxury restaurant doesn't dwell on the past. Come here for a perfectly measured haute-cuisine experience, since Savoy's several bistros have not lured him away from the kitchen. The artichoke soup with black truffles, sea bass with spices, and veal kidneys in mustard-spiked jus reveal the magnitude of his talent, and his mille-feuille is an instant classic. If the waiters see you're relishing a dish, they won't hesitate to offer second helpings. Generous half portions allow you to graze your way through the menu—unless you choose a blowout feast for set menus of €315 or €360—and reasonably priced wines are available (though beware the cost of wines by the glass). The €110 lunch special is a good way to sample some of this fine chef's inspired cooking. Best of all, the atmosphere is joyful, because Savoy knows that having fun is just as important as eating well. $ *Average main: €120* ✉ *18 rue Troyon, 17e, Champs-Élysées* ☎ *01–43–80–40–61* ⊕ *www.guysavoy.com* ✍ *Reservations essential* ⋔ *Jacket required* ☉ *Closed Sun., Mon., Aug., and 1 wk at Christmas. No lunch Sat.* Ⓜ *Charles-de-Gaulle–Étoile* ✛ *1:C3.*

$$$
JAPANESE

✕ **Kifune.** It's rare to see a non-Japanese face in the bistrolike dining room of Kifune, where you can sit at the bar and admire the sushi chef's lightning-quick skills or opt for a more intimate table. The crab-and-shrimp salad is a sublime starter, and the miso soup with clams is deeply flavored. To follow, you can't go wrong with the sashimi. A meal here will leave a dent in your wallet (though there is a €32 set menu at lunch), but some expats say you won't find anything closer to authentic Japanese cooking in Paris. With only 20 seats they often turn away would-be customers, so be sure to book. $ *Average main: €35* ✉ *44 rue St-Ferdinand, 17e, Champs-Élysées* ☎ *01–45–72–11–19* ✍ *Reservations essential* ☉ *Closed Sun. and Mon., 3 wks in Aug., 1 wk in Dec., and 2 wks in May* Ⓜ *Argentine* ✛ *1:A3.*

$$$
MODERN FRENCH

✕ **L'Arôme.** Eric Martins ran a popular bistro in the far reaches of the 15e arrondissement before opening this contemporary restaurant off the Champs-Élysées, and his background in haute cuisine—he worked at Ledoyen and Hélène Darroze, among others—makes this ambitious restaurant an easy transition. The chef, Thomas Boullaut, turns out seasonal dishes with a touch of finesse from the open kitchen: dishes like foie gras confit with rosemary-poached quince and wild rose jam, or scallops à la plancha with vanilla and spaghetti squash might be featured. There is no à la carte, and if the dinner menus seem steep at €69 and €79 (€155 with wine pairing), the lunch menu is a mere €39. Watch out for the pricey wines by the glass. $ *Average main: €45* ✉ *3 rue St-Philippe du Roule, 8e, Champs-Élysées* ☎ *01–42–25–55–98* ⊕ *www.larome.fr* ✍ *Reservations essential* ☉ *Closed weekends, Aug.* Ⓜ *St-Philippe du Roule* ✛ *1:E4.*

$$
SEAFOOD

✕ **L'Huîtrier.** If you have a single-minded craving for oysters, this is the place for you. The friendly owner will describe the many different kinds available, and you can follow with any of several daily fish specials—or opt for a full seafood platter for around €50. Mood lighting, blond wood and cream tones create a tranquil, stylish atmosphere. $ *Average main: €18* ⊠ *16 rue Saussier-Leroy, 17e, Champs-Élysées* ☎ *01–40–54–83–44* ⊕ *www.huitrier.fr/* ⊗ *Closed Mon., and Aug.* Ⓜ *Ternes* ✛ *1:C2.*

$$
BRASSERIE
✕ **La Fermette Marbeuf.** Graced with one of the most mesmerizing Belle Époque rooms in town—accidentally rediscovered during renovations in the 1970s—this is a favorite haunt of French celebrities, who adore the sunflowers, peacocks, and dragonflies of the Art Nouveau mosaic. The menu rolls out updated classics: try the snails in puff pastry, beef fillet with pepper sauce, and the Grand Marnier soufflé—but ignore the limited-choice €33 prix fixe (€23.50 at lunch) unless you're on a budget: the options are a notch below what you get à la carte. Popular with tourists and businesspeople at lunch, La Fermette becomes truly animated around 9 pm. $ *Average main: €25* ⊠ *5 rue Marbeuf, 8e, Champs-Élysées* ☎ *01–53–23–08–00* ⊕ *www.fermettemarbeuf.com* Ⓜ *Franklin-D.-Roosevelt* ✛ *1:D5.*

$$$$
MODERN FRENCH
✕ **La Table de Lancaster.** Operated by one of the most enduring families in French gastronomy (the Troisgros clan has run a world-famous restaurant in Roanne for three generations), this stylish boutique-hotel restaurant is the perfect setting for stellar cosmopolitan cuisine; try to sit in the stunning Asian-inspired courtyard with its red walls and bamboo. Often drawing on humble ingredients such as eel or pigs' ears, the food reveals fascinating flavor and texture contrasts, like silky sardines on crunchy melba toast or tangy frogs' legs in tamarind; the salmon with sorrel sauce is a classic Troisgros dish. There is also a seven-course menu for €145. Don't miss the desserts, such as not one but two slices of sugar tart, with grapefruit slices for contrast. On Sunday there's a special €65 lunch menu (€40 for kids). $ *Average main: €50* ⊠ *Hotel Lancaster, 7 rue de Berri, 8e, Champs-Élysées* ☎ *01–40–76–40–18* ⊕ *www.hotel-lancaster.fr* ⌕ *Reservations essential* ⊗ *No lunch Sat.* Ⓜ *George V* ✛ *1:D4.*

$$$$
MODERN FRENCH
✕ **Le Bristol.** After a rapid ascent at his own new-wave bistro, which led to his renown as one of the more inventive young chefs in Paris, Eric Frechon became head chef at the three-star Bristol, the home-away-from-home for billionaires and power brokers. Frechon creates masterworks—say, farmer's pork cooked "from head to foot" with truffle-enhanced crushed potatoes—that rarely stray far from the comfort-food tastes of bistro cuisine. The €130 lunch menu makes his cooking accessible not just to the palate but to many pocketbooks. No wonder his tables are so coveted. Though the two dining rooms are impeccable—an oval oak-panel one for fall and winter and a marble-floor pavilion overlooking the courtyard garden for spring and summer—they provide few clues to help the world-weary traveler determine which city this might be. $ *Average main: €110* ⊠ *Hôtel Bristol, 112 rue du Faubourg St-Honoré, 8e, Champs-Élysées* ☎ *01–53–43–43–00* ⊕ *www.hotel-bristol.com* ⌕ *Reservations essential* 🛏 *Jacket and tie* Ⓜ *Miromesnil* ✛ *1:F4.*

$$$$
MODERN FRENCH
Fodor'sChoice
★
✕ **Le Cinq.** Eric Briffard is not the most famous chef in Paris but he *is* one of the best, as proved by his smooth transition into the role of head chef in one of the city's most deluxe dining rooms. You'll find all the luxury products you might expect—lobster, truffles, game in season—but

14

treated with a light touch that often draws on Asian ingredients such as wasabi or cassia bark. A perfect example is his abalone, a rare shellfish prized by sushi chefs, prepared several ways: raw in a tartare, bathed in a creamy chicken bouillon, meunière-style in watercress sauce, and perched atop a bed of gingered kabocha squash. Desserts are ethereal and service is unfailingly thoughtful: really, the only problem with a meal here is that it has to end. Oh, and that it costs a small fortune—thankfully there is an €86 prix fixe at lunch. $ *Average main: €100* ⊠ *Hôtel Four Seasons George V, 31 av. George V, 8e, Champs-Élysées* ☎ *01–49–52–70–00* ⊕ *www.fourseasons.com/paris* 🖉 *Reservations essential* 🏠 *Jacket and tie* Ⓜ *George V* ✛ *1:D5.*

$$$ ✕ **La Cristal Room.** The success of this restaurant in the Baccarat museum-
MODERN FRENCH   boutique stems not only from the stunning decor by Philippe Starck—mirrors, patches of exposed-brick wall, and a black chandelier—but also from the culinary stylings of chef Guy Martin. The menu provides a taste of his ultra-refined style with dishes such as green asparagus soup with a lemon-poached egg, and sole meunière with grapefruit and an arugula flan. Plan on reserving a week or two ahead for dinner; lunch requires little advance notice and is a reasonable €29. $ *Average main: €40* ⊠ *11 pl. des États-Unis, 16e, Champs-Élysées* ☎ *01–40–22–11–10* ⊕ *www. baccarat.fr* 🖉 *Reservations essential* ☾ *Closed Sun.* Ⓜ *Kléber* ✛ *1:C5.*

$$$$ ✕ **Ledoyen.** Tucked away in the quiet gardens flanking the Champs-
MODERN FRENCH   Élysées, Ledoyen is a slightly faded study in the grandiose style of Napoléon III. Breton chef Christian Le Squer's menu is a treat, whether you opt for the lunchtime €88 prix fixe or the €199 tasting extravaganza (€299 with matching wines). He uses flawless ingredients, as showcased in *les coquillages* (shellfish), a delicious dish of herb risotto topped with lobster, langoustines, scallops, and grilled ham. The turbot with truffled mashed potatoes is excellent, too, and don't skip the superlative cheese trolley. $ *Average main: €100* ⊠ *1 av. Dutuit, on Carré des Champs-Élysées, 8e, Champs-Élysées* ☎ *01–53–05–10–01* 🖉 *Reservations essential* 🏠 *Jacket required* ☾ *Closed weekends and Aug. No lunch Mon.* Ⓜ *Concorde, Champs-Élysées–Clemenceau* ✛ *1:F6.*

$ ✕ **Le Hide.** Hide Kobayashi, known as "Koba," is one of several Japanese
BISTRO   chefs in Paris who trained with some of the biggest names in French cuisine before opening their own restaurants. With stints at Lenôtre, the Louis XV in Monaco, and Joël Robuchon under his belt, Koba had the brilliant idea of opening a great-value bistro near the Arc de Triomphe (the three-course prix fixe is €29). Not surprisingly, this little dining room with cream-color walls and red banquettes became instantly popular with locals as well as visiting Japanese and Americans who follow the food news. Generosity is the key to the cooking here, which steers clear of haute cuisine flourishes: both the monkfish fricassee with anchovy-rich tapenade and a classic veal kidney in mustard sauce, for instance, come with a heap of mashed potatoes. For dessert try the stunning *île flottante* (floating island), made with oven-baked meringue. Wines by the glass start at €2—unheard-of in this area. $ *Average main: €17* ⊠ *10 rue du Général Lanzerac, 8e, Champs-Élysées* ☎ *01–45–74–15–81* ⊕ *www.lehide.fr* 🖉 *Reservations essential* ☾ *Closed Sun. and 2 wks in Aug. No lunch Sat.* Ⓜ *Charles de Gaulle–Étoile* ✛ *1:B3.*

$$ ✕ **Mini Palais.** The new Mini Palais, inside the Grand Palais, has gotten
MODERN FRENCH it smashingly right. With silvery ceilings, dark wood, and faux clas-
sical marbles, it's among Paris's most stylish dining rooms, but the
menu—designed by superchef Eric Frechon of Le Bristol and executed
by protegé Stephane d'Aboville—is the real draw. The *burger de magret
et foie gras*, a flavorful mélange of tender duckling breast and duck foie
gras drizzled with truffled *jus* on a buttery brioche bun underscores
what's best about this place: a thoroughly modern cuisine with an old-
fashioned extravagance. For a summer meal or a cocktail, the majesti-
cally pillared terrace overlooking Pont d'Alexandre III must be the most
beautiful in Paris. What's more, it's open nonstop from 10 am to 2 am,
an oasis in a neighborhood short on conveniences. $ *Average main: €25*
✉ *3 av. Winston Churchill, 8e, Champs-Élysées* ☎ *01–42–56–42–42*
⊕ *www.minipalais.com* ✍ *Reservations essential* Ⓜ *Champs-Élysées–
Clemenceau* ✛ *1:F6.*

$$$$ ✕ **Pierre Gagnaire.** If you want to venture to the frontier of contempo-
MODERN FRENCH rary luxe cooking—and if money is no object—dinner here is a must.
Fodor's Choice Chef Pierre Gagnaire's work is at once intellectual and poetic, often
★ blending three or four unexpected tastes and textures in a single dish.
Just taking in the menu requires concentration (ask the waiters for
help), so complex are the multiline descriptions about the dishes' six or
seven ingredients. The Grand Dessert, a seven-dessert marathon, will
leave you breathless, though it's not as overwhelming as it sounds. The
businesslike gray-and-wood dining room feels refreshingly informal,
especially at lunch, but it also lacks the grandeur expected at this level.
The uninspiring prix-fixe lunch (€110) and occasional ill-judged dishes
(Gagnaire is a big risk taker, but also one of France's top chefs) linger
as drawbacks, and prices keep shooting skyward, so Pierre Gagnaire is
an experience best saved for the financial elite. $ *Average main: €110*
✉ *6 rue de Balzac, 8e, Champs-Élysées* ☎ *01–58–36–12–50* ⊕ *www.
pierre-gagnaire.com* ✍ *Reservations essential* ⊗ *Closed Sat., Aug., and
1 wk at Christmas. No lunch Sun.* Ⓜ *Charles-de-Gaulle–Étoile* ✛ *1:D4.*

$$$ ✕ **Rech.** Having restored the historic Paris bistros Aux Lyonnais
SEAFOOD and Benoît to their former glory, star chef Alain Ducasse turned his pierc-
Fodor's Choice ing attention to this seafood brasserie founded in 1925. His wisdom
★ lies in knowing what not to change: the original Art Deco chairs in the
main floor dining room; seafood shucker Malec, who has been a fix-
ture on this chic stretch of sidewalk since 1982; and the XL éclair (it's
supersize) that's drawn in locals for decades. Original owner Auguste
Rech believed in serving a limited selection of high-quality products—a
principle that suits Ducasse perfectly—and legendary 60-year-old chef
Jacques Maximin is now in the kitchen, turning out Med-inspired dishes
such as tomato cream with crayfish and fresh almonds or Niçoise-
style sea bass with thyme fritters. Save room for the whole farmer's
Camembert, another Rech tradition. A great-value €32 menu is available at lunch; the dinner menu is €54. $ *Average main: €32* ✉ *62 av.
des Ternes, 17e, Champs-Élysées* ☎ *01–45–72–29–47* ⊕ *www.rech.fr*
✍ *Reservations essential* ⊗ *Closed Sun., Mon., late July–late Aug., and
1 wk at Christmas* ✛ *1:B3.*

14

$$$ FRENCH FUSION 🍴 **Stella Maris.** A pretty Art Deco front window is the calling card for this pristine spot near the Arc de Triomphe. An expense-account crowd mixes with serious French gourmands here to dine on the subtle cuisine of likable Japanese chef Tateru Yoshino, who trained with Joël Robuchon. Yoshino rewrites his menu four times a year but you can always find hints of Japan in dishes—made with organic ingredients—such as eel blanquette with grilled cucumber, salmon prepared four ways (in salt, marinated with dill, smoked, and panfried), and a unique take on the French classic *tête de veau,* with turtle jus. Put your trust in the chef by opting for the tasting menu (€99 or €130), or keep your budget in check with the €49 lunch menu or €70 seasonal menu. [$] *Average main: €36* ✉ *4 rue Arsène-Houssaye, 8e, Champs-Élysées* ☎ *01–42–89–16–22* ✍ *Reservations essential* ⏲ *Closed Sun. No lunch Sat.* [M] *Étoile* ✣ *1:C4.*

$$$$ MODERN FRENCH 🍴 **Taillevent.** Perhaps the most traditional—for many diners this is only high praise—of all Paris luxury restaurants, this grande dame basks in renewed freshness under brilliant chef Alain Solivérès, who draws inspiration from the Basque country, Bordeaux, and Languedoc for his daily-changing menu. Traditional dishes such as scallops *meunière* (with butter and lemon) are matched with contemporary choices like a splendid spelt risotto with truffles and frogs' legs or panfried duck liver with caramelized fruits and vegetables. One of the 19th-century paneled salons has been turned into a winter garden, and contemporary paintings adorn the walls. The service is flawless, and the exemplary wine list is well priced. All in all, a meal here comes as close to the classic haute-cuisine experience as you can find in Paris. There's an €82 lunch menu and special wine "degustation" evenings, pairing food with exceptional wines from their legendary cave for €180. [$] *Average main: €110* ✉ *15 rue Lamennais, 8e, Champs-Élysées* ☎ *01–44–95–15–01* 🌐 *www.taillevent.com* ✍ *Reservations essential Jacket and tie* ⏲ *Closed weekends and Aug.* [M] *Charles-de-Gaulle–Étoile* ✣ *1:D4.*

EASTERN PARIS

BASTILLE/NATION

$$$ BISTRO 🍴 **Au Trou Gascon.** This classy establishment off Place Daumesnil—well off the beaten tourist track but worth the trip—is overseen by celebrated chef Alain Dutournier while his wife runs the dining room, which combines contemporary furnishings and beautiful ceiling moldings. Dutournier does a refined take on the cuisine of Gascony—a region renowned for its ham, foie gras, lamb, and duck. Most popular with the regulars are the surprisingly light cassoulet (all the meats are grilled before going into the pot) with big white Tarbais beans and a superb duck or goose confit. There is an ethereal dessert of raspberries, ice cream, and meringue. Prices are steep but there is a limited-choice lunch menu for €40 and a five-course tasting menu at dinner for €60. With some 1,100 wines and 130 Armagnacs to choose from, this is the place to splurge on vintage. [$] *Average main: €36* ✉ *40 rue Taine, 12e, Bastille/Nation* ☎ *01–43–44–34–26* 🌐 *www.autrougascon.com* ⏲ *Closed weekends, Aug., and 1 wk at Christmas* [M] *Daumesnil* ✣ *4:H4.*

$$ BRASSERIE 🍴 **Bofinger.** One of the oldest, loveliest, and most popular brasseries in Paris has generally improved in recent years, so stake out one of the tables dressed in crisp white linen under the glowing Art Nouveau glass cupola and enjoy classic brasserie fare: stick to trademark dishes such as the seafood, choucroute, steak tartare, or smoked haddock with spinach, as the seasonal specials can be hit-or-miss. Take advantage of the prix-fixe menus for €28.50 (two courses) and €33.50 (three courses) and all-day service beginning at noon on Sunday. [$] *Average main: €20* ✉ *5–7 rue de la Bastille, 4e, Bastille/Nation* ☎ *01–42–72–87–82* [M] *Bastille* ✣ *4:H2.*

$ CAFÉ Fodor's Choice ★ 🍴 **Jacques Genin.** Master chocolatier-pâtissièr Jacques Genin deserves the legion d'honneur for his efforts to restore great traditional French pastries to their classic form, particularly the august mille-feuille. Genin's stripped-down version disposes with the usual bells and whistles—fresh fruit, custard, chocolate—to achieve a scintillating clarity: layers of lightly caramelized pâte feuilletée, a buttery puff pastry, and an ethereal, barely sweet pastry cream in either vanilla, caramel, or praline. All of the glorious pastries in this tearoom, chocolate boutique, and pastry shop (probably the most beautiful in Paris, by the way) are available for takeaway, but this one is assembled to order and is best eaten fresh on the premises. Along with a cup of Genin's bittersweet hot chocolate, well, you get the picture. Oh, yes, and then there are the chocolates, some of Paris's finest. [$] *Average main: €8* ✉ *133 rue de Turenne, 3e, Bastille/Nation* ☎ *01–45–77–29–01* 🌐 *jacquesgenin.fr/* ⏲ *Closed Mon.* [M] *Filles du Calvaire* ✣ *2:G6.*

$ WINE BAR 🍴 **Jacques Mélac.** This wine bar has been in the family since 1938 and is named after the jolly second-generation owner who harvests grapes from the vine outside and bottles his own wines. Cheese is hacked from a giant hunk of Cantal, and much of the hearty bistro fare hearkens back to the Aveyron, a notable gastronomic region of France whence the Mélac family proudly hails. [$] *Average main: €17* ✉ *42 rue Léon-Frot, 11e, Bastille/Nation* ☎ *01–43–70–59–27* 🌐 *www.melac.fr* ⏲ *Closed Sun., Mon., and Aug.* [M] *Charonne* ✣ *4:H2.*

$$ BISTRO 🍴 **La Gazzetta.** This bistro epitomizes what makes Paris such an exciting culinary hub right now: a talented young chef serving inventive, market-driven food at an offbeat location. Chef Petter Nilsson began cooking in his native Sweden and honed his skills in Provence; both figure in the kind of dishes that have made this a foodie hot spot, where fish—often lightly cooked or smoked—and regional meats (like Pyrénées lamb) are featured. It's a set menu (one starter, one main, one dessert), and whether it's a velvety spinach pesto in a spelt risotto or a silky purée of celeriac with grilled eel, veggies are never just sidekicks. The Art Deco dining room and old-style zinc bar are especially atmospheric at dinnertime when the lights are low; the three-course €17 lunch menu is a steal. [$] *Average main: €23* ✉ *29 rue de Cotte, 12e, Bastille/Nation* ☎ *01–43–47–47–05* 🌐 *www.lagazzetta.fr* ✍ *Reservations essential* ⏲ *Closed Sun., Mon., Aug.* [M] *Ledru Rollin* ✣ *4:H4.*

$$ BISTRO 🍴 **La Table de Claire.** Just the kind of neighborhood bistro everyone wishes they had around the corner, La Table de Claire is inviting with its vintage tiles, Formica bar, contemporary light fixtures, and clientele

14

of locals who invariably greet the owners with handshakes or kisses. Serge Haguenauer runs the dining room while Claire Seban watches over bistro dishes such as rabbit confit in the style of duck, steamed cod with ginger butter and four vegetables, and blanc manger with berries. Lunch menus are a great deal at €13 and €16, and once a month, Claire and Serge host a chef d'un soir, usually a gifted amateur who, for two days, presents a menu of French or international dishes alongside the usual kitchen offerings. $ *Average main: €20* ⊠ *30 rue Émile Lepeu, 11e, Bastille/Nation* ☎ *01–43–70–59–84* ⊕ *www.latabledeclaire.fr* ⊗ *Closed Sun., Mon. and Aug.* Ⓜ *Charonne* ✛ *2:H5.*

$ ✕ **Le Baron Bouge.** Formerly Le Baron Rouge, this proletarian wine bar
WINE BAR   near the Place d'Aligre market is a throwback to another era, with a few tables and giant barrels along the walls for filling and refilling your take-home bottles. A fun time to come is Sunday morning (yes, morning) when it's packed with locals who have just been to the market or on a winter's day when oysters are shucked and slurped curbside. $ *Average main: €11* ⊠ *1 rue Théophile Roussel, 12e, Bastille/Nation* ☎ *01–43–43–14–32* ⊗ *Closed Mon.* Ⓜ *Ledru-Rollin* ✛ *4:H3.*

$$ ✕ **Le Bistrot Paul Bert.** Faded 1930s decor: check. Boisterous crowd:
BISTRO   check. Thick steak with real frites: check. Good value: check. The Paul Bert delivers everything you could want from a traditional Paris bistro, so it's no wonder its two dining rooms fill every night with a cosmopolitan crowd. Some are from the neighborhood, others have done their bistro research, but they've all come for the balance of ingredients that makes for a feel-good experience every time. The impressively stocked wine cellar helps, as does the cheese cart, the laid-back yet efficient staff, and hearty dishes such as monkfish with white beans and duck with pears. The reasonable prix fixe is three courses for €36, or you can order à la carte. If you're looking for an inexpensive wine, choose from the chalkboard rather than the wine list. $ *Average main: €22* ⊠ *18 rue Paul Bert, 11e, Bastille/Nation* ☎ *01–43–72–24–01* ⊴ *Reservations essential* ⊗ *Closed Sun., Mon., and Aug.* ✛ *4:H3.*

$$ ✕ **Le Repaire de Cartouche.** In this split-level, dark-wood bistro between
BISTRO   Bastille and République, chef Rodolphe Paquin applies a disciplined creativity to earthy French regional dishes. The menu changes regularly, but typical options are a salad of haricots verts topped with tender slices of squid; scallops on a bed of diced pumpkin; juicy lamb with white beans; game dishes in winter; and old-fashioned desserts like baked custard with tiny shell-shaped madeleines. In keeping with cost-conscious times, there is a bargain three-course lunch menu for €17 that doesn't skimp on ingredients—expect the likes of homemade pâté to start, followed by fried red mullet or hanger steak with french fries, and chocolate tart. The wine list is very good, too, with some bargain selections from small producers. $ *Average main: €24* ⊠ *99 rue Amelot, 11e, Bastille/Nation* ☎ *01–47–00–25–86* ⊴ *Reservations essential* ⊗ *Closed Sun., Mon., and Aug.* Ⓜ *Filles du Calvaire* ✛ *4:G1.*

$$ ✕ **Rino.** The unanointed might walk right by this modest storefront eat-
BISTRO   ery without an inkling of the gastronomic mecca within. Decor takes second place to the impressive cuisine that the welcoming Roman chef Giovani Passerini—Rino to his friends—consistently offers. Dishes like

tender mackerel ravioli alongside razor-thin slices of watermelon radish, briny bottarga, and a drizzle of bitter lemon aïoli, or lightly seared monkfish with tiny samplings of sea urchin and velvety bone marrow served with a rich squid-ink sauce highlight what this restaurant is about: top-notch ingredients, original pairings, and a rare simplicity. With a reasonable four- or six-course dinner menu (€38, €55) and lunch menus of two or three courses (€20, €25)—there is no à la carte—and a small but informed wine list, what's not to love? $ *Average main: €20* ✉ *46 rue Trousseau, 11e, Bastille/Nation* ☎ *01–48–06–95–85* ⚑ *Reservations essential* ⊘ *Closed Sun., Mon., Aug., and 1 week at Christmas. No lunch Tues.–Thurs.* Ⓜ *Charonne* ✛ *4:H3.*

$$$
ITALIAN

✗ **Sardegna a Tavola.** Paris might have more Italian restaurants than you can shake a noodle at, but few smack of authenticity like this out-of-the-way Sardinian spot with peppers, braids of garlic, and cured hams hanging from the ceiling. Dishes are listed in Sardinian with French translation—*malloredus* is a gnocchi-like pasta; Sardinian ravioli are stuffed with cheese and mint. Perhaps best of all are the clams in a spicy broth with tiny pasta and the orange-scented prawns with tagliatelle, though the choice of dishes changes with the seasons and the chef's imagination. $ *Average main: €32* ✉ *1 rue de Cotte, 12e, Bastille/Nation* ☎ *01–44–75–03–28* ⊘ *Closed Sun. and Aug. No lunch Mon.* Ⓜ *Ledru-Rollin* ✛ *4:H4.*

$$
BISTRO

✗ **Septime.** This is the kind of bistro we'd all love in our neighborhood—good food and a convivial atmosphere where diners crane to admire each other's plates. Bertrand Grébaut, the affable young chef, can often be found chatting away with guests in the cacophonous dining room. In a neighborhood where excellent bistro fare is ridiculously plentiful—thanks to several talented young chefs who've set up shop here in the last few years—this spot stands out. Seasonal ingredients, inventive pairings, excellent natural wines, plus dishes like creamy gnochetti in an orange rind–flecked gouda sauce sprinkled with coriander flowers; tender fillet of Landes hen in a mustard-peanut sauce, with braised endive and cabbage perfumed with lemon; fresh white asparagus with raspberries and blanched almonds, are sophisticated and satisfying. The €26 weekday lunch menu is a good place to begin. $ *Average main: €20* ✉ *80 rue de Charonne, 11e, Bastille/Nation* ☎ *01–43–67–38–29* ⊕ *www.septime-charonne.fr* ⚑ *Reservations essential* ⊘ *Closed Sat. lunch, Sun., Mon.* Ⓜ *Ledru Rollin, Charonne* ✛ *4:H3.*

$$
MODERN
ARGENTINE

✗ **Unico.** An architect and a photographer, both Parisians born in Argentina, teamed up to open one of Bastille's hottest restaurants—literally hot, too, since the Argentinean meat served here is grilled over charcoal—and good-looking young locals pile into the orange-tiled, vintage 1970s dining room or the covered terrace to soak up the party vibe. Whichever cut of beef you choose (the ultimate being *lomo*, or fillet), it's so melt-in-your-mouth that the sauces served on the side seem almost superfluous. Dessert probably won't be necessary, but banana in dulce de leche could satisfy the strongest sweet craving. If there's a wait for a table, head across the street to the eponymous *cave à vin* for an Argentine apéro and appetizer. $ *Average main: €24* ✉ *15 rue Paul-Bert, 11e, Bastille/Nation* ☎ *01–43–67–68–08* ⊕ *www.resto-unico.com*

14

🕐 *Closed Sun., 2 wks in Aug., Christmas. No lunch Mon.* Ⓜ *Faidherbe-Chaligny* ✛ *4:H3.*

BELLEVILLE

$$
BISTRO
🕐
Fodor's Choice
★

✕ **Le Baratin.** Le Baratin has been around for more than 20 years, but that hasn't stopped it from recently becoming one of the most fashionable out-of-the-way bistros in Paris. The key to its success is the combination of inventive yet comforting cooking by Argentinean-born chef Raquel Carena and a lovingly selected list of organic and natural wines from small producers, courtesy of her partner Philippe Pinoteau. He might seem brusque at first, but show an interest and he opens up like a vintage wine. Carena learned the art of making bouillons from none other than star Breton chef Olivier Roellinger, and uses them to bring out the best in any ingredient from fish to foie gras. ⓢ *Average main: €22* ✉ *3 rue Jouye Rouve, 20e, Ménilmontant* ☎ *01–43–49–39–70* 🍽 *Reservations essential* 🕐 *No lunch Sat., closed Sun., Mon., and Aug.* Ⓜ *Pyrénées, Belleville* ✛ *2:H3.*

CANAL ST-MARTIN

$
WINE BAR

✕ **Jeanne A.** This six-table épicerie-bistro-wine bar on a pretty cobbled street is just the thing for an uncomplicated lunch, dinner, or afternoon snack. Next door to the popular old-style bistro Astier, and run by the same owner, it's the kind of place where you can follow your pleasure—whether it's just a great glass of wine and a plate of artisanal charcuterie and/or cheese you're hungering for, or a full meal, the classic French fare is always very good. Tasty rotisserie chicken is served daily, along with another main, like *gigot d'agneau*, rabbit, or duck fresh from the kitchen next door, served up with creamy potato gratin, side salad or soup of the day, with a dense almond financier for dessert. All this for under €20, *pas mal!* The big table is great for groups of five or more. ⓢ *Average main: €10* ✉ *42 rue Jean-Pierre-Timbaud, 11e, République* ☎ *01–43–55–09–49* 🍽 *Reservations not accepted* 🕐 *Closed Tues., Wed.* Ⓜ *Parmentier, Oberkampf* ✛ *2:H5.*

$$$
MODERN FRENCH

✕ **Le Chateaubriand.** A chef who once presented a single, peeled apple pip (really) on a plate (at the museum restaurant Le Transversal outside Paris) has no ordinary approach to food. Self-taught Basque cook Inaki Aizpitarte is undeniably provocative, but he gets away with it because (a) he's young and extremely cool and (b) he has an uncanny sense of which unexpected ingredients go together, as in a combination of oysters and lime zest in chicken stock. The no-choice, €55 dinner menu is modern and deconstructed, and the vintage dining room buzzes with an artsy, black-dressed crowd. Open for dinner only. ⓢ *Average main: €40* ✉ *129 av. Parmentier, 11e, Canal St-Martin* ☎ *01–43–57–45–95* 🍽 *Reservations essential* 🕐 *Dinner only, closed Sun. and Mon.* Ⓜ *Goncourt* ✛ *2:H5.*

$
WINE BAR

✕ **Le Dauphin.** Avant-garde chef Inaki Aizpatarte has struck again, transforming (with a little help from Rem Koolhaas) a dowdy little café two doors from his acclaimed Le Chateaubriand into a sleek, if chilly, all-marble watering hole for late-night cuisinistas. Honing his ever-iconoclastic take on tapas, the dishes served here—along with a thoughtful selection of natural wines—are a great way to get an idea of what all the fuss is about. Offerings like sweetly delicate crabmeat punctuated with tart marinated radish and avocado puree, or a well-prepared lemon sole drizzled with hazelnut butter highlight what this chef can do with quality ingredients. Dishes are small, well-priced, and meant to be shared to maximize exposure to the food. [$] *Average main: €20* ✉ *131 av. Parmentier, 11e, Canal St-Martin* ☎ *01–55–28–78–88* ✍ *Reservations essential* 🕑 *Closed Sun., Mon. no lunch Sat.* [M] *Parmentier* ✥ *2:H5.*

$ WINE BAR 🍴 **Le Verre Volé.** Cyril Bordarier blazed a path with this minuscule bar à vins, which quickly became the ticket for hipsters seeking out exceptional, good-value natural wines with food to match. Nowadays you're as likely to be seated next to a table of American tourists or expats as a bunch of French wine aficionados. This is not so much due to the chic factor as to Bordarier's insistence on top-quality products. Wines are mostly organic, the charcuterie hails from top artisan producers, and the variety of small dishes alongside a few hearty main courses works just as well for lunch on the fly as for a leisurely dinner. This is a very popular spot, especially for Sunday brunch, so reserve ahead. [$] *Average main: €15* ✉ *67 rue de Lancry, 10e, Canal St-Martin* ☎ *01–48–03–17–34* ✍ *Reservations essential* [M] *République* ✥ *2:G4.*

$$ BISTRO 🍴 **Philou.** On a quiet street between Canal St-Martin and the historic Hôpital Saint-Louis, few places could be more pleasant than a sidewalk table at this most welcome addition to Paris's thriving bistro scene. On a cool day the red banquettes and Ingo Maurer chandelier cast a cozy glow, all the better to enjoy a hearty, well-priced selection of dishes, like slices of foie gras served atop crème de lentilles and sprinkled with garlicky croutons, ham clafoutis with girolle mushrooms, or a rosy beef entrecôte with roasted baby Yukon gold potatoes and mushrooms *de Paris*. In springtime, fat white asparagus is nicely paired with salty smoked haddock and spring peas. A wine list replete with well-chosen natural wines plus the reasonable €25 tasting menu at lunch and €34 at dinner make it one of more popular tables in town, so try to reserve ahead. [$] *Average main: €24* ✉ *12 av. Richerand, 10e, Canal St-Martin* ☎ *01–42–38–00–13* ✍ *Reservations essential* 🕑 *Closed Sun., Mon.* [M] *Jacques Bonsergent* ✥ *2:G4.*

$ BAKERY 🍴 **Véronique Mauclerc.** To really know Paris is to know her great boulangeries, a tradition in free fall since the advent of that notorious cricket bat, the industrial baguette. Thankfully there's an ever-growing group of bakers carrying the flame, literally. Véronique Mauclerc, one of the very best, makes her breads, classic viennoiserie (croissants, turnovers, pain au chocolat), and savory tarts on the premises in a traditional wood-fired oven using only organic flour and natural ferments for leavening. As if this weren't enough, her pastries are a triumph. The fine traditional Paris Brest—a slightly sweet, hazelnut cream–filled pâte à choux sprinkled with slivered almonds—sells out quickly, as do the excellent mini chocolate cakes and fruit strudels. Although out of the way, being two steps from the lovely Buttes Chaumont makes it picnic perfect. [$] *Average main: €5* ✉ *rue de Crimée, 19e, Canal St-Martin* ☎ *01–42–40–64–55* [M] *Botzaris* ✥ *2:H1.*

14

PÈRE LACHAISE

$ ✕ **La Boulangerie.** In a former bakery spruced up with a bread-theme
BISTRO mural, this bistro in the shabby-chic neighborhood of Ménilmontant
dishes up a great-value lunch menu for €14 (two courses) or €17 (three
courses). Dinner is a still-reasonable €32, and the quality of the ingredients is admirable, even if the cooking can be inconsistent. Expect
seasonal dishes like squash soup with spice-bread croutons, pot-roasted
veal with root vegetables, and *cannelés* (eggy, caramelized cakes) with
jasmine ice cream made on the premises. If you're exploring the area
around Père Lachaise, it would be hard to find a better French eatery. $ *Average main: €16* ⊠ *15 rue des Panoyaux, 20e, Père Lachaise*
☎ *01–43–58–45–45* ⚉ *Reservations essential* ⊘ *Closed Sun., Mon., 1
wk in July, 3 wks in Aug., and 1 wk at Christmas. No lunch Sat.* Ⓜ *Ménilmontant* ✛ *2:H5.*

$ ✕ **Dong Huong.** Dong Huong isn't a secret, but you wouldn't find it by
VIETNAMESE accident. These two undecorated dining rooms on a Belleville side street
are where the local Chinese and Vietnamese come for a reassuring bowl
of *pho* (noodle soup) or plate of grilled lemongrass-scented meat with
rice. Spicy, peanut-y *saté* soup is a favorite, and at this price (€6.50)
you can also spring for a plate of crunchy imperial rolls, to be wrapped
in accompanying lettuce and mint. Try one of the lurid nonalcoholic
drinks; they're surprisingly tasty. $ *Average main: €11* ⊠ *14 rue Louis-
Bonnet, 11e, Père Lachaise* ☎ *01–43–57–18–88* ⊘ *Closed Tues. and
3 wks in Aug.* Ⓜ *Belleville* ✛ *2:H4.*

RÉPUBLIQUE

$$ ✕ **Astier.** There are three good reasons to go to Astier: the generous
BISTRO cheese platter plunked on your table atop a help-yourself wicker tray,
☕ the exceptional wine cellar with bottles dating back to the 1970s, and
the French bistro fare, even if portions seem to have diminished over the
years. Dishes like marinated herring with warm potato salad, sausage
with lentils, and baba au rhum are classics on the frequently changing
set menu for €35, which includes a selection of no less than 20 cheeses.
The vintage 1950s wood-panel dining room attracts plenty of locals and
remains a fairly sure bet in the area, especially because it's open every
day (except in August). $ *Average main: €21* ⊠ *44 rue Jean-Pierre Tim-
baud, 11e, République* ☎ *01–43–57–16–35* ⊕ *www.restaurant-astier.
com* ⚉ *Reservations essential* ⊘ *Closed in Aug.* Ⓜ *Parmentier* ✛ *2:H5.*

$ ✕ **Au Passage.** This recently opened *bistrot à vins* has the lived-in look
BISTRO of a neighborhood eatery going 30 years strong. Which, in fact, it was
until two veterans of the raging Paris wine bar scene reinvented the
place, keeping the laid-back atmosphere and adding a serious foodie
menu that quickly became one of the best deals in town. For lunch, the
two-course €13 formule offers a choice of meat or fish, and at dinner the
menu shifts to a blackboard selection of small €4 to €8 tapas dishes—
including several house-made pâtés, fresh tomato or beet salad, a superb
seafood carpaccio, and artisanal charcuterie and cheeses. Four or more
diners can hack away at a crispy-succulent roasted lamb haunch, which
ours pretty much gnawed to the bone. The excellent wine list features
plenty of natural wines. It's a diverse and lively crowd of happy din-
ers who know they've found a very good thing. $ *Average main: €13*

✉ *1 bis, Passage Saint-Sébastien, 11e, République* ☎ *01–43–55–07– 52* ⌕ *Reservations essential* ⊗ *Closed Sun., Sat. lunch, Mon. dinner* Ⓜ *Saint Ambroise; Saint Sebastien Froissart; Richard Lenoir* ✛ *2:H6.*

$ ✗ **Chez Omar.** This is no longer the only trendy North African restau-
MOROCCAN rant in town, but during fashion week you still might see top models with legs like gazelles touching up their lipstick in front of the vintage mirrors—though that doesn't stop them from digging into huge plat-ters of couscous with grilled skewered lamb, spicy *merguez* sausage, lamb shank, or chicken, washed down with robust, fruity Algerian or Moroccan wine. Proprietor Omar Guerida speaks English and is famously friendly to all. The setting is that of a beautifully faded French bistro, complete with elbow-to-elbow seating, so be prepared to par-take of your neighbors' conversations. $ *Average main: €17* ✉ *47 rue de Bretagne, 3e, République* ☎ *01–42–72–36–26* ⌕ *Reservations not accepted* ▭ *No credit cards* ⊗ *No lunch Sun.* Ⓜ *Temple, République* ✛ *2:F6.*

$ ✗ **Le Martel.** Of the scads of neighborhood couscous joints in Paris, a few
MOROCCAN have become fashionable thanks to their host's magnetic personality and their stylish setting—and this converted bistro ranks among the more recent of that set. It's crowded, but the clientele of fashion designers, photographers, models, and media folk is as cool as it gets in this up-and-coming quartier. Everyone digs in to a mix of French standbys (such as artichokes with vinaigrette) and more exotic fare like lamb tagine with almonds, prunes, and dried apricots. $ *Average main: €17* ✉ *3 rue Martel, 10e, République* ☎ *01–47–70–67–56* ⊗ *Closed Sun. and 2 wks in Aug. No lunch Sat.* Ⓜ *Château d'Eau* ✛ *2:E4.*

LATIN QUARTER

$$$ ✗ **Fogòn St-Julien.** The most ambitious Spanish restaurant in Paris occu-
SPANISH pies an airy Seine-side space, avoiding tapas-bar clichés. The seasonal all-tapas menu, at €54 per person, is the most creative choice, but that would mean missing out on the seven different takes on paella that are available daily: perhaps saffron with seafood (which could be a bit more generous), inky squid, vegetable, or Valencia-style with rabbit, chicken, and vegetables. Finish up with custardy crème Catalan and a glass of muscatel. $ *Average main: €27* ✉ *45 quai des Grands-Augustins, 5e, Latin Quarter* ☎ *01–43–54–31–33* ⊕ *www.fogon.fr* ⌕ *Reservations essential* ⊗ *Closed Mon., 2 wks in Aug.–Sept., and 1 wk in Jan. No lunch Tues.–Fri.* Ⓜ *St-Michel* ✛ *4:C2.*

$$$ ✗ **Itinéraires.** Having paid his dues in the tiny kitchen of Le Temps au
BISTRO Temps near the Bastille, young Lyonnais chef Sylvain Sendra is now happily ensconced in the spacious former premises of the noted Chez Toutoune. The once-faded surroundings have been revitalized, and the taupe walls, a long *table d'hôtes* (shared table), and a bar for solo meals or tapas-style snacks are all new. Sendra's cooking, meanwhile, is as inspired as ever. Menu highlights include a tart of foie gras, duck confit, and nutmeg, cod poached in a vegetable and sage bouillon sprinkled with lemon "caviar," and a deconstructed lemon tart with a touch of celery. A good wine list with some reasonable bottles and a well-conceived selection of wines by the glass to pair with the meal. Prices

14

run the gamut from a €29 two-course lunch (€39 for three courses) and a €59 or €79 degustation menu at dinner. [$] *Average main: €25* ✉ *5 rue de Pontoise, 5e, Latin Quarter* ☎ *01–46–33–60–11* 🌐 *www.restaurantitineraires.com/* ✍ *Reservations essential* 🕓 *Closed Sun., Mon., and Tues. lunch* [M] *Maubert-Mutualité* ✥ *4:E4.*

$$ MODERN FRENCH 👶 🍴 **L'Avant-Goût.** Christophe Beaufront belongs to a generation of gifted bistro chefs who have rejected the pressure-cooker world of haute cuisine in favor of something more personal and democratic. The result: delighted and loyal customers. The three-course dinner prix-fixe costs €32, and there's a lunch menu for €14 (soup, main course, glass of wine, and coffee). Typical of his market-inspired cooking is his signature pot-au-feu *de cochon aux épices,* in which spiced pork stands in for the usual beef, and the bouillon is served separately. Homemade desserts and a good-value wine list round off a satisfying experience. Children get an especially warm welcome here. Drop into his *épicerie* across the street to browse the wine selection or order dinner to go, complete with a returnable cast-iron pot. [$] *Average main: €19* ✉ *26 rue Bobillot, 13e, La Butte aux Cailles* ☎ *01–53–80–24–00* 🌐 *www.lavantgout.com* ✍ *Reservations essential* 🕓 *Closed Sun., Mon.* [M] *Place d'Italie* ✥ *4:G6.*

$$ BISTRO 🍴 **L'Ourcine.** Sylvain Danière knows just what it takes to open a wildly popular bistro: choose an obscure location in a residential neighborhood, decorate it simply but cheerfully, work extremely hard, set competitive prices (€34 for three courses at dinner, €26 for two courses at lunch), and constantly reinvent your menu. The real key ingredient is talent, though, and Danière has plenty of it, as demonstrated by his updated duckling *au sang* (in blood sauce) with celery-root puree, and a popular *crémeux au chocolat* (chocolate pudding) to finish things off. Locals mingle with well-informed tourists from Texas or Toulouse in the red-and-cream dining room, and you can watch the chef hard at work in his small kitchen. The only flaw is the inconsistent—and sometimes brusque—service, but one of the small producers' wines should make that go down more easily. [$] *Average main: €19* ✉ *92 rue Broca, 13e, Latin Quarter* ☎ *01–47–07–13–65* 🕓 *Closed Sun., Mon., 3 wks in Aug, and 1 wk in Feb.* [M] *Les Gobelins* ✥ *4:D6.*

$$$$ MODERN FRENCH 🍴 **La Tour d'Argent.** La Tour d'Argent has had a rocky time in recent years with the loss of a Michelin star and the death of owner Claude Terrail, but chef Laurent Delarbre has found his footing, and there's no denying the splendor of the setting overlooking the Seine. If you don't want to splash out on dinner, treat yourself to the three-course lunch menu for a reduced price of €65; this entitles you to succulent slices of one of the restaurant's numbered ducks (the great duck slaughter began in 1919 and is now well past the millionth mallard, as your numbered certificate will attest). Don't be too daunted by the vast wine list—with the aid of the sommelier you can splurge a little (about €80) and perhaps taste a rare vintage Burgundy from the extraordinary cellars, which survived World War II. [$] *Average main: €90* ✉ *15–17 quai de la Tournelle, 5e, Latin Quarter* ☎ *01–43–54–23–31* 🌐 *www.latourdargent.com* ✍ *Reservations essential* 👔 *Jacket and tie* 🕓 *Closed Sun., Mon., and Aug.* [M] *Cardinal Lemoine* ✥ *4:E4.*

$$$ BISTRO

🍴 **Lapérouse.** Émile Zola, George Sand, and Victor Hugo were regulars here, and the restaurant's mirrors still bear diamond scratches from the days when mistresses didn't take jewels at face value. It's hard not to fall in love with this 17th-century Seine-side town house whose warren of intimate, woodwork-graced salons breathes history. A new chef, Christophe Guilbert, recently took over the kitchen; his cuisine seeks a balance between traditional and modern, often drawing on Mediterranean inspirations. For a truly intimate meal, reserve one of the legendary private *salons* where anything can happen (and probably has). You can also sample the restaurant's magic at lunch, when a bargain prix-fixe menu is served for €35–€45 in both the main dining room and the private salons. [$] *Average main: €45* ✉ *51 quai des Grands Augustins, 6e, Latin Quarter* ☎ *01–43–26–68–04* 🌐 *www.laperouse.fr* ✍ *Reservations essential* 🕑 *Closed Sun. and Aug. No lunch Sat.* [M] *St-Michel* ✣ *4:C2.*

$$ BRASSERIE 👍

🍴 **Le Balzar.** Regulars grumble about the uneven cooking at Le Balzar, but they continue to come back because they can't resist the waiters' wry humor and the dining room's amazing people-watching possibilities (you can also drop in for a drink on the terrace). The restaurant attracts politicians, writers, tourists, and local eccentrics—and remains one of the city's classic brasseries: the perfect stop before or after a Woody Allen film in a local art-house cinema. Don't expect miracles from the kitchen, but stick to evergreens like snails in garlic butter, onion soup, panfried veal liver with sautéed potatoes, and baba au rhum for dessert. Night owls congregate for the €21.50 menu, after 10 pm. [$] *Average main: €21* ✉ *49 rue des Écoles, 5e, Latin Quarter* ☎ *01–43–54–13–67* 🌐 *www.brasseriebalzar.com* ✍ *Reservations essential* [M] *Cluny–La Sorbonne* ✣ *4:C4.*

$$ BISTRO

🍴 **Le Buisson Ardent.** This charming Quartier Latin bistro with woodwork and murals dating from 1925 is always packed and boisterous. A glance at chef Arnaud Vansanten's €36 set menu—a bargain €20.90 at lunch for three courses—makes it easy to understand why. Dishes such as chestnut soup with spice bread, squid with chorizo and creamy quinoa, and quince Tatin (upside-down tart) with mascarpone and pink pralines put a fresh twist on French classics, and service is reliably courteous. Bread is made on the premises, and if you don't finish your bottle of wine, you can take it with you to savor the last drops. [$] *Average main: €23* ✉ *25 rue Jussieu, 5e, Latin Quarter* ☎ *01–43–54–93–02* 🌐 *www.lebuissonardent.fr* ✍ *Reservations essential* 🕑 *Closed Aug. No dinner Sun.* [M] *Jussieu* ✣ *4:E4.*

$$ MODERN FRENCH

🍴 **Le Pré Verre.** Chef Philippe Delacourcelle knows his cassia bark from his cinnamon thanks to a long stint in Asia. He opened this lively bistro with its purple-gray walls and photos of jazz musicians to showcase his unique culinary style, rejuvenating archetypal French dishes with Asian and Mediterranean spices. So popular has it proved, especially with Japanese visitors, that the restaurant opened a branch in Tokyo in late 2007. His bargain prix-fixe menus (€13.50 at lunch for a main dish, glass of wine, and coffee; €39.00 for three courses at dinner) change constantly, but his trademark spiced suckling pig with crisp cabbage is always a winner, as is his rhubarb compote with gingered white-chocolate mousse. Ask for advice in selecting wine from a list that

ON THE RUN

Eating on the run doesn't come naturally to the French, and you can easily spend two hours, albeit pleasantly, having lunch in a Paris café. If you're looking for something quicker, there's no point in trying to make a Parisian waiter move faster than he wants to; instead, head to a new breed of snack shop that puts speed first, without sacrificing quality. Prices can be high for what you get (expect to spend €10–€15 for a meal), but it's still a lot cheaper than most bistros.

Be. Star chef Alain Ducasse and wizard baker Eric Kayser make sandwiches a luxury item here; snag one of the handful of tables amid the heavenly bakery aromas. ⊠ *73 bd. de Courcelles, 17e* ☎ *01–46–22–20–20.*

Bob's Juice Bar. If you're strolling along Canal St-Martin, stop into this funky juice bar run by American Marc Grossman, aka Bob, for juices, organic salads, and muffins. Bob's also has a northern Marais offshoot called Kitchen ⊠ *74 rue des Gravilliers, 3e* ⊠ *15 rue Lucien Saimpax, 10e* ☎ *06–82–63–72–74.*

Cojean. This French-run chain takes an Anglo approach to healthful eating, with salads and sandwiches plus quick dishes available at the counter.

Così. This Italian sandwich shop in St-Germain, the original Così, piles imaginative fillings—like fig, Comté cheese, and arugula—onto delicious crusty bread baked in a brick oven. ⊠ *54 rue de Seine, 6e* ☎ *01–46–33–35–36.*

Le Pain Quotidien. Part bakery, part café, this Belgian chain with locations throughout the city serves fresh salads and sandwiches at lunch and is great for breakfast. It tends to be overrun with office workers at peak times.

Oh Poivrier! Specializing in open-face sandwiches, this is a long-established chain with several locations; some have terraces.

Oh Mon Cake. Linger in the comfy upstairs room or perch at the counter of this cheerful Anglo-inspired café near the Louvre to tuck into inventive wraps and salads. ⊠ *154 rue St-Honoré, 1er* ☎ *01–42–60–31–84.*

highlights small producers. $ *Average main: €18* ⊠ *8 rue Thénard, 5e, Latin Quarter* ☎ *01–43–54–59–47* ⊕ *www.lepreverre.com* ⌑ *Reservations essential* ☉ *Closed Sun. and Mon.* Ⓜ *Maubert-Mutualité* ✦ *4:D4.*

$$ ✕ **Les Papilles.** Part wineshop and épicerie, part restaurant, Les Papilles
WINE BAR has a winning formula—pick any bottle off the well-stocked shelf and pay a €7 corkage fee to drink it with your meal; or savor one of several superb wines by the glass at the classic zinc bar. The superb no-choice menu—made with top-notch, seasonal ingredients—usually begins with a luscious velouté, a velvety soup served from a large tureen, and proceeds with a hearty-yet-tender meat dish alongside perfectly cooked vegetables—well worth spending a little extra time for lunch or dinner. $ *Average main: €17* ⊠ *30 rue Gay-Lussac, 5e, Latin Quarter* ☎ *01–43–25–20–79* ⊕ *www.lespapillesparis.fr* ⌑ *Reservations essential* ☉ *Closed Sun., Mon., last wk of July and 2 wks in Aug.* Ⓜ *Cluny–La Sorbonne* ✦ *4:C5.*

$$ ✕ **Ribouldingue.** Find offal off-putting? Off-cuts take pride of place on
BISTRO the €28 prix fixe (there's no à la carte), but don't let that stop you from

trying this bistro near the ancient St-Julien-le-Pauvre church. You can avoid odd animal bits completely, if you must, and still have an excellent meal—opt for dishes like marinated salmon or veal rib with fingerling potatoes—or go out on a limb with the *tétine de vache* (thin breaded and fried slices of cow's udder) and *groin de cochon* (the tip of a pig's snout). This adventurous menu is the brainchild of Nadège Varigny, daughter of a Lyonnais butcher (*quel surprise*). She runs the front of the house while chef Amélie Darvas turns out the impeccable food—veal kidney with potato gratin is a house classic, and there are always three fish dishes. Don't miss the unusual desserts, like tangy ewe's-milk ice cream. $ *Average main: €21* ⊠ *10 rue St-Julien-le-Pauvre, 5e, Latin Quarter* ☎ *01-46-33-98-80* ⊘ *Closed Sun., Mon., 1 wk in spring, 3 wks in Aug., and 1 wk in winter* Ⓜ *St-Michel* ✥ *4:D3.*

14

$$$ ✕ **Sola.** Chef Hiroki Yoshitake was schooled in the kitchens of famed
ECLECTIC innovators Pascal Barbot of Astrance and William Ledeuil of Ze Kitchen Galerie before striking out on his own. Dishes like miso-lacquered foie gras, served with toasted pain de mie, or sake-glazed suckling pig—perfectly crisp on the outside and melting inside—pair traditional Japanese and French ingredients to wondrous effect. Plates are artfully arranged with a sprinkling of piquant shiso leaves or jewel-like roasted vegetables to please the eye and the palate. The excellent-value three-course, €32 lunch menu—it's prix fix only—offers a choice of fish or meat and finishes with Fukano Hirobu's stunning confections. Shoes stay on in the tranquil half-timbered dining room upstairs, but the vaulted room downstairs is totally traditional—and one of the loveliest in Paris. $ *Average main: €28* ⊠ *12 rue de l'Hôtel Colbert, 5e, Latin Quarter* ☎ *01-43-29-59-04* ⊕ *restaurant-sola.com* ⌚ *Reservations essential* ⊘ *Sun., Mon.* Ⓜ *Maubert-Mutualité* ✥ *4:D3.*

$$$ ✕ **Ze Kitchen Galerie.** William Ledeuil made his name at the popular
MODERN FRENCH Les Bouquinistes before opening this contemporary bistro in a loftlike
Fodor's Choice space. The name might not be inspired, but the cooking shows creativity
★ and a sense of fun: from a deliberately deconstructed menu featuring raw fish, soups, pastas, and *à la plancha* (grilled) plates, consider the roast and confit duck with a tamarind-and-sesame condiment and foie gras, or lobster with mussels, white beans, and Thai herbs. A tireless experimenter, Ledeuil buys heirloom vegetables direct from farmers and tracks down herbs and spices in Asian supermarkets. The menu changes monthly, and there are several different prix-fixe options at lunch, starting at €27. $ *Average main: €30* ⊠ *4 rue des Grands-Augustins, 6e, Latin Quarter* ☎ *01-44-32-00-32* ⊕ *www.zekitchengalerie.fr* ⌚ *Reservations essential* ⊘ *Closed Sun. No lunch Sat.* Ⓜ *St-Michel* ✥ *4:C2.*

CHINATOWN

$ ✕ **La Chine Massena.** With wonderfully overwrought rooms that seem
CHINESE draped in a whole restaurant-supply catalog's worth of Asiana (plus
☪ four monitors showing the very latest in Hong Kong music videos), this is a fun place. Not only is the pan-Asian food good and moderately priced, but the restaurant itself has lots of entertainment value—wedding parties often provide a free floor show, and on weekends Asian disco follows variety shows. Steamed dumplings, lacquered duck, and the fish and seafood you'll see swimming in the tanks are specialties, and

the oyster bar serves heaping seafood platters. For the best value come at noon on weekdays for the bargain lunch menus, starting at €12.20, or drop in for dim sum on weekends. $ *Average main: €12* ⊠ *Centre Commercial Massena, 13 pl. de Vénétie, 13e, Chinatown* ☎ *01–45–83–98–88* ⊕ *lachinemassena.free.fr* Ⓜ *Porte de Choisy* ✥ *4:F6.*

$ ✕ **Le Bambou.** The line-up outside this restaurant anytime after 7 pm is
VIETNAMESE   a sure sign that something exciting is going on in the kitchen. The small dining room is crowded and noisy, and service is more than brisk—the only thing missing is an eject button on your seat—but it's well worth it for some of the cheapest and most authentic Vietnamese food in town. If you find yourself in doubt about how to eat some of the dishes that involve wrapping meat and herbs in transparent rice paper or lettuce leaves, just spy on the regulars, many of them Vietnamese. Otherwise, go for one of the huge bowls of soup: tripe is popular, though there are plenty of other meat and seafood variations. $ *Average main: €9* ⊠ *70 rue Baudincourt, 13e, Chinatown* ☎ *01–45–70–91–75* ⊙ *Closed Mon. and 3 wks in Aug.* Ⓜ *Tolbiac or Olympiades* ✥ *4:F6.*

MARAIS

$$ ✕ **Au Bourguignon du Marais.** The handsome, contemporary look of this
BISTRO   Marais bistro and wine bar is the perfect backdrop for traditional fare and excellent Burgundies served by the glass and bottle. Unusual for Paris, food is served nonstop from noon to 11 pm, and you can drop by just for a glass of wine in the afternoon. Always on the menu are Burgundian classics such as *jambon persillé* (ham in parsleyed aspic jelly), escargots, and *boeuf bourguignon* (beef stewed in red wine). More up-to-date picks include a cèpe-mushroom velouté with poached oysters, though the fancier dishes are generally less successful. The terrace is busy in warmer months. $ *Average main: €22* ⊠ *52 rue François-Miron, 3e, Marais* ☎ *01–48–87–15–40* ⊙ *Closed Sun. and Mon., 3 wks in Aug., and 2 wks in Feb.* Ⓜ *St-Paul* ✥ *4:F2.*

$$$ ✕ **Benoît.** Without changing the vintage 1912 setting, superchef Alain
BISTRO   Ducasse and Thierry de la Brosse of L'Ami Louis have subtly improved
☾   the menu here, with dishes such as marinated salmon, frogs' legs in a morel-mushroom cream sauce, and an outstanding cassoulet served in a cast-iron pot. Wilfrid Hocquet keeps the kitchen running smoothly, and the waiters are charm incarnate. It's a splurge to be here, so go all the way and top off your meal with the caramelized tarte tatin or a rum-doused baba. $ *Average main: €35* ⊠ *20 rue St-Martin, 4e, Marais* ☎ *01–42–72–25–76* ⊕ *www.benoit-paris.com* ⊙ *Closed Aug. and 1 wk in Feb.* Ⓜ *Châtelet* ✥ *4:D1.*

$ ✕ **Breizh Café.** Eating a crêpe in Paris might seem a bit clichéd, until you
FRENCH   venture into this modern offshoot of a Breton crêperie. The pale-wood,
☾   almost Japanese-style decor is refreshing, but what really makes the difference are the ingredients—farmers' eggs, unpasteurized Gruyère, shiitake mushrooms, Valrhona chocolate, homemade caramel, and extraordinary butter from Breton dairy farmer Jean-Yves Bordier. You'll find all the classics among the galettes (buckwheat crêpes), but it's worth choosing something more adventurous like the *cancalaise* (traditionally smoked herring, potato, crème fraîche, and herring roe). You might also slurp

a few Cancale oysters, a rarity in Paris, and try one of the 20 artisanal ciders on offer. The nonstop serving hours from noon to 11 pm can be a lifesaver if you're shopping in the Marais. Weekends are hectic, so be sure to reserve. $ *Average main: €12* ⊠ *109 rue Vieille du Temple, 3e, Marais* ☎ *01–42–72–13–77* ⊕ *www.breizhcafe.com* ⌂ *Reservations essential* ⊘ *Closed Mon., Tues., and Aug.* Ⓜ *St-Sébastien–Froissart* ✛ *4:F1.*

$ ✕ **Bubar.** In summer look for the hip crowd spilling out the front of this
WINE BAR signless wine bar in the Marais. It's named for Jean-Paul, the bartender (*bubar* or *barbu* is French slang for "bearded"). The wine menu—with many selections available by the glass—features French wines and small-batch vintages from South Africa, Chile, and Argentina, along with small dishes and some lovely *tartines* (toasted bread with various toppings). $ *Average main: €12* ⊠ *3 rue des Tournelles, 4e, Marais* ☎ *01–40–29–97–72* ⊘ *7 days a week, 7 pm–2 am* Ⓜ *Bastille* ✛ *4:G2.*

$ ✕ **Café des Musées.** Warm and authentic, this bustling little bistro offers
BISTRO a convivial slice of Parisian life—and excellent value. Here traditional French bistro fare is adapted to a modern audience, and the best choices are the old tried-and-trues: hand-cut *tartare de boeuf*; rare entrecôte served with a side of perfect frites and homemade Béarnaise; and the classic *parmentier* with pheasant instead of the usual ground beef. Portions are ample, but save room for dessert: old-style favorites like *diplomate aux cherises,* a rum-soaked, cherry-laden sponge cake, or the terrine de chocolate with crème Anglaise are not to be missed. Fixed menus are a bargain at €14 for lunch and €22 at dinner. $ *Average main: €16* ⊠ *49 rue de Turenne, 3e, Marais* ☎ *01–42–72–96–17* ⌂ *Reservations essential* ⊘ *Closed Aug., 1 wk in Jan.* Ⓜ *St-Paul* ✛ *4:G2.*

$ ✕ **Cantine Merci.** Deep inside the city's latest concept store, whose pro-
MODERN FRENCH ceeds go to charities for women in India and Madagascar, lurks the perfect spot for a quick and healthy lunch between bouts of shopping. The brief menu of soups, salads, risottos, and a daily hot dish is more than slightly reminiscent of Rose Bakery—salads such as fava beans with radish and lemon wedges or melon, cherry tomato, and arugula are bright, lively, and crunchy, and you can order a freshly squeezed juice or iced tea with fresh mint to wash it all down. Delicious, homey desserts might include cherry clafoutis or raspberry and pistachio crumble. $ *Average main: €14* ⊠ *111 bd. Beaumarchais, 3e, Marais* ☎ *01–42–77–78–92* ⊕ *www.merci-merci.com* ⊘ *Closed Sun. No dinner* Ⓜ *St-Sébastien–Froissart* ✛ *2:G1.*

$$$ ✕ **Chez Julien.** This charming vintage bistro next to the Seine was easy to
BISTRO overlook until the Costes Brothers—famous for stylish brasseries such
☾ as Café Marly and Georges—worked their magic on it. With a terrace that now extends across the cobbled pedestrian street and a few modish touches in the turn-of-the-20th-century dining room that was once a boulangerie, Chez Julien is now one of the Marais's hippest spots. The steep prices for rather ordinary food reflect this transformation, so you might decide to skip the starters, linger over a thick steak with crisp shoestring fries or roast farmer's chicken with baby potatoes, then head into the Marais for ice cream or gelato. $ *Average main: €30* ⊠ *1 rue du Pont Louis-Philippe, 4e, Marais* ☎ *01–42–78–31–64* ⌂ *Reservations essential* ⊘ *Closed Sun. and Mon. lunch* Ⓜ *Pont Marie* ✛ *4:E2.*

14

$$ ✕ **L'Ambassade d'Auvergne.** A rare authentic Parisian bistro that refuses
BISTRO to change, the Ambassade claims one of the city's great restaurant char-
acters: the maître d' Francis Panek, with his handlebar mustache and
gravelly voice. Settle into the dining room in this ancient Marais house
to try rich dishes from the Auvergne, a sparsely populated region in
central France. Lighter dishes such as turbot with fennel are available,
but it would be missing the point not to indulge in a heaping serving of
the superb lentils in goose fat with bacon or the Salers beef in red wine
sauce with *aligot* (mashed potatoes with cheese). You might want to
loosen your belt for the astonishingly dense chocolate mousse, served
in a giant bowl that allows you to decide the quantity. The Auvergnat
wines come with appetizing descriptions, but don't expect anything
remarkable from this (justifiably) obscure wine region. A three-course,
€29 menu covers all the important bases. $ *Average main: €19* ⊠ *22
rue du Grenier St-Lazare, 3e, Marais* ☎ *01–42–72–31–22* ⊕ *www.
ambassade-auvergne.com* Ⓜ *Rambuteau* ⊕ *4:E1.*

$ ✕ **L'As du Fallafel.** Look no further than the fantastic falafel stands on the
MIDDLE EASTERN pedestrian Rue de Rosiers for some of the cheapest and tastiest meals in
☺ Paris. L'As (the Ace) is widely considered the best of the bunch, which
accounts for the lunchtime line that extends down the street, despite
the recent expansion of the dining room from 70 to 115 seats. A falafel
sandwich costs €5 to go, €7.50 in the dining room, and comes heaped
with grilled eggplant, cabbage, hummus, tahini, and hot sauce. The *sha-
warma* (grilled, skewered meat) sandwich, made with chicken or lamb,
is also one of the finest in town. Though takeout is popular, it can be
more fun (and not as messy) to eat off a plastic plate in one of the two
frenzied dining rooms. Fresh lemonade is the falafel's best match. $ *Av-
erage main: €10* ⊠ *34 rue des Rosiers, 4e, Marais* ☎ *01–48–87–63–60*
☺ *Closed Sat. No dinner Fri.* Ⓜ *St-Paul* ⊕ *4:F2.*

$$$ ✕ **Le Murano.** If you love Baccarat's Cristal Room, you'll adore the
MODERN FRENCH swank Murano Urban Resort's restaurant in the achingly chic north-
ern Marais. There's nothing subtle about the dining room, whose ceiling drips with white tubes of various lengths, so dress to the nines and
arrive with plenty of attitude (or brace yourself with three test tubes of
alcohol at the bar). The chef puts the emphasis on product, with dishes
like Breton sea bass with truffled asparagus ravioli. If you survive the
once-over at the door, surprisingly good-humored dining-room staff
add to the experience. $ *Average main: €45* ⊠ *13 bd. du Temple, 3e,
Marais* ☎ *01–42–71–20–00* ✑ *Reservations essential* Ⓜ *Filles du Calvaire* ⊕ *2:G6.*

$$ ✕ **Restaurant le Gaigne.** Mickaël Gaignon worked with Pierre Gagnaire
BISTRO and Frédéric Anton before opening this pocket-size plum-and-ivory
bistro in a quiet Marais street. His cooking shows the creativity of the
first master chef and the attention to ingredients of the second: each
dish highlights a single product, which is often organic. An example
is *l'oeuf bio,* three soft-boiled organic eggs filled with creamed veg-
etables and served with toast fingers for dipping. Best value is the €45
tasting menu (€64 with matching wines), which brings you five inven-
tive courses; there's also a weekday lunch menu for €18 (two courses)
or €24 (three courses). $ *Average main: €24* ⊠ *12 rue Pecquay, 4e,*

Marais ☎ *01–44–59–86–72* 🌐 *www.restaurantlegaigne.fr* ✍ *Reservations essential* ⏲ *Closed Sun., Mon., and Aug.* [M] *Rambuteau* ✥ *4:F1.*

MONTMARTRE

$$$ BISTRO 🍴 **Bistrot des Deux Théâtres.** This theater-lover's bistro with red-velour banquettes, black-and-white photos of actors, and a giant oil painting depicting celebrities, is always packed, and with good reason. The great-value prix-fixe menu for €39 (there's no à la carte) brings three courses, a bottle of unpretentious wine, and coffee. This isn't a place for modest eaters, so have foie gras or escargots to start, a meaty main such as the crackly crusted rack of lamb, and a potent baba au rhum or rustic lemon meringue tart for dessert. Waiters are jokey, English-speaking, and efficient. [$] *Average main: €30* ✉ *18 rue Blanche, 9e, Montmartre* ☎ *01–45–26–41–43* 🌐 *www.bistrocie.fr* ✍ *Reservations essential* [M] *Trinité* ✥ *2:A2.*

$$$ JAPANESE 🍴 **Guilo Guilo.** Already a star in Kyoto, Eiichi Edakuni created a sensation with his first Parisian restaurant, where 20 diners seated around the black bar can watch him at work each night. The no-choice, €45 set menu is a bargain given the quality and sophistication of the food: it changes every month, but you might come across dishes such as sea bream and wagyu beef on shiso leaves with ponzu sauce, or the chef's signature foie gras sushi, an idea that could easily fall flat but instead soars. If you can afford it, complement your meal with exceptional sakes by the glass, one of which is sparkling. Beware: the first seating gets very rushed, reserve the 9:30 seating if you want to linger. [$] *Average main: €45* ✉ *8 rue Garreau, 18e, Montmartre* ☎ *01–42–54–23–92* 🌐 *www.guiloguilo.com* ✍ *Reservations essential* ⏲ *No lunch, closed Mon.* [M] *Abbesses* ✥ *2:B1.*

$$ BRASSERIE 🍴 **La Mascotte.** Though everyone talks about the "new Montmartre," exemplified by a wave of chic residents and throbbingly cool cafés and bars, it's good to know that the old Montmartre is alive and well at the untrendy-and-proud-of-it Mascotte. This old-fashioned café-brasserie—which dates from 1889, the same year that saw the opening of the Tour Eiffel and the Moulin Rouge—is where you can find neighborhood fixtures such as the drag queen Michou (of the nearby club Chez Michou), who always wears blue. Loyalists come for the seafood platters, the excellent steak tartare, the warming *potée auvergnate* (pork stew) in winter, and the gossip around the *comptoir* (bar) up front. There is a two-course lunch menu for €25 and nonstop service on weekends. [$] *Average main: €24* ✉ *52 rue des Abbesses, 18e, Montmartre* ☎ *01–46–06–28–15* 🌐 *www.la-mascotte-montmartre.com* [M] *Abbesses* ✥ *2:B1.*

$$ BISTRO 👍 🍴 **Le Miroir.** Residents of Montmartre are breathing a sigh of relief: they no longer have to leave the neighborhood to find a good-value bistro. Run by a trio who honed their skills at Lavinia, La Tour d'Argent, and Aux Lyonnais, this red-and-gray bistro with a glass roof at the back serves just the kind of sophisticated comfort food everyone hopes to find in Paris. A meal might start with a plate of *cochonailles* (pâté, cured sausage, and deboned pig's trotter with onion jam) or perhaps a salad of whelks and white beans, before hearty main courses such as

a stunning beef rib for two with sautéed potatoes or duck breast with chanterelle mushrooms and a slice of panfried foie gras. To finish, it's hard to choose between the aged Beaufort cheese or the vanilla pot de crème, served with shortbread and chocolate *financiers* (almond cakes). $ *Average main: €19 ⊠ 94 rue des Martyrs, 18e, Montmartre* ☎ *01–46–06–50–73* ♨ *Reservations essential* ⊘ *Closed Mon., Sun. dinner and 3 wks in Aug.* Ⓜ *Abbesses* ✛ *2:B1.*

$$ ✕ **Rose Bakery.** On a street lined with French food shops selling produce,
BRITISH fish, bread, and cheeses, this British-run café-restaurant might easily go unnoticed—if it weren't for the frequent line out the door. Whitewashed walls, naïve art, and concrete floors provide the decor, and organic producers supply the ingredients for food so fresh and tasty it draws crowds to feast on fresh juices, salads, soups, and hot dishes, such as delicious risotto, followed by carrot cake, sticky toffee pudding, or lemon tarts. The nostalgic can buy homemade granola, British marmalade, or baked beans to take home. Rose Bakery also has its own cookbook in English, plus branches at 30 rue Debelleyme in the Marais and a new spot in the Bastille, inside the Galerie Maison Rouge, at 10 boulevard de la Bastille. Weekend brunch is popular, so plan to arrive early. $ *Average main: €14 ⊠ 46 rue des Martyrs, 9e, Montmartre* ☎ *01–42–82–12–80* ♨ *Reservations not accepted* ⊘ *Closed Mon. and 2 wks in Aug. No dinner* Ⓜ *Notre-Dame-de-Lorette* ✛ *2:C2.*

MONTPARNASSE

$$$ ✕ **L'Assiette.** David Rathgeber spent 12 years working for Alain Ducasse
BISTRO as chef of Aux Lyonnais and then Benoît before taking over this landmark restaurant, where he has created a new menu and welcomed a new clientele. Expect bourgeois classics with a subtle modern touch, perhaps white tuna steak with spinach, lemon, capers, and croutons, and crème caramel with salted butter—all executed with the precision you would expect of a Ducasse veteran. The excellent two-course lunch menu with coffee is a bargain at €23. Each month, the tea "tasting ateliers" span the globe via the world's great teas, pairing these grand cru's with French cuisine. $ *Average main: €27 ⊠ 181 rue du Château, 14e, Montparnasse* ☎ *01–43–22–64–86* ⊕ *www.restaurant-lassiette.com* ⊘ *Closed Mon., Tues., and Aug.* Ⓜ *Pernety, Mouton-Duvernet* ✛ *3:H6.*

$$ ✕ **La Cerisaie.** Cyril Lalanne belongs to a breed of young chefs who like
BISTRO to cook for a privileged few. And if you can nab a seat in this unremarkable yellow-and-red dining room (be sure to call ahead), you'll be rewarded with food whose attention to detail restores your faith in humanity. Foie gras makes several appearances on the chalkboard menu, since Lalanne is from southwest France, but you can also find freshly caught fish and perhaps farmer's pork from Gascony, a rarity in Paris. Lalanne does his own variation on baba au rhum—with Armagnac, another nod to his native region—and the wine list is strong on southwestern French bottles. $ *Average main: €18 ⊠ 70 bd. Edgar Quinet, 14e, Montparnasse* ☎ *01–43–20–98–98* ♨ *Reservations essential* ⊘ *Closed weekends, mid-July–mid-Aug., and 1 wk at Christmas* Ⓜ *Edgar Quinet* ✛ *4:A6.*

$$ ✕ **La Coupole.** This world-renowned cavernous spot with Art Deco
BRASSERIE murals practically defines the term *brasserie*. La Coupole might have
🕒 lost its intellectual aura since it was restored by the Flo restaurant
group, which has put its rather commercial stamp on many historic
Paris brasseries, but it's been popular since Jean-Paul Sartre and Simone
de Beauvoir were regulars, and it's still great fun. Today it attracts a
mix of bourgeois families, tourists, and lone diners treating themselves
to a dozen oysters. Recent additions to the classic brasserie menu are
a tart of caramelized apple and panfried foie gras, beef fillet flambéed
with cognac before your eyes, and profiteroles made with Valrhona
chocolate. You usually can't make reservations after 8 or 8:30, so be
prepared for a wait at the bar. $ *Average main: €21* ⊠ *102 bd. du Mont-
parnasse, 14e, Montparnasse* ☎ *01–43–20–14–20* ⊕ *www.flobrasseries.
com* Ⓜ *Vavin* ✛ *4:A6.*

$ ✕ **La Crêperie Josselin.** With lacey curtains, beamed ceilings, and murals,
MODERN FRENCH this is the closest you'll get to an authentic Breton crêperie without
🕒 heading to the coast. Tuck into a hearty buckwheat galette, perfectly
crisped on the edges and filled with, perhaps, a classic combo of country
ham, egg, cheese, and mushrooms accompanied by a pitcher of refresh-
ing dry Breton cider. For dessert, the traditional crêpe filled with crème
chataigne (chestnut) or the sublime *caramel au beurre salé* are not to be
missed. With a two-course lunch *formule* with beverage for €10, this is
a great place for a quick, satisfying, and thoroughly French meal. Extra
bonus: the kids will love it. $ *Average main: €10* ⊠ *67 rue du Mont-
parnasse, 14e, Montparnasse* ☎ *01–43–20–93–50* ▭ *No credit cards*
◷ *Closed Mon., Aug., and 1 wk in Jan.* Ⓜ *Vavin, Edgar Quinet* ✛ *3:H6.*

$$$ ✕ **Le Dôme.** Now a fancy fish brasserie serving seafood delivered fresh
BRASSERIE from Normandy every day, this restaurant began as a dingy meeting
place for exiled artists and intellectuals like Lenin and Picasso. Try
the *sole meunière* or the *bouillabaisse,* the ingredients of which are on
display in their raw form in the restaurant's sparkling fish shop next
door. You can still drop by the covered terrace for a cup of coffee or a
drink. $ *Average main: €34* ⊠ *108 bd. Montparnasse, 14e, Montpar-
nasse* ☎ *01–43–35–25–81* ◷ *Closed Sun. and Mon. in July and Aug.*
Ⓜ *Vavin* ✛ *4:A6.*

$$ ✕ **Le Timbre.** Working in a tiny open kitchen, Manchester native Chris
BISTRO Wright could teach many a French chef a thing or two about *la cuisine
française.* He uses only the finest suppliers to produce a constantly
changing seasonal menu that keeps the locals coming back: in fall you
might sample the *cochon noir de Bigorre* (a pedigreed pig from south-
west France) with marinated red cabbage, or blood sausage with french
fries. The signature mille-feuille is spectacular, but try not to miss *le
vrai et le faux fromage* (literally "the real and the fake cheese"): per-
haps a two-year-old British cheddar juxtaposed with a farmer's goat
cheese from the Ardèche. (The joke is that the English cheese is the
"real" cheese and the French cheese is fake—although French people
might read it the other way.) $ *Average main: €18* ⊠ *3 rue Ste-Beuve,
6e, Montparnasse* ☎ *01–45–49–10–40* ⊕ *www.restaurantletimbre.com*
🖋 *Reservations essential* ◷ *Closed Sun., Mon., Aug., and 10 days at
Christmas* Ⓜ *Vavin* ✛ *4:A5.*

14

OPÉRA/GRANDS BOULEVARDS

$$ BISTRO 🍴 **Aux Lyonnais.** With a passion for the old-fashioned bistro, Alain Ducasse resurrected this 1890s gem by appointing a terrific young chef to oversee the short, frequently changing, and reliably delicious menu of Lyonnais specialties. Dandelion salad with crisp potatoes, bacon, and a poached egg; watercress soup poured over parsleyed frogs' legs; and fluffy *quenelles de brochet* (pike-perch dumplings) show he is no bistro dilettante. The decor hews to tradition, too, with a zinc bar, an antique coffee machine, and original turn-of-the-20th-century woodwork. There's a limited-choice lunch menu for €28, but the cacophonous dining room is jammed with traders from nearby Bourse. Tables turn relatively quickly, so despite the gorgeous setting this is not a spot for a romantic meal. [$] *Average main: €24* ✉ *32 rue St-Marc, 2e, Opéra/Grands Boulevards* ☎ *01–42–96–65–04* 🌐 *www.auxlyonnais.com* 🕒 *Closed Sun., Mon., and 3 wks in Aug. No lunch Sat.* [M] *Bourse* ✣ *2:B4.*

$ BISTRO 👍 🍴 **Chartier.** This classic *bouillon* (a term referring to the Parisian soup restaurants popular among workers in the early 20th century) is a part of the Gérard Joulie group of bistros and brasseries, which discreetly updated the menu without changing the fundamentals. People come here more for the bonhomie and the stunning 1896 interior than the cooking, which could be politely described as unambitious—then again, where else can you find a plate of foie gras for €6.80? This cavernous restaurant—the only original fin-de-siécle *bouillon* to remain true to its mission of serving cheap, sustaining food to the masses—enjoys a huge following, including one regular who has come for lunch nearly every day since 1946. You may find yourself sharing a table with strangers as you study the old-fashioned menu of such standards as pot-au-feu and blanquette de veau. [$] *Average main: €11* ✉ *7 rue du Faubourg-Montmartre, 9e, Opéra/Grands Boulevards* ☎ *01–47–70–86–29* 🌐 *www.restaurant-chartier.com* ✍ *Reservations not accepted* 🕒 *Open 7 days a week* [M] *Montmartre* ✣ *2:C4.*

$$ BISTRO 🍴 **Chez Casimir.** Thierry Breton's bright, easygoing bistro is popular with polished Parisian professionals, for whom it serves as a sort of canteen—why cook when you can eat this well so affordably? The €32 dinner menu (€24 for two courses at lunch) covers lentil soup with fresh croutons, braised endive and andouille salad, and roast lamb on a bed of Paimpol beans, and there are 12 cheeses to choose from. Good, if not exceptional, desserts include *pain perdu,* a dessert version of French toast—here it's topped with a roasted pear or whole cherries. Drop in at lunchtime on the weekend for the great-value €26 buffet. There is no à la carte. [$] *Average main: €32* ✉ *6 rue de Belzunce, 10e, Opéra/Grands Boulevards* ☎ *01–48–78–28–80* 🕒 *Closed 3 wks in Aug. and 1 wk at Christmas. No dinner weekends* [M] *Gare du Nord* ✣ *2:E2.*

$$ MODERN FRENCH 👍 🍴 **Drouant.** Best known for the literary prizes awarded here since 1914, Drouant has shed its dusty image to become a forward-thinking restaurant. The man behind the transformation is Alsatian chef Antoine Westermann, who runs the hit bistro Mon Vieil Ami on Ile St-Louis. At Drouant the menu is more playful, revisiting the French hors d'oeuvres tradition with starters that come as a series of four plates. Diners can pick from themes such as French classics (like a deconstructed leek

salad) or convincing mini-takes on Thai and Moroccan dishes. Main courses similarly encourage grazing, with accompaniments in little cast-iron pots and white porcelain dishes. Even desserts take the form of several tasting plates. Pace yourself, since portions are generous and the cost of a meal quickly adds up. This is the place to bring adventurous young eaters, thanks to the €15 children's menu, and there's a special post-theater prix fixe (€42 for two courses, €54 for three) from 10:30 pm to midnight. The revamped dining room is bright and cheery, though the designer has gone slightly overboard with the custard-yellow paint and fabrics. $ *Average main: €18* ⊠ *16–18 pl. Gaillon, 2e, Opéra/ Les Halles* ☎ *01–42–65–15–16* ⊕ *www.drouant.com* ☽ *Open 7 days a week* Ⓜ *Pyramides* ✛ *2:B5.*

$$$
BISTRO

✗**Goupil le Bistro.** The best Paris bistros emit an air of quiet confidence, and this is certainly the case with Goupil, a triumph despite its out-of-the-way location not far from the Porte Maillot conference center. The dining room attracts dark suits at lunch and a festive crowd in the evenings, with a few well-informed English-speakers sprinkled into the mix. The tiny open kitchen works miracles with seasonal ingredients, transforming mackerel into luxury food (on buttery puff pastry with mustard sauce) and pan-frying monkfish to perfection with artichokes and chanterelles. Friendly waiters are happy to suggest wines by the glass. $ *Average main: €25* ⊠ *4 rue Claude Debussy, 17e, Opéra/ Grands Boulevards* ☎ *01–45–74–83–25* ⬧ *Reservations essential* ☽ *Closed weekends and 3 wks in Aug.* Ⓜ *Porte de Champerret* ✛ *1:B1.*

14

$
JAPANESE

✗**Higuma.** When it comes to steaming bowls of noodles, this no-frills dining room divided into three sections beats its many neighboring competitors. Behind the counter—an entertaining spot for solo diners—cooks toil over giant flames, tossing strips of meat and quick-fried vegetables, then ladling noodles and broth into giant bowls. A choice of *formules* (fixed price menu options) allows you to pair various soups and stir-fried noodle dishes with six delicious *gyoza* (Japanese dumplings), and the stir-fried dishes are excellent, too. Don't expect much in the way of service, but it's hard to find a more generous meal in Paris at this price. There is a more subdued annex (without the open kitchen) at 163 rue St-Honoré, near the Louvre. $ *Average main: €13* ⊠ *32 bis rue Ste-Anne, 1er, Opéra/Grands Boulevards* ☎ *01–47–03–38–59* Ⓜ *Pyramides* ✛ *2:B5.*

$$
MODERN FRENCH

✗**Julien.** Famed for its 1879 decor—think Art Nouveau stained glass and *La Bohème*–style street lamps hung with vintage hats—this Belle Époque dazzler in the up-and-coming neighborhood near Gare de l'Est certainly lives up to its oft-quoted moniker, "the poor man's Maxim's." Look for smoked salmon, stuffed roast lamb, cassoulet, and, to finish, profiteroles or the *coupe Julien* (ice cream with cherries). The scene here is lots of fun, and the restaurant has a strong following with the fashion crowd, so it's mobbed during the biannual fashion and fabric shows. Food is served until midnight, and there are various prix-fixe menus that start at €32 for a main course with a desert and a glass of wine. $ *Average main: €23* ⊠ *16 rue du Faubourg St-Denis, 10e, Opéra/Grands Boulevards* ☎ *01–47–70–12–06* ⊕ *www.julienparis.com* Ⓜ *Strasbourg St-Denis* ✛ *2:E4.*

$$ BRASSERIE 🍴 **Le Vaudeville.** Part of the Flo group of historic brasseries, Le Vaudeville tends to fill with journalists, bankers, and locals *d'un certain âge* who come for the good-value assortment of prix-fixe menus, starting at €26, and highly professional service. Shellfish, house-smoked salmon, foie gras with raisins, slow-braised lamb, and desserts like the floating island topped with pralines are particularly enticing. Enjoy the graceful 1920s decor—almost the entire interior of this intimate dining room is done in real or faux marble—and lively dining until 1 am on weeknights, midnight on Friday and Saturday. [$] *Average main: €22* ✉ *29 rue Vivienne, 2e, Opéra/Grands Boulevards* ☎ *01–40–20–04–62* 🌐 *www.vaudevilleparis.com* [M] *Bourse* ✣ *2:C5.*

$$ WINE BAR 🍴 **Racines.** The secret of the deceptively simple yet hearty food served here is top-quality ingredients and expert preparation. The wines are all natural—sulfite-free, hand-harvested, and unfiltered—so it's a great place to try out unusual, hard-to-find wines. The old tile floors, wood tables, and location in the atmospheric Passage des Panoramas, Paris's oldest covered arcade, only add to the ambience. It's packed at mealtimes, so be sure to reserve. [$] *Average main: €26* ✉ *8 passage des Panoramas, 2e, Opéra/Grands Boulevards* ☎ *01–40–13–06–41* ✍ *Reservations essential* ⏲ *Closed weekends, last 2 wks Aug. and at Christmas* [M] *Grands Boulevards, La Bourse* ✣ *2:C4.*

$$$ MODERN FRENCH 🍴 **Saturne.** It's no surprise that chef Sven Chartier, a veteran of famous produce-centric restaurants L'Arpege and Racines, would focus his restaurant around seasonal, locally sourced veggies, along with the freshest seafood and pedigreed meats. The luminous dining room, with a huge central skylight, pale wood, and industrial details, is as contemporary and devoid of ostentation as the food. Dishes tend to be fresh and minimally cooked, featuring unusual pairings of vegetables and greens—tender baby scallops served with slivered radish, tiny watercress leaves, crisp raw mushrooms, and shallot; or fillet of mackerel drizzled with arugula pesto, a tiny dollop of uni, a sprinkling of mustard seed and piquant purslane—that are sophisticated almost to the point of cerebral. Desserts are equally original, and a superb roster of natural wines insures that diners who care to broaden their horizons won't be disappointed. Open for lunch and dinner Monday through Friday. Prix fix only. [$] *Average main: €26* ✉ *17 rue Notre-Dame des Victoires, 2e, Opéra/Grands Boulevards* ☎ *01–42–60–31–90* ✍ *Reservations essential* ⏲ *Closed Sat., Sun.* [M] *Bourse* ✣ *2:C5.*

$$$ MODERN FRENCH 🍴 **Senderens.** Iconic chef Alain Senderens waited until retirement age to make a rebellious statement against the all-powerful Michelin inspectors, "giving back" the three stars he had held for 28 years and renaming his restaurant (it was Lucas Carton). He also updated the decor, juxtaposing curvy, white, new furnishings, against the splendid Art Nouveau interior. The fusion menu spans the globe, though Senderens also, happily, reintroduces the occasional Lucas Carton signature dish such as polenta with truffles in winter. Senderens takes his passion for food-and-drink matches to extremes, suggesting a glass of wine, whiskey, sherry, or even punch to accompany each dish. Hours are longer than the usual Paris restaurants, so you can enjoy a late lunch or linger as long as you like. Upstairs, Le Passage Bar serves tapas-style dishes for

less than €20 a plate, or €36 for four small courses. $ *Average main: €34* ✉ *9 pl. de la Madeleine, 8e, Opéra/Grands Boulevards* ☎ *01–42–65–22–90* ⊕ *www.senderens.fr* ✆ *Open 7 days a week* ✆ *Closed 3 wks in Aug.* Ⓜ *Madeleine* ✛ *1:H5.*

ST-GERMAIN-DES-PRÉS

$$ ✕ **Alcazar.** When Sir Terence Conran opened this impressive 300-seat
BRASSERIE restaurant, he promised to reinvent the Parisian brasserie, and he's come close. Alcazar's mezzanine bar is famed for its DJ, and with its slick decor and skylight roof, it feels more like London than the Rive Gauche. The kitchen may have started out rather uncertain of what it wanted to accomplish, but the food is now resolutely French with the occasional Mediterranean touch, plus the house classic fish-and-chips. Prices are reasonable: lunch menus range from €21 to €37, which includes a glass of wine and coffee; a dinner menu is €42. The chef seems to have found his groove with dishes such as salmon-and-ginger tataki and veal braised with morels. For dessert, it's hard to pass up the profiteroles, mille-feuille, or baba au rhum. Sunday brunch is popular, and the restaurant has introduced "lyric nights," with a piano-accompanied opera singer, the first Monday of the month, and is now the Paris venue for the TV show "Top Chef." $ *Average main: €27* ✉ *62 rue Mazarine, 6e, St-Germain-des-Prés* ☎ *01–53–10–19–99* ⊕ *www.alcazar.fr* Ⓜ *Odéon* ✛ *4:B2.*

$ ✕ **Au Sauvignon.** Edge your way in among the students and lively tipplers
WINE BAR at this homey, old-fashioned spot—one of Paris's oldest wine bars—with antique tiles and a covered terrace. The basic menu, which includes several small dishes, like charcuterie, terrine, or regional cheeses, makes ordering the right glass a breeze. $ *Average main: €15* ✉ *80 rue des Sts-Pères, 7e, St-Germain-des-Prés* ☎ *01–45–48–49–02* Ⓜ *Sèvres-Babylone* ✛ *4:A3.*

$$ ✕ **Boucherie Roulière.** If it's steak you're craving, put your faith in Jean-
BISTRO Luc Roulière, a fifth-generation butcher who opened this long, narrow bistro near St-Sulpice church in 2006. Partner Franck Pinturier is from the Auvergne region, which is also known for its melt-in-the-mouth meat, so start with truffle-scented ravioli or a rich marrow bone before indulging in a generous slab of Limousin or Salers beef, excellent veal kidney, or, for the meat-shy, perhaps lobster or sea bass. The minimalist cream-and-brown dining room with checkerboard floor tiles and black-and-white photos on the walls keeps the focus on the food, and waiters are of the professional Parisian breed. $ *Average main: €19* ✉ *24 rue des Canettes, 5e, St-Germain-des-Prés* ☎ *01–43–26–25–70* ✆ *Closed Mon. and Aug.* Ⓜ *Mabillon* ✛ *4:B3.*

$$ ✕ **Café de Flore.** Picasso, Chagall, Sartre, and de Beauvoir, attracted by
CAFÉ the luxury of a heated café, worked and wrote here in the early 20th century. Today you'll find more tourists than intellectuals, and prices are hardly aimed at struggling artists, but the outdoor terrace is great for people watching and popular with Parisians. The service is brisk and the food is fine, but nothing special. $ *Average main: €22* ✉ *172 bd. St-Germain, 6e, St-Germain-des-Prés* ☎ *01–45–48–55–26* ⊕ *www.cafedeflore.fr* Ⓜ *St-Germain-des-Prés* ✛ *4:A2.*

14

$ ✕ **Eggs & Co.** This cheerfully bright and tiny, wood-beamed dining
BISTRO room—there's more space in the loftlike upstairs—is devoted to the egg
in all its forms, and whether you like yours baked with smoked salmon,
whisked into an omelet with truffle shavings, or beaten into fluffy pan-
cakes, there will be something for you on the blackboard menu. It's
perfect for a late breakfast or light lunch on weekdays (it opens at
11:30 am), though rather mobbed for weekend brunch (11:30–4:30
pm). $ *Average main: €12* ✉ *11 rue Bernard Palissy, 6e, St-Germain-
des-Prés* ☎ *01–45–44–02–52* ⊕ *www.eggsandco.fr* ☉ *Open daily* Ⓜ *St-
Germain-des-Prés* ✛ *4:A3.*

$$$ ✕ **Gaya Rive Gauche.** If you can't fathom paying upward of €200 per
MODERN FRENCH person to taste the cooking of Pierre Gagnaire (the city's most avant-
garde chef) at his eponymous restaurant, book a meal here, at his fash-
ionable fish restaurant, instead. At Gaya Rive Gauche, Gagnaire uses
seafood as a palette for his creative impulses: expect small portions of
artfully presented food, as in a seafood gelée encircled by white beans
and draped with Spanish ham, or cod "petals" in a martini glass with
soba noodles, mango, and grapefruit. Don't miss the desserts, one of
Gagnaire's great strengths. Aim for the main-floor room, with its fish-
scale wall, natural lighting, and bar for solo diners. $ *Average main:
€28* ✉ *44 rue du Bac, 7e, St-Germain-des-Prés* ☎ *01–45–44–73–73*
⊕ *www.pierre-gagnaire.com* ⌕ *Reservations essential* ☉ *Closed Sun.
No lunch in Aug.* Ⓜ *Rue du Bac* ✛ *3:H2.*

$$$ ✕ **Hélène Darroze.** The most celebrated female chef in Paris is now cook-
MODERN FRENCH ing at the Connaught in London, but her St-Germain dining room is
an exclusive setting for her sophisticated take on southwestern French
food. Darroze's intriguingly modern touch comes through in such dishes
as a sublime duck foie gras confit served with an exotic-fruit chutney
or a blowout of roast wild duck stuffed with foie gras and truffles. If
the food, at its best, lives up to the very high prices, the service sometimes struggles to reach the same level. For a more affordable taste, try
the relatively casual Salon d'Hélène downstairs, which serves a very
reasonable €28 lunch "tray" that includes a glass of wine. $ *Average
main: €85* ✉ *4 rue d'Assas, 6e, St-Germain-des-Prés* ☎ *01–42–22–00–
11* ⊕ *www.helenedarroze.com* ⌕ *Reservations essential* ☉ *Closed Sun.
and Mon.* Ⓜ *Sèvres-Babylone* ✛ *4:A4.*

$$ ✕ **Huîtrerie Régis.** When the oysters are this fresh, who needs anything
SEAFOOD else? That's the philosophy of this bright 14-seat restaurant with crisp
white tablecloths and pleasant service, popular with the area's glit-
terati. If you find yourself puzzling over the relative merits of *fines de
claires, spéciales,* and *pousses en claires,* you can always go with the
€26 prix fixe that includes a glass of Muscadet, 12 No. 3 (medium)
oysters, and coffee—or ask the knowledgeable waiters for their advice.
You can supplement this simplest of meals with shrimp and perhaps
a slice of freshly made fruit pie. Because of the lack of space, there's a
minimum order of a dozen oysters per person. $ *Average main: €24*
✉ *3 rue de Montfaucon, 6e, St-Germain-des-Prés* ☎ *01–44–41–10–07*
⊕ *www.huitrerieregis.com* ☉ *Closed Mon. and mid-July to end of Sept.*
Ⓜ *Mabillon* ✛ *4:B3.*

$$
BISTRO

✕ **Josephine Chez Dumonet.** Theater types, politicos, and locals fill the moleskin banquettes of this venerable bistro, where the frosted-glass lamps and amber walls put everyone in a good light. Unlike most bistros, Josephine caters to the indecisive, since generous half portions allow you to graze your way through the temptingly retro menu. Try the excellent boeuf bourguignon, roasted saddle of lamb with artichokes, top-notch steak tartare prepared table-side, or anything with truffles in season; game is also a specialty in fall and winter. For dessert, choose between a mille-feuille big enough to serve three and a Grand Marnier soufflé that simply refuses to sink, even with prodding. The wine list, like the food, is outstanding if expensive. $ *Average main: €24* ✉ *117 rue du Cherche-Midi, 6e, St-Germain-des-Prés* ☎ *01–45–48–52–40* ⌷ *Reservations essential* ⊘ *Closed weekends* Ⓜ *Duroc* ✛ *3:G5.*

$$$
MODERN FRENCH

✕ **KGB.** After extravagant success with his Asian-infused cuisine at Ze Kitchen Galerie, master-chef William Ledeuil extended his artistry to annex KGB (Kitchen Galerie Bis) just down the street, this time with a different focus and gentler prices. For starters, the "zors-d'oeuvres" of two, four, or six mini-dishes—think cubes of foie gras *mi-cuit* (half-cooked) in duck consommé, tender pork won tons in coconut milk with a hint of galanga—allow for a deeper exploration of what makes Ledeuil's cooking so alluring. Main courses, like roasted monkfish with a prune-lemongrass relish or the superb braised veal cheek in teriyaki jus, showcase his wizardry. Top it all off with a banana cappucino with caramel glaze and coconut sorbet. At €34, the three-course lunch menu is a bargain in this neighborhood. $ *Average main: €28* ✉ *25 rue des Grands Augustins, 6e, St-Germain-des-Prés* ☎ *01–46–33–00–85* ⊕ *kitchengaleriebis.com* ⌷ *Reservations essential* ⊘ *Closed Sun., Mon., Aug.* Ⓜ *Odéon, St-Michel* ✛ *4:C3.*

$$$
MODERN FRENCH

✕ **L'Atelier de Joël Robuchon.** Famed chef Joël Robuchon retired from the restaurant business for several years before opening this red-and-black-lacquer space with a bento-box-meets-tapas aesthetic. High seats surround two U-shaped bars, and this novel plan encourages neighbors to share recommendations and opinions. Robuchon's devoted kitchen staff whip up small plates for grazing (€19–€75) as well as full portions, which can turn out to be the better bargain. Highlights from the oft-changing menu have included an intense tomato jelly topped with avocado puree and the thin-crusted mackerel tart, although his inauthentic (but who's complaining?) take on carbonara with cream and Alsatian bacon, and the *merlan* Colbert (fried herb butter) remain signature dishes. Reservations are taken for the first sittings only at lunch and dinner. $ *Average main: €36* ✉ *5 rue Montalembert, 7e, St-Germain-des-Prés* ☎ *01–42–22–56–56* ⊕ *joel-robuchon.net* Ⓜ *Rue du Bac* ✛ *4:A2.*

$$
BISTRO

✕ **L'Epigramme.** Great bistro food is not so hard to find in Paris, but only rarely does it come in a comfortable setting. At L'Epigramme, the striped orange-and-yellow chairs are softly padded, there's space between you and your neighbors, and a big glass pane lets in plenty of light from the courtyard. Chef Karine Camcian has an almost magical touch with meat: try her stuffed suckling pig with turnip choucroute, or seared slices of pink lamb with root vegetables in a glossy reduced sauce.

14

In winter the eleborate game dish *lièvre à la royale* (hare stuffed with goose or duck liver and cooked in wine) sometimes makes an appearance. Desserts are not quite as inspired, so try to take a peek at the plates coming out of the kitchen before making your choice. Ⓢ *Average main: €32* ✉ *9 rue de l'Eperon, 6e, St-Germain-des-Prés* ☏ *01-44-41-00-09* ⌕ *Reservations essential* ⊙ *Closed Sun., Mon., 3 wks in Aug., and 1 wk at Christmas* Ⓜ *Odéon* ✛ *4:C3.*

$$ ✕**La Bastide Odéon.** The open kitchen of this popular Provençal bis-
BISTRO tro near the Jardin du Luxembourg allows you to watch the cooks at work. Chef Pascal Mousset demonstrates an expert, loving, and creative hand with Mediterranean cuisine—expect unusual dishes such as aged Spanish ham with a grilled pepper pipérade and artichokes; mushroom-and-pea risotto with arugula; and duck breast with orange sauce, date puree, polenta, and wild asparagus. To finish things off, try the pear poached with lemon and saffron, served with a fromage blanc sorbet. Unusual for Paris, an entire section of the menu is devoted to vegetarian dishes. Ⓢ *Average main: €22* ✉ *7 rue Corneille, 6e, St-Germain-des-Prés* ☏ *01-43-26-03-65* ⊕ *www.bastide-odeon.com* Ⓜ *Odéon; RER: Luxembourg* ✛ *4:C4.*

$$ ✕**La Ferrandaise.** Portraits of cows adorn the stone walls of this bistro
BISTRO near the Luxembourg Gardens, hinting at the kitchen's penchant for meaty cooking (Ferrandaise is a breed of cattle). Still, there's something for every taste on the market-inspired menu, which always lists three meat and three fish mains. Dill-marinated salmon with sweet mustard sauce is a typical starter, and a thick, milk-fed veal chop might come with a squash pancake and spinach. The dining room buzzes with locals who appreciate the good-value €34 prix fixe—there is no à la carte—and the brilliant bento box–style €16 lunch menu, in which three courses are served all at once. Ⓢ *Average main: €24* ✉ *8 rue de Vaugirard, 6e, St-Germain-des-Prés* ☏ *01-43-26-36-36* ⊕ *www. laferrandaise.com* ⊙ *Closed Sun. and 3 wks in Aug. No lunch Mon. and Sat.* Ⓜ *Odéon, RER: Luxembourg* ✛ *4:C4.*

$$$ ✕**Le 21.** Paul Minchelli has always known that the best way to treat
MODERN FRENCH squeaky fresh seafood is to keep it as simple as possible. At his new, bistrolike space decorated in black and white, his cooking has become rather less austere, with dishes such as *gambas* (shrimp) with pasta and sweet tomato sauce (some might liken it to ketchup), or marinated herrings and mackerel. Popular with local gallery owners rather than tourists, this is a discreet spot for an intimate and rather expensive meal among the "gauche caviar" (well-off intellectuals) of St-Germain. Service is friendly and professional, though not always quick. Ⓢ *Average main: €36* ✉ *21 rue Mazarine, 6e, St-Germain-des-Prés* ☏ *01-46-33-76-90* ⊙ *Closed Sun., Mon., Aug., 2 wks at Christmas, and 1 wk at Easter* Ⓜ *Odéon* ✛ *4:B2.*

$$ ✕**Le Bouillon Racine.** Originally a *bouillon*—one of the Parisian soup res-
BRASSERIE taurants popular at the turn of the 20th century—this two-story restaurant is now a lushly renovated Belle Époque haven with a casual setting downstairs and a lavish room upstairs. The menu changes seasonally: lamb knuckle with licorice, wild boar *parmentier* (like a shepherd's pie, with mashed potatoes on top and meat underneath), and roast suckling

pig are warming winter dishes. For dessert, dig into crème brûlée with maple syrup or the *café liégois* (coffee-flavored custard topped with whipped cream), which comes in a jug. If you're on a budget, try the set menus ranging from €29 to €41. This is a good place to keep in mind for a late lunch or an early dinner, since it serves nonstop from noon until 11 pm, 7 days a week, and you can also drop in for a Belgian waffle and hot chocolate in the afternoon. [$] *Average main: €21* ✉ *3 rue Racine, 6e, St-Germain-des-Prés* ☎ *01–44–32–15–60* 🌐 *www.bouillon-racine.com* ⏲ *Open 7 days a week* [M] *Odéon* ✣ *4:C4.*

$$ BISTRO 🍴 **Le Comptoir du Relais Saint-Germain.** Run by legendary bistro chef Yves Camdeborde, this tiny Art Deco hotel restaurant is booked up well in advance for the single dinner sitting that comprises a five-course, €55 set menu of haute-cuisine food. On weekends from noon to 10 pm and before 6 pm during the week a brasserie menu is served and reservations are not accepted, resulting in long lines and brisk, sometimes shockingly rude, service. Start with charcuterie or pâté, then choose from open-faced sandwiches like a smoked salmon–and–comté cheese croque monsieur, gourmet salads, and a variety of hot dishes such as braised beef cheek, roast tuna, and Camdeborde's famed deboned and breaded pig's trotter. If you don't mind bus fumes, sidewalk tables make for prime people-watching in summer. Le Comptoir also runs Avant Comptoir next door; a minuscule stand-up zinc bar with hanging hams and sausages, where you can score a superb plate of charcuterie, a couple warm dishes, and an inky glass of Morgon. Quality crêpes and sandwiches are still served from the window out front. [$] *Average main: €22* ✉ *9 carrefour de l'Odéon, 6e, St-Germain-des-Prés* ☎ *01–44–27–07–50* [M] *Odéon* ✣ *4:B3.*

$$$ BISTRO 🍴 **Les Bouquinistes.** Showcasing the talents of Guy Savoy protégé Stéphane Perraud, this is the star chef Savoy's most popular "baby bistro," frequented by art dealers from the nearby galleries and the occasional *bouquiniste* (bookseller) from the quais across the street. Expect to hear more English than French in the cheery, contemporary dining room with its closely packed tables looking out onto the Seine, but the sophisticated seasonal cuisine—such as snails and mussels with gnocchi, followed by British Hereford beef with squash-stuffed rigatoni and a nougat crème brûlée—is as authentic as you could hope for. The €31 *menu du marché* (back from the market) lunch menu seems less imaginative than the pricier à la carte options—though it does include three courses and a glass of wine. The wine list is extensive, with 180 wines and 12 champagnes. [$] *Average main: €35* ✉ *53 quai des Grands-Augustins, 6e, St-Germain-des-Prés* ☎ *01–43–25–45–94* 🌐 *www.lesbouquinistes.com* ⏲ *Closed Sun. and Aug. No lunch Sat.* [M] *St-Michel* ✣ *4:C2.*

$$$ JAPANESE 🍴 **Yen.** If you're having what is known in French as a *crise de foie* (liver crisis), the result of overindulging in rich food, this chic Japanese noodle house with a summer terrace and a VIP room upstairs is the perfect antidote. The blond-wood walls soothe the senses, the staff is happy to explain proper slurping technique, and the *soba* (buckwheat noodles), served in soup or with a restorative broth for dipping, will give you the courage to face another round of caramelized foie gras. The soba noodles are made fresh on the premises every day, showing Parisians

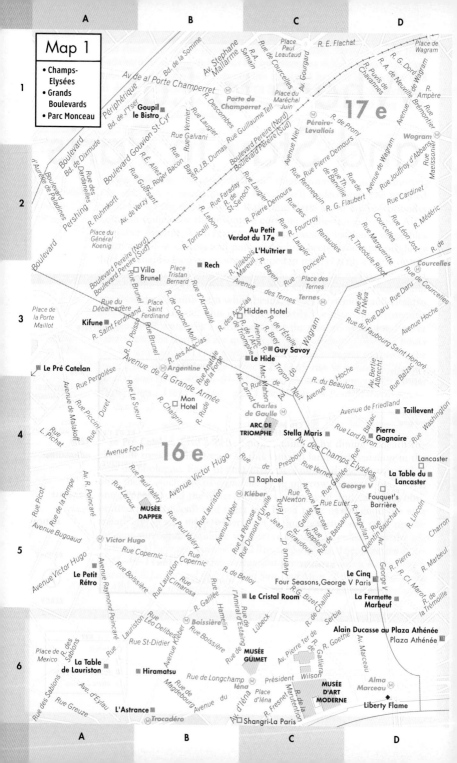

Map 1

- Champs-Elysées
- Grands Boulevards
- Parc Monceau

17e

16e

ARC DE TRIOMPHE

Charles de Gaulle

Goupil le Bistro

Au Petit Verdot du 17e

L'Huîtrier

Rech

Villa Brunel

Kifune

Hidden Hotel

Guy Savoy

Le Hide

Le Pré Catelan

Argentine

Mon Hotel

Stella Maris

Taillevent

Pierre Gagnaire

Lancaster

La Table du Lancaster

Raphael

Kléber

MUSÉE DAPPER

Victor Hugo

Le Petit Rétro

Fouquet's Barrière

Le Cinq

Four Seasons, George V Paris

La Fermette Marbeuf

Le Cristal Room

Alain Ducasse au Plaza Athénée

Plaza Athénée

La Table de Lauriston

Hiramatsu

MUSÉE GUIMET

L'Astrance

Trocadéro

MUSÉE D'ART MODERNE

Alma Marceau

Liberty Flame

Shangri-La Paris

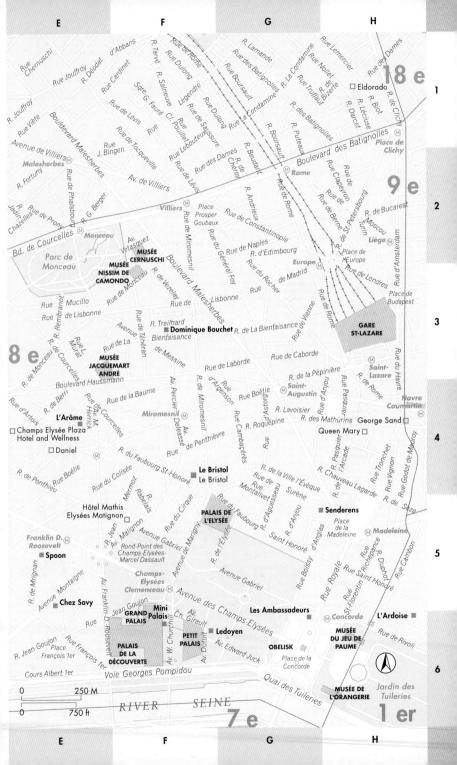

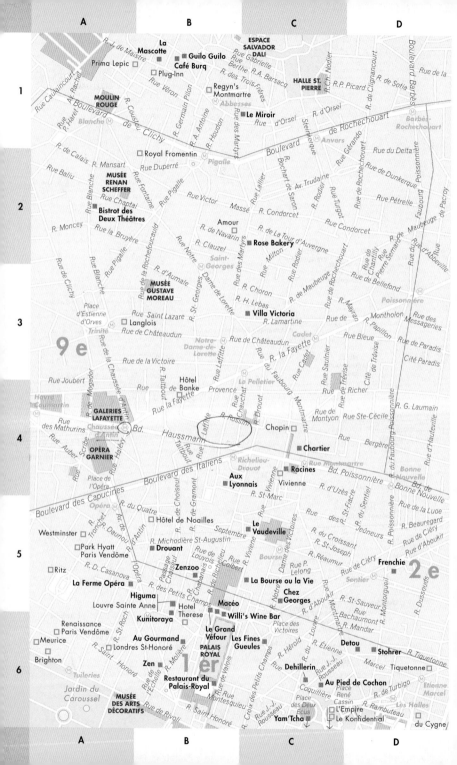

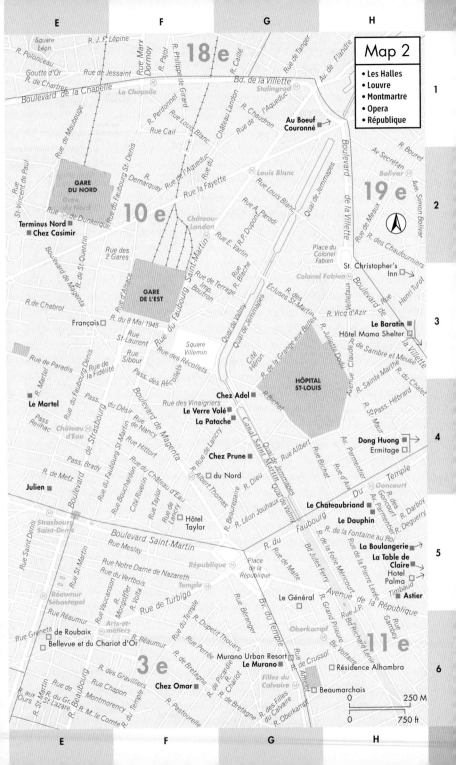

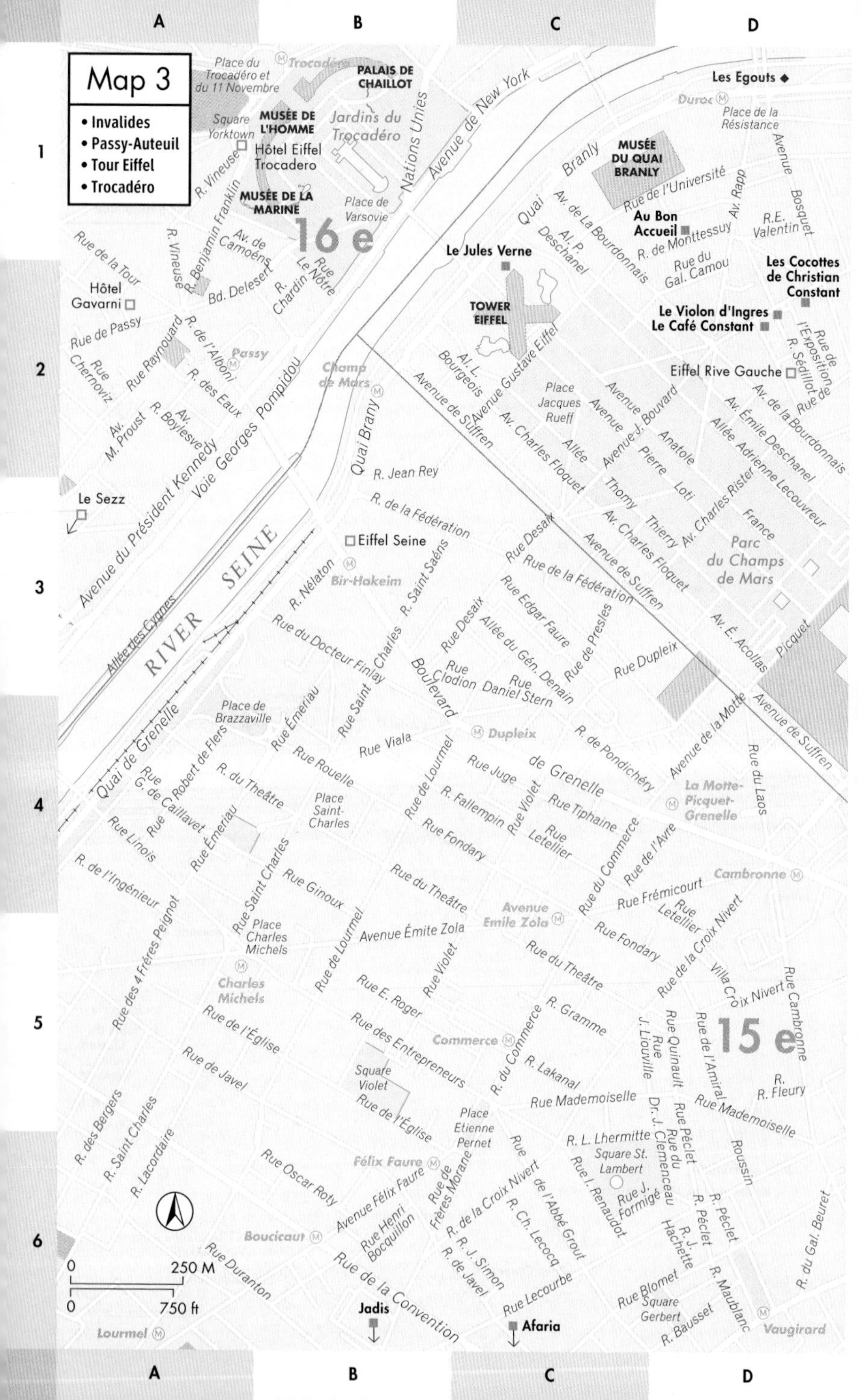

Map 3

- Invalides
- Passy-Auteuil
- Tour Eiffel
- Trocadéro

1

Place du Trocadéro et du 11 Novembre

Trocadéro

PALAIS DE CHAILLOT

MUSÉE DE L'HOMME

Jardins du Trocadéro

Square Yorktown

Hôtel Eiffel Trocadéro

R. Vineuse

R. Benjamin Franklin

Av. de Camoëns

MUSÉE DE LA MARINE

R. Vineuse

Bd. Delessert

R. Le Nôtre

R. Chardin

Place de Varsovie

16e

Nations Unies

Avenue de New York

Quai Branly

Av. de La Bourdonnais

Av. de l'Université

MUSÉE DU QUAI BRANLY

R. de Monttessuy

Au Bon Accueil

R. Rapp

Av. Bosquet

R.E. Valentin

Rue du Gal. Camou

Les Cocottes de Christian Constant

Duroc

Place de la Résistance

Les Egouts ◆

Av. Rapp

D

2

Hôtel Gavarni

Rue de la Tour

Rue de Passy

Rue Chernoviz

Rue Raynouard

R. de l'Alboni

R. des Eaux

Passy

Av. M. Proust

R. Boylesvedy

Av. du Président Kennedy

Voie Georges Pompidou

Champ de Mars

Quai Branly

Av. L. Bourgeois

Avenue Gustave Eiffel

Av. Charles Floquet

Avenue de Suffren

Le Jules Verne

TOWER EIFFEL

Al. P. Deschanel

Place Jacques Rueff

Allée Thomy Thierry

Avenue J. Bouvard

Anatole Pierre Loti

Avenue Charles Floquet

Av. Charles Risler

Le Violon d'Ingres
Le Café Constant

Eiffel Rive Gauche

Av. de l'Exposition de

R. Sédillot de

Av. Émile Deschanel

Allée Adrienne Lecouvreur

France

Av. de la Bourdonnais

Parc du Champs de Mars

Picquet

3

RIVER SEINE

Allée des Cygnes

Le Sezz

R. Nélaton

Bir-Hakeim

R. Saint Saëns

Rue du Docteur Finlay

Rue Desaix

Allée du Gén. Denain

Rue Edgar Faure

Rue de la Fédération

Rue de Presles

Rue Desaix

Rue de la Fédération

Avenue de Suffren

Rue Dupleix

Av. E. Acollas

Avenue de Suffren

Eiffel Seine

R. de la Fédération

R. Jean Rey

4

Quai de Grenelle

Rue Linois

R. de l'Ingénieur

Place de Brazzaville

Rue G. de Caillavet

Rue Robert de Flers

R. du Théâtre

Rue Émeriau

Rue Émeriau

Rue Rouelle

Rue Viala

Rue Saint Charles

Rue Clodion Boulevard

Rue Daniel Stern

Place Saint-Charles

Rue de Lourmel

R. Fallempin

Rue Juge

Rue Violet

Rue Letellier

Rue Tiphaine

Dupleix

de Grenelle

R. de Pondichéry

Rue du Commerce

Rue de l'Avre

Rue Frémicourt

Avenue de la Motte

Rue du Laos

La Motte-Picquet-Grenelle

Cambronne

Rue Letellier

Rue Fondary

Rue Fondary

5

R. des 4 frères Peignot

Rue Saint Charles

Rue Ginoux

Rue du Théâtre

Avenue Émile Zola

Rue de Lourmel

Place Charles Michels

Charles Michels

Rue de l'Église

Rue E. Roger

Rue des Entrepreneurs

Rue Violet

Rue du Théâtre

Rue Gramme

Commerce

R. Lakanal

R. du Commerce

Avenue Émile Zola

Rue Mademoiselle

Rue Quinault

Rue Péclet

Rue J. Liouville

Rue du Dr. J. Clemenceau

15e

Rue de l'Amiral

Villa Croix Nivert

Rue de la Croix Nivert

Rue Cambronne

R. Fleury

Rue Mademoiselle

Roussin

6

R. des Bergers

R. Saint Charles

R. Lacordaire

Rue de Javel

Rue Duranton

Rue Oscar Roty

Avenue Félix Faure

Félix Faure

Rue Henri Bocquillon

Boucicaut

Square Violet

Rue de l'Église

Place Étienne Pernet

Rue des Frères Morane

Rue de la Croix Nivert

R. Ch. Lecocq

R. RJ Simon

R. de Javel

Commerce

R. L. Lhermitte

Square St. Lambert

Rue J. Renaudot

Rue J. Formigé

R. de l'Abbé Groult

Rue Lecourbe

Rue Blomet

Square Gerbert

R. Bausset

Rue Péclet

R. du Clemenceau

Rue Péclet

R. Maublanc

R. Hachette

R. du Gal. Beuret

Vaugirard

0 ___ 250 M
0 ___ 750 ft

Lourmel

Jadis
↓

Afaria
↓

A   **B**   **C**   **D**

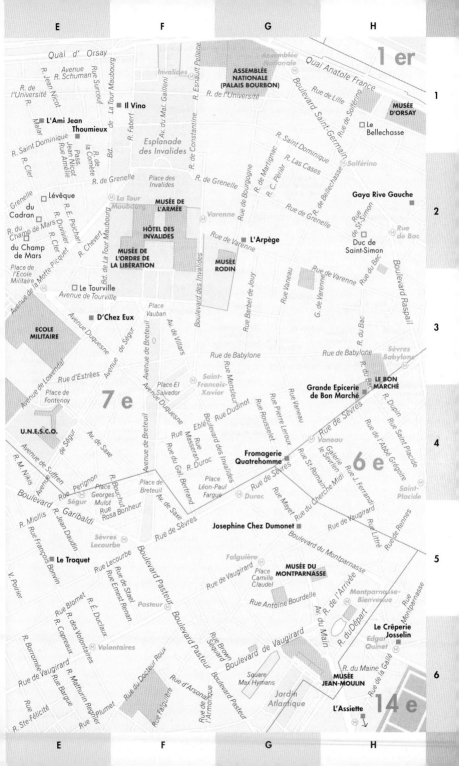

E   F   G   H

1 er

Quai d' Orsay

Avenue
R. Schuman
Rue Surcouf
Rue de La Tour Maubourg
Invalides
R. Esnault Pelterie
R. de Constantine
Assemblée Nationale
Quai Anatole France
Boulevard Saint-Germain
Rue de Lille
Rue de Solférino

MUSÉE D'ORSAY

R. Jean Nicot
R. de l'Université
R.
Malar
Av. du Mal. Galliéni
R. Fabert
R. de l'Université

■ Il Vino

ASSEMBLÉE NATIONALE (PALAIS BOURBON)

☐ Le Bellechasse

1

■ L'Ami Jean
Thoumieux

R. Saint Dominique
Rue Jean Nicot
Rue Amélie
R. Cler
Pass. Jean Nicot
R. de la Comète

Esplanade
des Invalides

R. Saint Dominique
R. de Martignac
R. C. Périer
R. Las Cases
R. de Bellechasse

Solférino

Place des Invalides

R. de Grenelle

R. de Grenelle

R. de Bourgogne

Gaya Rive Gauche ■

Grenelle
du
Cadran

☐ Lévêque

R. E. Psichari
R. Duvivier
R. Cler

La Tour Maubourg

MUSÉE DE L'ARMÉE

Varenne

Rue de Varenne

Rue de Grenelle

Rue St-Simon
de
☐ Duc de Saint-Simon

Rue du Bac

Boulevard Raspail

Rue de Bac

2

R. du
Champ de Mars

HÔTEL DES INVALIDES

■ L'Arpège

du Champ
de Mars

R. Chevert
Bd. de La Tour Maubourg

MUSÉE DE L'ORDRE DE LA LIBÉRATION

MUSÉE RODIN

Rue de Varenne

Place de
l'Ecole
Militaire

☐ Le Tourville
Avenue de Tourville

Boulevard des Invalides

Rue Barbet de Jouy

Rue Vaneau

G. de Varenne

Rue du Bac

3

Avenue de La Motte-Picquet

■ D'Chez Eux

Place
Vauban

Av. de Villars

Rue de Babylone

Rue de Babylone

Sèvres
Babylone

ECOLE MILITAIRE

Avenue Duquesne

Avenue de Ségur

Avenue de Breteuil

Place El
Salvador

Saint-
François-
Xavier

Rue Mensieur

Rue de Sèvres

LE BON MARCHÉ

R. Dupin

Rue d'Estrées

Avenue de Lowendal

Place de
Fontenoy

7 e

Avenue Duquesne

Rue Dudinot
Rue Pierre Leroux
Rue Rousselet

**Grande Epicerie
de Bon Marché**

R. Saint Placide

R. de l'Abbé Grégoire

4

U.N.E.S.C.O.

Av. de Saxe

Rue
Masseran
R. Duroc

**Fromagerie
Quatrehomme** ■

Vaneau

Galerie
le Sévier
Rue St-Romaine le Midi
Rue J. Ferrandi

6 e

Saint-
Placide

Av. de Ségur
R. M. Nikis
Avenue de Suffren
Rue Perignon

Place
Bouchut
Rue Bouchut
Georges
Mulot
Rue
Rosa Bonheur

Place de
Breteuil

Place
Léon-Paul
Fargue

Durac

Rue Mayet
Rue du Cherche Midi

Rue de Vaugirard

Rue Littré
Rue de Rennes

Boulevard Garibaldi

Ségur

Av. de Saxe

Rue de Sèvres

Josephine Chez Dumonet ■

Boulevard du Montparnasse

5

R. Miollis
Rue François Bonvin

■ Le Troquet

Rue Lecourbe
Rue de Staël
Rue Ernest Renan

Boulevard Pasteur

Rue de Vaugirard

Falguière

Place
Camille
Claudel

MUSÉE DU MONTPARNASSE

Av. du Maine

Rue Montparnasse

V. Poirier

Sèvres
Lecourbe

Pasteur

Rue Antoine Bourdelle

Montparnasse-
Bienvenue

Av. de R. de l'Arrivée

R. du Départ

**Le Crêperie
Josselin**

Edgar
Quinet

Rue de la Gaîté

Rue Blomet
R. É. Duclaux
Rue des Volontaires
R. Copreaux

Volontaires

Boulevard de Vaugirard

6

R. Borromée
Rue de Vaugirard
Rue Bargue
Rue Ste-Félicité

Rue du Docteur Roux
Rue Falguière

Rue Brown
Séquard
Boulevard Pasteur
Rue d'Arsonval
Boulevard Pasteur

Square
Max Hymans

R. du Maine

**MUSÉE
JEAN-MOULIN**

14 e

Jardin
Atlantique

L'Assiette

E   F   G   H

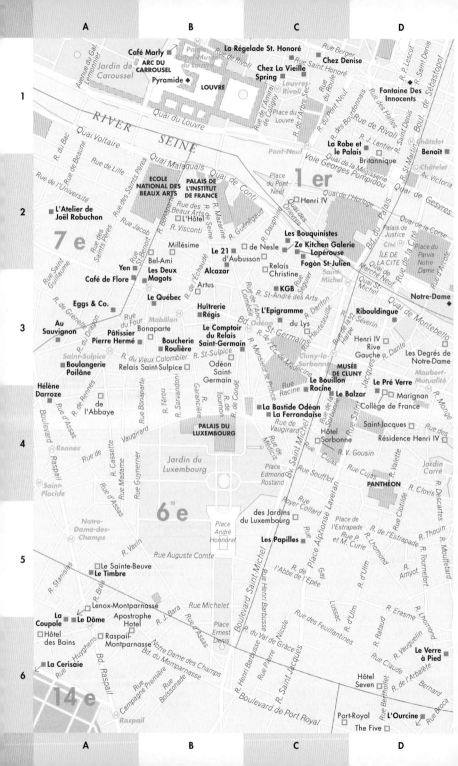

A

Café Marly
ARC DU CARROUSEL
Jardin du Carrousel
Palais Royal-Musée du Louvre
Pyramide ◆
LOUVRE

La Régelade St. Honoré
Rue de Rivoli
Rue Saint Honoré

Chez La Vieille
Spring

Chez Denise
Rue du Roule

Rue Berger
Rue du Pont Neuf

Rue P. Lescot
R. Saint Denis

1

Fontaine Des Innocents

Rue des Halles
Boul. de Sébastopol

RIVER
Quai du Louvre
Quai Voltaire
Quai de Beaune
R. du Bac

SEINE
Quai Malaquais
Quai de Conti

Pont-Neuf
Voie Georges Pompidou

La Robe et le Palais
Britannique

Benoît

Châtelet

Av. Victoria

R. de l'Université
Rue de Lille
Rue des Saints Pères

ECOLE NATIONAL DES BEAUX ARTS
PALAIS DE L'INSTITUT DE FRANCE

Place du Pont Neuf

Quai de l'Horloge

Palais de Justice

Quai de la Corse

1 er

2

L'Atelier de Joël Robuchon

Rue Jacob
Rue des Beaux Arts
L'Hôtel
R. Visconti

Millésime
Bel-Ami
Yen
Les Deux Magots
Café de Flore

Rue de Seine
R. Mazarine
R. Guénégaud
R. Dauphine

Le 21 d'Aubusson
de Nesle

Relais Christine

Les Bouquinistes
Ze Kitchen Galerie
Lapérouse
Fogón St-Julien

Quai des Grands Augustins
Quai St. Michel
Saint-Michel

ÎLE DE LA CITÉ
Quai du Marché Neuf

Place du Parvis Notre-Dame

Notre-Dame ◆

Quai de Montebello

7 e

Eggs & Co.

Rue de Grenelle
R. de l'Echaudé

Alcazar
Artus

Le Québec

Au Sauvignon

3

Rue du Four
Mabillon

Pâtissier Pierre Hermé
Bonaparte

Huîtrerie Régis

Boucherie Roulière

Le Comptoir du Relais Saint-Germain

R. St-Sulpice

Saint-Sulpice
Boulangerie Poilâne
R. du Vieux Colombier
Relais Saint-Sulpice

KGB

L'Epigramme
du Lys
Bd. St-Germain

R. St-André des Arts
R. de l'Ancienne Comédie
R. Hautefeuille
R. de l'Ec. de Médecine
R. Danton
R. St-Séverin
R. de la Harpe

Ribouldingue

Henri IV Rive Gauche
R. Dante

Les Degrés de Notre-Dame

Maubert-Mutualité

Odéon
Saint-Germain

R. Monsieur le Prince
R. de Condé
R. de Tournon

Cluny-la-Sorbonne
MUSÉE DE CLUNY

Le Bouillon Racine
Le Balzar

Le Pré Verre

Marignan

Collège de France

Rue Racine

R. St. Jacques

Hélène Darroze

R. de Rennes
de l'Abbaye

Boulevard Raspail

Rennes

R. Férou
R. Servandoni
Garancière
R. de Vaugirard

PALAIS DU LUXEMBOURG

La Bastide Odéon
La Ferrandaise

Hôtel Sorbonne
Place de Médicis

Rue Cujas
R. V. Gousin
Rue Cujas

Saint-Jacques
Résidence Henri IV

Jardin Carré

R. Clovis
R. Descartes

4

Saint-Placide

R. Cassette
R. Madame
Rue Guynemer
Rue d'Assas

Jardin du Luxembourg

6 e

Place Edmond Rostand

Place André Honnorat

Rue Soufflot

PANTHÉON

R. Clotilde

Notre-Dame-des-Champs

Rue Vavin
Rue Auguste Comte

des Jardins du Luxembourg

Boulevard Saint-Michel

Place Royer Collard

Les Papilles

Place de l'Estrapade
Rue P. et M. Curie

R. de l'Estrapade
R. Thouin
R. Mouffetard

5

R. Stanislas
R. Bréa

Le Sainte-Beuve
Le Timbre

Rue Michelet

R. J. Bara

Rue Henri Barbusse

R. de l'Abbé de l'Epée

Lussac
R. d'Ulm

R. Erasme
R. Lhomond

R. Amyot
R. Tournefort

La Coupole
Le Dôme

Hôtel des Bains

Lenox-Montparnasse
Apostrophe Hotel

Raspail-Montparnasse

Rue Huyghens

Place Ernest Denis

Notre Dame des Champs
Bd. du Montparnasse

R. du Val de Grâce
R. Pierre Nicole
R. Saint Jacques

Rue des Feuillantines

Rue Claude

R. Rataud

R. Vauquelin

Le Verre à Pied

6

La Cerisaie

Rue Raspail
Rue Campagne Première
Rue Boissonade

14 e

Raspail

Boulevard de Port Royal

Hôtel Seven

R. Berthollet
R. de l'Arbalète

R. Bernard

Port-Royal
The Five

L'Ourcine

R. Broca

A   **B**   **C**   **D**

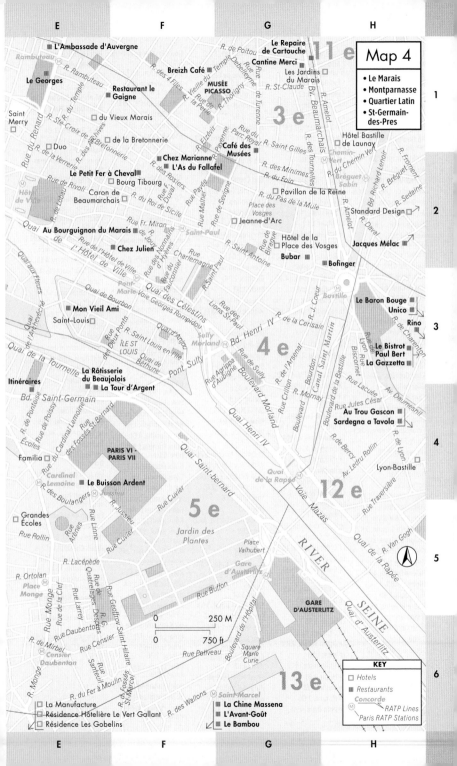

Map 4

- Le Marais
- Montparnasse
- Quartier Latin
- St-Germain-des-Pres

KEY

☐ Hotels
■ Restaurants
Concorde
Ⓜ RATP Lines
Paris RATP Stations

Where to Stay

WORD OF MOUTH

"We really liked staying in the St-Germain area, rue Jacob, and have done so a number of times. I like the cafes in that area at all hours; great to sit and people watch. I find the Quartier Latin a little too lively."

—Lexma90

Updated
by Heather
Stimmler-Hall

If your Parisian fantasy involves staying in a historic hotel with the smell of fresh-baked croissants gently rousing you in the morning, here's some good news: you need not be Ritz-rich to realize it. With more than 1,450 hotels, the City of Light gives visitors stylish options in all price ranges.

In terms of location, there are more hotels on the *Rive Droite* (the Right Bank) offering luxury—in terms of formality—than on the *Rive Gauche* (the Left Bank), where the hotels are frequently smaller and richer in old-fashioned charm. The Rive Droite's 1er, 8^e, and 16^e arrondissements are still the most exclusive, and the prices there reflect that. Some of these palatial hotels charge more than €500 a night without batting an eye. Less expensive alternatives on the Rive Droite can be found in the fashionable Marais quarter (3^e and 4^e arrondissements). The hotbed of chic hotels on the Rive Gauche is the 6^e arrondissement; choices get cheaper in the 5e and 7e. Some excellent budget deals can be found slightly off the beaten track in the 9e, 10e, and 13e arrondissements. Wherever possible, we've located budget hotels in more expensive neighborhoods—check out the handful of budget-priced sleeps in the shadow of Notre-Dame, St-Germain-des-Prés, and the Louvre.

Although historic charm is a given, space to stretch out is not. Even budget travelers can sleep under 200-year-old wooden beams, but if you're looking for enough room to spread out multiple suitcases, better book a suite in a four-star palace hotel. Indoor spaces—from beds to elevators—may feel cramped to those not used to life on a European scale. The no-smoking law went into effect in all public spaces in January 2008. Enforcement is not always perfect, but at least now you'll have a valid complaint if your room smells like stale smoke. Amenities have also improved, with virtually every hotel now equipped with cable TV (meaning CNN and BBC news in English), minibars, in-room safes, and wireless Internet access (though not always free). Another recent change is the increasing availability of air-conditioning, which can be saintly in July and August.

WHERE SHOULD I STAY?

	NEIGHBORHOOD VIBE	PROS	CONS
St-Germain and Montparnasse (6e, 14e, 15e)	The center of café culture and the emblem of the Rive Gauche; the mood is leisurely; attractions are well established, and the prices are high.	A safe, historic area with chic fashion boutiques, famous cafés and brasseries, and lovely side streets. Lively day and night.	Expensive. Noisy along the main streets. The area around the monstrous Tour Montparnasse is a soul-sucking tribute to commerce.
The Latin Quarter (5e)	The historic student quarter of the Rive Gauche; full of narrow, winding streets and major parks and monuments such as the Panthéon.	Plenty of cheap eats and sleeps, discount book and music shops, and noteworthy open-air markets. Safe area for wandering walks.	Touristy. No métro stations around the Panthéon. Student pubs can be noisy in summer. Hotel rooms tend to be smaller.
Marais and Bastille (3e, 4e, 11e)	Cute shops, museums, and laid-back bistros line the narrow streets of the Marais, home to both the gay and Jewish communities. Farther east, ethnic eats, and edgy shops.	Generally excellent shopping, sightseeing, dining, and nightlife in the supersafe Marais. Bargains aplenty at Bastille hotels. Several modern-design hotels, too.	The Marais's narrow sidewalks are always overcrowded, and rooms don't come cheap. It's noisy around the gritty boulevards of Place de la Bastille and Nation.
Montmartre and northeast Paris (18e, 19e, 20e)	The Rive Droite's hilltop district is known for winding streets leading from the racy Pigalle district to the stark-white Sacré-Coeur Basilica.	Amazing views of Paris, romantic cobblestone streets, easy access to Roissy-Charles de Gaulle airport.	Steep staircases, few métro stations, and Pigalle can be too seedy to stomach, especially late at night, when it can also be unsafe.
Champs-Élysées and Western Paris (8e, 16e, 17e)	The world-famous avenue is lively 24/7 with cinemas, high-end shops, and nightclubs, all catering to the moneyed jet set.	The home to most of the city's famous palace hotels, there's no shortage of luxurious sleeps here on the Rive Droite.	The high prices of this neighborhood, along with its Times Square tendencies, repel Parisians but lure pickpockets.
Around the Eiffel Tower (7e, 15e)	The impressive Eiffel Tower and monumental Palais de Chaillot at Trocadéro straddle the Seine River.	Safe, quiet, and relatively inexpensive Rive Gauche area of Paris with green spaces and picture-perfect views at every turn.	With few shops and restaurants, this district is quiet at night; long distances between métro stations.
Louvre, Les Halles, Ile de la Cité (1er, 2e, 8e)	The central Parisian district around the Tuileries gardens and Louvre museum is best known for shopping and sightseeing; Les Halles is a buzzing hub of commerce and mass transit.	Convenient for getting around Paris on foot, bus, or métro. Safe, attractive district close to the Seine and shops of all types. All the major métro and RER lines are right by Les Halles.	The main drag along Rue de Rivoli can be noisy with traffic during the day, and the restaurants cater mostly to tourists. Shops are tacky and fast food predominates around Les Halles.

15

PLANNING

APARTMENT RENTALS

See the Apartment Rentals box on p. 295

BREAKFAST

Almost all Parisian hotels charge extra for breakfast, with per-person prices ranging from €5 to more than €30. Continental breakfast—coffee, baguette, croissant, jam, and butter—is sometimes included in the hotel rate. This is noted as *breakfast*, in the meal plan section of the review. If you decide to eat elsewhere, inform the staff so breakfast won't be charged to your bill.

CHECKING IN

Typical check-in and check-out times are 2 pm and noon, respectively, although some properties allow check-in as early as noon and require check-out as early as 11 am. Many flights from North America arrive early in the morning, but having to wait six hours for a room after arriving jet-lagged at 8 am isn't the ideal way to start a vacation. Alert the hotel of your early arrival; larger establishments can often make special early check-in arrangements, but don't expect more than baggage storage.

CHILDREN

Most hotels in Paris allow children under the age of 12 to stay in their parents' room at no charge. Hotel rooms are often on the small side, so inquire about connecting rooms or suites.

HOTEL FEATURES

Unless stated in the review, hotels have elevators, and all guest rooms have air-conditioning, TV, telephone, and a private bathroom. In France the first floor is the floor above the ground floor, or *rez-de-chaussée*. The number of rooms listed at the end of each review reflects those with private bathrooms (which means they have a shower or a tub, but not necessarily both). Tubs don't always have fixed curtains or showerheads; how the French rinse themselves with the handheld nozzle without flooding the entire bathroom remains a cultural mystery. It's rare to find moderately priced places that expect guests to share toilets or bathrooms, but be sure you know what facilities you are getting when you book a budget hotel.

HOTEL QUALITY

Note that the quality of accommodations can vary from room to room. If you don't like the room you're given, ask to see another. The French star ratings can be misleading: official stars are granted for specific amenities and services rather than for ambience, style, or overall comfort, so you may find that a two-star hotel eclipses a three-star establishment. Many hotels prefer to remain "under-starred" for tax reasons.

LODGING STRATEGY

Where should we stay? With hundreds of Paris hotels, it may seem like a daunting question. But fret not—our expert writers and editors have done most of the legwork. The 100-plus selections here represent the best this city has to offer. Scan "Best Bets" on the following pages for top recommendations by price and experience. Or find a review quickly in the listings, which are arranged by arrondissement and then alphabetically.

RESERVATIONS

Make reservations as far in advance as possible, especially for May, June, September, and October. Calling works, but email (or fax) may be the easiest way to make contact, because hotel staff are more likely to read English than understand it over the phone. Specify arrival and departure dates; room size (single or double), room type (standard, deluxe, or suite); the number of people in your party; and whether you want a bathroom with a shower or bathtub (or both). Ask if a deposit is required, and what happens if you cancel.

WHAT IT COSTS

Often a hotel in a certain price category will have a few less expensive rooms; it's worth asking. In the off-season—mid-July, August, November, early December, and late January—rates can be considerably lower. You should also inquire about specials and weekend deals, and you may be able to get a better rate per night if you're staying a week or longer. There's a nominal city *taxe de séjour* ranging between €0.20 and €1.20 per person, per night, based on the hotel's star rating. Sometimes this tax is included in the room price, sometimes not.

If you're staying in Paris for more than just a few days, you might want to look into the increasingly popular option of renting an apartment. *Check out the Lodging Alternatives feature in this chapter.* Not only does this often save in nightly costs, but with your own kitchen you can save by living like a local and cooking some of your own meals. *Prices in the reviews are the lowest cost of a standard double room in high season.*

HOTEL REVIEWS

In alphabetical order by neighborhood. Use the coordinate (⊕ 1:B2) at the end of each review to locate a property on the corresponding map preceding this chapter.

AROUND THE EIFFEL TOWER

For expanded hotel reviews, visit Fodors.com.

$$$ HOTEL 🏨 **Eiffel Seine Hôtel.** This tiny boutique hotel near the Eiffel Tower mixes contemporary amenities and custom Art Nouveau decor. **Pros:** next door to the Eiffel Tower; easy métro access. **Cons:** not an easy walk to the center of town; minimal space in standard rooms; some street noise. **TripAdvisor:** "nice hotel in a great location," "met and exceeded our expectations," "convenience and cleanliness." [$] *Rooms from: €230* ✉ *3 bd. de Grenelle, 15e, Around the Eiffel Tower* ☎ *01–45–78–14–81* 🌐 *www.eiffelseine.com* 🛏 *45 rooms* [M] *Bir Hakeim* ⊕ *3:B3.*

$$ HOTEL 🏨 **Grand Hôtel Lévêque.** This budget hotel is nothing to look at, but the Eiffel Tower is around the corner and one of the city's finest street markets is just outside the front door. **Pros:** prime location; free Wi-Fi; budget singles if you don't mind a shared shower. **Cons:** only superior rooms have been recently renovated; air-conditioning available only

BEST BETS FOR PARIS LODGING

Fodor's offers a selective listing of high-quality lodging experiences at every price range, from the best budget options to the most sophisticated grande-dame hotel. *Below are our top recommendations by price and experience.*

Fodor's Choice ★

Four Seasons Hôtel George V Paris, p. 296

Hôtel Lancaster, p. 297

Hôtel Jules & Jim, p. 306

Hôtel d'Aubusson, p. 311

Hôtel du Cygne, p. 292

Hôtel Familia, p. 302

Hôtel Mama Shelter, p. 300

Hôtel Odéon Saint-Germain, p. 311

Hôtel Plaza Athénée, p. 297

Hotel Seven, p. 303

Hôtel Taylor, p. 300

Hôtel Thérèse, p. 296

Le Citizen Hôtel, p. 301

Shangri-La Paris, p. 292

St. Christopher's Inn, p. 300

By Price

$

Hôtel Tiquetonne, p. 294

Port-Royal Hôtel, p. 304

Hôtel du Champ de Mars, p. 291

Hôtel Familia, p. 302

Hôtel Marignan, p. 303

Hôtel Taylor, p. 300

Résidence Les Gobelins, p. 304

$$

Apostrophe Hotel, p. 307

Hôtel Langlois, p. 309

Hôtel Mama Shelter, p. 300

Hôtel Saint Merry, p. 292

Le Citizen Hôtel, p. 301

$$$

Hôtel Relais Saint-Sulpice, p. 312

Hôtel Jules & Jim, p. 306

Hôtel Thérèse, p. 296

Le Citizen Hôtel, p. 301

$$$$

Four Seasons Hôtel George V Paris, p. 296

Hôtel d'Aubusson, p. 311

Hôtel Duc de Saint-Simon, p. 311

Hôtel Odéon Saint-Germain, p. 311

Hôtel Recamier, p. 312

Hotel Seven, p. 303

Shangri-La Paris, p. 292

By Experience

MOST CHARMING

Hôtel d'Aubusson, p. 311

Hôtel des Jardins du Luxembourg, p. 302

Hôtel Notre Dame, p. 303

HISTORIC

Hôtel de la Place des Vosges, p. 305

Hôtel Odéon St-Germain, p. 311

Hôtel Saint Merry, p. 292

BEST DESIGN

The Five Hôtel, p. 304

Hotel Seven, p. 303

Le Bellechasse, p. 291

Hôtel Jules & Jim, p. 306

MOST CENTRAL

Hôtel Britannique, p. 292

Hôtel Henri IV, p. 312

Hôtel Le Crayon, p. 294

BUSINESS TRAVEL

Four Seasons Hôtel George V Paris, p. 296

Hôtel Lancaster, p. 297

Les Jardins du Marais, p. 300

Renaissance Paris Vendôme, p. 296

Renaissance Paris Arc de Triomphe, p. 299

BEST VIEWS

Hôtel Brighton, p. 294

Shangri-La Paris, p. 292

MOST ROMANTIC

Hôtel Recamier, p. 312

Hôtel Daniel, p. 297

Hotel Seven, p. 303

Le Konfidentiel, p. 296

L'Hôtel, p. 312

from June to September. **TripAdvisor:** "charming," "central location on Rue Cler," "small friendly hotel." [$] *Rooms from: €140* ✉ *29 rue Cler, 7e, Around the Eiffel Tower* ☎ *01–47–05–49–15* 🌐 *www.hotel-leveque.com* 🛏 *50 rooms, 45 with bath* [M] *École Militaire* ✥ *3:E2.*

$$$ HOTEL 🏨 **Hôtel du Cadran.** Completely redesigned in 2009, this hotel near the Rue Cler market has sleek, minimalist lines punctuated by bright shots of color and vintage clocks (*cadran* means clock). **Pros:** easy walk to Eiffel Tower, Les Invalides, and the market; free Wi-Fi; queen- and king-size beds. **Cons:** small rooms; prices at the high end for this area. **TripAdvisor:** "awesome décor and design," "clean with a good location," "great staff." [$] *Rooms from: €250* ✉ *10 rue du Champ de Mars, 7e, Around the Eiffel Tower* ☎ *01–40–62–67–00* 🌐 *www.cadranhotel.com* 🛏 *40 rooms, 1 suite* [M] *École Militaire* ✥ *3:E2.*

$ HOTEL 🏨 **Hôtel du Champ de Mars.** This hotel just off Rue Cler has an appealing down-home feel, with a vibrant Provence-inspired lobby and huge picture windows overlooking the street. **Pros:** free Wi-Fi; good value; walking distance to Eiffel Tower and Les Invalides. **Cons:** smallish rooms; no air-conditioning. **TripAdvisor:** "quiet," "beautiful little Parisian hotel," "convenient location." [$] *Rooms from: €115* ✉ *7 rue du Champ de Mars, 7e, Around the Eiffel Tower* ☎ *01–45–51–52–30* 🌐 *www.hotelduchampdemars.com* 🛏 *25 rooms* [M] *École Militaire* ✥ *3:E2.*

$$$ HOTEL 🏨 **Hôtel Eiffel Trocadéro.** This hotel between Trocadéro and the Eiffel Tower blends old-style French elegance (period antiques, Napoleonic draperies, classical plaster busts) with modern conveniences (flat-screen TVs, spa tubs, free Wi-Fi) and a new "green hotel" attitude. **Pros:** hillside views over the Eiffel Tower; upscale residential district; organic breakfast. **Cons:** not an easy walk to the center of town; some unrenovated rooms are rather small and cramped. **TripAdvisor:** "beautiful boutique hotel," "great location and great view," "nice people." [$] *Rooms from: €209* ✉ *35 rue Benjamin-Franklin, Around the Eiffel Tower* ☎ *01–53–70–17–70, 800/246–0041 in U.S.* 🌐 *www.hoteleiffeltrocadero.com* 🛏 *17 rooms* [M] *Trocadéro* ✥ *3:A1.*

$$$$ HOTEL 🏨 **Hôtel Le Tourville.** This cozy, upscale hotel near Invalides and the Eiffel Tower is a comfortable base for exploring Paris. **Pros:** good location; attentive service; soundproofed windows. **Cons:** no shower curtains for the bathtubs; standard rooms quite small; air-conditioning works only during summer months. **TripAdvisor:** "small but quaint," "chicest boutique hotel in Paris," "four star cleanliness and service." [$] *Rooms from: €295* ✉ *16 av. de Tourville, 7e, Around the Eiffel Tower* ☎ *01–47–05–62–62* 🌐 *www.hoteltourville.com* 🛏 *27 rooms, 3 suites* [M] *École Militaire* ✥ *3:E3.*

$$$$ HOTEL 🏨 **Le Bellechasse.** French designer Christian Lacroix helped decorate all 34 rooms of Le Bellechasse, a tiny boutique hotel just around the corner from the popular Musée d'Orsay. **Pros:** central location near top Paris museums; unique style; spacious and bright; Anne Semonin toiletries. **Cons:** street-facing rooms can be a bit noisy; open bathrooms lack privacy. **TripAdvisor:** "boutique hotel in superb location," "groovy little place," "beautiful property." [$] *Rooms from: €310* ✉ *8 rue de Bellechasse, 7e, Around the Eiffel Tower* ☎ *01–45–50–22–31* 🌐 *www.lebellechasse.com* 🛏 *33 rooms, 1 suite* [M] *Solferino* ✥ *3:H1.*

$$$$ HOTEL Fodor's Choice ★ 🏨 **Shangri-La Paris.** This impressive 19th-century mansion overlooking the Eiffel Tower from the Right Bank was once the stately home of Prince Roland Bonaparte, grandnephew of the Emperor himself. **Pros:** close to the metro and luxury shopping district; varied dining options for all tastes; TV screens in the bathrooms. **Cons:** expensive neighborhood that is somewhat lacking in charm. **TripAdvisor:** "stunning throughout," "beautiful hotel," "excellent staff." [$] *Rooms from: €850* ✉ *10 av. Iéna, 16e, Around the Eiffel Tower* ☎ *01–53–67–19–98* 🌐 *www.shangri-la.com* 🛏 *54 rooms, 27 suites.* [M] *Iéna* ✥ *1:B6.*

AROUND THE LOUVRE

For expanded hotel reviews, visit Fodors.com.

LES HALLES

$ HOTEL 🏨 **Hôtel Bellevue et du Chariot d'Or.** This Belle Époque time traveler is proud to keep its dingy chandeliers and faded gold trimming. **Pros:** large rooms great for families; easy walk to the Marais and Les Halles districts. **Cons:** busy, noisy street; not the most attractive part of central Paris; drab decor. **TripAdvisor:** "friendly," "convenient and comfortable," "great location." [$] *Rooms from: €79* ✉ *39 rue de Turbigo, 3e, Les Halles* ☎ *01–48–87–45–60* 🌐 *www.hotelbellevue75.com* 🛏 *59 rooms* 🍴 *Breakfast* [M] *Réaumur-Sébastopol, Arts et Métiers* ✥ *2:E6.*

$$$ HOTEL 🏨 **Hôtel Britannique.** Open since 1861 and a stone's throw from the Louvre, the Britannique blends courteous English service with old-fashioned French elegance. **Pros:** one of the city's most charming hotels; on a calm side street less than a block from the métro/RER station; attentive staff. **Cons:** smallish rooms; soundproofing between rooms could be better. **TripAdvisor:** "a little gem," "excellent room," "great location and staff." [$] *Rooms from: €198* ✉ *20 av. Victoria, 1er, Les Halles* ☎ *01–42–33–74–59* 🌐 *www.hotel-britannique.fr* 🛏 *39 rooms, 1 suite* [M] *Châtelet* ✥ *4:1D.*

$ HOTEL Fodor's Choice ★ 🏨 **Hôtel du Cygne.** Passed down from mother to daughter, "the Swan" is decorated with homey touches like hand-sewn curtains, country quilts, and white wood furniture. **Pros:** spotless rooms and bathrooms; central location on a pedestrian street; good value. **Cons:** old building with small rooms; no elevator; not the most attractive area of central Paris; can be intimidating after dark. **TripAdvisor:** "wonderfully clean," "very good location," "comfortable and convenient." [$] *Rooms from: €122* ✉ *3 rue du Cygne, 1er, Les Halles* ☎ *01–42–60–14–16* 🌐 *www.cygne-hotel-paris.com* 🛏 *18 rooms* [M] *Étienne Marcel, Les Halles* ✥ *2:D6.*

$$ HOTEL 🏨 **Hôtel Saint Merry.** Due south of the Centre Pompidou is this small and stunning Gothic hideaway, once the presbytery of the adjacent St-Merry church. **Pros:** unique medieval character; central location on a pedestrian street full of cafés and shops. **Cons:** no amenities; street-facing rooms can be too noisy to open windows in summer. **TripAdvisor:** "shabby chic," "atmospheric," "idiosyncratic charm." [$] *Rooms from: €150* ✉ *78 rue de la Verrerie, 4e, Les Halles* ☎ *01–42–78–14–15* 🌐 *www.hotelmarais.com* 🛏 *11 rooms, 1 suite* [M] *Châtelet, Hôtel de Ville* ✥ *4:E1.*

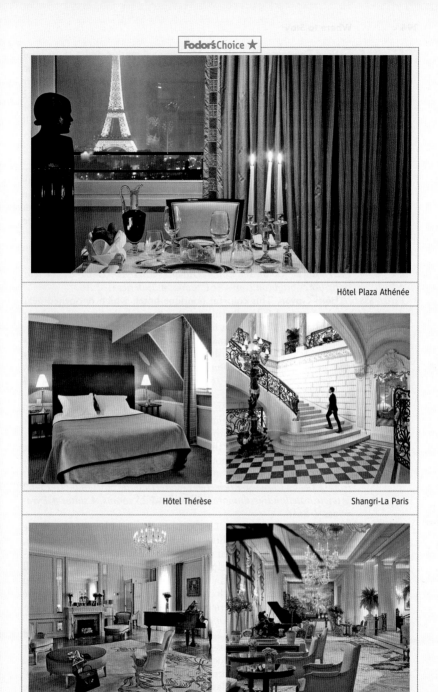

Hôtel Plaza Athénée

Hôtel Thérèse

Shangri-La Paris

Hôtel Lancaster

Four Seasons Hôtel George V Paris

$ HOTEL **Hôtel Tiquetonne.** Just off the Montorgueil market and a short hoof from Les Halles (and slightly seedy Rue St-Denis), this is one of the least expensive hotels in the city center. **Pros:** dirt-cheap rooms in the center of town; in a trendy shopping and nightlife area. **Cons:** minimal service and no amenities; noise from the street. **TripAdvisor:** "shabby exterior hides a little gem," "the nicest French you'll ever meet," "clean and well located." [$] *Rooms from: €60* ✉ *6 rue Tiquetonne, 2e, Les Halles* ☎ *01–42–36–94–58* 🛏 *45 rooms, 33 with bath* [M] *Étienne Marcel* ✣ *2:D6.*

LOUVRE/TUILERIES

$$$ HOTEL **Hôtel Brighton.** Many of Paris's most prestigious palace hotels face the Tuileries or Place de la Concorde, and while the Brighton breathes the same rarified air under the arcades, it does so for a fraction of the price. **Pros:** great views; central location in a prestigious neighborhood; free Wi-Fi. **Cons:** the busy street can make rooms with a view a bit noisy; variable quality in decor between rooms. **TripAdvisor:** "outstanding views," "perfect location," "charming rooms." [$] *Rooms from: €209* ✉ *218 rue de Rivoli, 1er, Louvre/Tuileries* ☎ *01–47–03–61–61* 🌐 *www.paris-hotel-brighton.com* 🛏 *61 rooms* [M] *Tuileries* ✣ *2:A6.*

$$$ HOTEL **Hôtel Crayon.** This colorful boutique hotel, which re-opened near the Louvre and Palais-Royal in 2011, has an eclectic pop-art decor mixed with real flea market finds. **Pros:** new decor; very friendly staff; excellent location. **Cons:** small bathrooms in standard rooms; no restaurant. **TripAdvisor:** "stylish and very friendly," "great hosts," "cozy and good location." [$] *Rooms from: €249* ✉ *25 rue du Bouloi, 1er, Louvre/Tuileries* ☎ *01–42–36–54–19* 🌐 *www.hotelcrayon.com* 🛏 *24 rooms* [M] *Louvre* ✣ *2:C6.*

$$ HOTEL **Hôtel Londres St-Honoré.** An appealing combination of character and comfort distinguishes this small, inexpensive hotel a five-minute walk from the Louvre. **Pros:** within walking distance of major sites; free Wi-Fi. **Cons:** small elevator that doesn't go to ground floor; small beds; upper rooms can get very hot in summer (fans are available). **TripAdvisor:** "terrific location," "quite pleased," "good service." [$] *Rooms from: €147* ✉ *13 rue St-Roch, 1er, Louvre/Tuileries* ☎ *01–42–60–15–62* 🌐 *www.hotellondresstbonore-paris.com* 🛏 *25 rooms, 4 suites* [M] *Pyramides* ✣ *2:A6.*

$$ HOTEL **Hôtel Louvre Sainte Anne.** This small but modern hotel between the Opéra and the Louvre has bright rooms decorated in a country theme, with little extras like heated towel racks and fluffy duvets. **Pros:** central location; free Wi-Fi; helpful staff. **Cons:** smallish rooms and dull decor; "Japanese" district can feel very un-Parisian. **TripAdvisor:** "good service," "quaint," "great location." [$] *Rooms from: €125* ✉ *32 rue Ste-Anne, 1er, Louvre/Tuileries* ☎ *01–40–20–02–35* 🌐 *www.louvre-ste-anne.fr* 🛏 *20 rooms* [M] *Pyramides* ✣ *2:B5.*

$$$$ HOTEL 👍 **Hôtel Meurice.** Since 1835 the Meurice has welcomed royalty and celebrities, from the Duchess of Windsor to Salvador Dalí. **Pros:** views over the gardens; central location, trendy public spaces. **Cons:** on a noisy street; popularity makes the public areas not very discreet. **TripAdvisor:** "luxurious first class decadence," "superb service," "divine opulence." [$] *Rooms from: €720* ✉ *228 rue de Rivoli, 1er, Louvre/*

CLOSE UP

Apartment Rentals

Many Fodorites rent apartments in Paris because they favor extra space plus that special sense of living like a local. Rentals can also offer savings, especially for groups.

Check out the **Paris Tourism Office** website (⊕ www.parisinfo.com) for reputable agency listings. Policies differ, but you can expect a minimum required stay from three to seven days; a refundable deposit payable on arrival; possibly an agency fee; and maid service. A great website with unbiased ratings of agencies and listing services is **Paris Apartment Info** (⊕ www.paris-apartment-info.com).

The following is a list of good-value residence hotels and apartment services: **Ah! Paris** (☎ 01–40–28–97–96 ⊕ www.ahparis.com) offers a large selection of rentals with reasonable all-inclusive rates and no additional fees. **Citadines Résidences Hôtelières** (☎ 08–25–33–33–32 ⊕ www.citadines. fr) is a chain of apartment-style hotel accommodations. They're somewhat generic, but offer many services and good value for short stays. **Lodgis Paris** (☎ 01–70–39–11–11 ⊕ www. lodgis.com) has one of the largest selections in Paris; however, the agency fee makes it cheaper to rent for more than one week. **Paris Vacation Apartments** (☎ 06–12–44–64–78 ⊕ www.parisvacationapartments. com) specializes in luxury rentals, with all-inclusive prices by the week. Agencies based in the United States can also help you find an apartment in Paris: **Rendez-vous à Paris** (✉ 1220 N. Market St., Suite 606, Wilmington, DE ⊕ www.rendez-vousaparis.com) has just a few properties, but all are in prime locations and are top quality at a reasonable price. **Rentals in Paris** (☎ 516/874–0474 ⊕ www.

rentals-in-paris.com) has two dozen centrally located rentals with all-inclusive weekly rates and last-minute special offers.

Additionally, **Fodorites** recommend these rental services:

"I rented . . . from **Rent Paris** (⊕ www. rentparis.com) last summer and had a great experience." —slangevar

"I always rent from **Paris Perfect** (⊕ www.parisperfect.com). All of their places are lovely." —gracejoan3

"**Vacation in Paris** (⊕ www. vacationinparis.com) is a great company and service, and one can pay in U.S. dollars. . . . One also gets the apartment keys mailed . . . no need to meet an agent to let one into the apartment." —Guenmai

"We rented from **Guest Apartment Services** (⊕ www.guestapartment. com) . . . Superlative experience. I stayed there with my mother and she is picky!" —Leely2

"We have rented three apartments in recent years from **Rothray** (www. rothray.com). I can't tell you how completely reliable Ray is and how nice his apartments are. . . . Look at his website and know he will help you with everything and is 100% honest." —MAP

"The English-speaking owners are a pleasure to deal with, and seem to have thought of everything. . . . See for yourself at **Rental Apartment Paris** (⊕ www.RentalApartmentParis. com)." —lregeo

"We have rented twice from Thierry at **Paris Best Lodge** (⊕ www. parisbestlodge.com). He is great . . . I would definitely trust him." —emsmom

15

Tuileries ☎ *01–44–58–10–09* ⊕ *www.lemeurice.com* ➼ *160 rooms, 36 suites* Ⓜ *Tuileries, Concorde* ✛ *2:A6.*

$$$
HOTEL
Fodor'sChoice
★
🛏 **Hôtel Thérèse.** Tucked away from the bustle of the Avenue de l'Opéra, Hotel Thérèse, named after the wife of the Sun King, Louis XIV, is a stone's throw from regal sites like the Louvre and the Palais Royal. **Pros:** great location; friendly staff; cozy rooms. **Cons:** expensive neighborhood; a bit small for the price. **TripAdvisor:** "perfect hotel," "lovely and warm staff," "cozy and classy." Ⓢ *Rooms from: €180* ⊠ *5/7 rue Thérèse, 1er, Louvre/Tuileries* ☎ *01–42–96–10–01* ⊕ *www.hoteltherese. com* ➼ *40 rooms, 3 suites* Ⓜ *Pyramides* ✛ *2:B6.*

$$$$
HOTEL
🛏 **Le Konfidentiel.** Sleep under the pre-guillotined head of Marie Antoinette or amid the turmoil of the Revolution in one of the six individually themed rooms. **Pros:** located next to the Louvre; comfortable rooms; great restaurant. **Cons:** can feel a bit enclosed or exclusive; showers only, no tubs. **TripAdvisor:** "trendy," "fantastic service," "beautiful hotel." Ⓢ *Rooms from: €350* ⊠ *64 rue de l'Arbre Sec, 1er, Louvre/ Tuileries* ☎ *01–55–34–40–40* ⊕ *www.konfidentiel-paris.com* ➼ *6 suites* Ⓜ *Louvre Rivoli* ✛ *2:C6.*

$$$$
HOTEL
🛏 **Renaissance Paris Vendôme.** Hiding behind a classic 19th-century facade is a fresh, contemporary hotel with subtle 1930s influences. **Pros:** posh location; trendy restaurant. **Cons:** as part of the Marriott group, it can feel a bit lacking in character. **TripAdvisor:** "excellent location," "big hotel comfort," "paradise in Paris." Ⓢ *Rooms from: €399* ⊠ *4 rue du Mont Thabor, 1er, Louvre/Tuileries* ☎ *01–40–20–20–00* ⊕ *www.renaissanceparisvendome.com* ➼ *82 rooms, 15 suites* Ⓜ *Tuileries* ✛ *2:A6.*

CHAMPS-ÉLYSÉES

For expanded hotel reviews, visit Fodors.com.

$$$$
HOTEL
�
Fodor'sChoice
★
🛏 **Four Seasons Hôtel George V Paris.** The George V is as poised and polished as the day it opened in 1928: the original Art Deco detailing and 17th-century tapestries have been restored, the bas-reliefs regilded, and the marble-floor mosaics rebuilt tile by tile. **Pros:** in the couture shopping district; courtyard dining in summer; guest-only indoor swimming pool. **Cons:** several blocks from the nearest métro; lacks the intimacy of smaller boutique hotels. **TripAdvisor:** "beyond my expectations," "elegant," "the definition of world class." Ⓢ *Rooms from: €815* ⊠ *31 av. George V, 8e, Champs-Élysées* ☎ *01–49–52–70–00, 800/332–3442 in U.S.* ⊕ *www.fourseasons.com/paris* ➼ *184 rooms, 61 suites* Ⓜ *George V* ✛ *1:D5.*

$$$
HOTEL
🛏 **Hidden Hotel.** The rough-hewn wood facade heralds the nature-friendly theme of this boutique hotel a block from the Arc de Triomphe, and the interior follows through with handcrafted glass, wood, stone, and ceramic decor in materials. **Pros:** organic toiletries in recycled packaging; free Wi-Fi; a block from main métro line and Champs-Élysées. **Cons:** rooms on the small side; open-plan bathrooms have little privacy for roommates. **TripAdvisor:** "very nice and clean rooms," "super mod," "fabulous staff." Ⓢ *Rooms from: €250* ⊠ *28 rue de*

l'Arc de Triomphe, 17e, Champs-Élysées ☎ *01–40–55–03–57* 🌐 *www.hiddenhotelparis.com* *23 rooms* ✥ *1:B3.*

$$$$ HOTEL **Hôtel Daniel.** A contemporary antidote to the minimalist trend, the Daniel is decorated in sumptuous fabrics and antique furnishings from France, North Africa, and the Far East. **Pros:** intimate, homey atmosphere; cell phones and PC available to borrow; close to the Champs-Élysées. **Cons:** across from a noisy bar; no fitness center. **TripAdvisor:** "charming and beautiful," "perfection in every detail," "haven of hospitality." $ *Rooms from: €420* ✉ *8 rue Frédéric Bastiat, 8e, Champs-Élysées* ☎ *01–42–56–17–00* 🌐 *www.hoteldanielparis.com* *17 rooms, 9 suites* Ⓜ *St-Philippe-du-Roule* ✥ *1:E4.*

$$$$ HOTEL **Hôtel Fouquet's Barrière.** This luxury hotel is above the legendary Fouquet's Brasserie at the corner of the Champs-Élysées and Avenue George V. **Pros:** many rooms overlooking the Champs-Élysées; bathroom TVs; métro right outside. **Cons:** anonymous decor; kids in pool heard in the spa. **TripAdvisor:** "high level of luxury," "very congenial staff," "genuinely passionate." $ *Rooms from: €730* ✉ *46 av. George V, 8e, Champs-Élysées* ☎ *01–40–69–60–00* 🌐 *www.fouquets-barriere.com* *87 rooms, 20 suites* Ⓜ *George V* ✥ *1:D4.*

15

$$$$ HOTEL Fodor'sChoice ★ **Hôtel Lancaster.** A complete historical renovation in 2011, a Michelin-star restaurant, and a courtyard garden make this former Spanish nobleman's town house a luxurious retreat. **Pros:** Sunday brunch with organic farm products; just steps away from the Champs-Élysées; hot chocolate menu in winter. **Cons:** size of rooms varies greatly; pricey room service. **TripAdvisor:** "sheer class," "sublime service," "wonderful hotel in a great location." $ *Rooms from: €650* ✉ *7 rue de Berri, 8e, Champs-Élysées* ☎ *01–40–76–40–76, 877/757–2747 in U.S.* 🌐 *www.hotel-lancaster.fr* *46 rooms, 11 suites* Ⓜ *George V* ✥ *1:D4.*

$$$$ HOTEL **Hôtel Le Bristol.** The Bristol ranks among Paris's most exclusive hotels and has the awards to prove it. **Pros:** large interior garden; luxury shopping street; new spa. **Cons:** a few blocks from the nearest métro; old-fashioned atmosphere may not be for everyone. **TripAdvisor:** "perfect classic elegance," "incredible Regency oak Parisian dining room," "a fantastic place." $ *Rooms from: €850* ✉ *112 rue du Faubourg St-Honoré, 8e, Champs-Élysées* ☎ *01–53–43–43–00* 🌐 *www.hotel-bristol.com* *121 rooms, 86 suites* Ⓜ *Miromesnil* ✥ *1:F4.*

$$$$ HOTEL Fodor'sChoice ★ **Hôtel Plaza Athénée.** Prime-time stardom as Carrie Bradshaw's Parisian pied-à-terre in the final episodes of *Sex and the City* boosted the street cred of this 1911 palace hotel. **Pros:** on a luxury shopping street; Dior spa; Eiffel Tower views; special attention to children. **Cons:** vast difference in style of rooms; easy to feel anonymous in such a large hotel. **TripAdvisor:** "quintessential Parisian luxury," "always high class," "great staff and location." $ *Rooms from: €650* ✉ *25 av. Montaigne, 8e, Champs-Élysées* ☎ *01–53–67–66–65, 866/732–1106 in U.S.* 🌐 *www.plaza-athenee-paris.com* *146 rooms, 45 suites* Ⓜ *Alma-Marceau* ✥ *1:D6.*

$$$$ HOTEL **Hôtel Raphael.** This discreet palace hotel was built in 1925 to cater to travelers spending a season in Paris, so every space is generously sized for long, lavish stays. **Pros:** a block from the Champs-Élysées and Arc de Triomphe; rooftop garden terrace; cozy hotel bar frequented by

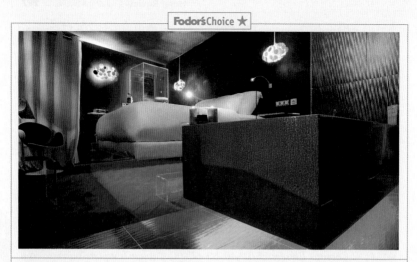

Hotel Seven

Le Citizen Hôtel

St. Christopher's Inn

Hôtel Taylor

Hôtel Mama Shelter

locals. **Cons:** old-fashioned Parisian decor; some soundproofing issues; the neighborhood can have a majestic yet cold atmosphere. **TripAdvisor:** "most romantic in Paris," "charming," "real classical beauty." $ *Rooms from: €650* ✉ *17 av. Kléber, 16e, Champs-Élysées* ☎ *01–53–64–32–00* ⊕ *www.raphael-hotel.com* ⤴ *53 rooms, 39 suites* Ⓜ *Kléber* ✛ *1:C4.*

$$$$
HOTEL
🏨 **Jays Paris.** Opened in 2009, the Jays Paris is a discrete, 19th-century mansion with just five suites, located between the Champs-Elysées and Eiffel Tower. **Pros:** Personalized service; three rooms can be connected for families; several lounge areas. **Cons:** No elevator; business district lacks charm. **TripAdvisor:** "truly remarkable," "absolutely amazing attention to detail," "wonderful hotel and staff." $ *Rooms from: €450* ✉ *6 rue Copernic, Champs-Élysée* ☎ *01–47–04–16–16* ⊕ *www.jays-paris.com* ⤴ *5 suites* Ⓜ *Boissière* ✛ *1:B5.*

$$$$
HOTEL
🏨 **Mon Hotel.** Contemporary design and modern comforts, just two blocks from the Arc de Triomphe and Champs-Élysées, are big draws for this stylish boutique hotel. **Pros:** unique contemporary decor; convenient to the Champs-Élysées. **Cons:** some rooms have limited closet space; no extra beds for children; inconvenient for walking to the center of Paris. **TripAdvisor:** "great service," "wonderful room," "intimate boutique hotel." $ *Rooms from: €440* ✉ *1 rue Argentine, 16e, Champs-Élysées* ☎ *01–45–02–76–76* ⊕ *www.monhotel.fr* ⤴ *37 rooms* Ⓜ *Argentine* ✛ *1:B4.*

$$$$
HOTEL
🏨 **Renaissance Paris Arc de Triomphe.** This modern, American-style hotel is located in a predominantly business district between the Arc de Triomphe and the Parc Monceau. **Pros:** Quiet; spacious; good discounts with Marriott points. **Cons:** Neighborhood lacks character; hotel hosts many business conferences. **TripAdvisor:** "modern hotel in a perfect location," "outstanding service," "chic Paris." $ *Rooms from: €379* ✉ *39 av. de Wagram, Champs-Élysées* ☎ *01–55–37–55–37* ⊕ *www.marriott.fr/hotels/travel/parwg-renaissance-paris-arc-de-triomphe-hotel/* ⤴ *84 rooms, 17 suites* Ⓜ *Ternes* ✛ *1:C3.*

$$$
HOTEL
🏨 **Villa Brunel.** This new hotel in a small 19th-century building between the Arc de Triomphe and Porte Maillot is an exceptional deal considering its rather aristocratic neighbors. **Pros:** close to the Champs-Élysées; suites good for families; quiet location. **Cons:** a bit off the beaten track; too far to walk to most sites. **TripAdvisor:** "a well-placed boutique hotel," "perfect location," "pleasant relaxed stay." $ *Rooms from: €200* ✉ *46 rue Brunel, 17e, Champs-Élysées* ☎ *01–45–74–74–51* ⊕ *www.villabrunel.com* ⤴ *32 rooms* Ⓜ *Argentine* ✛ *1:A3.*

EASTERN PARIS

For expanded hotel reviews, visit Fodors.com.

BASTILLE

$$
HOTEL
🏨 **Hôtel Bastille de Launay.** The no-frills decoration might seem too spartan at first, but this boutique hotel offers elegant comfort, modern amenities, and the perfect location just a few blocks from the regal Place des Vosges. **Pros:** homey; attentive service; reasonably spacious for the neighborhood. **Cons:** elevator and some rooms and bathrooms

very compact. **TripAdvisor:** "cozy charismatic hotel," "lovely décor," "friendly staff." [$] *Rooms from: €150* ✉ *42 rue Amelot, 11e, Bastille* ☎ *01–47–00–88–11* 🌐 *www.bastilledelaunay-hotel-paris.com* 🛏 *36 rooms* [M] *Chemin Vert* ⊕ *4:H1.*

$$ HOTEL Fodor's Choice ★ **Hôtel Mama Shelter.** The heir to the Club Med empire decided to do for the hotel industry what jeans did for fashion: democratize style. **Pros:** trendy design; easy access to airport; entertainment center in each room. **Cons:** on the edge of Paris; dark lighting; club across the street can be noisy. **TripAdvisor:** "funky and friendly," "a warm welcome," "cool hotel in cool area." [$] *Rooms from: €159* ✉ *109 rue de Bagnolet, 20e, Bastille* ☎ *01–43–48–48–48* 🌐 *www.mamashelter.com* 🛏 *172 rooms* ⊕ *2:H3.*

$$$$ HOTEL **Les Jardins du Marais.** Behind an unassuming facade on a narrow street, this rambling hotel's nine historic buildings (including Gustave Eiffel's old workshop) surround a spacious sculpture-garden courtyard. **Pros:** historic building; easy walk to the Marais and Bastille; all rooms face garden courtyard. **Cons:** often booked by groups; big difference between room decor and public areas; some rooms in these odd, old buildings have a pillar in the center. **TripAdvisor:** "helpful staff," "elegant quiet rooms," "practical hideaway." [$] *Rooms from: €269* ✉ *74 rue Amelot, 11e, Bastille* ☎ *01–40–21–20–00* 🌐 *www.homeplazza.com* 🛏 *205 rooms, 58 suites* [M] *St-Sébastien-Froissart* ⊕ *4:H1.*

$ HOTEL Fodor's Choice ★ **St. Christopher's Inn.** Overlooking the canal, near the Parc de la Villette, this British-run hostel is the first purpose-built hostel in Paris. **Pros:** very modern facilities; bike rentals; 24-hour reception. **Cons:** a bit far from the major sights; can be noisy since it attracts groups of young travelers. **TripAdvisor:** "youthful," "great views," "great hostel for partying." [$] *Rooms from: €36* ✉ *68 Quai de la Seine, 19e, Bastille* ☎ *01–40–34–34–40* 🌐 *www.st-christophers.co.uk* 🛏 *175 rooms* [M] *Riquet* ⊕ *2:H3.*

$$ HOTEL **Standard Design Hôtel.** It was about time for a design hotel to open in this alternative hipster corner of the Bastille district. **Pros:** trendy design style; personalized gift packs available (features are constantly changing, maybe flowers, or breakfast, or a massage, etc.; you get a choice of three); funky shopping and nightlife district. **Cons:** street noise; some rooms very small. **TripAdvisor:** "well decorated," "stylishly good value," "a wonderful stay." [$] *Rooms from: €175* ✉ *29 rue des Taillandiers, 11e, Bastille* ☎ *01–48–05–30–97* 🌐 *www.standard-hotel.com* 🛏 *36 rooms* [M] *Bastille* ⊕ *4:H2.*

CANAL ST-MARTIN

$ HOTEL Fodor's Choice ★ **Hôtel Taylor.** Tucked away on a tiny street between République and the Canal St Martin, the Hôtel Taylor offers spacious, spic-and-span rooms in the gentrified 10th arrondissement. **Pros:** close to the métro; spacious rooms; thoughtful amenities. **Cons:** street can seem intimidating at night in still-gentrifying neighborhood. **TripAdvisor:** "lovely place," "convenient," "romantic and central." [$] *Rooms from: €90* ✉ *6 rue Taylor, 10e, Canal St-Martin* ☎ *01–42–40–11–01* 🌐 *www.paristaylorhotel.com* 🛏 *37 rooms* [M] *République* ⊕ *2:F5.*

$$$ HOTEL Fodor's Choice ★ **Le Citizen Hôtel.** Minimalist cool decor, complimentary iPads, and views over the historic Canal St-Martin make the Citizen a great choice for those interested in checking out the hip East Paris vibe. **Pros:** trendy neighborhood far from tourists; all-inclusive breakfast and minibar snacks; friendly, attentive staff. **Cons:** smallest rooms are best for one person or short stays; noisy street; about 20 minutes by metro to the main tourist sites. **TripAdvisor:** "amazing staff," "cozy hotel," "fantastic rooms." [$] *Rooms from: €195* ✉ *96 quai de Jemmapes, Canal St-Martin* ☎ *01–83–62–55–50* 🌐 *lecitizenhotel.com* 🛏 *12* [M] *Jacques-Bonsergent* ✥ *2:G4.*

RÉPUBLIQUE

$ HOTEL **Hôtel du Nord.** Behind the rustic facade of this budget hotel that's just around the corner from Place de la République is a charming little lobby with clay-tile floors, exposed stone walls, and wooden beams. **Pros:** bike rental; close to East Paris nightlife districts. **Cons:** few amenities; busy Place de la République is noisy. **TripAdvisor:** "perfect getaway," "great shower," "loved the staff." [$] *Rooms from: €82* ✉ *47 rue Albert Thomas, 10e, République* ☎ *01–42–01–66–00* 🌐 *www.hoteldunord-leparivelo.com* 🛏 *24 rooms* [M] *République* ✥ *2:F4.*

$$$ HOTEL **Hôtel Gare de l'Est Français.** This Haussmann-era budget hotel faces historic Gare de l'Est and is two blocks from Gare du Nord and the popular Canal St-Martin district. **Pros:** convenient for Eurostar travelers; many amenities for the price. **Cons:** noisy street; unattractive neighborhood. **TripAdvisor:** "very convenient," "perfect location," "friendly service." [$] *Rooms from: €200* ✉ *13 rue du 8 Mai 1945, 10e, République* ☎ *01–40–35–94–14* 🌐 *www.hotelfrancais.com* 🛏 *71 rooms* [M] *Gare de l'Est* ✥ *2:E3.*

$ HOTEL **Hôtel Palma.** Just down the street from Père Lachaise cemetery, and a block from the Place de Gambetta, this off-the-beaten-path hotel may be far from the action, but the métro will get you where you need to go quickly and efficiently. **Pros:** recently renovated; close to métro. **Cons:** far from city center; lacks charm. [$] *Rooms from: €100* ✉ *77 av. Gambetta, 20e, République* ☎ *01–46–36–13–65* 🌐 *www.hotelparis20.fr* 🛏 *32 rooms* [M] *Gambetta* ✥ *2:H5.*

$ HOTEL **Hôtel Résidence Alhambra.** The white facade, rear garden, and flower-filled window boxes brighten this lesser-known neighborhood between the Marais and Rue Oberkampf. **Pros:** bright and colorful; popular nightlife district. **Cons:** small doubles; long walk to the center of town; no air-conditioning. **TripAdvisor:** "clean and comfortable rooms," "good service and location," "friendly staff." [$] *Rooms from: €92* ✉ *13 rue de Malte, 11e, République* ☎ *01–47–00–35–52* 🌐 *www.hotelalhambra.fr* 🛏 *58 rooms* [M] *Oberkampf* ✥ *2:H6.*

$$$ HOTEL **Le Général Hôtel.** Designer Jean-Philippe Nuel's sleek hotel was one of Paris's first budget design hotels. **Pros:** iPod docks; tea/coffeemaker in the room; in popular nightlife district. **Cons:** noisy neighborhood; not within easy walking distance of major tourist sites. **TripAdvisor:** "hip with some nice touches," "exceptional staff," "good business hotel." [$] *Rooms from: €230* ✉ *5–7 rue Rampon, 11e, République* ☎ *01–47–00–41–57* 🌐 *www.legeneralhotel.com* 🛏 *43 rooms, 3 suites* [M] *République* ✥ *2:G5.*

15

LATIN QUARTER

For expanded hotel reviews, visit Fodors.com.

$ 🛏 **Hôtel Collège de France.** Exposed-stone walls, wooden beams, and
HOTEL medieval artwork echo the style of the Musée Cluny, two blocks from
this small, family-run hotel. **Pros:** walking distance to major Rive
Gauche sights and the islands; free Wi-Fi; ceiling fans. **Cons:** big difference between renovated and unrenovated rooms; no air-conditioning;
thin walls between rooms. **TripAdvisor:** "unforgettable," "clean hotel
with all the basics," "great stuff." Ⓢ *Rooms from: €107* ✉ *7 rue Thénard, 5e, Latin Quarter* ☏ *01–43–26–78–36* ⊕ *www.hotelcdf.com*
➴ *29 rooms* Ⓜ *Maubert-Mutualité, St-Michel–Cluny–La Sorbonne*
✛ *4:D4.*

$$ 🛏 **Hôtel des Jardins du Luxembourg.** Blessed with a personable staff and a
HOTEL smart, stylish look, this hotel on a calm cul-de-sac a block away from the
Jardin du Luxembourg is an oasis for contemplation. **Pros:** quiet street
close to gardens and RER station; sauna; hot buffet breakfast. **Cons:**
extra charge to use Wi-Fi; some very small rooms; air-conditioning
not very strong. **TripAdvisor:** "quiet," "comfortable and cozy," "good
location." Ⓢ *Rooms from: €175* ✉ *5 impasse Royer-Collard, 5e, Latin
Quarter* ☏ *01–40–46–08–88* ⊕ *www.les-jardins-du-luxembourg.com*
➴ *26 rooms* Ⓜ *RER: Luxembourg* ✛ *4:C5.*

$$ 🛏 **Hôtel du Lys.** To jump into an inexpensive Parisian fantasy, just climb
HOTEL the stairway to your room (there's no elevator) in this former 17th-
century royal residence. **Pros:** central location on a quiet side street;
historic character; free Wi-Fi. **Cons:** old-fashioned decor is decidedly
outdated; perfunctory service, no air-conditioning. **TripAdvisor:** "comfortable room," "wonderful hotel and location," "clean and authentic."
Ⓢ *Rooms from: €125* ✉ *23 rue Serpente, 6e, Latin Quarter* ☏ *01–43–
26–97–57* ⊕ *www.hoteldulys.com* ➴ *22 rooms* ❖ *Breakfast* Ⓜ *St-
Michel, Odéon* ✛ *4:C3.*

$ 🛏 **Hôtel Familia.** Owners Eric and Sylvie continue to update and improve
HOTEL their popular budget hotel without raising the prices. **Pros:** attentive,
Fodor's Choice friendly service; great value; has all the modern conveniences. **Cons:** on
★ a busy street; some rooms are small; noise between rooms can be loud.
TripAdvisor: "good value in great location," "great staff," "charming."
Ⓢ *Rooms from: €112* ✉ *11 rue des Écoles, 5e, Latin Quarter* ☏ *01–43–
54–55–27* ⊕ *www.hotel-paris-familia.com* ➴ *30 rooms* ❖ *Breakfast*
Ⓜ *Cardinal Lemoine* ✛ *4:E4.*

$$ 🛏 **Hôtel Grandes Écoles.** Distributed among a trio of three-story build-
HOTEL ings, Madame Lefloch's rooms have a distinct grandmotherly vibe with
flowery wallpaper and lace bedspreads, but are downright spacious for
this part of Paris. **Pros:** large courtyard garden; close to Latin Quarter
nightlife spots; good value. **Cons:** uphill walk from the métro; some
noisy rooms; few amenities. **TripAdvisor:** "great experience," "charm-
ing," "cute and cozy." Ⓢ *Rooms from: €145* ✉ *75 rue du Cardinal, 5e,
Latin Quarter* ☏ *01–43–26–79–23* ⊕ *www.hotel-grandes-ecoles.com*
➴ *51 rooms* Ⓜ *Cardinal Lemoine* ✛ *4:E5.*

$$$ 🛏 **Hôtel Henri IV Rive Gauche.** From the ashes of the legendary dive bar
HOTEL Polly Magoo rose this smart new hotel back in 2003; it's 50 paces from
Notre-Dame and the Seine. **Pros:** elegant, comfortable decor; central

location close to major sights and RER station. **Cons:** on a busy street full of late-night bars; single rooms are small. **TripAdvisor:** "perfect position for visiting the city," "lovely," "friendly staff." [$] *Rooms from: €195 ✉ 9–11 rue St-Jacques, 5e, Latin Quarter ☎ 01–46–33–20–20 🌐 www.henri-paris-hotel.com 🛏 23 rooms [M] St-Michel ✣ 4:D3.*

$ HOTEL 👶 **Hôtel Marignan.** Not to be confused with the hotel of the same name near the Champs-Élysées, this Latin Quarter Marignan lies squarely between budget-basic and youth hostel (no TVs or elevator) and offers lots of communal conveniences—a fully stocked kitchen, free laundry machines, and copious tourist information. **Pros:** great value for the location; free kitchen and laundry facilities; free Wi-Fi. **Cons:** no elevator; room phones take only incoming calls; has a bit of a youth-hostel atmosphere. **TripAdvisor:** "very quaint spot," "lovely simply hotel," "comfy and fun." [$] *Rooms from: €95 ✉ 13 rue du Sommerard, 5e, Latin Quarter ☎ 01–43–54–63–81 🌐 www.hotel-marignan.com 🛏 30 rooms, 12 with bath 🍴 Breakfast [M] Maubert-Mutualité ✣ 4:D4.*

15

$$$$ HOTEL **Hôtel Notre Dame.** If you love the quirky and eclectic fashions of Christian Lacroix and don't mind hauling your bags up some stairs, this unique boutique hotel overlooking Notre Dame Cathedral and the Seine River is for you. **Pros:** decor by Christian Lacroix; views of Notre Dame and river; comfortable beds. **Cons:** stairs can be tricky with large bags; no minibar in rooms; some noise from busy street. **TripAdvisor:** "beautiful hotel," "lovely view," "cozy and perfectly placed." [$] *Rooms from: €270 ✉ 1 quai Saint-Michel, Latin Quarter ☎ 01–43–54–20–43 🌐 www.hotelnotredameparis.com 🛏 26 [M] St-Michel ✣ 4:D3.*

$$$$ HOTEL 👶 **Hôtel Résidence Henri IV.** This small Latin Quarter hotel on a quiet cul-de-sac is perfect for travelers, especially those with children, who need a home base where they can kick back and make their own meals. **Pros:** kitchenettes; close to Latin Quarter sights. **Cons:** closest métro is a few blocks away. **TripAdvisor:** "little treasure in Paris," "comfort and location," "good hotel for a short break." [$] *Rooms from: €260 ✉ 50 rue des Bernadins, 5e, Latin Quarter ☎ 01–44–41–31–81 🌐 www.residencehenri4.com 🛏 8 rooms, 5 apartments [M] Maubert-Mutualité ✣ 4:D4.*

$$ HOTEL **Hôtel Saint-Jacques.** Nearly every wall in this bargain Latin Quarter hotel is bedecked with faux-marble and trompe-l'oeil murals. **Pros:** unique Parisian decor; close to Latin Quarter sights; free Wi-Fi and free laptop to borrow. **Cons:** very busy street makes it too noisy to open windows in summer; thin walls between rooms. **TripAdvisor:** "classically French character," "lovely," "friendly staff." [$] *Rooms from: €168 ✉ 35 rue des Écoles, 5e, Latin Quarter ☎ 01–44–07–45–45 🌐 www.hotel-saintjacques.com 🛏 38 rooms [M] Maubert-Mutualité ✣ 4:D4.*

$$$$ HOTEL Fodor's Choice ★ **Hotel Seven.** The "seven" refers to the level of heaven you'll find at this extraordinary boutique hotel. **Pros:** copious breakfast buffet; quiet location near Mouffetard market street; interesting wine bar and cocktail selection at night. **Cons:** small closet space; several blocks to closest metro. **TripAdvisor:** "unique experience," "amazing funky hotel," "beautiful interior." [$] *Rooms from: €330 ✉ 20 rue Berthollet, 5e, Latin Quarter ☎ 01–43–31–47–52 🌐 www.sevenhotelparis.com 🛏 28 rooms, 7 suites [M] Censier-Daubentin ✣ 4:D6.*

$$$ ☐ **Hotel Sorbonne.** For what French students pay to study at the Sor-
HOTEL bonne, visitors can stay a few nights next door at this swanky design
hotel (yes, tuition is *that* cheap). **Pros:** centrally located; fun decor;
attentive service. **Cons:** tiny rooms for the price; small breakfast room.
TripAdvisor: "adorable hotel in a great neighborhood," "helpful staff,"
"clean and quiet." Ⓢ *Rooms from: €240* ✉ *6 rue Victor Cousin, 5e,
Latin Quarter* ☎ *01–43–54–01–52* ⊕ *www.hotelsorbonne.com* ⤶ *38
rooms* Ⓜ *Cluny La Sorbonne* ✛ *4:C4.*

$$ ☐ **Les Degrés de Notre-Dame.** On a quiet lane a few yards from the Seine,
HOTEL this diminutive budget hotel is lovingly decorated with the owner's flea-
market finds. **Pros:** breakfast included; attractive location in quiet part
of Latin Quarter; popular locals' restaurant. **Cons:** no air-conditioning;
street noise; no elevator. **TripAdvisor:** "old Paris," "very friendly staff,"
"great location." Ⓢ *Rooms from: €170* ✉ *10 rue des Grands Degrés, 5e,
Latin Quarter* ☎ *01–55–42–88–88* ⊕ *www.lesdegreshotel.com* ⤶ *10
rooms* ⏿ *Breakfast* Ⓜ *Maubert-Mutualité* ✛ *4:D3.*

$ ☐ **Port-Royal Hôtel.** The spotless rooms and extra-helpful staff at the
HOTEL Port-Royal are well above average for this price range. **Pros:** excellent
value for the money; attentive service; typical Parisian neighborhood
close to two major markets. **Cons:** not very central; on a busy street;
no a/c or Wi-Fi in rooms. **TripAdvisor:** "quaint," "perfect Parisian budget hotel," "excellent location." Ⓢ *Rooms from: €84* ✉ *8 bd. de Port-
Royal, 5e, Latin Quarter* ☎ *01–43–31–70–06* ⊕ *www.hotelportroyal.fr*
⤶ *46 rooms, 20 with bath* ⊟ *No credit cards* Ⓜ *Les Gobelins* ✛ *4:C6.*

$$ ☐ **Résidence Hôtelière Le Vert Galant.** In a little-known neighborhood west
☾ of Place d'Italie awaits a sincere welcome from Madame Laborde, the
HOTEL proprietress at this plain but proper hotel that encloses peaceful green
garden. **Pros:** quiet location with a garden; kitchenettes in some rooms;
safe residential district. **Cons:** not very central; no air-conditioning;
some noise between rooms. **TripAdvisor:** "lovely friendly hotel," "great
service," "beautiful and romantic." Ⓢ *Rooms from: €130* ✉ *41–43
rue Croulebarbe, 13e, Latin Quarter* ☎ *01–44–08–83–50* ⊕ *www.
vertgalant.com* ⤶ *15 rooms* Ⓜ *Les Gobelins* ✛ *4:E6.*

$ ☐ **Résidence Les Gobelins.** Wicker furniture and sunny colors warm up
HOTEL this small, simple hotel on a quiet side street between Place d'Italie and
the Latin Quarter, not far from the market street Mouffetard. **Pros:**
close to major métro and bus lines; friendly welcome; near shops and
cafés. **Cons:** 20-minute walk to the center of Paris; few amenities; no air-
conditioning. **TripAdvisor:** "clean and well located," "extremely helpful
staff," "a gem of a place." Ⓢ *Rooms from: €98* ✉ *9 rue des Gobelins,
13e, Latin Quarter* ☎ *01–47–07–26–90* ⊕ *www.hotelgobelins.com*
⤶ *32 rooms* Ⓜ *Les Gobelins* ✛ *4:E6.*

$$$ ☐ **The Five Hôtel.** Small is beautiful at this tiny design hotel on a quiet
HOTEL street near the Mouffetard market. **Pros:** stylish design; personalized
welcome; quiet side street. **Cons:** most rooms are too small for excessive
baggage; the nearest métro is a 10-minute walk. **TripAdvisor:** "trendy
hotel with friendly staff," "very nicely designed," "nice and quaint."
Ⓢ *Rooms from: €225* ✉ *3 rue Flatters, 5e, Latin Quarter* ☎ *01–43–
31–74–21* ⊕ *www.thefivehotel.com* ⤶ *24 rooms* Ⓜ *Gobelins* ✛ *4:D6.*

MARAIS

For expanded hotel reviews, visit Fodors.com.

$$$
HOTEL
Hôtel Bourg Tibourg. Scented candles and subdued lighting announce designer-du-jour Jacques Garcia's mix of haremlike romance and Gothic contemplation. **Pros:** right in the heart of trendy Marais district; luxurious style at moderate prices; great nightlife district. **Cons:** rooms are small and ill equipped for those with large suitcases; no hotel restaurant. **TripAdvisor:** "fantastic attention to detail," "great staff," "a discreet hideaway." $ *Rooms from: €250* ⌗ *19 rue Bourg Tibourg, 4e, Marais* ☎ *01–42–78–47–39* ⊕ *www.hotelbourgtibourg.com* ⤷ *29 rooms, 1 suite* Ⓜ *Hôtel de Ville* ✛ *4:E2.*

$$$
HOTEL
Hôtel Caron. This petite and contemporary boutique hotel on a Marais side street has typically small rooms, but they're well-equipped with many thoughtful freebies. **Pros:** excellent locatio in center of Paris; L'Occitane toiletries; friendly staff. **Cons:** only enough room for small suitcases; no hotel restaurant or bar; some noise from bar across the street. **TripAdvisor:** "a Paris gem," "excellent service," "incredible location." $ *Rooms from: €245* ⌗ *3 rue Caron, Marais* ☎ *01–40–29–02–94* ⊕ *www.hotelcaron.com* ⤷ *18* Ⓜ *Bastille or St-Paul* ✛ *4:G2.*

$$
HOTEL
Hôtel Caron de Beaumarchais. The theme of this intimate, romantic hotel is the work of former next-door neighbor Pierre-Augustin Caron de Beaumarchais, supplier of military aid to American revolutionaries and playwright who penned *The Marriage of Figaro* and *The Barber of Seville.* **Pros:** cozy, historic Parisian decor; breakfast in bed; easy walking distance to major monuments. **Cons:** small rooms; busy street of bars and cafés can be noisy. **TripAdvisor:** "quaint," "romantic little gem," "charming." $ *Rooms from: €165* ⌗ *12 rue Vieille-du-Temple, 4e, Marais* ☎ *01–42–72–34–12* ⊕ *www.carondebeaumarchais.com* ⤷ *19 rooms* Ⓜ *Hôtel de Ville* ✛ *4:F2.*

$$
HOTEL
Hôtel de la Bretonnerie. This small hotel is in a 17th-century *hôtel particulier* (town house) on a tiny street in the Marais, a few minutes' walk from the Centre Pompidou and the bars and cafés of Rue Vieille du Temple. **Pros:** central location and comfortable decor at a moderate price; typical Parisian character. **Cons:** quality and size of the rooms vary greatly; the in-your-face gay district location may not be to everyone's taste. **TripAdvisor:** "convenient and customer-friendly," "wonderful location," "an amazing period hotel." $ *Rooms from: €165* ⌗ *22 rue Ste-Croix-de-la-Bretonnerie, 4e, Marais* ☎ *01–48–87–77–63* ⊕ *www.bretonnerie.com* ⤷ *22 rooms, 7 suites* Ⓜ *Hôtel de Ville* ✛ *4:E1.*

$
HOTEL
Hôtel de la Place des Vosges. Despite a lack of amenities and an elevator that doesn't serve all floors, a loyal clientele swears by this small, historic hotel just off the 17th-century Place des Vosges. **Pros:** excellent location; fans on request; historic feel; new bathrooms. **Cons:** no air-conditioning; most rooms are very small; street-facing rooms can be noisy. **TripAdvisor:** "comfortable," "great neighborhood," "charming in its own way." $ *Rooms from: €110* ⌗ *12 rue de Birague, 4e, Marais* ☎ *01–42–72–60–46* ⊕ *www.hotelplacedesvosges.com* ⤷ *16 rooms* Ⓜ *Bastille* ✛ *4:G2.*

$$$
HOTEL
Hôtel Duo. This design hotel in the heart of the trendy Marais district has a fresh, contemporary style with bold colors and dramatic lighting;

15

some rooms have the original 16th-century beams integrated into the decor. **Pros:** central location near shops and cafés; walking distance to major monuments; good amentities. **Cons:** noisy street; service not always delivered with a smile. **TripAdvisor:** "boutique chic," "beautiful hotel," "nice staff." [$] *Rooms from: €230* ✉ *11 rue du Temple, 4e, Marais* ☎ *01–42–72–72–22* 🌐 *www.duoparis.com* 🛏 *58 rooms* [M] *Hôtel de Ville* ⊕ *4:E1.*

$ HOTEL 🏨 **Hôtel Jeanne-d'Arc.** You can get your money's worth at this hotel in an unbeatable location off the tranquil Place du Marché Ste-Catherine, one of the city's lesser-known pedestrian squares. **Pros:** charming street close to major sites; good value for the Marais; lots of drinking and dining options nearby. **Cons:** late-night revelers on the square can be noisy after midnight; minimal amenities; rooms have varying quality and size. **TripAdvisor:** "classic hotel," "friendly staff," "lots of charm." [$] *Rooms from: €96* ✉ *3 rue de Jarente, 4e, Marais* ☎ *01–48–87–62–11* 🌐 *www.hoteljeannedarc.com* 🛏 *35 rooms* [M] *St-Paul* ⊕ *4:G2.*

$$$ HOTEL Fodor's Choice ★ 🏨 **Hôtel Jules & Jim.** Opened in December 2011, this contemporary hotel in the less-traveled corner of the trendy Marais district feels almost like an art gallery. **Pros:** bright, stylish rooms; trendy bar attracts locals; up-and-coming neighborhood. **Cons:** the small "Jules" rooms are best for those traveling light or only staying a night; no restaurant; street full of wholesale shops closed to the public. [$] *Rooms from: €220* ✉ *11 rue des Gravilliers, Marais* ☎ *01–42–78–10–01* 🌐 *www.hoteljulesetjim.com* 🛏 *21 rooms, 2 duplexes* [M] *Arts-et-métiers* ⊕ *2:E6.*

$$$$ HOTEL 🏨 **Pavillon de la Reine.** This enchanting countrylike château is hidden off the regal Place des Vosges behind a stunning garden courtyard. **Pros:** typically Parisian historic character; proximity to the Place des Vosges without the noise; Carita spa treatments. **Cons:** expensive for the Marais and the size of the rooms; the nearest métro is a few blocks away. **TripAdvisor:** "incredible Paris perfection," "quiet stay," "tranquil retreat." [$] *Rooms from: €410* ✉ *28 pl. des Vosges, 3e, Marais* ☎ *01–40–29–19–19, 800/447–7462 in U.S.* 🌐 *www.pavillon-de-la-reine.com* 🛏 *31 rooms, 23 suites* [M] *Bastille, St-Paul* ⊕ *4:G2.*

MONTMARTRE

For expanded hotel reviews, visit Fodors.com.

$ HOTEL 🏨 **Ermitage Hôtel Sacré Coeur.** It's a bit of a hike from the nearest métro, but this family-run hotel in a Napoléon III–era building is friendly and filled with mirrored armoires, chandeliers, and other antiques. **Pros:** family-run atmosphere; charming Parisian neighborhood. **Cons:** not close to the métro station; no online reservations or credit cards accepted. **TripAdvisor:** "unique," "fabulous but with quirks," "excellent French environment and location." [$] *Rooms from: €105* ✉ *24 rue Lamarck, 18e, Montmartre* ☎ *01–42–64–79–22* 🌐 *www.ermitagesacrecoeur.fr* 🛏 *11 rooms* 💳 *No credit cards* 🍴 *Breakfast* [M] *Lamarck Caulaincourt* ⊕ *2:H4.*

$ HOTEL 🏨 **Hôtel Eldorado.** The unpretentious Eldorado, just west of Montmartre, is perfect for guests who are happy lying low without room phones, TVs, or an elevator. **Pros:** budget decor with character; leafy garden courtyard; hipster locals' hangout. **Cons:** far from the center of Paris; few amenities; courtyard can be noisy in summer. **TripAdvisor:** "clean rooms," "bohemian Paris style," "warm and welcoming." $ *Rooms from: €85* ✉ *18 rue des Dames, 17e, Montmartre* ☎ *01–45–22–35–21* ⊕ *www.eldoradohotel.fr* ⇱ *33 rooms, 23 with bath* Ⓜ *Place de Clichy* ✛ *1:H1.*

$$ 🛏 **Hôtel Regyn's Montmartre.** Lots of folks book the tiny Regyn's for the
HOTEL out-of-*Amélie* Place des Abbesses location; they're also pleased to find bright, warm colors and rooms with modern bathrooms, hair dryers, and radios. **Pros:** métro station right outside; great views over Paris; new mattresses. **Cons:** no air-conditioning; some street noise; tiny elevator. **TripAdvisor:** "quaint," "friendly and helpful staff," "authentic French experience." $ *Rooms from: €122* ✉ *18 pl. des Abbesses, 18e, Montmartre* ☎ *01–42–54–45–21* ⊕ *www.hotel-regyns-paris.com* ⇱ *22 rooms* Ⓜ *Abbesses* ✛ *2:B1.*

$$ 🛏 **Hôtel Royal Fromentin.** An old-world, historic budget hotel on the bor-
HOTEL der of Montmartre's now tamed red-light district, this former cabaret has much of its Art Deco wood paneling and theatrical trappings intact. **Pros:** spacious rooms for the price; historic absinthe bar; close to Sacré-Coeur. **Cons:** some guests may find neighborhood peep shows and sex shops disturbing; spotty Wi-Fi; far from the center of Paris. **TripAdvisor:** "room with a view," "Spartan but clean," "charming." $ *Rooms from: €150* ✉ *11 rue Fromentin, 9e, Montmartre* ☎ *01–48–74–85–93* ⊕ *www.hotelroyalfromentin.com* ⇱ *47 rooms* Ⓜ *Blanche* ✛ *2:B2.*

$ 🛏 **Plug-Inn.** This likable "boutique hostel" is on a quiet side street at the
HOTEL foot of Montmartre, near colorful Rue Lepic. **Pros:** flat-screen TVs in private rooms; free breakfast; some Eiffel Tower views. **Cons:** no air-conditioning; extremely small elevator; some street noise. **TripAdvisor:** "nice breakfast," "clean rooms," "tiny but well formed." $ *Rooms from: €101* ✉ *7 rue Aristide-Bruant, 18e, Montmartre* ☎ *01–42–58–13–44* ⊕ *www.plug-inn.fr* ⇱ *30 rooms* Ⓜ *Abbesses, Blanche* ✛ *2:B1.*

MONTPARNASSE

For expanded hotel reviews, visit Fodors.com.

$$ 🛏 **Apostrophe Hotel.** Those enamored of the artistic and literary history
HOTEL of Paris's Left Bank will appreciate this whimsical family-run hotel between Montparnasse and Luxembourg Gardens. **Pros:** friendly service; charming neighborhood close to the métro; free laptop and bike loans. **Cons:** limited closet space; the open bathroom plan offers little privacy from roommates. **TripAdvisor:** "serene simplicity," "small but perfectly formed," "great location and service." $ *Rooms from: €195* ✉ *3 rue de Chevreuse, 6e, Montparnasse* ☎ *01–56–54–31–31* ⊕ *www.apostrophe-hotel.com* ⇱ *16 rooms* ✛ *4:A6.*

$ 🛏 **Hôtel des Bains.** In a charming neighborhood, this hidden find has
HOTEL tastefully decorated rooms, satellite TV, and air-conditioning. **Pros:** close to Jardin du Luxembourg and St-Germain-des-Prés; garden courtyard; typical Parisian character. **Cons:** no online booking; streets can be noisy; some rooms very small. **TripAdvisor:** "a very Parisian experience," "comfortable large room," "charming." $ *Rooms from: €96*

15

✉ *33 rue Delambre, 14e, Montparnasse* ☎ *01–43–20–85–27* ⊕ *www. hotel-des-bains-montparnasse.com* ⬎ *34 rooms, 8 suites* Ⓜ *Vavin, Edgar Quinet* ✛ *4:A6.*

$$$ 🛏 **Hôtel Le Sainte-Beuve.** On a tranquil street between the Jardin du Lux-
HOTEL embourg and Montparnasse's timeless cafés and brasseries is the pleas-
ant Sainte-Beuve. **Pros:** stylish decor; upscale location without tourist
crowds; close to major métro lines. **Cons:** a good 10-minute walk to
the Latin Quarter or St-Germain-des-Prés; small rooms and elevator.
TripAdvisor: "a perfect stay," "charming small quiet hotel," "elegant."
Ⓢ *Rooms from: €242* ✉ *9 rue Ste-Beuve, 6e, Montparnasse* ☎ *01–45–
48–20–07* ⊕ *www.parishotelcharme.com* ⬎ *22 rooms* Ⓜ *Vavin* ✛ *4:A5.*

$$$ 🛏 **Hôtel Lenox-Montparnasse.** Proximity to the Jardin du Luxembourg
HOTEL and extra amenities such as free Wi-Fi are what make this hotel a
good value. **Pros:** lively district close to Montparnasse and St-Germain-
des-Prés; honesty bar. **Cons:** standard rooms are small; noisy street.
TripAdvisor: "comfortable and welcoming," "cozy with an excellent
location," "good staff." Ⓢ *Rooms from: €250* ✉ *15 rue Delambre, 14e,
Montparnasse* ☎ *01–43–35–34–50* ⊕ *www.paris-hotel-lenox.com* ⬎ *46
rooms, 6 suites* Ⓜ *Vavin* ✛ *4:A6.*

$$$ 🛏 **Hôtel Raspail-Montparnasse.** Capturing the spirit of Montparnasse in
HOTEL its heyday as the art capital of the world in the 1920s and '30s, rooms
in this hotel are named after some illustrious neighborhood stars like
Picasso, Chagall, and Modigliani. **Pros:** convenient to métro and bus;
many markets and cafés nearby; friendly staff. **Cons:** traffic noise;
some smallish rooms. **TripAdvisor:** "charming little hotel," "com-
fortable," "convenient and reasonably priced." Ⓢ *Rooms from: €185*
✉ *203 bd. Raspail, 14e, Montparnasse* ☎ *01–43–20–62–86* ⊕ *www.
hotelraspailmontparnasse.com* ⬎ *38 rooms* Ⓜ *Vavin* ✛ *4:A6.*

OPÉRA/GRANDS BOULEVARDS

For expanded hotel reviews, visit Fodors.com.

$$$$ 🛏 **Hôtel Banke.** Once a stately bank built in the early 20th century, this
HOTEL luxurious hotel lies in the heart of the Opera district, with its shops
and theaters. **Pros:** great location; spacious; excellent service. **Cons:**
pricey restaurant; cramped spa/gym; several blocks from the nearest
métro. **TripAdvisor:** "very kind staff," "beautiful contemporary hotel,"
"unique." Ⓢ *Rooms from: €280* ✉ *20 rue LaFayette, 9e, Opéra/Grands
Boulevards* ☎ *01–55–33–22–05* ⊕ *www.derbyhotels.com/banke-hotel-
paris* ⬎ *76 rooms, 18 suites* Ⓜ *Opéra* ✛ *2:B4.*

$ 🛏 **Hôtel Chopin.** The Chopin recalls its 1846 birth date with a creaky-
HOTEL floored lobby and aged woodwork, with basic but comfortable rooms
that overlook the Passage Jouffroy's quaint toy shops and bookstores.
Pros: unique location; close to major métro station; great nightlife dis-
trict. **Cons:** thin walls; single rooms are very small; few amenities. **Tri-
pAdvisor:** "classic French hotel," "unique experience," "friendly staff
and well located." Ⓢ *Rooms from: €114* ✉ *10 bd. Montmartre, 46
passage Jouffroy, 9e, Opéra/Grands Boulevards* ☎ *01–47–70–58–10*
⊕ *hotelchopin.fr/* ⬎ *36 rooms* Ⓜ *Grands Boulevards* ✛ *2:C4.*

$$$ HOTEL **Hôtel de Noailles.** With a nod to the work of postmodern designers like Putman and Starck, this style-driven boutique is both contemporary and cozy. **Pros:** a block from the airport bus; easy walk to the Louvre and Opéra. **Cons:** small elevator; no interesting views. **TripAdvisor:** "amazing style," "efficient and welcoming," "extremely comfortable." [$] *Rooms from: €255* ✉ *9 rue de Michodière, 2e, Opéra/Grands Boulevards* ☎ *01–47–42–92–90* 🌐 *www.hoteldenoailles.com* *57 rooms* [M] *Opéra* ✥ *2:B5.*

$$ HOTEL **Hôtel George Sand.** This family-run boutique hotel where the 19th-century writer George Sand once lived is fresh and modern, while preserving some original architectural details. **Pros:** next door to two department stores; historic atmosphere. **Cons:** noisy street; can hear métro rumble on lower floors; some rooms are quite small. **TripAdvisor:** "plenty of room," "perfect for a short weekend," "great staff." [$] *Rooms from: €200* ✉ *26 rue des Mathurins, 9e, Opéra/Grands Boulevards* ☎ *01–47–42–63–47* 🌐 *www.hotelgeorgesand.com* *20 rooms* [M] *Havre Caumartin* ✥ *1:H4.*

15

$$$ HOTEL **Hôtel Gramont Opéra.** This elegant and friendly family-owned boutique hotel near the Opéra and historic department stores has lots of little extras that make it a great value. **Pros:** Good breakfast buffet with eggs to order; friendly staff; connecting rooms for families. **Cons:** Singles have no desk; small bathrooms; elevator doesn't go to top floor rooms. **TripAdvisor:** "the friendliest and most efficient staff," "small but perfectly formed," "clean and very welcoming." [$] *Rooms from: €239* ✉ *22 rue Gramont, Grands Boulevards* ☎ *01–42–96–85–90* 🌐 *www.hotel-gramont-opera.com* *22 rooms, 3 suites* [M] *Quatre Septembre* ✥ *2:B4.*

$$ HOTEL Fodor's Choice ★ **Hôtel Langlois.** After starring in *The Truth About Charlie* (a remake of *Charade*), this darling hotel gained a reputation as one of the most atmospheric budget sleeps in the city. **Pros:** excellent views from the top floor; close to department stores and Opéra Garnier; historic decor. **Cons:** noisy street; off the beaten path; some sagging furniture. **TripAdvisor:** "character and homeliness," "very clean and comfortable," "an old and charming building." [$] *Rooms from: €150* ✉ *63 rue St-Lazare, 9e, Opéra/Grands Boulevards* ☎ *01–48–74–78–24* 🌐 *www.hotel-langlois.com* *24 rooms, 3 suites* [M] *Trinité* ✥ *2:A3.*

$$$ HOTEL **Hôtel Queen Mary.** This cheerfully cozy hotel is two blocks from Place de la Madeleine and Paris's famous department stores. **Pros:** close to high-end shopping streets and department stores; large beds; extra-attentive service. **Cons:** some rooms are quite snug; those on the ground floor and facing the street can be noisy. **TripAdvisor:** "loved the staff," "very charming," "fantastic location." [$] *Rooms from: €219* ✉ *9 rue Greffulhe, 8e, Opéra/Grands Boulevards* ☎ *01–42–66–40–50* 🌐 *www.hotelqueenmary.com* *36 rooms, 1 suite* [M] *Madeleine, St-Lazare, Havre Caumartin* ✥ *1:H4.*

$ HOTEL **Hôtel Vivienne.** The location near the Opéra Garnier and Grands Boulevards department stores make this a good bet for the price, even if the decor is a bit schizoid. **Pros:** good value for central Paris; a block from the métro station. **Cons:** a noisy street and late-night bar across the road can make it hard to keep windows open in summer; some rooms have minimal closet space and tiny showers. **TripAdvisor:** "great little Paris hotel," "as good as it gets," "very good hotel for a weekend." [$] *Rooms from: €100* ✉ *40 rue Vivienne, 2e, Opéra/Grands Boulevards* ☎ *01–42–33–13–26* 🌐 *www.hotel-vivienne.com* 🛏 *45 rooms, 35 with bath* [M] *Bourse, Richelieu-Drouot* ✥ *2:C4.*

$$$$ HOTEL 🏨 **Hôtel Westminster.** On one of the most prestigious streets in Paris, between the Opéra and Place Vendôme, this former inn was built in the mid-19th century, and happily retains its old-world feel. **Pros:** prestigious location; good-value promotional rates on the website; popular jazz bar. **Cons:** a bit too old-fashioned in decor; some views of air shaft; Internet access isn't free. **TripAdvisor:** "perfect," "nice staff," "lovely hotel in a good location." [$] *Rooms from: €320* ✉ *13 rue de la Paix, 2e, Opéra/Grands Boulevards* ☎ *01–42–61–57–46* 🌐 *warwickwestminsteropera.com* 🛏 *80 rooms, 22 suites* [M] *Opéra* ✥ *2:A5.*

$$$$ HOTEL 🏨 **Park Hyatt Paris Vendôme.** Understated luxury with a contemporary Zen vibe differentiates this Hyatt from its more classic neighbors between the Place Vendôme and Opéra Garnier. **Pros:** the latest hotel technology and stylish design; spa suites; popular bar and restaurant. **Cons:** as part of the Hyatt chain, can feel anonymous. **TripAdvisor:** "Paris elegance," "classy," "well serviced and spacious." [$] *Rooms from: €730* ✉ *3–5 rue de la Paix, 2e, Opéra/Grands Boulevards* ☎ *01–58–71–12–34* 🌐 *www.paris.vendome.hyatt.com* 🛏 *132 rooms, 36 suites* [M] *Concorde, Opéra* ✥ *2:A5.*

ST-GERMAIN-DES-PRÉS

For expanded hotel reviews, visit Fodors.com.

$$$$ HOTEL 🏨 **Artus Hôtel.** One of the best things about the Artus, aside from the sleek look, is the fact that it's smack in the middle of Rue de Buci in the St-Germain-des-Prés district. **Pros:** attentive service; excellent location on a market street; stylish design. **Cons:** rooms are small for the price; neighborhood is quite busy and at times noisy. **TripAdvisor:** "style and service," "all the comforts of home," "perfect location." [$] *Rooms from: €295* ✉ *34 rue de Buci, 6e, St-Germain-des-Prés* ☎ *01–43–29–07–20* 🌐 *www.artushotel.com* 🛏 *25 rooms, 2 suites* 🍴 *Breakfast* [M] *Mabillon* ✥ *4:B3.*

$$$$ HOTEL 🏨 **Hôtel Bel-Ami.** Just a stroll from Café de Flore, the Bel-Ami hides its past as an 18th-century textile factory behind contemporary veneer furnishings and crisply jacketed staff. **Pros:** upscale, stylish hotel; central St-Germain-des-Prés location; spacious fitness center and spa. **Cons:** some guests report loud noise between rooms; some very small rooms in lower price category. **TripAdvisor:** "fantastic service," "location is perfect," "great small hotel." [$] *Rooms from: €340* ✉ *7–11 rue St-Benoît, 6e, St-Germain-des-Prés* ☎ *01–42–61–53–53* 🌐 *www.hotel-bel-ami.com* 🛏 *113 rooms, 2 suites* [M] *St-Germain-des-Prés* ✥ *4:B2.*

$$ HOTEL 🏨 **Hôtel Bonaparte.** Services may be basic at this unpretentious hotel, but the location in the heart of St-Germain is fabulous. **Pros:** upscale shopping neighborhood; large rooms for the Rive Gauche; air-conditioning. **Cons:** outdated decor and some tired mattresses. **TripAdvisor:** "lovely staff," "great location and service," "unpretentious." [$] *Rooms from:*

€139 ✉ 61 rue Bonaparte, 6e, St-Germain-des-Prés ☎ 01–43–26–
⊕ www.hotelbonaparte.fr ⤸ 29 rooms ⦿ Breakfast Ⓜ St-Sulpice ✛

$$$$ 🏨 **Hôtel d'Aubusson.** The staff greets you warmly at this 17th-century
HOTEL town house and former literary salon in the heart of St-Germain-des-
Fodor's Choice Prés. **Pros:** central location near shops and market street; live jazz on
★ weekends; personalized welcome. **Cons:** some of the newer rooms lack
character; busy street; bar can be noisy on weekends. **TripAdvisor:**
"great location," "perfect service for a romantic break," "fun find in
Paris." Ⓢ Rooms from: €315 ✉ 33 rue Dauphine, 6e, St-Germain-des-
Prés ☎ 01–43–29–43–43 ⊕ www.hoteldaubusson.com ⤸ 49 rooms
Ⓜ Odéon ✛ 4:C2.

$$$$ 🏨 **Hôtel de l'Abbaye.** This hotel on a tranquil side street near St-Sul-
HOTEL pice welcomes you with a cobblestone ante-courtyard and cozy floral
fabrics. **Pros:** tranquil setting; upscale neighborhood; good value for
price. **Cons:** rooms differ greatly in size and style; some bathrooms
are quite small, with handheld shower heads. **TripAdvisor:** "a glorious French hotel," "charming," "absolute perfection." Ⓢ Rooms from:
€250 ✉ 10 rue Cassette, 6e, St-Germain-des-Prés ☎ 01–45–44–38–11
⊕ www.hotel-abbaye.com ⤸ 26 rooms, 8 suites ⦿ Breakfast Ⓜ St-
Sulpice ✛ 4:A4.

$$$$ 🏨 **Hôtel Duc de Saint-Simon.** An intimate hotel with a hidden location
HOTEL between Boulevard St-Germain and Rue de Bac offers traditionally
decorated rooms in floral chintz. **Pros:** upscale neighborhood close to
St-Germain-des-Prés; historic character. **Cons:** rooms in the annex are
smaller and have no elevator; small bathrooms. **TripAdvisor:** "small
and romantic," "beautiful setting," "pretty and peaceful." Ⓢ Rooms
from: €265 ✉ 14 rue St-Simon, 7e, St-Germain-des-Prés ☎ 01–44–39–
20–20 ⊕ www.hotelducdesaintsimon.com ⤸ 29 rooms, 5 suites Ⓜ Rue
du Bac ✛ 3:H2.

$$$$ 🏨 **Hôtel Millésime.** Step through the doors of this 17th-century city man-
HOTEL sion in St-Germain-des-Prés and you'll feel transported to the sunny
south of France. **Pros:** upscale shopping location; young, friendly staff;
well-appointed rooms. **Cons:** ground-floor rooms can be noisy; smoke
from courtyard when windows are open. **TripAdvisor:** "Left Bank
delight," "still great staff," "excellent service." Ⓢ Rooms from: €250
✉ 15 rue Jacob, 6e, St-Germain-des-Prés ☎ 01–44–07–97–97 ⊕ www.
millesimehotel.com ⤸ 20 rooms, 1 suite ⦿ Breakfast Ⓜ St-Germain-
des-Prés ✛ 4:B2.

$$$$ 🏨 **Hôtel Odéon Saint-Germain.** The exposed stone walls and original
HOTEL wooden beams give this 16th-century building typical Rive Gauche
Fodor's Choice character, and designer Jacques Garcia's generous use of striped taffeta
★ curtains, velvet upholstery, and plush carpeting imbues the family-run
hotel with the distinct luxury of St-Germain-des-Prés. **Pros:** Occitane
toiletries; free Internet; luxuriously appointed, historic building in an
upscale shopping district. **Cons:** small rooms aren't convenient for
those with extra-large suitcases; tiny elevator. **TripAdvisor:** "very comfortable," "comfortable surroundings," "charming hotel with good
service." Ⓢ Rooms from: €280 ✉ 13 rue St-Sulpice, 6e, St-Germain-des-
Prés ☎ 01–43–25–70–11 ⊕ www.paris-hotel-odeon.com ⤸ 22 rooms,
5 junior suites Ⓜ Odeon ✛ 4:B3.

$$$$ HOTEL 🏨 **Hôtel Recamier.** This discreet boutique hotel overlooking the Eglise St-Sulpice is perfect for those seeking a romantic and cozy nest in the St-Germain-des-Près district. **Pros:** Peaceful garden couryard; free Wifi and computer station; well-appointed bathrooms. **Cons:** Small closets and bathrooms; room service only until 11 pm. **TripAdvisor:** "cozy stylish hotel," "peaceful haven," "great décor and wonderful location." [$] *Rooms from: €260* ✉ *3 bis place St-Sulpice, St-Germain-des-Prés* ☎ *01–43–26–04–89* 🌐 *hotelrecamier.com/* 🛏 *24* [M] *Mabillon* ✥ *4:B3.*

$$$ HOTEL 🏨 **Hôtel Relais Saint-Sulpice.** A savvy clientele frequents this fashionable little hotel sandwiched between St-Sulpice and the Jardin du Luxembourg. **Pros:** chic location; close to two métro stations; bright breakfast room and courtyard; good value. **Cons:** smallish rooms in the lower category; noise from the street on weekend evenings. **TripAdvisor:** "great location," "lots of charm," "quiet little gem." [$] *Rooms from: €222* ✉ *3 rue Garancière, 6e, St-Germain-des-Prés* ☎ *01–46–33–99–00* 🌐 *www.relais-saint-sulpice.com* 🛏 *26 rooms* [M] *St-Germain-des-Prés, St-Sulpice* ✥ *4:B3.*

$$$$ HOTEL 🏨 **L'Hôtel.** Though sophisticated in every way, there's something just a bit naughty in the air at this eccentric and opulent boutique hotel. **Pros:** luxurious decor; elegant bar and restaurant; walking distance to the Orsay and the Louvre. **Cons:** some rooms are very small for the price; closest métro station is a few blocks away. **TripAdvisor:** "romantic restaurant," "luxury personified," "cozy hotel in a great location." [$] *Rooms from: €290* ✉ *13 rue des Beaux-Arts, 6e, St-Germain-des-Prés* ☎ *01–44–41–99–00* 🌐 *www.l-hotel.com* 🛏 *16 rooms, 4 suites* [M] *St-Germain-des-Prés* ✥ *4:B2.*

$$$$ HOTEL 🏨 **Relais Christine.** This exquisite property, once a 13th-century abbey, has an impressive stone courtyard and fireside honor bar in the lobby, decorated with rich fabrics, stone, wood paneling, and antiques. **Pros:** quiet location while still close to the action; historic character; Payot spa. **Cons:** thin walls in some rooms; no on-site restaurant. **TripAdvisor:** "stunning historic hotel," "a very private beautiful romantic location," "intimacy and excellent services." [$] *Rooms from: €398* ✉ *3 rue Christine, 6e, St-Germain-des-Prés* ☎ *01–40–51–60–80, 800/525–4800 in U.S.* 🌐 *www.relais-christine.com* 🛏 *33 rooms, 18 suites* [M] *Odéon* ✥ *4:C2/3.*

THE ISLANDS

For expanded hotel reviews, visit Fodors.com.

ILE DE LA CITÉ

$ HOTEL 🏨 **Hôtel Henri IV.** This 17th-century building, which once housed King Henri IV's printing presses on the Ile de la Cité, offers few comforts or amenities, but you'll be hard-pressed to find a more central hotel for this price. **Pros:** very quiet; top rooms have balconies; basic breakfast included. **Cons:** steep stairs and no elevator; few services or amenities; reservations by phone only. **TripAdvisor:** "very quaint with a nice atmosphere," "a royal experience," "friendly staff." [$] *Rooms from: €78* ✉ *25 pl. Dauphine, 1er* ☎ *01–43–54–44–53* 🌐 *www.henri4hotel.fr* 🛏 *15 rooms, 14 with bath* 🍴 *Breakfast* [M] *Cité, St-Michel, Pont Neuf* ✥ *4:C2.*

Hôtel d'Aubusson

Hôtel Langlois

Hôtel Odéon Saint-Germain

ILE ST-LOUIS

$$ HOTEL 🏨 **Hôtel Saint-Louis en L'Isle.** The location on the Ile St-Louis is the real draw of this recently renovated hotel, which retains many of its original 17th-century stone walls and wooden beams. **Pros:** romantic location on the tiny Ile St-Louis; ancient architectural details; freshly decorated rooms. **Cons:** the location makes the price high; métro stations are across the bridge; small rooms. **TripAdvisor:** "quaint," "very pleasant," "excellent location." [$] *Rooms from: €169* ✉ *75 rue St-Louis-en-l'Ile, 4e, Ile St-Louis* ☎ *01–46–34–04–80* 🌐 *www.saintlouisenlisle.com* 🛏 *20 rooms* [M] *Pont Marie* ✣ *4:E3.*

WESTERN PARIS

For expanded hotel reviews, visit Fodors.com.

$$$ HOTEL 🏨 **Hôtel Gavarni.** Considering the traditional, almot old-fashioned Parisian decor, it may come as a surprise to learn that this property, which is located in a chic residential neighborhood, is one of the first certified eco-hotels in Paris. **Pros:** organic breakfast; charming Parisian neighborhood; friendly welcome. **Cons:** a few blocks to the nearest metro;standard rooms quite small. **TripAdvisor:** "comfortable," "small ideal location," "nice and cute hotel." [$] *Rooms from: €200* ✉ *5 rue Gavarni, 16e, Passy, Western Paris* ☎ *01–45–24–52–82* 🌐 *www.gavarni.com* 🛏 *21 rooms, 4 suites* ✣ *3:A2.*

$$$$ HOTEL 🏨 **Le Sezz.** Created by French furniture designer Christophe Pillet in a chic residential district of Paris, Le Sezz mixes rough stone walls with flashes of bright color. **Pros:** sexy designer decor; huge bathtubs; quiet location. **Cons:** close to Eiffel Tower, not much else; services are limited for a hotel in this price range. **TripAdvisor:** "nothing but romance," "great rooms and staff," "quirky." [$] *Rooms from: €290* ✉ *6 av. Frémiet, 16e, Passy-Auteuil* ☎ *01–56–75–26–26* 🌐 *www.hotelsezz.com* 🛏 *13 rooms, 13 suites* [M] *Passy* ✣ *3:A3.*

Shopping

WORD OF MOUTH

"Le Bon Marché . . . lovely store! I could have spent forever at the perfume counters. But the Grande Epicerie was calling. Yep, I took pictures of the Ibérico ham on the shank and the langoustines. It is really something to see and makes the local Kroger look even more pitiful to me now!"

—denisea

CHAMPS-ÉLYSÉES AND AVENUE MONTAIGNE

Step into your Chanel suit, gird your loins, and plunge into Paris's most elegant and daunting hunting grounds, where royals, jet-setters, starlets, and other glitterati converge in pursuit of the luxurious life.

This elegant triangle—bordered by the avenues Montaigne and Georges V and the Champs-Élysées, with Rue François 1er in between—is home to pretty much all the luxury Goliaths with a few added lesser worthies. Once Paris's most elegant Grand Boulevard, the Champs-Élysées has suffered the blight of megastores, fast food, movie chains, and the like, but once off the avenue you'll get a sense of what it once was. Palatial old mansions now house embassies and boutiques, all with liveried doormen who will take your measure—and find you lacking. Not to worry, just hold your head high, flash your platinum card, and don't forget not to smile.

BEST TIME TO GO

Unlike other shopping meccas, these streets never get too wild, even during the semiannual sales. Although we advise weekday afternoons for most shopping areas—when crowds are tame—here you might want to consider a weekend visit.

BEST FIND FOR YOUR SISTER

If there's one place sure to give bang for the buck, it's **Petit Bateau**. Their comfy cotton and cotton-silk-blend T-shirts are highly prized among Parisian women and kids. Wardrobe staples include cardigans and V-necks, along with silky-soft nighties, loungewear, and undies in colors that change each season.

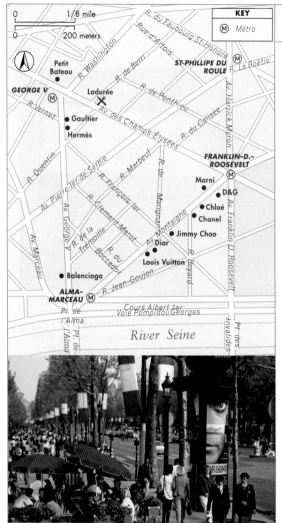

KEY

Ⓜ *Métro*

WHAT YOU'LL WANT

CLASSY COUTURE
Chanel. Elegant, classic looks, with sex appeal and lasting value.

Gaultier. Only his spectacular garments could outshine this fantasyland boutique.

IN-YOUR-FACE OPULENCE
Balenciaga. Fashion's darling, Nicolas Ghesquière, does futurism in nylon, patent leather, and fur.

Chloé. Sleek silhouettes in neutral colors without a use-by date.

Dior. Don't be fooled by the prim lavender exterior. Inside is pure vixen.

Dolce & Gabbana. Liberate your inner sex goddess. Everything here is meant to entice.

Marni. Dares to be different. Sort of an "upper crust slumming it" effect.

SHOES AND ACCESSORIES
Hermès. The go-to for those who prefer their logo discrete yet still crave instant recognition.

Jimmy Choo. Starlets adore his glitzy stilettos and fabulous flats.

Louis Vuitton. The Champs-Élysées megastore houses this ever-morphing line in a gorgeous space.

16

REFUELING

Not only is **Ladurée** one of the world's legendary *pâtisseries,* but the Champs-Élysées location also keeps great hours: from early breakfast (doors open at 7:30 am) to a post-theater snack, just amble over whenever the urge strikes. Whether you desire a cup of their famously rich hot chocolate; a refreshing raspberry, lychee, and rose-petal ice-cream sundae; a melt-in-your-mouth *mille-feuille;* or a gourmet club sandwich, you'll find plenty to choose from at fairly reasonable prices (it's still Paris, dahling), all perfectly scrumptious.

RUE ST-HONORÉ

You're just as likely to bump into a Saudi princess as a Japanese DJ on what is unarguably one of the world's great shopping streets. All the big names in luxury rub elbows here, along with scores of independents with loads of attitude and fashion cachet.

What really makes this street special, though, is the plenitude of its attractions. Turn the corner and there's the sweeping Place Vendôme, an ex-palace and haven for world-class jewelers. Enter the breathtaking Palais Royal gardens, whose noble mien has been invigorated by the arrival of American bad-boy designers Marc Jacobs and Rick Owens, eco-chic diva Stella McCartney, and other gems. With Place de la Concorde and the Tuileries flanking its borders, you'll know you're strolling Paris's most splendid shopping promenade.

BEST TIME TO GO

Weekends can get crowded, especially at the major draws, like Colette. But maybe that's the point: The fabulous seek to mull with their own kind, and aspirants can catch a few of their rays.

BEST FIND FOR THE BABYSITTER

If you can't drop a cool thousand at the oh-so-fabulous **Colette**, head straight for the checkout counter for the adorable tongue-in-chic items in every price range. Cartoon-character key chains and delicate silk-string bracelets (some with tiny diamonds) elate fashionistas—and it's all wrapped up in a Colette bag. *Sigh*.

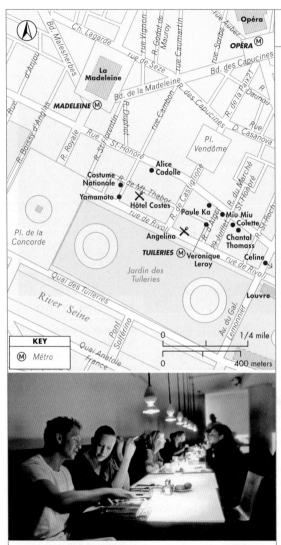

KEY

Ⓜ Métro

REFUELING

A cocktail at the **Hotel Costes** reassures that you, too, are one of the anointed. Beware: drop-dead-gorgeous waitresses tend to fluster the faint of heart. Chanel-suited dowagers know where to go for a luscious and restorative cup of hot chocolate. **Angelina,** like its quintessentially Parisian clientele, may be a bit frayed at the edges, but that only adds to its charm. Go at teatime for a truly sinful experience.

WHAT YOU'LL WANT

GLAMOUR AND GLITZ

Céline. Refined, elegant, streamlined; the go-to spot for Paris's fashion elite.

Costume Nationale. You are the rock star and his girlfriend: expensive looks, unbridled sex appeal.

Miu Miu. Shoes and accessories scream opulence; the clothes favor sleek refinement.

Paule Ka. Movie-star icons are her inspiration. Think Audrey—Hepburn and Tautou, that is.

Veronique Leroy. Bewitching colors and sexy contours with fur detailing have garnered serious clout among fashion mavens.

Yamamoto. This stark white boutique offsets exquisite designs for men and women.

LUXE DOWN UNDER

Alice Cadolle. Movie stars and society brides flock to Rue St-Honoré for bespoke perfection; there's ready-to-wear on Rue Cambon.

Chantal Thomass. From dominatrix to dewy ingénue—whatever your pleasure, you can find it here.

Erès. The most comfortable lingerie on the planet smoothes, shapes, and moves with the body. Sexy and smart, just the way we like it.

16

CANAL ST-MARTIN

"Off the beaten track" aptly describes this up-and-coming neighborhood, dotted with galleries, vintage shops, and iconoclastic boutiques.

Although you're not likely to forget you're in Paris, the pace here is noticeably slower. The canal's cobblestones, plane trees, and arched bridges provide the atmosphere, and its stone embankments make an excellent spot to take in the scene. Or, as Parisians do on temperate evenings, share a bite and a bottle of wine with friends. And the shopping: low-key cool reigns here, none of the high-wattage, high-profile designers that vie for the big bucks in Paris's tony neighborhoods. The area's hipster equivalent of mom-and-pop shops ensure a few choice finds that will be seen on you and only you. Walk along Avenue Beaurepaire, the area's shopping epicenter, toward the canal. From here you'll want to check out some of the smaller streets, especially Rue de Marseille and Rue de Lancry, and meander along the canal—a great way to discover a *quartier* that's still one of Paris's best-kept secrets.

BEST TIME TO GO

If you want to experience the neighborhood at its most tranquil, go on a weekday. If it's the scene you're after, plan on a Saturday afternoon visit.

BEST FIND FOR A PICKY HIPSTER

Cool, colorful bracelets and intricate Gothic-inspired chokers are all in rubber at **Idé Co**. Or, for the best-cut velour jeans this side of the Atlantic, go to **Boutique Renhsen**.

Rouge Kaki. Design-savvy accessories at Rouge Kaki, on Rue de Lancry, are so appealing you'll want one of everything.

WHAT YOU'LL WANT

UNDERGROUND CHIC
Antoine & Lili. An exuberant universe, with women's, kids', and housewares on the same block. Everything bursts with color, imagination, and charm.

Boutique Renhsen. Fashionistas swear by the jeans, comfy sportswear, and accessories.

Des Petits Hauts. Stylish, ultrafeminine separates make this line a smashing success, along with a small but chic selection of bags, shoes, and jewelry.

Dupleks. "Ethical designers" but no lack of design daring. Sexy micro-blazers and form-flattering tunics.

Liza Korn. Charmingly eccentric and original clothing, shoes, jewelry, and stylish kids' clothes.

MUST-HAVES
Bazar Éthic. This department store for equitable commerce champions sleek-and-chic designs in everything from tableware to clever clothes, accessories, and jewelry, too.

Idé Co. Witty items for the home and updates on all the French staples.

BRILLIANT BIJOUX
Médecine Douce. Whimsical, wearable baubles perfectly in tune with an avant-garde canal-side crowd.

16

REFUELING

To really immerse yourself in the scene, join the young designers and artists at **Chez Prune**. On warm days its canal-side spot makes it the place to be. Or drop in to **Le Verre Volé** for biodynamic wine, authentic charcuterie, and excellent company. For atmosphere and a little history to boot, lunch at the **Hotel du Nord** (movie buffs will know it from the eponymous 1938 Marcel Carné film).

THE MARAIS

The Marais has just about stolen the show as the city's hottest shopping spot—for sheer volume it can't be beat. Not to mention atmosphere: from the elegant Place des Vosges to the stately Musée Picasso, its irregular streets and ancient *hôtels particuliers* give it the air of Old Paris.

Rue des Francs Bourgeois is the shopping-central spine from which the upper and lower Marais branch out. As the Marais's popularity grows, so, too, does the variety of its attractions. The neighborhood's newest frontier is its northeastern edge—the haut Marais—where ultrastylish boutiques, over-the-top vintage stores, and design ateliers are found amid tiny centuries-old millinery shops. Between Rue de Bretagne and Boulevard du Temple to the east you can find à la mode boutiques too numerous to list (and still relatively undertouristed). Rue Charlot is one of the area's primary draws, along with upper Rue Vieille du Temple and Rue de Poitou in between. But this is by no means an exhaustive selection. The best idea is to get out there and wander, because in this lovely *quartier*, everywhere the eye rests, it rests happily.

BEST TIME TO GO

If being jostled by tourists and cranky Parisians isn't your thing, head over between Tuesday and Friday after 11 am. Remember, the Marais is one of the few places in Paris where shops open up on Sunday. If you're short on time or need a last-minute shopping fix, the Marais is your best bet.

BEST FIND FOR YOUR COWORKER

For those challenged in the gift-finding department, you'll think you've landed in heaven at **Muji**. This store has a flurry of fun, unusual items for the office, home, and bath; many are purse-size, so stuff your suitcase full and *finally* please everyone.

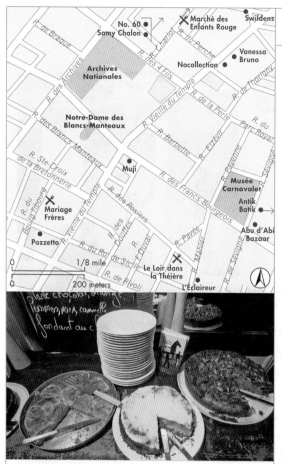

REFUELING

Lines are out the door for brunch at **Le Loir dans la Théière**, so go at teatime instead. The comfy, overstuffed chairs, large selection of teas, and glorious pastries provide the perfect late-afternoon pick-me-up. Join Paris aficionados at **Pozzetto** for some of the best artisanal gelato in the city and—finally—a superlative cup of Italian-style coffee. The *gianduja*, a luscious mix of chocolate and hazelnut, is heaven on a spoon. Nary a tourist lands here at Paris's oldest covered market, **Marché des Enfants Rouge**, where you can sit in the semi-outdoors under a translucent roof for a satisfying Italian or Japanese lunch or just an espresso.

WHAT YOU'LL WANT

SHOWSTOPPING CHIC
Abu d'Abi Bazaar. This is your one-stop outfitter with color-coded racks of the season's standouts.

Antik Batik. Diaphanous silks, vivid colors, and sparkling beadwork add up to thrilling pieces that look great day and night.

L'Éclaireur. Has been supplying high-concept fashion for 30 years.

No. 60. Slinky tops, avant-garde leather, and bottle-leg jeans add up to flattering rocker chic.

Nocollection. Oh-so-pretty silk dresses and separates in soft fabrics and romantic colors.

Samy Chalon. This designer works magic with handmade knitwear—refreshingly original and wondrously sexy.

Swildens. Timeless casuals with plenty of supple leather, chunky knits, and hip accessories.

Vanessa Bruno. Paris's "it" girl combines high style and wearability in her ultrapopular separates and accessories.

TEATIME
Mariage Frères. Elbow your way in for any and every kind of tea, as well as tea-scented jams, chocolates, and gorgeous teaware.

16

RIVE GAUCHE

Ever since the 1960s, when Yves Saint Laurent cashed in on the neighborhood's bohemian-artistic allure, the Rive Gauche has been synonymous with iconoclastic style.

All the major names in French fashion have since taken his lead, transforming the Rive Gauche into a bastion of Parisian chic. Trendsetters line the jumble of streets in the 6e arrondissement, around Rue Bonaparte, Rue du Four, Rue du Cherche Midi, and Boulevard St-Germain, and tons of exciting boutiques line the charming streets near St. Sulpice. In the 7e arrondissement there is the Rue de Grenelle, the venerable, treasure-lined Rue des Saints Pères, Rue du Bac, and that jewel of a department store, Le Bon Marché. To see it all would take weeks; with a well-drawn-out plan, however, you can see quite a lot in an afternoon or two. There's always the option of doing what Parisians do best: stroll, observe, discover.

BEST TIME TO GO

Although Tuesday through Friday afternoons are recommended, this area covers enough ground never to seem too overcrowded, even on weekends.

BEST FIND FOR A SWEET TOOTH

Ladurée's stylish boxes alone are worth the purchase; filled with their legendary lighter-than-air *macarons*—in flavors like salted caramel, rose, or cassis-violet—they make a celestial offering.

You can take it with you! Pierre Hermé, Paris's star *pâtissier*, offers a scrumptious, zesty lemon pound cake preboxed and dense enough to survive the trip home. Maybe.

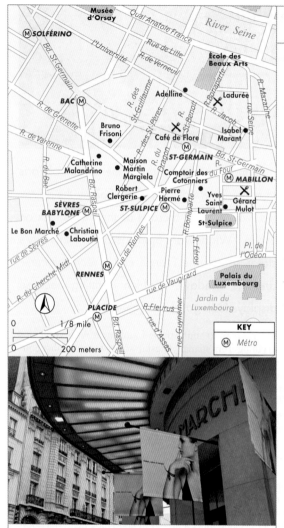

REFUELING

With the Luxembourg Gardens nearby, pick up picnic savories and sweets from the time-honored pâtisserie-traiteur-chocolatier **Gérard Mulot**. Try a yummy shrimp-salad sandwich or *paté en croute* topped off with a mini caramelized-orange tart or a few delectable *macarons*.

If you prefer to be served (however haughtily), the illustrious **Café de Flore** offers pretty good café fare with excellent opportunities for people-watching—inside and out.

WHAT YOU'LL WANT

CLOTHES À LA MODE
Catherine Malandrino. Smart sexy dresses, jackets, and skirts go easily from office to evening.

Comptoir des Cotonniers. Comfortable, affordable, and superchic clothes make this chain popular.

Isabel Marant. Bobo (bourgeois Bohemian) chic with supple leathers, fur, and sheer sweaters.

Maison Martin Margiela. You'll love the soft, flowing jersey tops and the edgier designs, too.

Yves Saint Laurent. Impeccable styling and consummate glamour—ever at fashion's vanguard.

EXCEPTIONAL GEMS
Adelline. A veritable treasure trove of modern, streamlined designs.

WELL-SHOD CHIC
Bruno Frisoni. Alluring and naughty, each shoe is a work of art.

Christian Louboutin. Sensational, vertiginous styles take glamour (and you) to new heights.

Le Bon Marché. A one-stop shop for all the top names in footwear.

Robert Clergerie. Shoes hailed for excellent craftsmanship and enduring style.

16

Updated
by Jennifer
Ditsler-Ladonne

Nothing, but nothing, can push you into the current of Paris life faster than a few hours of shopping. Follow the example of Parisians, who slow to a crawl as their eyes lock on a tempting display. Window-shopping is one of this city's greatest spectator sports; the French call it *lèche-vitrine*—literally, "licking the windows"—which is fitting because many of the displays look good enough to eat.

Store owners in Paris play to sophisticated audiences with voracious appetites for everything from spangly flagship stores to minimalist boutiques to under-the-radar spots in 19th-century glass-roofed passages. Parisians know that shopping isn't about the kill, it's about the chase: walking down cobblestone streets looking for items they didn't know they wanted, they're casual yet quick to pounce. They like being seduced by a clever display and relish the performance elements of browsing. Watching them shop can be almost as much fun as shopping yourself.

And nowhere is the infamous Parisian "attitude" more palpable than in the realm of fine shopping—and the more *haute* the more hauteur. Parisians are a proud bunch, and they value decorum. Look good; dress to make an impression. You must say *bonjour* upon entering a shop and *merci, au revoir* when leaving, even if it's to no one in particular. Think of it more as announcing your coming and going. Beyond this, protocol becomes less prescribed and more a matter of good judgment. If a salesperson is hovering, there's a reason; let him or her help you. To avoid icy stares once and for all, confidence and politeness go a long way.

As for what to buy, the sky's the limit in terms of choices. If your funds aren't limitless, however, take comfort in knowing that treasures can be found on a budget. And if you do decide to indulge, what better place to make that once-in-a-blue-moon splurge? When you get home and friends ask where you got those to-die-for shoes, with a shrug you'll casually say, "These? Oh . . . I bought them in Paris."

BATIGNOLLES

MONTMARTRE

LA VILLETTE

Av. de Clichy

Bd. de Clichy

18 e

Rue Marx Dormoy

Bd. de la Chapelle

Bd. des Batignolles

Bd. de Rochechouart

OPÉRA

Rue la Fayette

10 e

◀ **CHAMPS-ÉLYSÉES & AV. MONTAIGNE**
Megastores & haute couture

9 e

PIGALLE

Bd. Haussmann

CANAL ST-MARTIN
Cutting-edge & eclectic

8 e

Bd. des Italiens *Bd. Poissonnière* *Bd. de Bonne Nouvelle*

Rue Royale

RUE ST-HONORÉ
Extreme chic & serious glamour

PALAIS-ROYAL
Top-notch vintage & star designers

2 e

Rue de Turbigo

3 e

Av. des Champs-Élysées

Bd. Saint-Germain

Jardin des Tuileries

Quai des Tuileries

River

Seine

Quai Anatole France

Quai Voltaire

Place René Cassin

Boulevard de Sébastopol

Rue Beaubourg

LE MARAIS
Up-to-the-moment styles & trendsetters

◆ Louvre

1 er

Quai du Louvre

Voie Georges Pompidou

ÎLE DE LA CITÉ

Place des Vosges

7 e

6 e

Quai des Grands Augustins

Quai de l'Hôtel de Ville

4 e

INVALIDES

RIVE GAUCHE
Refined, sophisticated, & diverse

Bd. Saint-Germain

Quai de Montebello

ÎLE ST LOUIS

Quai de la Tournelle

Pont Sully

Voie Mazas

Rue de Sèvres

Bd. Raspail

Pr. Alphonse Laveran

Rue Monge

5 e

Jardin du Luxembourg

Bd. Saint-Michel

LATIN QUARTER

Jardin des Plantes

Bd. de Vaugirard

Bd. Edgar Quinet

MONTPARNASSE

15 e

Av. Denfert-Rochereau

Bd. Saint-Jacques

Av. des Gobelins

Bd. Auriol Vincent

0 ——— 500 meters

0 ——— 1,500 ft

PLANNING

BOOKS

The scenic open-air *bouquinistes* bookstalls along the Seine are stacked with secondhand books (mostly in French), prints, and souvenirs. French-language bookshops—specializing in art, film, literature, and philosophy—can be found in the scholarly Latin Quarter and the publishing district, St-Germain-des-Prés.

HOW TO DO DUTY-FREE

A value-added tax (V.A.T.; T.V.A. in French) of approximately 19.6% is imposed on most consumer goods. Non–EU residents can reclaim part of this tax. To qualify for a refund, you must purchase €175 of goods in the same shop on the same day, you must have stayed three months or less in the EU at the time of purchase, and you must have your passport validated by customs within three months after the date of purchase. Ask for a *détaxe* form at the time of purchase; smaller stores will fill it out for you, department stores have special *détaxe* desks.

FOOD MARKETS

Year-round and in any weather, the city's open-air food markets play an integral part of daily life, attracting the entire spectrum of Paris society, from the splendid matron, her minuscule dog in tow, to the mustachioed regular picking up his daily baguette. Although some markets are busier than others, there's not a market in Paris that doesn't captivate the senses. Each season has its delicacies: *fraises des bois* (wild strawberries) and tender asparagus in spring, squash blossoms and fragrant herbs in summer, saffron-tinted chanterelles in autumn, bergamot oranges in late winter. Year-round you can find pungent *lait cru* (unpasteurized) cheeses, charcuterie, and unfarmed game and fish. Many of the better-known open-air markets are in areas you'd visit for sightseeing. To get a list of market days in your area, ask your concierge or check the markets section on the website ⊕ *www.paris.fr/marches*.

If you're unused to the metric system, it may be helpful to know that *une livre* is French for a pound; *une demi-livre* is a half-pound. For cheese or meats, *un morceau* will get you a piece, *une tranche* a slice.

Most markets are open from 8 am to 1 pm three days a week year-round (usually the weekend and one weekday, but never Monday) on a rotating basis.

STORE HOURS

Store hours can be tricky in Paris. Aside from department stores, which keep slightly longer hours and are usually open late one weeknight, shops tend to open around 10 or 11 am and close around 7 pm. It's not unusual to find a "back at 3" sign taped on the doors of smaller boutiques at lunchtime. Plan to do most of your foraging between Tuesday and Saturday, as the majority of shops, including department stores, are closed Sunday and some on Monday as well. You can find areas—particularly the Marais—where stores are open on Sunday. However, if you're making a special trip somewhere, always call ahead to check hours.

SHOPPING IN PARIS

Reviews are alphabetical by neighborhood.

AROUND THE EIFFEL TOWER

BARGAIN SHOPPING

Le Dépôt Vente de Passy. Le Dépôt Vente de Passy specializes in barely worn designer ready-to-wear from big names, including Chanel, Dior, Hermès, Gucci, and Prada. Few can pass up one of last season's outfits at one-third the price, or forgo browsing the vast selection of accessories: bags, belts, scarves, shoes, and costume jewelry. ✉ *14 rue de la Tour, 16e, Around the Eiffel Tower* ☎ *01–45–20–95–21* Ⓜ *Passy* ✉ *109 rue de Courcelles, 17e, Champs-Élysées* ☎ *01–40–53–80–82* Ⓜ *Wagram.*

AROUND THE LOUVRE

FAUBOURG ST-HONORÉ

ANTIQUES AND COLLECTIBLES

Astier de Villatte. Come here for tongue-in-chic interpretations of 18th-century table settings and furniture; live out your Baroque or Empire fancies with milk-white china sets and lots of mahogany. Moody candles and incense complete the atmosphere. ✉ *173 rue St-Honoré, 1er, Louvre/Tuileries* ☎ *01–42–60–74–13* Ⓜ *Tuileries.*

BEAUTY

Annick Goutal. Annick Goutal sells its own line of signature scents, which come packaged in gilded gauze purses. Gardenia, Passion, Petite Chérie, and l'Eau d'Hadrien are perennial favorites. ✉ *14 rue de Castiglione, 1er, Louvre/Tuileries* ☎ *01–42–60–52–82* Ⓜ *Concorde.*

By Terry. This small, refined store is the brainchild of Terry de Gunzburg, Yves Saint Laurent's former director of makeup, whose brand of ready-to-wear makeup is a favorite of French actresses and socialites. Upstairs, specialists create what de Gunzburg calls *haute couleur*, exclusive made-to-measure makeup tailored for each client (very expensive; book far in advance). ✉ *36 Galerie Véro-Dodat, 1er, Louvre/Tuileries* ☎ *01–44–76–00–76* Ⓜ *Palais-Royal, Louvre.*

Fodor'sChoice ★ **Les Salons du Palais-Royal Shiseido.** This perfumerie douses its old-new *pharmacie* decor in shades of lilac. Every year Shiseido's creative genius, Serge Lutens, dreams up two new scents, which are then sold exclusively in this boutique. Each is compellingly original, from the strong *somptueux* scents, often with musk and amber notes, to intense florals (Rose de Nuit). ✉ *Jardins du Palais-Royal, 142 Galerie de Valois, 1er, Louvre/Tuileries* ☎ *01–49–27–09–09* Ⓜ *Palais-Royal.*

SUPER SHOPPING TIP

Galeries Lafayette and Au Printemps each offer 10%-off discount cards to foreign visitors. Some things, usually designer clothing and sale items, are excluded. To get one, go to the welcome desk on the main floor of either store. Remember to bring a passport or driver's license.

16

BEST BETS FOR PARIS SHOPPING

With thousands of shops to choose from, how will you decide where to go? Below you'll find some of Fodor's writers' and editors' favorites to help you get started. You can also search by category within each neighborhood for noteworthy shops and peruse the previous pages for spotlights on specific neighborhoods.

BEST WOMENSWEAR

Isabel Marant, p. 347
Marni, p. 345
Shine, p. 354
Spree, p. 356
Zadig & Voltaire, p. 355

BEST MENSWEAR

A.P.C., p. 363
BHV, p. 342
Boutique Renhsen, p. 349
Galeries Lafayette, p. 359
L'Eclaireur, p. 352
Le Bon Marché, p. 364

BEST SHOES

Bruno Frisoni, p. 366
Galeries Lafayette, p. 359
K. Jacques, p. 356
Pierre Hardy, p. 340
Roger Vivier, p. 340

BEST TRENDSETTING STYLE

Colette, p. 331
Isabel Marant, p. 347
L'Eclaireur, p. 352

Maison Martin Margiela, p. 334
Surface to Air, p. 354

BEST BARGAIN HUNTING

A.P.C., p. 356
Jamin Puech Inventaire, p. 349
L'Habilleur, p. 351
Monoprix, p. 358
Zadig & Voltaire, p. 351

BEST FOR BEAUTY

Anne Sémonin, p. 340
BHV, p. 342
By Terry, p. 329
Make Up For Ever, p. 343
Shu Uemura, p. 362

BEST VINTAGE

Didier Ludot, p. 332
La Jolie Garde-Robe, p. 353
Pretty Box, p. 353
Vintage Clothing Paris, p. 353

BEST HIGH FASHION

Azzedine Alaïa, p. 352
Catherine Malandrino, p. 363
Chloé, p. 331

BEST LINGERIE

Alice Cadolle, p. 337
Chantal Thomass, p. 337
Fifi Chachnil, p. 337
Sabbia Rosa, p. 366

BEST PERFUME

Annick Goutal, p. 329
Editions de Parfums Frédéric Malle, p. 362
Guerlain, p. 343
L'Artisan Parfumeur, p. 351
Les Salons du Palais-Royal Shiseido, p. 329

BEST JEWELRY

Adelline, p. 365
Agatha, p. 365
Dinh Van, p. 360
Médecine Douce, p. 347
Yves Gratas, p. 356

BEST HANDBAGS

Goyard, p. 339
Hermès, p. 339
Jérôme Dreyfuss, p. 366
Miguel Lobato, p. 356

BEST FOR THE WHOLE FAMILY

Agnès B, p. 340
BHV, p. 342
Eric Bompard, p. 358
Galeries Lafayette, p. 359
Le Bon Marché, p. 364
Monoprix, p. 358

BEST KIDS' CLOTHES

Alice à Paris, p. 363
Baghère, p. 363
Petit Bateau, p. 343
Wowo, p. 352

BEST BOOKSTORES

La Hune, p. 362
The Red Wheelbarrow, p. 351
Shakespeare & Company, p. 350
Taschen, p. 362
Tea & Tattered Pages, p. 362
Village Voice, p. 362

BEST SWEETS

Jacques Genin, p. 338
Jean-Paul Hévin, p. 338
Ladurée, p. 337
Meert, p. 355
Pierre Hermé, p. 338

BOOKS AND STATIONERY

W. H. Smith. This bookseller carries a multitude of travel and language books, cookbooks, and fiction for adults and children. It also has the best selection of foreign magazines and newspapers in Paris (which you're allowed to peruse without interruption—many magazine dealers in France aren't so kind). ⊠ *248 rue de Rivoli, 1er, Louvre/Tuileries* ☎ *01–44–77–88–99* Ⓜ *Concorde.*

CLOTHING

Alberta Ferretti. Sheer, flowing, and structured by turns, these super-feminine creations seek to enchant—and succeed. Sexy silk dresses mine past fashion tropes and make them new: 1940s noirish look or a flapperish gold-beaded mini dress. The well-loved (and more gently priced) diffusion line, Philosophy, is here, too, along with shoes, bags, and accessories. ⊠ *418 rue St-Honoré, 8e, Louvre/Tuileries* ☎ *01–42–60–14–97* Ⓜ *Madeleine/Concorde.*

Chloé. Chloé made a canny move in May 2011 when they tapped Clare Waight Keller to take the helm. Keller cut her teeth under Tom Ford at Gucci, but her most recent coup was to inject the century-old knitwear house, Pringle, with a much-needed dose of modernism. Keller's debut Spring 2012 was a triumph of the kind of flowing, feminine silhouettes the luxury house is known for but with a twist—a voluminous charmeuse skirt cut thigh-high; a transparent flapperesque silk dress over teeny silk shorts. ⊠ *44 av. Montaigne, 8e, Champs-Élysées* ☎ *01–47–23–00–08* Ⓜ *Franklin-D.-Roosevelt.*

Claudie Pierlot. This designer is deservedly lauded for her smart, urban clothes that unite youthful chic with solid designs; they also successfully transition over several seasons. The irresistible combination of classic looks, good tailoring, and affordability keeps loyal fans coming back year after year. ⊠ *1 rue du 29 Juillet, 1er, Louvre/Tuileries* ☎ *01–42–60–01–19* Ⓜ *Étienne Marcel* ⊠ *23 rue du Vieux Colombier, 6e, St-Germain-des-Prés* ☎ *01–45–48–11–96* Ⓜ *St-Sulpice* ⊠ *30 rue des Francs Bourgeois, 3e, Marais* ☎ *01–57–40–69–78* Ⓜ *St. Paul.*

★ **Colette.** This is the place for ridiculously cool fashion par excellence. So the staff barely deigns to make eye contact—who cares! There are ultramodern trinkets and trifles of all kinds: perfumes; an exclusive handful of cosmetics, including Malin+Goetz and Le Labo; and loads of superchic jewelry . . . and that's just the ground floor. The first floor has wares (clothes, shoes, and accessories) from every internationally known and unknown designer with trendy street cred, a small library, the latest out-there CDs, and an art display space. The basement has a water bar (because that's what models eat) and a small restaurant that's good for a quick bite. ⊠ *213 rue St-Honoré, 1er, Louvre/Tuileries* ☎ *01–55–35–33–90* Ⓜ *Tuileries.*

Costume National. Costume National is all about sharp styling and unerring sophistication. Ennio Capasa's flawlessly cut suits confer

16

CLOSE UP

Museum Stores

These days it seems that contemporary museum stores hawk their stock-in-trade images on everything from playing cards to neckties. *The boutiques below are an antidote to these "mug-and-tote" chains and—dare we say it—are worth the trip, whether you visit the museum or not.*

107 Rivoli. This is the consummate museum store, inside the Musée des Arts Décoratifs. The boutique carries books, jewelry, fashion accessories, paper products, toys, tableware, and objects inspired by the past but with an up-to-date design. Some of the contemporary pieces are limited editions. ⊠ *107 rue de Rivoli, 1er, Louvre/Tuileries* ☎ *01–42–60–64–94* Ⓜ *Louvre Rivoli, Châtelet.*

La Chalcographie du Louvre. More than 13,000 prints from the Louvre's collection can be had at the museum's own print shop for a relatively minor investment. The most popular images are in stock, easy to view, and can walk right out with you. ⊠ *Louvre museum store, 1er, Louvre/Tuileries* ☎ *01–40–20–59–35* Ⓜ *Palais-Royal/ Musée du Louvre.*

La Galerie de L'Opéra de Paris. This is every ballerina, ballerina wanabe, or ballet lover's dreamstore. The majestic landmark's soaring ceilings and marble pillars provide fitting drama for a treasure trove of ballet-inspired wares—Repetto slippers, Italian feathered masks and handmade ballet shoes, jewelry, featherweight cashmere sweaters, and, of course, tutus; along with fine Bernardaud porcelain depicting the Opera Garnier's famous Chagall ceilings. Plus an exceptional collection of CDs, DVDs, and books (many in English) for dance aficionados of all ages. ⊠ *8 rue Scribe, 9e, Opéra/Grands Boulevards* ☎ *01–53–43–03–97* Ⓜ *Opéra, Chaussée d'Antin La Fayette.*

Musée Baccarat. This gorgeous gallery is filled with contemporary crystal by top-name designers, as well as stemware, vases, tableware, jewelry, chandeliers, and even furniture. It's all here, it's all for sale, and it's all breathtaking. ⊠ *11 pl. des États-Unis, 16e, Trocadéro/Tour Eiffel* ☎ *01–40–22–11–00* Ⓜ *Iéna/Boissière.*

high-powered status, and teensy dresses with plunging necklines shoot for unabashed allure. Shoes and accessories are surprisingly versatile. ⊠ *5 rue Cambon, 1er, Louvre/Tuileries* ☎ *01–40–15–04–36* Ⓜ *Tuileries.*

Cotélac. Cotélac gives feminine shapes a bohemian edge in earthy tones from azure to deep aubergine. The figure-skimming and frillier separates beg to be layered. ⊠ *284 rue St-Honoré, 1er, Louvre/Tuileries* ☎ *01–47–03–21–14* Ⓜ *Tuileries* ⊠ *30 rue Montmartre, 1er, Les Halles* ☎ *01–40–28–13–84* Ⓜ *Les Halles* ⊠ *17 rue du Cherche Midi, 6e, St-Germain-des-Prés* ☎ *01–42–84–10–25* Ⓜ *Sèvres-Babylone.*

D&G. The Dolce & Gabbana sportswear line rocks the concept of day wear with leather, denim, and splashy florals spiked with lingerie details. There are clothes for men, women, and even kids. ⊠ *244 rue de Rivoli, 1er, Louvre/Tuileries* ☎ *01–42–86–00–44* Ⓜ *Concorde.*

★ **Didier Ludot.** Didier Ludot inspired the fervent craze for vintage couture and is an incredibly charming man to boot. (A tip: be nice to the dogs.)

TOP PARIS SHOPPING EXPERIENCES

Visiting Le Bon Marché. The city's chicest and oldest department store is a great first stop for an overview of the current season's pieces from all the top designers.

Shopping at the food markets. Year-round and in any weather, the city's open-air food markets are an integral part of daily Paris life.

The Marais. This is one of Paris's most charming places to stroll and shop, with tons of local boutiques and French-owned chains, along cobblestone streets.

Riffle through French couture from the 1920s to the '80s on the racks: wonderful Chanel suits, Balenciaga dresses, and Hermès scarves. He has three boutiques: No. 20 houses his amazing collection of vintage couture; No. 24 the vintage ready-to-wear; and across the way at No. 125 you can find his own vintage-inspired black dresses and his coffee-table book aptly titled *The Little Black Dress*. ⊠ *Jardins du Palais-Royal, 20 Galerie Montpensier, 1er, Louvre/Tuileries* ☎ *01–42–96–06–56* Ⓜ *Palais-Royal* ⊠ *24 Galerie Montpensier, 1er, Louvre/Tuileries* ⊠ *125 Galerie de Valois, 1er, Louvre/Tuileries.*

E2. This boutique, open by appointment only, houses a line by designers Michèle and Olivier Chatenet. You'll find their own label of ethnic-influenced fashion inspired by the 1930s through the '70s; impeccable vintage couture finds like Chanel, Pucci, Lanvin, and Hermès; plus clothing remade with their own special customizing method. They take tired fashion and transform it—for example, sewing emerald-green sequins into the pleats of an ordinary gray kilt. With one of these creations, you'll definitely be dressed like no one else. ⊠ *40 rue Coquillière, 1er, Louvre/Tuileries* ☎ *01–47–70–17–20* Ⓜ *Louvre Rivoli.*

Gabrielle Geppert. Gabrielle Geppert carries only the big guys: Chanel, Hermès, YSL, Vuitton, and what's here is exactly what Gabrielle likes: from a 1950s-era fully sequined cape and '60s jet-beaded minidress to an '80s number right at home under the disco ball. Geppert's personal line of shades, handbags, and jewelry is at the teensy boutique at No. 34. ⊠ *31–34 Galerie de Montpensier, 1er, Louvre/Tuileries* ☎ *01–42–61–53–52* Ⓜ *Palais Royal, Musée du Louvre.*

Galliano. Galliano, fittingly enough, landed an address with Revolutionary history for his namesake store. With all the hubbub surrounding his disgrace in early 2011, it's hard to know what will become of the shop or the man, who is, undeniably, a living hyperbole. ⊠ *384 rue St-Honoré, 1er, Louvre/Tuileries* ☎ *01–55–35–40–40* Ⓜ *Concorde.*

Jérôme L'Huillier. L'Huillier cut his teeth at the ateliers of Balmain and Givenchy, and it shows. A wizard with silk in all its iterations (the joyously colored prints are L'Huillier's own designs), you can find lively, sexy new interpretations of the wrap dress, along with rainbow-hue blouses, sexy empire-waist dresses, and velvet trench coats in jewel colors. ⊠ *138–139 Galerie de Valois, 1er, Louvre/Tuileries* ☎ *01–49–26–07–07* Ⓜ *Palais Royal Musée du Louvre.*

16

Loris Azzaro. Azzaro is a master of the dramatic dress: floor-length columns with jeweled collars and sheer gowns with strategically placed sequins. When he saw his 1970s designs, now collector's items, worn by stars like Nicole Kidman and Liz Hurley, he decided to update his best sellers. ✉ *65 rue de Faubourg St-Honoré, 8e, Louvre/Tuileries* ☎ *01–42–66–92–98* Ⓜ *Concorde.*

★ **Maison Martin Margiela.** This famously elusive Belgian designer has a devoted following for his avant-garde styling—sometimes oversize but never bulky—and for his innovative technique, from spiraling seams to deconstructed shirts. Look for Ligne 6, his secondary line of more casual (and less expensive) clothes for women. The Passage Potier location carries men's clothing only. ✉ *25 bis, rue de Montpensier, 1er, Louvre/Tuileries* ☎ *01–40–15–07–55* Ⓜ *Palais-Royal* ✉ *23 passage Potier, 1er, Louvre/Tuileries* ☎ *01–40–15–06–44* Ⓜ *Palais-Royal* ✉ *13 rue de Grenelle, 7e, St-Germain-des-Prés* ☎ *01–45–49–06–68* Ⓜ *St-Sulpice.*

Maje. Maje brings a certain ease to looking great. The designs are original, up-to-the-moment, and not wildly expensive—that's why the popular label has expanded exponentially. Seasonal collections include minis in every form: sequined, flouncy, leather; lean, peg-leg trousers in denim and leather; and some of the best outerwear around. ✉ *267 rue St-Honore, 2e, Louvre/Palais-Royal* ☎ *01–42–96–84–93* Ⓜ *Palais-Royal-Musée du Louvre* ✉ *49 rue Vieille du Temple, 3e, Marais* ☎ *01–42–74–63–77* Ⓜ *St. Paul* ✉ *42 rue du Four, 6e, St-Germain-des-Prés* ☎ *01–42–22–43–69* Ⓜ *St-Germain-des-Prés.*

Marc Jacobs. Marc Jacobs remains the darling of American style with his singular take on 20th-century American classics—from flapper-style (big flowers, unstructured lines, drop waists, flounces) to 1960s prom (empire waists, copious tulle) with a bit of motorcycle chic thrown in. Metallics appear in most every collection, as do breezy, feminine fabrics and lots of layers. Ready-to-wear is at Palais Royal. The secondary line Marc by Marc Jacobs is at Marché St-Honoré. Men's and accessories are at both. ✉ *56–62 Galerie de Montpensier, 1e, Louvre/Tuileries* ☎ *01–55–35–02–60* Ⓜ *Palais Royal Musée du Louvre* ✉ *19 place du Marché St-Honoré, 1er, Louvre/Tuileries* Ⓜ *Tuileries.*

Miu Miu. This St-Honoré boutique dispenses with the designer's Modernist ethos in favor of a neo-baroque sensibility—and it influences everything from the velvet wallpaper to, perhaps, a lavish pair of ruby slippers. Although the shoes and accessories scream glitz, the clothes still have a sleek refinement, with the designer's notorious tension between minimalism and opulence. ✉ *219 rue St-Honoré, 1er, Louvre/Tuileries* ☎ *01–58–62–53–20* Ⓜ *Tuileries.*

Rick Owens. Rick Owens expertly finessed the jump from L.A. rock-star chic to Paris offbeat elegance. Lately defined more by glamour than grunge, his lush fabrics and asymmetrical designs have evolved to a new level of artistry—and wearability. Owens still loves a paradox (shrouding while revealing), and mixes high luxury with a bit of the tooth and the claw. You'll also find shoes, furs, jewely, accessories, and his line of furniture here. ✉ *130–133 Galerie de Valois, 1er, Louvre/Tuileries* ☎ *01–40–20–42–52* Ⓜ *Palais Royal–Musée du Louvre.*

Stella McCartney. Stella McCartney has an uncanny knack for knowing what women want. After resuscitating the house of Chloé and then starting her own label in 2001, McCartney has steadily built on her success. Season after season, she channels the prevailing mood into innovative takes on classics like the boyfriend blazer, the silk sheath, and the cigarette jean. The clothes flatter real women, and the steep prices can be justified by their staying power (and the fact that nothing was killed in the making). ⊠ *114–121 Galerie de Valois, 1er, Palais Royal* ☏ *01–47–03–03–80* Ⓜ *Palais Royal–Musée du Louvre.*

Tara Jarmon. Tara Jarmon has her bases covered when it comes to that coveted French élan: sleek designs, excellent quality, luxe fabrics, and prices well within the stratosphere. With styles that vie with the high-profile designers, and accessories to match, this label is fast becoming the chic Parisian's wardrobe essential. ⊠ *400 rue St-Honoré, 1er, Louvre/Tuileries* ☏ *01–40–15–02–13* Ⓜ *Concorde* ⊠ *75 rue des Saints-Péres, 6e, St-Germain-des-Prés* ☏ *01–45–44–36–14* Ⓜ *St-Germain-des-Prés* ⊠ *73 av. des Champs-Élysées, 8e, Champs-Élysées* ☏ *01–45–63–45–41* Ⓜ *George V.*

★ **Vanessa Bruno.** Vanessa Bruno stirs up a new brew of feminine dressing: some androgynous pieces (skinny pants) plus delicacy (filmy tops) with a dash of whimsy (lace insets). Separates are coveted for their sleek styling, gorgeous colors, and unerring sexiness. Wardrobe staples include perfectly proportioned cotton tops and sophisticated dresses. Athé, the secondary or "diffusion" line, flies off the racks, so if you see something you love, grab it. Bruno's shoes and accessories are the cherry on the cake: her ultrapopular sequin-striped totes inspired an army of knockoffs. ⊠ *12 rue de Castiglione, 1er, Louvre/Tuileries* ☏ *01–42–61–44–60* Ⓜ *Pyramides* ⊠ *25 rue St-Sulpice, 6e, Latin Quarter* ☏ *01–43–54–41–04* Ⓜ *Odéon* ⊠ *100 rue Vieille du Temple, 3e, Marais* ☏ *01–42–77–19–41* Ⓜ *St-Sébastien-Froissart.*

16

Ventilo. Ventilo brings cool ethnic style to the city. Where else can you find a bright-fuchsia silk-velvet bolero jacket with sequin appliqué or a modern Mongol leather coat lined in fur? There's also room for classics to mix and match, such as handmade wool turtlenecks and a pleated raincoat that fit perfectly. ⊠ *27 bis, rue du Louvre, 2e, Louvre/Tuileries* ☏ *01–44–76–83–00* Ⓜ *Louvre* ⊠ *13–15 bd. de la Madeleine, 1er, Louvre/Tuileries* ☏ *01–42–60–46–40* Ⓜ *Madeleine.*

Veronique Leroy. Veronique Leroy highlights a woman's silhouette while paying close attention to details like open seam work and perfect draping. Slinky silk-jersey dresses, form-flattering sweaters in dusky hues, and lacy dresses with come-hither necklines help explain her current darling-of-the-fashion-world status. ⊠ *10 rue d'Alger, 1er, Louvre/Tuileries* ☏ *01–49–26–93–59* Ⓜ *Tuileries.*

Yves Saint Laurent. Yves Saint Laurent revolutionized women's wear in the 1970s, putting pants in couture shows for the first time. His safari jackets, "le smoking" suits, Russian-boho collections, and tailored *Belle de Jour* suits are considered fashion landmarks—and these are big shoes to fill. Stefano Pilati, successor to the ingenious Tom Ford, earned mixed praise in his ten year tenure, which ended in Spring 2012, leaving the brand temporarily leaderless. Not for long, no doubt. The menswear collection,

Jardin du Palais Royal

Paris's secret oasis no more. With the arrival of Marc Jacobs, Rick Owens, and Stella McCartney, the palace and gardens of the Jardin du Palais Royal officially join the ranks of fashion hot spots. Not that it ever lacked allure; those in the know have come here for fabulous shoes, artisanal perfumes, and vintage haute couture for years. Shopping in Paris is no common experience, but shopping at the Palais Royal—under its neat rows of lime and chestnut trees and vaulted arcades—is almost worship.

Entering the gardens from the Rue St-Honoré, you'll see the Colonnes de Buren, a series of sculpted columns, covering the first inner courtyard. Galerie de Montpensier is the long arcade to your left; Galerie de Valois flanks the gardens to your right.

GALERIE DE VALOIS

No. 156: **Pierre Hardy:** head-turning heels that tantalize while they flatter, with some of Paris's best bags to match (☎ 01–42–60–59–75).

No. 142: **Les Salons du Palais-Royal Shiseido:** Serge Lutens, nose par excellence, offers his renowned perfumes in this jewel of a boutique, along with some signature scents sold only here (☎ 01–49–27–09–09).

No. 138–139: **Jérôme l'Huillier:** color-saturated silks in sexy, mod styles, with sleek new takes on the wrap dress (☎ 01–49–26–07–07).

No. 130–133: **Rick Owens:** over-the-top rock-star glamour with an avant-garde edge, he makes serious fashion waves worldwide (☎ 01–40–20–42–52).

No. 128–129: **Maison Fabre:** has made some of the most beautiful gloves in the world since 1924. Styles in python, peccary, and crocodile fit like a second skin (☎ 01–42–60–75–88).

No. 124: **Acne Studio:** Swedish design for men and women who demand it all: style, fit, comfort, and plenty of cool (☎ 01–42–60–16–62).

No. 114–121: **Stella McCartney:** This warm, feminine boutique reflects her A-list creds, achieved over years of steady success. The wearable-yet-sexy separates are a must in any well-appointed wardrobe (☎ 01–47–03–03–80).

GALERIE DE MONTPENSIER

No. 63–64: **Maison de Vacances:** quilts, pillows, and other decor items in silk, marabou, cashmere, and washed leather, plus cheeky handbags and slippers (☎ 01–47–03–99–74).

No. 56–62: **Marc Jacobs:** from flapper to prom queen to motorcycle moll—iconic American style updated (☎ 01–55–35–02–60).

No. 43: **Avenches:** compelling jewels that make a statement; from the whimsical to the sculptural—every piece is a work of art (☎ 01–42–74–04–28).

No. 31: **Gabrielle Geppert:** vintage haut couture at its best: think Belle de Jour and Krystle Carrington—why buy a knockoff when you can have the original? Bags, jewelry, and sunglasses, too (☎ 01–42–61–53–52).

No. 20–24: **Didier Ludot:** this legend in vintage couture covers the greats in French fashion from the '20s to the '80s; his personal take on the little black dress can be found across the gardens at 125 Galerie de Valois (☎ 01–42–96–06–56).

at No. 32 rue du Faubourg St-Honoré, can be relied on for Saint Laurent's classic pinstripes and satin-lapel tuxes. ✉ *38 and 32 rue du Faubourg St- Honoré, 8e, Louvre/Tuileries* ☎ *01–42–65–74–59* Ⓜ *Concorde* ✉ *6 pl. St-Sulpice, 6e, St-Germain-des-Prés* ☎ *01–43–29–43–00* Ⓜ *St-Sulpice.*

FOOD AND TREATS

★ **Ladurée.** Founded in 1862, Ladurée oozes period atmosphere—even at the new, large Champs-Élysées branch—but nothing beats the original tearoom on Rue Royale, with its pint-size tables and frescoed ceiling. Ladurée claims a familial link to the invention of the *macaron*, and appropriately there's a fabulous selection of these cookies: classics like pistachio, salted caramel, and coffee, and, seasonally, violet–black currant, chestnut, and lime-basil. ✉ *16 rue Royale, 8e, Louvre/Tuileries* ☎ *01–42–60–21–79* Ⓜ *Madeleine* ✉ *75 av. des Champs-Élysées, 8e, Champs-Élysées* ☎ *01–40–75–08–75* Ⓜ *George V* ✉ *21 rue Bonaparte, 6e, Latin Quarter* ☎ *01–44–07–64–87* Ⓜ *Odéon.*

HOME DÉCOR

★ **E. Dehillerin.** E. Dehillerin has been around since 1820. Never mind the creaky stairs; their huge range of professional cookware in enamel, stainless steel, or fiery copper is gorgeous. Julia Child was a regular. ✉ *18–20 rue Coquillière, 1er, Louvre/Tuileries* ☎ *01–42–36–53–13* Ⓜ *Les Halles.*

Gien. Gien has been making fine china since 1821. The faience spans traditional designs, such as those inspired by Italian majolica or blue-and-white delftware, and French toile, as well as contemporary looks. ✉ *18 rue de l'Arcade, 8e, Louvre/Tuileries* ☎ *01–42–66–52–32* Ⓜ *Madeleine.*

JEWELRY AND ACCESSORIES

Cartier. Cartier flashes its jewels at more than half a dozen boutiques in the city. Longtime favorites such as the Trinity rings and Tank watches compete for attention with the newer Panthère, Love, and Caresse d'Orchidées collections. ✉ *23 pl. Vendôme, 1er, Louvre/Tuileries* ☎ *01–44–55–32–20* Ⓜ *Tuileries, Concorde* ✉ *154 av. des Champs-Élysées, 8e, Champs-Élysées* ☎ *01–58–18–17–78* Ⓜ *George V.*

Alice Cadolle. Alice Cadolle has been selling lingerie to Parisians since 1889, offering some of Paris's most sumptuous couture undergarments. Ready-to-wear bras, corsets, and sleepwear fill the Rue Cambon boutique; on Rue St-Honoré, Madame Cadolle offers made-to-measure service. ✉ *4 rue Cambon, 1er, Louvre/Tuileries* ☎ *01–42–60–94–22* Ⓜ *Concorde* ✉ *255 rue St-Honoré, 1er, Louvre/Tuileries* ☎ *01–42–60–94–94* Ⓜ *Concorde.*

Fodor's Choice ★ **Chantal Thomass.** The legendary lingerie diva is back with this *Pillow Talk*–meets–Louis XIV–inspired boutique. This is French naughtiness at its best, striking the perfect balance between playful and seductive. Sheer silk negligees edged in Chantilly lace and lascivious bra-and-corset sets punctuate the signature line. ✉ *211 rue St-Honoré, 1er, Louvre/Tuileries* ☎ *01–42–60–40–56* Ⓜ *Tuileries.*

Fifi Chachnil. Fifi Chachnil girls are real boudoir babes, with a fondness for quilted-satin bed jackets and lingerie in candyland colors. The look is cheerfully sexy, with checkered push-up bras, frilled white knickers, and peach-satin corsets. ✉ *231 rue St-Honoré, 1er, Louvre/Tuileries*

16

CLOSE UP

The Best Chocolate in Paris

The French take chocolate seriously. There are dozens of chocolatiers to choose from, but the purveyors listed here are unusually distinguished for excellence and originality.

Christian Constant. Christian Constant is deservedly praised for his exquisite ganaches, perfumed with jasmine, ylang-ylang, or verveine. ✉ *37 rue d'Assas, 6e, Luxembourg* ☎ *01–53–63–15–15* Ⓜ *St-Placide.*

Jacques Genin. Pared down to the essentials, Genin offers the essence of great chocolate: not too sweet, with handpicked seasonal ingredients for the velvety ganaches. Relax at the boutique-café for a creamy hot chocolate or chocolate sampler. ✉ *133 rue de Turenne, 3e, Marais* ☎ *01–45–77–29–01* Ⓜ *Oberkampf.*

Jean-Charles Rouchoux. Rouchoux makes three superb collections: the Ephemeral, with fresh fruit; Made-to-Measure, with animals and figurines; and the Permanent Collection of everyday favorites. ✉ *16 rue d'Assas, Luxembourg* ☎ *01–42–84–29–45* Ⓜ *Rennes.*

Jean-Paul Hévin. Jean-Paul Hévin has a formal tearoom at his Rue St-Honoré boutique, and there are "exhibits" of chocolates and pastries at Rue Vavin—Mr. Hévin hasn't earned his world-class chocolatier status because of his interiors, though: the 40 different varieties of chocolate each seem more delectable than the last. ✉ *231 rue St-Honoré, 1er, Louvre/Tuileries* ☎ *01–55–35–35–96* Ⓜ *Louvre/Tuileries* ✉ *3 rue Vavin, 6e, Luxembourg* ☎ *01–43–54–09–85* Ⓜ *Vavin.*

La Maison du Chocolat. This is chocolate's gold standard. The silky ganaches are renowned for subtlety and flavor. ✉ *19 rue de Sèvre, 6e, St-Germain-des-Prés* ☎ *01–45–44–20–40* Ⓜ *Sèvres-Babylone* ✉ *8 bd. de la Madeleine, 9e, Louvre/Tuileries* ☎ *01–47–42–86–52* Ⓜ *Madeleine* ✉ *225 rue du Faubourg St-Honoré, 8e, Louvre/Tuileries* ☎ *01–42–27–39–44* Ⓜ *Ternes.*

Michel Chaudun. This chocolatier is known for putting granules of cocoa beans into the chocolates to enhance intensity. His delicate *pavés*—squares of dark-chocolate truffle ganache topped with a dusting of cocoa—are fabulous. ✉ *149 rue de l'Université, 7e, Invalides* ☎ *01–47–53–74–40* Ⓜ *Invalides.*

Patrick Roger. Paris's bad-boy chocolatier likes to shock with provocative shapes and wicked humor. Everything is sinfully good. ✉ *108 bd. St-Germain, Latin Quarter* ☎ *01–43–29–38–42* Ⓜ *Odéon* ✉ *91 rue de Rennes, Luxembourg.*

Pierre Hermé. Hermé may be Paris's (or the world's) most renowned pâtissier, and his chocolate never wavers. Classics, like the dark-chocolate and orange-rind batons, are perennial favorites. ✉ *72 rue Bonaparte, 6e, Latin Quarter* ☎ *01–43–54–47–77* Ⓜ *Odéon* ✉ *4 rue Cambon, 1er, Louvre/Tuileries* ☎ *01–58–62–43–17* Ⓜ *Concorde* ✉ *185 rue de Vaugirard, 15e, Montparnasse* ☎ *01–47–83–29–72* Ⓜ *Pasteur.*

Pierre Marcolini. Pierre Marcolini proves it's all in the bean with his specialty *saveurs du monde* collection, made with a single cacao from a single location, such as Madagascar or Ecuador. ✉ *89 rue de Seine, 6e, St-Germain-des-Prés* ☎ *01–44–07–39–07* Ⓜ *Mabillon.*

☎ 01–42–61–21–83 Ⓜ *Tuileries* ✉ *68 rue Jean-Jacques Rousseau, 1er, Les Halles* ☎ 01–42–21–19–93 Ⓜ *Étienne Marcel.*

SHOPPING GALLERIES

★ **Galerie Véro-Dodat.** Galerie Véro-Dodat was built in 1826. At what is now the Café de l'Époque, just at the gallery's entrance, the French writer Gérard de Nerval took his last drink before heading to Châtelet to hang himself. The glass-ceilinged gallery has painted medallions and copper pillars and shops selling contemporary art, instruments, and leather goods. It's best known, though, for its antiques stores. ✉ *19 rue Jean-Jacques Rousseau, 1er, Louvre/Tuileries* Ⓜ *Louvre.*

SHOES, HANDBAGS, AND LEATHER GOODS

Causse. Causse dates back to a time when the quality of the gloves said it all. Supple python or cherry-lacquered lambskin may not have been the rage in 1892 when this eminent glove maker was founded, but its 100-plus years in the business add up to unparalleled style and fit. ✉ *12 rue de Castiglione, 1er, Louvre/Tuileries* ☎ 01–49–26–91–43 Ⓜ *Tuileries.*

Goyard. These colorful totes are the choice of royals, blue bloods, and the like (clients have included Sir Arthur Conan Doyle, Gregory Peck, and the Duke and Duchess of Windsor). Parisians swear by their durability and longevity; they're copious enough for a mile-long baguette, and durable enough for a magnum of champagne. What's more, they easily transition into ultrachic beach or diaper bags. ✉ *233 rue St-Honoré, 1er, Louvre/Tuileries* ☎ 01–42–60–57–04 Ⓜ *Tuileries.*

★ **Hermès.** Hermès was established as a saddlery in 1837 and went on to create the eternally chic Kelly (named for Grace Kelly) and Birkin (named for Jane Birkin) handbags. The silk scarves are legendary for their rich colors and intricate designs, which change yearly. Other accessories are also extremely covetable: enamel bracelets, dashing silk-twill ties, and small leather goods. During semiannual sales, in January and July, prices are slashed up to 50%, and the crowds line up for blocks. ✉ *24 rue du Faubourg St-Honoré, 8e, Louvre/Tuileries* ☎ 01–40–17–47–17 Ⓜ *Concorde* ✉ *42 av. Georges V, 8e, Champs-Élysées* ☎ 01–47–20–48–51 Ⓜ *George V.*

Maison Fabre. Until you've eased into an exquisite pair of gloves handcrafted by Fabre, you probably haven't experienced the sensation of having a second skin far superior to your own. Founded in 1924, this is one of Paris's historic *gantiers*. Styles range from classic to haute: that is, elbow-length croc leather, coyote-fur mittens, peccary driving gloves. ✉ *128–129 Galerie de Valois, 1er, Louvre/Tuileries* ☎ 01–42–60–75–88 Ⓜ *Palais Royal–Musée du Louvre* ✉ *60 rue des Sts-Pères, 7e, St-Germain-des-Prés* ☎ 01–42–22–44–86 Ⓜ *St-Germain-des-Prés.*

Michel Perry. This designer has branched out from his beloved mile-high shoes into more wearable styles, including sleek suede boots in shades like caramel and scarlet, along with his signature two-toned Oxford booties. Supersexy platforms still prevail. ✉ *243 rue St-Honoré, 1er, Louvre/Tuileries* ☎ 01–42–44–10–07 Ⓜ *Tuileries.*

Moynat. Designed to evoke a wheel, as in "we're going places, baby," this gleaming boutique showcases the new Moynat, while evoking the brand's 19th- and early 20th-century glory days, when Pauline Moynat was France and Britain's queen of luggage design. Women's bags are

16

sleek, expertly engineered, and exceedingly beautiful—the reversible leather tote in either bone/coral or mocha/taupe is an instant classic. Men's briefcases are convex on one side to avoid bumping legs, an ingenous design that harkens back to the advent of automobile travel, when Moynat's trunks were curved to hug a car roof. Crocodile bags, silk scarves, and a thriving bespoke service are cherries on the cake. ⊠ *348 rue St-Honoré, 1e, Louvre/Tuileries* ☎ *01–47–03–83–90* ⊕ *www. moynat.com* Ⓜ *Tuileries.*

★ **Pierre Hardy.** Pierre Hardy completes the triumvirate (with Frisoni and Louboutin) of anointed Paris shoe designers. Armed with a pedigree— Dior, Hermès, Balenciaga—Hardy opened his own boutique in 2003 and made serious waves. The shoes are unmistakable: sky-scraping platforms and wedges double as sculpture with their breathtaking details. His sensational bags, introduced in 2006, became instant classics. ⊠ *156 Galerie de Valois, Palais Royal Gardens, 1er, Louvre/Tuileries* ☎ *01–42–60–59–75* Ⓜ *Palais Royal Musée du Louvre.*

Rodolphe Ménudier. Rodolphe Ménudier spins a hard-edge sexiness, from its interior design—think sleek black windows, metal cupboards, and a wall covered in white crocodile leather—to its pointy-toe high heels. Stilettos with ankle straps? *Mais oui.* ⊠ *14 rue de Castiglione, 1er, Louvre/Tuileries* ☎ *01–42–60–86–27* Ⓜ *Tuileries.*

★ **Roger Vivier.** Known for decades for his Pilgrim-buckle shoes and inventive heels, Roger Vivier's name is being resurrected through the creativity of über-Parisienne Inès de la Fressange and the expertise of shoe designer Bruno Frisoni. The results are easily some of the best shoes in town: leather boots that mold to the calf perfectly, towering rhinestone-encrusted or feathered platforms for evening, and vertiginous crocodile pumps. ⊠ *29 rue du Faubourg St-Honoré, 8e, Louvre/Tuileries* ☎ *01–53–43–00–85* Ⓜ *Concorde.*

LES HALLES

BEAUTY

Anne Sémonin. Anne Sémonin sells skin-care products made out of seaweed and trace elements, as well as essential oils that are popular with fashion models. ⊠ *2 rue des Petits-Champs, 2e, Les Halles* ☎ *01–42–60–94–66* Ⓜ *Palais-Royal* ⊠ *108 rue du Faubourg St-Honoré, 8e, Champs-Élysées* ☎ *01–42–66–24–22* Ⓜ *Champs-Élysées–Clemenceau.*

CLOTHING

Agnès b. Agnès b embodies the quintessential French approach to easy but stylish dressing. There are many branches, and the clothes are also sold in department stores, but for the fullest range go to Rue du Jour, where Agnès takes up most of the street (women's wear at No. 6, children at No. 2, menswear at No. 3), or the newest store at Avenue George V. For women, classics include sleek black-leather jackets, flattering black jersey separates, and trademark wide-stripe T-shirts. Children love the two-tone T-shirts proclaiming their age. And the stormy-gray velour or corduroy suits you see on those slouchy, scarf-clad men? Agnès b. ⊠ *2, 3, and 6 rue du Jour, 1er, Les Halles* ☎ *01–42–33–04–13* Ⓜ *Châtelet Les Halles* ⊠ *6 rue Vieux Colombier, 6e,*

Pierre Hardy makes some of the most sought-after shoes and purses in Paris.

Germain-des-Prés ☎ *01–44–39–02–60* Ⓜ *St-Sulpice* ✉ *38 av. George V, 8e, Champs-Élysées* ☎ *01–40–73–81–10* Ⓜ *George V.*

Et Vous Stock. This is a great alternative to the regular boutiques because the clothes are still very much in style and are 50% off. You'd never know you were in a stock store if you walked in off the street. There are accessories, too. ✉ *17 rue Turbigo, 2e, Les Halles* ☎ *01–40–13–04–12* Ⓜ *Étienne Marcel.*

G-Star Store. This is a haven for fans of raw denim. It, uniquely, stocks the designs of the Dutch-based label G-Star, whose highly desirable jeans have replaced Levi's as the ones to be seen in. There are also military-inspired clothing, bags, and T-shirts. ✉ *46 rue Étienne Marcel, 2e, Les Halles* ☎ *01–42–21–44–33* Ⓜ *Étienne Marcel.*

Paul & Joe. Paul & Joe is designer Sophie Albou's eclectic, girlish blend of modern trends. There's a retro feel to the diaphanous blouses, A-line jackets with matching short shorts, and swingy felt coats. In summer she'll mix in a little hippie chic. The secondary line, Paul & Joe Sister—with a decidedly younger clientele—brings a slouchy, casual edge to the line. ✉ *46 rue Étienne Marcel, 2e, Les Halles* ☎ *01–40–28–03–34* Ⓜ *Étienne Marcel* ✉ *2 av. Montaigne, 8e, Champs-Élysées* ☎ *01–47–20–57–50* Ⓜ *George V* ✉ *66 rue des Sts-Pères, 7e, St-Germain-des-Prés* ☎ *01–42–22–47–01* Ⓜ *St-Germain-des-Prés.*

Yohji Yamamoto. Yohji Yamamoto made his name in the 1980s as a master of the drape, fold, and twist. The design legend favors predominantly black clothes that are both functional and edgy. A canny fashion investment—these pieces never go out of style. You'll find ready-to-wear for men and women at the Louvre boutique, along with the Y's sportswear line; at rue Cambon, the Yoji label for men and women and the Noir line for women only. ✉ *25 rue du Louvre, 1er, Les Halles* ☎ *01–42–21–42–93* Ⓜ *Étienne Marcel* ✉ *4 rue Cambon, 1er, Louvre/ Tuileries* ☎ *01–40–20–00–71* Ⓜ *Concord.*

DEPARTMENT STORES

BHV. BHV, short for Bazar de l'Hôtel de Ville, houses an enormous basement hardware store that sells everything from doorknobs to cement mixers and has to be seen to be believed. The fashion offerings for men, women, and kids have been totally revamped, with many of the top labels and a fabulous and not-too-crowded lingerie department on the second floor. But BHV is most noteworthy for its huge selection of high-quality household goods, home-decor material, electronics, and office supplies. If you're looking for typically French household items (those heavy, gold-rimmed café sets, gorgeous French linen, or Savon de Marseille), this is your ticket. The extensive men's store is across the street at 36 rue de la Verrerie. ✉ *52–64 rue de Rivoli, 4e, Les Halles* ☎ *01–42–74–90–00* Ⓜ *Hôtel de Ville.*

FNAC. Parisians flock to this high profile French "cultural" department store for the huge selection of music and books, as well as photo, TV, and audio equipment. ✉ *Forum des Halles, 1er, Les Halles* ☎ *01–40–41–40–00* Ⓜ *Les Halles* ✉ *74 av. des Champs-Élysées, 8e, Champs-Élysées* ☎ *01–53–53–64–64* Ⓜ *Franklin-D.-Roosevelt* ✉ *136 rue de Rennes, 6e, Montparnasse* ☎ *01–49–54–30–00* Ⓜ *St-Placide.*

HOME DÉCOR

A. Simon. This is where Parisian chefs come for their kitchen needs— from plates and glasses to pans, dishes, and wooden spoons. The quality is excellent and the prices reasonable. ✉ *48 rue Montmartre, 2e, Les Halles* ☎ *01–42–33–71–65* Ⓜ *Étienne Marcel.*

LINGERIE

Princesse Tam Tam. Princesse Tam Tam is the go-to for affordable and beguiling bra-and-panty sets that combine sex appeal and playfulness. Designed for mileage as much as allure, the softer-than-soft cotton wrap tops and nighties, lace-edged silk tap pants, camisoles, slips, and adorable separates for the boudoir are comfortable *and* comely. ✉ *5 rue Montmartre, 1er, Les Halles* ☎ *01–45–08–50–69* Ⓜ *Les Halles* ✉ *53 rue Bonaparte, 6e, St-Germain-des-Prés* ☎ *01–43–29–01–91* Ⓜ *St-Germain-des-Prés* ✉ *20 rue St-Antoine, 4e, Marais* ☎ *01–42–77–27–38* Ⓜ *Bastille.*

MARKETS

Rue Montorgueil. This old-fashioned market street has evolved into a chic *"bobo"* (bourgeois bohemian) zone; its stalls now thrive amid stylish cafés and the oldest oyster counter in Paris. ✉ *1er, Les Halles* Ⓜ *Châtelet Les Halles.*

SHOES, HANDBAGS, AND LEATHER GOODS

★ **Christian Louboutin.** These shoes carry their own red carpet with them, in their trademark crimson soles. Whether tasseled, embroidered, or strappy, in Charvet silk or shiny patent leather, these heels are always perfectly balanced. No wonder they set off such legendary legs as Tina Turner's and Gwyneth Paltrow's. ✉ *19 rue Jean-Jacques Rousseau, 1er,*

Les Halles ☎ *01–42–36–53–66* Ⓜ *Palais-Royal* ✉ *38–40 rue de Grenelle, 7e, St-Germain-des-Prés* ☎ *01–42–22–33–07* Ⓜ *Sèvres-Babylone.*

SHOPPING GALLERIES

Passage du Grand-Cerf. Passage du Grand-Cerf has regained the interest
of Parisians. La Parisette, a small boudoir-pink space at No. 1, sells
fun accessories, and Marci Noum, at No. 4, riffs on street fashion. Silk
bracelets, crystals, and charms can be nabbed at Eric & Lydie and Satellite. ✉ *145 rue St-Denis, 2e, Les Halles* Ⓜ *Étienne Marcel.*

CHAMPS-ÉLYSÉES

BEAUTY

Guerlain. Guerlain has long resided at this opulent address, a befitting
home for the world-class perfumer. Still the only Paris outlet for legendary perfumes like Shalimar and L'Heure Blue, they've added several
new signature scents (Rose Barbare, Cuir Beluga), and the perfume
"fountain" allows for personalized bottles in several sizes to be filled
on demand. Or, for a mere €30,000, a customized scent can be blended
just for you. Also here are makeup, scented candles, and a spa featuring their much-adored skin-care line. ✉ *68 av. des Champs-Élysées, 8e,
Champs-Élysées* ☎ *01–45–62–52–57* Ⓜ *Franklin-D.-Roosevelt.*

Make Up For Ever. This store, at the back of a courtyard, is a must-
stop for makeup artists, models, actresses, and divas of all stripes. The
riotous color selection includes hundreds of hues for foundation, eye
shadow, powder, and lipstick. ✉ *5 rue de la Boétie, 8e, Grands Boulevards* ☎ *01–53–05–93–31* Ⓜ *St-Augustin* ✉ *5 rue des Francs Bourgeois,
Marais* ☎ *01–42–71–23–19.*

Parfums de Nicolaï. This perfumerie is run by a member of the Guerlain
family: Patricia de Nicolaï. Children's, women's, and men's perfumes
are on offer (including some unisex), as well as sprays for the home
and scented candles. ✉ *69 av. Raymond Poincaré, 16e, Champs-Élysée*
☎ *01–47–55–90–44* Ⓜ *Victor-Hugo* ✉ *80 rue de Grenelle, 7e, Around
the Eiffel Tower* ☎ *01–45–44–59–59* Ⓜ *Dupleix* ✉ *28 rue de Richelieu,
1er, Louvre/Tuileries* ☎ *01–44–55–02–02* Ⓜ *Palais-Royal.*

CHILDREN'S CLOTHING

Fodor's Choice ★ **Bonpoint.** Bonpoint is for the prince or princess in your life (royalty
does shop here). Yes, prices are high, but the quality is exceptional.
The mini-duds couldn't be more stylish (or adorable) with items such
as a perfect emerald-green hand-smocked silk dress, a mini leopard-
print jacket, or a midnight-blue velvet suit for Little Lord Fauntleroy.
✉ *64 av. Raymond Poincaré, 16e, Champs-Élysées* ☎ *01–47–27–60–81*
Ⓜ *Trocadéro* ✉ *15 rue Royale, 8e, Louvre/Tuileries* ☎ *01–47–42–52–
63* Ⓜ *Madeleine.*

★ **Petit Bateau.** Petit Bateau provides a fundamental part of the classic
French wardrobe from cradle to teen and beyond: the T-shirt, cut close
to the body, with smallish shoulders (they work equally well with
school uniforms or vintage Chanel). The high-grade cotton clothes follow designs that haven't changed in decades—onesies and pajamas for
newborns, T-shirts that change color for every season, underwear sets,

16

and dresses with tiny straps for summer; and now lines in cotton-silk or cotton-cashmere. Stock up—if you can find this brand back home, the prices are sure to be higher. ✉ *116 av. des Champs-Élysées, 8e, Champs-Élysées* ☎ *01–40–74–02–03* Ⓜ *George V* ✉ *53 bis, rue de Sèvres, 6e, St-Germain-des-Prés* ☎ *01–45–49–48–38* Ⓜ *Sèvres-Babylone.*

CLOTHING

Balenciaga. Balenciaga was completely revamped in 1997 by Nicolas Ghesquière, who electrified the fashion world with his singular vision. Known for playing with volume (bubbling skirts, stovepipe pants) and references (robot, futuristic) the rigorous architectural clothes consistently earn the highest marks from fashion editors. The accessories and menswear are often more approachable, like the perfectly tooled leather bags and narrow suits. Women's wear is at Avenue George V and menswear at Rue de Varennes. ✉ *10 av. George V, 8e, Champs-Élysées* ☎ *01–47–20–21–11* Ⓜ *Alma-Marceau* ✉ *5 rue de Varennes, 7e, St-Germain-des-Prés* ☎ *01–42–22–00–56* Ⓜ *Sèvres-Babylone.*

Céline. Céline was venerable and dusty before designer Michael Kors showed up in the late '90s with his version of Jackie O, "the Greek magnate years" and put Céline back on the map. Phoebe Philo gave the brand a jolt in 2009, drawing raves from critics for her focused approach. Classic tailoring and minute attention to details underlie the seeming simplicity of the styles. ✉ *36 av. Montaigne, 8e, Champs-Élysées* ☎ *01–56–89–07–91* Ⓜ *Franklin-D.-Roosevelt.*

★ **Chanel.** Chanel is helmed by Karl Lagerfeld, whose collections are steadily vibrant. The historic center is at the Rue Cambon boutique, where Chanel once perched high up on the mirrored staircase watching audience reactions to her collection debuts. Great investments include all of Coco's favorites: the perfectly tailored tweed suit, a lean, soigné black dress, or a quilted bag with a gold chain. ✉ *42 av. Montaigne, 8e, Champs-Élysées* ☎ *01–47–23–74–12* Ⓜ *Franklin-D.-Roosevelt* ✉ *31 rue Cambon, 1er, Louvre/Tuileries* ☎ *01–42–86–26–00* Ⓜ *Tuileries.*

Christian Dior. Christian Dior installed the flamboyantly talented John Galliano in 1997 and embarked on a wild ride to fashion's highest pinnacle before the designer's infamous crash landing in spring 2011. The forward-thinking house will no doubt reinvent itself with all the flair and panache that have defined it since Dior founded the label back in 1947. ✉ *30 av. Montaigne, 8e, Champs-Élysées* ☎ *01–40–73–54–44* Ⓜ *Franklin-D.-Roosevelt* ✉ *16 rue de l'Abbé, 6e, St-Germain-des-Prés* ☎ *01–56–24–90–53* Ⓜ *St-Germain-des-Prés.*

Dolce & Gabbana. Dolce & Gabbana offers a sexy, young-Italian-widow vibe with a side of moody boyfriend. Svelte silk dresses, sharply tailored suits, and plunging necklines are made for drama. Women's clothes are at Avenue Montaigne; men's are at Rue St-Honoré. ✉ *54 av. Montaigne, 8e, Champs-Élysées* ☎ *01–42–25–68–78* Ⓜ *Alma-Marceau* ✉ *3 rue Faubourg St-Honoré, 8e, Louvre/Tuileries* ☎ *01–44–94–95–95* Ⓜ *Concorde.*

Jean-Paul Gaultier. Jean-Paul Gaultier first made headlines with his celebrated corset with the ironic iconic breasts for Madonna but now sends fashion editors into ecstasies with his sumptuous haute-couture creations. Designer Philippe Starck spun an *Alice in Wonderland* fantasy for the boutiques, with quilted cream walls and Murano mirrors. Make no mistake, though, it's all about the clothes. ⊠ *44 av. George V, 8e, Champs-Élysées* ☎ *01–44–43–00–44* Ⓜ *George V* ⊠ *6 rue Vivienne, 2e, Opéra/Grands Boulevards* ☎ *01–42–86–05–05* Ⓜ *Bourse.*

Le66. Finding just the right totally chic, totally black anything is a breeze here. This impossibly hip concept store, comprised of three boutiques on two levels (including shoes, jewelry, accessories, and men's), lines up all the top names that you know, along with those that you may not but should. Diffusion lines of the major labels, like See by Chloé, mingle with Acne, Helmut Lang, Ilaria Mistri, Heimstone, Dolfie, and nearly 200 others, all hand-picked to ensure fabulousness. If pressed for time, it's a good bet for all-around satisfaction. ⊠ *66 av. des Champs-Élysées, 8e, Champs-Élysées* ☎ *01–53–53–33–80* Ⓜ *Franklin-D.-Roosevelt.*

★ **Marni.** Marni started out as a little Italian label with a quirky take on the classics—retro-ish prints and colors (citron-yellow, seaweed-green), funky fabrics (rubberized cotton, filmy silks)—and has evolved into a major player on the edgy fashion scene. Each season has something new to say: a new take on bold ethnic prints, ingenious knits, or eloquent color schemes. Sought-after shoes and jewelry never make it to sale time. ⊠ *57 av. Montaigne, 8e, Champs-Élysées* ☎ *01–56–88–08–08* Ⓜ *Franklin-D.-Roosevelt.*

Nina Ricci. Nina Ricci appeals to the leather-and-lace sensibility in surprising ways; that is, the lace might be in leather. After fashion-favorite Olivier Theyskins's departure in 2009, Peter Copping (lately of Marc Jacobs–Louis Vuitton) grabbed the wheel, outdoing past Ricci designers in archly feminine touches: bows, ruffles, perforated leather, pastel silks, delicate florals, and frothy colors, along with sensuous lingerie touches. The airy white-on-white boutique remains one of Paris's dreamiest. ⊠ *39 av. Montaigne, 8e, Champs-Élysées* ☎ *01–40–88–67–60* Ⓜ *Franklin-D.-Roosevelt.*

Prada. Prada spins gold out of fashion straw. Knee-length skirts, peacock colors, cardigan sweaters, geometric prints; the waiting lists cross continents. Shoes, bags, and other accessories for men and women perennially become cult items. ⊠ *10 av. Montaigne, 8e, Champs-Élysées* ☎ *01–53–23–99–40* Ⓜ *Alma-Marceau* ⊠ *6 rue du Faubourg St-Honoré, 8e, Louvre/Tuileries* ☎ *01–58–18–63–30* Ⓜ *Concorde* ⊠ *5 rue de Grenelle, 6e, St-Germain-des-Prés* ☎ *01–45–48–53–14* Ⓜ *St-Sulpice.*

Réciproque. Réciproque is Paris's largest and most exclusive swap shop. Savings on designer wear—Hermès, Dior, Chanel, and Louis Vuitton—are significant, but prices aren't as cheap as you might expect, and there's not much in the way of service or space. The shop at No. 101 specializes in leather goods. Both locations are closed Sunday and Monday. ⊠ *89, 92, 93, 95, and 101 rue de la Pompe, 16e, Champs-Élysées* ☎ *01–47–04–30–28* Ⓜ *Rue de la Pompe.*

16

HOME DÉCOR

Laguiole. This is France's most famous brand of knives. Today designers like Philippe Starck and Sonia Rykiel have created special models for the company. ⊠ *29 rue Boissy d'Anglas, 8e, Champs-Élysées* ☎ *01–40–06–09–75* Ⓜ *Concorde.*

★ **Maison de Baccarat.** This museum and crystal store was once the home of Marie-Laure de Noailles, known as the Countess of Bizarre. Philippe Starck revamped the space with his signature cleverness—yes, that's a chandelier floating in an aquarium and, yes, that crystal arm sprouting from the wall alludes to Jean Cocteau (a friend of Noailles). Follow the red carpet to the jewelry room, where crystal baubles hang from bronze figurines, and to the immense table stacked with crystal items for the home. ⊠ *11 pl. des États-Unis, 16e, Champs-Élysée* ☎ *01–40–22–11–00* Ⓜ *Trocadéro.*

JEWELRY AND ACCESSORIES

Dior Joaillerie. Dior Joaillerie got a big dollop of wit and panache when it signed on young designer Victoire de Castellane to create Dior's first line of fine jewelry. She does oversize rings, hoop earrings, and bracelets swinging with diamonds, and—lest you forget the amped-up spirit at Dior house—white-gold death's-head cufflinks. ⊠ *28 av. Montaigne, 8e, Champs-Élysées* ☎ *01–47–23–52–39* Ⓜ *Franklin-D.-Roosevelt* ⊠ *8 pl. Vendôme, 1er, Opéra/Grands Boulevards* ☎ *01–42–96–30–84* Ⓜ *Opéra.*

SHOES, HANDBAGS, AND LEATHER GOODS

Berluti. Berluti has been making exquisite and expensive men's shoes for more than a century. "Nothing is too beautiful for feet" is Olga Berluti's motto; she even exposes her creations to the moonlight to give them an extra-special patina. One model is named after Andy Warhol; other famous clients of the past include the Duke of Windsor, Fred Astaire, and James Joyce. ⊠ *26 rue Marbeuf, 8e, Champs-Élysées* ☎ *01–53–93–97–97* Ⓜ *Franklin-D.-Roosevelt.*

Giuseppe Zanotti Design. Every pair of shoes here is fetish worthy, if not downright dangerous. Mile-high spike heels, buckle stilettos, slinky python booties, and jewel-encrusted black-satin pumps beg to be noticed. More toned-down models, like over-the-knee leather flats, can be had, too. ⊠ *12 av. Montaigne, 8e, Champs-Élysées* ☎ *01–47–20–07–85* Ⓜ *Franklin-D.-Roosevelt* ⊠ *233 rue St-Honoré, 1er, Louvre/Tuileries* ☎ *01–47–03–02–60* Ⓜ *Tuileries* ⊠ *22 rue de Grenelle, 7e, St-Germain-des-Prés* ☎ *01–42–22–04–18* Ⓜ *Rue du Bac.*

Jimmy Choo. This is the place for vampy platforms and strappy flats. Beautiful bags, clutches, and small leather items in animal print, reptile, and metallics are deservedly popular. Choo's fashion creds went platinum after *Sex and the City*, yet recent collaborations with Hunter boots (fabulous) and UGG (ugh!) have made them a household name. ⊠ *34 av. Montaigne, 8e, Champs-Élysées* ☎ *01–47–23–03–39* Ⓜ *Franklin-D.-Roosevelt* ⊠ *376 rue St-Honoré, 1er, Louvre/Tuileries* ☎ *01–58–62–50–40* Ⓜ *Concord.*

Fodor'sChoice **Louis Vuitton.** Louis Vuitton has spawned a voracious fan base from Texas
★ to Tokyo with its mix of classic leather goods and the saucy revamped versions orchestrated by Marc Jacobs. Jacobs's collaborations, such as

with Japanese artist Takashi Murakami, have become instant collectibles (and knockoffables). This soaring cathedral-esque paean to luxury (and consumption) is unsurpassed. ⊠ *101 av. des Champs-Élysées, 8e, Champs-Élysées* ☎ *08–10–81–00–10* Ⓜ *George V* ⊠ *6 pl. St-Germain-des-Prés, 6e, St-Germain-des-Prés* ☎ *08–10–81–00–10* Ⓜ *St-Germain-des-Prés* ⊠ *22 av. Montaigne, 8e, Champs-Élysées* ☎ *08–10–81–00–10* Ⓜ *Franklin-D.-Roosevelt.*

Robert Clergerie. Robert Clergerie knows that the shoes make the woman. Styles combine visionary design, first-rate craftsmanship, and wearability with rare staying power. Plus, they're still a relative bargain on this side of the Atlantic. ⊠ *18 av. Victor Hugo, 16e, Champs-Élysées* ☎ *01–45–01–81–30* Ⓜ *Charles de Gaulle–Étoile* ⊠ *5 rue du Cherche-Midi, 6e, St-Germain-des-Prés* ☎ *01–45–48–75–47* Ⓜ *St-Sulpice.*

EASTERN PARIS

BASTILLE/NATION
CLOTHING
★ **Isabel Marant.** This rising design star is a honeypot of bohemian rockstar style. Her separates skim the body without constricting: layered miniskirts, loose peek-a-boo sweaters ready to slip from a shoulder, teeny-weeny hot pants, and super fox-fur jackets in lurid colors. Look for the secondary line, Étoile, for a less expensive take. ⊠ *16 rue de Charonne, 11e, Bastille/Nation* ☎ *01–49–29–71–55* Ⓜ *Ledru-Rollin* ⊠ *1 rue Jacob, 6e, St-Germain-des-Prés* ☎ *01–43–26–04–12* Ⓜ *St-Germain-des-Prés* ⊠ *47 rue Saintonge, 3e, Marais* ☎ *01–42–78–19–24* Ⓜ *Filles du Calvaire.*

MARKETS
Marché d'Aligre. Arguably the most locally authentic market, Marché d'Aligre is open until 1 every day except Monday. Don't miss the covered hall on the Place d'Aligre, where you can stop by a unique olive-oil boutique for bulk and prebottled oils from top producers. ⊠ *Rue d'Aligre, 12e, Bastille/Nation* Ⓜ *Ledru-Rollin.*

Marché Bastille. Paris's largest market is as much an event as a place to shop, with blocks of specialized stalls—including rare wines, regional cheeses, game, and seafood and flowers—catering to a large swath of Paris chefs and epicures. Open Sunday 7 am–3 pm. ⊠ *Bd. Richard Lenoir, between rues Amelot and St-Sabin, 11e, Bastille/Nation* Ⓜ *Ledru-Rollin.*

CANAL ST-MARTIN
JEWELRY AND ACCESSORIES
Médecine Douce. Médecine Douce proffers sculptural pieces that combine leather, suede, rhinestones, sheered agate, or resin with whimsical themes: orbs, owls, pom-poms, and a saucy monkey. The wildly popular lariat necklace can be looped and dangled according to the mood du jour. ⊠ *10 rue de Marseille, 10e, Canal St-Martin* ☎ *01–48–03–57–28* Ⓜ *République.*

Viveka Bergström. Viveka Bergström leads the ranks of designers who thumb their noses at the pretensions of traditional costume

16

Notable Neighborhoods, Select Streets

Paris's legendary shopping destinations draw people the world over, but perhaps a deeper allure lies in the lesser-known attractions: the city harbors scores of hidden neighborhoods and shopping streets—some well traveled, others just emerging—that brim with treasure. Each carries its own distinct style that reflects the character of the particular *quartier*. Here are a few of Paris's most satisfying and *très branché* (very trendy) enclaves.

Rue Keller, Rue Charonne (11ᵉ). These streets are a haven for young clothing designers with panache. Stylish housewares, kids' clothes, jewelry, and art galleries augment the appeal. Start at the end of Rue Keller where it intersects with Rue de la Roquette: walk the length of this short street, then make a right onto Rue Charonne and meander all the way to Rue du Faubourg St-Antoine to discover a trove of great boutiques.

Rue Oberkampf (11ᵉ). At the outer edge of the Marais, this street is well known among young fashionistas for its eclectic atmosphere and bohemian flavor. High-end jewelry and of-the-minute boutiques are clustered amid stylish wine bars and comfy cafés.

Rue des Abbesses, Rue des Martyrs (18ᵉ and 9ᵉ). In the shadow of lofty Sacré-Coeur, the Rue des Abbesses is studded with shops—from vintage jewelry and unique clothing to antiques and upscale gardening. Turn onto the Rue des Martyrs and discover one of Paris's hottest emerging scenes, with trendy boutiques scattered among inviting cafés.

Rues Étienne Marcel, du Jour, du Louvre, and Montmartre (2ᵉ). Just around the corner from teeming Les Halles, this area is jam-packed with big names (Yamamoto, Agnès b, Barbara Bui), but it also boasts multitudes of smaller boutiques (Madame à Paris, Shine, Gas by Marie) popular with hip young Parisians.

Rue du Bac (7ᵉ). After browsing at Le Bon Marché turn the corner at the Grand Epicerie and stroll down this most bountiful of shopping streets. Old and well established, this is where the Paris *beau monde* finds everything from elegant linens and home furnishings to any item of apparel a grownup or child could possibly want.

Rue Vavin (6ᵉ). One of Paris's epicenters for outfitting those hopelessly chic Parisian children, this street is lined with boutique after boutique for tots. If you have the kids in tow, follow up with a pony ride at the Luxembourg Gardens (weekends and Wednesday afternoon only). Jewelry, clothing, Savon de Marseille, and J.P. Hevin, one of Paris's top chocolatiers, give adults plenty to love, too.

Rue Pont Louis Philippe (4ᵉ). Long enjoyed for its multitude of elegant paper and stationery shops, here you can also find antiques, musical instruments, artisan jewelry, and classy clothing. A great spot for window-shopping en route from the Marais to the Ile St-Louis.

Rue Francois Miron (from St-Paul métro to Place St-Gervais, 4ᵉ). Many shoppers overlook this lovely street at the Marais's Seine-side fringes, but there's plenty here to make a wander worthwhile. Parisians in the know head here for spices, top-notch designs for the home, antiques, jewelry, pretty cafés, and much more. Bonus: Two of the oldest houses in Paris are here; they're the medieval half-timbered ones.

jewelry—these baubles just want to have fun! Whether it's a bracelet of gigantic rhinestones, a ring of fluorescent pink resin, or a pair of floating angel wings on a necklace, each piece proffers an acute sense of style while not taking itself too seriously. ⊠ *23 rue de la Grange aux Belles, 10e, Canal St-Martin* ☎ *01–40–03–04–92* Ⓜ *République.*

SHOES, HANDBAGS, AND LEATHER GOODS

Jamin Puech Inventaire. These are last season's models, but no one will guess; savings are 30% to 60%. ⊠ *61 rue d'Hauteville, 10e, Canal St-Martin* ☎ *01–40–22–08–32* Ⓜ *Poisonnière.*

RÉPUBLIQUE

CLOTHING

Antoine & Lili. This bright, fuchsia-colored store is packed with eclectic objects from around the world and its own line of clothing. The fantasy seems to work for the French, because these boutiques are always hopping. There's an ethnic rummage-sale feel, with old Asian posters, small lanterns, and basket upon basket of inexpensive doodads, baubles, and trinkets for sale. The clothing itself has simple lines, and there are always plenty of picks in raw silk. ⊠ *95 quai de Valmy, 10e, République* ☎ *01–40–37–41–55* Ⓜ *Jacques-Bonsergent* ⊠ *90 rue des Martyrs, 18e, Montmartre* ☎ *01–42–58–10–22* Ⓜ *Abbesses.*

Boutique Renhsen. This boutique is popular for its jeans: slender and ultraflattering, but those in the know also come for the stylish separates—many from the fetching French label Sessùn—in natural fibers and a range of must-have accessories, including Patricia Blanchet's sensational booties in cherry-red patent, metallic black, or glittery fuchsia leather. ⊠ *22 rue Beaurepaire, 10e, République* ☎ *01–48–04–01–01* Ⓜ *République.*

Des Petits Hauts. Des Petits Hauts charmed its way into the local fashion idiom with chic yet beguilingly feminine styles. Fabrics are soft; styles are casual with a tiny golden star sewn into each garment for good luck. ⊠ *21 rue Beaurepaire, 10e, République* ☎ *01–40–40–95–47* Ⓜ *République* ⊠ *24 rue de Sévigné, 4e, Marais* ☎ *01–48–04–77–25* Ⓜ *St-Paul* ⊠ *70 rue Bonaparte, 6e, St-Germain-des-Prés* ☎ *01–43–29–40–46* Ⓜ *St-Germain-des-Prés.*

Liza Korn. Liza Korn is that rare designer who seems to do it all and do it well; whether it's rock 'n' roll (grommeted leather baseball jackets), asymmetry (slant-necked minidresses), and classic (tailored blazers over stovepipe trousers), she raises the bar on eclecticism. Her togs for stylish tots are refreshingly childlike, and her home and baby linens are simply beautiful. ⊠ *19 rue Beaurepaire, 10e, République* ☎ *01–42–01–36–02* Ⓜ *République.*

DEPARTMENT STORES

Bazar Éthic. Bazar Éthic may be a "department store" for eco-friendly, ethical commerce, but that doesn't mean they can't have fun. Smart contemporary design is found in everything from candles and cashmere pillows to leather-alternative bags and deconstructed scarves. Luscious Tibetan cashmere dresses and sweaters for women and adorable kids clothes are both à la mode *and* virtuous. ⊠ *25 rue Beaurepaire, 10e, République* ☎ *01–42–00–15–73* Ⓜ *République* ⊠ *9 rue de Rivoli, 4e, Marais* ☎ *01–44–07–22–28* Ⓜ *St-Paul.*

16

HOME DÉCOR

Idé Co. Idé Co. offers small items for the home in a riot of color. You'll find kitchen staples, cappuccino bowls, and fabulous rubber jewelry and funky stuff for kids big and small. ⊠ *19 rue Beaurepaire, 10e, République* ☎ *01–42–01–00–11* Ⓜ *République.*

LATIN QUARTER

BOOKS AND STATIONERY

Abbey Bookshop. Paris's Canadian bookstore has books on Canadian history as well as new and secondhand Québécois and English-language novels. The Canadian Club of Paris also organizes regular poetry readings and literary conferences here. ⊠ *29 rue de la Parcheminerie, 5e, Latin Quarter* ☎ *01–46–33–16–24* Ⓜ *Cluny–La Sorbonne.*

Shakespeare & Company. This sentimental Rive Gauche favorite is named after the bookstore whose American owner, Sylvia Beach, first published James Joyce's *Ulysses.* Nowadays it specializes in expat literature. Although the eccentric and beloved owner, George Whitman, passed away in 2011, his daughter Sylvia has taken up the torch. You can still count on a couple of characters lurking in the stacks, a sometimes spacey staff, the latest titles from British presses, and hidden secondhand treasures in the odd corners and crannies. Poets give readings upstairs on Monday at 8 pm; there is also music and special workshops. ⊠ *37 rue de la Bûcherie, 5e, Latin Quarter* ☎ *01–43–25–40–93* Ⓜ *St-Michel.*

HOME DÉCOR

Avant-Scène. Avant-Scène is good for original, poetic furniture. Owner Elisabeth Delacarte commissions limited-edition pieces from artists like Mark Brazier-Jones, Franck Evennou, Elizabeth Garouste, and Hubert Le Gall. ⊠ *4 pl. de l'Odéon, 6e, Latin Quarter* ☎ *01–46–33–12–40* Ⓜ *Odéon.*

★ **Le Monde Sauvage.** Le Monde Sauvage is a must-visit for home accessories—reversible silk bedspreads in rich colors, velvet throws, hand-quilted bed linens, silk floor cushions, colorful rugs, and the best selection of hand-embroidered curtains in silk, cotton, linen, or velvet. ⊠ *11 rue de l'Odéon, 6e, Latin Quarter* ☎ *01–43–25–60–34* Ⓜ *Odéon.*

JEWELRY AND ACCESSORIES

Peggy Huynh Kinh. Peggy Huynh Kinh is a former architect who's now behind the structural line of bags at Cartier. She shows her own line of accessories at this eponymous boutique—understated totes, shoulder bags, wallets, and belts in high-quality leather, as well as a line of office accessories. ⊠ *11 rue Coëtlogon, 6e, Latin Quarter* ☎ *01–42–84–83–82* Ⓜ *St-Sulpice.*

MARKETS

Rue Mouffetard. This market, near the Jardin des Plantes, reflects its multicultural neighborhood; vibrant, with a laid-back feel that still smacks of old Paris. It's best on weekends. ⊠ *5e, Latin Quarter* Ⓜ *Monge.*

MARAIS

ANTIQUES AND COLLECTIBLES

Village St-Paul. This clutch of streets, in the beautiful historic nether-world tucked between the fringes of the Marais and the banks of the Seine, has many antiques shops. ⊠ *Enter from Rue St-Paul, 4e, Marais* Ⓜ *St-Paul.*

BARGAIN SHOPPING

L'Habilleur. L'Habilleur is a favorite with the fashion press and anyone looking for a deal. For women there's a great selection from designers like Firma, Stefano Mortari, Paul & Joe, and Giorgio Brato. Men can find suits from Roberto Collina and Paul & Joe at slashed prices. ⊠ *44 rue de Poitou, 3e, Marais* ☎ *01–48–87–77–12* Ⓜ *St-Sébastien Froissart.*

Zadig & Voltaire Stock. Here you'll find new unsold stock from last season. There's a great selection of beautiful cashmere sweaters, silk slip dresses, rocker jeans, and leather jackets, all in their signature luscious colors for 30%–70% off. ⊠ *22 rue Bourg Tibourg, 4e, Marais* ☎ *01–44–59–39–62* Ⓜ *Hôtel de Ville.*

BEAUTY

L'Artisan Parfumeur. L'Artisan Parfumeur is known for its own brand of scents for the home and perfumes with names like Méchant Loup (Big Bad Wolf). ⊠ *32 rue du Bourg Tibourg, 4e, Marais* ☎ *01–48–04–55–66* Ⓜ *Hôtel de Ville.*

BOOKS AND STATIONERY

Comptoir de l'Image. This is where designers John Galliano, Marc Jacobs, and Emanuel Ungaro stock up on old copies of *Vogue, Harper's Bazaar,* and *The Face.* You'll also find trendy magazines like *Dutch, Purple,* and *Spoon;* designer catalogs from the past; and rare photo books. ⊠ *44 rue de Sévigné, 3e, Marais* ☎ *01–42–72–03–92* Ⓜ *St-Paul.*

Ofr. Ofr gets magazines from the most fashionable spots in the world before anyone else. The store is messy, but you can rub shoulders with photo and press agents and check out the latest in underground, art, and alternative monthlies. ⊠ *20 rue du petit Thouars, 3e, Temple* ☎ *01–42–45–72–88* Ⓜ *St-Paul.*

★ **The Red Wheelbarrow.** This is *the* Anglophone bookstore: if it was written in English, you can get it here. The store also has a collection of special-edition historical reads, and a great selection of children's books. Check out its flyers for info on English-language readings, given at least once a month; local artists and visiting authors pitch in on events. ⊠ *22 rue St-Paul, 4e, Marais* ☎ *01–48–04–75–08* Ⓜ *St-Paul.*

CHILDREN'S CLOTHING

Bonton. Bonton takes the prize for most-coveted duds among those who like to think of the child as fashion accessory. (Moms may find some useful wardrobe pointers, too.) Sassy separates in saturated colors layer beautifully, look amazing and manage to be perfectly kid-friendly. Bonton sells toys and furniture, too. ⊠ *5 bd. des Filles du Calvaire, 3e, Marais* ☎ *01–53–63–14–41* Ⓜ *Filles du Calvaire* ⊠ *82 rue de Grenelle, 7e, St-Germain-des-Prés* ☎ *01–44–39–09–20* Ⓜ *Rue du Bac.*

16

Wowo. Wowo is an original line of stylish well-made clothes for children from three months to preteen. Designer Elizabeth Relin blends her fashion sensibility and love of color with her respect for the world of childhood—no pop tarts here. ⊠ *5 rue Froissart, 3e, Marais* ☎ *01–53–40–84–80* Ⓜ *République.*

CLOTHING

AB33. AB33 is like a sleek boudoir—complete with comfy chair and scented candles—and the clothes here are unabashedly feminine: separates in luxury fabrics from top designers, irresistible silk lingerie, dainty jewelry, and a selection of accessories celebrate that certain French *je ne sais quoi.* ⊠ *33 rue Charlot, 3e, Marais* ☎ *01–42–71–02–82* Ⓜ *Filles du Calvaire.*

Abou d'Abi Bazar. This shop organizes its collection of up-to-the-moment designers on color-coordinated racks that highlight the asymmetrical design of this opulent boutique. Artsy and bohemian all at once, there is plenty to covet here, from frothy Isabel Marant silk-organza blouses to sumptuous cashmere-blend tunics and satin shirtwaist dresses. Reasonably priced picks make it a desirable destination. ⊠ *125 rue Vieille du Temple, 3e, Marais* ☎ *01–42–71–13–26* Ⓜ *Filles du Calvaire* ⊠ *15 rue Soufflot, 5e, Latin Quarter* ☎ *01–42–77–96–98* Ⓜ *Cluny la Sorbonne* ⊠ *33 rue du Temple, Marais* ☎ *01–44–61–37–24* Ⓜ *St-Paul.*

Azzedine Alaïa. Alaïa is one of the darlings of the fashion set with his perfectly proportioned "king of cling" dresses. And you don't have to be under 20 to look good in one of his dresses; Tina Turner wears his clothes well, as does every other beautiful woman with the courage and the curves. His boutique/workshop/apartment is covered with artwork by Julian Schnabel and is not the kind of place you casually wander into out of curiosity: the sales staff immediately makes you feel awkward in that distinctive Parisian way. ⊠ *7 rue de Moussy, 4e, Marais* ☎ *01–42–72–19–19* Ⓜ *Hôtel de Ville.*

Comptoir des Cotonniers. Comptoir des Cotonniers is a star for its smart, wearable styles that stress ease and comfort over fussiness. Separates in natural fibers—cotton, silk, and cashmere blends—can be light and breezy or cozy and warm, but are always soft, flattering, and in a range of beautiful colors. Styles for moms and daughters age four and up. ⊠ *33 rue des Francs-Bourgeois, 4e, Marais* ☎ *01–42–76–95–33* Ⓜ *St-Paul* ⊠ *12 pl. St-Sulpice, 6e, St-Germain-des-Prés* ☎ *01–56–81–00–18* Ⓜ *St-Sulpice* ⊠ *342 rue St-Honoré, 1er, Louvre/Tuileries* ☎ *01–42–60–10–75* Ⓜ *Tuileries.*

COS. COS, which stands for Collection of Style, is the H&M group's answer to fashion sophisticates, who flock here in droves for high-concept, minimalist design with serious attention to quality tailoring and fabrics at a reasonable price. Classic accessories and shoes look more expensive than they are. Best of all, the clothes for men, women, and kids (2–8) can't be found in the States—yet. ⊠ *4 rue des Rosiers, 4e, Marais* ☎ *01–44–54–37–70* Ⓜ *St-Paul.*

L'Eclaireur. This boutique is Paris's touchstone for edgy, up-to-the-second styles. L'Eclaireur's knack for uncovering new talent and championing established visionaries is legendary—no surprise after 30 years in the

CLOSE UP

Vintage Marais

The Marais is fast becoming Paris's vintage central. The many *friperies* (secondhand clothing stores) scattered about the neighborhood run the gamut from rag-picker's paradise to treasure troves of top-quality vintage couture. The shops listed below stand out either for quality, originality, or both. Most boutiques are open five days a week, afternoons only. To be on the safe side, go Tuesday through Saturday, between 2 and 7 pm.

Free 'P' Star. Don't let the chaos at Free 'P' Star discourage you—there's gold in these bins. Determined seekers on a budget can reap heady rewards—at least according to the young hipsters that flock here for anything from a floor-sweeping peasant skirt to a cropped chinchilla cape. Best of all, there's not one but two branches, both equally stuffed to the gills. Happy hunting! ⊠ *8 rue Sainte Croix de la Bretonnerie, 4e, Marais* ☎ *01-42-76-03-72* Ⓜ *Hôtel de Ville.*

La Jolie Garde-Robe. Could that minutely pleated, full-length black organdy gown prominently displayed front and center really be a genuine, circa 1955 Madame Grès couture gown? Yes! And a steal at $2,000. There's plenty more to tempt at this pretty boutique, specializing in ready-to-wear and designer styles from the '40s to the '80s. While the collection isn't huge, it's chosen with a connoisseur's eye. ⊠ *15 rue Commines, 3e, Marais* ☎ Ⓜ *Filles du Calvaire.*

Pretty Box. The owners of Pretty Box have scoured Europe for unique pieces from the '20s through the '80s. Women love the super-stylish belts, shoes, and bags—many in reptile—sold here for a fraction of what they'd cost new, along with an eccentric

selection of cool separates and Betty Page–era lingerie. The men's collection includes vintage French military coats and riotously patterned '70s Pierre Cardin shirts. ⊠ *46 rue de Saintonge, 3e, Marais* ☎ *01-48-04-81-71* Ⓜ *Saint-Sébastien.*

Studio W. If you're nostalgic for the days of Studio 54, sashay over to Studio W, where a rare Loris Azzaro gold-chain top or a plunging Guy Laroche beaded couture dress in crimson mousseline have Liza and Bianca written all over them. With plenty of jewelry, shoes, bags, and even gloves to match, this elegant boutique is a must-see for fashion divas that don't mind spending little more for sublimity. ⊠ *Rue du Pont aux Choux, 3e, Marais* ☎ *01-44-78-05-02* Ⓜ *St.-Sébastien Froissart.*

Vintage Clothing Paris. It's worth a detour to the Marais's outer limits to drop by Vintage Clothing Paris, whose racks read like an A-list of designer greats—Yves Saint Laurent, Hermès, Balman, Valentino, Lagerfeld, Mugler, just to name a few. Brigitte Petit's minimalist shop is the fashion insider's go-to spot for rare pieces that stand out in a crowd—even a Parisian crowd—like a circa 1985 Alaiia suede skirt with peek-a-boo grommets and zip-up front ($200) and a jaunty Yves Saint Laurent Epoch Russe hooded cape. ⊠ *10 rue de Crussol, 11e, Marais* ☎ *01-48-07-16-40* Ⓜ *Filles du Calvaire, Oberkampf.*

16

business. Hard-to-find geniuses, like leather wizard Isaac Sellam and British prodigy Paul Harnden, cohabit with luxe labels such as Ann Demeulemeester, Haider Ackermann, and Lanvin. Women's wear is in one shop with men's around the corner. ⊠ *40 rue de Sevigné, 3e, Marais* ☎ *01–48–87–10–22* Ⓜ *St-Paul* ⊠ *12 rue Mahler, 4e, Marais* ☎ *01–44–54–22–11* Ⓜ *St-Paul.*

Et Vous. Et Vous takes its cue from the catwalk, turning out affordable, extremely well-cut clothing: pants (low waist/slim hip), knee-skimming skirts, chunky sweaters, and classic work wear with individual details. ⊠ *17 rue de Sévigné, 4e, Marais* ☎ *01–44–54–94–14* Ⓜ *St-Paul* ⊠ *271 rue St-Honoré, 1er, Louvre/Tuileries* ☎ *01–47–03–00–31* Ⓜ *Tuileries.*

Nocollection. Nocollection incorporates ravishing colors with flattering styles and soft fabrics to create a collection of up-to-the-moment styles that make a statement while still allowing for plenty of sensuality and, best of all, comfort. A choice selection of exceptional—and well-priced—coats and shoes flies out of the stores, so get there early in the season. ⊠ *96 rue Vieille du Temple, 3e, Marais* ☎ *01–40–26–57–80* Ⓜ *Filles du Calvaire.*

Paule Ka. Paule Ka has that movie-star glamour down pat. For daytime, perfectly cut silk, belted shirtdresses with matching coats, for evening, gemstone-studded gowns and furs. Both Audrey and Katherine would have made this their second home. ⊠ *20 rue Malher, 4e, Marais* ☎ *01–40–29–96–03* Ⓜ *St-Paul* ⊠ *192 bd. St-Germain, 7e, St-Germain-des-Prés* ☎ *01–45–44–92–60* Ⓜ *St-Germain-des-Prés* ⊠ *223 rue St-Honoré, 1er, Louvre/Tuileries* ☎ *01–42–97–57–06* Ⓜ *Tuileries.*

Samy Chalon. Samy Chalon brings handknits into the 21st century with inspired shapes and colors. Updates on the classics are never bulky and ever flattering. Form-fitting cashmeres, long mohair wrap coats in deep crimson or indigo, along with light-as-air skirts and summer dresses made from vintage designer silk scarves. ⊠ *24 rue Charlot, 3e, Marais* ☎ *01–44–59–39–16* Ⓜ *Filles du Calvaire.*

Shine. Even in its hip Marais location, this boutique lives up to its name. Retro and übermodern, it deals in only the sharper edge of chic (with a clientele to match): Marc by Marc Jacobs, See by Chloé, Carven, and Helmut Lang. ⊠ *15 rue de Poitou, 3e, Marais* ☎ *01–48–05–80–10* Ⓜ *Filles du Calvaire* ⊠ *65 rue Montmartre, 2e, Les Halles* ☎ *01–42–33–65–68* Ⓜ *Les Halles.*

Surface to Air. Promoting itself as a style lab and art gallery rather than a straight-on boutique, Surface to Air has become the hipster's label of choice. The focus here is on cool, understated design with an air of counterculture chic. Women's separates range from metallic jeans to asymmetrical minidresses, along with cool shoes and accessories; menswear includes enigmatic T-shirts, streamlined jeans, and cropped leather jackets. ⊠ *108 rue Vieille du Temple, 3e, Marais* ☎ *01–44–61–76–27* Ⓜ *St-Sébastien-Froissart.*

Swildens. Swildens pioneered the trendy haut Marais and has since gained an ardent following of street-smart twenty- and thirtysomethings who insist as much on comfort as they do on cool. Slouchy separates in natural fibers and fetching colors are punctuated by pieces in leather and shearling, along with belted cardigans and long, drapey sweaters that can be worn almost year-round. The clothes accomplish that rare feat of being both of-the-moment and timeless. ⊠ *22 rue de Poitou, 3e, Marais* ☎ *01–42–71–19–12* Ⓜ *St-Sébastien Froissart* ⊠ *38 rue Madame, 6e, St-Germain-des-Prés* ☎ *01–45–44–66–20* Ⓜ *St-Sulpice.*

Fodor'sChoice
★
Zadig & Voltaire. Zadig & Voltaire rocks the young fashionistas, offering street wear at its best: racy camisoles, cashmere sweaters in gorgeous colors, cropped leather jackets, and form-fitting pants to cosset those tiny French derrieres. ⊠ *42 rue des Francs Bourgeois, 3e, Marais* ☎ *01–44–54–00–60* Ⓜ *St-Paul* ⊠ *118 rue Vieille du Temple, 3e, Marais* ☎ *01–42–78–69–92* Ⓜ *St-Sébastien Froissart* ⊠ *1–3 rue du Vieux Colombier, 6e, St-Germain-des-Prés* ☎ *01–43–29–18–29* Ⓜ *St-Sulpice.*

FOOD AND TREATS

Izraël. Izraël is not called the "épicerie du monde" for nothing. It's the one-stop shop for any spice under the sun, plus those hard-to-find items you'd spend days tracking down, all under one roof. Overflowing bins of every variety of candied fruit, nuts, beans, olives, pickles, and preserved fish and the perfume of exotic spices give this tiny shop the air of an exotic bazaar. You'll also find all manner of canned goods, candies, rare spirits, and baking necessities. ⊠ *30 rue François Miron, 4e, Marais* ☎ *01–42–72–66–23* Ⓜ *St-Paul.*

Le Palais des Thés. Le Palais des Thés is a comprehensive experience—white tea, green tea, black tea, tea from China, Japan, Indonesia, South America, and more. Try one of the flavored teas such as Hammam, a traditional Turkish recipe with date pulp, orange flower, rose, and red berries. ⊠ *64 rue Vieille du Temple, 3e, Marais* ☎ *01–48–87–80–60* Ⓜ *St-Paul.*

Mariage Frères. Mariage Frères, with its colonial *charme* and wooden counters, has 100-plus years of tea purveying behind it. Choose from more than 450 blends from 32 countries, not to mention teapots, teacups, books, and tea-flavor biscuits and candies. Both tearooms serve high tea and a light lunch, although the St-Germain location is considerably less frenzied. ⊠ *30 rue du Bourg-Tibourg, 4e, Marais* ☎ *01–42–72–28–11* Ⓜ *Hôtel de Ville* ⊠ *13 rue des Grands-Augustins, 6e, St-Germain-des-Prés* ☎ *01–40–51–82–50* Ⓜ *Mabillon, St-Michel.*

Meert. This is the first Paris offshoot of the famous patisserie and tea salon in Lille—one of France's oldest—specializing in the *gauffre,* a delicate waffle handmade in the original 19th-century molds and wrapped in gilt-paper packages. Native to Belgium and northern France, Meert's version—whose recipe is a strict secret—is treasured for its light cream center perfumed with Madagascar vanilla. There are also chocolates, pastries, and flavored *guimauves,* the light-as-air French marshmallows. ⊠ *16 rue Elzévir, Marais* ☎ *01–49–96–56–94* Ⓜ *St. Paul.*

HOME DÉCOR

★ **Muji.** Muji runs on the concept of *kanketsu,* or simplicity, and the resulting streamlined designs are all the rage in Europe. Must-haves include a collection of mini-necessities—travel essentials, wee office gizmos, purse-size accoutrements, and the best notebooks and pens around—so useful and adorable you'll want them all. ⊠ *47 rue des Francs Bourgeois, 4e, Marais* ☎ *01–49–96–41–41* Ⓜ *St-Paul* ⊠ *27 and 30 rue St-Sulpice, 6e, St-Germain-des-Prés* ☎ *01–46–34–01–10* Ⓜ *Odéon.*

16

★ **Sentou.** Sentou knocked the Parisian world over the head with its fresh designs. Avant-garde furniture, rugs, and a variety of home accessories line the cool showroom. Look for the April Vase, old test tubes linked together to form different shapes, or the oblong suspended crystal vases and arty tableware. ⊠ *29 rue Francois Miron, 4e, Marais* ☎ *01–42–78– 50–60* Ⓜ *Tuileries* ⊠ *26 bd. Raspail, 7e, St-Germain-des-Prés* ☎ *01–45– 49–00–05* Ⓜ *Rue du Bac.*

Van der Straeten. Paris designer Hervé van der Straeten started out creating jewelry for Saint Laurent and Lacroix, designed a perfume bottle for Christian Dior, and moved on to making rather baroque and often wacky furniture. In his loft gallery-cum-showroom, furniture, jewelry, and startling mirrors are on display. ⊠ *11 rue Ferdinand Duval, 4e, Marais* ☎ *01–42–78–99–99* Ⓜ *St-Paul.*

JEWELRY AND ACCESSORIES

Yves Gratas. Yves Gratas has a knack for pairing gems of varying sizes, brilliance, and texture, allowing each stone to influence the design. Whether it's a spectacular necklace of sapphire beads to be worn long or doubled, or a simple agate sphere tipped in gold and dangling like a tiny planet, the pieces feel like one organic whole. ⊠ *9 rue Oberkampf, 11e, Marais* ☎ *01–49–29–00–53* Ⓜ *Oberkampf.*

SHOES, HANDBAGS, AND LEATHER GOODS

K. Jacques. K. Jacques has shod everyone from Brigitte Bardot to Drew Barrymore. The famous St-Tropez–based maker of strappy leather-soled flats has migrated to the big time while still keeping designs classic and comfortable. From gladiator-style to lightweight cork platforms, metallics to neutrals, these are perennial favorites. ⊠ *16 rue Pavée, 4e, Marais* ☎ *01–40–27–03–57* Ⓜ *St-Paul.*

Miguel Lobato. This is a sweet little boutique with accessories for the woman who wants it all. Beautiful high heels by Balenciaga, Chloé, and Pierre Hardy and fabulous bags by Martin Margiela, Jil Sander, and Costume National are just the start. ⊠ *6 rue Malher, 4e, Marais* ☎ *01–48–87–68–14* Ⓜ *St-Paul.*

MONTMARTRE

CLOTHING

A.P.C. A.P.C. opened its surplus store steps away from Sacré-Coeur. No need to wait for the sales; their funky classics can be found here for a whopping 50% off. ⊠ *20 rue André del Sarte, 18e, Montmartre* ☎ *01–42–62–10–88* Ⓜ *Château Rouge.*

Spree. When Spree first opened, its mission was to give young designers a venue; it has since branched out to include fashion elites like Margiela, Isabel Marant, Comme des Garçons, and Tsumori Chisato. The expertly chosen inventory seems almost curated. A great selection of accessories and jewelry, along with cool furniture and a revolving exhibition of artwork by local artists, complete the gallery feel. ⊠ *16 rue la Vieuville, 18e, Montmartre* ☎ *01–42–23–41–40* Ⓜ *Abesses.*

MARKETS

Marché aux Puces St-Ouen. Also referred to as Clignancourt, this market, on Paris's northern boundary, still attracts the crowds when it's open—Saturday to Monday, from 9 to 6—but its once-unbeatable prices are now a relic. The century-old labyrinth, packed with antiques dealers' booths and *brocante* stalls, sprawls for more than a square mile. Old Vuitton trunks, ormolu clocks, 1930s jet jewelry, and vintage garden furniture sit cheek by jowl. Arrive early to pick up the most worthwhile loot. Be warned—if there's one place in Paris where you need to know how to bargain, this is it! If you're arriving by métro, walk under the overpass and take the first left at the Rue de Rosiers to reach the center of the market. Around the overpass huddle stands selling dodgy odds and ends (think designer knockoffs and questionable gadgets). These blocks are crowded and gritty; be careful with your valuables.

Le Soleil. If you need a breather, stop for a bite in one of the rough-and-ready cafés. A good pick is Le Soleil. ⊠ *109 av. Michelet* ☎ *01–40–10–08–08* ⊕ *www.parispuces.com* Ⓜ *Porte de Clignancourt.*

MONTPARNASSE

BARGAIN SHOPPING

Mi-Prix. Mi-Prix is a jumble of end-of-series designer shoes and accessories from the likes of Michel Perry, Rodolph Ménudier, and some of the big-name Italian labels priced at up to 70% below retail. ⊠ *27 bd. Victor, 15e, Montparnasse* ☎ *01–48–28–42–48* Ⓜ *Porte de Versailles.*

Rue d'Alésia. Rue d'Alésia, in the 14e arrondissement, is the main place to find shops selling last season's fashions at a discount. Be forewarned: most of these shops are much more downscale than their elegant sister shops; dressing rooms are not always provided. Ⓜ *Alésia.*

MARKETS

Porte de Vanves. This smaller flea market, which lies at the southern side of the city, is a hit with the fashion and design set and specializes in smaller objects—mirrors, textiles, glassware, clothing, and collectables—as well as books, posters, antique wallpapers, and postcards. With tables sprawling along both sides of the sidewalk, there's an extravagant selection, but be sure to bargain. It's open weekends only from 8 to 5, but arrive early if you want to find a bargain: the good stuff goes fast, and stalls are liable to be packed up before noon. Ⓜ *Porte de Vanves.*

OPÉRA/GRANDS BOULEVARDS

ANTIQUES AND COLLECTIBLES

Drouot auction house. This world-famous auction house draws all the top dealers as well as savvy novices and those who just love the chase. You can find advance information on all auctions online with catalogs detailing the objects on offer. ⊠ *9 rue Drouot, 9e, Opéra/Grands Boulevards* ☎ *01–48–00–20–20* Ⓜ *Richelieu Drouot.*

BARGAIN SHOPPING

Monoprix. With branches throughout the city, this is *the* French dime store par excellence, stocking everyday items like French cosmetics, groceries, toys, typing paper, and kitchen wares—a little of everything. It also has a line of stylish, inexpensive, basic wearables for the whole family—particularly adorable kids clothes—and isn't a bad place to stock up on French chocolate, jams, or *confit de canard* at reasonable prices. ⊠ *21 av. de l'Opéra, 1er, Opéra/Grands Boulevards* ☎ *01–42–61–78–08* Ⓜ *Opéra* ⊠ *20 bd. de Charonne, 20e, Bastille/Nation* ☎ *01–43–73–17–59* Ⓜ *Nation* ⊠ *50 rue de Rennes, 6e, St-Germain-des-Prés* ☎ *01–45–48–18–08* Ⓜ *St-Germain-des-Prés.*

CLOTHING

Anouschka. Anouschka has set up shop in her apartment (by appointment only, Monday to Saturday) and has rack upon rack of vintage clothing dating from the 1930s to the '80s. It's the perfect place to find a '50s cocktail dress in mint condition or a mod jacket for him. A former model herself, she calls this a "designer laboratory," and teams from top fashion houses often pop by looking for inspiration. ⊠ *6 av. du Coq, 9e, Opéra/Grands Boulevards* ☎ *01–48–74–37–00* Ⓜ *St-Lazare, Trinité.*

Charvet. Charvet is the Parisian equivalent of a Savile Row tailor: a conservative, aristocratic institution famed for made-to-measure shirts, exquisite ties, and accessories; for garbing John F. Kennedy, Charles de Gaulle, and the Duke of Windsor; and for its regal address. Although the exquisite silk ties, in hundreds of colors and patterns, and custom-made shirts for men are the biggest draw, refined pieces for women and girls, as well as adorable miniatures for boys, round out the collection. ⊠ *28 pl. Vendôme, 1er, Opéra/Grands Boulevards* ☎ *01–42–60–30–70* Ⓜ *Opéra.*

Eric Bompard. Eric Bompard provides stylish Parisians with luxury cashmeres in every color, style, and weight; yarns range from light as a feather to a hefty 50-ply for the jaunty caps. The store caters to men and women (there are some kids' models, too). Styles are updated seasonally yet tend toward the classic. ⊠ *75 bd. Haussmann, 8e, Opéra/Grands Boulevards* ☎ *01–42–68–00–73* Ⓜ *Miromesnil* ⊠ *31 rue du Bac, 7e, Germain-des-Prés* ☎ *01–40–20–11–41* Ⓜ *Rue du Bac* ⊠ *91 av. des Champs-Élysées, 8e, Champs-Élysées* ☎ *01–53–57–89–60* Ⓜ *George V.*

DEPARTMENT STORES

Au Printemps. Au Printemps is actually three major stores: Printemps de la Maison (home furnishings), Printemps de l'Homme (menswear—six floors of it), and the brilliant Printemps de la Mode (fashion, fashion, fashion), which has everything from cutting-edge to the teeny bopper. Be sure to check out the beauty area, with the Nuxe spa, hairdressers, and seemingly every beauty product known to woman under one roof. Fashion shows are held on Tuesday (all year) and Friday (April–October) at 10 am under the cupola on the seventh floor of La Mode and are free. (Reservations can be made in advance by calling ☎ *01–42–82–63–17*; tickets can also be obtained on the day of the show at the service desk on the first floor.) ⊠ *64 bd. Haussmann, 9e, Opéra/Grands Boulevards* ☎ *01–42–82–50–00* Ⓜ *Havre Caumartin, Opéra, and RER: Auber.*

★ **Galeries Lafayette.** Galeries Lafayette is one of those places that you wander into unawares, leaving hours later a poorer and humbler person. At the flagship store at 40 boulevard Haussmann, a Belle Époque stained-glass dome caps the world's largest perfumery. The store bulges with thousands of designers; free fashion shows are held Friday at 3 pm in the upstairs café (reservations are a must: call ☎01–42–82–36–40 or email ✉*welcome@galerieslafayette.com*). A big draw is the comestibles department, stocked with everything from herbed goat cheese to Iranian caviar. Just across the street at 35 boulevard Haussmann is Galeries Lafayette Maison. The Montparnasse branch is a pale shadow of the Boulevard Haussmann behemoths. ✉*35–40 bd. Haussmann, 9e, Opéra/Grands Boulevards* ☎*01–42–82–34–56* Ⓜ*Chaussée d'Antin, Opéra, Havre Caumartin* ✉*Centre Commercial Montparnasse, 14e, Montparnasse* ☎*01–45–38–52–87* Ⓜ*Montparnasse Bienvenüe.*

FOOD AND TREATS

À la Mère de Famille. This enchanting shop is well versed in French regional specialties and old-fashioned bonbons, sugar candy, and more. ✉*35 rue du Faubourg-Montmartre, 9e, Opéra/Grands Boulevards* ☎*01–47–70–83–69* Ⓜ*Cadet.*

À l'Étoile d'Or. This is the quintessential dream of a candy shop. This whimsical confectionary will delight children of all ages, not to mention chocoholics, as it stocks some famously hard-to-find chocolates (like Bernachon, from Lyon). Dedicated to the candies of France, it's a walk back in time, with classic sweets from every Gallic region. Although a tad out of the way, it's worth the trip. ✉*30 rue Pierre Fontaine, 9e, Montmartre* ☎*01–48–74–59–55* Ⓜ*Pigalle.*

Fauchon. Fauchon remains the most iconic of Parisian food stores. It's expanding globally, but the flagship is still behind the Madeleine church. Established in 1886, it sells renowned pâté, honey, jelly, tea, and private-label champagne. Expats come for hard-to-find foreign foods (U.S. pancake mix, British lemon curd); those with a sweet tooth make a beeline for the *macarons* (airy, ganache-filled cookies) in the pâtisserie. There's a café for a quick bite. Prices can be eye-popping—marzipan fruit for €95 a pound? ✉*26 pl. de la Madeleine, 8e, Opéra/Grands Boulevards* ☎*01–70–39–38–00* Ⓜ*Madeleine.*

Hédiard. Hédiard, established in 1854, was famous in the 19th century for its high-quality imported spices. These—along with rare teas and beautifully packaged house brands of jam, mustard, and cookies—continue to be popular gifts for self and others. ✉*21 pl. de la Madeleine, 8e, Opéra/Grands Boulevards* ☎*01–43–12–88–88* Ⓜ*Madeleine.*

HOME DÉCOR

Christofle. Christofle, founded in 1830, has fulfilled all kinds of silver wishes, from a silver service for the *Orient Express* to a gigantic silver bed. Come for timeless table settings, vases, jewelry boxes, and more. ✉*24 rue de la Paix, 2e, Opéra/Grands Boulevards* ☎*01–42–65–62–43* Ⓜ*Opéra* ✉*9 rue Royale, 8e, Louvre/Tuileries* ☎*01–55–27–99–13* Ⓜ*Concorde, Madeleine.*

Kitchen Bazaar. This shop gleams with an astonishing array of culinary essentials for the novice and professional. Don't be surprised at the urge

16

The interior of the Galeries Lafayette department store—especially the ceiling—almost outshines the fabulous merchandise.

to replace every utensil in your kitchen with these up-to-the-minute designs. ✉ *4 rue de Bretagne, 3e, Marais* ☎ *01–44–78–97–04* Ⓜ *Filles du Calvaire.*

JEWELRY AND ACCESSORIES

Alexandre Reza. One of Paris's most exclusive jewelers, Alexandre Reza is first and foremost a gemologist. He travels the world looking for the finest stones and then works them into stunning pieces, many of which are replicas of jewels of historical importance. ✉ *21 pl. Vendôme, 1er, Opéra/Grands Boulevards* ☎ *01–42–61–51–21* Ⓜ *Opéra.*

Chanel Jewelry. Chanel Jewelry feeds off the iconic design elements of the pearl-draped designer: quilting (reimagined for gold rings), camellias (now brooches), and shooting stars (used for her first jewelry collection in 1932, now appearing as diamond rings). ✉ *18 pl. Vendôme, 1er, Opéra/Grands Boulevards* ☎ *01–55–35–50–00* Ⓜ *Tuileries, Opéra.*

Dinh Van. Dinh Van, just around the corner from Place Vendôme's titan jewelers, thumbs its nose at in-your-face opulence. The look here is refreshingly spare. Best sellers include a hammered gold orb necklace and leather-cord bracelets joined with geometric shapes in white or yellow gold, some with pavé diamonds. ✉ *16 rue de la Paix, 2e, Opéra/ Grands Boulevards* ☎ *01–42–61–74–49* Ⓜ *Opéra* ✉ *22 rue François 1 er, 8e, Champs-Élysées* ☎ *01–56–64–09–91* Ⓜ *Franklin-D.-Roosevelt* ✉ *58 rue Bonaparte, 6e, St-Germain-des-Prés* ☎ *01–56–24–10–00* Ⓜ *St-Germain-des-Prés.*

MARKETS

Rue Lévis. This market, near Parc Monceau, has Alsatian specialties and a terrific cheese shop. It's closed Sunday afternoon and Monday. ⊠ *17e, Parc Monceau* Ⓜ *Villiers.*

SHOPPING GALLERIES

Fodor'sChoice
★
Galerie Vivienne. Galerie Vivienne, between the Bourse and the Palais-Royal, is home base for a range of interesting and luxurious shops as well as the lovely tearoom, A Priori Thé, and a terrific wineshop, Cave Legrand. Don't leave without checking out the Jean-Paul Gaultier boutique. ⊠ *4 rue des Petits-Champs, 2e, Opéra/Grands Boulevards* Ⓜ *Bourse.*

Passage des Panoramas. Passage des Panoramas, opened in 1800, is the oldest arcade extant; it's especially known for its stamp shops. ⊠ *11 bd. Montmartre, 2e, Grands Boulevards* Ⓜ *Opéra/Grands Boulevards.*

16

Passage Jouffroy. Passage Jouffroy is full of shops selling toys, Oriental furnishings, and cinema books and posters. Pain D'épices, at No. 29, has dollhouse decor, and Au Bonheur des Dames, at No. 39, has all things embroidery. ⊠ *12 bd. Montmartre, 9e, Grands Boulevards* Ⓜ *Grands Boulevards.*

Passage Verdeau. Passage Verdeau, across from Passage Jouffroy, has shops carrying antique cameras, comic books, and engravings. ⊠ *4–6 rue de la Grange Batelière, 9e, Opéra/Grands Boulevards* Ⓜ *Grands Boulevards.*

WINE

★
Lavinia. Lavinia has the largest selection of wine in one spot in Europe—more than 6,000 wines and spirits from all over the world, ranging from the simple to the sublime. On-site there are expert English-speaking sommeliers to help you sort it all out, as well as a wine-tasting bar, a bookshop, and a restaurant. ⊠ *3–5 bd. de la Madeleine, 1er, Opéra/Grands Boulevards* ☎ *01–42–97–20–20* Ⓜ *St-Augustin.*

Les Caves Augé. Les Caves Augé, one of the best wine shops in Paris since 1850, is just the ticket, whether you're looking for a rare vintage, a select Bordeaux, or a seductive champagne for a tête-à-tête. English-speaking Marc Sibard is a well-known aficionado and an affable adviser. ⊠ *116 bd. Haussmann, 8e, Opéra/Grands Boulevards* ☎ *01–45–22–16–97* Ⓜ *St-Augustin.*

TOYS

Pain d'Epices. This shop has anything you can imagine for the French home (and garden) in miniature, including Lilliputian croissants, wine decanters, and minuscule instruments in their cases. Build-it-yourself dollhouses include a 17th-century town house and a *boulangerie* storefront. Upstairs are do-it-yourself teddy-bear kits and classic toys. ⊠ *29 Passage Jouffroy, 9e, Grands Boulevards* ☎ *01–47–70–08–68* Ⓜ *Grands Boulevards.*

ST-GERMAIN-DES-PRÉS

ANTIQUES AND COLLECTIBLES

Fodor'sChoice **Carré Rive Gauche.** Carré Rive Gauche is where you'll find museum-quality
★ pieces. Head to the streets between Rue du Bac, Rue de l'Université, Rue
de Lille, and Rue des Sts-Pères to find more than 100 associated shops,
marked with a small, blue square banner on their storefronts. ⊠ *Between
St-Germain-des-Prés and Musée d'Orsay, 6e, St-Germain-des-Prés* Ⓜ *St-
Germain-des-Prés, Rue du Bac.*

BEAUTY

★ **Editions de Parfums Frédéric Malle.** This perfumerie is based on a simple
concept: take the nine most famous noses in France and have them
edit singular perfumes. The result? Exceptional, highly concentrated
fragrances. Le Parfum de Thérèse, for example, was created by famous
Dior nose Edmond Roudnitska for his wife. Monsieur Malle has devised
high-tech ways to keep each smelling session unadulterated. At the Rue
de Grenelle store, individual scents are released in glass columns; stick
your head in and sniff. The Avenue Victor Hugo boutique has a glass-
fronted "wall of scents"; at the push of a button a selected fragrance
mists the air. ⊠ *37 rue de Grenelle, 7e, St-Germain-des-Prés* ☎ *01–42–
22–76–40* Ⓜ *Rue du Bac* ⊠ *140 av. Victor Hugo, 16e, Trocadéro/Tour
Eiffel* ☎ *01–45–05–39–02* Ⓜ *Victor Hugo* ⊠ *21 rue du Mont Thabor,
1er, Louvre/Tuileries* ☎ *01–42–22–16–89* Ⓜ *Tuileries.*

Shu Uemura. Shu Uemura has enhanced those whose faces are their fortune for decades. Models swear by the cleansing oil; free samples are prof-
fered. A huge range of colors, every makeup brush imaginable, and the
no-pinch eyelash curler keep fans coming back. ⊠ *176 bd. St-Germain,
6e, St-Germain-des-Prés* ☎ *01–45–48–02–55* Ⓜ *St-Germain-des-Prés.*

BOOKS AND STATIONERY

★ **La Hune.** Sandwiched between the Café de Flore and Les Deux Magots,
La Hune is a landmark for intellectuals. French literature is downstairs,
but the main attraction is the comprehensive collection of international
books on art and architecture upstairs. You can hang out until midnight
with all the other genius-insomniacs. ⊠ *170 bd. St-Germain, 6e, St-
Germain-des-Prés* ☎ *01–45–48–35–85* Ⓜ *St-Germain-des-Prés.*

Taschen. Perfect for night owls, Taschen is open until midnight on Friday
and Saturday. The Starck-designed shelves and desks hold glam titles
on photography, fine art, design, fashion, and fetishes. ⊠ *2 rue de Buci,
6e, St-Germain-des-Prés* ☎ *01–40–51–79–22* Ⓜ *Mabillon.*

Tea & Tattered Pages. This is the place for bargains: cheap secondhand
paperbacks plus new books (publishers' overstock) at low prices. Tea
and brownies are served, and browsing is encouraged. ⊠ *24 rue Mayet,
6e, St-Germain-des-Prés* ☎ *01–40–65–94–35* Ⓜ *Duroc.*

Fodor'sChoice **Village Voice.** This bookstore is a heavy hitter in Paris's ever-thriving
★ expat literary scene. It's known for its excellent current and classic
book selections, frequent book signings, and readings by authors of
legendary stature along with up-and-comers, all run by a knowledgeable and friendly staff. There's always a fresh stash of English-language

periodicals and magazines. ✉ *6 rue Princesse, 6e, St-Germain-des-Prés* ☎ *01–46–33–36–47* Ⓜ *Mabillon.*

CHILDREN'S CLOTHING

Alice à Paris. Alice à Paris stocks inventive, stylish, affordable and, above all, kid-proof clothing. These adorable outfits, for children from birth to 10 years old, are functional takes on classic styles in durable cottons and woolens. ✉ *9 rue de l'Odeon, 6e, St-Germain-des-Prés* ☎ *01–42–22–53–89* Ⓜ *St-Placide* ✉ *64 rue Condorcet, 9e, Montmartre/Pigalle* ☎ *01–48–78–17–31* Ⓜ *Pigalle.*

★ **Baghère.** Baghère is a favorite of movie-star moms. Designer Sylvie Loussiers's meticulous care with fabrics and cuts ensures supremely elegant clothing for kids from birth to age 8. Whether a charming pair of top-stitched overalls with dainty shell buttons, a tiny cashmere cardigan, or a winsome dress in a charming Liberty print cotton, each piece is of heirloom quality. ✉ *17 rue de Tournon, 6e, St-Germain-des-Prés* ☎ *01–43–29–37–21* Ⓜ *Odéon.*

Pom d'Api. Pom d'Api lines up footwear for babies and preteens in quality leathers and vivid colors. Expect well-made, eye-catching fashion—bright gold sneakers and fringed suede boots, as well as classic Mary Janes in shades of silver, pink, and gold. There are also utility boots for boys and sturdy rain gear. ✉ *28 rue du Four, 6e, St-Germain-des-Prés* ☎ *01–45–48–39–31* Ⓜ *St-Germain-des-Prés.*

CLOTHING

Antik Batik. Antik Batik has a wonderful line of ethnically inspired clothes. There are row upon row of beaded and sequined dresses, Chinese silk tunics, short fur jackets and fur-lined anoraks, flowing organza separates, and some of Paris's most popular sandals and giant scarves. Stores feature maxi- and mini-versions for mothers-to-be and adorable mini-versions for girls ages 2 to 14, too. ✉ *26 rue St-Sulpice, 6e, St-Germain-des-Prés* ☎ *01–44–07–68–53* Ⓜ *Odéon, Marais* ✉ *18 rue de Turenne, 4e, Marais* ☎ *01–44–78–02–00* Ⓜ *St-Paul.*

A.P.C. A.P.C. may be antiflash, but a knowing eye can always pick out their jeans in a crowd. The clothes are rigorously well-made; prime wardrobe pieces include dark indigo and black denim, zip-up cardigans, and peacoats. ✉ *38 rue Madame, 6e, St-Germain-des-Prés* ☎ *01–42–22–12–77* Ⓜ *St-Sulpice* ✉ *112 rue Vieille du Temple, 3e, Marais* ☎ *01–42–78–18–02* Ⓜ *Filles du Calvaire.*

Catherine Malandrino. Catherine Malandrino designs for the urban sophisticate, expertly combining glamour, smarts, and allure in her office-to-soirée styles. Glam separates include fur-lined cocoon coats, body-hugging cropped leather jackets, slinky dresses with peekaboo detailing, and black-silk harem pants. ✉ *10 rue de Grenelle, 6e, St-Germain-des-Prés* ☎ *01–42–22–26–95* Ⓜ *Sèvres-Babylone.*

Carven. This label dropped off the fashion map until its 2009 revival with artistic director Guillaume Henry at the helm. A veteran of Givenchy and Paule Ka, Henry took a mere two years to catapult the label into the major leagues. Inspired by the true-to-life movie heroines of Chabrol and Cassavetes, Henry injects the line with a vibrant sex appeal that's smart and wearable. What you get is couture quality at half the

16

price. ✉ *36 rue St-Sulpice, St-Germain-des-Prés* ☎ *01–44–61–02–07* Ⓜ *St-Sulpice, Odéon.*

Lucien Pellat-Finet. Lucien Pellat-Finet does cashmere that shakes up the traditional world of cable knits—here, sweaters for men, women, and children come in punchy colors and cheeky motifs. A psychedelic marijuana leaf may bounce across a sky-blue crewneck; a crystal-outlined skull could grin from a sleeveless top. The cashmere's wonderfully soft—and the prices are accordingly high. ✉ *231 rue St-Honoré, 1er, Louvre/Rivoli* ☎ *01–42–22–22–77* Ⓜ *Tuileries.*

Sonia Rykiel. Sonia Rykiel has been designing insouciant knitwear since the 1960s. Sweaters drape and cling by turns and her color combinations (she's partial to stripes) are lovely. Opulent silks, furs, accessories dotted with rhinestones, and soft leather bags punctuate the collection. Sonia by Sonia Rykiel, the secondary line, is playful, smart, and targets a slightly younger crowd. ✉ *175 bd. St-Germain, 6e, St-Germain-des-Prés* ☎ *01–49–54–60–60* Ⓜ *St-Germain-des-Prés* ✉ *70 rue du Faubourg St-Honoré, 8e, Louvre/Tuileries* ☎ *01–42–65–20–81* Ⓜ *Concorde.*

DEPARTMENT STORES

Fodor'sChoice
★
Le Bon Marché. Founded in 1852, Le Bon Marché has emerged as the city's chicest department store. Long a hunting ground for linens and other home items, the store got a face-lift that brought fashion to the fore. The ground floor sets out makeup, perfume, and accessories; this is where celebs duck in for essentials while everyone pretends not to recognize them. Upstairs, do laps through labels chichi (Burberry, Sonia Rykiel) and überhip (Martin Margiela, Comme des Garçons). Menswear, under the moniker Balthazar, keeps pace with designers like Yves Saint Laurent, and Paul Smith. Zip across the second floor walkway to the mode section (above the next-door *épicerie*), home to streetwise designers and edgy secondary lines (and a funky café). French favorites include Athé by Vanessa Bruno, Zadig & Voltaire, Manoush, Isabel Marant's Étoile line, and Madame à Paris. Best of all, this department store isn't nearly as crowded as those near the Opéra. Don't miss La Grande Épicerie next door; it's the haute couture of grocery stores. Artisanal jams, olive oils, and much more make great gifts, and the luscious pastries and fruit beg to be chosen for a snack. ✉ *24 rue de Sèvres, 7e, St-Germain-des-Prés* ☎ *01–44–39–80–00* Ⓜ *Sèvres-Babylone.*

FOOD AND TREATS

Debauve & Gallais. The two former chemists who founded Debauve & Gallais in 1800 became the royal chocolate purveyors and were famed for their "health chocolates," made with almond milk. Test the benefits yourself with ganache, truffles, or *pistols* (flavored dark-chocolate disks). ✉ *30 rue des Sts-Pères, 7e, St-Germain-des-Prés* ☎ *01–45–48–54–67* Ⓜ *St-Germain-des-Prés.*

Huilerie Artisanale J. Leblanc et Fils. This *huilerie* corrals everything you need for the perfect salad dressing into its small space: aged vinegars, *fleur de sel* (unprocessed sea salt), and more than 15 varieties of oils pressed the old-fashioned way, with a big stone wheel, from olives, hazelnuts, pistachios, or grape seed. ✉ *6 rue Jacob, 6e, St-Germain-des-Prés* ☎ *01–46–34–61–55* Ⓜ *Mabillon.*

HOME DÉCOR

Alexandre Biaggi. Alexandre Biaggi specializes in 20th-century Art Deco and also commissions designs from such talented designers as Patrick Naggar and Hervé van der Straeten. ✉ *14 rue de Seine, 6e, St-Germain-des-Prés* ☎ *01–44–07–34–73* Ⓜ *St-Germain-des-Prés.*

Catherine Memmi. This trendsetter in pared-down housewares also sells lamps, furniture, and home accessories. ✉ *11 rue St-Sulpice, 6e, St-Germain-des-Prés* ☎ *01–44–07–02–02* Ⓜ *St-Sulpice.*

Cire Trudon. Cire Trudon has illuminated the great palaces and churches of Paris since the 1700s. Nowadays they provide the atmosphere for tony restaurants and exclusive soirees. The all-vegetal, atmospherically scented candles come in elegant black glass, pillars of all sizes, or busts of clientele past: Napoleon, Marie Antoinette. ✉ *78 rue de Seine, 6e, St-Germain-des-Prés* ☎ *01–43–26–46–50* Ⓜ *Odéon.*

Conran Shop. This is the brainchild of British entrepreneur Terence Conran. The shop carries expensive contemporary furniture, beautiful bed linens, and items for every other room in the house—all marked by a balance of utility with not-too-sober style. Conran makes even shower curtains fun. ✉ *117 rue du Bac, 7e, St-Germain-des-Prés* ☎ *01–42–84–10–01* Ⓜ *Sèvres-Babylone.*

16

Diptyque. This shop is famous for its candles and eaux de toilettes and now body care in sophisticated scents like myrrh, fig tree, and quince. They're delightful but not cheap; the candles, for instance, cost nearly $1 per hour of burn time. ✉ *34 bd. St-Germain, 5e, St-Germain-des-Prés* ☎ *01–43–26–77–44* Ⓜ *Maubert-Mutualité* ✉ *8 rue des Francs Bourgeois, Marais* ☎ *01–48–04–95–57* Ⓜ *St-Paul.*

R&Y Augousti. R&Y Augousti are two Paris-based designers who make furniture and objects for the home from nacre, ostrich, palm wood, and parchment. Also for sale are their hand-tooled leather bags and wallets. ✉ *103 rue du Bac, 7e, St-Germain-des-Prés* ☎ *01–42–22–22–21* Ⓜ *Sèvres-Babylone.*

JEWELRY AND ACCESSORIES

Adelline. This jewelry shop creates the effect of having landed in Ali Baba's cave: each piece is more gorgeous than the last, and the bounty of beautiful shapes and styles satisfies a large range of tastes. Huge cabochon rings, jeweled cuffs in a web of gold, and simple cord-and-gem bracelets cannot fail to make a statement. ✉ *54 rue Jacob, 6e, St-Germain-des-Prés* ☎ *01–47–03–07–18* Ⓜ *St-Germain-des-Prés.*

Agatha. This is the perfect place to buy a moderately priced piece of fun jewelry. Agatha's line of earrings, rings, hair accessories, bracelets, necklaces, watches, brooches, and pendants is ever popular with Parisians. Styles change quickly, but classics include charm bracelets and fine gold necklaces with whimsical pendants. ✉ *45 rue Bonaparte, 6e, St-Germain-des-Prés* ☎ *01–46–33–20–00* Ⓜ *St-Germain-des-Prés.*

Alexandra Sojfer. Alexandra Sojfer, the proprietress, is the queen of walking sticks. The late president François Mitterrand bought his at this tiny shop—open since 1834—which also has an amazing range of umbrellas. ✉ *218 bd. St-Germain, 7e, St-Germain-des-Prés* ☎ *01–42–22–17–02* Ⓜ *Rue du Bac.*

Arthus-Bertrand. Arthus-Bertrand, which dates back to 1803, has glass showcases full of designer jewelry and numerous objects to celebrate births. ⊠ *6 pl. St-Germain-des-Prés, 6e, St-Germain-des-Prés* ☎ *01–49–54–72–10* Ⓜ *St-Germain-des-Prés.*

Marie Mercié. Marie Mercié is one of Paris's most fashionable hat makers. Her husband, Anthony Peto, makes men's hats and has a store at 56 rue Tiquetonne. ⊠ *23 rue St-Sulpice, 6e, St-Germain-des-Prés* ☎ *01–43–26–45–83* Ⓜ *Mabillon, St-Sulpice.*

LINGERIE

Sabbia Rosa. You could easily walk straight past this discreet, boudoir-like boutique. It is, however, one of the world's finest lingerie stores and the place where actresses Catherine Deneuve and Isabelle Adjani (and others who might not want to reveal their errand) buy superb French silks. ⊠ *71–73 rue des Sts-Pères, 6e, St-Germain-des-Prés* ☎ *01–45–48–88–37* Ⓜ *St-Germain-des-Prés.*

MARKETS

Boulevard Raspail. Boulevard Raspail, between Rue du Cherche-Midi and Rue de Rennes, is the city's major *marché biologique,* or organic market, bursting with produce, fish, and eco-friendly products every Sunday. The market is also open on Tuesday and Friday with nonorganic products. ⊠ *6e, St-Germain-des-Prés* Ⓜ *Rennes.*

Rue de Buci. Vendors at this market often tempt you with tastes of their wares: slices of sausage, slivers of peaches. It's closed Sunday afternoon and Monday. ⊠ *6e, St-Germain-des-Prés* Ⓜ *Odéon.*

SHOES, HANDBAGS, AND LEATHER GOODS

Fodor'sChoice ★ **Bruno Frisoni.** Bruno Frisoni has an impressive pedigree, most lately as art director for Roger Vivier. His first boutique for women is lined with ultrasexy, ultrasophisticated shoes and bags in vivid colors. The vertiginous tapered heels, lean platforms, and delicately conceived flats mix glamour with a hint of S&M. ⊠ *34 rue de Grenelle, 7e, St-Germain-des-Prés* ☎ *01–42–84–12–30* Ⓜ *St-Germain-des-Prés.*

★ **Jamin Puech.** Jamin Puech thinks of its bags not just as a necessity, but as jewelry. Nothing's plain Jane here—beaded bags swing from thin link chains, fringes flutter from dark embossed-leather totes, small evening purses are covered with shells, oversize sequins, or hand-dyed crochet. The collections fluctuate with the seasons but never fail to be whimsical, imaginative, and highly coveted. ⊠ *43 rue Madame, 6e, St-Germain-des-Prés* ☎ *01–45–48–14–85* Ⓜ *St-Sulpice* ⊠ *68 rue Vieille-du-Temple, 3e, Marais* ☎ *01–48–87–84–87* Ⓜ *St-Paul* ⊠ *26 rue Cambon, 1er, Louvre/Tuileries* ☎ *01–40–20–40–28* Ⓜ *Concord.*

Jérôme Dreyfuss. Jérôme Dreyfuss is the newest star in Paris's many splendored handbag universe, having captivated *le tout Paris* with his artsy take on the hobo, Birkin, and messenger bags. Unique styles, like the delicious twee-mini, in myriad shades—ochre, stormy gray, violet, and evergreen—verge on the sublime and the luxe matte-python bags are worth taking out a second mortgage. ⊠ *1 rue Jacob, 6e, St-Germain-des-Prés* ☎ *01–43–54–70–93* Ⓜ *St-Germain-des-Prés* ⊠ *127 Galerie de Valois, Louvre/Tuileries* ☎ *01–42–60–38–76* Ⓜ *Palais-Royal.*

CLOSE UP

Worth a Look

There are some stores that are worth visiting, whether or not you're going to make a purchase; check these out for a priceless slice of Parisian life.

Deyrolle. This fascinating 19th-century taxidermist has long been a stop for curiosity seekers. A fire in 2008 destroyed what was left of the original shop, but it has been lavishly restored and remains a cabinet of curiosities par excellence. ✉ *46 rue du Bac, 7e, St-Germain-des-Prés* ☎ *01-42-22-30-07* Ⓜ *Rue du Bac.*

Hervé Gambs. For elegant decorating on a smaller scale, Hervé Gambs has the chutzpah to vie with Mother Nature. Take home one of his all-silk floral creations—think a no-care stem of orchids or a stunning monster leaf—and dazzle your houseguests. Seasonal and holiday-appropriate displays change every few months. Gambs's own pedestal candles, home fragrances, and sculptural vases styled from natural forms make great gifts. ✉ *60 bd. Beaumarchais, 11e, Marais* ☎ *01-55-28-65-50* Ⓜ *St-Sébastien Froissart* ✉ *21 rue St-Sulpice, 6e, St-Germain-des-Prés* ☎ *01-70-08-09-08* Ⓜ *Odéon.*

Merci. This is the world's most gorgeous charity shop, put together by Marie-France and Bernard Cohen of the luxury kid's line, Bonpoint. Everything here—designer and vintage clothes, furniture, antiques, jewelry, and housewares—has been plucked straight from many top-tier designers and is offered at a discount. Five percent of the proceeds are earmarked to aid disadvantaged children in Madagascar. ✉ *111 bd. Beaumarchais, 3e, Marais* ☎ *01-42-77-00-33* Ⓜ *St-Sebastien-Froissart.*

Zuber. Have you always wanted to decorate your home like the grand homes of Paris? Zuber has operated nonstop for more than two centuries as the world's oldest producer of prestige hand-printed wallpapers, renowned for their magnificent panoramic scenes. Warning: with only one scene produced per year, the wait can be nearly 10 years long. They appear at Sotheby's, too, from time to time. Opulent Restoration-era wallpapers (including metallics, silks, velvets, and pressed leather) make modern statements and can be purchased in 32-foot rolls for slightly less than a king's ransom. ✉ *3 rue des Saints-Pères, 6e, St-Germain-des-Prés* ☎ *01-42-77-95-91* Ⓜ *St-Germain-des-Prés.*

16

Michel Perry Collector. This shop is a mixed bag with reliably great finds: among those unsellable gladiator numbers you might turn up delicate silvery-pink pumps; you have to look to make the finds. Season-old collections of Michel Perry shoes are half off; during sales the store practically gives them away. The staff is helpful and fun. ✉ *42 rue de Grenelle, 7e, St-Germain-des-Prés* ☎ *01-42-84-12-45* Ⓜ *Rue du Bac.*

TOYS

FNAC Junior. Anything this chain lacks charm, it makes up with variety. Some of the famous old names in French toys can be found here, including the much-loved wooden toys from Vilac, but the impressive collection is mostly contemporary (for kids from birth to age 12). ✉ *19 rue Vavin, 6e, St-Germain-des-Prés* ☎ *01-56-24-03-46* Ⓜ *Vavin.*

WINE

La Dernière Goutte. This inviting *cave* (literally wine store or wine cellar) focuses on wines by small French producers. Each is handpicked by the owner, along with a choice selection of estate champagnes, Armagnac, and the classic Vieille Prune (plum brandy). The friendly English-speaking staff makes browsing a pleasure. Don't miss the Saturday afternoon tastings with the wine-makers. ⊠ *6 rue de Bourbon le Château, 6e, St-Germain-des-Prés* ☎ *01–46–29–11–62* Ⓜ *Odéon.*

Ryst-Dupeyron. Ryst-Dupeyron specializes in fine wines and liquors, with port, calvados, and Armagnacs that date from 1878. A great gift idea: find a bottle from the year of a friend's birth and have it labeled with your friend's name. Personalized bottles can be ordered and delivered on the same day. ⊠ *79 rue du Bac, 7e, St-Germain-des-Prés* ☎ *01–45–48–80–93* Ⓜ *Rue du Bac.*

Nightlife

WORD OF MOUTH

"Go to an old, rowdy jazz club such as Caveau de la Huchette [not pictured above], pay 10 euros to the guy in the tiny ticket window because you can already hear how good the music is . . . enter the 'caveau,' an ancient stone room with vaulted ceilings . . . and watch the trombonist fill his cheeks. Fantastique."

—dekoder

Updated by
Paige Donner

You haven't seen Paris until you've seen the city at night. Throngs fill popular streets and the air fills with the melody of French conversation and the clinking of glasses. This is when Parisians let down their hair and reveal their true bonhomie, laughing and dancing, flirting and talking. Parisians love to savor life together: they dine out, drink endless espressos, offer innumerable toasts, and are often so reluctant to separate that they party all night.

Parisians go out weekends and weeknights, late and early. And they tend to frequent the same places once they've found spots they like: it could be a wine bar, corner café, or hip music club, and you can often find a welcoming "the gang's all here" atmosphere. A wise way to spend an evening is to pick an area in a neighborhood that interests you, then give yourself time to browse. Parisians love to bar-hop, and the energy shifts throughout the evening, so be prepared to follow the crowds all night.

Nightlife hot spots are scattered throughout the city, with each neighborhood offering a unique vibe. If you prefer clinking drinks with models and celebrities, check out the Champs-Élysées or St-Germain-des-Prés areas, but be prepared to shell out *beaucoup* bucks and stare down surly bouncers. Easygoing, bohemian-chic revelers can be found in the northeastern districts like Canal St-Martin and Belleville, while students tend to pour into the Bastille and the Quartier Latin. Gays and party-hearty types can nail a wild time nearly every night in the Marais. The Grands Boulevards and Rue Montorgueil, just north of Les Halles, are party central for young professionals and the fashion crowd, and the Pigalle/Montmartre area is always hopping with plenty of theaters, cabarets, bars, and concert venues. Warmer months draw the adventurous to floating clubs and bars moored along the Seine from Bercy to the Eiffel Tower.

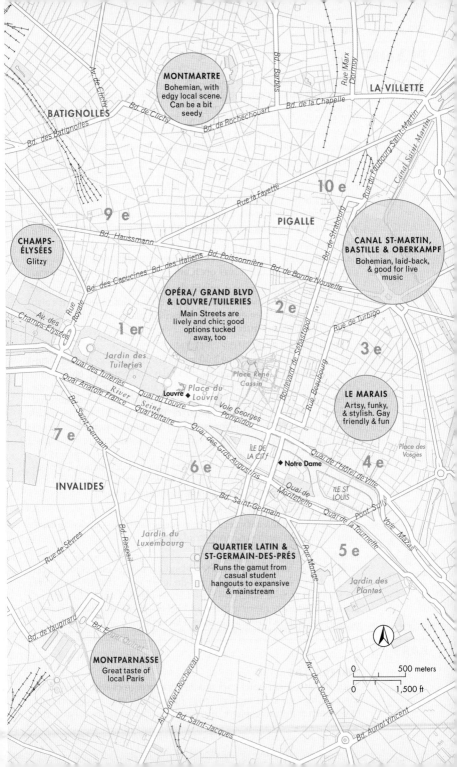

MONTMARTRE
Bohemian, with edgy local scene. Can be a bit seedy

LA VILLETTE

BATIGNOLLES

Bd. des Batignolles

Av. de Clichy

Bd. de Clichy

Bd. de Rochechouart

Bd. de la Chapelle

Rue Marx Dormoy

Rue la Fayette

Rue du Faubourg Saint-Martin

Canal Saint-Martin

10 e

9 e

PIGALLE

Bd. de Strasbourg

Bd. Haussmann

CHAMPS-ÉLYSÉES
Glitzy

Bd. des Capucines

Bd. des Italiens

Bd. Poissonnière

Bd. de Bonne Nouvelle

CANAL ST-MARTIN, BASTILLE & OBERKAMPF
Bohemian, laid-back, & good for live music

Bd. des Capucines

Rue Royale

Av. des Champs-Élysées

OPÉRA/ GRAND BLVD & LOUVRE/TUILERIES
Main Streets are lively and chic; good options tucked away, too

2 e

Rue de Turbigo

3 e

1 er

Jardin des Tuileries

Quai des Tuileries

Quai du Louvre

Place René Cassin

Boulevard de Sébastopol

Rue de Beaubourg

LE MARAIS
Artsy, funky, & stylish. Gay friendly & fun

River Seine

Quai Anatole France

Quai Voltaire

Louvre ◆

Place du Louvre

Voie Georges Pompidou

Quai des Gras Augustins

Bd. Saint-Germain

7 e

ÎLE DE LA CITÉ

Place des Vosges

4 e

6 e

◆ Notre Dame

Quai de l'Hôtel de Ville

INVALIDES

Bd. Saint-Germain

Quai de Montebello

ÎLE ST LOUIS

Quai de la Tournelle

Voie Mazas

Pont Sully

Rue de Sèvres

Bd. Raspail

Jardin du Luxembourg

QUARTIER LATIN & ST-GERMAIN-DES-PRÉS
Runs the gamut from casual student hangouts to expansive & mainstream

Rue Monge

5 e

Jardin des Plantes

Bd. de Vaugirard

Bd. Edgar Quinet

MONTPARNASSE
Great taste of local Paris

Av. Denfert-Rochereau

Bd. Saint-Jacques

Av. des Gobelins

Bd. Auriol Vincent

0   500 meters
0   1,500 ft

PLANNING

GETTING PAST THE BOUNCER

It shouldn't surprise any nightlife lover that the more *branché* (literally, "plugged-in" or trendy) the spot, the knottier the door-entry problem will be. Most bars aren't a problem, but when it comes to clubbing, don't assume you're going to get in just because you show up. This is particularly true at the hot spots near the Champs-Élysées. A limo at your disposal and global fame aren't essential to pass muster, but you absolutely must have a cocky yet somehow simultaneously polite attitude and look fabulous. Having a high female quotient in your party definitely helps (fashion models are a particular plus). Solo men—or, worse, groups of men—are going to have a tougher time, unless they are high rollers and have reserved a table (bottle purchase *obligatoire*).

HOURS

Bars tend to stay open until between midnight and 2 am, with no specific last call. Clubs often stay open until 4 am, and many until dawn.

If you want to hit bars at a relatively quiet hour, go for an *apéritif* around 6 pm. Many places offer drink specials at this time, and it's also when Parisians congregate to make late-night plans. Many bars charge slightly higher prices after 10.

LATE-NIGHT TRANSPORTATION

The last métro runs between 12:30 am and 1 am Monday through Sunday, but there is late-night service on Friday and Saturday until 2 am. After that, you can take a cab, but it can be extremely difficult to find one in the wee hours. Taxi stands are plagued with long lines for few cabs, and calling Taxi Bleu (☎ 08–91–70–10–10) or Taxi G-7 (☎ 01–47–39–47–39 or 01–41–27–66–99 for English-speaking operator) is unpredictable on weekends. Another option is the Noctilien, the sometimes rowdy night-bus system *(see By Bus in Paris Travel Smart)*. Another option is the Vélib', if you stay within biking distance of chosen destinations, though after a few champagnes it may be better to do like the Parisians and just stay out until the métro starts running again at 5:45 am.

TABLE SERVICE, OR NON?

Some bars have table service; at others (designated by "Service au Bar" signs), you must fetch your own drinks.

WHAT TO WEAR

Parisians are chic, so if you want to blend in (and get into clubs), dress up. Men, you can wear your jeans—designer jeans, that is—but leave the sneakers at your hotel and try adding a blazer. Ladies, dressing up doesn't necessarily mean a dress and heels—Parisian girls manage to look like a million bucks in jeans and a chic top.

BARS

HOTEL BARS

Some of Paris's best hotel bars mix historic pedigrees with hushed elegance; others go for a modern, edgy luxe. They offer an opportunity to experience the atmosphere of some of the chicest spots in Paris. But high prices and the fickle Parisian fashion pack ensure that only the latest, highly hyped bars draw in locals regularly.

WINE BARS
Wine bars are different from regular bars in that they serve simple meals and snacks (charcuterie, cheese) as well as wine; they usually close earlier than full-fledged bars—somewhere between 10 and midnight. *For reviews of bars à vins, see the Where to Eat chapter.*

CABARETS

Paris's cabarets range from boîtes once haunted by Picasso and Piaf to those sinful showplaces where *tableaux vivants* offer acres of bare female flesh. Some of these places, like the Lido, are more Vegas than the petticoat vision re-created by Hollywood in Baz Luhrmann's *Moulin Rouge*—but the rebirth of burlesque is making some of the old-school venues more popular. You can dine at many cabarets, but the food isn't the attraction. Prices range from about €24 (admission plus one drink) to more than €130 (dinner plus show).

CLUBS

Paris's hyped *boîtes de nuit*—more often referred to as simply *boîtes* (nightclubs)—tend to be expensive and exclusive. If you're friends with a regular or you've modeled in *Vogue*, you'll have an easier time getting through the door. Cover charges at some spots push the €20 range, with drinks at the bar starting at €10 for a beer. Others are free to enter, but getting past the doorman can still be an issue. Locals looking to dance tend to stick to the smaller clubs, where the cover ranges from free (usually on slower weekdays) to €15 and the focus is on the music and upbeat atmosphere. Club popularity depends on the night or event, as Parisians are more loyal to certain DJs than venues and often hit two or three spots before ending up at one of the many after-parties, which can last until noon the next day.

GAY AND LESBIAN BARS AND CLUBS

Gay and lesbian bars and clubs are mostly concentrated in the Marais and include some of the hippest addresses in the city. Keep in mind, however, that many of these sites fall in and out of favor at lightning speed. The best way to find out what's hot is by picking up a copy of *Têtu* or *2X*, the free "agendas" (listings for hot spots and events) that can be found in any of the bars listed here.

PUBS

Pubs wooing English-speaking clients with selections of British and Irish beers are becoming increasingly popular with Parisians. They're also good places to find reasonably priced food at off hours.

17

NIGHTLIFE IN PARIS

Reviews are alphabetical by neighborhood.

AROUND THE LOUVRE

LES HALLES

BARS

Chacha Club. Behind a nondescript facade you'll find a 1930s-style bar-club-restaurant arranged like a private home, with a series of rooms on three floors—including a special smoking lounge—and lots of corners where the casually stylish cool cats of Paris get cozy until the wee hours. ⊠ *47 rue Berger, 1er, Les Halles* ☎ *01–40–13–12–12* Ⓜ *Châtelet-Les Halles.*

Experimental Cocktail Club. Experimental Cocktail Club fashioned itself as a speakeasy on a tiny brick-paved street that seems like it should be lighted by gas lamps. The show is all about the *alcool,* and colorful, innovative cocktails like the Lemon Drop are mixed with aplomb by hunky, friendly bartenders. By 11 pm it's packed with a diverse mix of locals, professionals, and fashionistas, who occasionally dress up like characters from a Toulouse-Lautrec painting on special costume nights. ⊠ *37 rue Saint-Sauveur, 2e, Les Halles* ☎ *01–45–08–88–09* Ⓜ *Réamur-Sébastopol.*

Jefrey's. The custom DJ'd music track, the love seats, and the inventive cocktails make this a sophisticated and easy choice for intimate evening in good company and stylish surroundings. Great for return customers, Jefrey's lets you keep your bottle stored on the shelf, with your name on it, for next time. ⊠ *14 rue Saint-Sauveur, Les Halles* ☎ *01–42–33–60–77* ☻ *Tues.–Sat. 7 pm–2 am.*

Le Café Noir. Le Café Noir lures Parisians from Bobos to *pompiers* (fire fighters) to its elegantly worn digs that feature a pipe-smoking papier-mâché fish, a leopard-print-covered old motorbike, cool *alcool,* and friendly staff. (The restaurant with the same name is unrelated.) ⊠ *65 rue Montmartre, 2e, Les Halles* ☎ *01–40–39–07–36* Ⓜ *Étienne Marcel.*

Le Truskel. Le Truskel—what looks and sounds and feels like an English pub but kicks booty like a punk club? Le Trusk, whose basement showcases gigs by the globe's hottest new alternative acts while a loud, happy Parisian rocker crowd staggers around the roomy bar. ⊠ *12 rue Feydeau, 2e, Les Halles* ☎ *01–40–26–59–97* Ⓜ *Bourse.*

GAY AND LESBIAN BARS AND CLUBS

Banana Café. Banana Café draws a trendy and scantily clad mixed crowd, and offers show tunes in the cellar, where dancing on tables is the norm. Monday night is the "soirée sans interdit" (where nothing is forbidden)—ooh la la! ⊠ *13 rue de la Ferronnerie, 1er, Les Halles* ☎ *01–42–33–35–31* Ⓜ *Châtelet–Les Halles.*

★ **Bar d'Art/Le Duplex.** Bar d'Art/Le Duplex throbs with young tortured-artist types who enjoy the frequent art exhibitions, alternative music, and mood-inspiring ambient lighting. ⊠ *25 rue Michel-Le-Comte, 3e, Les Halles* ☎ *01–42–72–80–86* Ⓜ *Rambuteau.*

An evening at Au Lapin Agile, one of Paris's original cabarets (founded in 1860), consists of live music, satire, and singing, unlike the racier cabaret shows.

Le Dépôt. Le Dépôt is a cruising bar, club, and the largest back room in Europe. The ever-popular Gay Tea Dance spices up Sunday afternoon. ✉ *10 rue aux Ours, 3e, Les Halles* ☎ *01–44–54–96–96* Ⓜ *Étienne Marcel.*

JAZZ CLUBS

Le Sunset. Le Sunset hosts French and American musicians, with an accent on electronic jazz fusion and groove. ✉ *60 rue des Lombards, 1er, Les Halles* ☎ *01–40–26–46–60* Ⓜ *Châtelet Les Halles.*

Le Sunside. Le Sunside, connected to Le Sunset, specializes in classic jazz and swing. ✉ *60 rue des Lombards, 1er, Les Halles* ☎ *01–40–26–46–60* Ⓜ *Châtelet–Les Halles.*

LOUVRE

BARS

Bar 8. Since this monolitic marble bar at the Mandarin Oriental Hotel opened its doors, it has been the "in" game in town. There's an extensive champagne menu, and the terrace was an instant hit with the Fashion Week gang. ✉ *251 rue St-Honoré, Louvre/Tuileries* ☎ *01–70–98–78–88.*

Bar 228. Hôtel Meurice converted its ground-floor Fontainebleau library into the intimate Bar 228, with wood paneling and huge murals depicting the royal hunting forests of Fontainebleau. Its loyal fashion crowd is continually wooed by Philippe Starck decor updates and lubricated with the bar's famous Bellinis. ■TIP➜ Try the Meurice Millennium cocktail, made with champagne, rose liqueur, and Cointreau. ✉ *228 rue de Rivoli, 1er, Louvre* ☎ *01–44–58–10–66* Ⓜ *Tuileries.*

L'Assaggio Bar. At this bar, in Chanel's old neighborhood, you can order tea and macarons until midnight—in addition to cocktails. ✉ *33–37 rue Cambon, Louvre/Tuileries* ☎ *01–44–58–44–58.*

★ **Le Fumoir.** Le Fumoir is an oh-so-reliably ultrachic charmer across from the Louvre where fashionable neighborhood gallery owners and professionals meet for late-afternoon wine, early-evening cocktails, or dinner. It features a super-stocked bar in the front, an ample multilingual library in the back, and chess boards for the clientele to use while sipping martinis. ✉ *6 rue de l'Amiral-Coligny, 1er, Louvre* ☎ *01–42–92–00–24* Ⓜ *Louvre.*

CLUBS

Cab. Cab is a popular fashion-centric club across from the Louvre, where models, photographers, and stylists bypass the lesser beings at the velvet rope. If you make it inside, you'll appreciate the chic Space Odyssey atmosphere. Depending on the night, you'll hear funk, hip-hop, electro, or house. ✉ *2 pl. du Palais-Royal, 1er, Louvre* ☎ *01–58–62–56–25* Ⓜ *Palais-Royal.*

Kong. Kong is glorious not only for its panoramic skyline views, but for its exquisite manga-inspired decor, the top-shelf DJs for weekend dancing, and its kooky, disco-ball-and-kid-sumo-adorned bathrooms. It was featured as a chic eatery in *Sex and the City*; need we say more? ✉ *1 rue du Pont-Neuf, 1er, Louvre* ☎ *01–40–39–09–00* Ⓜ *Pont-Neuf.*

Soirée Bus. Traveling with a tribe? You and up to 60 of your closest friends can drink and dance in this private disco on wheels—with a DJ *and* a bouncer—while touring Paris sights such as the Eiffel Tower, the Champs Élysées, and Place Vendôme. ✉ *Louvre/Palais-Royal* ☎ *06–32–62–14–34.*

VIP Room. Although it's no longer on the Champs Élysées, this temple of bling still attracts the latest DJs, beautiful people, and . . . VIPs! Check the website for the latest soirée: usually R&B/hip-hop/top 40 crowd pleasers. There's a gift shop, a ground floor café, and a pricey Italian restaurant on the top floor. Dress to impress. ✉ *188 bis, rue de Rivoli, 1er, Louvre* ☎ *01–58–36–46–00* Ⓜ *Palais-Royal.*

GAY CLUBS

Club 18. Club 18 takes gay pride to the heart of the Louvre district on the weekends. This elegant spot is the oldest gay club in Paris and boasts a well-earned reputation as a "friendly party scene." ✉ *18 rue de Beaujolais, 1er, Louvre* ☎ *01–42–97–52–13* Ⓜ *Palais Royale.*

CHAMPS-ÉLYSÉES

BARS

★ **Apicius.** Apicius offers sublime elegance mere steps from the Champs-Élysées. Wander through the luxe front garden and château restaurant to the sleekly modern black bar where couture cocktails are concocted to suit any cultured taste. Closed weekends. ✉ *20 rue d'Artois, 8e, Champs-Élysées* ☎ *01–43–80–19–66* Ⓜ *George V.*

Bar Metropolitan. This cozy spot, which seats 25 at most, has one of the best bar views of the Eiffel Tower in town. It also serves delicious champagne cocktails dreamed up by the head bartender, who is only too happy to practice his American on you. ✉ *10 place de Mexico, Trocadéro/Tour Eiffel* ☎ *01–56–90–40–04* Ⓜ *Trocadéro.*

Buddha Bar. Buddha Bar is past its prime with Parisians, but visitors can't seem to get enough of the high-camp towering gold Buddha that holds court over giant palm fronds, red satin walls, colorful chinoiserie, and a spacious mezzanine bar that, in turn, overlooks a dining room serving pan-Asian fare. ✉ *8 rue Boissy d'Anglas, 8e, Champs-Élysées* ☎ *01–53–05–90–00* Ⓜ *Concorde.*

English Bar. You might find diplomats and other dignitaries discussing state affairs at this plush red den of masculinity at L'hôtel Raphael, a stone's throw from the Arc de Triomphe. ■ TIP→ The hotel's Rooftop Bar, a well-guarded Parisian secret, was voted the best bar in Europe in recent years. ✉ *17 av. Kleber, Champs-Élysée* ☎ *01–53–64–32–00* Ⓜ *Kleber, Champs-Élysées, Étoile.*

Flute Bar. A Paris offshoot of the original Flûte bar in New York, Flûte L'Etoile is just off the Champs in the chic 17th. In a country where you might expect to find champagne bars on every corner, Flûte is one of only a handful that serve a serious selection by the glass or bottle. ✉ *19 rue de l'Étoile, Champs-Élysées* ☎ *01–45–72–10–14.*

Hotel Daniel. A quiet haven off the Champs-Élysées? Doesn't exist, you say? At Hotel Daniel you can install yourself on overstuffed silk couch or divan and sip on a flute of champagne while having a quiet conversation until late into the night. Really. ✉ *8 rue Frédéric Bastiat, Champs-Élysée* ☎ *01–42–56–17–00* Ⓜ *George V.*

Hôtel Le Bristol. Hôtel Le Bristol attracts the rich and powerful. Cocktails are stellar, and the music is an ultrachic blend of jazz–lounge. For a pre-cocktail treat, check out the occasional mini-runway shows at teatime on the first Monday of the month. At this writing, a smaller, cosier alcove bar was due to open by 2012. ■ TIP→ Try the famous Crazy Horse cocktail or their signature raspberry puree and champagne, the Dolce Vita. ✉ *112 rue du Faubourg St-Honoré, 8e, Champs-Élysées* ☎ *01–53–43–43–00* Ⓜ *Miromesnil.*

Hôtel Plaza Athenée. Hôtel Plaza Athenée is Paris's perfectly chic chillout spot, with a sexy, glowing bar designed by Philippe Starck protégé Patrick Jouin. Gather here for an apéritif to stoke your energy before hitting the nearby club scene. It's party central during Paris Fashion Week. ■ TIP→ You'll find one of the most inventive cocktail lists in town here: try the acclaimed Rose Royale, with Alain Ducasse champagne and freshly crushed raspberries. ✉ *25 av. Montaigne, 8e, Champs-Élysées* ☎ *01–53–67–66–00* Ⓜ *Alma-Marceau.*

Le Bar. The Shangri-La Hotel's popular bar serves cocktails with a signature Asian touch. On Tuesdays and Wednesdays La Bauhinia, the hotel's restaurant, has well-attended jazz nights. ✉ *10 av. d'Iéna, Trocadéro* ☎ *01–53–67–19–98* Ⓜ *Iéna.*

Le Bar at George V. Le Bar at George V is an ultraluxe, clubby hideaway in the Four Seasons Hotel, perfect for star-gazing from the plush wine-red armchairs, cognac in hand. The charm still lures the glitterati, especially during fashion weeks. Be sure to notice the hotel's signature—and stunning—flower arrangements. ✉ *31 av. George V, 8e, Champs-Élysées* ☎ *01–49–52–70–00* Ⓜ *George V.*

17

Les Jardins du Trocadéro. Nestled in the eaves of the Trocadéro, this white and jewel-toned bar/lounge gives the monumental Place a chic new updo. Champagne by the glass, intimate seating, tasteful lighting, and light, locally-sourced, organic snacks offer a stylish alternative to the centuries-old bistros that otherwise dot the Troc. ⊠ *35 rue Benjamin-Franklin, Trocadéro/Tour Eiffel* ☎ *01–53–70–17–70* Ⓜ *Trocadéro.*

Saint James Club Paris. Like a library room out of Harry Potter, the bar at the Saint James Club Paris is studiously inviting. It's very French, and open to non-members only after 7 pm or during Sunday brunch. The owners are a venerable old Bordeaux family; accordingly, you'll find a respectable selection of champagnes and wines. ⊠ *43 av. Bugeaud, Passy, Western Paris* ☎ *01–44–05–81–82* Ⓜ *Porte Dauphine.*

White Room. The White Room is a very-of-the-moment dance club and drinks lounge in a—you guessed it—white room. Its outdoor terrace is one of the most impressive in the city, with direct views of the Eiffel Tower. ⊠ *At Maison Blanche restaurant, 15 av. Montaigne, 8e, Champs-Élysées* ☎ *01–47–23–55–99* Ⓜ *Alma-Marceau.*

CABARET

★ **Crazy Horse.** Crazy Horse has honed striptease to an elegant art. Founded in 1951 and renovated in 2007, it's renowned for gorgeous dancers and raunchy routines characterized by lots of humor and few clothes. Burlesque artist extraordinaire and fashion show regular Dita von Teese has been known to perform here, elevating the reputation of this haunt. ⊠ *12 av. George V, 8e, Champs-Élysées* ☎ *01–47–23–32–32* Ⓜ *Alma-Marceau.*

Lido. Lido stars the supercalifragilisticexpialidelicious Blubell Girls, in feathers, spangles, boas, and lots of skin. The owners claim that no show this side of Vegas rivals it for special effects. ⊠ *116 bis, av. des Champs-Élysées, 8e, Champs-Élysées* ☎ *01–40–76–56–10* Ⓜ *George V.*

CLUBS

Black Calavados. Black Calavados, known as "BC" to its trendsetting devotees, is a sleek bar where the party starts late (don't bother coming before 1 am) and lasts until morning. Ring the buzzer out front for the doorman to assess your worth—this is a celebrity hangout. Inside, try the Black Kiss, a shot of black vodka served on ice with sugar-cube lips. ■TIP➔ If all else fails, head upstairs to the smaller but equally sexy Blitz tequila bar. ⊠ *40 av. Pierre 1er de Serbie, 8e Champs-Élysées* ☎ *01–47–20–77–77* Ⓜ *Alma-Marceau or George V.*

★ **Le Baron.** Le Baron, formerly a seedy "hostesse" bar, didn't bother to update its decadent cabaret decor (red banquettes, mirror ball, and baronial top-hat sign) when it opened in 2004—and it didn't need to. Models, musicians, and Oscar winners party until morning while indulging in the bar's classic cocktail: a mix of red fruits, champagne, and vodka called the Baron Deluxe. It's notoriously difficult to get in. ⊠ *6 av. Marceau, 8e, Champs-Élysées* ☎ *01–47–20–04–01* Ⓜ *Alma-Marceau.*

Le Duplex. Le Duplex offers three rockin' rooms, all underground, each with its own character and music, from techno to vintage disco. The hot spot draws a mixed-aged group of friendly locals. ⊠ *2 bis, av. Foch, 16e, Champs-Élysées* ☎ *01–45–00–45–00* Ⓜ *Charles de Gaulle-Étoile.*

Queen. This mythic gay club of the '90s is not quite as monumental as it once was, but it still packs 'em in and the doors are still difficult to get through, especially—inevitably—on weekends. Proudly hosting a fantastic roster of top DJs, it's known for its campy soirées. These days it attracts a gay-straight mix of international partygoers eager to dance on podiums. ⊠ *102 av. des Champs-Élysées, 8e, Champs-Élysées* ☎ *01–53–89–08–90* Ⓜ *George V.*

Sens. Sens is all about the music, with a superb sound system and meticulous house DJs who spin a mix of techno and disco. Saved by its always slightly off-peak popularity, it nurtures a kind of retro superiority that continues to attract models and trendies. ⊠ *23 rue de Ponthieu, 8e, Concorde* ☎ *01–42–25–95–00.*

Showcase. Showcase takes the gold medal for best location: under the golden Pont Alexandre bridge. Inside, a long bar, two VIP sections, and a stage that hosts a diverse range of talented groups and DJs makes this a mandatory stop on any night of clubbing. ⊠ *Pont Alexandre III, 8e, Concorde* ☎ *01–45–61–25–43.*

JAZZ CLUBS
Lionel Hampton Jazz Club. Lionel Hampton Jazz Club, named for the American vibraphonist adored by Parisians, hosts a roster of international jazz musicians in a classy set of rooms. Check out the Sunday afternoon jazz brunch buffet. ⊠ *Méridien Hotel, 81 bd. Gouvion–St-Cyr, 17e, Champs-Élysées* ☎ *01–40–68–30–42* Ⓜ *Porte Maillot.*

17

EASTERN PARIS

BASTILLE/NATION
BARS
Bar Sans Nom. Bar Sans Nom is a cozy getaway in the increasing hubbub of the Bastille. The warm, red decor exudes a sultry glow, and hip lounge music adds to the charm. The flaming Kucaracha shot will turn up the heat. ⊠ *49 rue de Lappe, 11e, Bastille* ☎ *01–48–05–59–36* Ⓜ *Bastille.*

Barrio Latino. Barrio Latino rocks the rafters for adventurers who love to indulge in Latin cultures from Brazilian to Cuban in the middle of Paris. The quirky four-story hacienda-resto, two dance bars, and top-floor nightclub fuel the devoted who shake to salsa and samba beats all night. The pricey €20 weekend entrance fee includes a drink. ⊠ *46–48 rue du Faubourg St-Antoine, 12e, Bastille* ☎ *01–55–78–84–75* Ⓜ *Bastille.*

CLUBS
La Scène Bastille. La Scène Bastille is one of the more refreshing venues in the Bastille club scene, with a laid-back, eclectic crowd and a cozy (if uncreatively decorated) lounge atmosphere. A variety of theme nights keep this place interesting, especially the "Techno Sweet Peak" and "In Funk We Trust." Gay nights also attract a lively crowd. ⊠ *2 bis, rue des Taillandiers, 11e, Bastille/Nation* ☎ *01–48–06–50–70* Ⓜ *Bastille.*

Le Balajo. Le Balajo, a casual dance club in an old ballroom, has been around since 1936. Latin groove, funk, and R&B disco are the standards, with old-style musette Sunday afternoons, salsa on Tuesday and Thursday nights. Saturday is ladies' night with half-price entrance charge. ⊠ *9 rue de Lappe, 11e, Bastille* ☏ *01–47–00–07–87* Ⓜ *Bastille.*

BERCY

BARS

Folie en Tête. Folie en Tête, or "Lunacy in the Head," is a former mainstay of the Paris '70s punk scene. The comfortable interior is decorated with percussion instruments, comic books, and old skis. It's known for its reggae and jazz, not to mention the traffic light in the toilet that lets you know when it's safe to enter. ⊠ *33 rue de la Butte aux Cailles, 13e, Bercy/Tolbiac* ☏ *01–45–80–65–99* Ⓜ *Corvisart, Place d'Italie.*

CLUBS

★ **Le Batofar.** Le Batofar is an old tugboat refitted as a hip bar and concert venue. Music at this trendy yet reasonably priced spot is eclectic, from live world-beat to electronic and techno. ■**TIP**➜ (Stylish) sneakers are recommended on the slippery deck. ⊠ *Port de la Gare, 13e, Bercy/Tolbiac* ☏ *09–71–25–50–61* Ⓜ *Bibliothèque.*

Le Djoon. Le Djoon attracts a devoted dance crowd—it's not the place to stand around. With inspiration from the '80s New York house scene, the DJ mixes afro, disco, and funk. It's a taxi ride away from everywhere, but a fun diversion from the normally cramped clubs. Open Friday and Saturday from 11:30 to 5 am, and Sunday from 6 to 1 am. ⊠ *22 bd. Vincent Auriol, 13e, Bercy/Tolbiac* ☏ *01–45–70–83–49* Ⓜ *Quai de la Gare.*

CANAL ST-MARTIN

BARS

Hôtel du Nord. Hôtel du Nord starred in the classic Marcel Carné film of the same name. It's been spiffed up but still maintains its cool with a vibrant lounge-bar (and restaurant) scene in the hipster trendy Canal St-Martin district. ⊠ *102 quai de Jemmapes, 10e, Canal St-Martin* ☏ *01–40–40–78–78* Ⓜ *Goncourt.*

La Patache. La Patache On the Rue Lancry, which is loaded with bars and eateries, this bar has a wide selection of wines in a retro-inspired ambience fueled by a jukebox and candlelight that illuminates the vintage photos on the wall. ⊠ *60 rue Lancry, 10e, Canal St-Martin* ☏ *01–42–08–14–35* Ⓜ *Jacques-Bonsergent.*

OBERKAMPF

BARS

★ **Café Charbon.** Café Charbon seduces neighborhood bohos with its warm wooden Belle Époque charm and floor-to-soaring-ceiling mirrors. The attached Nouveau Casino offers cutting-edge live performances. ⊠ *109 rue Oberkampf, 11e, Oberkampf* ☏ *01–43–57–55–13* Ⓜ *St-Maur, Parmentier.*

PÈRE LACHAISE

BARS

Flèche d'Or. A bastion of rock concerts and other musical performances, this venue is just across the street from Mama Shelter, in a neighborhood some like to call the Brooklyn of Paris. ⊠ *102 bis rue Bagnolet, Père Lachaise* ☏ *01–44–64–01–02.*

Canal St-Martin

The Canal St-Martin area is one of the latest neighborhoods to become a cultural hub for up-and-coming young Parisians, offering an enriching nightlife away from the sometimes overwhelming intensity of overly hyped locations. It's a lovely residential area with a lazy charm spiced with offbeat bars, buzzy cafés, and eclectic shops. The best spots are clustered along the tree-lined canal built by Napoléon I, where barges still pass under mini-pedestrian bridges, and friends share bottles of wine along the banks. The nabe, just northeast of the Marais, is easy to get to via métro: the 3, 5, 8, 9, and 11 lines all converge at the République station.

Chez Prune was the groundbreaking establishment here, with a corner location making it perfect for people-watching. Across the canal, **Hôtel du Nord** is the current bar-restaurant hot

ticket where you might find fashion designer Christian Lacroix or graffiti artist André. It's noirishly atmospheric, with a zinc bar and velvet curtains. Note that the food is just okay; the bar is where it's at.

Bizz'Art. The Bizz'Art presents inexpensive soul concerts and renowned tango soirées every Sunday in a New York loft atmosphere. ✉ *167 quai de Valmy, 10e* ☎ *01-40-34-70-00* Ⓜ *Louis Blanc.*

Point Ephémère. The city-sponsored, vast arts center Point Ephémère helps cultivate local talent and hosts late-night electro parties once a month. The former loading dock and Art Deco warehouse offers gallery exhibits, dance performances, and young bands that are hot in every possible sense. ✉ *200 quai de Valmy, 10e* ☎ *01-40-34-02-48* Ⓜ *Jaurés/Louis Blanc.*

17

Mama Shelter. Hip Paris makes the pilgrimage to visit the Island Bar at this hotel, the happeningest spot around. Beautiful people flock here for solid cocktails, foosball, and even an adjacent pizza bar. It's always packed, but lines will be out the door on Saturdays, when DJs and other international artists perform. ✉ *109 rue de Bagnolet, Père Lachaise* ☎ *01-43-48-48-48* Ⓜ *Alexandre Dumas.*

CABARET

Le Bellevilloise. Le Bellevilloise is a multi-use exhibition space that functions as a bar, dance club, restaurant, and performance venue, with concerts, and burlesque shows. ✉ *19, 21 rue Boyer, 20e, Eastern Paris* ☎ *01-46-36-07-07* Ⓜ *Gambetta, Ménilmontant.*

RÉPUBLIQUE

BARS

Chez Prune. Chez Prune epitomizes the effortless cool so elemental to the arty hipdom that reigns in this nabe. The lively glowing, golden getaway offers the designers, architects, and journalists who gather here a prime terrace for gazing out at the fun footbridges of Canal St-Martin and the funkier locals. Open daily until 2 am. ✉ *36 rue Beaurepaire, 10e, République* ☎ *01-42-41-30-47* Ⓜ *Jacques Bonsergent.*

★ **Favela Chic.** This popular Latin cocktail bar took the scene early, forging Oberkampf's hip reputation. Back behind courtyard gates you'll find caipirinhas and mojitos, guest DJs presenting an eclectic mix of samba, soul, and hip-hop, and a nonstop dance scene. ⊠ *18 rue du Faubourg du Temple, 11e, République* ☎ *01–40–21–38–14* Ⓜ *République.*

CLUBS

La Java. La Java, the spot where Piaf and Chevalier made their names, has reinvented itself as a dance club with rock–pop and soul music. Also hosts inexpensive performances by up-and-coming bands. ⊠ *105 rue du Faubourg du Temple, 10e, République* ☎ *01–42–02–20–52* Ⓜ *Belleville, Goncourt.*

Le Gibus. Le Gibus is one of Paris's most famous music venues. More than 6,500 concerts (including the Police, Deep Purple, and Billy Idol) have packed in fans for more than 30 years. Today the Gibus's cellars are *the* place for trance, techno, and especially hip-hop. ⊠ *18 rue du Faubourg du Temple, 11e, République* ☎ *01–47–00–78–88* Ⓜ *République.*

★ **Le Nouveau Casino.** Le Nouveau Casino is a concert hall and club tucked behind the Café Charbon. Pop and rock concerts prevail during the week, with clubbing on Friday and Saturday from midnight until dawn. Electronic, house, disco, and techno DJs are the standard. ⊠ *109 rue Oberkampf, 11e, République* ☎ *01–43–57–57–40* Ⓜ *Parmentier.*

Pop-In. On a back street just off the Boulevard Beaumarchais (which links the Bastille to République), this dark, hard-partying boho playhouse has a pronounced English-rocker feel. ⊠ *105 rue Amelot, 4e, République* ☎ *01–48–05–56–11* Ⓜ *St-Sebastien–Froissart.*

LATIN QUARTER

BARS

Cap Rouge. Eighties pop music plays in the glowing red interior and a young crowd rushes the bar for happy-hour specials until 10. Three-euro pints and an array of classic cocktails lead to dancing in the cellar where the DJ takes over. ⊠ *23 rue Mouffetard, 5e, Latin Quarter* ☎ *01–47–07–61–02* Ⓜ *Place Monge.*

Curio Parlor. Hidden away on a quiet street on the eastern end of the Latin Quarter, this low-lit speakeasy created by the team from the Experimental Cocktail Club has that establishment's same creative libations, in an Art Deco setting of emerald velour, curtained niches, and taxidermied animals. Regular Japanese whiskey tastings in the lower level bar. ⊠ *16 rue des Bernadins, 5e, Latin Quarter* ☎ *01–44–07–12–47* Ⓜ *Maubert.*

Delmas. Delmas attracts a buzzing crowd with its comfy leather couches, exposed brick walls, and trompe l'oeil bookcases inside this bar-café-resto. ⊠ *2/4 pl. de la Contrescarpe, 5e, Latin Quarter* ☎ *01–43–26–51–26* Ⓜ *Cardinal Lemoine.*

Qui Êtes-Vous, Polly Maggoo?. Qui Êtes-Vous, Polly Maggoo? is a convivial hangout legendary as the student rioters' unofficial HQ during the May '68 uprising and named after the satirical French art-house movie about a supermodel. Weekends are wild, with drinks at the wacky tile bar and live Latino music that keeps the party thumping until morning. ⊠ *3–5 rue du Petit Pont, 5e, Latin Quarter* ☎ *01–46–33–33–64* Ⓜ *St-Michel.*

CABARET

★ **Paradis Latin.** Paradis Latin peppers its quirky show with acrobatics and eye-popping lighting effects, in a building by Gustav Eiffel, making it the liveliest and trendiest cabaret on the Left Bank. It's closed Tuesday. ✉ *28 rue du Cardinal Lemoine, 5e, Latin Quarter* ☎ *01–43–25–28–28* Ⓜ *Cardinal Lemoine.*

JAZZ CLUBS

Caveau de la Huchette. Caveau de la Huchette is one of the few surviving cellar clubs from the 1940s. It boasts the "best boppers" in the city, and packs 'em in for swing dancing and Dixieland tunes. It's a killer jazz spot for everyone but claustrophobics. The music continues till dawn Thursday to Saturday. ✉ *5 rue de la Huchette, 5e, Latin Quarter* ☎ *01–43–26–65–05* Ⓜ *St-Michel.*

Le Petit Journal. Le Petit Journal, with two locations, has long attracted great French and international jazz names. It specializes in big band (Montparnasse) and Dixieland (St-Michel) jazz, with dinner served from 8:30 to midnight. ✉ *71 bd. St-Michel, 5e, Latin Quarter* ☎ *01–43–26–28–59* Ⓜ *Luxembourg* ✉ *13 rue du Commandant-Mouchotte, 14e, Montparnasse* ☎ *01–43–21–56–70* Ⓜ *Montparnasse–Bienvenüe.*

MARAIS

17

BARS

Andy Wahloo. Andy Wahloo has a hip crowd and an Andy Warhol-meets-*Casablanca* decor. Fans of the ginger-rum Wahloo *spéciales* relax on oversize paint-can stools beneath high-kitsch silk-screened Moroccan coffee ads, and listen to funky Arabic Raï remixes. Dancing to DJs starts later in the night. ✉ *69 rue des Gravilliers, 3e, Marais* ☎ *01–42–71–20–38* Ⓜ *Arts et Métiers.*

Auld Alliance. Auld Alliance has Scottish shields on the walls, and the bar staff dresses in kilts for special events. There are more than 120 whiskeys, Scottish beer, soccer, and rugby on TV, and sometimes live music. ✉ *80 rue François Miron, 4e, Marais* ☎ *01–48–04–30–40* Ⓜ *St-Paul.*

La Belle Hortense. La Belle Hortense is heaven for anyone who ever wished they had a book in a bar (or a drink in a bookstore). The *bar litteraire* is the infamous spot where gal-about-town Catherine M. launched her *vie sexuelle* that became a baudy bestseller. ✉ *31 rue Vielle-du-Temple, 4e, Marais* ☎ *01–48–04–74–60* Ⓜ *St-Paul.*

★ **La Perle.** La Perle is a bustling, buzzy Marais masterpiece, where straights, gays, and lesbians of all types come to mingle. The crowd makes this place interesting, not the neon lights, diner-style seats, or stripped-down decor. It continues to pack in some of the city's fashion movers and shakers from midafternoon on. ✉ *78 rue Vielle-du-Temple, 3e, Marais* ☎ *01–42–72–69–93* Ⓜ *Chemin-Vert.*

Le Trésor. Le Trésor is lively and sophisticated, with mismatched Baroque furnishings in a large space and a chill vibe on a tiny street a tad separate from the sometimes madding crowd of the Marais. ✉ *7 rue du Trésor, 4e, Marais* ☎ *01–42–71–35–17* Ⓜ *St-Paul.*

Max y Jeremy. Just up the street from the old-world Carreau du Temple covered market is the second location of this hip tapas bar (the first is at 30 rue St-Saveur, 2e, 01–40–28–03–81). Inside, an almost-too-cool crowd can be found in the red emberlike interior, drinking cocktails and eating the sultry bite-sized *pintxos* of the Basque country. There's a distinctly party atmosphere, which can spill into the street, especially in summer. ⊠ *6 rue Dupuis, 3e, Marais* 🕾 *01–42–78–00–68* Ⓜ *Temple.*

GAY AND LESBIAN BARS AND CLUBS

3W Kafé. 3W, as in "Women With Women," is a pillar of the lesbian scene. ⊠ *8 rue des Ecouffes, 4e, Marais* 🕾 *01–48–87–39–26* Ⓜ *St-Paul.*

Café Cox. Café Cox is a prime gay pickup joint. Behind the frosted glass windows of the fire-engine red hotspot, men appraise the talent. ⊠ *15 rue des Archives, 4e, Marais* 🕾 *01–42–72–08–00* Ⓜ *Hôtel de Ville.*

★ **L'Open Café.** L'Open Café is a relaxed, packed Marais favorite with a disco-café vibe that draws suits to punks and is less of a gay meat market than neighboring Café Cox. ⊠ *17 rue des Archives, 4e, Marais* 🕾 *01–42–72–26–18* Ⓜ *Hôtel de Ville.*

Les Bains-Douches. Les Bains-Douches is an institution that has evolved into one of the hottest gay clubs in the city on Friday through Sunday nights—think Studio 54 à la gay français. There are theme nights and guest DJs; be prepared for a wild time. ⊠ *7 rue du Bourg-l'Abbé, 3e, Marais* 🕾 *01–53–01–40–60* Ⓜ *Étienne Marcel.*

Raidd Bar. Raidd Bar is popular and friendly, with a darker downstairs bar and potent drinks. The men are hot, and so is the steamy shower show presented after 11 pm—not for timid voyeurs. ⊠ *23 rue du Temple, 3e, Marais* 🕾 *01–42–77–04–88* Ⓜ *Hôtel de Ville, St-Paul.*

So What!. So What! is a happening lesbian bar that welcomes all comers (including small groups of men) to this popular spot in the heart of the gay district. The DJ in the tiny basement cooks on Friday and Saturday nights. ⊠ *30 rue du Roi de Sicile, 4e, Marais* Ⓜ *St-Paul.*

Tango. Tango has carefully safeguarded its dance-hall origins and lures a friendly mixed crowd of gays, lesbians, and "open minded" heteros. Late-night music is mostly French and American pop, but before midnight, the DJ plays classic chansons (French torch songs), so arrive early to waltz and swing! ⊠ *11 rue au Maire, 3e, Marais* 🕾 *01–42–72–17–78* Ⓜ *Arts et Métiers.*

MONTMARTRE

BARS

Café la Fourmi. Café la Fourmi is one of Pigalle's trendiest addresses, with a funky spacious bar-café where cool locals party. ⊠ *74 rue des Martyrs, 18e, Montmartre* 🕾 *01–42–64–70–35* Ⓜ *Pigalle.*

★ **Chào Bà Café.** Chào Bà Café transports colonial French Indochine to the foot of Montmartre with a glam gold interior, comfy bamboo chairs on two floors, and exotic drinks like the popular Kamikaze. DJs mix it up with techno and lounge music weekends. ⊠ *22 bd. de Clichy, 18e, Montmartre* 🕾 *01–46–06–72–90* Ⓜ *Pigalle.*

The Paradis Latin cabaret is one of the liveliest spots on the Left Bank.

Le Rendez-Vous Des Amis. Le Rendez-Vous Des Amis is an intriguing midway breather if you climb the hill of Montmartre by foot. There's a jovial staff, eclectic music, and a century's worth of previous patrons immortalized in photos. ⊠ *23 rue Gabrielle, 18e, Montmartre* ☎ *01–46–06–01–60* Ⓜ *Abbesses.*

Le Sancerre. Le Sancerre, a café by day, turns into an essential watering hole for Montmartrois and artists at night, with Belgian beers on tap and an impressive list of cocktails. It was spruced up in 2007 but still maintains its traditional old-school vibe. ⊠ *35 rue des Abbesses, 18e, Montmartre* ☎ *01–42–58–08–20* Ⓜ *Abbesses.*

CABARET

Fodor's Choice ★ **Au Lapin Agile.** Au Lapin Agile is an authentic survivor from the 19th century, and considers itself the doyen of cabarets. Founded in 1860, it still inhabits a modest house, once a favorite subject of painter Maurice Utrillo. It became the home-away-from-home for Braque, Modigliani, Apollinaire, and Picasso—who once paid for a meal with one of his paintings, then promptly exited and painted another that he named after this place. There are no topless dancers—this is a genuine French cabaret with songs, poetry, and humor (in French) in a publike setting. Entry €24. ⊠ *22 rue des Saules, 18e, Montmartre* ☎ *01–46–06–85–87* Ⓜ *Lamarck Caulaincourt.*

Michou. Michou presents an over-the-top show by the always-decked-out-in-blue owner Michou. The show features "tranformiste" men on stage in extravagant drag, performing with high camp for a radically different cabaret experience. Dinner shows are €105 and €135, or you can watch from the bar for €35, which includes a drink. ⊠ *80 rue des Martyrs, 18e, Montmartre* ☎ *01–46–06–16–04* Ⓜ *Pigalle.*

Moulin Rouge. Moulin Rouge offered a circuslike atmosphere when it opened in 1889, and lured Parisians of all social stripes including, of course, the famous Toulouse-Lautrec, who immortalized the venue and the dancers in his paintings. Think elephants, donkey rides for the ladies, and the incomparable French cancan revue. Today the cancan is still a popular highlight of what is now a classy version of a Vegas-y show, starring 100 dancers, acrobats, ventriloquists, and contortionists, and more than 1,000 costumes. Dinner starts at 7, revues at 9 and 11 (arrive 30 minutes early). Men are expected to wear a jacket and tie. Prices range from €95 for just a revue to €200 for luxe dinner and a show. ⊠ *82 bd. de Clichy, 18e, Montmartre* ☎ *01–53–09–82–82* Ⓜ *Blanche.*

CLUBS
L'Élysée Montmartre. L'Élysée Montmartre rocks the rafters of an old concert hall with music that runs the gamut of hits from the 1940s to 1980s (emphasis on the latter); the DJ is backed by a 10-piece orchestra. ⊠ *72 bd. de Rochechouart, 18e, Montmartre* ☎ *01–44–92–45–47* Ⓜ *Anvers.*

Le Folie's Pigalle. This former cabaret is decorated like a '30s-era bordello. It cultivates a decadent ambience, with music that ranges from house and techno to R&B and electro. After-parties hop on Sunday morning. ⊠ *11 pl. Pigalle, 9e, Montmartre* ☎ *01–48–78–55–25* Ⓜ *Pigalle.*

GAY AND LESBIAN BARS AND CLUBS
Chez Moune. Chez Moune is the former lesbian cabaret now run by the same team as Le Baron—expect the same strict door policy—with regular DJs and aftershow parties that keep the devoted dancing until dawn. ⊠ *54 rue Jean-Baptise Pigalle, 9e, Pigalle* ☎ *01–45–26–64–64* Ⓜ *Pigalle.*

JAZZ CLUBS
Bar le Houdon. Bar le Houdon transforms from humdrum café to warm jazz venue Friday and Saturday. The musicians are top-notch and the price is right. ⊠ *5 rue des Abbesses, 18e, Montmartre* ☎ *01–42–62–21–34* Ⓜ *Abbesses.*

MONTPARNASSE

BARS
★ **American Bar at La Closerie des Lilas.** American Bar at La Closerie des Lilas lets you drink in the swirling action of the adjacent restaurant and brasserie at a piano bar hallowed by plaques honoring such former habitués as Man Ray, Jean-Paul Sartre, Samuel Beckett, and Ernest Hemingway, who talks of "the Lilas" in *A Moveable Feast.* ⊠ *171 bd. du Montparnasse, 6e, Montparnasse* ☎ *01–40–51–34–50* Ⓜ *Montparnasse.*

Le Rosebud. Step into Le Rosebud through the Art Nouveau front door of this one-time haunt of Jean-Paul Sartre and you're instantly immersed in the dark, moody, fourth dimension of Old Montparnasse, where white-jacketed servers and red-lacquered tables transport you into the past. ⊠ *11 bis, rue Delambre, 14e, Montparnasse* ☎ *01–43–35–38–54* Ⓜ *Vavin.*

CLUBS

La Coupole. La Coupole, the gorgeous dance hall beneath the famous brasserie, has "Latin Fever" nights on Friday from 7:45 pm (for beginners) until dawn. Saturday has the popular "Re-Definition" night of hip-hop, R&B, and afro-zouk from 11:30. ☒ *100 bd. du Montparnasse, 14e, Montparnasse* ☎ *01–43–20–14–20* Ⓜ *Vavin.*

Le Red Light. Le Red Light has two giant dance floors playing mainly house and electronic music by big-name, international DJs every Friday and Saturday from midnight until dawn. It draws a casual, mixed crowd. ☒ *34 rue du Départ, 15e, Montparnasse* ☎ *01–42–79–94–53* Ⓜ *Montparnasse Bienvenüe.*

OPÉRA/GRANDS BOULEVARDS

BARS

Barramundi. Barramundi lures the city's nouveau-riche chic, who chill to electro-lounge tunes and world music in the cool gold ambience, and sip tropical drinks like piña coladas and the exotically dubbed "sex on the beach" cocktail at the long copper bar. ☒ *3 rue Taitbout, 9e, Opéra/ Grands Boulevards* ☎ *01–47–70–21–21* Ⓜ *Richelieu Drouot.*

Café Oz. Café Oz zips you Down Under to big-screen soccer and rugby games amid Aussie expats. There are several locations around Paris. ☒ *8 bd. Montmartre, 9e, Grands Boulevards* ☎ *01–47–70–18–52* Ⓜ *Grands Boulevards.*

★ **Corcoran's Irish Pub.** This roomy pub, with several locations in central Paris, has an ample menu, a gorgeous bar, and old-timey photos and quotations on the walls—such as "He who opens his mouth most is the one who opens his purse least." Conversation turns to dancing at night with a regulated guy-to-girl ratio, so men shouldn't try coming alone. ☒ *23 bd. Poissonière, 2e, Grands Boulevards* ☎ *01–40–39–00– 16* Ⓜ *Grands Boulevards.*

Fodor'sChoice **Delaville Café.** Delaville Café cultivates a funky baroque ambience, with
★ its huge, heated sidewalk terrace, Belle Époque mosaic-tile bar, graffiti'd walls, and swishy lounge. It's the anchor of the bustling Grands Boulevards scene, so arrive early on weekends if you want a seat. ☒ *34 bd. Bonne Nouvelle, 10e, Opéra/Grands Boulevards* ☎ *01–48–24–48–09* Ⓜ *Bonne Nouvelle, Grands Boulevards.*

Duke's Bar. A favorite not just for its prestige location between Opéra and Place Vendôme, but also for its worn leather chairs and English private club feel, the Westminster Hotel's bar offers drinks like the "James Bond" and "Duke's Martini." At times you get the feeling that Mr. Hercule Poirot is lurking just behind that wingback chair. ☒ *13, rue de la Paix, Opéra* ☎ *01–42–61–55–11* Ⓜ *Opéra.*

★ **Harry's New York Bar.** Harry's New York Bar is a cozy, wood-paneled hangout decorated with dusty college pennants; it's popular with expatriates and American-loving French people who welcome the ghosts of Ernest Hemingway and F. Scott Fitzgerald, who drank himself unconscious here. Bartenders mix a mean Bloody Mary. The legendary spot was founded in 1911, and Gershwin composed "An American in Paris"

17

CLOSE UP

After-Hours Restaurants

Craving steak au poivre after a post-midnight party? Most late-night brasseries and 'round-the-clock restaurants don't need reservations. Here are some of the best.

Á la Cloche d'Or. This Paris classic, whose traditional French dishes satisfied the likes of the late president François Mitterrand and Moulin Rouge dancers (though not together), is open until 4 am every day but Sunday. It also shuts down in August. ⊠ *3 rue Mansart, 9e, Montmartre* ☎ *01–48–74–48–88* Ⓜ *Place de Clichy.*

Au Chien Qui Fume. Au Chien Qui Fume, open until 2 am, is a picturesque spot founded in 1740 and decorated with drôle, old master–style paintings of smoking dogs. Traditional French cuisine and seafood platters are served until closing. ⊠ *33 rue du Pont-Neuf, 1er, Louvre/Tuileries* ☎ *01–42–36–07–42* Ⓜ *Les Halles.*

Au Pied de Cochon. Au Pied de Cochon once catered to the all-night workers at the adjacent Les Halles food market. Its Second Empire carvings have been restored, and traditional dishes like pig's trotters and chitterling sausage still grace the menu. And you haven't tasted pig's trotters until you've tasted them at 6 am. This place is nothing less than an institution, and it's open 24 hours daily. ⊠ *6 rue Coquillière, 1er, Beaubourg/Les Halles* ☎ *01–40–13–77–00* Ⓜ *Les Halles.*

Grand Café Capucines. Grand Café Capucines has an exuberant pseudo–Belle Époque dining room that matches the bustling mood of the neighboring Opéra; it serves excellent oysters, fish, and meat dishes at hefty prices, and is open around the clock. ⊠ *4 bd. des Capucines, 9e, Opéra/* Grands Boulevards ☎ *01–43–12–19–00* Ⓜ *Opéra.*

Le Bienvenu. Le Bienvenu doesn't look like much (notice the kitsch mural on the back wall), but it serves simple French food and couscous in the wee hours of the morning until 6 am. ⊠ *42 rue d'Argout, 2e, Louvre/Tuileries* ☎ *01–42–33–31–08* Ⓜ *Louvre.*

Le Théâtre Saint-Germain. This two-story rococo salon, formerly Le Lup, is sultry and intimate, with red velvet and soft lights. The Asian-influenced French cuisine lures the post-opera and theater set, and there's a resident DJ on weekends. ⊠ *2–4 rue du Sabot, 6e, St-Germain-des-Prés* ☎ *01–45–48–86–47.*

Le Tambour. Le Tambour wins hands-down for wackiness and flea-market charm. The eye-catching decor includes everything but the proverbial kitchen sink. The food's especially fine here—think onion soup, foie gras, steak tartare, and confit de canard. Open 6 pm–6 am; last dinner service at 3:30 am. ⊠ *41 rue Montmartre, 2e, Beaubourg/Les Halles* ☎ *01–42–33–06–90* Ⓜ *Étienne Marcel, Les Halles.*

Les Coulisses. Les Coulisses, near picturesque Place du Tertre, has more character than most late-night restaurants, with red banquettes and 18th-century Venetian mirrors that make it look like an Italian theater. The food—traditional French—is served until 2 am. There's a club in the basement, open Thursday to Saturday, where dancers work up a late-night appetite. ⊠ *1 rue St-Rustique, 18e, Montmartre* ☎ *01–42–62–89–99* Ⓜ *Abbesses.*

in the piano bar downstairs. ✉ *5 rue Daunou, 2e, Opéra/Grands Boulevards* ☎ *01–42–61–71–14* Ⓜ *Opéra.*

Kitty O'Shea's. Kitty O'Shea's is an ever-popular Irish pub near the Place Vendôme that draws a posh after-work crowd as well as salt-of-the-earth punters. Authentic trimmings like stained glass and Gaelic street signs are decor highlights, and a hearty restaurant serves burgers and fish-and-chips. There are rugby games on the big screen in season, as well as quiz night every Wednesday, and other theme nights. ✉ *10 rue des Capucines, 2e, Opéra* ☎ *01–40–15–00–30* Ⓜ *Opéra.*

Le Bar Long. At the Royal Monceau's innovative bar your mixologist will fix your drink right next to you at the illuminated long table. The collection of glasses on the walls isn't just decoration—you may choose which to drink from, if you wish. ✉ *37 av. Hoche, Parc Monceau* ☎ *01–42–99–88–00.*

No Comment. This newly renovated nightclub is housed in a former swinger's club and boasts that it has retained the libertine vibe without the libertine ways. Only the trendiest seem to go . . . and get in. ✉ *36 rue de Ponthieu, 8e, Champs-Élysées* ☎ *01–43–59–23–95.*

Silencio Club. David Lynch named his nightclub after a reference to his Oscar hit, *Mulholland Drive.* Silencio Club, whose buzzwords are secret and mysterious, made a splash from the start. The club, which puts up concerts, films, and other performances, is open only to members and their guests until midnight; after that, theoretically, everyone is allowed. ✉ *142 rue Montmartre, Grands Boulevards.*

17

CABARET

★ **Le Limonaire.** Le Limonaire oozes Parisian charm and serves food until 10 pm Tuesday–Sunday before giving way to the singing of traditional French songs of "expression," with musical accompaniment *bien sûr.* There's no entrance fee; musicians pass the hat. ✉ *18 cité Bergère, 9e, Opéra/Grands Boulevards* ☎ *01–45–23–33–33* Ⓜ *Grands Boulevards.*

CLUBS

★ **Le Rex.** Le Rex is a temple of techno and house, popular with students and open Wednesday through Sunday. One of France's most famous DJs, Laurent Garnier, is sometimes at the turntables. ✉ *5 bd. Poissonnière, 2e, Opéra/Grands Boulevards* ☎ *01–42–36–10–96* Ⓜ *Grands Boulevards.*

Scop Club. Formerly le Scopitone and re-christened le Scop Club in late 2011, the venue hosts rock concerts, electro-rock, and folk bands as well as DJ sets until 5 am most nights. Their motto: "We eat, we listen, we look." ✉ *5 av. de l'Opéra, 2e, Opéra* ☎ *01–42–60–64–45* Ⓜ *Pyramides.*

JAZZ CLUBS

Fodor's Choice ★ **New Morning.** New Morning is the premier spot for serious fans of avant-garde jazz, folk, and world music. The look is spartan, the mood reverential. ✉ *7 rue des Petites-Ecuries, 10e, Opéra/Grands Boulevards* ☎ *01–45–23–51–41* Ⓜ *Château d'Eau.*

CLOSE UP

Jazz Clubs

The French fell hard for jazz nearly a century ago, during World War I, but the real *coup de foudre*—literally "lightning bolt" or figuratively "love at first sight"—came after the war when Yank sax man Sidney Bechet and 19-year-old song-and-dance vamp Josephine Baker of St. Louis joined a European tour of the Revue Nègre musical. Baker, or the "Black Venus that haunted Baudelaire," as she was known by French critics, instantly became the sweetheart of Paris. Note: a larger-than-life picture of Baker wearing only a smile, a string of pearls, and a thigh-high skirt today adorns a wall of historic photographs along the platform of the Tuileries métro.

By 1934 France had created its own impressive claim to jazz fame, the all-string Quintette du Hot Club de France, which featured Gypsy guitarist Django Reinhardt and his partner, violinist Stéphane Grappelli. They, in turn, influenced string players from country musicians to Carlos Santana. Reinhardt performed throughout much of World War II in the underground French jazz scene. In the 1950s Paris grew to become a major destination of the bebop diaspora, and expat jazz musicians including Bechet, Bud Powell, and Dexter Gordon played the venues along with such jazz greats as Dizzy Gillespie, Charlie Parker, and Miles Davis. France embraced the evolving jazz sound that many Americans were still struggling to accept and provided a worshipful welcome to musicians battling discrimination at home. In Paris, Davis said, he was "treated like a human being."

WANT TO EXPERIENCE A NIGHT OF JAZZ YOURSELF?
The French obsession with jazz continues to this day, and travelers seeking a quintessential Parisian experience have the opportunity to hear jazz artists from all over the world nearly any night of the week. Aficionados can choose from traditional jazz to the latest experimental efforts, in clubs ranging from casual to chichi, sedate to hopping. Many venues present a wide range of music: a good option is the double club on Rue des Lombards near Les Halles: Le Sunside specializes in more traditional jazz, and its downstairs sister, Le Sunset, features edgier options.

Music generally begins after 9 pm, so plan accordingly. You can dine at some of the clubs, including Le Petit Journal Montparnasse, or in the Hotel Méridien on the Champs-Élysées, which houses the classy Lionel Hampton Jazz Club.

As everywhere else in the city, the French folks at the clubs tend to dress more stylishly than the average traveler with a limited wardrobe, but they're generally a tolerant bunch, particularly in venues frequented by students and in the heart of tourist areas like Caveau de la Huchette, a hot cellar dance club across the river from Notre-Dame. Keep in mind, though, that the French are serious about their jazz: with a few exceptions, the audience is generally focused and quiet during performances.

Recognizable names to watch for include expat Yank flute and sax man Bobby Rangell and singer Sara Lazarus, and much-loved French musicians like the pianists Alain Jean-Marie and Pierre de Bethman, sax man Didier Malherbe, and Olivier Ker Ourio on the harmonica. You might want to check out a jazz style you're less likely to find at home, though, like the latest iteration of Gypsy musette—a distinctive, swing-infused interpretation of old Paris dance music—presented by virtuosos like accordionist Richard Galliano, violinist Didier Lockwood, and the guitar-picking Ferre brothers, Boulou and Elios. Look for them at Duc Des Lombards.

The best place to find out what's playing and even purchase tickets is at ⊕ www.infoconcert.com or on club websites, some of which offer English versions. *Pariscope, Jazz Magazine,* and *Jazz Hot,* available at newsstands, also have listings in French. Reservations can be critical, especially for leading U.S. jazz musicians.

Entrance charges are rarely more than €20 and often less. Some venues have free jam sessions, depending on the night, so check listings. Drink prices can be sky-high, but most table staff won't harass budget-conscious customers nursing a single drink.

Another way to experience a variety of top-quality jazz is by attending world-renowned Paris festivals that run from early spring through September, including the **Banlieues Bleues** (☎ 01–49–22–10–10 ⊕ www. banlieuesbleues.org), the **Paris Jazz Festival** (☎ 01–48–72–32–97 ⊕ www. parisjazzfestival.fr), and the **Villette Jazz Festival** (☎ 01–44–84–44–84 ⊕ www.citedelamusique.fr).

WORD OF MOUTH
"OK, if I were hip . . . and wanted jazz . . . I'd stay in the 10th and find my way to New Morning jazz club."
—SuzieC

17

ST-GERMAIN-DES-PRÉS

BARS

★ **Alcazar.** Alcazar is Sir Terence Conran's makeover of a 17th-century Parisian *jeu de paume* court that features a stylish mezzanine-level bar under a greenhouse-glass roof. The vibe changes from Wednesday to Saturday as spicy DJs spin mixes into the wee hours. ⊠ *62 rue Mazarine, 6e, St-Germain-des-Prés* ☎ *01–53–10–19–99* Ⓜ *Odéon.*

Bar du Marché. Bar du Marché is a local legend where waiters wearing red overalls and revolutionary "Gavroche" hats serve drinks every day of the week, with particular zeal around happy hour. With bottles of wine at about €25, it draws a quintessential Left Bank mix of expat locals, fashion-house interns, and even some professional rugby players. Sit outside on the terrace and enjoy the prime corner location. ⊠ *16 rue de Buci, 6e, St-Germain/Buci* ☎ *01–43–26–55–15* Ⓜ *Mabillon/Odeon.*

Chez Georges. Chez Georges has been serving red wine, pastis, and beer for the past 60-odd years in pretty much the same *caveau* that still packs in devotees today. Older students and locals fill sofas and crowd around tiny tables glowing with candles in the cellar bar before grinding to pulsing world music all night. ⊠ *11 rue de Canettes, 6e, St-Germain-des-Prés* ☎ *01–43–26–79–15* Ⓜ *Mabillon.*

★ **L'Hôtel.** L'Hôtel offers an exquisite, hushed Baroque hideaway bar that makes for the perfect discreet rendezvous. Designed in typically jaw-dropping Jacques Garcia style, it boasts a photo of a louche Keanu Reeves on the wall and evokes the decadent spirit of one-time resident Oscar Wilde. ⊠ *13 rue des Beaux-Arts, 6e, St-Germain-des-Prés* ☎ *01–44–41–99–00* Ⓜ *St-Germain-des-Prés.*

CLUBS

Chez Castel. Chez Castel is the swankiest of private Paris clubs: a three-story gold-and-red-velvet mansion with vaulted ceilings where celebrities like Monica Bellucci and Vincent Cassel cavort far from the St-Germain tourists. Making reservations at the two dining rooms (one more formal than the other) will ease your entry. ⊠ *15 rue Princesse, 6e, St-Germain-des-Prés* ☎ *01–40–51–52–80* Ⓜ *St-Germain-des-Prés, Mabillon.*

Le Montana. Notoriously difficult to get past the doorman since it opened with a redesign by Vincent Darre during Fashion Week in 2009, this sleek St-Germain club owned by French nightlife king André (Le Baron) has a Studio 54 vibe and enormous cocktails. It's frequented by models, actors, artists, and Parisian playboys. ⊠ *28 rue St-Benoît, 6e, St-Germain-des-Prés* ☎ *01–44–39–71–00* Ⓜ *St-Germain-des-Prés, Mabillon.*

WAGG. WAGG is tucked beneath the popular bar-resto Alcazar, in a vaulted stone cellar that was Jim Morrison's hangout back in its '70s incarnation as the Whiskey-a-Go-Go. It's now a welcoming dance club featuring vintage disco, funk, groove, and salsa (the latter on Sunday nights, with classes that start at 3:30 pm, with state-of-the-art sound, lighting, and guest DJs. ⊠ *62 rue Mazarine, 6e, St-Germain-des-Prés* ☎ *01–55–42–22–01* Ⓜ *Odéon.*

Performing Arts

WORD OF MOUTH

"If you're interested in the Garnier opera house you might want to see a performance. There's a wide variety of ticket prices including cheap ones. Usually it's ballets at the Garnier but they do operas there occasionally as well as musical concerts."

—Apres_Londee

Updated by
Paige Donner

The performing-arts scene in Paris runs the gamut from highbrow to lowbrow, cheap (or free) to break-the-bank expensive. Venues are indoors and outdoors, opulent or spartan, and dress codes vary accordingly. Regardless of the performance you choose, it's unlikely to be like anything you've seen before. Parisians have an audacious sense of artistic adventure and a stunning eye for scene and staging. An added bonus in this city of classic beauty is that many of the venues themselves—from the opulent interior of the Opéra Garnier to the Art Deco splendor of the Théâtre des Champs-Élysées—are a feast for the eyes.

One thing that sets Paris apart in the arts world is the active participation of the Ministry of Culture, which sponsors numerous concert halls and theaters, like the Comédie Française, that tend to present less commercial, though artistically captivating, productions. Other theaters, like the Théâtre de Marigny and Palais de Chaillot, are known for sold-out shows and decade-long production runs.

Most performances are in French, although you can find English theater productions. English-language movies are often presented undubbed, with subtitles. Of course, you don't need to speak the language to enjoy opera, classical music, dance, or the circus.

PLANNING

FESTIVALS

The music and theater season generally runs from September to June, but summer is packed with all sorts of performing arts festivals.

Orangerie de Bagatelle. The annual Chopin Festival is a highlight at the picturesque Orangerie de Bagatelle in late June and early July. ⊠ *Parc* *de Bagatelle, Allée de Longchamp, 16e, Bois de Boulogne* ☎ *01–45– 00–22–19* ✉ *Free; €5 special exhibits* ⊙ *Open year round* Ⓜ *Porte Maillot, then Bus 244.*

Parc Floral. Free outdoor classical concerts lure fans to the Parc Floral of the Bois de Vincennes on August and September weekends at 4 (entrance to the park is €5). This is also the spot that hosts the Paris Jazz Festival each weekend in summer. ☎ *01–49–57–24–84* ⊕ *www. parcfloraldeparis.com.*

Quartier d'Eté. The Quartier d'Eté festival in July and August, held throughout Paris, attracts international stars of dance, classical music, and jazz. ☎ *01–44–94–98–00* ⊕ *www.quartierdete.com.*

Rock-en-Seine. Rock-en-Seine is a three-day rock festival held every August on the outskirts of Paris. It's one of the largest of its kind in France; past international headliners include Massive Attack, My Chemical Romance, Arcade Fire, Offspring, and Foo Fighters. ✉ *Domaine National de St-Cloud, Parc de St-Cloud* ⊕ *www.rockenseine.com.*

Villette Jazz Festival. The annual Villette Jazz Festival is held at the Parc de La Villette every fall. ✉ *211 av. Jean-Jaurès* ☎ *01–40–03–75–75* ⊕ *www.villette.com.*

TICKET PRICES AND DISCOUNTS

As anywhere it's best to buy event tickets in advance.

Events range in price from about €5 for standing room at the Opéra Bastille or €7 for a circus performance to upward of €180 for an elaborate National Opéra production. Most performances, however, are in the €15–€25 range. Discounts are often available for limited-visibility seats, students, and senior citizens. Movies cost about €6–€10.50, but many cinemas have reduced rates on Monday or Wednesday.

Kiosques Théâtre. Half-price tickets for same-day theater performances are available at the Kiosques Théâtre, open Tuesday to Saturday 12:30 to 8 and Sunday 12:30 to 4. ✉ *Across from 15 pl. de la Madeleine, Opéra/Grands Boulevards* Ⓜ *Madeleine* ✉ *Outside Gare Montparnasse, Pl. Raoul Dautry, Montparnasse* Ⓜ *Montparnasse, Bienvenüe* ✉ *Pl. des Ternes, Champs-Élysées* Ⓜ *Ternes.*

Half-price tickets are also available at many theaters during the first week of each new show, and inexpensive tickets are often available at the last minute.

FNAC (⊕ *www.fnacspectacles.com*) and Virgin Megastores (⊕ *www. virginmega.fr*) sell tickets in stores and online. Both have locations on the Champs-Élysées and branches in other neighborhoods.

WHERE TO GET INFO

Detailed entertainment listings in French can be found in the weekly magazines *Pariscope* and *L'Officiel des Spectacles*, available at newsstands and in bookstores; in the Wednesday entertainment insert *Figaroscope*, in the *Figaro* newspaper (⊕ *www.scope.lefigaro.fr/ theatres-spectacles*); and in the weekly *À Nous Paris*, distributed free in the métro. The webzine *Paris Voice* (⊕ *www.parisvoice.com*) offers superb highlights in English. Most performing arts venues also have their own websites, and many include listings and other helpful information in English.

The website of the Paris Tourist Office (⊕ *www.parisinfo.com*) has theater and music listings in English.

CIRCUS

Italian Antonio Franconi helped launch the first Cirque Olympique, considered the start of the modern circus, in Paris in 1783—and the French have been hooked ever since. Circus acts are cherished as high art in Paris—for all ages. The city boasts a 19th-century permanent circus theater and sprouts tents in every major park to present spectacles from the sublime to the quirky.

CONCERTS

There's something majestic about listening to classical music under the airy roof of a medieval stained-glass church, where many free or almost-free lunchtime and evening concerts are performed. Check weekly listings and flyers posted at the churches for information.

Museums also host classical concerts; tickets are usually sold separately from admission. The Auditorium du Louvre presents chamber music, string quartets, and a special series of promising new musicians on Thursday; the Musée du Moyen-Age stages medieval music concerts between October and July, including the free *l'Heure Musicale* on Sunday at 4 and Monday at 12:30; and the Musée d'Orsay often offers small-scale concerts in the lower-level auditorium.

DANCE

Classical ballet takes the stage in Paris in places as varied as the historic Opéra Garnier and the Grand Palais. More avant-garde or up-and-coming choreographers tend to show their works off in the smaller performance spaces of the Bastille and the Marais, and in theaters in nearby suburbs. And of course there's the Centre National de Danse.

MOVIES

The French call films the *septième art* (seventh art), and discuss the latest releases with the same intensity as they do gallery openings or theatrical debuts. Most theaters run English-language films undubbed, with subtitles. VO means *version originale*; films that are dubbed are VF (*version française*). First-run cinemas are clustered around the principal tourist areas, such as the Champs-Élysées, Boulevard des Italiens near the Opéra, Bastille, Châtelet, and Odéon. For listings online check ⊕ *www.allocine.fr*.

THEATER

A number of theaters line the Grands Boulevards between the Opéra and République, but there is no Paris equivalent of Broadway or the West End. Shows are mostly in French, with a few notable exceptions listed here. English-language theater groups playing in various venues throughout Paris and its suburbs include the **International Players** (⊕ *www.internationalplayers.co.uk*). Broadway-scale singing-and-dancing musicals are generally staged at either the Palais des Sports or the Palais des Congrès.

THE PERFORMING ARTS IN PARIS

Listings are alphabetical by neighborhood.

AROUND THE EIFFEL TOWER

INVALIDES

Fodor's Choice **La Pagode.** La Pagode —where else but in Paris would you find movies
★ screened in an antique pagoda? A Far Eastern fantasy, this structure was built in 1896 as a ballroom for the wife of the owner of Le Bon Marché department store. In the 1970s it was slated for demolition but saved by a grassroots wave of support spearheaded by director Louis Malle. Though the fare is standard, the surroundings are enchanting. Come early for tea in the garden (summer only). ⊠ *57 rue de Babylone, 7e, Invalides* ☎ *01–46–34–82–54* Ⓜ *St-François Xavier.*

TROCADERO

Théâtre National de Chaillot. Théâtre National de Chaillot is an imposing neoclassic building overlooking the Eiffel Tower, with two theaters dedicated to drama and dance. Major dance companies like the Ballet Royal de Suède and William Forsythe's company also visit regularly. ⊠ *1 pl. du Trocadéro, 16e, Trocadéro/Tour Eiffel* ☎ *01–53–65–30–00* Ⓜ *Trocadéro.*

18

AROUND THE LOUVRE

LES HALLES

IRCAM. IRCAM organizes contemporary and classical music concerts, as well as dance and other modern art performances, in its own theater and at the Centre Pompidou next door for only €14. ⊠ *1 pl. Igor-Stravinsky, 4e, Beaubourg/Les Halles* ☎ *01–44–78–48–43* ⊕ *www.ircam.fr* Ⓜ *Châtelet, Les Halles, Hôtel de Ville.*

Le Forum des Images. Le Forum des Images, emerging from a massive state-of-the-art renovation, organizes thematic screenings, often presenting directors or a film expert for discussion beforehand, along with archival films and videos, workshops, and lectures. Entry starts at €5; €8 for festivals. ⊠ *Forum des Halles, Porte St-Eustache entrance, 1er, 2 rue du Cinéma, Beaubourg/Les Halles* ☎ *01–44–76–63–00* ⊙ *12:30–11:30 Mon.–Fri; 2–11:30 Sat.–Sun.* Ⓜ *Les Halles.*

Théâtre de la Ville. Théâtre de la Ville is *the* top venue for contemporary dance. Troupes like Anne-Teresa de Keersmaeker's Rosas company are presented here. Book early; shows sell out quickly. ⊠ *2 pl. du Châtelet, 4e, Beaubourg/Les Halles* ☏ *01–42–74–22–77* Ⓜ *Châtelet.*

Théâtre du Châtelet. Also known as Théâtre Musical de Paris, this venue presents some of the finest opera productions in the city and regularly attracts international divas like Cecilia Bartoli and Anne-Sofie von Otter. It also hosts classical concerts, dance performances, classic Broadway musicals, and the occasional play. ⊠ *Pl. du Châtelet, 1er, Beaubourg/Les Halles* ☏ *01–40–28–28–40* ⊕ *www.chatelet-theatre. com* Ⓜ *Châtelet.*

LOUVRE/TUILERIES

Fodor's Choice
★ **Comédie Française.** Comédie Française dates from 1680 and is the most hallowed institution in French theater. It specializes in splendid classical French plays by the likes of Racine, Molière, and Marivaux. ■TIP➜ Buy tickets at the box office, by telephone, or online. If the theater is sold out, turn up an hour before the performance and wait in line for very inexpensive last-minute tickets. ⊠ *Salle Richelieu, Pl. Colette, 1er, Louvre* ☏ *08–25–10–16–80* Ⓜ *Palais-Royal–Musée du Louvre* ⊠ *Studio Théâtre, Galerie du Carrousel du Louvre, 99 rue de Rivoli, 1er, Louvre* ☏ *01–44–58–98–58* Ⓜ *Palais-Royal* ⊠ *Théâtre du Vieux Colombier, 21 rue Vieux Colombier, 6e, St-Germain-des-Prés* ☏ *01–44–39–87–00* Ⓜ *St-Sulpice.*

Théâtre du Palais-Royal. Théâtre du Palais-Royal is a sumptuous 750-seat Italian theater bedecked in gold and purple in the former residence of Cardinal Richelieu. ⊠ *38 rue Montpensier, 1er, Louvre* ☏ *01–42–97–40–00* ⊕ *www.theatrepalaisroyal.com* Ⓜ *Palais-Royal.*

CHAMPS-ÉLYSÉES

Comédie des Champs-Élysées. Comédie des Champs-Élysées offers intriguing productions in its small theater, next door to the larger Théâtre des Champs-Élysées. ⊠ *15 av. Montaigne, 8e, Champs-Élysées* ☏ *01–53–23–99–19* Ⓜ *Alma-Marceau.*

Le Balzac. Le Balzac often presents directors' talks before film screenings and features concerts as well as live music for silent classics. ⊠ *1 rue Balzac, 8e, Champs-Élysées* ☏ *01–45–61–10–60* Ⓜ *George V.*

Salle Gaveau. Salle Gaveau is a small, perfectly appointed gold-and-white hall of 1,200 seats with a distinctly Parisian allure and remarkable acoustics. It hosts chamber music, piano, and vocal recitals. ⊠ *45-47 rue la Boétie, 8e, Champs-Élysées* ☏ *01–49–53–05–07* ⊕ *www.sallegaveau. com* Ⓜ *Miromesnil.*

Salle Pleyel. Salle Pleyel features varied musical presentations from international stars like Lionel Hampton and directors of the New York Philharmonic as well as repeat performances by the Orchestre de Paris. ⊠ *252 rue du Faubourg-St-Honoré, 8e, Concorde* ☏ *01–42–56–13–13* ⊕ *www.sallepleyel.fr* Ⓜ *Ternes.*

Théâtre des Champs-Élysées. Théâtre des Champs-Élysées was the scene of the famous Battle of the Rite of Spring in 1913, when police had to be called in after the audience ripped up the seats in outrage at Stravinsky's *Le Sacre du Printemps* and Nijinsky's choreography. Today this elegantly restored and plush performance temple is worthy of a visit if only for one of the most striking examples of Art Deco architecture in Paris. It also hosts top-notch opera, dance performances, jazz, world music, and orchestra and chamber concerts. ⊠ *15 av. Montaigne, 8e, Champs-Élysées* ☎ *01–49–52–50–50* Ⓜ *Alma-Marceau.*

Théâtre Marigny. Théâtre Marigny offers top-flight theater, often with a big-name French star topping the bill. ⊠ *Carré Marigny, 8e, Champs-Élysées* ☎ *01–53–96–70–30* Ⓜ *Champs-Élysées–Clemenceau.*

EASTERN PARIS

BASTILLE/NATION

Opéra de la Bastille. Opéra de la Bastille, the mammoth ultramodern facility designed by architect Carlos Ott and built in 1989, long ago took over the role of Paris's main opera house from the Opéra Garnier (although both operate under the same Opéra de Paris umbrella). Like the building, performances tend to be on the avant-garde side—you're as likely to see a contemporary adaptation of *La Bohème* as you are to hear Kafka set to music. Tickets for Opéra de Paris productions range from €5 to €200 and generally go on sale at the box office a month before shows, earlier by phone and online. The opera season usually runs September through July, and the box office is open Monday–Saturday 11–6:30. ■ **TIP→** You can buy tickets (€12) for guided tours of the opera house at the box office. Call for dates and times. ⊠ *Pl. de la Bastille, 12e, Bastille/Nation* ☎ *08–92–89–90–90, 01–40–01–19–70 Tours* ⊕ *www.operadeparis.fr* Ⓜ *Bastille.*

Théâtre de la Bastille. Théâtre de la Bastille merits mention as an example of the innovative activity in the Bastille area; it has an enviable record as a launching pad for tomorrow's modern-dance stars. ⊠ *76 rue de la Roquette, 11e, Bastille/Nation* ☎ *01–43–57–42–14* Ⓜ *Bastille.*

BERCY/TOLBIAC

Fodor's Choice ★ **Cinémathèque Française.** Cinémathèque Française is a mecca for cinephiles brought up on Federico Fellini, Igmar Bergman, and Alain Resnais. Its spectacular home, in the former American Center designed by Frank Gehry, opened in October 2005 and includes elaborate museum exhibitions as well as four cinemas and a video library. ⊠ *51 rue de Bercy, 12e, Bercy* ☎ *01–71–19–33–33* ⊕ *www.cinematheque.fr* Ⓜ *Bercy.*

MK2 Bibliothèque. MK2 Bibliothèque is a slick, 14-*salle* cineplex in the shadow of Mitterrand's National Library, with trademark scarlet-red two-person chairs—they fit two people without a divider; sort of like watching a movie at home on your couch—as well as four restaurants and music and DVD shops. ⊠ *128–162 av. de France, 13e, Tolbiac* ☎ *08–92–69–84–84* Ⓜ *Quai de la Gare, Bibliothèque.*

UGC Ciné-Cité Bercy. UGC Ciné-Cité Bercy is a mammoth 18-screen complex in the Bercy Village shopping area. For sound and seating, it's one of the best. ⊠ *2 cour St-Emilion, 12e, Bercy* ☎ *08–92–70–00–00* Ⓜ *Cour St-Emilion.*

18

CANAL ST-MARTIN

Le Manoir de Paris. Let yourself be enchanted and frightened as talented performers bring Paris legends to life. As you walk through this Parisian mansion, the history of the Bloody Baker, the Phantom of the Opera, and Catherine de Medici's hired assassin are acted out . . . on you! ■ TIP→ If you are in Paris during Halloween, this is just about the best game in town. ⊠ *18 rue de Paradis, Eastern Paris* ☎ Ⓜ *Chateau d'Eau.*

Théâtre des Bouffes du Nord. Théâtre des Bouffes du Nord is the wonderfully atmospheric, slightly decrepit home of English director Peter Brook, who regularly delights with his quirky experimental productions in French and, sometimes, English, too. ⊠ *37 bis, bd. de la Chapelle, 10e, Stalingrad/La Chapelle* ☎ *01–46–07–34–50* Ⓜ *La Chapelle.*

LA VILLETTE

Circus Arts at the Parc de la Villette. Circus Arts at the Parc de la Villette features an *Espace Chapiteaux*, a high-tech circus-tent complex that hosts innovative circus performers including students from the National Circus Arts Center. It focuses on contemporary performance art—not to be missed by "new circus" fans. ⊠ *211 av. Jean-Jaurès, 20e, La Villette* ☎ *01–40–03–75–75* Ⓜ *Porte de Pantin.*

Cité de la Musique. Cité de la Musique presents a varied program of classical, experimental, and world-music concerts in a postmodern setting. ⊠ *In Parc de La Villette, 221 av. Jean-Jaurès, 19e, La Villette* ☎ *01–44–84–45–00* ⊕ *www.cite-musique.fr/anglais* Ⓜ *Porte de Pantin.*

La Géode. La Géode screens wide-angle Omnimax films—including kid-friendly documentaries—on a gigantic spherical surface. ⊠ *At Cité des Sciences et de l'Industrie, Parc de La Villette, 26 av. Corentin-Cariou, 19e, La Villette* ☎ *01–40–05–79–99* Ⓜ *Porte de La Villette.*

Parc de La Villette. Parc de La Villette shows free open-air movies in July and August. Most people take along a picnic. You can rent deck chairs and blankets by the entrance. ⊠ *In Prairie du Triangle at Parc de La Villette, 221 av. Jean-Jaurès, 19e, La Villette* ☎ *01–40–03–75–75* Ⓜ *Porte de Pantin, Porte de La Villette.*

Théâtre Darius Milhaud. Théâtre Darius Milhaud presents classics by Camus and Baudelaire, as well as occasional productions in English and shows for children. ⊠ *80 allée Darius Milhaud, 19e, La Villette* ☎ *01–42–01–92–26* Ⓜ *Porte de Pantin.*

RÉPUBLIQUE

Cirque d'Hiver Bouglione. Cirque d'Hiver Bouglione brings together two famous circus institutions: the beautiful Cirque d'Hiver hall, constructed in 1852, and the Bouglione troupe, known for its rousing spectacle of acrobats, jugglers, clowns, trapeze artists, tigers, and housecats that leap through rings of fire. ⊠ *110 rue Amelot, 11e, République* ☎ *01–47–00–28–81* ⊕ *www.cirquedhiver.com* Ⓜ *Filles du Calvaire.*

LATIN QUARTER

Accatone. Accatone features a steady stream of European art films. ⊠ *20 rue Cujas, 5e, Latin Quarter* ☎ *01–46–33–86–86* Ⓜ *Cluny–La Sorbonne, Luxembourg.*

The Frank Gehry–designed Cinémathèque Française presents an ever-changing range of films and exhibitions.

Action Écoles. Action Écoles specializes in American classics and cult films for only €8! ✉ *23 rue des Écoles, 5e, Latin Quarter* ☎ *01–43–25–72–07* Ⓜ *Maubert–Mutualité.*

St-André-des-Arts. St-André-des-Arts, one of a number of popular cinemas near the Sorbonne, is also one of the best cinemas in Paris. It hosts an annual festival devoted to a single director, such as Bergman or Tarkovski. ✉ *30 rue St-André-des-Arts, 6e, Latin Quarter* ☎ *01–43–26–48–18* Ⓜ *St-Michel.*

Théâtre de la Huchette. Théâtre de la Huchette is a tiny Rive Gauche theater that has been staging the titanic Romanian-French writer Ionesco's *The Bald Soprano* and *The Lesson* since 1957, and also stages other productions. (The box office is open Monday–Saturday 5 pm–9 pm.) ✉ *23 rue de la Huchette, 5e, Latin Quarter* ☎ *01–43–26–38–99* Ⓜ *St-Michel.*

MARAIS

Café de la Gare. Café de la Gare offers a fun opportunity to experience a particularly Parisian form of theater, the *café-théâtre*—part satire, part variety revue, jazzed up with slapstick humor and performed in a café salon. ■TIP➔ You'll need a good grasp of French slang and current events to keep up with the jokes. ✉ *41 rue du Temple, 4e, Marais* ☎ *01–42–78–52–51* Ⓜ *Hôtel de Ville.*

MONTMARTRE

Cinéma des Cinéastes. Cinéma des Cinéastes shows previews of feature films, as well as documentaries, films for kids, short films, and rarely shown movies; it's in an old cabaret transformed into a movie theater and wine bar. ⊠ *7 av. de Clichy, 17e, Montmartre* ☎ *08–92–68–97–17* Ⓜ *Place de Clichy.*

Sudden Theatre. Sudden Theatre is a tiny, contemporary theater and acting academy offering regular English-language productions. ⊠ *14 bis, rue Ste-Isaure, 18e, Montmartre* ☎ *01–42–62–35–00* Ⓜ *Jules Joffrin.*

Théâtre des Abbesses. Théâtre des Abbesses Part of the Théâtre de la Ville, this 400-seat theater in Montmartre opened in 1996 to feature lesser-known acts and up-and-coming choreographers who often make it to the program in the Théâtre de la Ville the following year. ⊠ *31 rue des Abbesses, 18e, Montmartre* ☎ *01–42–74–22–77* Ⓜ *Abbesses.*

> ## PUPPET SHOWS
>
> On most Wednesday, Saturday, and Sunday afternoons, the Guignol—the French equivalent of Punch and Judy—can be seen launching their hilarious puppet battles in most of Paris's larger parks. Look for performance spaces called *Théâtre de Marionnettes.* Entrance is usually about €3.50; performances are in French.

MONTPARNASSE

♻ **Le Lucernaire.** Le Lucernaire wins a standing ovation as far as cultural centers are concerned. With two theaters (eight performances a night), three movie screens, an art gallery, a bookstore, a lively bar, and the equally lively surrounding neighborhood of Vavin, it caters to young intellectuals—and, thanks to the puppet shows (Wednesday and Saturday), their children, too. ⊠ *53 rue Notre-Dame-des-Champs, 6e, Montparnasse* ☎ *01–42–22–26–50* Ⓜ *Notre-Dame-des-Champs.*

Théâtre de la Cité Internationale. Théâtre de la Cité Internationale is a complex of three theaters in the heart of the Cité Internationale Universitaire de Paris, an international student residence community and park. It hosts young avant-garde companies and is also the main venue for the Presqu'Iles de la Danse festival in February. ⊠ *17 bd. Jourdan, 14e, Parc Montsouris* ☎ *01–43–13–50–50* Ⓜ *RER: Cité Universitaire.*

OPÉRA/GRANDS BOULEVARDS

Casino de Paris. Casino de Paris, once a favorite of the immortal Serge Gainsbourg, has a horseshoe balcony, a cramped, cozy music-hall feel, and performances by everyone from Dora the Explorer to the Scissor Sisters! This is where Josephine Baker performed in the early '30s with her leopard, Chiquita. ⊠ *16 rue de Clichy, 9e, Opéra/Grands Boulevards* ☎ *08–92–69–89–26* ⊕ *www.casinodeparis.fr* Ⓜ *Trinité.*

Opéra Comique. Opéra Comique is a gem of an opera house whose reputation was forged by its former director, enfant terrible Jérôme

Savary. As well as staging operettas, the hall hosts modern dance, classical concerts, and vocal recitals. Tickets usually range from €6 to €50 and can be purchased at the theater, by mail, online, or by phone. ⊠ *5 rue Favart, 2e, Opéra/Grands Boulevards* ☎ *08–25–01–01–23* ⊕ *www. opera-comique.com* Ⓜ *Richelieu–Drouot.*

Fodor's Choice
★
Opéra Garnier. Opéra Garnier, the magnificent and magical former haunt of the Phantom of the Opera, painter Edgar Degas, and any number of legendary opera stars, still hosts performances of the Opéra de Paris, along with a fuller calendar of dance performances, as the theater is the official home of the Ballet de l'Opéra National de Paris. The grandest opera productions are usually mounted at the Opéra de la Bastille, whereas the Garnier now presents smaller-scale operas such as Mozart's *La Clemenza di Tito* and *Così Fan Tutte*. Gorgeous and intimate though the Garnier is, its tiara-shaped theater means that many seats have limited visibility, so it's best to ask specifically what the sight lines are when booking (partial view in French is *visibilité partielle*. ■TIP→ The cheaper seats are often those with partial views. Seats generally go on sale at the box office a month before any given show, earlier by phone and online; you must appear in person to buy the cheapest tickets. Last-minute discount tickets, if available, are offered 15 minutes before a performance for senior citizens and anyone under 28. The box office is open 11–6:30 daily, but you should get in line up to two hours in advance. Individual and group tours (€9–13.50) are available; check the website for details. ⊠ *Pl. de l'Opéra 9e, Opéra/Grands Boulevards* ☎ *08–92–89–90–90* ⊕ *www.operadeparis.fr* Ⓜ *Opéra.*

Fodor's Choice
★
Salle Cortot. Salle Cortot is an acoustic gem built by Auguste Perret in 1918. At the time he promised to construct "a hall that sounds like a Stradivarious." Jazz and classical concerts are held here. ■TIP→ Free student recitals are offered at 12:30 on Tuesday and Thursday from October to April. ⊠ *78 rue Cardinet, 17e, Parc Monceau* ☎ *01–47–63–47–48* ⊕ *www.ecolenormalecortot.com* Ⓜ *Malesherbes.*

Théâtre de la Renaissance. This theater was put on the map by Belle Époque superstar Sarah Bernhardt (she was the manager from 1893 to 1899). Big French stars often perform here. ⊠ *20 bd. St-Martin, 10e, Opéra/Grands Boulevards* ☎ *01–42–02–47–35* Ⓜ *Strasbourg St-Denis.*

Théâtre Mogador. Théâtre Mogador, one of Paris's most sumptuous theaters, features musicals and other productions with a pronounced popular appeal (think *Mamma Mia!*). ⊠ *25 rue de Mogador, 9e, Opéra/ Grands Boulevards* ☎ *08–20–88–87–86* Ⓜ *Trinité.*

ST-GERMAIN-DES-PRÉS

Ateliers Berthier. Ateliers Berthier is the outlying atelier for the more illustrious Théâtre de l'Odéon. Its location in the 17e is a bit off the beaten path but on Tuesdays and Saturdays they often show 3 pm afternoon matinees in addition to the 8 pm show. ⊠ *Bd. Berthier's corner, 1 rue André Suarès, Parc Monceau* ☎ *01–44–85–40–40* Ⓜ *Porte de Clichy.*

Odéon–Théâtre de l'Europe. Odéon–Théâtre de l'Europe was once home to the Comédie Française. This venue focuses on pan-European theater, offering a variety of European-language productions in Paris for no more than €32. ⊠ *Pl. de l'Odéon, 6e, St-Germain-des-Prés* ☎ *01–44–85–40–40* Ⓜ *Odéon.*

OUTSIDE PARIS

Centre National de la Danse. After being sidelined by politics and budget problems for a decade, this dance center opened in a former administrative center of the Pantin suburb of Paris. The space is dedicated to supporting professional dancers, with classes, rehearsal studios, and a multimedia dance library. A regular program of performances, expositions, and conferences is also open to the public. ⊠ *1 rue Victor Hugo, Pantin* ☎ *01–41–83–98–98* ⊕ *www.cnd.fr* Ⓜ *Hoche or RER: Pantin.*

La Cartoucherie. This complex of five theaters (Théâtre du Soleil, Théâtre de l'Aquarium, Théâtre de la Tempête, Théâtre de l'Epée de Bois, and the Théâtre du Chaudron) in a former munitions factory lures cast and spectators into an intimate theatrical world. Go early for a simple meal; actors often help serve "in character." ⊠ *In Bois de Vincennes, route du Champ de manoeuvre* ☎ *01–43–74–88–50, 01–43–74–87–63* Ⓜ *Château de Vincennes, then shuttle bus or Bus 112.*

Maison des Arts de Créteil. This popular dance venue just outside Paris often attracts top-flight international and French companies, such as Blanca Li, Bill T. Jones, and the cutting-edge annual EXIT Festival. ⊠ *Pl. Salvador Allende, Creteil* ☎ *01–45–13–19–19* ⊕ *www.maccreteil.com* Ⓜ *Créteil-Préfecture.*

WESTERN PARIS

18

Cirque National Alexis Gruss. Cirque National Alexis Gruss, founded in 1854, remains an avowedly old-fashioned production with showy horseback riders, trapeze artists, and clowns. It runs November through February, with performances Saturday (including a dinner show for €90), Sunday, and Wednesday. ⊠ *Rte. de l'Hippodrome, 16e, Bois de Boulogne* ☎ *01–45–01–71–26* ⊕ *www.alexis-gruss.com* Ⓜ *Ranelagh.*

Side Trips from Paris

WITH VERSAILLES, DISNEYLAND PARIS, AND CHARTRES

WORD OF MOUTH

"I wouldn't buy a ticket to Versailles ahead of time. It's very easy to get there from Paris, so choose your day with good weather to fully enjoy the lovely gardens."

—TPAYT

Updated
by Jennifer
Ditsler-Ladonne

With so much to see in Paris, it may seem hard to justify a side trip. But just outside the city is the rest of the fabled region known as Ile-de-France, where, along with gorgeous countryside and quiet towns, you can find spectacular Versailles, the immense Chartres cathedral, and a little region unto itself where a mouse named Mickey is king.

Plan to spend an entire day at **Versailles** (at least), enjoying the gorgeously manicured gardens—one of the largest parks in Europe—as well as touring the palace, which includes the Hall of Mirrors, and Marie-Antoinette's private retreat in an enclave of the royal park. **Chartres** is a charming town that makes a lovely day or half-day side trip from Paris. Its main attraction is Cathédrale de Chartres, an awe-inspiring Gothic cathedral that looms like a great fantasy ship on the horizon and is world-renowned for its stained-glass windows. **Disneyland Paris** arrived in 1992, but the magic was slow to take effect. The resort opened with the uninspiring name of EuroDisney and further baffled the French, for whom no meal is complete without wine, with its ban on alcohol. After the ban was lifted in the park's sit-down restaurants and the park's name was changed, Disneyland Paris became France's leading tourist attraction, drawing sellout crowds of Europeans seeking a kitschy glimpse of the American Dream—and of American families stealing a day from their museum schedule. A second park, Walt Disney Studios, opened in 2002.

PLANNING

TOUR OPTIONS
Cityrama (☏ *01–44–55–60–00* ⊕ *www.cityrama.com*) and **Paris Vision** (☏ *01–42–60–30–01* ⊕ *www.parisvision.com*) run half- and full-day trips to Versailles (€54–€115). **Paris Euroscope** (☏ *01–56–03–56–81* ⊕ *www.euroscope.fr*) operates half-day guided excursions to Chartres (€88).

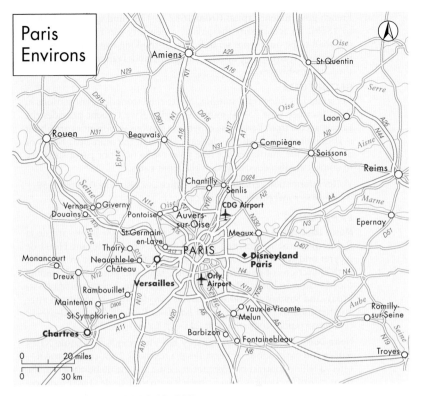

Paris
Environs

TRAIN VERSUS CAR

Traveling to Chartres, Disneyland Paris, and Versailles from Paris is easy. Although each side trip is within an hour's drive, we *strongly* recommend taking the train from the city rather than renting a car. If Disneyland is your destination and you don't plan to visit Paris, there are shuttle buses that will take you directly from the airports to the park.

TIMING TIPS

The château of Versailles is closed on Monday.

Disneyland Paris gets extremely crowded on summer weekends, so plan your trip during the week, and early, if possible.

VERSAILLES

16 km (10 miles) west of Paris via A13.

Fodor'sChoice ★ It's hard to tell which is larger at **Château de Versailles**—the world-famous château that housed Louis XIV and 20,000 of his courtiers, or the mass of tour buses and visitors standing in front of it. The grandest palace in France remains one of the marvels of the world (⇨ *Its full story is covered in the special photo feature on the château in this chapter, "Gilt Trip: A Tour of Versailles"*). But this edifice was not just home to the Sun King, it was also to be the new headquarters of the

French government capital (from 1682 to 1789 and again from 1871 to 1879). To accompany the palace, a new city—in fact, a new capital—had to be built from scratch. Tough-thinking town planners took no prisoners, dreaming up vast mansions and avenues broader than the Champs-Élysées.

GETTING HERE

Versailles has three train stations, all reached from different stations in Paris (journey time 25–40 mins). Versailles Rive Gauche provides the easiest access from Paris. The other two stations in Versailles are about a 10-minute walk from the château, although the municipal Bus B or a summertime shuttle service (use your métro ticket or pay a small fee in coins) can also deposit you at the front gates.

Visitor Information Versailles Tourist Office ✉ *2 bis, av. de Paris* ☎ *01–39–24–88–88* ⊕ *www.versailles-tourisme.com.*

EXPLORING

Musée Lambinet. Around the back of Notre-Dame, on Boulevard de la Reine (note the regimented lines of trees), are the elegant Hôtel de Neyret and the Musée Lambinet, a sumptuous mansion from 1751, with collections of paintings, weapons, fans, and porcelain (including the Madame du Barry "Rose"). The new tearoom, open Thursday, Saturday, and Sunday afternoons, provides an elegant way to refresh after an afternoon of sightseeing. ✉ *54 bd. de la Reine* ☎ *01–39–50–30–32* ⊕ *www.versailles-tourisme.com* 🖃 *€4* ⊙ *Sat.–Thurs. 2–6.*

Notre-Dame. If you have any energy left after exploring Louis XIV's palace and park, a tour of Versailles—a textbook 18th-century town—offers a telling contrast between the majestic and the domestic. From the front gate of Versailles's palace turn left onto the Rue de l'Independence-Américaine and walk over to Rue Carnot past the stately Écuries de la Reine—once the queen's stables, now the regional law courts—to octagonal Place Hoche. Down Rue Hoche to the left is the powerful Baroque facade of Notre-Dame, built from 1684 to 1686 by Jules Hardouin-Mansart as the parish church for Louis XIV's new town.

Place du Marché-Notre-Dame. Passage de la Geôle, a cobbled alley lined with quaint antiques shops, climbs up to Place du Marché-Notre-Dame, with an open-air morning market on Tuesday, Friday, and Sunday that is famed throughout the region (note the four 19th-century timber-roof halls). Fresh fruit and vegetables from the palace's own kitchen garden, *le potager du roi*, can be purchased on market days.

$$$$
FRENCH
Fodor's Choice
★

✕**Gordon Ramsay au Trianon.** Gordon Ramsay, the ebullient "bad boy de la cuisine anglaise," has already amassed a string of restaurants worldwide, including three in New York, a three-star restaurant in London, and a consistent two stars for this establishment. Although he cut his culinary teeth in the kitchens of master chefs Guy Savoy and Joël Robuchon, this is his first eatery on French soil. The delicious results—overseen by his longstanding London number two, Simone Zanoni—are predictably conversation-worthy: raviolo of langoustines and lobster cooked in a Riesling bisque with Petrossian caviar and lime consommé; or the Périgord foie gras done "2 ways," roasted with a beetroot tart and pressed with green apple and sauternes, are two top main dishes.

Desserts are marvels, too, with chocolate meringue with vanilla ice cream, candied pear, and black currant vying for top honors with the raspberry soufflé with chocolate and tarragon ice cream. The Trianon's more casual, 60-seat Véranda restaurant is now also under Ramsay's sway, and in its black-and-white contemporary setting you can opt for Ramsay's "light, modern take" on such bistro novelties as radicchio and Parmesan risotto with chorizo oil or the fillet of sole in a parsley crust, cepes, and sautéed artichokes. Teatime provides a delightful (and reasonable) restorative for weary château-goers, with a French take on high tea: scones, madeleines, and heavenly macaroons. $ *Average main: €150* ☒ *1 bd. de la Reine* ☎ *01–30–84–55–56* ⊕ *www.gordonramsay. com/grautrianon* ⬥ *Reservations essential* 🏛 *Jacket required* ☉ *Closed Sun. and Mon. Lunch available Fri. and Sat. only.*

$$$

FRENCH

★

✕ **L'Angelique.** After the stellar success of his first Michelin-starred restaurant, L'Escarbille (in Meudon), chef Régis Douysset's newest venture confirms his commitment to refined-yet-unfussy French cuisine. The dining room, in a restored 17th-century town house, is serene and comfortable, with white walls, wood-beam ceilings, dark wood paneling, and tasteful artwork—a handsome setting in which to relax into one of the best meals in town. The seasonally changing menu offers a good balance of seafood, game, and meat: a delicate perch filet with spaghettis *de mer* in a shellfish bouillon or the venison shoulder with grilled turnips and a spätzle of girolle mushrooms. Desserts are not to be missed—the tart *feuilletée,* with candied peaches, cardamom, and peach sorbet is ethereal. Having earned a Michelin star in 2010, this spot is justifiably popular, so reserve well in advance. $ *Average main: €28* ☒ *27 av. de Saint-Cloud* ☎ *01–30–84–98–85* ⊕ *www.langelique.fr* ☉ *Closed Sun. and Mon.*

WHERE TO STAY

For expanded hotel reviews, visit Fodors.com.

$

HOTEL

🏨 **Le Cheval Rouge.** This unpretentious old hotel, built in 1676, is in a corner of the town market square, close to the château and strongly recommended if you plan to explore the town on foot. **Pros:** great setting in town center; good value for Versailles. **Cons:** bland public areas; some rooms need renovating. **TripAdvisor:** "great location," "very good value," "a bit of history." $ *Rooms from: €82* ☒ *18 rue André-Chénier* ☎ *01–39–50–03–03* ⊕ *www.chevalrougeversailles.fr* ⬦ *40 rooms* ⏐◎⏐ *No meals.*

$$$$

HOTEL

★

🏨 **Trianon Palace.** A modern-day Versailles, this deluxe hotel is in a turn-of-the-20th-century, creamy white creation of imposing size, filled with soaring rooms (including the historic Salle Clemenceau, site of the 1919 Versailles Peace Conference), palatial columns, and with a huge garden close to the château park. **Pros:** palatial glamour; wonderful setting right by château park; Gordon Ramsay. **Cons:** lack of a personal touch after recent changes of ownership. **TripAdvisor:** "beyond words," "service was top notch," "très beautiful." $ *Rooms from: €250* ☒ *1 bd. de la Reine* ☎ *01–30–84–50–00* ⊕ *www.trianonpalace.com* ⬦ *199 rooms, 23 suites* ⏐◎⏐ *Breakfast.*

19

Continued on page 421

GILT TRIP
A TOUR OF VERSAILLES

By Robert I.C. Fisher

Louis XIV's Hall of Mirrors

A two-century spree of indulgence in the finest bling-bling of the age by the consecutive reigns of three French kings produced two of the world's most historic artifacts: gloriously, the Palace of Versailles and, momentously, the French Revolution.

Less a monument than an entire world unto itself, Versailles is the king of palaces. The end result of 380 million francs, 36,000 laborers, and enough paintings, if laid end to end, to equal 7 miles of canvas, it was conceived as the ne plus ultra expression of monarchy by Louis XIV. As a child, the king had developed a hatred for Paris (where he had been imprisoned by a group of nobles known as the Frondeurs), so, when barely out of his teens, he cast his cantankerous royal eye in search of a new power base. Marshy, inhospitable Versailles was the stuff of his dreams. Down came dad's modest royal hunting lodge and up, up, and along went the minion-crushing, Baroque palace we see today.

Between 1661 and 1710, architects Louis Le Vau and Jules Hardouin Mansart designed everything his royal acquisitiveness could want, including a throne room devoted to Apollo, god of the sun (Louis was known as *le roi soleil*). Convinced that his might depended upon dominating French nobility, Louis XIV summoned thousands of grandees from their own far-flung châteaux to reside at his new seat of government. In doing so, however, he unwittingly triggered the downfall of the monarchy. Like an 18th-century Disneyland, Versailles kept its courtiers so richly entertained they all but forgot the murmurs of discontent brewing back home.

As Louis XV chillingly foretold, "After me, the deluge." The royal commune was therefore shocked—shocked!—by the appearance, on October 5, 1789, of a revolutionary mob from Paris ready to sack Versailles and imprison Louis XVI. So as you walk through this awesome monument to splendor and excess, give a thought to its historic companion: the French Revolution. A tour of Versailles's grand salons inextricably mixes pathos with glory.

CROWNING GLORIES:
TOP SIGHTS OF VERSAILLES

Versailles from the outside

Seducing their court with their self-assured approach to 17th- and 18th-century art and decoration, a trinity of French kings made Versailles into the most vainglorious of châteaux.

Galerie des Glaces (Hall of Mirrors). Of all the rooms at Versailles, none matches the magnificence of the Galerie des Glaces (Hall of Mirrors). Begun by Mansart in 1678, this represents the acme of the Louis Quatorze (Louis-XIV) style. Measuring 240 feet long, 33 feet wide, and 40 feet high, it is ornamented with gilded candlesticks, crystal chandeliers, and a coved ceiling painted with Charles Le Brun's homage to Louis XIV's reign.

Detail of the ceiling

In Louis's day, the Galerie was laid with priceless carpets and filled with orange trees in silver pots. Nighttime galas were illuminated by 3,000 candles, their blaze doubled in the 17 gigantic mirrors that precisely echo the banner of windows along the west front. Lavish balls were once held here, and you can still get the full royal treatment at the Serenade Royale. This reenacts one of Louis XIV's grand soirées with dancers in period costumes. The 45-minute spectacle is held at 6:45 and 7:45 pm, from mid-June to September. (☎ €39, €27 ages 6–18 ⊕ www.chateauversailles-spectacles.fr ☎ 01–30–83–78–98).

Hall of Mirrors

The Grands Appartements (State Apartments). Virtual stages for ceremonies of court ritual and etiquette, Louis XIV's first-floor state salons were designed in the Baroque style on a biceps-flexing scale meant to one-up the lavish Vaux-le-Vicomte château recently built for Nicolas Fouquet, the king's finance minister.

Inside the Apollo Chamber

Flanking the Hall of Mirrors and retaining most of their bombastic Italianate Baroque decoration, the Salon de la Guerre (Salon of War) and the Salon de la Paix (Salon of Peace) are ornately decorated with gilt stucco, painted ceilings, and marble sculpture. Perhaps the most extravagant is the Salon d'Apollon (Apollo Chamber), the former throne room.

Hall of Battles

Appartements du Roi (King's Apartments). Completed in 1701 in the Louis-XIV style, the king's state and private chambers comprise a suite of 15 rooms set in a "U" around the east facade's Marble Court. Dead center across the sprawling cobbled forecourt is Louis XIV's bedchamber—he would awake and rise (just as the sun did, from the east) attended by members of his court and the public. Holding the king's chemise when he dressed soon became a more definitive reflection of status than the possession of an entire province. Nearby is Louis XV's magnificent Cabinet Intérieur (Office of the King), shining with gold and white boiseries; in the center is the most famous piece of furniture at Versailles, Louis XV's roll-top desk, crafted by Oeben and Riesener in 1769.

Louis XIV

King's Apartments

Chambre de la Reine (Queen's Bedchamber). Probably the most opulent bedroom in the world, this was initially created for Marie Thérèse, first wife of Louis XIV, to be part of the Queen's Apartments. For Marie Antoinette, however, the entire room was glammed up with silk wall-hangings covered with Rococo motifs that reflect her love of flowers. Legend has it that the gardens directly beyond these windows were replanted daily so that the queen could enjoy a fresh assortment of blossoms each morning. The bed, decked out with white ostrich plumes *en panache*, was also redone for Louis XVI's queen. Nineteen royal children were born in this room.

VINTAGE BOURBON

Versailles was built by three great kings of the Bourbon dynasty. Louis XIV (1638–1715) began its construction in 1661. After ruling for 72 years, Louis Quatorze was succeeded by his great grandson, Louis XV (1710–74), who added the Royal Opera and the Petit Trianon to the palace. Louis XVI (1754–93) came to the throne in 1774 and was forced out of Versailles in 1789, along with Marie Antoinette, both guillotined three years later.

Queen's Bedchamber

Petits Appartements (Small Apartments). As styles of decor changed, Louis XIV's successors felt out of sync with their architectural inheritance. Louis XV exchanged the heavy red-and-gilt of Italianate Baroque for lighter, pastel-hued Rococo. On the top floor of the palace, on the right side of the central portion, are the apartments Louis XV commissioned to escape the wearisome pomp of the first-floor rooms. Here, Madame de Pompadour, mistress of Louis XV and famous patroness of the Rococo style, introduced grace notes of intimacy and refinement. In so doing, she transformed the daunting royal apartments into places to live rather than pose.

Parc de Versailles. Even Bourbon kings needed respite from Versailles's endless maze, hence the creation of one of Europe's largest parks. The sublime 250-acre grounds (☏ 01–30–83–77–88 for guided tour) is the masterpiece of André Le Nôtre, presiding genius of 17th-century classical French landscaping. Le Nôtre was famous for his "green geometries": ordered fantasies of clipped yew trees, multicolored flower beds (called *parterres*), and perspectival allées cleverly punctuated with statuary, laid out between 1661 and 1668. The spatial effect is best admired from inside the palace, views about which Le Nôtre said, "Flowers can only be walked on by the eyes."

Ultimately, at the royal command, rivers were diverted—to flow into more than 600 fountains—and entire forests were imported to ornament the park, which is centered around the mile-long Grand Canal. As for the great fountains, their operation costs a fortune in these democratic days, and so they perform only on Saturday and Sunday afternoons (⊘ 3:30–5:30) from mid-April through mid-October; admission to the park during this time is €8. The park is open daily 8 AM–8:30 PM.

LIGHTING UP THE SKY

The largest fountain at Versailles, the Bassin de Neptune, becomes a spectacle of rare grandeur during the Grandes Eaux Nocturnes, a light show to the strains of Baroque music, held Saturdays from the end of June through August at 9 pm, with fireworks at 11. Tickets are €23, €19 ages 6–18, and free for children under 6. ⊕ www.chateauversailles-spectacles.fr ☏ 01–30–83–78–98.

Dauphin's Apartments

Bassin de Neptune

Chapel and Opéra Royal: In the north wing of the château are three showpieces of the palace. The solemn white-and-gold Chapelle was completed in 1710—the king and queen attended daily mass here seated in gilt boxes. The Opéra Royal (Opera House), entirely constructed of wood painted to look like marble, was designed by Jacques-Ange Gabriel for Louis XV in 1770. Connecting the two, the 17th-century Galeries have exhibits retracing the château's history.

Opéra Royal

VERSAILLES: FIRST FLOOR, GARDENS & ADJACENT PARK

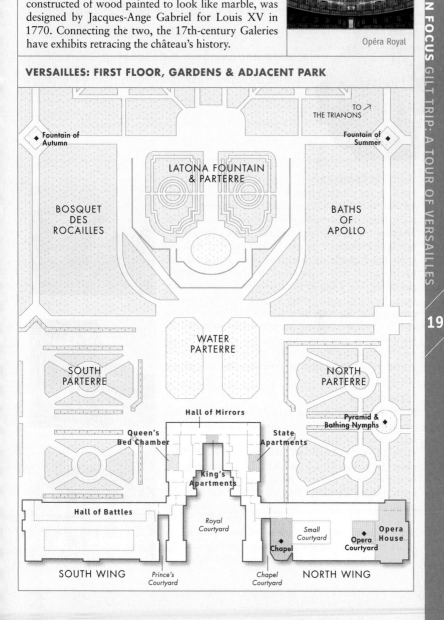

TO ↗
THE TRIANONS

◆ Fountain of
Autumn

Fountain of
Summer ◆

LATONA FOUNTAIN
& PARTERRE

BOSQUET
DES
ROCAILLES

BATHS
OF
APOLLO

WATER
PARTERRE

SOUTH
PARTERRE

NORTH
PARTERRE

Pyramid &
Bathing Nymphs ◆

Hall of Mirrors

Queen's
Bed Chamber

State
Apartments

King's
Apartments

Hall of Battles

Royal
Courtyard

Small
Courtyard

Opera
House

◆ Chapel

Opera
Courtyard

SOUTH WING

Prince's
Courtyard

Chapel
Courtyard

NORTH WING

LET THEM EAT CRÊPE:
MARIE ANTOINETTE'S ROYAL LAIR

Was Marie Antoinette a luxury-mad butterfly flitting from ball to costume ball? Or was she a misunderstood queen who suffered a loveless marriage and became a prisoner of court etiquette at Versailles? Historians now believe the answer was the latter and point to her private retreats at Versailles as proof.

R.F.D. VERSAILLES?

Here, in the northwest part of the royal park, Marie Antoinette (1755–93) created a tiny universe of her own: her comparatively dainty mansion called Petit Trianon and its adjacent "farm," the relentlessly picturesque Hameau ("hamlet"). In a life that took her from royal cradle to throne of France to guillotine, her happiest days were spent at Trianon. For here she could live a life in the "simplest" possible way; here the queen could enter a salon and the game of cards would not stop; here women could wear simple gowns of muslin without a single jewel. Toinette only wanted to be queen of Trianon, not queen of France. And considering the horrible, chamber-pot-pungent, gossip-infested corridors of Versailles, you can almost understand why.

TEEN QUEEN

From the first, Maria-Antonia (her actual name) was ostracized as an outsider, "l'Autrichienne"—the Austrian "bitch." Upon arriving in France in 1770—at a mere 14 years of age—she was married to the Dauphin, the future King Louis XVI. But shamed by her initial failure to deliver a royal heir, she grew to hate overcrowded Versailles and escaped to the Petit Trianon. Built between 1763 and 1768 by Jacques-Ange Gabriel for Madame de Pompadour, this bijou palace was a radical statement: a royal residence designed to be casual and unassuming. Toinette refashioned the Trianon's interior in the sober Neoclassical style.

Hameau

Queen's House

Temple of Love

Petit Trianon

Marie Antoinette

"THE SIMPLE LIFE"

Just beyond Petit Trianon lay the storybook Hameau, a mock-Norman village inspired by the peasant-luxe, simple-life daydreams caught by Boucher on canvas and by Rousseau in literature. With its water mill, thatched-roof houses, pigeon loft, and vegetable plots, this make-believe farm village was run by Monsieur Valy-Busard, a farmer, and his wife, who often helped the queen—outfitted as a Dresden shepherdess with a Sèvres porcelain crook—tend her flock of perfumed sheep.

As if to destroy any last link with reality, the queen built nearby a jewel-box theater (open by appointment). Here she acted in little plays, sometimes essaying the role of a servant girl. Only the immediate royal family, about seven or so friends, and her personal servants were permitted entry; disastrously, the entire official-dom of Versailles society was shut out—a move that only served to infuriate courtiers. This is how fate and destiny close the circle. For it was here at Trianon that a page sent by Monsieur de Saint-Priest found Marie-Antoinette on October 5, 1789, to tell her that Paris was marching on an already half-deserted Versailles.

Was Marie Antoinette a political traitor to France whose execution was well merited? Or was she the ultimate fashion victim? For those who feel that this tragic queen spent—and shopped—her way into a revolution, a visit to her relatively modest Petit Trianon and Hameau should prove a revelation.

LES BEAUX TRIANONS

A mile from the château, the Grand Trianon was created by Hardouin Mansart in 1687 as a retreat for Louis XIV; it was restored in the early 19th century, with Empire-style salons. It's a memorable spot often missed by foot-weary tourists exhausted by the château, but well worth the effort. A special treat is Marie Antoinette's hideaway nearby, the Petit Trianon, presumably restored to how she left it before being forced to Paris by an angry mob of soon-to-be revolutionaries.

TAKING ON VERSAILLES (WITHOUT LOSING YOUR HEAD)

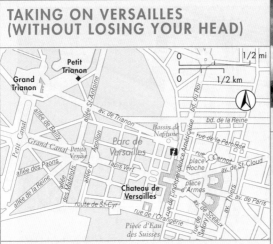

Statue of King Louis XIV

✉ Place d'Armes, Versailles

🌐 www.chateauversailles.fr

☎ 01–30–83–78–00

🎫 A €25 day Passport gets you into almost all sites, with audio-guide Grand Eaux, €18 in low season.

Château only is €18. Petit and Grand Trianons (joint ticket) €10; Parc de Versailles free; Grand Eaux Musicale fountain show's €23; Serenade Royale, €39.

🕐 The château is open Apr.–Oct., Tues.–Sun. 9–6:30; Nov.–Mar., Tues.–Sun, 9–5:30. Trianons Tues.–Sun. noon–6:30, Nov.–Mar. Park open daily 8–8:30.

Ⓜ RER Line C from Paris to Versailles–Rive Gauche station (closest to the Palace) or SNCF trains from Paris's Gare St-Lazare to Versailles–Rive Droite and Gare Montparnasse to Versailles.

Train tickets are €17. The best bargain (and a line-dodging time saver) is to buy a Forfait Loisirs Château de Versailles ticket (€22) that includes round-trip transportation from Paris and entrance to the main Versailles sights. Tickets are available at SNCF transilien train stations.

TOURING THE PALACE

The army of 20,000 noblemen, servants, and sycophants who moved into Louis XIV's huge Château de Versailles is matched today by the battalion of 3 million visitors a year. You may be able to avoid the modern-day crowds if you arrive here at 9 AM and buy your ticket in advance at FNAC or SNCF or online. The main entrance is near the top of the courtyard to the right; there are different lines depending on tour, physical ability, and group status. Frequent English guided tours visit the private royal apartments. More detailed hour-long tours explore the opera house (now reopened after a spectacular renovation; book a tour or concert ticket online) or Marie Antoinette's private parlors. You can wander the grandest rooms—including the Hall of Mirrors—without a group tour. To figure out the system, pick up a brochure at the information office for details.

TOURING THE PARK

If the grandeur of the palace begins to overwhelm, the Parc de Versailles is the best place to come back down to earth. The distances of the park are vast—the Trianons themselves are more than a mile from the château—so you might want to climb aboard the train (🎫€6.80 round-trip ☎01–39–54–22–00), or rent a bike from Petite-Venise (🎫€6.50 per hr or €17 for 6 hrs ☎01–39–66–97–66). You can hire a rowboat on the Grand Canal (🎫€15 per hr) or drive to the Trianons and canal through the Grille de la Reine (🎫€5.50 per car).

NIGHTLIFE AND THE ARTS

Académie du Spectacle Equestre. Directed by Bartabas, the Académie du Spectacle Equestre stages spectacular, hour-long shows on weekend afternoons of horses and their riders performing to music in the converted 17th-century Manège (riding school) at the Grandes Écuries opposite the palace. ⊠ *Av. Rockefeller* ☎ *01–39–02–07–14* ⊕ *www. acadequestre.fr.*

Centre de Musique Baroque. The Centre de Musique Baroque presents concerts of Baroque music in the château's Opéra Royal and chapel. ⊕ *www.cmbv.com.*

The Mois Molière. In June the Mois Molière heralds a program of concerts, drama, and exhibits inspired by the famous playwright. ☎ *01– 30–97–84–48.*

Théâtre Montansier. A nicely packed annual calendar here usually features a full program of plays. ⊠ *13 rue des Réservoirs* ☎ *01–39–20–16–00* ⊕ *www.theatremontansier.com.*

SHOPPING

Aux Colonnes. A highly rated *confiserie* (candy shop), Aux Colonnes has a cornucopia of chocolates and candies. It's closed Monday. ⊠ *14 rue Hoche.*

Les Délices du Palais. Everybody heads here to shop for the makings for an impromptu picnic (cold cuts, cheese, salads); it's closed Monday. ⊠ *4 rue du Maréchal-Foch.*

Passage de la Geôle. Open Friday–Sunday 9–7, this is close to the town's stupendous market and houses several good antiques shops.

CHARTRES

39 km (24 miles) southwest of Rambouillet via N10 and A11, 88 km (55 miles) southwest of Paris.

If Versailles is the climax of French secular architecture, Chartres is its religious apogee. All the descriptive prose and poetry that have been lavished on this supreme cathedral can only begin to suggest the glory of its 12th- and 13th-century statuary and stained glass, somehow suffused with burning mysticism and a strange sense of the numinous. Chartres is more than a church—it's a nondenominational spiritual experience.

GETTING HERE

Both regional and main-line (Le Mans–bound) trains leave Paris's Gare Montparnasse for Chartres (50–70 mins); tickets are around €27 roundtrip. Chartres's train station on Place Pierre-Sémard puts you within walking distance of the cathedral.

Visitor Information Chartres Tourist Office ⊠ *Pl. de la Cathédrale* ☎ *02–37– 18–26–26* ⊕ *www.chartres-tourisme.com.*

EXPLORING

If you arrive in summer from Maintenon across the edge of the Beauce, the richest agrarian plain in France, you can see Chartres's spires rising up from oceans of wheat. The whole town, with its old houses and quaint streets, is worth a leisurely exploration. From Rue du Pont-St-Hilaire there's an intriguing view of the rooftops below the cathedral. Ancient streets tumble down from the cathedral to the river, lined most weekends with bouquinistes selling old books and prints. Each year on August 15 pilgrims and tourists flock here for the Procession du Vœu de Louis XIII, a religious procession through the streets commemorating the French monarchy's vow to serve the Virgin Mary.

"Chartres en Lumieres," Chartres's festival of lights, is well worth lingering in town until dusk, when 28 of the city's most revered monuments, including the majestic Notre-Dame Cathedral, are transformed into vivid light canvases. Thematically based on the history and purpose of each specific site, the animated projections are organized into a city walk that covers a wide swath of the old town's cobbled streets and bridges. The spectacle is free and occurs nightly from April through September. A train tour of the illuminated city operates several times a night, from July 6 until August 25.

Fodor'sChoice
★

Cathédrale Notre-Dame. Worship on the site of the Cathédrale Notre-Dame, better known as Chartres Cathedral, goes back to before the Gallo-Roman period—the crypt contains a well that was the focus of druid ceremonies. In the late 9th century Charles II (known as "the Bald") presented Chartres with what was believed to be the tunic of the Virgin Mary, a precious relic that went on to attract hordes of pilgrims. The current cathedral, the sixth church on the spot, dates mainly from the 12th and 13th centuries and was erected after the previous building, dating from the 11th century, burned down in 1194. A well-chronicled outburst of religious fervor followed the discovery that the Virgin Mary's relic had miraculously survived unsinged. Princes and paupers, barons and bourgeoisie gave their money and their labor to build the new cathedral. Ladies of the manor came to help monks and peasants on the scaffolding in a tremendous resurgence of religious faith that followed the Second Crusade. Just 25 years were needed for Chartres Cathedral to rise again, and it has remained substantially unchanged since.

The lower half of the facade survives from the earlier Romanesque church: this can be seen most clearly in the use of round arches rather than the pointed Gothic style. The **Royal Portal** is richly sculpted with scenes from the life of Christ—these sculpted figures are among the greatest created during the Middle Ages. The taller of the two spires (380 feet versus 350 feet) was built at the start of the 16th century, after its predecessor was destroyed by fire; its fanciful Flamboyant intricacy contrasts sharply with the stumpy solemnity of its Romanesque counterpart (access €3, open daily 9:30–noon and 2–4:30). The **rose window** above the main portal dates from the 13th century, and the three windows below it contain some of the finest examples of 12th-century stained-glass artistry in France.

DID YOU KNOW?

Chartres's beautiful Clocher Neuf ("New Bell-tower") was completed in 1134, well before the Clocher Vieux ("Old Bell-tower"), on the right, which was built between 1145 and 1165.

As spiritual as Chartres is, the cathedral also had its more-earthbound uses. Look closely and you can see that the main nave floor has a subtle slant. This was built to provide drainage, as this part of the church was often used as a "hostel" by thousands of overnighting pilgrims in medieval times.

Your eyes will need time to adjust to the somber interior. The reward is seeing the gemlike richness of the stained glass, with the famous deep Chartres blue predominating. The oldest window is arguably the most beautiful: **Notre-Dame de la Belle Verrière** (Our Lady of the Lovely Window), in the south choir. The cathedral's windows are gradually being cleaned—a lengthy, painstaking process—and the contrast with those still covered in the grime of centuries is staggering. ■TIP➜ It's worth taking a pair of binoculars along with you to pick out the details. If you wish to know more about stained-glass techniques and the motifs used, visit the small exhibit in the gallery opposite the north porch. Since 2008, the cathedral has been undergoing an ambitious renovation—to the tune of a staggering €270 million (about $350 million)—that will continue through 2015. As of 2011, two major chapels (the chapels of the Martyrs and the Apostles) have been completely restored, as have the two bays of the nave and the lower choir. For those who remember these dark recesses before the restoration the transformation is nothing short of miraculous, with an estimated 160,000 square feet of original plasterwork now visible and many of the sublime details for which the cathedral is famous returned to their original 13th-century glory. For even more detail, try to arrange a tour (in English) with local institution Malcolm Miller, whose knowledge of the cathedral's history is formidable. (He leads tours twice a day Monday through Saturday, April–October, once a day November–March at noon. *You can reach him at the telephone number below, or at: ✎ millerchartres@aol.com.*) The vast black-and-white labyrinth on the floor of the nave is one of the few to have survived from the Middle Ages; the faithful were expected to travel along its entire length (some 300 yards) on their knees. Guided tours of the **Crypte** start from the Maison de la Crypte opposite the south porch. You can also see a fourth-century Gallo-Roman wall and some 12th-century wall paintings. ⊠ *16 cloître Notre-Dame* ☎ *02–37–21–75–02* ⊕ *www.chartres-tourisme.com* ☞ *Crypt €3. Tours €10* ☾ *Cathedral daily 8:30–7:30; guided tours of crypt Apr.–Oct., daily at 11, 2:15, 3:30, and 4:30; Nov.–Mar., daily at 11 and 4:15.*

Musée des Beaux-Arts (*Fine Arts Museum*). Just behind the famed cathedral, the town art museum is housed in a handsome 18th-century building that once used to serve as the bishop's palace. Its varied collection includes Renaissance enamels, a portrait of Erasmus by Holbein, tapestries, armor, and some fine (mainly French) paintings from the 17th, 18th, and 19th centuries. There's also a room devoted to the forceful 20th-century landscapes of Maurice de Vlaminck, who lived in the region. ⊠ *29 cloître Notre-Dame* ☎ *02–37–90–45–80* ☞ *€3.20; €5.20 with special exhibit* ☾ *Tues.–Sat. 10–noon and 2–6, Sun. 2–5.*

St-Aignan. Exquisite 17th-century stained glass can be admired at the church of St-Aignan, around the corner from St-Pierre. ⊠ *Rue des Grenets.*

St-Pierre. The Gothic church of St-Pierre, near the Eure River, has magnificent medieval windows from a period (circa 1300) not represented at the cathedral. The oldest stained glass here, portraying Old Testament worthies, is to the right of the choir and dates from the late 13th century. ✉ *Rue St-Pierre.*

WHERE TO EAT AND STAY

For expanded hotel reviews, visit Fodors.com.

$$$ FRENCH 🍴 **La Vieille Maison.** Just 100 yards from the cathedral, in a pretty 14th-century building with a flower-decked patio, this restaurant is a fine choice for either lunch or dinner. Chef Bruno Letartre changes his menu regularly, often including such regional specialties as asparagus, rich duck pâté, and superb homemade foie gras along with seafood and game in season. Prices, though justified, can be steep, but the "suggested" lunch menu ($$$) served on summer weekdays is a good bet. [$] *Average main: €31* ✉ *5 rue au Lait* ☎ *02–37–34–10–67* 🌐 *www.lavieillemaison.fr* ⏲ *No dinner Sun. Closed Mon. and Tues.*

$$ FRENCH 🍴 **Moulin de Ponceau.** Ask for a table with a view of the River Eure, with the cathedral looming above, at this 16th-century converted water mill. Better still, on sunny days you can eat outside, beneath a parasol on the stone terrace by the water's edge—an idyllic setting. Choose from a regularly changing menu of French stalwarts such as rabbit terrine, trout with almonds, and tarte tatin, or splurge on "la trilogie" of scallops, foie gras, and langoustine. [$] *Average main: €24* ✉ *21 rue de la Tannerie* ☎ *02–37–35–30–05* 🌐 *www.moulindeponceau.fr* ⏲ *No dinner Sun. Closed Mon.*

$$ HOTEL ★ 🏨 **Best Western Le Grand Monarque.** On Chartres's main town square not far from the cathedral, this is a delightful option with interiors that remain seductively and warmly redolent of the 19th century—it was originally built as a coaching inn—with many guest rooms attractively outfitted with brick walls, wood antiques, lush drapes, and modern bathrooms; the best are in a separate turn-of-the-20th-century building overlooking a garden, while the most atmospheric are tucked away in the attic. **Pros:** its old-fashioned charm still works today; the spanking new spa and fitness center offers beauty treatments and massage. **Cons:** best rooms are in an annex; uphill walk to cathedral. **TripAdvisor:** "central location," "good value," "atmospheric hotel." [$] *Rooms from: €120* ✉ *22 pl. des Épars* ☎ *02–37–18–15–15* 🌐 *www.bw-grand-monarque.com* 🛏 *55 rooms* 🍽 *Breakfast.*

$$$$ HOTEL Fodor's Choice ★ 🏨 **Château d'Esclimont.** On the way south from Rambouillet to Chartres, the town of St-Symphorien is famed for one of France's most spectacular château-hotels; with pointed turrets, *pièces d'eau* (moated pools), and a checkerboard facade, the 19th-century Esclimont domaine—built by La Rochefoucaulds—is well worth seeking out if you wish to eat and sleep like an aristocrat in luxuriously furnished guest rooms (many are loftily dimensioned, others snug in corner turrets) adorned with reproduction 18th-century French pieces. **Pros:** the grand style of a country château; wonderful rural setting. **Cons:** service can be pompous; off the beaten path and not easy to find. **TripAdvisor:** "fairy tale castle," "restored Bourbon relic," "fantastic prices." [$] *Rooms from: €240* ✉ *2 rue du Château-d'Esclimont, 24 km (15 miles) northeast of Chartres*

19

via N10/D18, St-Symphorien-le-Château ☎ *02–37–31–15–15* ⊕ *www. esclimont.com* ↪ *48 rooms, 5 suites* ○! *Some meals.*

DISNEYLAND PARIS

68 km (40 miles) southwest of Pierrefonds via D335, D136, N330, and A4; 38 km (24 miles) east of Paris via A4.

Originally called Euro Disney, Disneyland Paris is probably not what you've traveled to France to experience. But if you have a child in tow, the promise of a day here may get you through an afternoon at Versailles or Fontainebleau. If you're a dyed-in-the-wool Disney fan, you'll want to make a beeline for the park to see how it has been molded to appeal to the tastes of Europeans (Disney's "Imagineers" call it their most lovingly detailed park). And if you've never experienced this particular form of Disney showmanship, you may want to put in an appearance if only to see what all the fuss is about.

GETTING HERE

Take the RER from central Paris (stations at Étoile, Auber, Les Halles, Gare de Lyon, and Nation) to Marne-la-Vallée–Chessy, 100 yards from the Disneyland entrance. Journey time is around 40 minutes, and trains operate every 10–30 minutes, depending on the time of day. Note that a TGV (Train à Grande Vitesse) station links Disneyland to Lille, Lyon, Brussels, and London (via Lille and the Channel Tunnel). Disneyland's hotel complex offers a shuttle-bus service to Orly and Charles de Gaulle airports for €21.

Visitor Information Disneyland Paris reservations office ⌂ *B.P. 100, cedex 4, Marne-la-Vallée 77777* ☎ *01–60–30–60–90, 407/939–7675 in U.S.* ⊕ *www.disneylandparis.com.*

EXPLORING

☺   **Disneyland Paris.** Disneyland Paris, a slightly downsized version of its
Fodor's Choice   United States counterpart, is nevertheless a spectacular sight, created
★   with an acute attention to detail. Disney never had quite the following here as it did Stateside, so when it opened, few turned up. Today, however, the place is jammed with crowds with families from around the world reveling in the many splendors of the Disney universe.

Some of the rides can be a bit scary for little kids, but tots adore Alice's Maze, Peter Pan's Flight, and especially the whirling Mad Hatter's Teacups. Also getting high marks are the afternoon parades, which feature music and introductions in five languages and huge floats swarming with all of Disney's most beloved characters—just make sure to stake your place along Main Street in advance for a good spot (check for posted times). There's a lot here, so pace yourself: kids can easily feel overwhelmed with the barrage of stimuli or frustrated by extra-long waits at the rides. (Also be aware that there are size restrictions for some rides.) The older the child, the more they will enjoy Walt Disney Studios, a cinematically driven area, where many of the newer Disney character-themed rides can be found.

Disneyland Park, as the original theme park is styled, consists of five "lands": Main Street U.S.A., Frontierland, Adventureland, Fantasyland, and Discoveryland. The central theme of each land is relentlessly echoed in every detail, from attractions to restaurant menus to souvenirs. The park is circled by a railroad, which stops three times along the perimeter. **Main Street U.S.A.** goes under the railroad and past shops and restaurants toward the main plaza; Disney parades are held here every afternoon and, during holiday periods, every evening.

Top attractions at **Frontierland** are the chilling Phantom Manor, haunted by holographic spooks, and the thrilling runaway mine train of Big Thunder Mountain, a roller coaster that plunges wildly through floods and avalanches in a setting meant to evoke Utah's Monument Valley. Whiffs of Arabia, Africa, and the Caribbean give **Adventureland** its exotic cachet; the spicy meals and snacks served here rank among the best food in the park. Don't miss the Pirates of the Caribbean, an exciting *mise-en-scène* populated by eerily humanlike, computer-driven figures, or Indiana Jones and the Temple of Doom, a breathtaking ride that re-creates some of this luckless hero's most exciting moments.

Fantasyland charms the youngest parkgoers with familiar cartoon characters from such classic Disney films as *Snow White, Pinocchio, Dumbo,* and *Peter Pan.* The focal point of Fantasyland, and indeed Disneyland Paris, is Le Château de la Belle au Bois Dormant (Sleeping Beauty's Castle), a 140-foot, bubblegum-pink structure topped with 16 blue- and gold-tipped turrets. Its design was allegedly inspired by illustrations from a medieval Book of Hours—if so, it was by way of Beverly Hills. The castle's dungeon conceals a 2-ton scaly green dragon that rumbles in its sleep and occasionally rouses to roar—an impressive feat of engineering, producing an answering chorus of shrieks from younger children. **Discoveryland** is a futuristic eye-knocker for high-tech Disney entertainment. Robots on roller skates welcome you on your way to Star Tours, a pitching, plunging, sense-confounding ride based on the *Star Wars* films. In Le Visionarium, a simulated space journey is presented by 9-Eye, a staggeringly realistic robot. One of the park's newest attractions, the Jules Verne–inspired **Space Mountain Mission 2,** pretends to catapult *exploronauts* on a rocket-boosted, comet-battered journey through the Milky Way.

Disneyland Paris is peppered with places to eat, ranging from snack bars and fast-food joints to five full-service restaurants—all with a distinguishing theme. If your child has his or her heart set on a specifically themed restaurant, say, Pirates of the Caribbean—a dark corsair's lair that looks over the ride itself—or the Auberge de Cendrillon (Cinderella's Inn), where the nasty stepmother and sisters themselves bustle through the aisles, make sure to make reservations in advance (which can be done online). In addition, Walt Disney Studios, Disney Village, and Disney Hotels have restaurants open to the public. But since these are outside the park, it's not recommended that you waste time traveling to them for lunch. Disneyland Paris has relaxed its no-alcohol policy and now serves wine and beer in the park's sit-down restaurants, as well as in the hotels and restaurants outside the park.

19

Walt Disney Studios opened next to the Disneyland Park in 2002. The theme park is divided into four "production zones." Beneath imposing entrance gates and a 100-foot water tower inspired by the one erected in 1939 at Disney Studios in Burbank, California, **Front Lot** contains shops, a restaurant, and a studio re-creating the atmosphere of Sunset Boulevard. In **Animation Courtyard,** Disney artists demonstrate the various phases of character animation; Animagique brings to life scenes from *Pinocchio* and *The Lion King*, while the Genie from *Aladdin* pilots Flying Carpets over Agrabah. **Production Courtyard** hosts the Walt Disney Television Studios; Cinémagique, a special-effects tribute to U.S. and European cinema; and a behind-the-scenes Studio Tram tour of location sites, movie props, studio interiors, and costuming, ending with a visit to Catastrophe Canyon in the heart of a film shoot. **Back Lot** majors in stunts. At Armageddon Special Effects you can confront a flaming meteor shower aboard the Mir space station, then complete your visit at the giant outdoor arena with a Stunt Show Spectacular involving cars, motorbikes, and Jet Skis. ☎ *01–60–30–60–90* 🌐 *www.disneylandparis.com* 🎟 *€59, or €153 for 3-day Passport; includes admission to all individual attractions within Disneyland or Walt Disney Studios, but not meals; tickets for Walt Disney Studios are also valid for admission to Disneyland during last 3 opening hrs of same day* 🕓 *Disneyland mid-June–mid-Sept., daily 9 am–10 pm; mid-Sept.–Dec. 19 and Jan. 5–mid-June, weekdays 10–8, weekends 9–8; Dec. 20–Jan. 4, daily 9–8. Walt Disney Studios daily 10–6.*

WHERE TO EAT AND STAY

For expanded hotel reviews, visit Fodors.com.

$$$$ HOTEL 🏨 **Sequoia Lodge.** Ranging from superluxe to still-a-pretty-penny, Disneyland Paris has 5,000 rooms in five hotels, but your best bet on all counts may be the Sequoia Lodge, just a few minutes' walk from the theme park, where the mood—a grand recreation of an American mountain lodge—is quite different from the other, glitzier big hotels here. **Pros:** package deals include admission to theme park; cozy, secluded feel; great pools. **Cons:** restaurants a bit ho-hum; many rooms do not have lake view; room rates are 400 euros and up (and this is considered "mid-range" in Disney land). **TripAdvisor:** "not so magical," "average hotel," "would go again." [$] *Rooms from: €400* 📫 *Centre de Réservations, B.P. 100, cedex 4, Marne-la-Vallée 77777* ☎ *01–60–30–60–90, 407/939–7675 in U.S.* 🌐 *www.disneylandparis.com* 🍴 *All meals.*

UNDERSTANDING PARIS

BOOKS AND MOVIES

VOCABULARY

BOOKS AND MOVIES

Books

Fiction. Think of writers in Paris, and the romanticized expat figures of the interwar "lost generation" often come to mind: Ernest Hemingway (*The Sun Also Rises*), F. Scott Fitzgerald, Ezra Pound, and Gertrude Stein just to name a few. Further back in time are classics like Charles Dickens's *A Tale of Two Cities*, set during the Revolution, and Henry James's novels *The American* and *The Ambassadors*, both tales of Americans in Europe. The expats of World War II set the scene for future Americans in Paris: James Baldwin's life in the city in the 1950s informed novels such as *Giovanni's Room*, and the denizens of the so-called Beat Hotel (Allen Ginsberg, William Burroughs, and Henry Miller) squeezed in some writing among their less salubrious activities. The Canadian writer Mavis Gallant, who published many stories in *The New Yorker*, also began her tenure in Paris in the '50s; her collection *Paris Stories* is a delight.

Recent best sellers with a Paris setting include, of course, Dan Brown's *The Da Vinci Code*, as well as Diane Johnson's *Le Divorce* and *Le Mariage*, Anita Brookner's *Incidents in the Rue Laugier*, and Patrick Suskind's *Perfume: The Story of a Murderer*. Paul LaFarge's *Haussmann, or the Distinction* spins historical detail about the ambitious city planner into a fascinating period novel. For literary snacking, *Paris in Mind* pulls together excerpts from books by American authors.

For Children. Who doesn't remember Miss Clavel and her 12 young students in two straight lines? Ludwig Bemelmans' beloved *Madeleine* series about the namesake heroine is also illustrated with the author's drawings of Paris landmarks such as the Opéra and the Jardins du Luxembourg. *Eloise in Paris*, by Kay Thompson, also has illustrations, these by Hilary Knight (look for his take on Christian Dior). The *Anatole* books by Eve Titus are classics, starring a Gallic mouse. Playful, bright illustrations drive Maira Kalman's *Ooh-la-la (Max in Love)*; the singsong language, smattered with French, is perfect for reading aloud. Joan MacPhail Knight wrote a pair of books about an American girl visiting France in the late 1800s: *Charlotte in Giverny* and *Charlotte in Paris*.

History. Recent studies devoted to the capital include Philip Mansel's *Paris Between Empires: Monarchy and Revolution*; Jill Harsin's *Barricades: War on the Streets in Revolutionary Paris*; and Johannes Willms's *Paris: Capital of Europe*, which runs from the Revolution to the Belle Époque. Simon Schama's *Citizens* is a good introduction to the French Revolution. Alistair Horne's *Seven Ages of Paris* skips away from standard historical approaches, breaking the city's past into seven eras and putting a colorful spin on the Renaissance, the Revolution, Napoléon's Empire, and other periods.

Biographies and autobiographies of French luminaries and Paris residents can double as satisfying portraits of the capital during their subjects' lifetimes. Works on Baron Haussmann are especially rich, as the 19th-century prefect so utterly changed the face of the city. For a look at American expatriates in Paris between the wars, pick up *Sylvia Beach and the Lost Generation*, by Noel R. Fitch. Tyler Stovall's *Paris Noir: African-Americans in the City of Light* examines black American artists' affection for Paris during the 20th century; *Harlem in Montmartre*, by William A. Shack, homes in on expat jazz culture. Walter Benjamin's *The Arcades Project* uses the 19th century as a point of intersection for studies on advertising, Baudelaire, the Paris Commune, and other subjects.

Memoirs, Essays, and Observations. Ernest Hemingway's *A Moveable Feast*, the tale of his 1920s expat life in Paris as a struggling writer, grips from its opening lines. Gertrude Stein, one of Hemingway's friends, gave her own version of the era in *The Autobiography of Alice B. Toklas*.

In *The Secret Paris of the '30s*, Brassaï put into words the scenes he captured in photographs. Joseph Roth gave an exile's point of view in *Report from a Parisian Paradise*. Art Buchwald's funny yet poignant *I'll Always Have Paris* moves from the postwar GI Bill days through his years as a journalist and adventurer. Stanley Karnow also drew on a reporter's past in *Paris in the Fifties*. Henry Miller's visceral autobiographical works such as *The Tropic of Cancer* reveal a grittier kind of expat life. Janet Flanner's incomparable *Paris Journals* chronicle the city from the 1940s through 1970, and no one has yet matched A.J. Liebling at table, as described in *Between Meals*.

More recent accounts by Americans living in Paris include Edmund White's *Our Paris: Sketches with Memory* (White is also the author of a brief but captivating wander through the city in *The Flâneur*), Alex Karmel's *A Corner in the Marais: Memoir of a Paris Neighborhood*, Thad Carhart's *The Piano Shop on the Left Bank*, and the very funny *Me Talk Pretty One Day*, by David Sedaris. Adam Gopnik, a *New Yorker* writer who lived in Paris in the 1990s, intersperses articles on larger French issues with descriptions of daily life with his wife and son in *Paris to the Moon*. Gopnik also edited the anthology *Americans in Paris*, a collection of observations by everyone from Thomas Jefferson to Cole Porter.

Works in Translation. Many landmarks of French literature have long been claimed as classics in English as well—Victor Hugo's great 19th-century novels, including *The Hunchback of Notre-Dame* and *Les Misérables*, spin elaborate descriptions of Paris. Other 19th-century masterpieces include Gustave Flaubert's *Sentimental Education*, set against the capital's 1848 uprisings, and Honoré de Balzac's *Human Comedy*, a series of dozens of novels, many set in Paris.

Marcel Proust's masterpiece *À la Recherche du Temps Perdu* (*In Search of Lost Time*) describes fin-de-siècle Paris's parks, glittering aristocratic salons, and dread during the Great War. Colette was another great chronicler of the Belle Époque; her short works include *Chéri* and the Claudine stories.

Simone de Beauvoir's *The Prime of Life*, the second book in her autobiographical trilogy, details her relationship with the existentialist philosopher Jean-Paul Sartre in the context of 1930s and '40s Paris, when the Rive Gauche cemented its modern bohemian reputation in its cafés and jazz clubs.

Movies

Drama. One of the most talked-about movies of 2006 was Sofia Coppola's lavish *Marie Antoinette*; it might not have been a box office hit, but it's an interesting take on life at Versailles. Previous to that, the film version of *The Da Vinci Code* (2006), starring Tom Hanks and Audrey Tautou, was talked about for months preceding its release, although some were disappointed. The heist film *Ronin* (1998) pairs Robert De Niro and Jean Reno with a hyperkinetic chase through the streets of Paris; and in *Frantic* (1987) Harrison Ford plays an American doctor visiting Paris when his wife disappears, and director Roman Polanski shoots the city to build suspense and dread. The Palais-Royal gets an equally tense treatment in the Audrey Hepburn–Cary Grant thriller *Charade* (1963); the 2002 remake, *The Truth About Charlie*, doesn't hold a candle to the original. In *Before Sunset* (2004), Ethan Hawke meets Julie Delpy in Paris in the sequel to *Before Sunrise*.

French Films. One of the biggest hits out of France was *Amélie* (2001), which follows a young woman determined to change people's lives. There's a love angle, *bien sûr*, and the neighborhood of Montmartre is practically a third hero, although Parisians sniffed that it was a sterilized version of the raffish quartier.

Jean-Luc Godard's *Breathless* (1960) and François Truffaut's *The 400 Blows* (slang for "raising hell"; 1959) kicked off the New Wave cinema movement. Godard eschewed traditional movie narrative techniques, employing a loose style—including improvised dialogue and hand-held camera shots—for his story about a low-level crook (Jean-Paul Belmondo) and his girlfriend (Jean Seberg). Truffaut's film is a masterwork of innocence lost, a semiautobiographical story of a young boy banished to juvenile detention.

Catherine Deneuve is practically a film industry in and of herself. Her movies span the globe; those shot in Paris range from *Belle de Jour* (1967)—Luis Buñuel's study of erotic repression—to *Le Dernier Métro* (1980), a World War II drama.

Classic film noir and contemporary crime dramas are also highlights of French cinema: for a taste, rent *Rififi* (1955), with its excruciatingly tense 33-minute heist scene; *Le Samouraï* (1967), in which Alain Delon plays the ultimate cool assassin; or Robert Bresson's *Pickpocket* (1959). *La Casque d'Or* (1952) looks back to the underworld of the early 1900s, with Simone Signoret as the title irresistible blond. French director Luc Besson introduced a sly female action hero with *La Femme Nikita* (1990), in which Jean Reno chills as the creepy "cleaner" you don't want making house calls.

Filmed during the Occupation, *The Children of Paradise* (1945) became an allegory for the French spirit of resistance: the love story was set in 1840s Paris, thereby getting past the German censors. Other romantic films with memorable takes on Paris include *Cyrano de Bergerac* (1990), with Gérard Depardieu as the large-schnozzed hero; the comedy *When the Cat's Away* (1996); the talk-heavy films of Eric Rohmer; *Camille Claudel* (1988), about the affair between Rodin and fellow sculptor Claudel; and the gritty *The Lovers on the Bridge* (1999), the flaws balanced by the bravado of Juliette Binoche waterskiing on the Seine surrounded by fireworks. *The Red Balloon* (1956) is also a love story of a sort: a children's film of a boy and his faithful balloon.

Musicals. Love in the time of Toulouse-Lautrec? Elton John songs? Baz Luhrmann's *Moulin Rouge* (2001) whirls them together and wins through conviction rather than verisimilitude. John Huston's 1952 film of the same name is also well worth watching. Gene Kelly pursues Leslie Caron through postwar Paris in *An American in Paris* (1951); the Gershwin-fueled film includes a stunning 17-minute dance sequence. Caron reappears as the love interest—this time as a young girl in training to be a courtesan—in *Gigi* (1958). *Funny Face* (1957) stars Fred Astaire and Audrey Hepburn, and there's an unforgettable scene of Hepburn descending the staircase below the *Winged Victory* in the Louvre.

VOCABULARY

One of the trickiest French sounds to pronounce is the nasal final n sound (whether or not the n is actually the last letter of the word). You should try to pronounce it as a sort of nasal grunt—as in "huh." The vowel that precedes the n will govern the vowel sound of the word, and in this list we precede the final n with an h to remind you to be nasal.

Another problem sound is the ubiquitous but untransliterable eu, as in bleu (blue) or deux (two), and the very similar sound in je (I), ce (this), and de (of). The closest equivalent might be the vowel sound in "put," but rounded. The famous rolled r is a glottal sound. Consonants at the ends of words are usually silent; when the following word begins with a vowel, however, the two are run together by sounding the consonant. There are two forms of "you" in French: vous (formal and plural) and tu (a singular, personal form). When addressing an adult you don't know, vous is always best.

	ENGLISH	FRENCH	PRONUNCIATION
BASICS			
	Yes/no	Oui/non	wee/nohn
	Please	S'il vous plaît	seel voo play
	Thank you	Merci	mair-**see**
	You're welcome	De rien	deh ree-**ehn**
	Excuse me, sorry	Pardon	pahr-**don**
	Good morning/ afternoon	Bonjour	bohn-**zhoor**
	Good evening	Bonsoir	bohn-**swahr**
	Good-bye	Au revoir	o ruh-**vwahr**
	Mr. (Sir)	Monsieur	muh-**syuh**
	Mrs. (Ma'am)	Madame	ma-**dam**
	Miss	Mademoiselle	mad-mwa-**zel**
	Pleased to meet you	Enchanté(e)	ohn-shahn-**tay**
	How are you?	Comment allez-vous?	kuh-mahn-tahl-ay **voo**
	Very well, thanks	Très bien, merci	tray bee-ehn, mair-**see**
	And you?	Et vous?	ay voo?
NUMBERS			
	one	un	uhn
	two	deux	deuh
	three	trois	twah

ENGLISH	FRENCH	PRONUNCIATION
four	quatre	**kaht**-ruh
five	cinq	sank
six	six	seess
seven	sept	set
eight	huit	wheat
nine	neuf	nuf
ten	dix	deess
eleven	onze	ohnz
twelve	douze	dooz
thirteen	treize	trehz
fourteen	quatorze	kah-**torz**
fifteen	quinze	kanz
sixteen	seize	sez
seventeen	dix-sept	deez-**set**
eighteen	dix-huit	deez-**wheat**
nineteen	dix-neuf	deez-**nuf**
twenty	vingt	vehn
twenty-one	vingt-et-un	vehnt-ay-**uhn**
thirty	trente	trahnt
forty	quarante	ka-**rahnt**
fifty	cinquante	sang-**kahnt**
sixty	soixante	swa-**sahnt**
seventy	soixante-dix	swa-sahnt-**deess**
eighty	quatre-vingts	kaht-ruh-**vehn**
ninety	quatre-vingt-dix	kaht-ruh-vehn-**deess**
one hundred	cent	sahn
one thousand	mille	meel

COLORS

black	noir	nwahr
blue	bleu	bleuh

ENGLISH	FRENCH	PRONUNCIATION
brown	brun/marron	bruhn/mar-**rohn**
green	vert	vair
orange	orange	o-**rahnj**
pink	rose	rose
red	rouge	rouge
violet	violette	vee-o-**let**
white	blanc	blahnk
yellow	jaune	zhone

DAYS OF THE WEEK

Sunday	dimanche	dee-**mahnsh**
Monday	lundi	luhn-**dee**
Tuesday	mardi	mahr-**dee**
Wednesday	mercredi	mair-kruh-**dee**
Thursday	jeudi	zhuh-**dee**
Friday	vendredi	vawn-druh-**dee**
Saturday	samedi	sahm-**dee**

MONTHS

January	janvier	zhahn-vee-**ay**
February	février	feh-vree-**ay**
March	mars	marce
April	avril	a-**vreel**
May	mai	meh
June	juin	zhwehn
July	juillet	zhwee-**ay**
August	août	ah-**oo**
September	septembre	sep-**tahm**-bruh
October	octobre	awk-**to**-bruh
November	novembre	no-**vahm**-bruh
December	décembre	day-**sahm**-bruh

ENGLISH	FRENCH	PRONUNCIATION

USEFUL PHRASES

ENGLISH	FRENCH	PRONUNCIATION
Do you speak English?	Parlez-vous anglais?	par-lay **voo** ahn-**glay**
I don't speak . . .	Je ne parle pas . . .	zhuh nuh parl pah . . .
French	français	frahn-**say**
I don't understand	Je ne comprends pas	zhuh nuh kohm-**prahn** pah
I understand	Je comprends	zhuh kohm-**prahn**
I don't know	Je ne sais pas	zhuh nuh say **pah**
I'm American/ British	Je suis américain/ anglais	zhuh sweez a-may-ree-**kehn**/ ahn-**glay**
What's your name?	Comment vous appelez-vous?	ko-mahn vooz a-pell-ay-**voo**
My name is . . .	Je m'appelle . . .	zhuh ma-**pell** . . .
What time is it?	Quelle heure est-il?	kel air eh-**teel**
How?	Comment?	ko-**mahn**
When?	Quand?	kahn
Yesterday	Hier	yair
Today	Aujourd'hui	o-zhoor-**dwee**
Tomorrow	Demain	duh-**mehn**
Tonight	Ce soir	suh **swahr**
What?	Quoi?	kwah
What is it?	Qu'est-ce que c'est?	kess-kuh-**say**
Why?	Pourquoi?	poor-**kwa**
Who?	Qui?	kee
Where is . . .	Où est . . .	oo ay
the train station?	la gare?	la gar
the subway station?	la station de métro?	la sta-**syon** duh may-**tro**
the bus stop?	l'arrêt de bus?	la-ray duh booss
the post office?	la poste?	la post
the bank?	la banque?	la bahnk

ENGLISH	FRENCH	PRONUNCIATION
the . . . hotel?	l'hôtel . . .?	lo-**tel**
the store?	le magasin?	luh ma-ga-**zehn**
the cashier?	la caisse?	la **kess**
the . . . museum?	le musée . . .?	luh mew-**zay**
the hospital?	l'hôpital?	lo-pee-**tahl**
the elevator?	l'ascenseur?	la-sahn-**seuhr**
the telephone?	le téléphone?	luh tay-lay-**phone**
Where are the	Où sont les	oo sohn lay
restrooms?	toilettes?	twah-**let**
(men/women)	(hommes/femmes)	(**oh**-mm/**fah**-mm)
Here/there	Ici/là	ee-**see**/la
Left/right	A gauche/à droite	a goash/a draht
Straight ahead	Tout droit	too drwah
Is it near/far?	C'est près/loin?	say pray/lwehn
I'd like . . .	Je voudrais . . .	zhuh voo-**dray**
a room	une chambre	ewn **shahm**-bruh
the key	la clé	la clay
a newspaper	un journal	uhn zhoor-**nahl**
a stamp	un timbre	uhn **tam**-bruh
I'd like to buy . . .	Je voudrais acheter . .	zhuh voo-**dray ahsh**-tay
cigarettes	des cigarettes	day see-ga-**ret**
matches	des allumettes	days a-loo-**met**
soap	du savon	dew sah-**vohn**
city map	un plan de ville	uhn plahn de **veel**
road map	une carte routière	ewn cart roo-tee-**air**
magazine	une revue	ewn reh-**vu**
envelopes	des enveloppes	dayz ahn-veh-**lope**
writing paper	du papier à lettres	dew pa-pee-**ay** a **let**-ruh
postcard	une carte postale	ewn cart pos-**tal**
How much is it?	C'est combien?	say comb-bee-**ehn**

ENGLISH	FRENCH	PRONUNCIATION
A little/a lot	Un peu/beaucoup	uhn peuh/bo-**koo**
More/less	Plus/moins	plu/mwehn
Enough/too (much)	Assez/trop	a-say/tro
I am ill/sick	Je suis malade	zhuh swee ma-**lahd**
Call a . . .	Appelez un . . .	a-play uhn
doctor	docteur	dohk-**tehr**
Help!	Au secours!	o suh-**koor**
Stop!	Arrêtez!	a-reh-**tay**
Fire!	Au feu!	o fuh
Caution!/Look out!	Attention!	a-tahn-see-**ohn**

DINING OUT

A bottle of . . .	une bouteille de . . .	ewn boo-**tay** duh
A cup of . . .	une tasse de . . .	ewn tass duh
A glass of . . .	un verre de . . .	uhn vair duh
Bill/check	l'addition	la-dee-see-**ohn**
Bread	du pain	dew panh
Breakfast	le petit-déjeuner	luh puh-**tee** day-zhuh-**nay**
Butter	du beurre	dew burr
Cheers!	A votre santé!	ah **vo**-truh sahn-**tay**
Cocktail/aperitif	un apéritif	uhn ah-pay-ree-**teef**
Dinner	le dîner	luh dee-**nay**
Dish of the day	le plat du jour	luh plah dew **zhoor**
Enjoy!	Bon appétit!	bohn a-pay-**tee**
Fixed-price menu	le menu	luh may-**new**
Fork	une fourchette	ewn four-**shet**
I am diabetic	Je suis diabétique	zhuh swee dee-ah-bay-**teek**
I am vegetarian	Je suis végétarien(ne)	zhuh swee vay-zhay-ta-ree-**en**
I cannot eat . . .	Je ne peux pas manger de . . .	zhuh nuh puh pah mahn-**jay** deh

ENGLISH	FRENCH	PRONUNCIATION
I'd like to order	Je voudrais commander	zhuh voo-**dray** ko-mahn-**day**
Is service/the tip included?	Est-ce que le service est compris?	ess kuh luh sair-**veess** ay comb-**pree**
It's good/bad	C'est bon/mauvais	say bohn/mo-**vay**
It's hot/cold	C'est chaud/froid	say sho/frwah
Knife	un couteau	uhn koo-**toe**
Lunch	le déjeuner	luh day-zhuh-**nay**
Menu	la carte	la cart
Napkin	une serviette	ewn sair-vee-**et**
Pepper	du poivre	dew **pwah**-vruh
Plate	une assiette	ewn a-see-**et**
Please give me . . .	Donnez-moi . . .	doe-nay-**mwah**
Salt	du sel	dew sell
Spoon	une cuillère	ewn kwee-**air**
Sugar	du sucre	dew **sook**-ruh
Waiter!/Waitress!	Monsieur!/ Mademoiselle!	muh-**syuh**/ mad-mwa-**zel**
Wine list	la carte des vins	la cart day vehn

MENU GUIDE

FRENCH	ENGLISH

GENERAL DINING

Entrée	Appetizer/Starter
Garniture au choix	Choice of vegetable side
Plat du jour	Dish of the day
Selon arrivage	When available
Supplément/En sus	Extra charge
Sur commande	Made to order

FRENCH	ENGLISH

PETIT DÉJEUNER (BREAKFAST)

Confiture	Jam
Miel	Honey
Oeuf à la coque	Boiled egg
Oeufs sur le plat	Fried eggs
Oeufs brouillés	Scrambled eggs
Tartine	Bread with butter

POISSONS/FRUITS DE MER (FISH/SEAFOOD)

Anchois	Anchovies
Bar	Bass
Brandade de morue	Creamed salt cod
Brochet	Pike
Cabillaud/Morue	Fresh cod
Calmar	Squid
Coquilles St-Jacques	Scallops
Crevettes	Shrimp
Daurade	Sea bream
Ecrevisses	Prawns/Crayfish
Harengs	Herring
Homard	Lobster
Huîtres	Oysters
Langoustine	Prawn/Lobster
Lotte	Monkfish
Moules	Mussels
Palourdes	Clams
Saumon	Salmon
Thon	Tuna
Truite	Trout

FRENCH	ENGLISH

VIANDE (MEAT)

French	English
Agneau	Lamb
Boeuf	Beef
Boudin	Sausage
Boulettes de viande	Meatballs
Brochettes	Kabobs
Cassoulet	Casserole of white beans, meat
Cervelle	Brains
Chateaubriand	Double fillet steak
Choucroute garnie	Sausages with sauerkraut
Côtelettes	Chops
Côte/Côte de boeuf	Rib/T-bone steak
Cuisses de grenouilles	Frogs' legs
Entrecôte	Rib or rib-eye steak
Épaule	Shoulder
Escalope	Cutlet
Foie	Liver
Gigot	Leg
Porc	Pork
Ris de veau	Veal sweetbreads
Rognons	Kidneys
Saucisses	Sausages
Selle	Saddle
Tournedos	Tenderloin of T-bone steak
Veau	Veal

METHODS OF PREPARATION

French	English
A point	Medium
A l'étouffée	Stewed
Au four	Baked
Ballotine	Boned, stuffed, and rolled

FRENCH	ENGLISH
Bien cuit	Well-done
Bleu	Very rare
Frit	Fried
Grillé	Grilled
Rôti	Roast
Saignant	Rare

VOLAILLES/GIBIER (POULTRY/GAME)

Blanc de volaille	Chicken breast
Canard/Caneton	Duck/Duckling
Cerf/Chevreuil	Venison (red/roe)
Coq au vin	Chicken stewed in red wine
Dinde/Dindonneau	Turkey/Young turkey
Faisan	Pheasant
Lapin/Lièvre	Rabbit/Wild hare
Oie	Goose
Pintade/Pintadeau	Guinea fowl/Young guinea fowl
Poulet/Poussin	Chicken/Spring chicken

LÉGUMES (VEGETABLES)

Artichaut	Artichoke
Asperge	Asparagus
Aubergine	Eggplant
Carottes	Carrots
Champignons	Mushrooms
Chou-fleur	Cauliflower
Chou (rouge)	Cabbage (red)
Laitue	Lettuce
Oignons	Onions
Petits pois	Peas
Pomme de terre	Potato
Tomates	Tomatoes

FRENCH	ENGLISH

FRUITS/NOIX (FRUITS/NUTS)

FRENCH	ENGLISH
Abricot	Apricot
Amandes	Almonds
Ananas	Pineapple
Cassis	Black currants
Cerises	Cherries
Citron/Citron vert	Lemon/Lime
Fraises	Strawberries
Framboises	Raspberries
Pamplemousse	Grapefruit
Pêche	Peach
Poire	Pear
Pomme	Apple
Prunes/Pruneaux	Plums/Prunes
Raisins/Raisins secs	Grapes/Raisins

DESSERTS

FRENCH	ENGLISH
Coupe (glacée)	Sundae
Crème Chantilly	Whipped cream
Gâteau au chocolat	Chocolate cake
Glace	Ice cream
Tarte tatin	Caramelized apple tart
Tourte	Layer cake

DRINKS

FRENCH	ENGLISH
A l'eau	With water
Avec des glaçons	On the rocks
Bière	Beer
Blonde/brune	Light/dark
Café noir/crème	Black coffee/with steamed milk
Chocolat chaud	Hot chocolate
Eau-de-vie	Brandy

FRENCH	ENGLISH
Eau minérale	Mineral water
gazeuse/non gazeuse	carbonated/still
Jus de . . .	. . . juice
Lait	Milk
Sec	Straight or dry
Thé	Tea
Au lait/au citron	with milk/lemon
Vin	Wine
Blanc	white
Doux	sweet
Léger	light
Brut	very dry
Rouge	red

Travel Smart Paris

WORD OF MOUTH

"I suffer really bad jetlag coming from the U.S. to France. If you can, avoid a nap on your first day—that's a good idea. Have an early dinner and go to bed so you can get a good night's sleep and wake up feeling ready to go on the next day. I think walking outdoors in the fresh air will be the best thing to keep you on your toes. When you get tired, stop at a café, drink some coffee, and do some people watching. You can even sit outside at many cafes [in winter], as sometimes they have outdoor heaters to keep you warm."

—FrenchMystiqueTours

GETTING HERE AND AROUND

Addresses in Paris are fairly straight-forward: there's the number, the street name, and the zip code designating one of Paris's 20 *arrondissements* (districts); for instance, in Paris 75010, the last two digits "10" indicates that the address is in the 10^e. The large 16^e arrondissement has two numbers assigned to it: 75016 and 75116. *For the layout of Paris's arrondissements, see the What's Where map in the Experience chapter.*

The arrondissements are laid out in a spiral, beginning from the area around the Louvre (1er arrondissement), then moving clockwise through the Marais, the Latin Quarter, St-Germain, and then out from the city center to the outskirts to Ménilmontant/Père-Lachaise (20e arrondissement). Occasionally you may see an address with a number plus *bis*—for instance, 20 bis, rue Vavin. This indicates the next entrance or door down from 20 rue Vavin. Note that in France you enter a building on the ground floor, or *rez-de-chaussée* (RC or 0), and go up one floor to the first floor, or *premier étage*. General address terms used in this book are *av.* (avenue), *bd.* (boulevard), *carrefour* (crossway), *cours* (promenade), *passage* (passageway), *pl.* (place), *quai* (quay/wharf/pier), *rue* (street), and *sq.* (square).

▌ AIR TRAVEL

Flying time to Paris is 7 hours from New York, 9½ hours from Chicago, and 11 hours from Los Angeles. Flying time from London to Paris is 1½ hours.

The French are notoriously stringent about security, particularly for international flights. Don't be surprised by the armed security officers patrolling the airports, and be prepared for very long check-in lines. Peak travel times in France are between mid-July and September, during the Christmas–New Year's holidays in late December and

early January, and during the February school break. During these periods airports are especially crowded, so allow plenty of extra time. Never leave your baggage unattended, even for a moment. Unattended baggage is considered a security risk and may be destroyed.

Airline and Airport Links.com. Airline and Airport Links.com has links to many of the world's airlines and airports. ⊕ *www.airlineandairportlinks.com.*

Airline Security Issues Transportation Security Administration. Transportation Security Administration has answers for almost every question that might come up. ⊕ *www.tsa.gov.*

AIRPORTS

The major airports are Charles de Gaulle (CDG, also known as Roissy), 26 km (16 mi) northeast of Paris, and Orly (ORY), 16 km (10 mi) south of Paris. Both are easily accessible from Paris. Whether you take a car or bus to travel from Paris to the airport on your departure, always allot an extra hour because of the often horrendous traffic tie-ups in the airports themselves (especially in peak seasons and at peak hours). Free light rail connections (Orlyval and CDGval) available between the major terminals are one option for avoiding some of the traffic mess, but still give yourself enough time to navigate your way through these busy airports. Check the Aéroports de Paris Live! function on the website (or smartphone application) for more up-to-date details and real time news from the airports.

Airport Information **Charles de Gaulle/ Roissy and Orly** ☎ *0033–1–70–36–39–50 outside of France (3950* in English)* ⊕ *www.adp.fr.*

GROUND TRANSPORTATION

By bus from CDG/Roissy: Roissybus, operated by the RATP (Paris Transit Authority), runs between Charles de Gaulle and the Opéra every 20 minutes from 6 am to 11 pm; the cost is €10. The trip takes about 45 minutes in regular traffic, about 90 minutes in rush-hour traffic.

By shuttle from CDG/Roissy: The Air France shuttle service is a comfortable option to get to and from the city—you don't need to have flown the carrier to use it. Line 2 goes from the airport to Paris's Charles de Gaulle Étoile and Porte Maillot from 5:45 am to 11 pm. It leaves every 20 minutes and costs €15, which you can pay on board. Line 4 goes to Montparnasse and the Gare de Lyon from 7 am to 9 pm. Buses run every 30 minutes and cost €16.50. Passengers arriving in Terminal 1 need to take Exit 34; Terminals 2A and 2C go to exit C2; 2B and 2D take exit B1; Terminals 2E and 2F, Exit 3.

A number of van services serve both Charles de Gaulle and Orly airports. Prices are set so there are no surprises even if traffic is a snail-pace nightmare. To make a reservation, call or fax your flight details at least one week in advance to the shuttle company and an air-conditioned van with a bilingual chauffeur will be waiting for you upon your arrival. Confirm the day before. These vans sometimes pick up more than one party, though, so you may have to share the shuttle with other passengers. Likewise, when taking people to the airport these shuttles usually pick up a couple of groups of passengers. This adds at least 20 minutes to the trip.

By taxi from CDG/Roissy: Taxis are generally the least desirable mode of transportation into the city. If you're traveling at peak hours, journey times (and prices) are unpredictable. At best, the journey takes 30 minutes, but it can be as long as one hour.

NAVIGATING PARIS

Paris is a walker's city, but public transportation is excellent when your feet get tired. The métro and bus systems are extensive and easy to use.

There are many landmarks in Paris to orient yourself by—churches, the Opéra, the Tour Eiffel, and so on. Choose one near your hotel, for example, and if you get lost, it'll be easy to get back on track.

As with any city that's not laid out in a numbered grid, it can be confusing to find what you're looking for—especially in a foreign language; don't hesitate to ask for help. Most people are happy to give assistance, especially if you try out some French (like *bonjour*).

By train from CDG/Roissy: The least expensive way to get into Paris from CDG is the RER-B line, the suburban express train, which runs from 5 am to 11:30 pm daily. There are two RER stations at CDG "RER B Aéroport Charles de Gaulle 1" for Terminals 1 (via CDGval) and 3 (via a covered walkway). "RER B Aéroport Charles de Gaulle 2" serves Terminal 2, accessible via walkways or by the free N1 shuttle. Trains to central Paris (Les Halles, St-Michel, Luxembourg) depart every 15 minutes. The fare (including métro connection) is €9.25, and journey time is about 45 minutes.

By bus from Orly: Air France buses run from Orly to Les Invalides, Charles de Gaulle Étoile, and Montparnasse; these run every 15 minutes from 6 am to 11 pm. (You need not have flown on Air France to use this service.) The fare is €11.50, and journey time is between 30 and 45 minutes, depending on traffic. To find the bus, take Exit L if you've arrived in Orly South, or Exit B-C from Orly West. RATP's Orlybus is yet another option; buses leave every 15 minutes for the Denfert-Rochereau métro station in Montparnasse from Exit H in Orly South and Exit G in Orly West. The cost is €6.90. The cheapest bus is the

RATP city bus 183, which shuttles you from Metro Porte de Choisy (Line 7) to Orly South for just €3.70, every 30 minutes from 5:30 am to 8:30 pm. Travel time is approximately 50 minutes.

By train from Orly: The cheapest way to get into Paris by train is to take the shuttle bus from Exit F at Orly South or Exit G at Orly West to the station RER-C Pont de Rungis–Aéroport d'Orly into Paris. Trains to Paris leave every 15 minutes. The fare is €2.60 (Shuttle) plus €3.95 (RER), and journey time is about 35 minutes. Another slightly faster option is to take RATP's monorail service, Orlyval, which runs between the Antony RER-B station and Orly Airport daily every four to eight minutes from 6 am to 11 pm. Passengers arriving in the South Terminal should use Exit K; take Exit W if you've arrived in the West Terminal. The fare to downtown Paris is €10.90 and includes the RER transfer.

TRAVEL TO CENTRAL PARIS		
From	CDG	Orly
Taxi	45 mins–75 mins; €40–€70	20 mins–45 mins; €30–€50
Bus	45 mins–90 mins; €10–€16.50	30 mins–50 mins; €3.70–€11.50
Airport Shuttle	1 hr–2 hrs; €25–€45	45 mins–90 mins; €25–€45
RER	45 mins–1 hr; €9.25	25 mins–40 mins; €6.40

TRANSFERS BETWEEN AIRPORTS
To transfer between Paris's airports, there are several options. *See the "By Train" options above:* The RER-B travels from CDG to Orly with Paris in the middle, so to transfer, just stay on. Travel time is about 50–70 minutes and costs €18.20. The Air France Bus line 3 also runs between the airports for €19 one-way, every 30 minutes, with about 50 minutes travel time. Taxis are available but expensive: from €60 to €80, depending on traffic.

Contacts Air France Bus ☎ *08–92–35–08–20 recorded information in English, €0.34 per min* ⊕ *www.cars-airfrance.com.* **SuperShuttle Paris** ☎ *01–41–47–13–00* ⊕ *www.supershuttle.fr.* **Paris Airports Services** ☎ *01–55–98–10–80* ⊕ *www.parisairportservice.com.* **RATP (including Roissybus, Orlybus, Orlyval)** ☎ *3246 €0.34 per min* ⊕ *www.ratp.com.*

FLIGHTS
As one of the premier destinations in the world, Paris is serviced by a great many international carriers and a surprisingly large number of U.S.-based airlines. Air France (which partners with Delta) is the French flag carrier and offers numerous direct flights (often several per day) between Paris's Charles de Gaulle Airport and New York City's JFK Airport; Newark, New Jersey; Washington's Dulles Airport; and the cities of Boston, Philadelphia, Atlanta, Cincinnati, Miami, Chicago, Houston, Seattle, San Francisco, Los Angeles, Toronto, Montréal, and Mexico City. Most other North American cities are served through Air France partnerships with Delta and Continental Airlines. American-based carriers are usually less expensive, but offer, on the whole, fewer nonstop direct flights. United Airlines has nonstop flights to Paris from Chicago, Denver, Los Angeles, Miami, Philadelphia, Washington, and San Francisco. American Airlines offers daily nonstop flights to Paris's Charles de Gaulle Airport from numerous cities, including New York City's JFK, Miami, Chicago, and Dallas/Fort Worth. Northwest has a daily departure to Paris from its hub in Detroit. In Canada, Air France and Air Canada are the leading choices for departures from Toronto and Montréal; in peak season departures are often daily. From London, Air France, British Airways, and British Midland are the leading carriers, with up to 15 flights daily in peak season. In addition, direct routes link Manchester, Edinburgh, and Southampton with Paris. Ryanair, easyJet, CityJet, Aer Lingus, and BMI Baby offer direct service from Paris to Dublin, Birmingham,

London, Glasgow, Amsterdam, Cardiff, Zurich, and Brussels, to name just a few destinations. Tickets are available on the Web only and need to be booked well in advance to get the best prices—a one-way ticket from Paris to Dublin costs a mere €45, for example.

Airline Contacts Air Canada ☎ *888/247-2262 in U.S. and Canada, 0825-882-900 in France* ⊕ *www.aircanada.com.* **Air France** ☎ *800/237-2747 in U.S., 3654 [€0.34min]* ⊕ *www.airfrance.com.* **American Airlines** ☎ *800/433-7300, 08-26-460-950 in France* ⊕ *www.aa.com.* **British Airways** ☎ *800/247-9297 in U.S., 08-25-82-54-00 in France [€0.15min]* ⊕ *www.britishairways.com.* **Continental Airlines** ☎ *800/523-3273 for U.S. and Mexico reservations, 800/231-0856 for international reservations, 01-71-23-03-35 in France* ⊕ *www.continental.com.* **Delta Airlines** ☎ *800/221-1212 for U.S. reservations, 800/241-4141 for international reservations, 08-11-64-00-05 in France* ⊕ *www.delta.com.* **Northwest Airlines** ☎ *800/225-2525, 00-890-710-710 in France* ⊕ *www.nwa.com.* **United Airlines** ☎ *800/864-8331 for U.S. reservations, 800/538-2929 for international reservations, 08-10-72-72-72 in France* ⊕ *www.united.com.* **US Airways** ☎ *800/428-4322 for U.S. and Canada reservations, 800/622-1015 for international reservations, 08-10-63-22-22 in France* ⊕ *www.usairways.com.*

Discount Airlines BMI Baby ☎ *01-41-91-87-04 in France* ⊕ *www.bmibaby.com.* **CityJet** ☎ *3654 in France, 0044/871-66-33-777 from US* ⊕ *www.cityjet.com.* **easyJet** ☎ *08-20-42-03-15 in France* ⊕ *www.easyjet.com.* **Ryan Air** ☎ *08-92-78-02-10 in France* ⊕ *www.ryanair.com.*

Within Europe Air France ☎ *0845/242-9242 in U.K., 3272 in France* ⊕ *www.airfrance.com.* **British Airways** ☎ *0870/850-9850 in U.K., 08-25-82-54-00 in France* ⊕ *www.britishairways.com.* **British Midland** ☎ *0844/724-099 in U.K., 01-41-91-87-04 in France* ⊕ *www.flybmi.com.*

▮ BOAT TRAVEL

Linking France and the United Kingdom, a boat or ferry trip across the Channel can range from 35 minutes (via hovercraft) to 95 minutes (via ferryboat). Trip length also depends on departure point: popular routes link Boulogne and Folkestone, Le Havre, and Portsmouth, and, the most booked passage, Calais and Dover. DirectFerries.fr groups the sites for several ferry–land hovercraft crossings to make reservations more streamlined.

P&O European Ferries links Dover, England, with Calais (75 minutes). P&O has up to three sailings a day. Seafrance operates up to 15 sailings a day from Dover to Calais; the crossing takes 70 or 90 minutes, depending on the ship.

The driving distance from Calais to Paris is 290 km (180 mi). The fastest routes to Paris from each port are via N43, A26, and A1 from Calais and the Channel Tunnel; and via N1 from Boulogne.

Information DirectFerries.fr ☎ *08-92-23-08-58 from France* ⊕ *www.directferries.fr.* **P&O European Ferries** ☎ *0871/664-2121 in U.K., 0825/120-156 in France* ⊕ *www.poferries.com.* **Seafrance** ☎ *44845/458-0666 from France* ⊕ *www.seafrance.net.*

▮ BUS TRAVEL

ARRIVING AND DEPARTING PARIS

The excellent national train service in France means that long-distance bus service in the country is practically nonexistent; regional buses are found where train service is spotty. Local bus information to the rare rural areas where trains do not have access can be obtained from the SNCF (⇨ *see By Train, below*).

The largest international operator is Eurolines France, whose main terminal is in the Parisian suburb of Bagnolet (a half-hour métro ride from central Paris, at the end of métro Line 3). Eurolines runs international routes to more than 1,500 cities in Europe.

It's possible to take a bus (via ferry) to Paris from the United Kingdom; just be aware that what you save in money will almost certainly cost you in time—the bus trip takes about seven hours as opposed to the three it takes on the Eurostar train line (St-Pancras Station–Gare du Nord). In general, the price of a round-trip bus ticket is 50% less than that of a plane ticket and 25% less than that of a train ticket, so if you have the time and the energy, this is a good way to cut the cost of travel. Eurolines also offers a 15-day (€210–€350) or 30-day (€315–€460) pass if you're planning on doing the grand European tour. Ask about one of the Circle tours that depart from Paris (for example, via London, Amsterdam, then back to Paris again). Eurolines operates a service from London's Victoria Coach Station, via the Dover–Calais ferry, to Paris's Porte de Bagnolet. There's an 8 am departure that arrives in Paris at 4:30 pm, a noon departure that arrives at 9:30 pm, and the overnight trips at 9:30 pm, which arrive in Paris at 7:15 am, and the 10:30 pm departure, which arrives at 7:30 am. Fares are €70 round-trip (an under-25 youth pass is €65). Other Eurolines routes include Amsterdam (7 hours, 73), Barcelona (15 hours, €146), and Berlin (14 hours, €144), though prices do vary. There are also international-only arrivals and departures from Avignon, Bordeaux, Lille, Lyon, Toulouse, and Tours.

Eurolines accepts all major credit cards but does not accept traveler's checks.

Reservations for an international bus trip are essential. Be sure to check the Eurolines website for special discounts or incentives. Avoid buying your ticket at the last minute, when prices are highest.

IN PARIS

With dedicated bus lanes now in place throughout the city—allowing buses and taxis to whiz past other traffic mired in tedious jams—taking the bus is an appealing option. Although nothing can beat the métro for speed, buses offer great city views, and the new ones are equipped with air-conditioning—a real perk on those sweltering August days.

Paris buses are green and white; the route number and destination are marked in front, major stopping places along the sides. Brown bus shelters contain time-tables and route maps; note that buses must be hailed at these larger bus shelters, as they service multiple lines and routes. Smaller stops are designated simply by a pole bearing bus numbers.

More than 200 bus routes run throughout Paris, reaching virtually every nook and cranny of the city. On weekdays and Saturday, buses run every five minutes (as opposed to the 15- to 20-minute wait you'll have on Sunday and national holidays). One ticket will take you anywhere within the city and is valid for one transfer within 90 minutes.

A map of the bus system is on the flip side of every métro map, in all métro stations, and at all bus stops. Maps are also found in each bus. A recorded message announces the name of the next stop. To get off, press one of the red buttons mounted on the silver poles that run the length of the bus, and the *arrêt demandé* (stop requested) light directly behind the driver will light up. Use the rear door to exit.

The Balabus, an orange-and-white public bus that runs on Sunday and holidays between mid-April and September, gives an interesting 50-minute tour around the major sights. You can use your Paris-Visite or Mobilis pass (⇨ *by Métro*), or one to three bus tickets, depending on how far you ride. The route runs from La Défense to the Gare de Lyon.

The RATP has also introduced above-ground tram lines: two (T-1 and T-2) operate in the suburbs, and the T-3 tram, which connects the 13e, 14e, and 15e arrondissements, running from the Porte d'Ivry (Chinatown) to the Parc Montsouris, Porte d'Orléans, and the Paris Expo–Porte de Versailles. Trams take the same tickets as buses and the métro, with one ticket good for the entire line.

Regular buses accept métro tickets. Your best bet is to buy a *carnet* of 10 tickets for €12.70 at any métro station, or you can buy a single ticket on board (exact change appreciated) for €1.80. If you have individual tickets, you should be prepared to punch your ticket in the gray machines at the entrance of the bus. You need to show (but not punch) Paris-Visite tickets to the driver. Tickets can be bought on buses, in the métro, or in any bar–tabac store displaying the lime-green métro symbol above its street sign.

Most routes operate from 7 am to 8:30 pm; some continue to midnight. After midnight you must either take the métro or one of the 35 Noctilien lines (indicated by a separate signal at bus stops). These bus lines operate every 10–60 minutes (12:30 am–5:30 am) between Châtelet, major train stations, and various nearby suburbs; they can be stopped by hailing them at any point on their route. The Noctilien uses the same tickets as the métro and regular bus.

Bus Information Eurolines ☎ *08-92-89-90-91 in France, 08705–808080 in U.K.* ⊕ *www.eurolines.fr or www.eurolines-pass.com.* **Noctilien** ⊕ *www.noctilien.fr.* **RATP** ☎ *3246 €0.34 per min* ⊕ *www.ratp.com.*

∎ CAR TRAVEL

We can't say it too many times: unless you have a special, compelling reason, do yourself a favor and **avoid driving in Paris.** But if you've decided to do it anyway, there are some things to know. France's roads are classified into five types; they are numbered and have letter prefixes: A (*autoroute,* expressways), N (*route nationale*), D (*route départmentale*), and the smaller C or V. There are excellent links between Paris and most French cities. When trying to get around Ile-de-France, it's often difficult to avoid Paris—just try to steer clear of rush hours (7–9:30 and 4:30–7:30). A *péage* (toll) must be paid on most expressways outside Ile-de-France: the rate varies but can be steep. Certain booths allow you to pay with a credit card.

The major ring road encircling Paris is called the *périphérique,* with the *périphérique intérieur* going counterclockwise around the city, and the *périphérique extérieur,* or the outside ring, going clockwise. Up to five lanes wide, the périphérique is a major highway from which *portes* (gates) connect Paris to the major highways of France. The names of these highways function on the same principle as the métro, with the final destination as the determining point in the direction you must take.

Heading north, look for Porte de la Chapelle (direction Lille and Charles de Gaulle Airport); east, for Porte de Bagnolet (direction Metz and Nancy); south, for Porte d'Orléans (direction Lyon and Bordeaux); and west, for Porte d'Auteuil (direction Rouen and Chartres) or Porte de St-Cloud.

GASOLINE

There are gas stations throughout the city, but they can be difficult to spot; you can often find them in the underground tunnels that cross the city and in larger parking garages. Gas is expensive and prices vary enormously, ranging from about €1.35 to €1.70 per liter. If you're on your way out of Paris, save money by waiting until you've left the city to fill up. All gas stations accept credit cards.

PARKING

Finding parking in Paris is tough. Both meters and parking-ticket machines use parking cards (*cartes de stationnements*), which you can purchase at any café posting the red tabac sign; they're sold in two denominations: €10 and €30. Parking in the capital runs €2.50 per hour. Insert your card into the nearest meter, choose the approximate amount of time you expect to stay, and receive a green receipt. Place it on the dashboard on the passenger side; make sure the receipt's clearly visible to the meter patrol. Parking tickets are expensive, and there's no shortage of blue-uniformed parking police. Parking lots, indicated by a blue sign with a white "P", are usually underground and are generally expensive (charging €1.20

to €3 per hour, or €9 to €23 per day). One bright spot: you can park for free on Sunday, national holidays, and in certain residential areas in August. Parking meters with yellow circles indicate the free parking zone during August.

ROAD CONDITIONS

Chaotic traffic is a way of life in Paris. Some streets in the city center can seem impossibly narrow; street signs are often hard to spot; jaded city drivers often make erratic, last-minute maneuvers without signaling; and motorcycles often weave around traffic. Priority is given to drivers coming from the right, so watch for drivers barreling out of small streets on your right. Traffic lights are placed to the left and right of crosswalks, not above, so they may be blocked from your view by vehicles ahead of you.

There are a few major roundabouts at the most congested intersections, notably at *L'Étoile* (around the Arc de Triomphe), the Place de la Bastille, and the Place de la Concorde. Watch oncoming cars carefully and stick to the outer lane to make your exit. The *périphériques* (ring roads) are generally easier to use, and the quais that parallel the Seine can be a downright pleasure to drive when there's no traffic. Electronic signs on the périphériques and highways post traffic conditions: *fluide* (clear) or *bouchon* (jammed).

Some important traffic terms and signs to note: *sortie* (exit), *sens unique* (one way), *stationnement interdite* (no parking), *impasse* (dead end). Blue rectangular signs indicate a highway; triangles carry illustrations of a particular traffic hazard; speed limits are indicated in a circle, with the maximum speed circled in red.

ROADSIDE EMERGENCIES

If your car breaks down on an expressway, pull your car as far off the road as quickly as possible, set your emergency indicators, and, if possible, take the emergency triangle from the car's trunk and put it at least 30 yards behind your car to warn oncoming traffic; then go to a roadside

emergency telephone. These phones put you in direct contact with the police, automatically indicating your exact location, and are available every 3 km (2 mi). If you have a breakdown anywhere else, find the nearest garage or contact the police. There are also 24-hour assistance hotlines valid throughout France (available through rental agencies and supplied to you when you rent the car), but do not hesitate to call the police in case of any roadside emergency, for they are quick and reliable and the phone call is free.

Emergency Services Police ☎ *17, 112.*

RULES OF THE ROAD

You must always carry vehicle registration documents and your personal identification. The French police are entitled to stop you at will to verify your ID and your car—such spot checks are frequent, especially at peak holiday times. In France you drive on the right and give priority to drivers coming from the right (this rule is called *priorité à droite*).

The driver and all passengers in vehicle must wear seat belts, and children under 12 may not travel in the front seat. Children under 10 need to be in a car seat or specific child-restraining device, always in the back seat. Speed limits are designated by the type of road you're driving on: 130 kph (80 mph) on expressways (*autoroutes*), 110 kph (70 mph) on divided highways (*routes nationales*), 90 kph (55 mph) on other roads (*routes*), 50 kph (30 mph) in cities and towns (*villes et villages*). These limits are reduced by 10 kph (6 mph) in rainy, snowy, and foggy conditions. Drivers are expected to know these limits, so signs are generally posted only when there are exceptions to these rules. Right-hand turns are not allowed on a red light.

The use of handheld cellular phones while driving is forbidden; the penalty is a €60 fine. Alcohol laws have become quite tough—a 0.05% blood alcohol limit (a lower limit than in the United States).

▌MÉTRO TRAVEL

Taking the métro is the most efficient way to get around Paris. Métro stations are recognizable either by a large yellow *M* within a circle or by the distinctive curly green Art Nouveau railings and archway bearing the full title (Métropolitain). *See the Métro map on the inside back cover of this book.*

Fourteen métro and five RER (Réseau Express Régional, or the Regional Express Network) lines crisscross Paris and the suburbs, and you are seldom more than 500 yards from the nearest station. The métro network connects at several points in Paris with the RER, the commuter trains that go from the city center to the suburbs. RER trains crossing Paris on their way from suburb to suburb can be great time-savers, because they make only a few stops in the city (you can use the same tickets for the métro and the RER within Paris).

It's essential to know the name of the last station on the line you take, as this name appears on all signs. A connection (you can make as many as you like on one ticket) is called a *correspondance.* At junction stations, illuminated orange signs bearing the name of the line terminus appear over the correct corridors for each correspondence. Illuminated blue signs marked *sortie* indicate the station exit. Note that tickets are valid only inside the gates, or *limites.*

Access to métro and RER platforms is through an automatic ticket barrier. Slide your ticket in and pick it up as it pops out. **Keep your ticket during your journey;** you'll need it to leave the RER system and in case you run into any green-clad ticket inspectors, who will impose a hefty fine if you can't produce your ticket.

Métro service starts at 5:30 am and continues until 1 am Sunday through Thursday, and until 2 am on Friday and Saturday, when the last train on each line reaches its terminus. Some lines and stations in Paris are a bit risky at night, in particular lines 2 and 13, and the mazelike stations at Les Halles and République. But in general, the métro is relatively safe throughout, providing you don't travel alone late at night or walk around with your wallet hanging out of your back pocket.

TICKET/PASS	PRICE
Single Fare	€1.70 (€1.80 if purchased on bus)
Daily Mobilis Pass	€6.40
Paris Visit One-Day Pass	€9.75
10-Ticket Carnet	€12.70
Paris Visit Two-Day Pass	€15.85
Paris Visit Three-Day Pass	€21.60
Paris Visit Five-Day Pass	€31.15
Pass Navigo Découverte Weekly	€19.15
Pass Navigo Découverte Monthly	€62.90

All métro tickets and passes are valid not only for the métro but also for all RER, tram, and bus travel within Paris. Métro tickets cost €1.70 each; a *carnet* (10 tickets for €12.70) is a better value. The *Carte Navigo* replaced the weekly Carte Orange in March 2008. Receive a Pass Navigo Découverte at any ticket window for €5 plus the subscription for weekly (€19.15, valid Monday–Sunday) or monthly (€62.90, beginning the first of the month) service. Be sure to immediately attach a passport-size photo and sign your name. This magnetic swipe card allows you to zoom through the turnstiles and can be kept for years; just recharge it at any purple kiosk in the métro stations. Visitors can also purchase the one-day (Mobilis) and two- to five-day (Paris-Visite) tickets for unlimited travel on the entire RATP (Paris transit authority) network: métro, RER, bus, tram, funicular (Montmartre), and Noctilien (night bus). The Mobilis and Paris-Visite passes are valid starting any day of the week. Paris-Visite also gives you discounts on a few museums and attractions, too. Mobilis tickets cost €6.40. Paris-Visite is €9.75 (one day), €15.85 (two days), €21.60 (three days), and €31.15 (five days) for Paris only.

Métro Information Any RATP window in the métro sells tickets and provides maps, but if you're looking to purchase RATP souvenirs, you can find them at the main office near the Gare de Lyon. **RATP.** RATP, open daily 9–5. ✉ *54 quai de la Rapée, 12e* ⊕ *www.ratp.fr.*

∎ TAXI TRAVEL

Taxi rates are based on location and time. Daytime rates, denoted A (7 am–7 pm), within Paris are €0.96 per kilometer (½ mile), and nighttime rates, B, are €1.21 per kilometer. Suburban zones and airports, C, are €1.47 per kilometer. There's a basic hire charge of €2.40 for all rides, a €1 supplement per piece of luggage, and a €0.70 supplement if you're picked up at an SNCF (the French rail system) station. Waiting time is charged at around €30 per hour. The easiest way to get a taxi is to ask your hotel or a restaurant to call one for you, or go to the nearest taxi stand (you can find one every couple of blocks)—they're marked by a square, dark blue sign with a white T in the middle. ∎TIP→ People waiting for cabs often form a line, but will jump at any available taxi; be firm and don't let people cut in front of you. A taxi is available when the entire sign is lighted up, and taken when just the little bulb at the bottom of the sign is lighted. They'll accept a fourth passenger for an average supplement of €2.95. It's customary to tip the driver about 10% (⇨ *Tipping*).

Taxi Companies Airport Taxi ☏ *0825–560–320.* **Taxis Bleus** ☏ *08–91–70–10–10.* **Taxi G7** ☏ *01–47–39–47–39.*

∎ TRAIN TRAVEL

The SNCF, France's rail system, is fast, punctual, comfortable, and comprehensive. There are various options: local trains, overnight trains with sleeping accommodations, and the high-speed TGV, or Trains à Grande Vitesse (averaging 255 kph [160 mph] on the Lyon/southeast line and 300 kph [190 mph] on the Lille and Bordeaux/southwest lines).

The TGVs, the fastest way to get around the country, operate between Paris and Lille/Calais, Paris and Lyon/Switzerland/Provence, Paris and Angers/Nantes, Paris and Tours/Poitiers/Bordeaux, Paris and Brussels, and Paris and Amsterdam. As with other mainline trains, a small supplement may be assessed at peak hours.

Paris has six international rail stations: Gare du Nord (northern France, northern Europe, and England via Calais or Boulogne); Gare St-Lazare (Normandy, England via Dieppe); Gare de l'Est (Strasbourg, Luxembourg, Basel, and central Europe); Gare de Lyon (Lyon, Marseille, Provence, Geneva, Italy); Gare d'Austerlitz (Loire Valley, southwest France, Spain); and Gare Montparnasse (Brittany, Aquitaine, TGV-Atlantique service to the west and south of France, Spain). Until 2005 there were smoking and no-smoking cars on the trains, including the TGVs, but smoking is now prohibited on all trains in France.

There are two classes of train service in France: *première* (first class) or *deuxième* (second). First-class seats have 50% more legroom and nicer upholstery than those in second class, and the first-class cars tend to be quieter. First-class seats on the TGV have computer connections. First-class fares are nearly twice as much as those for second-class seats.

Fares are cheaper if you avoid traveling at peak times (around holidays and weekends), purchase tickets at least 15 days in advance (look for the *billet Prem's*), or find your destination among the last-minute offers online every Tuesday.

You can call for train information or reserve tickets in any Paris station, irrespective of destination, and you can access the multilingual computerized schedule information network at any Paris station. You can also make reservations and buy your ticket while at the computer. Go to the Grandes Lignes counter for travel within France and to the Billets Internationaux desk if you're heading out of the country. Note that calling the SNCF's 08 number costs €0.35 per minute; to save this cost, go to the nearest station and make the reservations in person or visit the SNCF website, ⊕ *www.sncf.fr*.

If you plan to travel outside Paris by train, consider purchasing a France Rail Pass, which allows three days of unlimited train travel in a one-month period. If you travel solo, first class will run you $303 and second class is $245; you can add up to six days on this pass for $46 a day for first class, $39 a day for second class. For two people traveling together on a Saver Pass, the first-class cost is $258, and in second class it's $211; additional days (up to six) cost $40 each for first class, $33 each for second class. Other options include the France Rail 'n Drive Pass (combining rail and rental car).

France is one of 21 countries in which you can use EurailPasses, which provide unlimited first-class rail travel in all the participating countries for the duration of the pass. If you plan to rack up the miles, get a standard pass. These are available for 15 days ($752), 21 days ($971), one month ($1,196), two months ($1,686), and three months ($2,079). If your travels will be more limited, the Eurail Selectpass gives you first-class travel over a two-month period in three to five bordering countries in 21 Eurail network countries. The Selectpass starts at $312 for five days of travel within three countries. Another option is the Regional Pass, which covers rail travel in and between pairs of bordering countries over a two-month period. Unlike most Eurail passes, Regional Passes are available for first- or second-class travel.

Costs begin at $402 (first class) and $345 (second class) for four days of travel; up to six extra days can be purchased.

In addition to standard EurailPasses, there are the Eurail Youthpass (for those under age 26, with second-class travel), the Eurail Saver Pass (which gives a discount for two or more people traveling together), the Eurail Flexipass (which allows a certain number of travel days within a set period), and the Euraildrive Pass (train and rental car). ■TIP➜ Remember that you must purchase your Eurail passes at home before leaving for France. You can purchase Eurail passes through the Eurail website as well as through travel agents.

Another option is to purchase one of the discount rail passes available for sale only in France from SNCF.

When traveling together, two people (who don't have to be a couple) can save money with the Prix Découverte à Deux. You'll get a 25% discount during *périodes bleus* (blue periods: weekdays and periods not on or near any holidays). Note that you have to be with the person you said you would be traveling with.

Reduced fares are available if you're a senior citizen (over 60), for children under 12, and up to four accompanying adults, and if you're under 26.

If you purchase an individual ticket from SNCF in France and you're under 26, you automatically get a 25% reduction (a valid ID such as an ISIC card or your passport is necessary). If you're going to be using the train quite a bit during your stay in France and if you're under 26, consider buying the Carte 12–25 (€50), which offers unlimited 50% reductions for one year (provided that there's space available at that price; otherwise you'll just get the standard 25% discount).

If you don't benefit from any of these reductions and you plan on traveling at least 200 km (132 miles) round-trip and don't mind staying over a Saturday night, look into the Prix Découverte Séjour. This ticket gives you a 25% reduction.

■TIP➜ A rail pass does not guarantee you a seat on the train you wish to ride. You need to book seats ahead even if you have a pass.

Seat reservations are required on TGVs and are a good idea on trains that may be crowded—particularly in summer and during holidays on popular routes. You also need a reservation for sleeping accommodations.

THE CHANNEL TUNNEL

Short of flying, taking the Channel Tunnel is the fastest way to cross the English Channel: 35 minutes from Folkestone to Calais, 60 minutes from motorway to motorway, or 2 hours and 15 minutes from London's St. Pancras Station to Paris's Gare du Nord, with stops in Lille, Calais, Ashford (U.K.), and Ebbsfleet (U.K.). The Belgian border is just a short drive northeast of Calais. High-speed Eurostar trains use the same tunnels to connect London's St. Pancras Station directly with Midi Station in Brussels in around 2 hours.

There's a vast range of prices for Eurostar—round-trip tickets range from €450 for first class (with access to the Philippe Starck–designed Première Class lounge) to €85 for second class, depending on when you travel. It's a good idea to make a reservation if you're traveling with your car on a Chunnel train; cars without reservations, if they can get on at all, are charged 20% extra.

British Rail also has four daily departures from London's Victoria Station, all linking with the Dover–Calais/Boulogne ferry services through to Paris. There's also an overnight service on the Newhaven–Dieppe ferry. Journey time is about eight hours. Credit-card bookings are accepted by phone or in person at a British Rail Travel Centre.

Information Rail Europe ☎ *800/622-8600 in U.S.* ⊕ *www.raileurope.com.* **SNCF** ✉ *88 rue St-Lazare* ☎ *08-92-35-35-35 €0.35 per min* ⊕ *www.Voyages-sncf.fr.*

Channel Tunnel Car Transport Eurotunnel ☎ *0870/535-3535 in U.K., 0810/630304 in France* ⊕ *www.eurotunnel.com.* **French Motorail/Rail Europe** ☎ *08448/484-051* ⊕ *www.raileurope.co.uk/frenchmotorail.*

Channel Tunnel Passenger Service BritRail Travel ☎ *866/938-7245 in U.S.* ⊕ *www.britrail.com.* **Eurostar** ☎ *08-92-35-35-39 in France, 0044/1233 617 575 in U.K.* ⊕ *www.eurostar.co.uk.* **Rail Europe** ☎ *888/382-7245 in U.S., 0870/584-8848 in U.K. inquiries and credit-card bookings* ⊕ *www.raileurope.com.*

ESSENTIALS

▐ COMMUNICATIONS

INTERNET AND WI-FI

Getting online in Paris is rarely a problem, as free and pay-as-you-go (via credit card) Wi-Fi service is available in most of the city's cafés, public spaces, and hotels through providers like SFR and Orange. Note that you may pick up a signal for "Free Wi-Fi," but this is the name of a French Internet provider and its network is open only to paying clients. Paris has made a big push in going wireless in recent years, and Wi-Fi (called WIFI) is available in more than 260 public parcs and civic centers like the Centre Pompidou and many libraries. Access is free and unlimited for anyone. Cafés will usually have a WIFI sticker on their window if there is wireless available, but always verify before ordering a drink; McDonald's also has free Wi-Fi spaces (sometimes disabled during peak dining hours). Many hotels have business services with Internet access, in-room modem lines, or high-speed wireless access. ▐ TIP➔ You will, however, need an adapter for your computer for the European-style plugs. If you're traveling with a laptop, carry a spare battery and adapter. Never plug your computer into any socket before asking about surge protection.

PHONES

The good news is that you can now make a direct-dial telephone call from virtually any point on earth. The bad news? You can't always do so cheaply. Calling from a hotel is almost always the most expensive option; hotels usually add huge surcharges to all calls, particularly international ones. In some countries you can phone from call centers or even the post office. Calling cards usually keep costs low, but only if you buy them locally. And then there are mobile phones (➔ below), which are sometimes more prevalent than landlines; as expensive as mobile phone calls can be, they are still usually a much cheaper option than calling from your hotel.

The country code for France is 33. The first two digits of French numbers are a prefix determined by zone: Paris and Ile-de-France, 01; the northwest, 02; the northeast, 03; the southeast, 04; and the southwest, 05. Pay close attention to numbers beginning with 08. Calls that begin with 08 followed by 00 are toll-free, but calls that begin with 08 followed by 36—like the information lines for the SNCF, for example—cost €0.35 per minute. Numbers that begin with 06 are reserved for cell phones.

Note that when dialing France from abroad, you should drop the initial 0 from the telephone number (all numbers listed in this book include the initial 0, which is used for calling *from within* France). To call a number in Paris from the United States, dial 011–33 plus the phone number, but minus the initial 0 listed for the specific number in Paris. In other words, the local number for the Louvre is 01–40–20–51–51. To call this number from New York City, dial 011–33–1–40–20–51–51. To call this number from within Paris, dial 01–40–20–51–51. To call France from the United Kingdom, dial 00–33, then dial the number in France minus the initial 0 of the specific number.

CALLING CARDS

French pay phones are operated by *télécartes* (phone cards), which you can buy from post offices, tabacs, and magazine kiosks. The ones you insert into pay phones have a "puce" microchip—a small copper square—that you can see on the card. There are as many phone cards these days as bakeries, so to be safe, request the *télécarte international*, which, despite its name, allows you to make either local or international calls and offers greatly reduced rates. Instructions are in English, and the cost is €9 for 60 units and €18 for 120 units. You may also request the simple *télécarte,* which allows you to make calls in France (the cost is €8 for 50 units, €15 for 120 units). You can use your credit card in much the same way as a télécarte, but there's a minimum €20 charge. You have 30 days after the first call on your credit card to use the €20 credit.

There are also international calling cards that work on any phone (including your hotel phone) because you dial a free number and punch in a code; these do not have the "puce" microchip. Don't hesitate to invest in one if you plan on making calls from your hotel, as hotels often levy service charges and also have the most expensive rates.

CALLING OUTSIDE FRANCE

Good news—telephone rates are actually decreasing in France because the France Telecom monopoly now has some stringent competition. As in most countries, the highest rates fall between 8 am and 7 pm and average out to a hefty €0.22 per minute to the United States, Canada, and the closer European countries, including Germany and Great Britain. Rates are greatly reduced from 7 pm to 8 am, costing an average of €0.10 per minute.

To make a direct international call out of France, dial 00 and wait for the tone; then dial the country code (1 for the United States and Canada, 44 for the United Kingdom, 61 for Australia, and 64 for New Zealand) and the area code (minus any initial 0) and number.

To call with the help of an operator, dial the toll-free number 08–00–99–00 plus the last two digits of the country code. Dial 08–00–99–00–11 for the United States and Canada, 08–00–99–00–44 for England, and 08–00–99–00–61 for Australia.

Access Codes AT&T Direct ☎ 08–00–99–00–11, 08–00–99–01–11, 800/222–0300 *for information.* **MCI WorldPhone** ☎ 08–00–99–00–19, 800/444–4444 *for information.* **Sprint International Access** ☎ 08–00–99–00–87, 900/446–2900 *for information.*

CALLING WITHIN FRANCE

For telephone information in France, you need to call one of the dozen or so six-digit *renseignement* numbers that begin with 118. Some of the better-known ones are 118–008 for the Pages Jaunes, or 118–711 for France Telecom. The number 118–247 is a bilingual option, run in partnership with the Paris tourism office. The average price for one of these calls is about €1.

Since all local numbers in Paris and the Ile-de-France begin with a 01, you must dial the full 10-digit number, including the initial 0. A local call costs €0.15 for every three minutes.

To call from region to region within France, dial the full 10-digit number, including the initial 0.

Public telephone booths can almost always be found in post offices, train stations, bus stops, and in some cafés, as well as on the street.

MOBILE PHONES

If you have a multiband phone (some countries use different frequencies than what's used in the United States) and your service provider uses the world-standard GSM network (as do T-Mobile, AT&T, and Verizon), you can probably use your phone abroad. Roaming fees can be steep, however: 99¢ a minute is considered reasonable. And overseas you normally pay the toll charges for incoming calls. It's almost always cheaper to send a text message than to make a call, since text messages have a very low set fee (often less than 5¢).

If you just want to make local calls, consider buying a new SIM card (note that your provider may have to unlock your phone for you to use a different SIM card) and a prepaid service plan in the destination. You'll then have a local number and can make local calls at local rates. If your trip is extensive, you could also simply buy a new cell phone in your destination, as the initial cost will be offset over time.

LOCAL DO'S AND TABOOS

CUSTOMS OF THE COUNTRY

The French like to look at people—that's half the point of cafés and fashion, so get used to being looked at; it's as natural here as breathing. They'll look at your shoes or your watch, check out what you're wearing or reading. What they will not do is maintain steady eye contact or smile. If a stranger of the opposite sex smiles at you, it's best to do as the French do and return only a blank look before turning away. If you smile back, you might find yourself in a Pepé Le Pew–type situation.

Visitors' exuberance—and accompanying loud voices—may cause discreet Parisians to raise their eyebrows or give a deep chesty sigh. They're not being rude, but they're telling you that they think you are. Be aware of your surroundings and lower your voice accordingly, especially in churches, museums, restaurants, theaters, cinemas, and the métro.

When entering and leaving a shop, greet and say good-bye to the staff. A simple *bonjour, monsieur/madame,* and *au revoir, merci* are considered a virtual necessity for politeness. Other basic pleasantries in French include *bonne journée* (have a nice day); *bonne soirée* (have a nice evening); *enchanté* (nice to meet you); *s'il vous plaît* (please); and *je vous en prie* (you're welcome). When asking for directions or other help, be sure to preface your request with a polite phrase such as *excusez-moi de vous déranger, madame/ monsieur* (excuse me for bothering you, ma'am/sir).

GREETINGS

When meeting someone for the first time, whether in a social or a professional setting, it's appropriate to shake hands. Other than that, the French like to kiss. For the Parisians, it's two *bisous,* which are more like air kisses with your cheeks touching lightly—don't actually smack your lips onto the person's face!

OUT ON THE TOWN

When visiting a French home, don't expect to be invited into the kitchen or to take a house tour. The French have a very definite sense of personal space, and you'll be escorted to what are considered the guest areas. If you're invited to dinner, be sure to bring a gift, such as wine, flowers, or chocolates.

Table manners are often considered a litmus test of your character or upbringing. When dining out, note that the French fill wineglasses only until half full—it's considered bad manners to fill it to the brim. They never serve themselves before serving the rest of the table. During a meal, keep both hands above the table, and keep your elbows off the table. Bread is broken, never cut, and is placed next to the plate, never on the plate. When slicing a cheese, don't cut off the point (or "nose"). Coffee or tea is ordered after dessert, not with dessert. (In fact, coffee and tea usually aren't ordered with any courses during meals, except breakfast.) Eating on the street is generally frowned on—though with the onslaught of Starbucks you can sometimes see people drinking coffee on the go.

LANGUAGE

One of the best ways to avoid being an Ugly American is to learn a bit of the local language.

The French may appear prickly at first to English-speaking visitors, but it usually helps if you make an effort to speak a little French. A simple, friendly *bonjour* (hello) will do, as will asking if the person you're greeting speaks English (*parlez-vous anglais?*). Be patient, and speak English slowly—but *not* loudly. *See the French Vocabulary and Menu Guide at the back of the book.*

A phrase book and language-tape set can help get you started. *Fodor's French for Travelers* (available at bookstores everywhere) is excellent.

■TIP➔ If you travel internationally frequently, save one of your old mobile phones or buy a cheap one on the Internet; ask your cell-phone company to unlock it for you, and take it with you as a travel phone, buying a new SIM card with pay-as-you-go service in each destination.

Cell phones are called *portables,* and most Parisians have one. British standard cell phones work in Paris, but for North Americans only triband phones work. If you'd like to rent a cell phone for your trip, reserve one at least four days before your departure, as most companies will ship it to you before you travel. Cellular Abroad rents cell phones packaged with prepaid SIM cards that give you a French cell-phone number and calling rates. Planetfone rents GSM phones, which can be used in more than 100 countries, but the per-minute rates are expensive. You can also buy a disposable "BIC" prepaid phone or a MobiKit pay-as-you-go phone from Orange if you want the best rates.

Contacts Cellular Abroad ☎ *800/287-5072* ⊕ *www.cellularabroad.com.* **Mobal.** Mobal rents mobiles and sells GSM phones (starting at $49) that will operate in 140 countries. Per-call rates vary throughout the world. ☎ *888/888-9162* ⊕ *www.mobalrental.com.* **Planet Fone** ☎ *888/988-4777* ⊕ *www.planetfone.com.*

▮ CUSTOMS AND DUTIES

You're always allowed to bring goods of a certain value back home without having to pay any duty or import tax. But there's a limit on the amount of tobacco and liquor you can bring back duty-free, and some countries have separate limits for perfumes; for exact figures, check with your customs department. The values of so-called "duty-free" goods are included in these amounts. When you shop abroad, save all your receipts, as customs inspectors may ask to see them as well as the items you purchased. If the total value of your goods is more than the duty-free limit, you'll have to pay a

tax (most often a flat percentage) on the value of everything beyond that limit.

If you're coming from outside the European Union (EU), you may import the following duty-free: (1) 200 cigarettes or 100 cigarillos or 50 cigars or 250 grams of tobacco; (2) 2 liters of wine and, in addition, (a) 1 liter of alcohol over 22% volume (most spirits) or (b) 2 liters of alcohol under 22% volume (fortified or sparkling wine) or (c) 4 more liters of table wine; (3) 50 ml of perfume and 250 ml of eau de toilette; (4) 200 grams of coffee, 100 grams of tea; and (5) other goods to the value of about €182 (€91 for ages 14 and under).

If you're arriving from an EU country, you may be required to declare all goods and prove that anything over the standard limit is for personal consumption. But there is no limit or customs tariff imposed on goods carried within the EU except on tobacco (800 cigarettes, 200 cigars, 1 kg of tobacco) and alcohol (10 liters of spirits, 90 liters of wine, with a maximum of 60 liters of sparkling wine, 110 liters of beer).

Any amount of euros or foreign currency may be brought into France, but foreign currencies converted into euros may be reconverted into a foreign currency only up to the equivalent of €769.

PETS

Any pet coming to France must have recent rabies shots (no less than 30 days before departure), all standard vaccinations, and must be older than three months. Be sure to have all paperwork on hand at the airport, where customs officials will inspect the animal in question.

Information in Paris Direction des Douanes ☎ *01-40-40-39-00, 0033/01-72-40-78-0 From US* ⊕ *www.douane.gouv.fr.*

U.S. Information U.S. Customs and Border Protection ⊕ *www.cbp.gov.*

ELECTRICITY

The electrical current in Paris is 220 volts, 50 cycles alternating current (AC); wall outlets take continental-type plugs, with two round prongs.

Consider making a small investment in a universal adapter, which has several types of plugs in one lightweight, compact unit. Most laptops and mobile phone chargers are dual voltage (i.e., they operate equally well on 110 and 220 volts), so require only an adapter. These days the same is true of small appliances such as hair dryers. Always check labels and manufacturer instructions to be sure. Don't use 110-volt outlets marked "For Shavers Only" for high-wattage appliances such as hair dryers.

EMERGENCIES

The French National Health Care system has been organized to provide fully equipped, fully staffed hospitals within 30 minutes of every resident in Paris. A sign of a white cross in a blue box appears on all hospitals. This book does not list the major Paris hospitals, as the French government prefers that an emergency operator assign you the best and most convenient option for your emergency. Note that if you're able to walk into a hospital emergency room by yourself, you are often considered "low priority," and the wait can be interminable. So if time is of the essence, it's best to call the fire department (☎ 18 or 112); a fully trained team of paramedics will usually arrive within five minutes. You may also dial for a Samu ambulance (☎ 15); there's usually an English-speaking physician available who will help you assess the situation and either dispatch an ambulance immediately or advise you about your best course of action. Be sure to check with your insurance company before your trip to verify that you are covered for medical care in other countries.

In a less urgent situation, do what the French do and call SOS Doctor or SOS Dental services; like magic, in less than an hour a certified, experienced doctor or dentist arrives at the door, armed with an old leather doctor case filled with the essentials for diagnosis and treatment (at an average cost of €65). The doctor or dentist may or may not be bilingual, but, at worst, will have a rudimentary understanding of English. This is a very helpful 24-hour service to use for common symptoms of benign illnesses that need to be treated quickly for comfort, such as high fever, toothache, or upset stomachs (which seem to have the unfortunate habit of announcing themselves late at night).

The American Hospital and the Hertford British Hospital both have 24-hour emergency hotlines with bilingual doctors and nurses who can provide advice. For small problems, go to a pharmacy, marked by a green neon cross. Pharmacists are authorized to administer first aid and recommend over-the-counter drugs, and they can be very helpful in advising you in English or sending you to the nearest English-speaking pharmacist.

Call the police (☎ 17) if there has been a crime or an act of violence. On the street, some French phrases that may be needed in an emergency are *Au secours!* (Help!), *urgence* (emergency), *samu* (ambulance), *pompiers* (firemen), *poste de station* (police station), *médecin* (doctor), and *hôpital* (hospital).

A hotline of note is SOS Help for English-language crisis information, open daily 3 pm–11 pm.

Doctor and Dentist Referrals SOS Dentiste ☎ *01-43-37-51-00.* **SOS Médecin** ☎ *01-47-07-77-77.*

Foreign Embassies U.S. Embassy Consular Section. U.S. Embassy Consular Section ✉ *4 av. Gabriel, 8e* ☎ *01-43-12-22-22 , appointments required (online form) except for lost or stolen passports and emergencies* Ⓜ *Concorde.*

General Emergency Contacts Ambulance ☎ *15.* **Fire Department** ☎ *18.* **General**

emergency services for police, fire, and ambulance (like 911) ☎ *112.* **Police.** These numbers are toll-free and can be dialed from any phone. ☎ *17.*

Hospitals and Clinics The American Hospital ✉ *63 bd. Victor-Hugo, Neuilly* ☎ *01–46–41–25–25.* **The Hertford British Hospital** ✉ *3 rue Barbès* ☎ *01–46–39–22–22.*

Hotline SOS Help ☎ *01–46–21–46–46.*

Pharmacies Dhéry. Dhéry is open 24 hours. ✉ *Galerie des Champs, 84 av. des Champs-Élysées, 8e* ☎ *01–45–62–02–41.* **Pharmacie des Arts.** Pharmacie des Arts is open daily until midnight. ✉ *106 bd. Montparnasse, 14e* ☎ *01–43–35–44–88.* **Pharmacie Internationale.** Pharmacie Internationale is open Monday–Saturday until midnight. ✉ *5 pl. Pigalle, 9e* ☎ *01–48–78–38–12.* **Pharmacie Matignon.** Pharmacie Matignon is open daily until 2 am. ✉ *2 rue Jean-Mermoz, at Rond-Point de Champs-Élysées, 8e* ☎ *01–45–62–79–16.*

∎ HOLIDAYS

With 11 national holidays (*jours feriés*) and five weeks of paid vacation, the French have their share of repose. In May there's a holiday nearly every week, so be prepared for stores, banks, and museums to shut their doors for days at a time. If a holiday falls on a Tuesday or Thursday, many businesses *font le pont* (make the bridge) and close on that Monday or Friday as well. Some exchange booths in tourist areas, small grocery stores, restaurants, cafés, and bakeries usually remain open. Bastille Day (July 14) is observed in true French form. Celebrations begin on the evening of the 13th, when city fire fighters open the doors to their stations, often classed as historical monuments, to host their much-acclaimed all-night balls and finish the next day with the annual military parade and air show.

Note that these dates are for the calendar year 2013: January 1 (New Year's Day); March 31–April 1 (Easter Sunday–Monday); May 1 (Labor Day); May 8 (VE Day); May 19 (Pentecost Sunday); May 9 (Ascension); July 14 (Bastille Day); August 15 (Assumption); November 1 (All Saints' Day); November 11 (Armistice); December 25 (Christmas).

∎ HOURS OF OPERATION

On weekdays banks are open generally 9–5 (note that the Banque de France closes at 3:30), and some banks are also open Saturday 9–5. In general, government offices and businesses are open 9–5. *See Mail, below, for post office hours.*

Most museums are closed one day a week—usually Monday or Tuesday—and on national holidays. Generally, museums and national monuments are open from 10 to 5 or 6. A few close for lunch (noon–2) and are open only in the afternoon on Sunday. Many of the large museums have one *nocturne* (nighttime) opening per week, when they are open until 9:30 or 10. Pharmacies are generally open Monday–Saturday 8:30–8. Nearby pharmacies that stay open late, for 24 hours, or Sunday, are listed on the door.

Generally, large shops are open from 9:30 or 10 to 7 or 8 Monday to Saturday and remain open through lunchtime. Many of the large department stores stay open until 10 on Wednesday or Thursday, and new laws passed in 2009 allow them to open on Sunday. Smaller shops and many supermarkets often open earlier (8 am) but take a lengthy lunch break (1–3) and generally close around 8 pm; small food shops are often open Sunday morning 9–1. There is typically a small corner grocery store that stays open late, usually until 11, if you're in a bind for basic necessities like diapers, bread, cheese, and fruit. Note that prices are substantially higher in such outlets than in the larger supermarkets. Not all shops stay open on Sunday, except in the Marais, where shops that stand side by side on Rue des Francs Bourgeois, from antiques dealers to chic little designers, open their doors to welcome hordes of Sunday browsers. The

Bastille, the Quartier Latin, the Champs-Élysées, Ile St-Louis, and the Ile de la Cité also have shops that open Sunday.

MAIL

Post offices, or PTT, are scattered throughout every arrondissement and are recognizable by a yellow "La Poste" sign. They're usually open weekdays 8–7, Saturday 8–noon. Airmail letters or postcards usually take at least five days to reach North America. When shipping home antiques or art, request assistance from the dealer, who can usually handle the customs paperwork for you or recommend a licensed shipping company.

Airmail letters and postcards to the United States and Canada cost €0.89 for 20 grams, €1.75 for 50 grams, and €2.35 for 100 grams. Stamps can be bought in post offices and cafés displaying a red "Tabac" sign.

If you're uncertain where you'll be staying, have mail sent to American Express (if you're a card member) or to "poste restante" at any post office.

Main Branches Champs-Élysées office.
Champs-Élysées office, Monday to Saturday, open until 7 pm. ⊠ 10 rue Balzar, 8e. **Main office.** Main office, open 24 hours, 7 days a week. ⊠ 52 rue du Louvre, 1er.

SHIPPING PACKAGES

Sending overnight mail from Paris is relatively easy. Besides DHL, Federal Express, and UPS, the French post office has an overnight mail service called Chronopost that has special prepaid boxes for international use (and also boxes specifically made to mail wine). All agencies listed can be used as drop-off points, and all have information in English.

Express Services DHL ⊠ 6 rue des Colonnes, 2e ☎ 08–20–20–25–25 ⊕ www.dhl. com ⊠ 59 av. Iéna, 16e ☎ 01–45–01–91–00. **Federal Express** ⊠ 63 bd. Haussmann, 8e ☎ 01–40–06–90–16 ⊕ www.fedex.com/fr. **UPS** ⊠ 34 bd. Malesherbes, 8e ☎ 08–21–23–38–77

⊕ www.ups.com ⊠ 107 rue Réaumur, 2e ☎ 08–00–87–78–77.

MONEY

Although a stay in Paris is far from cheap, you can find plenty of affordable places to eat and shop, particularly if you avoid the obvious tourist traps. Prices tend to reflect the standing of an area in the eyes of Parisians; the touristy area where value is most difficult to find is the 8e arrondissement, on and around the Champs-Élysées. Places where you can generally be certain to shop, eat, and stay without overpaying include the St-Michel/Sorbonne area on the Rive Gauche; the mazelike streets around Les Halles and Le Marais in central Paris; in Montparnasse south of the boulevard; and in the Bastille, République, and Belleville areas of eastern Paris.

In cafés, bars, and some restaurants you can save money by eating or drinking at the counter instead of sitting at a table. Two prices are listed—*au comptoir* (at the counter) and *à salle* (at a table)—and sometimes a third for the terrace. A cup of coffee, standing at a bar, costs from €1.50; if you sit, it will cost €2 to €7. A glass of beer costs from €2 standing and from €2.50 to €7 sitting; a soft drink costs between €2 and €5. A ham sandwich will cost between €3 and €6.

Expect to pay €7–€10 for a short taxi ride. Museum entry is usually between €4 and €11.50, though there are hours or days of the week when admission is reduced or free.

Prices throughout this guide are given for adults. Substantially reduced fees are almost always available for children, students, and senior citizens.

■TIP➔ Banks never have every foreign currency on hand, and it may take as long as a week to order. If you're planning to exchange funds before leaving home, don't wait until the last minute.

ATMS AND BANKS

Your own bank will probably charge a fee for using ATMs abroad; the foreign bank you use may also charge a fee. Nevertheless, you can usually get a better exchange rate at an ATM than at a currency-exchange office. And extracting funds as you need them is a safer option than carrying around a large amount of cash. Be sure to know your withdrawal limit before taking out cash, and note that French ATMs sometimes restrict how much money you can take out.

ATMs are one of the easiest ways to get euros. Although transaction fees may be higher abroad than at home, banks usually offer excellent wholesale exchange rates through ATMs. You may, however, have to look around for Cirrus and Plus locations; it's a good idea to get a list of locations from your bank before you go. Note, too, that you may have better luck with ATMs if you're using a credit card or debit card that is also a Visa or MasterCard rather than just your bank card.

The largest bank in France, BNP Paribas, has agreements with both Barclay's and Bank of America, among others, that allow no-fee withdrawals between affiliated ATMs. In these cases, a withdrawal of 20 euros would equal the direct exchange value in your home currency. Check with your local bank to see if it has an agreement with a French bank.

■TIP➜ To get cash at ATMs in Paris, your PIN must be four digits long. If yours has five or more, remember to change it before you leave. If you're having trouble remembering your PIN, do not try more than twice, because at the third attempt the machine will eat your card, and you will have to go back the next morning to retrieve it.

CREDIT CARDS

It's a good idea to inform your credit-card company before you travel, especially if you're going abroad and don't travel internationally very often. Otherwise, the credit-card company might put a hold on your card owing to unusual activity—not a good thing halfway through your trip. Record all your credit-card numbers— as well as the phone numbers to call if your cards are lost or stolen—in a safe place, so you're prepared should something go wrong. Both MasterCard and Visa have general numbers you can call (collect if you're abroad) if your card is lost, but you're better off calling the number of your issuing bank, since MasterCard and Visa usually just transfer you to your bank; your bank's number is usually printed on your card.

If you plan to use your credit card for cash advances, you'll need to apply for a PIN at least two weeks before your trip. Although it's usually cheaper (and safer) to use a credit card abroad for large purchases (so you can cancel payments or be reimbursed if there's a problem), note that some credit-card companies *and* the banks that issue them add substantial percentages to all foreign transactions, whether they're in a foreign currency or not. Check on these fees before leaving home, so there won't be any surprises when you get the bill.

Also be warned that most non-European cards lack a *puce*, the microchip found in most French credit cards. While waiters and store vendors will have no problem swiping your card, buying métro cards from a machine or renting a Vélib' public bicycle at stations are impossible without a European card (though Vélib' subscriptions can be purchased online).

■TIP➜ Before you charge something, ask the merchant whether he or she plans to do a dynamic currency conversion (DCC). In such a transaction the credit-card *processor* (shop, restaurant, or hotel, not Visa or MasterCard) converts the currency and charges you in dollars. In most cases you'll pay the merchant a 3% fee for this service in addition to any credit-card company and issuing-bank foreign-transaction surcharges.

Reporting Lost Cards American Express
☎ 800/528–4800 in U.S., 336/393–1111 collect from abroad ⊕ www.americanexpress.

com. Diners Club ☎ 800/234-6377 in U.S., 0810-314-159 in France ⊕ www.dinersclub. com. MasterCard ☎ 800/627-8372 in U.S., 0800-90-1387 in France ⊕ www.mastercard. com. Visa ☎ 800/847-2911 in U.S., 0800-90-1179 in France ⊕ www.visa.com.

CURRENCY AND EXCHANGE

In 2002 the single European Union (EU) currency, the euro, became the official currency of the 12 (now 16) countries participating in the European Monetary Union (with the notable exceptions of Great Britain, Denmark, and Sweden). The euro system has eight coins: 1 and 2 euros, plus 1, 2, 5, 10, 20, and 50 cents. All coins have one side that has the value of the euro on it, whereas the opposite side is adorned with each country's own unique national symbol. There are seven colorful notes: 5, 10, 20, 50, 100, 200, and 500 euros. Notes have the principal architectural styles from antiquity onward on one side and the map and the flag of Europe on the other and are the same for all countries. Also be aware that because of their high nickel content, euro coins can pose problems for people with an allergic sensitivity to the metal.

If you've brought some rumpled francs from home this trip, you can still exchange them. You had until midnight February 17, 2012, to change notes at the Banque de France. A fixed rate of exchange was established: 1 euro equaling 6.55957 French francs. Now, however, you may as well frame those remaining francs and hang them on the wall for posterity, not prosperity.

At this writing, 1 euro equaled approximately US$1.27 and $1.2 Canadian.

The easiest way to get euros is through ATMs; you can find them in airports, train stations, and throughout the city. ATM rates are excellent because they are based on wholesale rates offered only by major banks. ■TIP➜ It's a good idea to bring some euros with you from home so you don't have to wait in line at the airport. At exchange booths always confirm the rate with the teller before exchanging money. You won't do as well at exchange booths in airports or rail and bus stations, in hotels, in restaurants, or in stores. French banks only exchange the money of their own clients.

▌PACKING

You'll notice it right away: in Paris the women dress well to go shopping, to go to the cinema, to have a drink; the men look good when they're fixing their cars. The Parisians still wear hats to the races and well-cut clothes for fine meals; you will not see them in sweats unless they're doing something *sportif*. So don't wear shorts, sweats, or sneakers if you want to blend in. Good food in good settings deserves good clothing—not necessarily a suit and tie, but a long-sleeved shirt and pants for him, something nice for her. Trendy nightclubs usually refuse entrance to men who are wearing sandals.

Be sure to bring rain gear, a comfortable pair of walking shoes, and a sweater or shawl for cool churches and museums. You can never tell about the weather, so a small, foldable umbrella is a good idea. If you'd like to scrutinize the stained glass in churches, bring a pair of small binoculars. A small package of tissues is always a good idea for the occasional rustic bathroom in cafés, airports, and train stations. An additional note: if you're the kind of person who likes a washcloth in the bathroom, bring your own; they're not something you'll find in Paris hotels.

▌PASSPORTS AND VISAS

All citizens of Canada and the United States, even infants, need only a valid passport to enter France for stays of up to 90 days. If you lose your passport, call the nearest embassy or consulate and the local police immediately.

▌ RESTROOMS

Use of public toilet facilities in cafés and bars is usually reserved for customers, so you may need to buy a little something first. Bathrooms are often downstairs and are unisex, which may mean walking by a men's urinal to reach the cubicle. Turkish-style toilets—holes in the ground with porcelain pads for your feet—are still found (though they are becoming scarcer). Stand as far away as possible when you press the flushing mechanism to avoid water damage to your shoes. In certain cafés the lights will not come on in the bathroom until the cubicle door is locked. These lights work on a three-minute timer to save electricity. Simply press the button again if the lights go out. Clean public toilets are available in fast-food chains, department stores, and public parks. You can also find free toilet units on the street, in the larger métro stations, town halls, and in all train stations.

There are restroom attendants in train and métro stations and some of the nicer restaurants and clubs, so always bring some coins to the bathroom. Attendants in restaurants and clubs are in charge of cleaning the bathrooms and perhaps handing you a clean towel; slip some small change into the prominently placed saucer.

Find a Loo The Bathroom Diaries. The Bathroom Diaries is flush with unsanitized info on restrooms the world over—each one located, reviewed, and rated. ⊕ *www.thebathroomdiaries.com.*

▌ SAFETY

Paris is one of the safest big cities in the world, but as in any big city, be streetwise and alert. Certain neighborhoods are more seedy than dangerous, thanks to the night trade that goes on around Les Halles and St-Denis and on Boulevard Clichy in Pigalle. Some off-the-beaten-path neighborhoods—particularly the outlying suburban communities around Paris—may warrant extra precaution. When in doubt, stick to the boulevards and well-lighted, populated streets, but keep in mind that even the Champs-Élysées is a haven for pickpockets.

The métro is quite safe overall, though some lines and stations, in particular lines 2 and 13, get dodgy late at night. Try not to travel alone late at night, memorize the time of the last métro train to your station, ride in the first car by the conductor, and just use your common sense. If you're worried, spend the money on a taxi. Pickpocketing is the main problem, day or night. Be wary of anyone crowding you unnecessarily or distracting you. Pickpockets often work in groups; on the métro they usually strike just before a stop so that they can leap off the train as it pulls into the station. Be especially careful if taking the RER from Charles de Gaulle/Roissy airport into town; disoriented or jet-lagged travelers are vulnerable to sticky fingers. Pickpockets often target laptop bags, so keep your valuables on your person.

A tremendous number of protest demonstrations are held in Paris—scarcely a week goes by without some kind of march or public gathering. Most protests are peaceful, but it's best to avoid them. The CRS (French riot police) carefully guard all major demonstrations, directing traffic and preventing violence. They are armed and use tear gas when and if they see fit.

Report any thefts or other problems to the police as soon as possible. There are three or four police stations in every arrondissement in Paris and one police station in every train station; go to the police station in the area where the event occurred. In the case of pickpocketing or other theft, the police will give you a Déclaration de Perte ou de Vol (receipt for theft or loss). Police reports must be made in person, but the process is generally quite streamlined. In the case of theft, valuables are usually unrecoverable, but identity documents have been known to resurface. You may need a receipt of theft or loss to replace stolen train or plane tickets, passports, or traveler's checks; the receipts may also be useful for filing insurance claims.

Although women traveling alone sometimes encounter troublesome comments and the like, *dragueurs* (men who persistently profess their undying love to hapless female passersby) are a dying breed in this increasingly politically correct world. Note that smiling automatically out of politeness is not part of French culture and can be quickly misinterpreted. If you encounter a problem, don't be afraid to show your irritation. Completely ignoring the *dragueur* should be discouragement enough; if the hassling doesn't let up, don't hesitate to move quickly away.

■ **TIP→** Distribute your cash, credit cards, IDs, and other valuables between a deep front pocket, an inside jacket or vest pocket, and a hidden money pouch. Don't reach for the money pouch once you're in public.

■ TAXES

All taxes must be included in affixed prices in France. Prices in restaurants and hotel prices must by law include taxes and service charges. ■ **TIP→** If these appear as additional items on your bill, you should complain.

V.A.T. (value-added tax, known in France as TVA) at a standard rate of 21.2% (33% for luxury goods, or 5.5% for food in restaurants) is included in the price of many goods, but foreigners are often entitled to a refund. To be eligible for V.A.T. refund, the item (or items) that you have purchased must have been bought in a single day in a participating store (look for the "Tax-Free" sticker on the door) and must equal or exceed €182. The V.A.T. for services (restaurants, theater, etc.) is not refundable.

When making a purchase, ask for a V.A.T. refund form and find out whether the merchant gives refunds—not all stores do, nor are they required to. Have the form stamped like any customs form by customs officials when you leave the country or, if you're visiting several European

WORD OF MOUTH

"We've been very confused on tipping in the cafés and restaurants. All the guidebooks we read (and many menus) say that service is included. However, whenever we get a bill, it only gives the food prices and TVA. When we ask if 'the service est compris'?, they say no, so we have been leaving tips. Are we double-tipping?"
—beachgirl86

"Are you double-tipping? Absolutely. Service is included in the menu prices. As a general rule, if we're very happy with the service—or it's a place we go to often—we leave one or two euros."
—PBProvence

Union countries, when you leave the EU. After you're through passport control, take the form to a refund-service counter for an on-the-spot refund (which is usually the quickest and easiest option), or mail it to the address on the form (or the envelope with it) after you arrive home. You receive the total refund stated on the form, but the processing time can be long, especially if you request a credit-card adjustment.

Global Refund is a Europe-wide service with 225,000 affiliated stores and more than 700 refund counters at major airports and border crossings. Its refund form, called a Tax Free Check, is the most common across the European continent. The service issues refunds in the form of cash, check, or credit-card adjustment.

V.A.T. Refunds Global Refund ☎ *866/706–6090* ⊕ *www.globalrefund.com.*

■ TIME

The time difference between New York and Paris is six hours (so when it's 1 pm in New York, it's 7 pm in Paris). The time difference between London and Paris is one hour.

The European format for abbreviating dates is day/month/year, so 7/5/06 means May 7, not July 5.

TIPPING GUIDELINES FOR PARIS	
Bellhop	€1–€2, depending on the level of the hotel
Hotel Concierge	€5 or more, if he or she performs a service for you
Hotel Doorman	€1–€2 if he helps you get a cab
Hotel Maid	€1–€2 a day (either daily or at the end of your stay, in cash)
Hotel Room-Service Waiter	€1–€2 per delivery, even if a service charge has been added
Taxi Driver	10%, or just round up the fare to the next euro amount
Tour Guide	10% of the cost of the tour
Valet Parking Attendant	€1–€2, but only when you get your car
Waiter	Round up for small bills, 5% for more expensive meals
Restroom Attendant	Restroom attendants in more expensive restaurants expect small change or €1

▌ TIPPING

Bills in bars and restaurants must by law include service (despite what entrepreneurial servers may tell you), but it is customary to round your bill with small change unless you're dissatisfied. The amount varies—from €0.20 for a beer to €1–€2 after a meal. In expensive restaurants it's common to leave an additional 5% on the table.

Tip taxi drivers and hairdressers 10% of the bill. Give theater ushers €0.50. In some theaters and hotels cloakroom attendants may expect nothing (watch for signs that say *pourboire interdit*—tipping forbidden); otherwise, give them €0.75. Washroom attendants usually get €0.30, though the sum is often posted.

If you stay more than two or three days in a hotel, leave something for the chambermaid—about €1.50 per day. Expect to pay €1.50 (€0.75 in a moderately priced hotel) to the person who carries your bags or hails a taxi for you. In hotels providing room service, give €1 to the waiter (unless breakfast is routinely served in your room). If the chambermaid does pressing or laundering for you, give her €1.50–€2 on top of the bill. If the concierge has been helpful, leave a tip of €8–€16.

Museum guides should get €1.50–€3 after a guided tour. It's standard practice to tip long-distance bus drivers about €2 after an excursion.

▌ TOURS

Guided tours are a good option when you don't want to do it all yourself. And not all guided tours are an if-it's-Tuesday-this-must-be-Belgium experience. A knowledgeable guide can take you places that you might never discover on your own, and you may be pushed to see more than you would have otherwise. Tours aren't for everyone, but they can be just the thing for trips to places where making travel arrangements is difficult or time-consuming (particularly when you don't speak the language). Whenever you book a guided tour, find out what's included and what isn't. Also, in most cases prices in tour brochures don't include fees and taxes. And remember that you'll be expected to tip your guide (in cash) at the end of the tour.

BIKE AND SEGWAY TOURS

Cycling is a wonderful way to get a different view of Paris and work off all those three-course "snacks." A number of companies organize bike tours around Paris and its environs (Versailles, Chantilly, and Fontainebleau); these tours always include bikes, helmets, and an English-speaking guide. Costs start at around €25 for a half day; reservations are recommended.

Fat Tire Bike Tours is the best-known anglophone group. In addition to a general orientation bike tour, they organize a nighttime cycling trip that includes a boat cruise on the Seine. Paris à Vélo, C'est Sympa offers thematic tours; the Paris Wakes Up tour, for instance, is a unique spin through Montmartre at 6:30 am.

Information Fat Tire Bike Tours ⊠ *24 rue Edgar Faure, 15e* ☎ *01–56–58–10–54* ⊕ *www. fattirebiketoursparis.com.* **Paris à Vélo, C'est Sympa** ⊠ *22 rue Alphonse Baudin, 11e* ☎ *01– 48–87–60–01* ⊕ *www.parisvelosympa.com.*

BOAT TOURS

There are several boat tour companies operating cruises of one hour to a half-day of sightseeing (and even dining) on the Seine. See the In-Focus on the Seine for more information. Canauxrama organizes leisurely tours year-round in flat-bottom barges along the Canal St-Martin in east Paris. There are four daily departures; the trips last about 2½ hours and have live commentary in French and English. Reservations are required. Paris Canal runs 2½-hour trips with live bilingual commentary between the Musée d'Orsay and the Parc de La Villette from April to mid-November. Reservations are required. Yachts de Paris organizes romantic 2½-hour "gourmand cruises" (for about €198) year-round. Yachts set off every evening at 7:45; you'll be served a three-course meal.

Cruising the Seine on the Batobus is a convenient way to travel between all of the major sites along the river including Notre-Dame, the Louvre, and the Eiffel Tower. A ticket for one day of unlimited hop-on hop-off travel costs €15.

Information Batobus ☎ *08–25–05–01–01* ⊕ *www.batobus.com.* **Canauxrama** ☎ *01–42– 39–15–00* ⊕ *www.canauxrama.com.* **Paris Canal** ☎ *01–42–40–96–97* ⊕ *www.pariscanal. com.* **Yachts de Paris** ☎ *01–44–54–14–70* ⊕ *www.yachtsdeparis.fr.*

BUS TOURS

The two largest bus-tour operators are Cityrama, with 90-minute double-decker tours for €29, and Paris Vision, a two-hour luxury coach tour for €18. Both have headsets for commentary in more than a dozen languages. For a more intimate—albeit expensive—tour of the city, Paris Vision also runs minibus excursions with a multilingual tour operator from €63. Paris L'OpenTour gives tours in a London-style double-decker bus with English or French commentary over individual headsets. You can catch the bus at any of 50 pickup points; tickets cost €29 for one day, €32 for unlimited use for two days. Les Cars Rouges also has hop-on-hop-off tours on double-decker London-style buses, but with only nine stops. A ticket good for two consecutive days costs €26.

Low-cost Foxity tours depart from the Madeleine and offer a 90-minute tour for €14. Headphones provide a guided visit in one of nine languages. With both day and night tours, the tour takes visitors around most of central Paris and offers rare handicap access. For a more economical and commentary-free trip, take a regular Parisian bus for a mere €1.70 per ticket. A special Montmartrobus (€1.70) runs from the Anvers métro station to the top of Montmartre's winding streets. The RATP's Balabus goes from Gare du Lyon to the Grand Arche de la Défense, passing by dozens of major sights on the way. The Balabus runs from mid-April through September; tickets are €1.70 each, with one to three tickets required, depending on how far you travel.

Information Cityrama ⊠ *4 pl. des Pyramides, 1er* ☎ *01–44–55–61–00* ⊕ *www.ecityrama. com.* **Foxity** ⊠ *9 pl. de la Madeleine, 8e* ☎ *01-40-17-09-22* ⊕ *www.foxity.com.* **Les Cars Rouge** ☎ *01–53–95–39–53* ⊕ *www. carsrouges.com.* **Paris L'OpenTour** ☎ *01–42– 66–56–56* ⊕ *www.parislopentour.com.* **Paris Vision** ⊠ *214 rue de Rivoli, 1er* ☎ *01–44–55– 60–00* ⊕ *www.parisvision.com.* **RATP** ☎ *3246 €0.34 per min* ⊕ *www.ratp.fr.*

MINIBUS TOURS

Paris Trip and Paris Major Limousine organize tours of Paris and environs by limousine, Mercedes, or minibus (for 4–15 passengers) for a minimum of four hours. Chauffeurs are bilingual. The price varies from €260 to €400.

Information Paris Major Limousine ⊠ 6 pl. de la Madeleine, 8e ☎ 01–44–52–50–00 ⊕ www.1st-limousine-services.com. **Paris Trip** ⊠ 2 Cité de Pusy, 17e ☎ 01–56–79–05–23 ⊕ www.paris-trip.com.

SPECIAL-INTEREST AND WALKING TOURS

Has it been a while since Art History 101? Paris Muse can help guide you through the city's museums; with its staff of art historians (all native English-speakers) you can crack the Da Vinci code or gain a new understanding of hell in front of Rodin's sculpted gates. Rates run from €90 to €280, including museum admission.

If you'd like a bit of guidance flexing your own artistic muscles, catch a themed photography tour with Paris Photo Tours. Run by the transplanted Texan Linda Mathieu, these relaxed tours are perfect for first-time visitors and anyone hoping to improve their photography abilities.

Sign up with Chic Shopping Paris to smoothly navigate the city's shopping scene. You can choose a set tour, such as Shabby Chic (vintage–secondhand places) or Made in France (unique French products), or ask for an itinerary tailor-made to your interests. Tours start at €100.

Edible Paris, the brainchild of food writer and Fodor's updater Rosa Jackson, is a customized itinerary service for food-oriented visitors. Submit a wish list of your interests and guidelines for your tastes, and you'll receive a personalized itinerary, maps, and restaurant reservations on request. Prices start around €125 per half day. If you'd like a behind-the-scenes look at food in the capital, contact Culinary Concepts; Stephanie Curtis's tours will take you to Rungis, the gigantic professional food market on the outskirts

of Paris, at €120 per person. The Rungis trip starts at 5 am and must be booked a month ahead with a minimum of three people. Or try the bread, cheese, and wine walking tour for €120, which takes you into cheese and wine cellars and to the wood-burning ovens at the celebrated Poîlane bakery.

Paris by Mouth, the most popular English-language website about eating and drinking in Paris, offers tasting tours led by local food writers. Group tours, which run every day of the week, are available for groups of two to six people (€75 euros per person). Private tours and larger group tours are available upon request; you can also add on a wine tasting, shared lunch, or baguette-making class.

The team at Paris Walking Tours offers a wide selection of tours, from neighborhood visits to museum tours and theme tours such as Hemingway's Paris, and the Marais, Montmartre, and Latin Quarter itineraries. The guides are knowledgeable, taking you into less trammeled streets and divulging interesting stories about even the most unprepossessing spots. A two-hour group tour costs €12. For a more intimate experience, Context Paris offers specialized in-depth tours of the city's art and architecture by English-speaking architects and art historians. Prices range from €40 per person for a two-hour general tour, to €75 per person for a three-hour Medieval Architecture tour; private tours range from €170 per group (maximum five people) for a two-hour Introductory Paris walk, to €550 for a group visit plus €90 per person for a four-hour gourmet lunch and history of French gastronomy tour.

Black Paris Tours offers tours exploring the places made famous by African-American musicians, writers, artists, and political exiles. Tours include a four- to five-hour walking-bus-métro tour (€90) that offers first-time visitors a city orientation and a primer on the history of African-Americans in Paris. For those interested in getting behind the scenes at the Château de Versailles, French Links has more than 150 fully customizable themed tours, including Jewish Paris, Normandy Beaches, and Champagne Houses, from €575 per half day. Secrets of Paris offers a Naughty Paris theme tour for ladies, with visits to female-friendly adult toy and racy lingerie boutiques, erotic art galleries, the city's sexiest cocktail bars, and recommendations for naughty cabarets and couples-only clubs, as well as personally designed walking tours throughout Paris's neighborhoods and the surrounding areas including Chantilly and other sites.

A list of walking tours is also available from the Caisse Nationale des Monuments Historiques, in the weekly magazine *Pariscope,* and in *L'Officiel des Spectacles,* which lists walking tours under the heading *"Conférences"* (most are in French, unless otherwise noted). The magazines are available at the press kiosk.

Information **Black Paris Tours** ☎ *01-46-37-03-96* ⊕ *www.tomtmusic.com/id24.htm.* **Centre des monuments nationaux** ✉ *Bureau des Visites/Conférences, Hôtel de Sully, 62 rue St-Antoine, 4e* ☎ *01-44-61-21-00.* **Chic Shopping Paris** ☎ *06-77-65-08-01* ⊕ *www.chicshoppingparis.com.* **Context Paris** ☎ *01-72-81-36-35* ⊕ *www.contexttravel. com.* **Culinary Concepts** ✉ *10 rue Poussin* ☎ *01-45-27-09-09* ✐ *stecurtis@aol.com.* **Edible Paris** ⊕ *www.edible-paris.com.* **French Links** ☎ *01-45-77-01-63* ⊕ *www.frenchlinks. com.* **Paris by Mouth** ✐ *parisbymouth@ gmail.com* ⊕ *parisbymouth.com.* **Paris Muse** ☎ *06-73-77-33-52* ⊕ *www.parismuse.com.* **Paris Photo Tours** ☎ *01-44-75-83-80* ⊕ *parisphototours.com.* **Paris Walking Tours** ☎ *01-48-09-21-40* ⊕ *www.paris-walks.com.* **Secrets of Paris** ☎ *01-43-36-69-85* ⊕ *www. secretsofparis.com.*

▌ VISITOR INFORMATION

A Tout France is the international arm of the French tourism ministry; through its newsletters, brochures, and website you can pick up plenty of informa-

tion on Paris attractions, special events, promotions, and more.

Once you're in Paris, you can turn to the branches of the tourist information office. The longtime main tourist office that was on the Champs-Élysées moved to Rue des Pyramides (near the Opéra) in 2004, and a half-dozen visitor bureaus are stationed at the city's most popular tourist sights. It's often easier to visit one of these branches in person than to call the hotline, because on the phone you'll have to wait through long stretches of generic recorded information at €0.34 per minute. Most are open daily; the Gare de Lyon and Gare de l'Est branches, however, are open Monday through Saturday. The tourism bureaus have friendly, efficient, and multilingual staff. You can gather info on special events, local transit, hotels, tours, excursions, and discount passes. Extra kiosks pop up in the summer by Notre Dame, Hotel de Ville, the Champs-Elysées and Bastille.

Contacts **A Tout France** ☎ *310/271-6665 in U.S.* ⊕ *www.franceguide.com.*

Local Tourism Information **Office du Tourisme de la Ville de Paris Gare du Lyon** ✉ *Arrivals, 20 bd. Diderot* Ⓜ *Gare du Lyon.* **Office du Tourisme de la Ville de Paris Gare du Nord** ✉ *18 rue de Dunkerque* Ⓜ *Gare du Nord.* **Office du Tourisme de la Ville de Paris Opéra-Grands Magasins** ✉ *11 rue Scribe* Ⓜ *Opéra.* **Office du Tourisme de la Ville de Paris Pyramides** ✉ *25 rue des Pyramides* Ⓜ *Pyramides.* **Office du Tourisme de la Ville de Paris Montmartre** ✉ *72 bd. Rochechouart, Montmartre* Ⓜ *Anvers.*

ONLINE RESOURCES
ALL ABOUT PARIS

Besides the tourist office websites ⊕ *en. parisinfo.com* and ⊕ *www.PIDF.com,* there are several other helpful government-sponsored sites. The Paris mayor's office site, ⊕ *www.paris.fr,* covers all kinds of public cultural attractions, student resources, park and market info, and more. On the French Ministry of Culture's site, ⊕ *www.culture.fr,* you can search by theme (contemporary art, cinema, music, theater, etc.) or by region (Paris is in the Ile-de-France). The Réunion des Musées Nationaux (RMN), a consortium of public museums, hosts a group site for 32 national institutions: ⊕ *www.rmn.fr*. Fourteen of these museums are in Paris proper, including the Louvre, the Musée Rodin, and the Musée d'Orsay. The site has visitor info and an exhibition calendar for current and upcoming shows.

A useful website for checking Paris addresses is the phone and address directory, Les Pages Jaunes (⊕ *www. pagesjaunes.fr*). Input a specific address, and you get not just a street map but a photo.

The team at Paris by Mouth (⊕ *paris-bymouth.com*) will give you the latest on the food scene in Paris from expats like food journalist Alexander Lobrano. Also check Lobrano's site (⊕ *www. hungryforparis.com*) for his latest dining reviews, his articles published in the late *Gourmet* magazine, and his favorite Paris food links. DiningInFrance.com (⊕ *www. dininginfrance.com*) has a special section on Paris, with a selection of recent newspaper and magazine articles published on the capital's food scene.

Secrets of Paris (⊕ *www.secretsofparis. com*) is a free online newsletter of tips on dining, nightlife, accommodations, and sightseeing off the beaten path put together by Fodor's updater Heather Stimmler-Hall.

Paris-Anglo.com (⊕ *www.paris-anglo. com*) includes directories of cooking schools, galleries, language classes, and more, plus a biweekly column on various *la vie parisienne* topics. Though not entirely dedicated to Paris, the journal *France Today* (⊕ *www.francetoday.com*) often covers Paris-related news, arts events, and the like. And of course there are all sorts of Paris-related blogs that can be great sources of information and travel inspiration. Some of our faves are Paris Daily Photo (⊕ *www.parisdailyphoto. com*), a fun blog with cool photos from around the city, and Do It in Paris (⊕ *www.doitinparis.com*), a bilingual site covering fashion, shopping, dining, and fun things to do in Paris. French Word-a-Day (⊕ *www.french-word-a-day.typepad. com*) is an engaging slice of life, with a vocabulary bonus.

INDEX

PHOTO CREDITS

1, Sam Gillespie/Alamy. 3, SuperStock/age fotostock. Chapter 1: Experience: 6-7, Bildarchiv Monheim/age fotostock. 8-13 (all) and 14 (left), Joanne Rosensweig. 14 (top center), Bryan Busovicki/Shutterstock. 14 (bottom center), Bensliman/Shutterstock. 14 (top right), Jan Kranendonk/Shutterstock. 14 (bottom right), Ferenc Cegledi/Shutterstock. 15 (top left), wikipedia.org. 15 (bottom left), José Fuste Raga/age fotostock. 15 (top center), Jan Kranendonk/Shutterstock. 15 (bottom center), Joanne Rosensweig. 15 (right), travelstock44/Alamy. 16, Rob Knight/iStockphoto. 17 (left), Joanne Rosensweig. 17 (right), Steven Allan/iStockphoto. 18, Jan Kranendonk/Shutterstock. 19 (left), Photofrenetic/Alamy. 19 (right), Jochem Wijnands/age fotostock. 22, Francesco Dazzi/Shutterstock. 23 (left), Joanne Rosensweig. 23 (right), alysta/Shutterstock. 24, Joanne Rosensweig. 26, hsinli wang/iStockphoto. 27 (left), Joanne Rosensweig. 27 (right), claude thibault/Alamy. 28, Joseph Cesare/wikipedia.org. 29 (left), Fpinault/wikipedia.org. 29 (right), Raphael Frey/wikipedia.org. 30, Franck Chazot/Shutterstock. 31 (top), Paul Hahn/laif/Aurora Photos. 31 (bottom), SuperStock/age fotostock. 32 (top), Galina Barskaya/Shutterstock. 32 (bottom), Renaud Visage/age fotostock. 33 (top left), Stevan Stratford/iStockphoto. 33 (top right), Robert Haines/Alamy. 33 (bottom), Paul Hahn/Laif /Aurora Photos. 34 (left), Renaud Visage/age fotostock. 34 (right), Carsten Madsen/iStockphoto. 35 (top left), xc/Shutterstock. 35 (top right), Mehdi Chebil/Alamy. 35 (bottom), Corbis. 36, Elena Elisseeva/Shutterstock. Chapter 2: The Islands, Ile de la Cité and Ile St-Louis: 37, Jonathan Larsen/Shutterstock. 39, ImageGap/Alamy. 40, ImageGap/Alamy. 43, SuperStock/age footstock. 45, Joanne Rosensweig. 46, Fabien1309/wikipedia.org. 47, Renaud Visage/age fotostock. 48, (left), Frank Peterschroeder/Bilderberg/Aurora Photos. 48, (right), ostill/Shutterstock.. Chapter 3: Around the EIffel Tower: 49, Sean Nel/Shutterstock. 51, Patrick Hermans/Shutterstock. 52, Cristina CIOCHINA/Shutterstock. 53, tkachuk/Shutterstock. 56, Pline/wikipedia.org. 58, Directphoto.org/Alamy. 60, and 61, (left), Directphoto.org/Alamy. Chapter 4: The Champs-Elysées: 63, Art Kowalsky/Alamy. 65, Clay McLachlan/Aurora Photos. 66, dalbera/Flickr. 67, fabio chironi/age fotostock. 69, Lazar Mihai-Bogdan/Shutterstock. 73, dalbera/Flickr. Chapter 5: Around the Louvre: 77, blickwinkel/Alamy. 79, Sylvain Grandadam/age fotostock. 80, David A. Barnes/Alamy. 82, Travel Pix Collection/age fotostock. 84, pandapaw/Shutterstock. 90-91, Fischer/Bilderberg/Aurora Photos. 91 (top), Public Domain. 92 (top left, top right, bottom left, bottom 2nd from left, bottom 3rd from left, and right), Public Domain. 92 (4th from left), Toño Labra/age fotostock. 93 (top left), Visual Arts Library (London)/Alamy. 93 (top right), SPC 5 James Cavalier, US Military/wikipedia.org. 93 (bottom left), Hideo Kurihara/Alamy. 93 (bottom 2nd from left), Directphoto.org/Alamy. 93 (bottom 3rd from left, bottom 4th from left, and bottom right), Public Domain. 94, Rough Guides/Alamy. 95 (top), Peter Horree/Alamy. 95 (2nd from top), Public Domain. 95 (3rd from top), Timothy McCarthy/Art Resource. 95 (bottom), INTERFOTO Pressebildagentur/Alamy. 96, PCL/Alamy. 97 (top), The Bridgeman Art Library. 97 (2nd from top), Toño Labra/age fotostock. 97 (3rd from top), legge/Alamy. 97 (bottom), Public Domain. 98, SuperStock/age fotostock. 99 (top, 2nd from top, and bottom), Public Domain. 99 (3rd from top), Hideo Kurihara/Alamy. Chapter 6: Les Grand Boulevards: 103, Kevin George/Alamy. 105, Tristan Deschamps/Alamy. 106, iStockphoto. 110, Frank Herholdt/Alamy. 111 (top left), Luciana Pampalone/age fotostock. 111 (center left), Repetto. 111 (bottom left), Directphoto.org/Alamy. 111 (top right), eddie linssen/Alamy. 111 (center right), Vanessa Bruno. 111 (bottom right), keith van-Loen/Alamy. 112 (top left), Cartier. 112 (center left), Lamarthe. 112 (bottom left), Oliver Knight/Alamy. 112 (top right), Agnes B. 112 (center right), Longines. 112 (bottom right), Cacharel. 113 (top left), Cartier. 113 (center left), Directphoto.org/Alamy. 113 (bottom left), Roger Vivier. 113 (top right), Kevin George/Alamy. 113 (bottom right), Cartier. 114 (bottom left), PCL/Alamy. 114 (bottom right), Jean-Luc Morales/Alamy. Chapter 7: Montmartre: 119, Hemis/Alamy. 121, Matthew Bergheiser/Shutterstock. 122, Jon Arnold Images/Alamy. 123, rfx/SHutterstock. 126, L F File/Shutterstock. 127, Rough Guides/Alamy. Chapter 8: Le Marais: 131, Oliver Knight/Alamy. 133, Berndt Fischer/age fotostock. 134, David Jordan/age fotostock. 136-37, Marisa Allegra Williams/iStockphoto. 140, M & M Valledor/age fotostock. 145, tbkmedia.de/Alamy. 147, Timothy Ball/iStockphoto. Chapter 9: Eastern Paris: 149, Bob Handelman/Alamy. 151, Berndt Fischer/age fotostock. 152, f1 online/Alamy. 155, Boris Karpinski / Alamy. 158, Alex Segre/Alamy. Chapter 10: The Latin Quarter: 165, Danita Delimont/Alamy. 167, AA World Travel Library/Alamy. 168, Renaud Visage/age fotostock. 169, adam eastland/Alamy. 172, Aschaf/Flickr. Chapter 11: St-Germain-des-Pres: 177, Robert Harding Picture Library Ltd/Alamy. 179, Robert Harding Picture Library Ltd/Alamy. 180, Ian Dagnall/Alamy. 181, David Noton Photography/Alamy. 184, Sylvain Grandadam/age fotostock. 186, Public Domain. 188, Mark Edward Smith/age fotostock. Chapter 12: Montparnasse: 191, Berndt Fischer/age fotostock. 193 and 194, Berndt Fischer/age fotostock. Chapter 13: Western Paris: 199, Eddie Gerald/Alamy. 201, Brian Yarvin/age fotostock. 202, tbkmedia.de/Alamy. 204, Directphoto.org/Alamy. Chapter 14: Where to Eat: 209, Directphoto.org/Alamy. 210, Dana Ward/Shutterstock. 216, Les Deux Magots. 217 (top),

NOTES

NOTES

NOTES

ABOUT OUR WRITERS

When writer-editor **Jennifer Ditsler-Ladonne** decided it was time to leave her longtime home, Manhattan, there was only one place to go: Paris. Her insatiable curiosity—which earned her a reputation in New York for knowing just the right place to go for just the right anything—has found the perfect home in the inexhaustible streets of Paris. An avid cook and wine lover, she's a frequent contributor on wine and travel and a monthly columnist for the magazine *France Today*. Whether you're looking for the best neighborhood bistros or the perfect little black dress, she's the person to ask, as we did for our dining and shopping updates.

Paige Donner first moved to Paris with her husband in the '90s and worked as an entertainment reporter for *Variety*. She maintains a vibrant relationship with Paris's cultural offerings, be they dance, theater, opera, music, cinema, poetry, books, fashion, food, and wine. Her articles about travel, entertainment, and the environment have appeared in the *International Herald Tribune, New York Times, Los Angeles Times, Huffington Post,* and *Bonjour Paris*. Through her website/blog, Local Food And Wine, Paige organizes day-trips to Champagne and Paris tasting tours. Contact her at ⊕ *about.me/paigedonner*.

Journalist and photographer **Linda Hervieux** has explored most corners of Paris since moving to the City of Light in 2004. Her writing has appeared in the *New York Times*, the *International Herald Tribune,* and the *New York Daily News,* among others. For Fodor's *Paris,* she's scoped out more than 100 museums and galleries, taking particular care to document her favorite: the mighty Musée du Louvre, where she studied art history. Contact her at ⊕ *www.lindahervieux.com*.

After a short stint with a travel magazine in New York, **Bryan Pirolli** decided to leave the office in 2008 and actually travel, settling in Paris, conveniently near two major train stations. While delivering pizzas by bicycle, pulling coffee shots, and working as a tour guide, he has spent countless hours exploring Parisian neighborhoods for Fodor's, enjoying cafés and pastries along the banks of the Canal and chocolate shops and crepes in the Latin Quarter. Bryan is also pursuing a degree at the Sorbonne, where he absorbs recommendations from French students.

Heather Stimmler-Hall came to Paris as a university student in 1995 and was almost immediately put to work by family and friends back home who were asking for hotel recommendations. Over 15 years later she's made a career out of reading between the lines of glossy hotel brochures and talking even the grumpiest receptionist into letting her poke around their rooms. She's reviewed hundreds of hotels for international publications such as *France* magazine, *Hotelier International,* her own monthly e-newsletter, ⊕ *www.secretsofparis.com*, *Naughty Paris: A Lady's Guide to the Sexy City*. Although she's not too jaded to appreciate the city's gorgeous five-star palace and design-boutique hotels, what really gets her excited are the hidden budget hotels with a uniquely Parisian character.